International Business Strategy
Rethinking the Foundations of Global Corporate Success

Third Edition

Now in its third edition, this core textbook for advanced undergraduate, graduate, and postgraduate students combines analytical rigour and managerial insight on the functioning and strategy of large multinational enterprises (MNEs). Verbeke and Lee develop an original conceptual model that supports student learning by providing an integrated perspective, rooted in theory and practice. The discussion also includes unique commentaries on seventy-four seminal articles published in the *Harvard Business Review*, the *Sloan Management Review*, and the *California Management Review* over the past four decades, demonstrating how the key insights can be applied to real businesses engaged in international expansion programmes, especially as they venture into high-distance markets. This third edition has been thoroughly updated and features new sections on multinational entrepreneurship, strategic challenges in the new economy, and international business strategy during globally disruptive events, including the COVID-19 pandemic. Students will benefit from updated case studies, improved learning features, and a wide range of online resources.

International Business Strategy

Rethinking the Foundations of Global Corporate Success

Third Edition

ALAIN VERBEKE
University of Calgary

I. H. IAN LEE
Loyola University Chicago

CAMBRIDGE
UNIVERSITY PRESS

CAMBRIDGE
UNIVERSITY PRESS

University Printing House, Cambridge CB2 8BS, United Kingdom

One Liberty Plaza, 20th Floor, New York, NY 10006, USA

477 Williamstown Road, Port Melbourne, VIC 3207, Australia

314–321, 3rd Floor, Plot 3, Splendor Forum, Jasola District Centre, New Delhi – 110025, India

103 Penang Road, #05–06/07, Visioncrest Commercial, Singapore 238467

Cambridge University Press is part of the University of Cambridge.

It furthers the University's mission by disseminating knowledge in the pursuit of education, learning, and research at the highest international levels of excellence.

www.cambridge.org
Information on this title: www.cambridge.org/9781108488037
DOI: 10.1017/9781108768726

First edition © Alain Verbeke 2009
Second edition © Alain Verbeke 2013
Third edition © Alain Verbeke and I. H. Ian Lee 2022

First published 2009
7th printing 2012
Second edition 2013
9th printing 2018
Third edition 2022

Printed in the United Kingdom by TJ Books Limited, Padstow Cornwall, 2022

A catalogue record for this publication is available from the British Library.

ISBN 978-1-108-48803-7 Hardback
ISBN 978-1-108-73837-8 Paperback

Additional resources for this publication at www.cambridge.org/verbeke-lee

Contents

Figures

Tables

About the Authors

Alain Verbeke

Dr Alain Verbeke is a Professor of International Business Strategy and holds the McCaig Research Chair in Management at the Haskayne School of Business (HSB), University of Calgary (Canada). In 2014, Dr Verbeke was elected as the Inaugural Alan M. Rugman Memorial Fellow at the Henley Business School, University of Reading (United Kingdom). In 2019, he was appointed as a Dean's Circle Distinguished Research Fellow, College of Business, Florida International University (United States). He is also an Adjunct Professor at the Solvay Business School, University of Brussels (VUB, Belgium) and was previously associated with Templeton College (now Green Templeton), University of Oxford (United Kingdom). He is the Editor-in-Chief of the *Journal of International Business Studies* or *JIBS* (2017–2022).

Dr Verbeke's academic research agenda consists of rethinking and augmenting the core paradigms in strategic management and international business, especially internalization theory, which is a joint transaction cost economics and resource-based view of the firm, focused on the governance of new resource combinations. He has particular expertise in the management of headquarters–subsidiary relationships and broader governance challenges in large multinational enterprises. Dr Verbeke has authored or edited forty books and more than 200 refereed publications, including many articles in leading scholarly journals such as the *Journal of International Business Studies*, the *Strategic Management Journal*, and the *Journal of Management Studies*.

Dr Verbeke is an Elected Fellow of both the Academy of International Business (AIB) and the European International Business Academy (EIBA). He is the recipient of the double Gold Medal for scholarly contributions and scholarly service to *JIBS*. He is also an Honorary Guest Professor at the University of International Business and Economics, Beijing (China).

In the realm of managerial practice, Dr Verbeke has personally directed 150 consulting projects, many of these related to the economic and strategic evaluation of large-scale capital investments.

I. H. Ian Lee

Dr Inhyeock 'Ian' Lee is currently an Associate Professor of International Business and Strategy at the Quinlan School of Business, Loyola University Chicago (United States). He received his PhD in Business (Major: International Business/Strategy and Minor: Entrepreneurship) from the Kelley School of Business, Indiana University in 2007.

Dr Lee's primary research interests relate to the location strategies of multinational enterprises and the contributions of entrepreneurial firms to cluster formation and performance. Another area of interest is how regional strategies of multinational enterprises and international new ventures can affect firm performance.

Dr Lee has published in leading journals such as *Regional Studies, Journal of International Management, International Business Review, Small Business Economics, Journal of Business Research*, and *IEEE Transactions on Engineering Management*, among others. He currently serves as an editorial board member for the *Journal of International Management, Entrepreneurship Theory & Practice*, and *Asian Business & Management*.

Prior to joining academia, Dr Lee served for eight years as a Deputy Director at the Ministry of Trade, Industry & Energy in South Korea. He was the recipient of the 2018–2019 Alan M. Rugman Visiting Research Fellowship at the Henley Business School, University of Reading (United Kingdom).

Foreword

Too many international business strategy textbooks slavishly adhere to mainstream conceptual models. The publication of those models in prestigious practitioner journals such as the *Harvard Business Review* seems to shelter them from scholarly criticism. The problem is that the policy recommendations derived from these models, while sometimes insightful, are all too often based on implicit and restrictive assumptions. They are frequently oversimplified and seldom based on a rigorous analytical framework that assesses the opportunity costs of following the recommended paths, that is the costs of foregoing alternative strategies.

In this textbook of unusual depth and scope, Alain Verbeke and Ian Lee provide a critical reassessment of Theodore Levitt's famous edicts on global marketing, Michael Porter's diamond, Prahalad and Hamel's core competence, Bartlett and Ghoshal's transnational solution, and many other conceptual models that have until now been treated as almost sacrosanct. These mainstream views are not analyzed in isolation, but systematically within the context of a simple but insightful conceptual framework, which synthesizes several decades of scholarly research on multinational enterprise strategy.

In addition to solid conceptual foundations, this book provides a rich empirical background. Every concept is illustrated with examples drawn from actual managerial practice. The tight link between theory and practice makes for a powerful intellectual toolkit, which can be directly used by senior managers as they weigh alternative global strategies.

As a scholar engaged in the comparative institutional analysis of multinational enterprises, I am struck by the ad hoc quality of much of the advice offered to senior managers. Too often, such advice makes short shrift of the considerable body of theoretical insights and empirical evidence that has been amassed by international business researchers over the last decades. Not so with this book, which shows, once again, that 'nothing is more practical than a good theory'.

Jean-François Hennart
Fellow of the Academy of International Business
Fellow of the European International Business Academy
Professor of International Management
Tilburg University (The Netherlands), Politecnico di Milano
(Italy), and Aalborg University, (Denmark)

Acknowledgements

It has been a privilege to work on the third edition of this book with Valerie Appleby at Cambridge University Press.

Alain Verbeke is pleased to acknowledge the generous financial support of the McCaig family in Calgary, Canada. The family's leadership in funding the McCaig Research Chair in Management allowed writing the third edition of this textbook. Alain Verbeke also acknowledges valuable financial support from the Social Sciences and Humanities Research Council (SSHRC) in Canada, and intellectual guidance from distinguished colleagues at the Henley Business School, University of Reading (UK) and the Solvay Business School, Vrije Universiteit Brussel (Belgium).

Ian Lee acknowledges the unwavering support of the late Alan M. Rugman, Professor of international business strategy and one of the founders of the modern field of international business. Professor Rugman acted as Ian Lee's doctoral supervisor, at the Kelley School of Business – Indiana University, and he provided unparalleled opportunities for intellectual, professional, and personal growth. This third edition of the book, as the fruit of collaboration between the two authors, was possible only because of Professor Rugman's vision on the future of the field of IB and his focus on good theory and on parsimonious explanations of extraordinarily complex phenomena such as multinational enterprise functioning.

The authors express their gratitude to Professor Wenlong Yuan, who co-drafted most of the cases in the book's earlier editions. He also updated and extended all cases as online materials.

Professor Sjoerd Beugelsdijk, a well-known business scholar, developed a substantial body of excellent online materials while using the book at the University of Groningen in the Netherlands. We are very grateful to him for making these available to other instructors adopting the book.

The authors would also like to thank the many members of the Academy of International Business (AIB) and European International Business Academy (EIBA) who shared their valuable research insights, as good as hundreds of senior managers from around the globe who conveyed their dreams of international growth for the companies they cherish.

Abbreviations

3-D	Three-dimensional
3M	Minnesota Mining and Manufacturing Company
3R	Recover, reuse, recycle
5G	5th generation
ACLA	Acer Computec Latino America
AI	Artificial intelligence
AIB	Academy of International Business
AIDS	Acquired immune deficiency syndrome
AIOC	Anglo-Iranian Oil Company
AM	Additive manufacturing
AOL	America Online, Inc.
API	Application Programming Interface
APOC	Anglo-Persian Oil Company
ASA	Alliance-specific advantage
AST	Albert Safi Thomas
AT&T	American Telephone and Telegraph
ATM	Automated teller machine
B2B	Business-to-business
B2C	Business-to-consumer
BAA	British Airports Authority
BASF	Badische Anilin und Soda Fabrik (German for Baden Aniline and Soda Factory)
BBVA	Banco Bilbao Vizcaya Argentaria
BELF	Break-even load factor
BMW	Bayerische Motoren Werke (German for Bavarian Motor Works)
BP	British Petroleum
BRIC	Brazil, Russia, India, and China
C&C	Computers and communications
CAD	Computer-aided design
CAGE	Cultural, administrative, geographic, and economic
CAM	Computer-aided manufacturing
CAT	Computerized axial tomography

CD	Compact disc
CE	Circular economy
CEO	Chief executive officer
CES	Corporate environmental sustainability
CMC	Chemistry, manufacturing, and control
CMR	*California Management Review*
CNOOC	China National Offshore Oil Corporation
CNPC	China National Petroleum Corporation
CO_2	Carbon dioxide
COI	Cluster of innovation
COVID-19	Coronavirus disease 2019
CSAs	Country-specific advantages
CSR	Corporate social responsibility
CVC	Citicorp Venture Capital
DHL	Dalsey, Hillblom, and Lynn
EDCs	European Distribution Centres
EDGC	Economic Development Group Corp.
EIBA	European International Business Academy
EIP	Eco-industrial park
EMI	Electric and Musical Industries
EMNEs	Emerging economy multinational enterprises
ERP	Enterprise resource planning
ESG	Environment, social, and governance
ESGD	Environmental, social, governance, and data
EU	European Union
FDA	Food and Drug Administration
FDI	Foreign direct investment
FDX	FedEx
FSAs	Firm-specific advantages
FX	Foreign exchange
GAAP	Generally Accepted Accounting Principles
GAMs	Global account managers
GATT	General Agreement on Tariffs and Trade
GCM	Global customer management
GDP	Gross domestic product
GE	General Electric
GM	General Motors
GTE	General Telephone & Electronics
H&C	Harrisons & Crosfield
HBR	*Harvard Business Review*
HIV	Human immunodeficiency virus

HP	Hewlett-Packard
HRM	Human resources management
HSB	Haskayne School of Business
HSBC	Hongkong and Shanghai Banking Corporation
IB	International business
IBM	International Business Machines
ICT	Information and communications technology
IDV	Individualism
IE	International entrepreneurship
IKEA	Ingvar Kamprad, Elmtaryd, and Agunnaryd
INEOS	Inspec Ethylene Oxide Specialities
INSEAD	Institut européen d'administration des affaires (French for European Institute of Business Administration)
INVs	International new ventures
iOS	iPhone operating system
IPR	Intellectual property rights
IR	Investor relations
IR4	4th Industrial Revolution
IT	Information technology
JIBS	*Journal of International Business Studies*
JIT	Just-in-time
JV	Joint venture
KFC	Kentucky Fried Chicken
KKR	Kohlberg Kravis Roberts & Co.
KME	*Kabelmetal* AG and Stolberger Metallwerke GmbH (Germany), Tréfimétaux SA (France), and *Europa* Metalli SpA (Italy)
KPI	Key performance indicator
LAN	Línea Aérea Nacional (Spanish for National Airline)
LA	Location advantage
LATAM	Latin American
LB FSAs	Location-bound firm-specific advantages
LCA	Lifecycle analysis
LG	Lucky GoldStar
LLC	Limited liability company
LNG	Liquefied natural gas
LSID	Lake Stevens Instrument Division
LTO	Long-Term Orientation
LVMH	Moët Hennessy Louis Vuitton
M&As	Mergers and acquisitions
MAS	Masculinity
MBA	Master of Business Administration

MDC	Micro distribution centre
MIT	Massachusetts Institute of Technology
MNE	Multinational enterprise
MTN	Mobile Telephone Networks
NAFTA	North American Free Trade Agreement
NCR	National Cash Register
NEC	Nippon Electric Limited Partnership
NGOs	Non-governmental organizations
NJCIP	Nanjing Chemical Industrial Park
NLB FSAs	Non-location-bound firm-specific advantages
ODM	Original design manufacturing
OEM	Original equipment manufacturing/manufacturer
P&G	Procter & Gamble
P2P	Peer-to-peer
PC	Personal computer
PCB	Printed circuit board
PCD	Personal Computer Division
PDI	Power Distance
PI	Performance impact
PPE	Personal protective equipment
PWC	PricewaterhouseCoopers
R&D	Research and development
rDNA	recombinant DNA (deoxyribonucleic acid)
REI	Risk exposure index
RTU	Remote terminal unit
SAP SE	Systems, Applications & Products System Environment
SBU	Strategic business unit
SCI	Space Craft, Incorporated
SGS	Società Generale Semiconduttori
SK	Sunkyong
SMART	Simple, maintenance-friendly, affordable, reliable, and timely-to-market
SMBC	Sumitomo Mitsui Banking Corporation
SMI	Società Metallurgica Italiana
SMR	*Sloan Management Review*
SND	Suzhou New District
SSA	Subsidiary-specific advantage
SSTEC	Sino-Singapore Tianjin Eco-City
STI	Schneider Toshiba Inverter
TCO	Total cost of ownership
TED	Technology, entertainment, and design

TM	Traditional manufacturing
TRW	Thompson Ramo Wooldridge
TSX	Toronto Stock Exchange
TTR	Time to recovery
TV	Television
UAI	Uncertainty Avoidance
UBS	Union Bank of Switzerland
UK	United Kingdom
UN	United Nations
UNCTAD	UN Conference on Trade and Development
UNCTC	UN Centre on Transnational Corporations
US	United States
USA	United States of America
USMCA	United States–Mexico–Canada Agreement
UTZ	Universal Trade Zone
VCR	Video Cassette Recorder
VET	Vocational education and training
VLSI	Very Large Scale Integration
VUB	University of Brussels
WTO	World Trade Organization
YES	Yield, Ease, and Sustainability
ZF	Zahnradfabrik (German for Cogwheel Factory)

Chapter 1

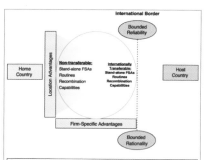

The triangle in the model represents the 'pyramidal' nature of the firm's advantages. Upon the broad base of home country external location advantages (LAs), i.e., the vertical rectangle on the left-hand side in the home country space, the MNE selectively builds a narrower and distinct set of FSAs that are location-bound (LB; the middle space in the pyramid), and then a typically even narrower initial set of FSAs that are non-location-bound (NLB; the top of the pyramid pointing to the international border). The circle represents the actual usage of the company-level FSAs in the home country milieu. Bounded rationality and bounded reliability constraints will influence the firm's strategy for transferring, deploying, and exploiting effectively its non-location-bound FSAs across borders (e.g., operating mode choices).

International Business Strategy presents, interprets, and critiques seventy-four seminal articles from the *Harvard Business Review, MIT Sloan Management Review,* and *California Management Review*. It synthesizes the practical knowledge contained in these articles into a unifying framework of seven key concepts for successful global business. These concepts are analyzed in detail in Chapter 1.

Case Examples

Case example In 1996, Kao was Japan's largest consumer goods company, with a quarter of the shampoo market, three-quarters of the bleach market, and half of the laundry detergent market.

One of the main reasons for Kao's dominant domestic position was its control of a comprehensive distribution system within Japan. Kao owned Hansha, a wholesale distributor, which distributed only Kao's products. As a result, Kao was able to supply small shops easily and also prevent outsiders from entering the market. Moreover, Hansha allowed Kao to gain privileged information on consumers' shopping habits. However, 'in Europe and America Kao has failed to build the comprehensive distribution system that it has in Japan'.[41] In 1996, around 20 per cent of Kao's sales came from overseas markets; by 2019, the percentage of foreign sales had risen to nearly 37 per cent, in ascending order of proportion from Europe, North America, and Asia/Oceania. Kao has still not been able to replicate fully its domestic success abroad.[42] ∎

Case example The immobility of domestic networks has also brought tremendous challenges to many foreign retail banks in Japan, such as Citibank (now Citigroup). Despite its leading position in the US retail banking industry and a large network of branches in the United States, Citibank found it difficult to access Japanese customers when it decided to target individual consumers in 1984. It took Citi-Japan a full ten years to break into the Japanese market. According to Citibank, 'retail banking . . . is like the petrol-station business: you've got to have your pumps in all the right locations. In Japan, the best spots are hard to get'.[43] In Japan, land prices were extremely high, and building a profitable retail network required large-scale investments and substantial time to establish the network. Moreover, Japanese consumers tended to view foreign banks as less trustworthy than local banks.

By 1990, Citibank was 'the last of 83 foreign banks in Japan still interested in retail banking'.[44] The number of its retail branches in Japan had grown from six in 1985 to nineteen in 1993, but it was still a minor player: the smallest Japanese retail bank had forty-one branches in 1985.[45]

Chapter 1 includes a wide range of both classic and recent, mini-case examples featuring high-profile multinational firms. The case examples illustrate aspects of each of the seven key concepts of successful business strategy in practice.

Management Insights

Applying the concepts developed in Chapter 1, we see that Prahalad and Hamel's notion of core competencies is largely equivalent to the higher-order FSA concept, with a strong focus on routines and recombination capabilities. Recombination capabilities are especially critical for Prahalad and Hamel, but, as they correctly point out, these can be difficult to define exactly or to deconstruct. These FSAs are also affected by the administrative infrastructure or heritage that has evolved over the life of the company. However, the key ingredients are similar to the ones described in Chapter 1: an *entrepreneurial attitude* of senior corporate-level managers and competence carriers, critical to identifying and pursuing new *market opportunities* and to uncovering *resources that are not yet fully utilized* and can be deployed in other markets, and an *organizational ability* to meld extant and new resources in novel ways.

In terms of the patterns of FSA development discussed in Chapter 1, the authors paradoxically focus largely on Pattern I (see Figure 1.7 in Chapter 1),

MANAGEMENT INSIGHTS

A rigorous and in-depth analysis of articles drawn from the leading practitioner journals. Their content is fully explored in terms of the key concepts in international business strategy, as well as recent real-world examples.

In addition to discussing classic articles from the *Harvard Business Review, MIT Sloan Management Review*, and *California Management Review*, the authors also analyze state-of-the-art contributions throughout the book. These latter contributions address the new strategic and digital challenges facing the MNE in today's complex, global economy. The analysis applies the book's key concepts in terms of MNEs successfully adapting to the changing external environment, wherein new business models and digital tools appear to be particularly significant.

Strategic Challenges in the New Economy

For lecturers and students:
- Cases that allow applying the framework developed in the book. This set will be updated and will grow over time.
- Links to useful databases and other electronic sources of useful information relevant to international business strategy.

For lecturers:
- Downloadable PowerPoint slides for every chapter and all figures.
- The answers to the case study questions (password protected).
- Multiple choice questions to test student understanding.

Web Materials

Introduction and Overview of the Book's Framework

Senior managers in multinational enterprises (MNEs) have a healthy appetite for knowledge that will improve their firm's performance. They want to know which models from the international business strategy literature can actually be applied in their own firm.

Rethinking the Classics in International Business Strategy

Many MNE senior managers hold (or pursue) MBA or executive MBA degrees, and they certainly read whatever is of use in publications such as the *Financial Times*, the *Wall Street Journal*, *The Economist*, *Business Week*, and *Fortune*. When these managers seek practical advice on improving multinational operations, however, one publication stands out: the *Harvard Business Review* (HBR).

For at least the past thirty years, *HBR* has published the frontier knowledge on everything that really matters to senior MNE managers. This explains why so many classroom readers include reprints of *HBR* articles, and why so many international management teachers use *HBR* articles in their classes. Apart from the *Harvard Business Review*, two other academic publications are highly relevant to managers: the *MIT Sloan Management Review* (SMR), published by the Massachusetts Institute of Technology (MIT), and the *California Management Review* (CMR), published by the Haas School of Business at the University of California at Berkeley.

The first articles on globalization and its impact on MNE strategy appeared in the early 1980s. The growing economic interdependence between nations – especially the rise of the Triad of the United States, Europe, and Japan (replacing post-World War II US hegemony) – drove much of this work. Subsequently, emerging economies became more important, most notably China with its own hegemonic ambitions. Since the early 1980s, *HBR* has published several outstanding and now classic research papers on how to improve MNE strategy. The two other key journals, *SMR* and *CMR*, have also published useful, complementary perspectives on the same international business subjects. Senior managers like these articles because they are well written, insightful and practical: they lead directly to improved managerial practice.[1]

Although we have used these articles with great success in our own MBA and Executive MBA classes, both students and MNE executives think there is great value in a general, unifying framework that managers can use to interpret and synthesize the valuable, practical knowledge contained in the articles. This book tries to provide such a framework; it is a synthesis of the best ***practitioner-oriented*** work in international business.

Such a synthesis might seem to be an impossible task, as there are as many views on international business strategy as there are people writing about it.[2] Nevertheless, we think that most of international business strategy can be captured by just a few simple concepts. Differences among authors are usually just variations on these central themes.

The structure of the book is as follows. In Chapter 1, we lay out the main building blocks of the unifying framework used throughout the book. This framework should allow MNE senior managers to grasp the essence, in strategy terms, of what happens in a complex international business setting.

In addition to describing managers' possible strategies, the framework of Chapter 1 also makes normative suggestions about which strategies are most effective. Most notably, the framework suggests how to improve MNE performance in two areas: value creation and satisfying stakeholder goals across borders. This normative approach is warranted because many MNEs can learn substantially in the short run from best practices adopted by other companies, and in the long run only firms adopting such best practices will survive. As much as possible, we try to specify the preconditions that must be fulfilled for these specific normative suggestions to be valid, often informed by our own research and consulting experience with senior MNE managers. Insufficient specification of when particular normative suggestions will actually improve performance, and when they will not, is probably the most common criticism voiced against articles published in *HBR*, *SMR*, and *CMR*. This is a trap we try to avoid in the present book.

In Chapters 2 to 17, we discuss what we consider to be the best international business articles published in *HBR*, *SMR*, and *CMR* since the early 1980s, and we systematically refer to the unifying framework. After starting each chapter by discussing a classic article in one of the practitioner journals, we then extend the analysis by describing the additional insights gained from articles published in the other journals. We think that this extensive use of practitioner-oriented journal articles has produced a book that is more practitioner-friendly than most of the existing books on international business strategy.

The book is divided into three parts: core concepts (Chapters 1 to 5), functional issues (Chapters 6 to 10), and the dynamics of global strategy (Chapters 11 to 17).

Chapter 17 has two distinct parts. Both parts address the broader responsibilities of MNEs, beyond satisfying the demands of their three main stakeholder groups (shareholders, customers, and employees). Part A addresses corporate social responsibility. Part B discusses MNE environmental sustainability. In the book's Conclusion, we briefly address a few key implications of the book's analysis for MNE managers to help them respond better to both the challenges and the unprecedented opportunities of managing international operations.

This book does not limit itself to a specific country or industry context. Such context is obviously important, as suggested by the many examples from practice, but managers should be able to apply the key concepts developed in this book to a wide variety of country and industry settings.

We assume that the reader has a basic understanding of strategic management concepts as developed for domestic contexts. Our purpose, however, is not simply to add an incremental 'international dimension' to the discussion of a set of conventional strategy problems. Our goal is to explain what lies at the heart of a successful international business strategy, through rethinking a large number of classic articles in international management, and thereby the foundations of global corporate success.

Five Changes in the Third Edition

We have made a number of changes to the book while preparing this third edition, based on the suggestions made by senior scholars who have adopted it in their courses at leading business schools. We would like to highlight the following five changes.

First, we have replaced our discussion of sixteen articles from the second edition with analysis of newer articles published during the 2010–2019 period that appeared more relevant to the present practice of management in internationally operating firms.

Second, we have added a new section, entitled 'Strategic Challenges in the New Economy', at the end of each chapter. In these sections, we discuss twenty-one new articles (eighteen from *HBR*, two from *SMR*, and one from *CMR*) with a particular focus on new challenges in international business strategy. Many of these address complexities arising from the growth of the digital economy and from the deployment of more complex business models across borders.

Third, at the end of each chapter from Part I on core concepts (Chapters 1 to 5), we have included a new section, entitled 'International Business Strategy During Globally Disruptive Events'. Our writing of these sections was informed mainly by the 2020 COVID-19 pandemic, but we draw insights from this pandemic that are relevant to preparing for other global environmental shocks.

Fourth, we have added a new Chapter 16 entitled 'Multinational Entrepreneurship', to analyze the phenomenon of small and young firms' early internationalization from the perspective of international business strategy.

Fifth, all the case studies from the second edition have been updated where relevant, but we have placed these cases online to complement the third edition, thereby allowing easy further updating, where relevant.

Definition of International Business Strategy

International business strategy means effectively and efficiently matching an MNE's internal strengths (relative to competitors) with the opportunities and challenges found in geographically dispersed environments that cross international borders. Such matching is a precondition to creating value and satisfying stakeholder goals, both domestically and internationally.

The above definition focuses on the MNE, a firm with economic operations located in at least two countries. This book will also note some of the special opportunities and challenges that arise when doing business across regions, such as those created by the European Union (EU) and the United States–Mexico–Canada Agreement (USMCA). 'Matching' does not mean that this book proposes a set of easy how-to-do-it prescriptions. Rather, this book intends to educate and further sharpen the intuition of MNE senior managers, when faced with strategic opportunities and challenges in international environments. As regards the relevant stakeholders, we consider satisfying the requirements of the firm's shareholders, its customers, and its employees (including managers) as equally important, though there may obviously be conflicts among the goals of each stakeholder group, and within each stakeholder group – especially between domestic and foreign stakeholders. Many stakeholder groups other than shareholders, customers, and employees may be relevant in terms of their potential impact on value creation, but we consider them secondary as compared to the three main groups. Shareholders and employees provide the inputs most critical to the MNE's functioning, and success can ultimately only be achieved if customers purchase the firm's products. However, a key feature of the new digital economy is that the boundaries between primary and secondary stakeholders sometimes become blurred. For example, many contributors to innovation in digital companies may not be formal employees, but can still be long-term partners of the MNE.

The Seven Concepts of the Unifying Framework – a Brief Overview

Most complex issues in international business strategy revolve around just seven concepts (Figure I.1). Differences among authors are usually just variations on these central themes. These seven concepts form a unifying framework that constitutes the essence of international business strategy, and reflects the foundations of global corporate success:

1. Internationally transferable (or non-location-bound) firm-specific advantages (FSAs)
2. Non-transferable (or location-bound) FSAs
3. Location advantages
4. Investment in – and value creation through – recombination
5. Complementary resources of external actors (not shown explicitly in Figure I.1)
6. Bounded rationality
7. Bounded reliability

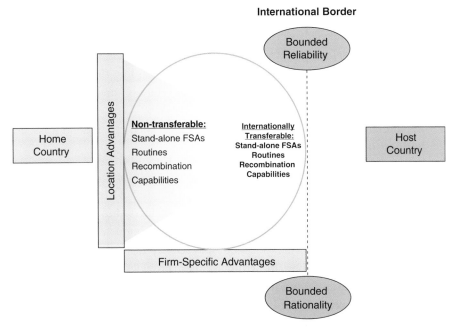

Figure I.1
Core concepts

The triangle in the model represents the 'pyramidal' nature of the firm's advantages. Upon the broad base of home country external location advantages (LAs), i.e., the vertical rectangle on the left-hand side in the home country space, the MNE selectively builds a narrower and distinct set of FSAs that are location-bound (LB; the middle space in the pyramid), and then a typically even narrower initial set of FSAs that are non-location-bound (NLB; the top of the pyramid pointing to the international border). The circle represents the actual usage of the company-level FSAs in the home country milieu. Bounded rationality and bounded reliability constraints will influence the firm's strategy for transferring, deploying, and exploiting effectively its non-location-bound FSAs across borders (e.g., operating mode choices).

The *first three concepts* above (*internationally transferable FSAs, non-transferable FSAs*, and *location advantages*), as a set, reflect the distinct resource base available to the firm, critical to achieving success in the marketplace.

In this book, the firm is viewed as essentially a bundle of resources under common governance.[3]

Expressed in practical, managerial terms, this resource base has various components, either owned by – or accessible to – the firm:

1. Physical resources, including natural resources, buildings, plant equipment, etc.
2. Financial resources, including access to equity and loan capital.
3. Human resources, including both individuals and teams. These individuals and teams have both entrepreneurial and operational (or efficiency-related) skills.
4. Upstream knowledge, including sourcing knowledge, as well as product- and process-related technological knowledge.
5. Downstream knowledge, critical to the interface with customers, and related to marketing, sales, distribution, and after-sales service activities.
6. Administrative (governance-related) knowledge regarding the functioning of the organizational structure, organizational culture, and organizational systems.
7. Reputational resources, including brand names, a good reputation for honest business dealings, etc.

A firm can have FSAs – i.e., strengths relative to rival companies – in each of the above resource areas. The nature, level, and contestability of these strengths vis-à-vis rivals is not always fully understood by outsiders, but these strengths should, in principle, be identifiable through a properly conducted benchmarking exercise. The firm's particular location may contribute significantly to this distinct resource base, especially if this location provides privileged access to specific resources external to the firm itself. Thus, FSAs and location advantages can be intimately related. For example, FSAs such as patents in the upstream knowledge area, or brand names in the reputational resource area, confer value only if supported by a favourable property rights regime (patent laws, trademark protection, etc.) that protects proprietary knowledge. The specifics of the property rights regime are different in each nation, and can thus represent a location advantage for firms with substantial proprietary knowledge and operating in countries with a favourable regime, in this case institutionalized through government intervention.

Routines reflect the distinct ability to combine further the above resources, in unique ways valued by the firm's stakeholders. Routines are stable patterns of decisions and actions that coordinate the productive use of resources, and thereby generate value, whether domestically or internationally. The combination ability expressed in routines is a higher-order FSA, because routines are more complex than an FSA derived from distinct but stand-alone resources. Therefore, rival companies face more difficulties imitating or otherwise acquiring it.

Case example Consider the classic example of Federal Express' mail delivery system. Frederick W. Smith founded Federal Express in 1971, based on his innovation of the 'hub-and-spoke' approach to mail delivery. In a change from the traditional direct shipping from origin to destination, Federal Express developed a new routine: it first gathered all mail in its hub in Memphis, Tennessee, sorted the mail there, and then shipped it from the hub to a variety of final destinations. Using this hub-and-spoke routine, the company was able to provide overnight delivery services with fewer trucks and planes.

Building upon this simple hub-and-spoke concept, Federal Express created multiple business processes, such as a sophisticated tracking and tracing system to monitor the routing of each item, a customized weather forecasting system to aid in-flight scheduling, fleet management systems for its planes and trucks, and a distinct management approach to its network of distributors. Although many competitors tried to copy these routines in the 1980s, Federal Express remained the industry leader.[4] It is important to understand that early entrepreneurial judgement was critical here. Mr Smith invented the hub-and-spoke model in an undergraduate essay he wrote at Yale University, and the idea of combining fleets of aircraft and trucks to create seamless logistics chains came from his service with the US Marines, which combined air and ground equipment in their military operations.[5]

Federal Express also applied the above routines when expanding internationally. For example, when Federal Express entered China, it rolled out its key routines, covering the entire upstream and downstream areas of the firm's value chain. It transferred its prevailing management systems, bought its own planes for this market, acquired its own air routes, and tried to establish its own network of distributors. As noted by T. Michael Glenn, Executive Vice President for marketing at FedEx's parent, FDX Corp, 'We've got a pretty good formula for attacking any market . . . Whether it's China or Japan or Germany, it really doesn't make any difference.'[6]

Compared with an FSA derived from a single, stand-alone resource, a capability to combine resources may be more flexible and durable, because it often involves substituting one resource (such as a high-quality human resource or a type of equipment) for another, similar, one without loss of long-term productive value. The combination capability may also guarantee the continued control over distinct, stand-alone resources, such as human resources, when it allows both higher productivity benefiting the firm and higher rewards to these distinct resources than they could earn outside of the firm.

Transferring and exploiting a routine across borders may pose problems, however, if the routine is not fully understood by either the source in the home country or the recipient in the host country, even if it has been deployed frequently and reliably in the home country. Failure to fully understand a routine typically occurs if the routine has a 'cultural' component. In such cases, the routine relies on a distinct, national cultural characteristic which may not be present in host country environments. ■

Case example As another classic example, Cisco, headquartered in the United States, is the world's largest networking equipment manufacturer. In 1994, it began the implementation of an enterprise resource planning (ERP) system and by 1998 was poised to focus its attention on the Chinese market. Cisco had garnered first-mover advantages and continued to maintain a considerable reputation with a single system image on a completely Web-based platform throughout the world.[7]

However, the local management in China identified a number of issues of local adaptation that could threaten the effective adoption of the common system platform and damage Cisco's market reputation (e.g., a need for Chinese character-based financial statements). Cisco listened to the advice of its local representatives and ultimately adapted successfully to the idiosyncratic requirements of the local Chinese workplace by, among other things, producing Chinese character-based financial statements. ∎

The simple point made by this last example is that knowledge management systems themselves, though at the heart of knowledge transfer within MNEs, may face a variety of problems when diffused throughout the MNE network. Importantly, the failure to transfer these types of routines effectively may have broader spillover effects on the MNE as a whole.

International transfer difficulties in part reflect the presence of generic differences, including cultural differences, between home and host countries (these differences require adaptation and a recombination capability, as explained below). In addition, another common transfer difficulty is that those supposed to implement a practice abroad lack a crucial piece of experiential knowledge. This problem is sometimes compounded by the lack of sufficient attention to the routine's tacit knowledge attributes by those supposed to transfer the practice from the source country.

The **fourth concept, recombination**, constitutes the heart of international business strategy: international corporate success requires more than just routines, whether internationally transferable or location-bound ones, that allow for stable and predictable patterns in combining resources. The highest-order FSA is the ability not just to combine reliably the MNE's existing resources, but to recombine its resources in novel ways, usually including newly accessed resources, whether in a limited geographic space (in which case the firm engages in domestic product diversification or innovation) or internationally. In the international context, MNEs must engage in the artful orchestration of resources, especially knowledge bundles, as a response to differences between national and foreign environments, and to satisfy new stakeholder demands in these foreign environments. In practical terms, entrepreneurial judgement is at the heart of the MNE's recombination capability: individuals inside the MNE act as entrepreneurs and craft new ways of combining and deploying the resources under their control as a response to perceived business opportunities. It is important to understand that recombination does not just mean adding new resources and managerial practices to existing ones: recombination means by definition foregoing at least some standard resources and standard practices before a new business opportunity can successfully be acted upon. A resource recombination capability is thus a precondition to value creation and satisfying stakeholder needs when operating in complex international settings.

The *fifth concept*, *complementary resources of external actors*, represents the additional resources, provided by external actors but accessible to the MNE, which may be necessary to fill resource gaps and achieve success in the marketplace. This book will focus solely on the complementary resources provided by external actors that are critical to international success.

Finally, the **sixth** and **seventh concepts**, **bounded rationality** and **bounded reliability**, reflect the behavioural characteristics (of both senior MNE managers and other relevant economic actors) that may impede international success. Bounded rationality implies limits to the capacity of individuals to absorb, process, and act upon complex and often incomplete information. Bounded reliability implies insufficient effort to deliver on promised behaviour or performance. As this book will demonstrate, acute problems of bounded rationality and bounded reliability characterize many international business decisions and actions.

This book discusses in much more detail the complexities associated with each of these seven concepts, as well as the sometimes subtle linkages among them.

PART I

CORE CONCEPTS

1 → Conceptual Foundations of International Business Strategy

Five Learning Objectives

1. To develop an understanding of the seven concepts of this book's unifying framework.
2. To link specific types of transfers of firm-specific advantages (FSAs) across borders with the four corresponding multinational enterprise (MNE) archetypes of administrative heritage.
3. To describe the various motivations for foreign direct investment (FDI) and to explain the linkages among non-location-bound (or internationally transferable) FSAs, location-bound (or non-transferable) FSAs, and location advantages within each of the four MNE archetypes.
4. To define the ten often-observed patterns of FSA development and resource recombination in international business.
5. To explain the need for complementary resources of external actors, including those in the MNE's stakeholder network and ecosystem, and the potential reasons for bounded rationality and bounded reliability when doing international business.

In this chapter, we will look in greater detail at each of the seven concepts of this book's unifying framework. Here is a brief introduction to these seven concepts, as also shown in Figure 1.1:

1. *Non-location-bound firm-specific advantages (FSAs)*. We will use the words 'internationally transferable' FSAs interchangeably with 'non-location-bound' FSAs, but it should be clear that when using the former, we also assume that the internationally transferred FSAs can be effectively deployed and profitably exploited in foreign locations. In other words, 'international transferability' in this book involves more than the mere technical transfer across borders of knowledge and other company strengths. This concept thus reflects an arsenal of strengths vis-à-vis rival companies when operating abroad.
2. *Location-bound FSAs*. Here, we will use the words 'non-transferable' FSAs as synonymous with 'location-bound' FSAs, thereby not only referring to technical transfer difficulties, but also to the totality of challenges, facing the

13

company in the realm of technical transfer, effective deployment, and profitable exploitation of FSAs across borders.

3. *Location advantages (LAs).* These are typically external to the MNE.
4. *Investment in – and value creation through – recombination.* Recombining resources is not the same as combining resources. Recombination or *novel combination* means that some resources used in an initial combination need to be dropped, and distinct new resources are added. For example, recombination could refer to something as simple as changing the packaging of products and as complex as completely reconfiguring a firm's logistics system to meet the requirements of foreign customers.
5. *Complementary resources of external actors* (not shown explicitly in Figure 1.1) that may be instrumental to effective resource recombination.
6. *Bounded rationality.*
7. *Bounded reliability.*

Figure 1.1
Core concepts

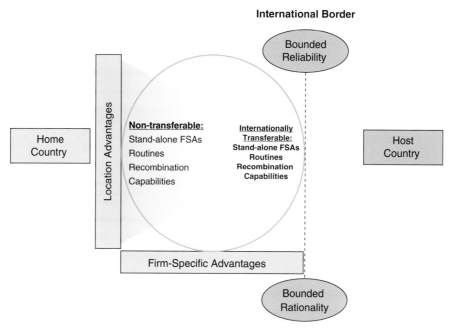

The triangle in the model represents the 'pyramidal' nature of the firm's advantages. Upon the broad base of home country external location advantages (LAs), i.e., the vertical rectangle on the left-hand side in the home country space, the MNE selectively builds a narrower and distinct set of FSAs that are location-bound (LB; the middle space in the pyramid), and then a typically even narrower initial set of FSAs that are non-location-bound (NLB; the top of the pyramid pointing to the international border). The circle represents the actual usage of the company-level FSAs in the home country milieu. Bounded rationality and bounded reliability constraints will influence the firm's strategy for transferring, deploying, and exploiting effectively its non-location-bound FSAs across borders (e.g., operating mode choices).

Let us start by describing a few key dimensions of the global economy, using statistical data on MNEs and their international business activities.

International Business, MNEs, and Their Activities in the Global Economy

The world economy has experienced an era of rapid and deep integration during the past half century. Some basic data on the world economy in Table 1.1 help us better understand the growing importance of international business (IB) during this era, and the role of the multinational enterprise in the process of globalization at the macro-level. We define an MNE as a firm that conducts economic transactions across national borders, and that owns assets in at least one other country than the home country.

The total volume of world merchandise exports has seen a more than hundredfold increase from $157 billion to $17.2 trillion over the period of 1963–2017[1] and they have more than doubled in the 2003–2017 period. The average annual growth rate of 4.1 per cent in the volume of world merchandise exports has been greater than the 2.5 per cent growth rate of world gross domestic product (GDP) over the same period.[2] In 2017, the top five exporting countries in world merchandise trade were China ($2.3 trillion), the United States of America ($1.5 trillion), Germany ($1.4 trillion), Japan ($698 billion), and the Netherlands ($652 billion). The top five importing countries in that same year were the United States of America ($2.4 trillion), China ($1.8 trillion),

Table 1.1 Basic data on world economy*

	2003	2017
World Merchandise Exports[1]	$7.4 trillion	$17.2 trillion
World Exports in Commercial Services[2]	$1.8 trillion	$5.3 trillion
World FDI Outflows[3]	$0.6 trillion	$1.4 trillion
World FDI Outbound Stocks[4]	$8.2 trillion	$30.8 trillion

* The exports and outbound FDI data from the countries of origin can also be given a 'mirror-image' interpretation, taking the form of imports and inbound FDI by the destination or recipient countries.

[1] WTO, *World Trade Statistical Review 2018* (Geneva, Switzerland: WTO, 2018).

[2] Ibid.; WTO, *International Trade Statistics 2004* (Geneva, Switzerland: WTO, 2004).

[3] UNCTAD, *World Investment Report 2018: Investment and New Industrial Policies* (New York and Geneva: United Nations Conference on Trade and Development, 2018); UNCTAD, *World Investment Report 2004: The Shift toward Services* (New York and Geneva: United Nations Conference on Trade and Development, 2004).

[4] Ibid.

Germany ($1.2 trillion), Japan ($672 billion), and the United Kingdom ($644 billion). These countries together account for more than one-third of the total volume of world merchandise trade.

The total volume of world exports in commercial services has also been rising from $1.8 trillion in 2003 to $5.3 trillion in 2017, with an average annual growth rate of 5 per cent. In 2017, the top five exporting countries for commercial services were the United States of America ($762 billion), the United Kingdom ($347 billion), Germany ($300 billion), France ($248 billion), and China ($226 billion). The top five importing countries for commercial services in the same year were the United States of America ($516 billion), China ($464 billion), Germany ($322 billion), France ($240 billion), and the Netherlands ($211 billion). As in the case of world merchandise trade, these leading countries accounted for more than one-third of the total volume of world exports and imports in commercial services.

The rapid and deep integration process of the world economy also becomes evident from annual statistics on foreign direct investment. In terms of FDI flows, the world FDI outflows for all countries were just $0.6 trillion in 2003, but jumped to $1.4 trillion in 2017, i.e., a more than twofold increase. In terms of FDI stocks in the world, the total values of outbound stocks of FDI were just $8.2 trillion in 2003, but skyrocketed to $30.8 trillion in 2017, reflecting an almost fourfold increase during this period. In 2017, the top five home countries of FDI outflows were the United States of America ($342 billion), Japan ($160 billion), China ($125 billion), the United Kingdom ($100 billion), and Hong Kong ($83 billion). The top five host countries for FDI inflows in the same year were the United States of America ($275 billion), China ($136 billion), Hong Kong ($104 billion), Brazil ($63 billion), and Singapore ($62 billion). These leading countries accounted for 56.6 and 44.8 per cent of the total FDI outflows and inflows, respectively, in the world economy.

MNEs have been at the centre of the integration process of the world economy, partly because trade and FDI are the two main vehicles used by these firms to conduct transactions across national borders. Trade represents the sale of products and services, and sometimes the rights to produce (as with licensing or manufacturing contracts) to foreign countries, and it includes exports and imports depending on the direction of the flow of these products, services, and rights. In contrast, FDI represents establishing or acquiring operations abroad. FDI involves more than the measured value of the financial resources transferred. It typically also entails the transfer of multiple, intermediary resources across borders, such as equipment, people, and especially intangible knowledge and reputational assets (such as a reputation for honest business dealings).

MNEs typically enter foreign markets via two modes – exports and outbound FDI. When the MNE chooses to export its products or services as its entry mode to enter a foreign market, the physical production process (including finished and intermediary products) takes place within the boundaries of its home country. The MNE then simply serves its foreign customers by transferring domestically produced goods and services across borders. However, when the MNE chooses outbound FDI to enter a foreign market, it typically first transfers abroad intermediary resources from its home country. In the case of a foreign acquisition, this might entail sending expatriates and transferring managerial practices. The MNE then conducts the physical production process of goods and services inside the foreign market, thereby mobilizing additional location-specific resources in the host environment. Considering the distinct characteristics of trade versus FDI as MNE entry mode choices, FDI activities of MNEs have been referred to as contributing to 'deep' integration of the global economy, whereas trade activities of MNEs supposedly contribute more to 'shallow' integration.

How many MNEs are currently operating in the world economy? A 2015 study suggested 85,000 MNEs as a conservative estimate,[3] and this number is likely to have grown even further in recent years. The present book focuses mainly on the largest and most successful MNEs, which are typically included in the *Fortune Global 500* list of companies. The world's 500 largest MNEs have been responsible for over 50 per cent of the world's trade and over 90 per cent of the world's stock of FDI in the past decades.[4] According to Fortune, the 2018 *Global 500* list[5] contributed $30 trillion of revenues and $1.9 trillion of profits to the global economy in the previous year (2017). The 500 largest MNEs play a critical role in the global economy: a single company's annual revenues can be greater than some countries' GDP.[6] For example, Walmart, the top MNE on the 2018 *Fortune Global 500* list, generated $500 billion in revenues in 2017, which is greater than the Austrian GDP at $474 billion in the same year.[7] Apple, the most profitable MNE on the same list, had more than $229 billion of revenues in 2017, which is greater than $194 billion of GDP generated by New Zealand in the same year.[8] It should be noted that the world's 500 largest MNEs are not spread equally around the world: instead, they are highly clustered around the triad, i.e., the three key trade and investment blocks of North America, the European Union (twenty-eight members until January 2020, when the United Kingdom left the Union), and the Asia-Pacific. The question arises whether these firms are truly global in terms of the distribution across the world of their assets, employees, sales, etc., or whether they have remained more oriented towards their home region in spite of their size. The empirical reality suggests a preponderance of regional multinationals. For example, among the 386 MNEs with publicly disclosed geographic sales segments on the *Fortune Global 500* list from 2017, 286 (74.1 per cent) were home-region-oriented MNEs. These firms made over 50 per cent of their annual sales within their home region of the triad. There were only thirty-six global MNEs on the list that made at least 20 per cent of their annual sales in each of the triad markets.[9]

In spite of their significant role in the global economy, the world's 500 largest MNEs remain vulnerable to strong competition in the international marketplace.[10] Twenty MNEs on the 2018 *Fortune Global 500* list were newcomers, meaning that twenty firms included in the previous list had disappeared. Substantial changes in the ranks of the 500 MNEs are also frequently observed: for example, Alibaba Group made a big jump from 462nd place in 2017 to 300th place in 2018, and Facebook moved up from 393rd place to 274th place during the same period. The number of MNEs from emerging economies in the *Fortune Global 500* has also been rising in recent years: a 2015 study reported that in 1990 around 5 per cent of the world's 500 largest MNEs were headquartered in emerging economies. This number had jumped to 26 per cent in the 2013 list, and was projected to increase further to more than 45 per cent by 2025.[11]

Our goal is to help readers better understand the importance of IB in the global economy, and the critical role of MNEs in international, economic integration processes. To achieve this goal, we will focus especially on the strategic decision making and functioning of (mainly large) MNEs. In the next section, we describe the seven key concepts of the unifying framework that is used throughout the book.

Internationally Transferable FSAs and the Four MNE Archetypes

The MNE creates value and satisfies stakeholder needs by operating across national borders. When crossing its home country border to create value in a host country, the MNE is, almost by definition, at a disadvantage as compared to rivals from the host country, because these firms possess a knowledge base that is more appropriately matched to local stakeholder requirements. The MNE incurs additional costs of doing business abroad, resulting from cultural, economic, institutional, and spatial distance between home and host country environments. MNE managers often find it particularly difficult to anticipate the liability of foreignness resulting from the cultural and institutional differences with their home country environments, even though these may be reduced over time as the firm learns and gains increased legitimacy in the host country.[12] We should note that, depending on the situational context, relevant rivals might include not only host country firms, but also more broadly host region rivals (e.g., when a European MNE enters China and must compete with Asian rivals that may be more attuned to the Chinese environment) and even global competitors, whether established firms or new entrants relevant to the MNE's profitability and growth across borders.

In order to overcome these additional costs of doing business abroad, the MNE must have proprietary internal strengths, such as technological, marketing, or administrative (governance-related) knowledge, as well as strengths in relationships with outside actors (e.g., long-established linkages with home country suppliers, buyers, government agencies, or family connections in the case of family firms, etc. that can be leveraged abroad). This set of MNE internal strengths, the availability of which both allows and constrains the scope of the firm's expansion across borders, is called the **non-location-bound FSAs**. These FSAs do not stop creating value when the border is crossed between the home and the host country, though their precise value may be somewhat different in the two countries.[13] In principle, the MNE can transfer, deploy, and exploit these FSAs successfully across borders. Non-location-bound FSAs can be embodied in final products, for example when the MNE exports goods and services that are valued highly by host country customers. Think of an automobile such as a Toyota car, exported from Japan to the United States. The exported vehicle itself embodies the outstanding production quality, characteristic of Toyota products, that results from superior manufacturing processes and quality control systems.

Alternatively, when faced with natural or government-imposed trade barriers, the MNE may transfer some FSAs abroad directly, as 'intermediate' products. In the Toyota case, the FSAs in manufacturing and quality control will then be deployed and exploited abroad through an affiliate in the host country, which will produce and market the automobiles itself, building on the knowledge bundles it receives from the parent company. The exploitation of FSAs transferred abroad can also be done by external actors (such as licensees), or by network partners (such as joint venture partners or distributors), who may add their own complementary resources to the foreign operation and thereby strengthen the MNE's position in the foreign marketplace by filling resource gaps.[14]

The paradox of an internationally transferable FSA is the following: if the FSA consists of easily codifiable knowledge (i.e., if it can be articulated explicitly, as in a handbook or blueprint), then it can be cheaply transferred, and effectively deployed and exploited abroad, but it can also be easily imitated by other firms. In other words, the costs of FSA transfer, deployment, and exploitation may be relatively low, but the potential value that can be derived from actually deploying and exploiting the FSA may also be relatively low, namely if competitors can easily imitate what the MNE is best at.

In contrast, MNEs face great difficulty transferring, deploying, and exploiting FSAs that consist of tacit knowledge. Tacit knowledge is difficult to transfer, deploy, and exploit abroad because it cannot be fully replicated through simple communication channels (e.g., technical manuals). Employing tacit knowledge requires person-to-person communication, and is necessarily associated with sending human resources abroad, building up experience over time, learning by doing, etc. If the tacit knowledge is collective knowledge, embedded in a team of individuals rather than a single person, it may be necessary to re-embed this knowledge in a foreign team. Though it is expensive and time-consuming to transfer, deploy, and exploit tacit knowledge across borders, the benefit to the MNE is that this knowledge is also difficult to imitate. Therefore, tacit knowledge is often a key source of competitive advantage when doing business abroad.

Perhaps the most important bundle of tacit knowledge is contained in the MNE's administrative heritage: the key routines developed by the firm since its inception. These are often 'imprinted' as the result of the founder's vision and the firm's particular set of external circumstances (e.g., 'this is the way we do things in this company'). At a general level, and when looking at the early history of large numbers of MNEs, we can distinguish among four archetypes of administrative heritage, each associated with a specific routine of international FSA transfer.[15]

First, the **centralized exporter**: this home-country-managed firm builds upon a tradition of selling products internationally, out of highly cost-efficient or exceptional-quality-generating facilities in the home country (e.g., as found in large steel firms and luxury leather goods producing family firms respectively), and with only minor, usually customer-oriented, value-creating activities abroad. *Standardized products manufactured at home embody the company's FSAs (themselves developed on the basis of a favourable home country environment, including local clustering) and make the exporting firm successful in international markets*. The foreign subsidiaries act largely as facilitators of efficient home country production. Multinational activities occur primarily in the downstream end of the value chain, and are related to marketing, distribution, and related logistics operations. Many large Japanese MNEs have this type of heritage. They became serious about international expansion in the 1960s, in an era of declining trade barriers, communication, and transport costs. For example, the introduction of the container as a cargo unit in maritime transport in the mid-1960s greatly facilitated international trade in manufactured goods.[16]

Case example A historical example of a centralized exporter is Nippon Electric Limited Partnership (NEC), established in 1899. In 1929, NEC developed the A-type switching system, the first of this type of radio communication systems, and supplied it to Japan's Ministry of Communications. In 1939, NEC established a fully fledged research laboratory, leading to successful new product development, including the first crossbar switching system adopted in Japan.

NEC's international expansion was characterized by the export of products that had already been successful domestically. As early as 1934, NEC provided the Chinese Xinjing station with a radio broadcasting system. However, extensive international expansion only started in the 1960s, when sales subsidiaries such as NEC de Mexico, NEC do Brasil, NEC Australia, and NEC Electronics (Europe) were established. At that stage, NEC also exported satellite communication systems to the United States, Switzerland, China, etc. NEC started to open foreign plants during the so-called 'C&C' era. C&C refers to the integration of computers and communications technologies from 1978 to 1989. This expansion included a telephone systems plant in the United States and a VLSI (Very Large Scale Integration) plant in the United Kingdom, capable of placing hundreds of thousands of electronic components on a single chip. In 2012, manufacturing was geographically dispersed: NEC had fifty-four plants in Japan, including five plants in or near Tokyo, and fifty-eight manufacturing plants overseas, meaning that NEC is no longer a 'pure' centralized exporter.[17]

In spite of its extensive international operations, NEC still functions with relatively centralized domestic R&D capabilities, and with half of its scientists being Japanese nationals. But it now also operates several international laboratories, for example, in Heidelberg (Germany), Beijing (China), Princeton and San Jose (United States), Singapore, Mumbai (India), and Herzliya Pituach (Israel). NEC is active at present in R&D domains such as data sciences, and more specifically in artificial intelligence (AI), with a focus on visualization, analysis, and prescription, for example in high-speed-camera object recognition technology and fibre optic sensors. It also conducts research on ICT platforms, for example, in the realm of cyber security and data distribution. Despite the broad geographic spread of its R&D facilities, NEC maintains central laboratories and innovation centres for all its R&D niches in Japan.[18] These domestic facilities are responsible for most of NEC's new products.[19] The domestic concentration, though diminished, of formal new knowledge development suggests the continued relevance of the firm's longstanding administrative heritage as a centralized exporter. ■

Case example Motion picture studios are often centralized exporters, and thus their final products incorporate all of the companies' FSAs. Motion pictures are typically exported from the place where they are created. Warner Bros. Pictures, a major US motion picture studio, has done very well in attracting foreign customers. Through its international offices in more than thirty countries, the company distributes films to more than 120 territories outside of North America. As one typical example of the importance of foreign markets, the 2019 movie 'Joker' grossed over a US $1 billion worldwide and over 68 per cent of the theatrical performances came from the international box office.[20] ■

The second archetype of administrative heritage is the *international projector*: this firm builds upon a tradition of transferring its proprietary knowledge developed in the home country to foreign subsidiaries, which are essentially clones of the home operations. Many American MNEs fit this model, as they expand internationally based upon a large and sophisticated home country market, as well as proprietary technology and unique management practices. *Knowledge-based FSAs developed in the home country are transferred to subsidiaries in host countries. The international projector MNE seeks international expansion by projecting its home country success recipes abroad.* To the extent that international projection requires the systematic and continuous transfer of tacit knowledge to multiple locations (particularly when the product offering contains a large service component), this firm relies on an extensive cadre of professional managers who can act as expatriates or repositories/transfer agents of the home country success recipes.

Case example As a historical example, the US automobile manufacturer Ford is a well-known case of a firm with an administrative heritage dominated by international projection. Ford, established in 1903, rapidly started to export cars to Canada and Europe through export agents.

In Canada, for example, Ford essentially cloned its American operations. In 1904, Gordon McGregor, a Canadian from Walkerville, Ontario, suggested the creation of a new company to manufacture the Model A in Canada. The anticipated significant tariff savings and new capability of rapid response to Canadian demand, as well as local financing possibilities, motivated Ford to sign the agreement that established Ford Canada. Ford agreed to 'furnish it with patents, plans, drawings, and specifications needed to build automobiles',[21] but Ford United States would retain control of Canadian operations, with 51 per cent of equity.

As a latecomer in internationalization as compared to the Olds Motor Company and the Cadillac Automobile Company, Ford benefited from strengths in the extensive use of machine tools as compared with the European automakers, but also faced the challenge of widespread prejudice against American cars sold in Europe.

At first, Ford exported to Great Britain through agents. Ford did not bear any duties on automobiles exported to Britain, and its low prices helped its expansion into the British market. However, other European countries imposed protective import duties, which complicated Ford's expansion into these markets. The rising sales in Britain, especially with the introduction of the Model T, made it attractive to establish an assembly plant in Britain, in order to reduce shipping and other transaction costs associated with exports. The Ford Motor Company Ltd (England) was established in March 1911. The manufacturing plant in Manchester followed the American production pattern almost exactly, with obvious exceptions such as right-hand drive: 'Variations at the factory were rare', and 'in production and purchasing techniques the resemblance between Manchester and Detroit was also close'.[22]

By 1921, Ford had opened plants in France, Denmark, Ireland, and Argentina. All these affiliates operated as branch plants, receiving 'the same general letters of instruction, the same communications about accounting, sales, production, and purchasing'. Marketing was also done according to 'the Ford Bible' emanating from Detroit.[23] ∎

Case example As another historical example, Disney opened Disneyland, its first theme park, in Anaheim, California (United States), in 1955. The park's success helped the company to open a second theme park, Walt Disney World, in Orlando, Florida (United States), in 1971. It then opened Tokyo Disneyland (Japan) in 1983, Disneyland Paris (France) in 1992, Hong Kong Disneyland in 2005, and Shanghai Disney Resort (Mainland China) in 2016.

Disney is an international projector, and Tokyo Disneyland, Disneyland Paris, and Hong Kong Disneyland cloned the original park in Anaheim. For example, except for some subtle local adaptations, Hong Kong Disneyland mirrored the Anaheim park, 'from Main Street, USA to the Space Mountain roller coaster to Sleeping Beauty's castle'.[24] As noted by Wing Chao, Vice Chairman for the Asia Pacific development of Disney parks: '(T)he Disney American spirit is in the architecture and the whole ambiance . . . We're bringing Disney America . . . to Hong Kong.'[25] All the face characters in these international parks are played by 'white actors who speak only English'.[26]

However, planting the US approach in Hong Kong without an in-depth understanding of the Hong Kong situation 'left Mickey Mouse looking like Cinderella's stepmother'.[27] Nasty headlines clouded the opening period. In addition to labour relations problems, a Disney official prevented government food inspectors from entering Disney until they removed their caps and badges to be indistinguishable from other visitors; Hong Kong pop stars filming promotional videos for the park for free were enraged by impolite treatment.

Disney's unfamiliarity with the local culture was exemplified by Disney's failure to host unanticipated larger numbers of visitors during the Chinese New Year holidays in late January and early February 2006. Disney sold discounted and undated one-day tickets, which allowed holders to visit Disney any time in the next six months except special days designated by Disney. Hong Kong had a four-day public holiday for the Chinese New Year, but mainland China had a one-week holiday. Disney designated only the Hong Kong public holidays as special days, and failed to anticipate the large number of mainlanders who were brought by Chinese tour agencies. Faced with swelling visitors beyond its size to host, Disney turned away thousands of visitors who had bought tickets. Ultimately, Disney's enragement of its visitors led the Hong Kong government to ask the firm to improve its ticketing.

In September 2006, Hong Kong Disneyland celebrated its first anniversary. Attendance exceeded 5 million, poorer than the expected 5.6 million visitors. After a sharp decline of attendance in the second year, visitor numbers again increased over time, reaching similar attendance as in the opening year. Hong Kong Disneyland clearly needed time to understand fully customers from Hong Kong and mainland China.[28] ∎

The third archetype of administrative heritage is the ***international coordinator***: this centrally managed firm's international success does not build primarily on home country FSAs embodied in products exported internationally (as was the case with the centralized exporter), nor does it simply transfer FSAs to foreign subsidiaries to replicate home country success (as was the case with the international projector). The international coordinator builds upon a tradition of managing international operations, both upstream and downstream, through a tightly controlled but still flexible logistics function. ***International operations are specialized in specific value-added activities and form vertical value chains across borders. The MNE's key FSAs are in efficiently linking these geographically dispersed operations through seamless logistics***. Many large MNEs in natural resources industries fit this archetype. They search for relevant resources internationally, manufacture in the most cost-efficient locations, and sell their products wherever there is demand for them.

Case example As a historical example, the oil major BP plc (formerly the British Petroleum Company plc) was established as the Anglo-Persian Oil Company (APOC) in 1909, to develop the oilfield in southwest Persia. Anglo-Persian soon constructed a refinery at Abadan on the Shatt-al-Arab waterway in 1913 and started to sell fuel oil to the British navy. In 1914, the British government bought a controlling interest in order to ensure an oil supply for the British navy. In these early days, the expertise of Anglo-Persian was its ability to link its oil supply in Persia with its customers in Britain. After World War I, however, Anglo-Persian expanded into new markets, building refineries around the world. By 1938, its products were sold in Europe, Africa, the Middle East, India, and Australia. However, prior to World War II, Anglo-Iranian Oil Company (AIOC, renamed from Anglo-Persian in 1935) still had only two major sources for oil: Iraq and Iran.

Over time, BP (which had another name change, from AIOC to British Petroleum Company plc in 1954) diversified its sources of oil, finding oil in the United Kingdom (the North Sea), the United States (Alaska), Abu Dhabi, Australia, Colombia, Kuwait, Norway, Papua New Guinea, and Qatar. Today, BP's businesses in seventy-eight countries include a wide variety of activities in exploration and production of crude oil and natural gas; refining and marketing oil and gas; and manufacturing and marketing petrochemicals. Almost all of the company's activities rely on trans-border coordination.

For example, because of the long distances between natural gas fields and many major markets such as the United States, the United Kingdom, Japan, and South Korea, BP's liquefied natural gas (LNG) business operates its own vessels as a 'mobile pipeline' to serve its customers. In BP's words: 'LNG bridges the gap: gas is lifted from underground, chilled to liquid, transported on ships from one part of the world to another, and then warmed back into gas to fuel a power plant, factory or home.' Further, BP also manages long-term, point-to-point contracts to integrate supply coming from specific production sites with demand in specific markets. For example, in Guangdong, China, BP operates an LNG import facility, which is supplied from the North West Shelf project in Australia.[29] ∎

Case example As another historical example, Logitech, a firm with a Swiss heritage and the world-leading mouse manufacturer, is also an international coordinator that has been very effective in piloting its various operations dispersed around the globe. The company has a manufacturing site in Suzhou (China), many distribution centres in Europe, North America, and Asia, and engineering centres, specializing in different technologies, located in Romanel-sur-Morges (Switzerland), California (United States), Texas (United States), Utah (United States), Chennai (India), Hsinchu (Taiwan), Vancouver (Canada), Mississauga (Canada), and Munich (Germany).[30]

To a large extent, Logitech's success depends on the international coordination of its activities. For example, its Swiss engineering centre develops new products in cooperation with several external design partners such as Design Partners, located in Ireland. Designs are sent to Fremont, California (Logitech's operating headquarters), for approval, after which the Hsinchu engineering centre in Taiwan performs pilot runs to check for any potential manufacturing problems. Finally, the products are moved to Suzhou, China, for high-volume manufacturing, and transported to distributors and large retailers around the world. The distribution centres also perform product localization functions, such as adding local language manuals and software CDs. Similarly, most new products designed at other R&D centres are tested in Hsinchu, Taiwan, manufactured in Suzhou, China, and subsequently shipped to distributors, retailers, and consumers.[31] ■

The fourth and final archetype of administrative heritage is the *multi-centred MNE*: this firm's international success does not build primarily on knowledge-based FSAs developed in the home country. *The multi-centred MNE consists of a set of entrepreneurial subsidiaries abroad, which are key to knowledge-based FSA development. National responsiveness is the foundation of the international strategy. The non-location-bound FSAs that hold these firms together are minimal: common financial governance and the identity and specific business interests of the founders or main owners (typically entrepreneurial families or financial investors).* Ultimately, the multi-centred MNE should be viewed as a portfolio of largely independent businesses. Many older European MNEs fit this mould. Unlike many of the large Japanese MNEs, these European MNEs expanded internationally before the second half of the twentieth century, in an era of trade, transport, and communication barriers. They operated with highly independent local production facilities to satisfy local market needs, and wealthy financial investors provided the required financial resources in an environment of poorly functioning financial markets.

Case example As a historical example, in 1891, the two Philips brothers, Gerard and Anton, established the Philips company in order to manufacture incandescent light bulbs in the Netherlands. The small size of the home country soon forced Philips to export its products to foreign countries. In 1921, Philips started to establish sales affiliates in the United States, Canada, France, etc.

However, after World War I, rising trade protectionism also forced Philips to establish factories in countries where it wished to sell. In Europe, most nations imposed import duties and quotas, aiming to protect domestic industry. As a result, Philips expanded its manufacturing operations in Czechoslovakia, Yugoslavia, Romania, Hungary, and Poland during this period. Philips ran its affiliates as semi-autonomous organizations because high cultural differences among the host countries acted as a major barrier to a more centralized or coordinated approach.

After World War II, the 'daughter companies had become [even] more independent',[32] mainly because the affiliates had continued to operate without much contact between the headquarters and the affiliates during the war. Consequently, Philips had to decide 'whether to revert to the pre-war system, or to continue on the road which the separate parts had already taken'.[33] It decided to stick with the newly established, decentralized course.

In the 1950s, Philips continued to set up new plants as a result of both trade barriers and the need to adapt its products to local conditions. At that stage, it manufactured in more than fifty countries and sold in more than seventy. Yet, it did not even have any specific department to monitor overseas operations, but only coordinators at the headquarters to maintain connections with the foreign affiliates. The management board was informed about overseas conditions through both direct reporting from its affiliates and personal travelling by board members all over the world. In 1954, Philips established the International Concern Council, consisting of all the principal managers from around the world and the management board, to review the past year, plan for the future, provide opportunities for personal contacts, arrange promotions, etc. ∎

Case example As another historical example, Lafarge Group (now LafargeHolcim, established after a 2015 merger with the Swiss cement company Holcim), a firm with French roots and one of the largest manufacturers of building materials, had largely adopted a multi-centred approach, while also encouraging knowledge sharing within the company.

The company's official goals were: 'first, to ensure total cohesion within a major multi-national Group present in 75 different countries; and second, to encourage the exchange of best practices, yet leave operating units with a high degree of autonomy'.[34]

To meet these goals, Lafarge was organized into three levels, as a 'multi-local' organization: the corporate level, the divisional level, and the business unit level. 'The Corporate level defines the Group's long-term strategies and ensures they are implemented', '[t]he Divisions are responsible for enhancing performance and for the long-term success of their respective business segment', and '[the business unit] most often corresponds to a Division's business segment or to a business segment in a given country or geographical area'.[35] Examples of business units included: Lafarge Gypsum Korea, the Business Unit of the Gypsum Division in South Korea; Fabrica Nacional de Cementos, the Business Unit of the Cement Division in Venezuela; Lafarge Bétons, the concrete Business Unit in France; Lafarge Aggregates, the Aggregates Business Unit in the United Kingdom; and Lafarge Dachsysteme, the Roofing Business Unit in Germany.[36]

Lafarge provided the following rationale for its decentralized organization: 'Each of our businesses is primarily a local business: our products cannot economically be transported over significant distances, construction markets have strong local characteristics, proximity is important to our customers, relationships with local communities are key, and much of our know-how originates from local experience.'[37] ∎

Is the above set of four MNE archetypes a complete set, given the large variety of MNE governance forms in practice? No: although the four archetypes probably describe the bulk of most large MNEs, especially the *Fortune Global 500* ones, there are other types. **However, the commonality among all these types is the transfer of at least some FSAs across borders.**

A *first example* from the late nineteenth century, not included in the above archetypes, is that of freestanding companies: companies that were set up abroad – mainly by British and Dutch investors – often in their home country's colonies, without a prior domestic production base. Harrisons & Crosfield, the Hong Kong and Shanghai Bank, and Rio Tinto Zinc were all established in this way.[38] These cases went beyond the simple financing of foreign operations (in fact, simple financing, in the sense of portfolio investment, often appeared impossible, given the inefficiency of the capital markets at that time). Here, entrepreneurial judgement and sound (though rather basic) governance were deployed internationally. The prior (macro-level) institutional linking of home and host countries through colonial relationships greatly facilitated this micro-level process. In other words, public policy and institutional convergence greatly reduced the additional costs of doing business abroad, and provided home country entrepreneurs with more direct access to the location advantages of the host countries involved. The coordination skills of the home country entrepreneurs thereby allowed for the establishment of easy linkages between abundant financial resources and project-management skills in the colonial power and abundant raw materials or cheap labour in the host country. The focus on coordination suggests at least some similarity with the international coordinator archetype, discussed above. To the extent that freestanding companies were actually part of larger business networks, the value of entrepreneurial coordination skills and other managerial services (in addition to the obvious value of substituting for imperfect capital markets) was even more apparent.

A *second example* of firms that may not fit the above archetypes includes many emerging economy MNEs (EMNEs). These firms typically do not derive their strengths primarily from advanced technology, brand names, or a sophisticated logistics apparatus. Rather, building upon generally available resources in their home country such as low-cost labour and various forms of government support (e.g., access to capital, usage of the government international trade and investment apparatus, etc.), these firms thrive on recombining whatever FSAs they may possess with resources accessed abroad. Many of these firms' initial FSAs when crossing borders revolve around – or result from – entrepreneurial judgement, knowledge borrowed from advanced economy MNEs, and disciplined execution of a firm-level strategy. Even when supported by cheap home country resources and an activist home nation government with deep pockets, international success will only materialize if the EMNE can effectively link new knowledge and other assets sourced abroad, with a set of internal strengths.

EMNE FSAs identified in the literature and facilitating international expansion in early stages include:[39]

- Entrepreneurial quality of management (e.g., in the Taiwanese company Acer);
- Management capabilities in effective strategy execution (e.g., in the Mexican cement company Cemex);
- Learned technologies, resulting from a role as licensee or subcontractor for technology-rich MNEs from developed economies, as in the context of out-sourcing strategies in offshore locations (e.g., Indian software development companies in the ICT business);
- Learned knowledge from early alliance formation with other MNEs, whereby the EMNE may have provided strengths in government relations or access to local resources to the alliance (e.g., the Chinese company Haier with various partners);
- Privileged access to home country resources (e.g., Venezuelan resource companies);
- Cost innovations/operational excellence, sometimes as the result of func-tioning in adverse environmental circumstances and ill-functioning external markets (valid for most EMNEs);
- Ability to adapt technology/products to emerging economy needs (e.g., as suggested by the Tata Group's Nano car).

Whatever archetype an MNE falls under, history suggests that the MNE will usually overestimate the international transferability from a mere technical standpoint, the potential for foreign deployment, and the profitable exploitation of its FSAs. Even when knowledge transfer across borders is achieved rather easily, contextual variables change: first, the forces that reflect extended rivalry (relevant competitors, suppliers, customers, potential entrants, and substitutes); second, government regulation and other non-market forces, such as environ-mental pressure groups; and third, the other relevant stakeholders in the broader business and economic environment. What may constitute an FSA in the home country – whether a set of distinct stand-alone resources, a routine, or even a recombination capability – does not necessarily confer the same value in a foreign context. Whereas upstream resource bundles – such as a superior sourcing system or unique product technology – may have universal, transfer-able appeal, this usually does not hold for more downstream strengths, where the interface with the customer is key to successful sales and profit performance. Here, substantial investments may be required to allow the deployment and profitable exploitation of the firm's existing FSAs, which may have limited international exploitation potential without such investments. More specifically, if many FSAs developed at home are actually location-bound, the MNE's challenge is to develop a new set of location-bound FSAs in host countries that permit successful operations there.[40]

Non-Transferable (or Location-Bound) Firm-Specific Advantages

Let us turn now to the second concept of this book's unifying framework: location-bound or non-transferable firm-specific advantages. These FSAs cannot be easily transferred, deployed, and exploited in foreign markets. There are four main types of location-bound FSAs. *First,* stand-alone resources linked to location advantages, such as a network of privileged retail locations leading to a dominant market share in the home market (as often found in retail banking), are immobile, and therefore inherently non-transferable. The immobility of domestic networks is a key reason why Japan-based Kao has had only little success in penetrating foreign markets.

Case example In 1996, Kao was Japan's largest consumer goods company, with a quarter of the shampoo market, three-quarters of the bleach market, and half of the laundry detergent market.

One of the main reasons for Kao's dominant domestic position was its control of a comprehensive distribution system within Japan. Kao owned Hansha, a wholesale distributor, which distributed only Kao's products. As a result, Kao was able to supply small shops easily and also prevent outsiders from entering the market. Moreover, Hansha allowed Kao to gain privileged information on consumers' shopping habits. However, 'in Europe and America Kao has failed to build the comprehensive distribution system that it has in Japan'.[41] In 1996, around 20 per cent of Kao's sales came from overseas markets; by 2019, the percentage of foreign sales had risen to nearly 37 per cent, in ascending order of proportion from Europe, North America, and Asia/Oceania. Kao has still not been able to replicate fully its domestic success abroad.[42] ■

Case example The immobility of domestic networks has also brought tremendous challenges to many foreign retail banks in Japan, such as Citibank (now Citigroup). Despite its leading position in the US retail banking industry and a large network of branches in the United States, Citibank found it difficult to access Japanese customers when it decided to target individual consumers in 1984. It took Citi-Japan a full ten years to break into the Japanese market. According to Citibank, 'retail banking . . . is like the petrol-station business: you've got to have your pumps in all the right locations. In Japan, the best spots are hard to get'.[43] In Japan, land prices were extremely high, and building a profitable retail network required large-scale investments and substantial time to establish the network. Moreover, Japanese consumers tended to view foreign banks as less trustworthy than local banks.

By 1990, Citibank was 'the last of 83 foreign banks in Japan still interested in retail banking'.[44] The number of its retail branches in Japan had grown from six in 1985 to nineteen in 1993, but it was still a minor player: the smallest Japanese retail bank had forty-one branches in 1985.[45]

However, things changed in the mid-1990s, as a result of both Japan's financial turmoil and Citibank's new strategies. In the early 1990s, Citibank hired Masamoto Yashiro from Exxon to head Citi-Japan. With his extensive knowledge of Exxon's retail gas stations, Yashiro saw the need for a large local distribution channel in Japan. Rather than building branches or purchasing a local retailing bank, Yashiro came up with the idea of linking Citi-Japan's financial network with the ATMs of Japanese commercial banks. Although this idea did not come to fruition, Japanese regulators did allow Citi-Japan to affiliate with the Japanese Postal System in 1999. In this way, Citi-Japan gained access to more than 20,000 branches of the Post Office and its ATMs. In return, the Post Office was provided the opportunity to learn about Citi-Japan's funds management capability. This learning was viewed as particularly useful, because the Japanese Post Office was expanding into the banking and insurance business.[46]

When many Japanese banks then encountered severe financial problems, Japanese consumers stopped viewing Citigroup as inferior to Japanese banks. Its affiliation with the Post Office even created the perception that Citigroup was more trustworthy, as the Post Office was widely viewed as the safest institution for deposits in Japan. After decades of operation, Citi-Japan did gain some market share in Japan thanks to the above partnership. In 2014, the bank operated thirty-two retail branches and had 740,000 retail customers throughout the country, and it had attracted Yen 2.44 trillion (approximately US $20 billion) in deposits. However, as compared to the performance of Citi's other foreign subsidiaries, the retail banking business of Citi-Japan was less profitable due to not having a large and wholly owned, dedicated network of retail outlets as in the United States, i.e., a location-bound FSA. In 2015, Citigroup Inc. sold Citi-Japan's retail banking operation to Sumitomo Mitsui Banking Corporation (SMBC), the third-largest commercial bank in Japan, for approximately Yen 40 billion (US $333 million). 'This decision furthers Citi's global strategy of focusing our resources where we feel we have a competitive advantage, which includes our Institutional Clients Group businesses in Japan', said Citi-Japan CEO Peter Eliot in a statement that rationalized the firm's failure in retail banking.[47] ▪

The **second** kind of non-transferable FSA: other resources such as local marketing knowledge and reputational resources (e.g., brand names). These may not have the same value across borders, either because they are not applicable to a host country context, or because they are simply not valued to the same extent by foreign stakeholders.

Case example As a historical example, we can illustrate the importance of reputational resources with the example of the Polo Ralph Lauren Company, a leading company in so-called 'opulent lifestyle products'. In North America, its brands – such as Polo by Ralph Lauren – have long been viewed as reflecting a 'classic American gentry style'. In Europe, by contrast, Ralph Lauren has built up a reputation as a high-quality sportswear manufacturer, known for high-quality sports shirts and golf jackets with the distinct Polo logo.

When the company decided it wanted to expand more rapidly in Europe in 2002, especially by pushing one of its brands that was representative of its upper-class American style, the difference between its European and American reputational resources became very apparent. According to one leading men's fashion news magazine, 'Europeans see [Ralph] Lauren as classic sportswear – the epitome being his polo shirt. This typecast won't be easy to overcome'.[48] ∎

Third, local best practices (i.e., routines considered highly effective and efficient in one country, such as incentive systems for highly skilled workers or buyer–supplier relations) may not be considered as such abroad by a variety of stake-holders, and may even be deemed illegal.

Case example A historical example in this context is the assessment of service quality in the hotel industry in locations such as Hong Kong versus the United States. Hong Kong-based hotel groups such as the Peninsula have developed a high quality of services, partially because of Hong Kong's location characteristics as a regional business centre and travelling site. This quality of services is manifested by a high ratio of employees to rooms, among other factors.

However, when these firms bought US hotels in the late 1980s, such practices were not appropriate, simply because labour in the United States is more expensive than in Hong Kong. Therefore, maintaining the same high ratio of employees to rooms, though viewed as a best practice in Hong Kong luxury hotels, was inefficient in US luxury hotels. As a result, the Hong Kong hotel groups had to rely more on other methods to assess and improve the quality of services in their US subsidiaries, such as a focus on more in-house training and the recruiting of more enthusiastic and younger staff.[49] ∎

The *fourth* kind of non-transferable FSA includes a firm's domestic recombin-ation capability. While this may have led to a dominant market share and superior expansion rate in the home country market, as the firm engaged in product diversification or innovation, and thereby increased its geographic market coverage domestically, this domestic capability may not be adept enough to confront the additional complexities of foreign markets.

Case example Office Depot, the leading office supply retailer in the United States, entered the Japanese market in 1997. Trying to follow its American retailing style, Office Depot found it hard to attract Japanese customers. Office Depot opened stores in Japan following the American format: more than 20,000 square feet in size, wide aisles, signs in English, etc. In other words, the firm's initial focus was on transferring its domestic routines rather than its recombination capabilities.

However, such an American format not only significantly increased the operating costs of the stores, but also failed to meet the habits of Japanese customers.[50] On the one hand, both the personnel costs and the rents in Japan were significantly higher than in the United States, resulting in excessive operating costs. On the other hand, Japanese customers did not value the American format: the large size gave them an unfavourable warehouse impression, as they were used to narrow aisles. In addition, the English signs confused them. On top of these problems, Office Depot needed to provide Japanese-style office products, different from

American ones, which it had to purchase from local suppliers, who did not necessarily offer them the best possible prices.

More recently, the company has tried to use its recombination ability to adapt to the idiosyncrasies of the Japanese market. For example, it started to operate both large and small stores, and strengthened its delivery capabilities.[51] However, the company only achieved limited success. In 2010, Office Depot sold all its retail operations in Japan to Tokyo-based retailer Kakuyasu, but continued to participate in this market through licensing agreements. 'We believe the combination of Office Depot's brand, merchandising and sourcing capabilities, coupled with Kakuyasu's multi-channel business, distribution network and local experience, will significantly strengthen our competitive position in this market,' said Mr Charlie Brown, President of the International Division of Office Depot to rationalize the firm's failure.[52] In 2016, the firm decided to eliminate its international division because of disappointing performance, and by 2018 the firm had divested most of its international operations in Europe, Asia (South Korea and China), and Oceania. It does still have trading and procurement operations in Asia. ∎

One of the most interesting aspects of all four of these kinds of location-bound FSAs (immobile resources linked to location advantages, local marketing knowledge and reputational resources, local best practices in the form of routines, and a domestic recombination ability) is that the corresponding FSA in each host country will need to be created or acquired from third parties operating in these foreign markets. Linking investments (such as Citigroup's affiliation with the Japanese Post Office, above) may be required to allow the matching of the MNE's internationally transferable FSAs with the relevant characteristics in host countries and regions. These linking investments can be viewed as investments in host country or host region responsiveness.[53]

Case example As a historical example, the Taiwanese computer manufacturer Acer Inc. engaged in such linking investments when it entered Mexico in 1989. An experienced original equipment manufacturer for IBM and other top international PC companies, Acer did not have a distribution network in Mexico, nor did it benefit from strong brand recognition. Acer therefore contracted out its distribution and marketing activities to Computec de Mexico, a local Mexican distributor, and, in 1992, formed Acer Computec Latino America (ACLA), a joint venture between Acer and Computec. Acer manufactured the PCs, but Computec (and later ACLA) was given high autonomy at the downstream end of the value chain in Mexico. They focused on small businesses and home PCs, and continued to invest in TV advertisements and other marketing media even during the 1994 peso collapse.

This strategy paid off: by 1992, Acer's linking investments had made it the dominant brand in Mexico.[54] After having been listed on the Mexican Stock Exchange for a period of four years, in 2000 ACLA was privatized as 'part of Acer's group-wide re-engineering effort that seeks to increase synergy between the group companies and the Taiwanese parent'.[55] ∎

Location Advantages

Having discussed transferable and non-transferable FSAs, *let us turn now to the third concept of the unifying framework: location advantages*. The MNE's economic success does not occur in a spatially homogeneous environment: location matters. Specifically, many firms are successful internationally because they take advantage of a favourable local environment. Location advantages represent the entire set of strengths characterizing a specific location, and useable by firms operating in that location.[56] These strengths should always be assessed relative to the useable strengths of other locations. Such strengths are really stocks of resources accessible to firms operating locally, and not accessible, or less so, to firms lacking local operations. Location advantages are often instrumental to the type of FSAs that can be developed by locally operating firms relative to firms operating elsewhere.

For example, abundant natural resources may help the creation of successful firms in the natural resource industry.

Case example Consider the example of natural resources in Canada. Domestic firms have been able to leverage domestic natural endowments to compete successfully in the resource industry. Ranking fourth in the world in terms of natural resources reserves (subsoil assets and timber resources) behind only Saudi Arabia, Norway, and Venezuela, Canada has significant reserves of wood, water, natural gas, oil, gold, coal, copper, iron ore, nickel, potash, uranium, and zinc. In 2019, the Toronto Stock Exchange (TSX) and TSX Venture Exchange had 1,138 mining companies listed, representing 50 per cent of the world's public mining companies, ranging from emerging explorers to world-class producers.[57] As of 2019, the five largest Canadian mining companies included: Barrick Gold Corporation, the second-largest gold mining company in the world; Nutrien Ltd, the largest producer of potash in the world, created in 2016 through merging PotashCorp and Agrium Inc.; Agnico Eagle Mines Ltd, a producer of precious metals with mines in Finland, Mexico, and Canada; Teck Resources Ltd, the largest producer of steelmaking coal in North America and the world's second-largest exporter of seaborne steelmaking coal; and Kirkland Lake Gold Ltd, one of the world's foremost gold mining companies, formed in 2016 through a merger of Canada's Kirkland Lake Gold and Australia's Newmarket Gold.[58] ■

A superior educational system – another location advantage – will support firms that build upon sophisticated human resource skills.

Case example As a historical example, in Germany, the dual system for vocational education and training (VET) has historically provided a stable source of highly skilled workers for German firms, and has helped these firms build a reputation for high product quality. VET covers several hundred occupations and focuses on the majority of young Germans who will not pursue university-level studies. The responsibility for training is shared by both public training schools and private companies. Such VET programmes, specialized in printing, optics, automotive assembly, hydraulics, etc., have historically led to 'highly skilled, technologically competent graduates who are thoroughly familiar with the flexible manufacturing systems typical of today's industry'.[59] VET programmes have thereby played an important role in helping a large number of German firms (Siemens, BASF, Volkswagen, etc.) retain their competitiveness in product performance and quality. ∎

For similar reasons, the presence of a demanding and sophisticated local market for specific products will likely foster local innovation in the relevant industry.

Case example Consider the history of the Japanese home appliances industry. With limited natural resources and a large population, Japan has long been characterized by high energy costs, high living expenses, and small dwellings, mainly apartments.

Customer needs regarding home appliances have reflected these housing conditions. Air conditioners, washing machines, etc. need to be compact, convenient, quiet, and energy-efficient in order to fit into small apartments and use minimal energy. Such requirements have historically led Japanese firms to respond in innovative ways. For example, in the 1980s:

> when market surveys revealed that workers living in apartments tend to do their laundry early in the morning or late at night – and that the sound irritated their neighbours – Japanese washing-machine makers came up with high-tech solutions. Their steel suppliers came up with noise-absorbent sheets – a layer of resin or polymer sandwiched between two thin steel plates. The new technique, also used to quiet noisy refrigerators, has led to a buying boom in two markets which had experienced virtually zero growth for several years.[60] ∎

Location advantages do not confer an equal strength to all locally operating firms vis-à-vis firms operating elsewhere. Rather, the more effective and efficient use of location advantages by some firms – usually the combination of these location advantages with specific proprietary resources – may confer to them an additional FSA over other locally operating firms. This may explain why only a few firms from world-renowned domestic industries, such as the French perfume industry, have been able to grow internationally.

Case example As a classic example, in France, almost half of the perfume business has historically been concentrated in and around Grasse, a small town in southern France with 'the largest concentration on earth of the most fragrant species of flowers'.[61] Such unique natural resources and three centuries of experience in the perfume business have helped French firms develop world-class processing capabilities and craft skills in perfume development.

However, only a handful of French perfume firms have grown into large-scale MNEs. These firms, such as Moët Hennessy Louis Vuitton (LVMH), were best able to combine generally available, localized knowledge with modern product development processes. Traditionally, perfume firms relied on a 'nose' – a fragrance expert – to determine the right combination of fragrances to be included in a new perfume. However, most successful perfume developers – such as LVMH – now develop products 'backwards': they start with a concept, then design an ad campaign, and finally focus on the actual perfume to be produced.[62] ∎

Location advantages can vary widely in their geographical scope. In some cases, a location advantage accrues to all firms operating in a particular country, for example if the government has created a favourable tax regime for specific economic activities, or general business incentives for skill upgrading of human resources.

Case example Consider India's location advantages. The impressive growth of India over the past three decades has been attributed to a series of country-specific factors after the economic reforms in 1991, including the abolishment of barriers to international trade and investment, tax reforms, deregulation, and the promotion of privatization. In addition, India offers a large supply of skilled workers with university degrees and proficiency in English. All these factors have boosted the Indian economy and have led to an impressive GDP growth rate during the past thirty years. The development of country-specific advantages in India has helped Indian firms go abroad to exploit their FSAs through outward FDI. From 2000 to 2018, outward FDI from Indian firms has grown from only US $514 million to around US $11 billion.[63] A number of other emerging economies in Asia might want to follow the Indian formula for success, but this will be challenging, as it is almost impossible to replicate the trajectory over time of the entire portfolio of parameters that led to India's success at the macro-level. ∎

In some cases, location advantages accrue only to firms operating in part of a country. Economic clusters, for example, are usually located in only part of a country. The physical locations of the firms that constitute the heart of the cluster determine the cluster boundaries.

Case example The United States, as the leading country for biotechnology innovation, has a number of established and emerging biotechnology clusters – small, distinct regions that have been called 'self-perpetuating centres of innovation and, hopefully, profit'.[64] Based upon data about research funding, lab space, the number of patents, the amount of venture capital funding, and workforce size, the Greater Boston cluster is ranked first, followed by clusters in the San Francisco Bay Area, the region of New York/New Jersey, the BioHealth Capital Region (Washington DC, Maryland, Virginia), and San Diego.[65]

A successful biotech cluster requires four pillars: at least one large, non-profit research university with a strong biomedical curriculum; venture capitalists who provide funding to biotech companies; local governmental support in creating a favourable environment for biotech firms; and a few publicly traded biotech companies.[66]

Firms tend to invest in established clusters to get close to the research environment there. One well-documented historical example was the shift of the command centre for global research at Novartis AG from Switzerland to the campus of the Massachusetts Institute of Technology, to be close to 'the centre of genetic research in the US',[67] and 'to parlay the knowledge gleaned from gene hunting into the next generation of innovation treatments'.[68] As noted by Daniel Vasella, CEO from 1996 to 2010, 'basing its research headquarters alongside the Boston area's booming biotechnology industry, academic institutions and their pools of scientific talent will play a critical role in discovering those drugs'.[69]

Before this shift, Novartis had already established its US base in New Jersey, and had sited the Novartis Institute for Functional Genomics in La Jolla, California. The newly established command centre was close to the Greater Boston cluster, the operation in New Jersey is close to the New York/New Jersey/Connecticut 'Pharm Country', and the institute in California is close to the San Diego cluster. ■

In other cases, location advantages reach across country borders. The creation of cross-border location advantages is one of the key purposes of most regional trading and investment agreements, intended at least partly to confer a location advantage to insiders at the expense of outsiders.

Case example The North American Free Trade Agreement (NAFTA) and its successor (as of 2020), the United States–Mexico–Canada Agreement (USMCA), have changed the distribution of trade. The sharp increase of trade among the NAFTA countries was partly the result of changes in trade patterns:

> the NAFTA may have deflected trade internally that would otherwise have taken place between individual North American countries and [the rest of the world] (the NAFTA dealt Mexico and Canada a price advantage over other countries and produced incentives for US customers not only to shift from domestic goods to imports, but to substitute imports from Mexico and Canada for imports from elsewhere).[70] ■

Another way to classify location advantages, as opposed to classifying by geographical scope (which may extend to a narrow cluster, a broader region within a country, a country, or a region spanning more than a country), is to classify them by what motivates a firm to conduct economic activity in that location. Because most of the book's examples to this point concerned *home country* location advantages (e.g., Canada's abundant natural resources conferring an advantage to domestic resource-based industries), the following discussion and classification of a firm's motivations will, for balance, focus on *host country* location advantages.

Why would an MNE want to engage in FDI in a host country? First of all, a key definition: **foreign direct investment** is the allocation of resource bundles (combinations of physical, financial, human, knowledge, and reputational resources) by an MNE in a host country, with the purpose of performing business activities over which the MNE retains strategic control in that country. The answer is that an MNE should engage in FDI only if the host country confers a location advantage relative to the home country. In each case, the value proposition of the foreign activity must be more attractive than alternative value propositions at home. We can distinguish among four motivations to perform activities in a host country rather than at home.[71]

The first motivation, **natural resource seeking**, entails the search for physical, financial, or human resources in host countries. These resources are in principle not proprietary, and their availability in host countries (which constitutes the location advantage of those countries) means that investment abroad leads to higher value creation than investment at home. A precondition to such investment is that the host country institutional environment actually allows foreign MNEs to access these resources.

Case example Faced with the continuing growth in the demand for energy, oil companies like ExxonMobil are striving to replenish their reserves by developing or buying new oilfields around the world. ExxonMobil, the largest refiner and one of the largest publicly traded companies by market capitalization in the world, has been expanding its access to new reserves through various forms of FDI in the past several years.

For example, in 2012, the Nigerian subsidiaries of ExxonMobil, Total SA, Chevron Petroleum, and Nexen Petroleum (now CNOOC Petroleum North America, which is Chinese owned) formed a joint venture for oil exploration from the coast of Nigeria.[72] As of 2016, the joint venture had found a reservoir which potentially holds 1 billion barrels of oil under 2 miles of ocean floor.[73] A few years earlier, in 2014, ExxonMobil established a joint venture with Hess and China's CNOOC to explore oil resources in Guyana. As of early 2019, the ExxonMobil-led joint venture had announced thirteen discoveries of oil reserves off the coast of Guyana, which increased ExxonMobil's recoverable oil to 5.5 billion barrels of oil equivalent.[74] ∎

The second motivation, **market seeking**, reflects the search for customers in host countries. Firms are market seeking when they conclude that deploying productive activities and selling in the foreign market confers higher value to the firm than engaging in alternative investment projects at home. The host country location advantage is the presence of customers willing and able to purchase the firm's products. Note that market seeking is not the same as mere exporting: market seeking involves business activities in the host country, based on resource bundles transferred there over which the MNE retains strategic control.

Case example With a population of more than 1.4 billion people in 2019 and a continuously growing middle class, China has become an attractive market for many US food services brands, including Kentucky Fried Chicken (KFC), McDonald's, Dairy Queen, and Pizza Hut.

As a classic case, KFC was the first US food services company to invest in China, opening the first unit in Beijing in 1987. 'From the opening day the Beijing unit has served an average of 9,000 customers a day. Its astounding popularity has broken all the company's world sales records.'[75] Individual restaurants had sales as high as US $4 million per year, and the margins in China were more than twice the US average.[76]

Another early success story has been McDonald's. As early as 1994, its huge 700-seat outlet in Beijing was reportedly serving '20,000 McDonald's customers a day, and as many as 50,000 on holidays'.[77] ∎

Case example With the world's second-largest population (1.39 billion people in 2019) and a rapidly increasing number of internet users, India represents a promising market for online e-commerce retailers, such as Amazon and Walmart.

Amazon entered India with the launch of its shopping website junglee.com in 2012,[78] which was replaced in 2017 by Amazon.in.[79] The website offers more than 12 million products from over 14,000 Indian and global brands, covering clothing, electronics, toys, jewellery, books, and video games. Amazon had approximately 150 million registered users in India and was the second-largest online retailer with a market share of 31.2 per cent, just behind Flipkart with a market share of 31.9 per cent,[80] in India's $33 billion e-commerce market in 2018.[81] At the same time, Amazon was trying to gain access to physical retailers. For example, Amazon acquired 49 per cent of Future Coupon, a subsidiary of Future Retail, India's second-largest retail chain in 2019. Future Retail operates more than 1,500 stores in India and owns several supermarket brands.[82]

Another company with a strong e-commerce arm that entered the Indian market is Walmart. Walmart entered India in 2007 through a joint venture with Bharti Enterprises, a local retailer.[83] In 2018, Walmart expanded into bookselling and acquired 77 per cent of Flipkart for $16 billion. Flipkart, founded by two former Amazon employees in 2007, was at that time India's largest online bookseller.[84] This acquisition allowed Walmart to compete more effectively with Amazon in the Indian market. ∎

The third motivation for an MNE to invest abroad, *strategic resource seeking*, is the desire to gain access to advanced resources in the sphere of upstream knowledge, downstream knowledge, administrative knowledge, or reputational resources. These resources, which constitute the host country location advantages, are in principle not generally accessible, in contrast to the resources sought with natural resource seeking and market seeking. Therefore, this type of FDI typically involves taking over other companies, engaging in alliance activity, or becoming an insider in foreign knowledge clusters. The underlying reasons to engage in strategic resource seeking often include the goal to become an established industry player in a set of strategically important knowledge development centres or output markets.

Case example As a historical example, the Korean firm Samsung Electronics is now viewed as one of the world's leading companies in consumer electronics and has made up for the years of trying to catch up with foreign technologies in consumer electronics.

From the early 1970s to the early 1990s, Samsung was able to reduce to less than one year its new product development gap behind the leading MNEs from the United States and Japan. However, it realized it still needed additional access to advanced foreign technologies. To accomplish this, Samsung strengthened its in-house R&D and acquired/invested in high-tech companies such as LUX, a Japanese producer of high-end audio systems, and the US firm AST Research. Access to the latter firm's technical know-how and patented technology allowed Samsung to reduce its technology sourcing and licensing dependence on IBM and other large firms. ■

Case example As a classic case, Lenovo, a China-based personal computer (PC) manufacturer, was founded in Beijing in 1984. It took Lenovo close to twenty years to transform itself from an unknown small Chinese firm into one of the largest PC manufacturers in the world.[85] The critical turning point in its history was the acquisition of IBM's PC unit. In 2005, Lenovo acquired IBM's highly reputed Personal Computer Division (PCD) for $1.25 billion.[86] The company thereby gained a wide variety of knowledge-based resources, including brand reputation, a refined global service system, innovative designs and products, customer loyalty, and some of the best corporate governance practices in industry. Before the acquisition, Lenovo was mainly a Chinese company with limited overseas activities, and with several foreign PC rivals such as Dell operating in its home market. With the acquisition, the company doubled its number of employees, and five US directors joined its Board. ■

Finally, ***efficiency seeking*** is a firm's desire to capitalize on environmental changes that make specific locations in the MNE's international network of operations more attractive than before for the consolidation or concentration of specific activities. Such environmental changes may include technological breakthroughs allowing greater scale economies; an increased industry focus on innovation, triggering higher required R&D investments; customer-induced, shorter product cycles; and the reduction of trade and investment barriers through regional agreements such as NAFTA (and its successor USMCA) and the European Union. Here, the location advantages of the various relevant countries may change relative to one another, making one more attractive than another and therefore more likely to receive new FDI.[87]

Case example We already introduced Logitech, the American-Swiss, leading mouse and computer peripheral manufacturer earlier in the chapter. It established its first manufacturing plant in Switzerland in 1981. It then established three foreign plants in the United States, Ireland, and Taiwan to serve US and European PC manufacturers who wanted their suppliers to be nearby, and to benefit from lower costs and manufacturing design capabilities in Taiwan. After establishing its Irish plant, Logitech closed its Swiss plant.

However, in the first half of the 1990s, Logitech suffered from inefficient manufacturing and an unclear customer focus. In order to remain competitive in an environment focused on cost cutting, it engaged in efficiency-seeking FDI, and started production in 1994 at a plant in Suzhou, China. It simultaneously closed its Irish and US factories, and retained only a small production line for pilot runs in Taiwan. Logitech subsequently reinforced its manufacturing base in Suzhou, China by launching a new factory in 2005. In 2020, half of Logitech's manufacturing was done at its Suzhou plants, with the other half outsourced to suppliers in Asia, including Taiwan, Hong Kong, Malaysia, Vietnam, and Thailand.[88] ∎

In some cases, it should be noted that mixed entry motivations can be observed. For example, MNEs may combine **natural resource seeking** in one host country with **strategic resource seeking** in another host country through an acquisition as governance instrument.

Case example China's demand for oil and gas has increased dramatically because of its increasing population and economic development since 1978.[89] To meet the rapidly growing domestic demand, Chinese oil and gas companies have been actively searching for natural resources, as well as advanced knowledge assets abroad. The country's 'go out' policy, starting in 1999, has supported outward FDI.[90]

As the largest state-owned oil company in China, the China National Petroleum Corporation (CNPC) acquired PetroKazakhstan in Kazakhstan for $4.18 billion in 2005, which was the most significant overseas Chinese acquisition at the time.[91] PetroKazakhstan, a Canadian oil company (based in Calgary, Alberta) with substantial reserves in Kazakhstan, was an integrated international energy company with upstream and downstream operations covering oil and gas exploration, development, refining, and marketing of refined products. It had eleven oilfields, five exploration blocks, and a transportation and sales network consisting of sales companies and service stations in Cyprus and Kazakhstan. Acquiring PetroKazakhstan gave CNPC access to PetroKazakhstan's proven and estimated oil and natural gas reserves, while at the same time gaining control over the acquired company's knowledge-based FSAs.[92] Here, natural resource seeking in one host country was combined with strategic asset seeking in another host country through an acquisition. When one observes this type of mixed FDI motivations of an acquirer, it is not always entirely clear which motivation dominates, or whether the acquisition of the strategic assets involved would have made economic sense if the natural resources held by the acquisition target had been located in a different host country. ∎

Now that location advantages have been discussed, all the pieces are in place for a visual representation of the essence of international business strategy.

Figure 1.2 shows the basic linkages among internationally transferable FSAs, location-bound FSAs, and location advantages. On the left-hand side of Figure 1.2, as noted above, location-bound FSAs in the home country often result from privileged access to location advantages, or from a more efficient and effective use thereof as compared to other companies. The location advantages themselves may in principle be generally available to all firms operating in a specific location, and therefore only reflect an advantage vis-à-vis firms operating elsewhere. In general, a domestically operating firm may have both routines and even recombination capabilities that lead to great business success domestically, but are only partially useable in an international context.

Why is there a circle on the right-hand side of Figure 1.2? This circle represents the usage of the MNE's FSAs in the host country's macro-level milieu. A firm's success abroad depends on its ability to link its internationally transferable FSAs derived from the home country with location advantages (whether valuable inputs or attractive market conditions) in host countries, which are the reasons why the MNE expanded there in the first place. This linking process often requires developing new, location-bound FSAs in the host country. As a result, the existing base of internationally transferable FSAs derived from the home country space is extended with a location-bound component, thereby improving its deployment and exploitation potential in the host country. This is a common resource recombination activity per-formed by the MNE. In other words, the new location-bound FSA bundle improves access to the location advantages of the host country. However, such national responsiveness is often difficult to achieve and may require substan-tial investments. The newly created location-bound FSAs are shown in the middle section of the triangle in the host country circle on the right-hand side of Figure 1.2. At the same time, the host country where the needed linkages are successfully established, has now de facto expanded (but obviously without direct or proprietary access) its base of resources to include the MNE's internationally transferred FSAs, which explains why its circle intersects with the home country circle. Here, the MNE as a micro-level actor performs the role of 'connector' of two macro-level milieus. We should emphasize again that recombining resources entails more than just 'adding' new location-bound FSAs to a set of internationally transferable ones. Recombination also requires 'letting go' of existing assets and capabilities that could be effectively deployed and profitably exploited in the home country, but less so in the host country.

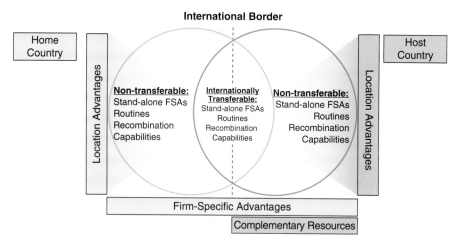

Figure 1.2
The essence of international business strategy

The middle section of the host country triangle, on the right-hand side, illustrates the importance of developing new LB FSAs in the host country. These LB FSAs complement the FSAs the firm has transferred from the home country, and are critical to achieve the firm's goals, in terms of accessing and benefiting from the location advantages (LAs) of the host country. If the firm commands insufficient FSAs internally to access and benefit from these LAs, it may draw upon complementary resources of external economic actors to achieve its goals in the host country. The NLB FSAs allow the MNE to connect the two countries' milieus, as described by the two circles.

Figures 1.3, 1.4, 1.5, and 1.6 take the basic template of Figure 1.2 and visualize how a *centralized exporter*, an *international projector*, an *international coordinator*, and a *multi-centred MNE* typically address the problem of partial rather than full usability at an international level of its stand-alone FSAs, routines, and recombination capabilities. In each case, the triangle within the host country circle on the right-hand side shows the most critical linkages to be established with the non-location-bound FSAs transferred from the home country (top of the pyramid on the left-hand side). This bundle of internationally transferable FSAs from the home country can be embodied in a centralized exporter's final products or, in the case of the other archetypes, transferred as intermediate goods.

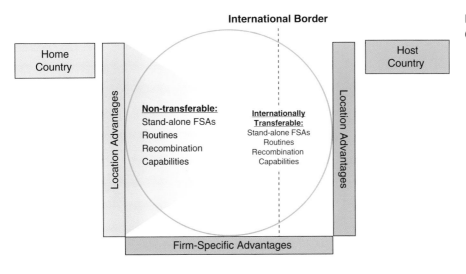

International Border

Home Country

Host Country

Location Advantages

Location Advantages

Non-transferable:
Stand-alone FSAs
Routines
Recombination
Capabilities

Internationally
Transferable:
Stand-alone FSAs
Routines
Recombination
Capabilities

Firm-Specific Advantages

Figure 1.3
Centralized exporter

The home-country-based circle and related pyramid connect directly with the location advantages in the host country. This represents the direct link between home country NLB FSAs and the host country's LAs (i.e., the foreign market), without development of new LB FSAs in the host country or formal transfer of existing NLB FSAs to the host country (the NLB FSAs are embodied in the centralized exporter's products). No host country circle is drawn here, as FSAs are not explicitly transferred to – nor actively developed and used in – the host country milieu. Exported products will in many cases simply be consumed, but especially in B2B transactions, these products may still lead to longer-term impacts in the host country milieu, for example, through productivity improvements (as is the case with sales of advanced manufacturing equipment).

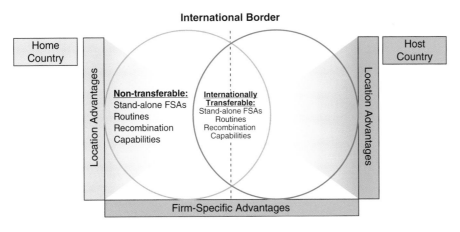

International Border

Home Country

Host Country

Location Advantages

Location Advantages

Non-transferable:
Stand-alone FSAs
Routines
Recombination
Capabilities

Internationally
Transferable:
Stand-alone FSAs
Routines
Recombination
Capabilities

Firm-Specific Advantages

Figure 1.4
International projector

The home and host country circles intersect as a result of the NLB FSAs that the MNE has transferred to its foreign operations, and which are now shared by – and utilized in – the two geographic milieus. The blank area of LB FSAs in the middle section of the host country triangle on the right reflects the international projector *not* developing LB FSAs in the host country, where operations simply clone those prevailing in the home country. Extant NLB FSAs suffice to success and benefit from host country LAs.

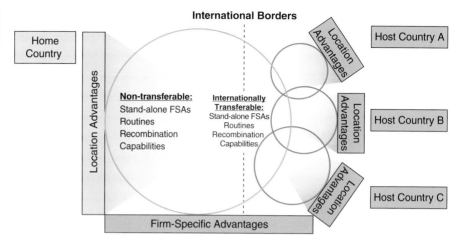

Figure 1.5
International coordinator

The different sizes of the overlapping areas between the home country circle and each of the (smaller) host country circles reflect the different types and levels of selected home country NLB FSAs to be transferred to different host environments as a function of the LAs the firm wishes to access. The large circle links together the various countries involved, which highlights the international coordinator's strengths in putting together a value chain based upon access to the coveted LAs of each country where the firm operates. The blank areas of LB FSAs in the middle sections of the host country triangles on the right, reflect the MNE *not* developing LB FSAs in these host countries.

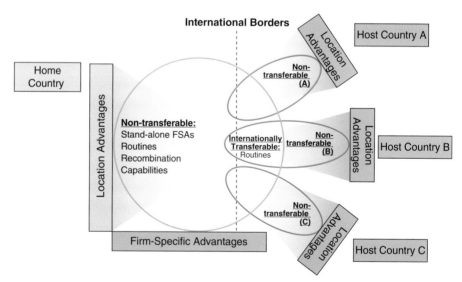

Figure 1.6
Multi-centred MNE

The multi-centred MNE typically transfers only key routines (managerial practices) from the home country to host countries. The middle sections of the triangles in the host countries represent the need to build distinct LB FSAs in each host country. The non-overlapping ovals reflect the independent nature of each MNE host country operation, whereby substantial investment in LB FSAs permits access to the coveted host country's LAs, whether at the input or output side.

The *centralized exporter* is essentially a market seeker: its internationally transferable FSAs are embodied in its final products, and the host country location advantage is simply the presence of customers willing and able to purchase the firm's products. In the 'ideal' case, there is minimal need to develop location-bound FSAs in the host country because of the products' desirability in host environments.

The *international projector* clones its home operations in the host country, replicating its internationally transferable FSAs. In the 'ideal' case, the host country operations directly access the local customers, without much need to develop new location-bound knowledge, again because of the desirability of the MNE's products.

The *international coordinator*'s main transferable FSA is its ability to coordinate the location advantages accessed in multiple host countries. In some host countries, it may still be necessary to transfer substantial resource bundles to the host country operations, so as to gain access to the host's location advantages (e.g., production capacity to access abundant natural resources). In other countries, there may be little need for this, namely if inputs can be accessed largely through third parties, such as the owners of natural resources or integrated logistics services providers. The actual coordination may occur largely in the home country or may be shared by a variety of locations.

The decentralized *multi-centred MNE*, recognizing that each host country operation needs to build upon its own distinct location-bound FSAs, transfers only core routines (e.g., in the area of financial management and administrative best practices) to each host country operation.

Value Creation through Recombination

Having discussed transferable FSAs, non-transferable FSAs, and location advantages – as well as the corresponding four archetypes of MNEs – *let us turn now to the fourth concept of the unifying framework: value creation through recombination.* Value creation through recombination means that the firm is able to grow by innovating and diversifying. This means combining in novel ways existing resources, often in conjunction with newly accessed resources. In this process, managers find new profitable ways – in this case across borders – to use excess resources at a relatively low marginal cost and to meld these with newly accessed resources. Resource recombination is both a key driver and a key constraint of firm growth.

In any organization, resource recombination requires three things: *first*, entrepreneurial skills possessed by managers and other employees that can be deployed in the face of new productive opportunities; *second*, slack or unused productive resources, beyond those needed for the efficient functioning of current operations; *third*, the willingness and capacity to let go of some resources embedded in extant FSAs, and to replace these by resources with higher value, creating potential in host environments. Here, the newly accessed resources in each host environment should be melded with existing resources.

Resource recombination in general – and knowledge recombination in particular – is critical to creating value and satisfying customer demand, because all MNEs, even the largest firms included in the *Fortune Global 500* list, have rivals who are trying to capture market share. Continuous innovation and effective exploitation of innovation is required to stay ahead of the competition.

Case example As a historical example, Carrefour, the world's second-largest and most internationalized retailer, has been challenged by competitors both at home and abroad.

For instance, in its French home market, Carrefour has lost market share to Aldi and Lidl, two German chains that have competed successfully based on their private label products and low prices. Carrefour has been unable to match these rivals' lower prices, as French regulations limit the extent to which retailers can reduce prices for branded products.

In Japan, Carrefour has had difficulties in purchasing land suited for new stores and in understanding Japanese consumers' needs. In 2005, it decided to leave Japan by selling its eight stores to Aeon Co., a local Japanese retailer. In the same year, it sold its Mexican operations, which failed to gain a sufficient market share after ten years of operation.[93]

In China, Carrefour failed to understand Chinese customers' changing preferences, following the rapid digitalization in the country after 2010. In response to the shift in Chinese customers' purchasing habits from in-store purchases to online shopping, and the increase in rental costs for physical space in the country's leading cities, Carrefour had closed all of its eighteen stores in China by the end of 2018. And in 2019, Carrefour exited entirely from the Chinese market, the world's largest e-commerce market, after twenty-four years of operation.[94]

The above illustrates Carrefour facing severe challenges when trying to recombine resources, whether in the home market or overseas. ■

When faced with competition, the MNE's most important strengths are usually not its physical, financial, or human resources as stand-alone items. Instead, the MNE's key strengths are its valuable, often proprietary knowledge, particularly its routines and recombination capabilities. Here, competitiveness results from the combination of stand-alone resources into bundles of location-bound and non-location-bound FSAs in technology, marketing, and reputation, and from the capability to recombine these knowledge bundles with newly accessed resources to produce goods and services that meet stakeholder needs internationally. Because the MNE is to a large extent a repository of knowledge bundles that can be deployed and recombined across borders, the firm's recombination capability can itself become the MNE's most important strength. Recombination, especially critical when satisfying stakeholder needs abroad, requires more than stand-alone knowledge bundles or existing routines. The MNE's recombination capability leads to processes and products that embody 'integrated bundles' of knowledge, meaning melded bundles of old and newly accessed knowledge.

The recombination capability is the MNE's highest-order FSA. This capability means the firm can not only transfer abroad its existing set of FSAs, but also create new knowledge, integrate it with the existing knowledge base, and exploit the resulting, new knowledge bundles across geographic space, in ways that satisfy stakeholder needs.

Effective recombination requires more than simply superior technology on the upstream side, market research skills on the downstream side, recognized brand names at the reputational side, the competent administration of current operations, etc. Instead, it requires entrepreneurial skills, because recombination cannot be easily planned beforehand, but requires the capability to adapt to new circumstances, especially when setting up a new business in a host country. It also requires unused or slack resources that can be deployed to develop new knowledge and perform the actual recombination. Finally, in host environments, it usually entails melding selectively existing resources with newly accessed resources so as to overcome the 'distance' between existing operations and the host environment. One paradox needs to be noted here: strong routines, though a critical component of the MNE's FSAs, can sometimes be detrimental to recombination, and thus to the MNE's recombination capability. There is a fine line between routines being helpful to international business strategy, by contributing to economies of scope (sharing of knowledge across borders), and these same routines becoming detrimental to further resource recombination, thereby impeding national responsiveness or even the creation of new, non-location-bound FSAs.

Figure 1.7 shows ten common patterns of FSA development and resource recombination in international business. The horizontal axis shows the two generic FSA types: FSAs are either internationally transferable (whereby we refer to the possibility of technical transfer, effective deployment, and profitable exploitation abroad of these FSAs) or location-bound. The vertical axis identifies the three possible geographic sources of an FSA: an FSA can be developed in a home country operation, in a host country operation, or by a network of MNE units.

The resulting matrix allows the identification of ten different patterns of FSA development, nine of which involve recombination and only one of which (Pattern I) does not involve recombination. The MNE's ability to carry out these patterns in real-world situations defines its recombination capability. Note that firms can – and usually do – carry out more than one pattern of FSA development at any given time.

Pattern I An internationally transferable FSA is developed in the home country and can be utilized across borders without any need for adaptation. This pattern is typical for stand-alone, advanced technical knowledge, which is valuable across borders (because it satisfies the objectives of shareholders, customers, and employees), and is not affected much by international differences in property rights regimes.

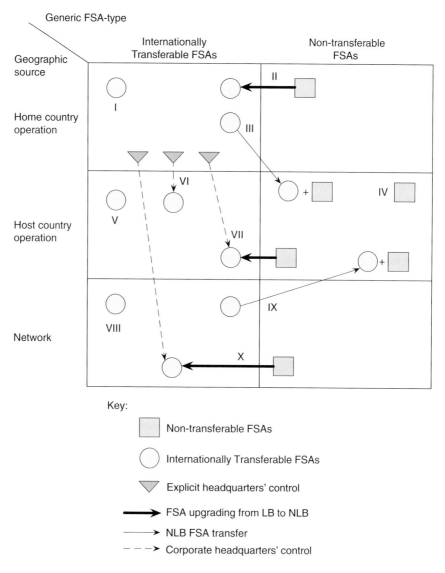

Figure 1.7
Ten patterns of FSA
development
in MNEs

Key:

■ Non-transferable FSAs

○ Internationally Transferable FSAs

▽ Explicit headquarters' control

➡ FSA upgrading from LB to NLB

→ NLB FSA transfer

- - -▷ Corporate headquarters' control

As this FSA development pattern does not require recombination, it will not be discussed in detail, but it lies at the heart of FSA transfer in the **centralized exporter**, **international projector**, and **international coordinator** archetypes.

Pattern II A location-bound FSA is developed domestically, in the home country, and is then upgraded so as to become internationally transferable. The upgrading draws on the firm's recombination capability, which may be helped by favourable location advantages at home.

Such an FSA upgrading pattern may occur at both the upstream and downstream ends of the value chain, as shown by respectively the development of new, proprietary drugs at Ranbaxy, and the development of a firm-specific sensitivity to local tastes at Jollibee. As noted earlier, recombination implies both 'adding' and 'letting go'. It does not suffice simply to add resources to an existing 'recipe'; the challenge is also to eliminate the 'ingredients' that will not lead to successful resources deployment and exploitation.

Case example As a historical example, Ranbaxy, India's largest pharmaceutical MNE, was incorporated in 1961. It quickly developed as a low-cost medicine manufacturer by leveraging the Indian intellectual property rights regime from the early 1970s to 2005, a regime that recognized process patents, but not product patents.

Using reverse engineering, Ranbaxy figured out how to duplicate existing molecules using its own innovative processes. As long as it used its own newly discovered manufacturing processes, it could legally manufacture and sell existing drugs that were still 'on patent' elsewhere in the world.

However, Ranbaxy realized that this domestic haven of loose intellectual property restrictions would not last forever. Furthermore, the firm realized that its reverse-engineering skills were not an internationally deployable FSA: those skills would not suffice for international expansion into markets with stronger intellectual property rights protection, such as the United States. In 1994, its new research centre at Gurgaon (near Delhi, India) started to extend its knowledge base from mere reverse engineering and copying towards developing new, proprietary drugs. This centre was staffed by both domestic researchers and Indian-origin researchers who were 'poached from [US] and European companies'.[95] (By 1999, twenty of the eight-five members in the new drug development team were such Indian-origin researchers, reflecting a reverse brain drain towards India.) In 1996, Ranbaxy launched fifteen of its own branded generic drugs in the United States, building upon its newly developed upstream transferable FSAs back in India. In 1999, 'it sold to Bayer AG an advanced formulation of one of the German company's most profitable drugs, ciprofloxacin ... The tablet conceived by Ranbaxy enable[d] patients to take only one dose a day, instead of several, by discharging the drug over a prolonged period of time'.[96] ∎

Case example As another historical example, but more at the downstream end of the value chain, Jollibee, the largest food chain in the Philippines and known as 'the company that beat McDonald's',[97] has upgraded its recombination skills to conform to local tastes in host markets around the world. This firm, incorporated in 1978, had only a few burger kitchens when McDonald's opened its first outlet in Manila in 1981.

From the outset, the company's founder, Tony Tan Caktiong, combined the US fast-food approach with a high sensitivity to local tastes. Jollibee had in-store playgrounds with costumed characters, as did McDonald's. At Jollibee, burgers were sweet and juicy, and spaghetti was saccharine. To most Filipinos, the food at Jollibee tasted better than that at McDonald's. Further, Jollibee's marketing reflected its local roots. For example, its advertising campaign in 1998 was linked to the country's centennial. By 2010, Jollibee had captured 65 per cent of local fast-food sales, about twice of McDonald's sales, and it has now become the largest quick-service-restaurant operator in the Philippines.[98]

The expansion to overseas markets targeted Filipinos abroad. To succeed, the company had to upgrade its non-transferable FSA – sensitivity to Filipino tastes in the Philippines – into a transferable FSA: sensitivity to Filipino tastes in each host country. As explained by a former general manager of Jollibee's international division: '[W]e have come up with dishes that are popular in the country we're in, and we make the burgers suitable to their palate'.[99] For instance, Jollibee makes a spicy and sweet Heavyweight Champ hamburger in Guam, a distinctive chicken curry in Indonesia, and a special spicy chicken dish in China.[100] By 2019, Jollibee operated over 250 outlets in foreign markets, including China, Brunei, Hong Kong, Oman, Kuwait, Qatar, Saudi Arabia, Vietnam, Singapore, and the United States.[101] ∎

This last example demonstrates that learning at home may create an internationally transferable FSA, in this case built around a high sensitivity to Filipino tastes in each host country. Such recombination capability may make it easier to understand what location-bound FSAs must be developed or otherwise accessed abroad (e.g., leading to the Heavyweight Champ hamburger sold by Jollibee in Guam) and to use those in conjunction with the company's other non-location-bound FSAs when penetrating foreign markets. The next pattern explicitly focuses on this creation of location-bound FSAs in host countries.

Pattern III An internationally transferable FSA is developed at home, but, in order to exploit it profitably in host countries, location-bound knowledge must be added to it, in the various host countries where the MNE operates. This is an expression of the philosophy 'think globally, act locally'. In this case, investments in location-bound FSAs complement the extant, internationally transferable FSAs, thereby allowing national responsiveness. When using Pattern III, the MNE is trying to achieve simultaneously both the benefits of integration and the benefits of national responsiveness. Similar to Pattern II, Pattern III may relate to either upstream or downstream activities. Again, the process of 'adding' new knowledge typically also implies 'discarding' extant knowledge that worked well in the home country, but less so across borders.

Case example As a historical example, Whirlpool Corporation, one of the world's leading manufacturers and marketers of major home appliances, successfully recombined its internationally transferable design and marketing skills with location-bound knowledge of consumer preferences in India.

Indian customers have a comparative preference for white garments, associated with purity and hygiene. However, frequent machine-washing in local water often discolours white fabrics. After learning about local preferences, Whirlpool designed washing machines that are particularly effective on white fabrics.[102]

In addition to appropriate product design, Whirlpool also produced a supporting TV commercial that appealed to Indian customers. It shows the daydream of a mother, in which her daughter dressed as Snow White wins a beauty contest against other contestants dressed in grey. At the end of the commercial, the mother awakes and 'glances proudly at her Whirlpool White Magic washing machine'.[103]

From 2005 to 2011, Whirlpool's sales in India nearly tripled, and it became the leading brand in India for fully automatic washing machines. ∎

Case example Disney company has opened four overseas Disneyland theme parks, namely in Tokyo (1983), Paris (1992), Hong Kong (2005), and Shanghai (2016). In each case, profitable growth required combining US-based, non-location-bound FSAs with newly crafted, location-bound FSAs, to accommodate especially local cultural requirements.[104]

In the Disneyland Shanghai project, which was the latest venture, the park was made more attractive to Chinese consumers by introducing the Garden of the Twelve Friends, whereby each animal in the Chinese zodiac was associated with a Disney character. For example, the 'Year of the Pig' was matched with Hamm, the wisecracking plastic piggy bank character from the movie Toy Story. The gardens were designed as a 'selfies paradise' so as to actively cater to the desire for self-portrait photos (taken with the camera held at arm's length), together with the animal that represents each individual's birth year. It was noted that 'Shanghai Disney Resort is the first Disneyland engineered with social media sharing in mind'.[105] More generally, creating location-bound FSAs did not come naturally for Disney and required years of meticulous planning: 'Shanghai Disney Resort here has suffered none of the cultural missteps that marred Disney openings in France and Hong Kong over the decades.'[106] By gathering and utilizing effectively contextual intelligence about the Chinese culture, Disney was able to move away from its conventional, International Projector approaches. ∎

Pattern IV Location-bound FSAs are developed in each host country where the MNE operates, and these FSAs are exploited locally, usually by autonomous affiliates. Does this involve recombination? Yes, it will almost always involve some recombination, as by definition the foreign affiliate can develop the new FSA only by recombining prior knowledge (for which the MNE as a whole acts as repository) with local knowledge. Why? Any foreign subsidiary exists only because of prior FDI and related transfer of resource bundles. When the foreign subsidiary starts developing its own FSAs, there must, by definition, be recombination. While this is particularly the case with greenfield FDI (i.e., direct investment in new facilities or the expansion of existing facilities), it will even be the case when the host country operation is acquired through a merger or acquisition, because the acquisition presumably makes sense only if the MNE feels that it can usefully combine its own knowledge with that of the merger partner or acquired company in the host country. This would typically entail replacing the accounting systems, ICT tools, and a variety of governance mechanisms that prevailed in the formerly independent firm, even if the content of strategic decision making such as choices in the realm of new product development and branding are left to the new unit's management.

If the new affiliate is indeed an existing company acquired by the MNE so as to achieve national responsiveness in the host market, the resistance to any imposed resources recombination in the realm of strategy content can be intense. This is a typical pattern for technological knowledge development in **multi-centred MNEs**.

This pattern is manifested in the cases of US-based Parke-Davis and the Dutch MNE Philips. The degree to which the FSAs were location-bound is evident by the immense resistance each company met when it tried to recombine the company's resources by integrating the autonomous subsidiaries.

Case example As a historical example, in 1970, the pharmaceutical company Warner-Lambert (since purchased by Pfizer) acquired US-based Parke-Davis in order to expand its international market coverage. At the time of acquisition, Parke-Davis operated manufacturing plants in the United Kingdom, France, Italy, Spain, Germany, Belgium, and Ireland. Responsible for blending and packaging to meet local needs, these national subsidiaries 'had historically enjoyed considerable autonomy and had developed substantial competences'.[107]

The Parke-Davis administrative heritage of autonomous subsidiaries and location-bound FSAs became obvious in the mid-1980s when, faced with the single European market, Warner-Lambert tried to restructure its operations by closing some plants and specializing the others along non-geographic lines. 'Fearful of losing power, and convinced that the parent was overestimating the impact of globalization, subsidiary managers fought back.'[108] Only after three years of intense debate did rationalization finally occur. ∎

Case example As another historical example, Philips relied on the extant capabilities of its national subsidiaries when the management board at Philips decided to reorganize the firm after World War II.

This autonomy facilitated flexible responses needed for each host environment, leading to specific technical skills developed at the national subsidiary level. For example, the firm's UK subsidiary developed the world's first teletext TV, its Canadian subsidiary designed the company's first colour TV, and its Australian subsidiary built the world's first stereo TV. In each case, the FSA was driven by local opportunities, often in the form of sophisticated local demand that did not exist elsewhere at the same time.

By the 1960s, however, such separate capabilities struck senior management as inadequate to meet the challenges brought by the development of the European common market. For Philips, the multi-centred administrative heritage was so ingrained that the reorganization efforts to gain control over its national subsidiaries spanned more than two decades. ∎

Pattern V An internationally transferable FSA is developed autonomously in a host country affiliate and then diffused internationally, either as an intermediate good, or embodied in finished products. Though this pattern looks similar to Pattern I, there are two key differences. First, the FSA is developed in the host country rather than the home country. Second, as discussed immediately above with regard to Pattern IV, Pattern V will almost always involve recombination, namely when the transfer of resource bundles overseas requires cooperation with other affiliates in the MNE that will have their say in the development or marketing of the product. Pattern V thus usually describes only part of a broader capability development process.

As described below, the European affiliate of US-based Goodyear and the Canadian affiliate of US-based Hewlett-Packard (HP) developed such internationally transferable FSAs in response to their local environments. At Goodyear, the design knowledge was transferred from the European affiliate to the US design centre; at HP, the product was developed in the Canadian affiliate, but sold to customers around the world. Whereas the Goodyear case involved the transfer of design knowledge, the HP case included the development of a product.

Case example As a historical example, in the mid-1960s, the French tyre manufacturer Michelin expanded to the United States with its radial tyre, which 'lasted far longer and provided better gas mileage than conventional bias-ply tires'.[109] Goodyear, a major US tyre manufacturer, still produced conventional tyres, and was unable to compete in its home market.

As a response, Goodyear's European affiliate developed its own radials, after observing Michelin's success in Europe. The engineers at the European technical centre 'took work done [in Europe] on radials and built on that base in the US'.[110] That base included 'tire-building machines and rubber compounds, which are different for radials than for bias-ply tires, and expertise in making steel-wire belts, which aren't used at all in conventional tires'.[111]

In 1984, the two technical centres coordinated to design a new radial truck tyre, the first time the two centres worked together. ▪

Case example As another historical example, in 1985, Johann Stich, the HP district sales manager in Calgary (Canada) identified the need for remote terminal units (RTUs) among some of his customers in the oil and gas industry. As one of the world's major centres for the oil and gas industry, Calgary hosts many oil and gas firms that need to monitor wells dispersed across a variety of remote environments. With support from the Canadian executive group, Stich established his RTU team in 1986. By mid-1988, the team started to test some components of the product at the site of a local customer. At the same time, the Calgary team won the charter from HP's corporate level against an internal competitor, as the product in Calgary was close to completion and Shell Oil had committed to buy the product.

The product sold well in Canada and, by 1990, also sold well in Europe. In 1993, the Calgary team, as well as the product, became part of HP's Lake Stevens Instrument Division (LSID), based near Seattle.[112] ▪

Pattern VI As with the previous pattern, the foreign affiliate develops an internationally transferable FSA, but in this case guided by corporate headquarters in the home country. The recombination capability is co-located in the home and the host country. It is actually relatively rare for subsidiary initiatives to unfold as Pattern V processes. In most cases, the corporate head office will be involved, thereby leading to Pattern VI.

Case example 3M, formerly known as Minnesota Mining and Manufacturing Company (3M), was founded in 1902. It gradually diversified into the customer market and became one of the world's leading innovators with widely known brands such as Scotch and Nexcare. Health care is its main business segment, representing more than 20 per cent of total sales. 3M's main driver of fast growth is its investments in technologies. All of 3M's seven business segments (including health care) and foreign subsidiaries have full access to its technologies.

The company's subsidiary in Taiwan is one example of a foreign operation developing an internationally transferable FSA guided by the parent company. This operation, 3M Taiwan, established in 1969 in Taipei City, had seen an expansion of its charter as of 1984, from marketing products developed at the head office to conducting its own product development.

In 2004, 3M Taiwan initiated a project named Acne Dressing development, augmenting the firm's hydrocolloid dressing technology as a response to local market needs. The head office performed a guiding role in the new product development process. It sent a US-based engineer to 3M Taiwan to provide training, and employees from different units within the 3M health care business segment were assigned to the subsidiary's project team.[113] The subsidiary recombined the parent's existing hydrocolloid dressing technology with its own location-specific knowledge about Taiwanese customers' preferences for an easy and effective acne treatment. This recombination process resulted in the launch of Acne Dressing as a new product.

More generally, 3M Taiwan operates an R&D centre in Yangmei City that has led to several innovations and associated FSAs. Examples include innovations related to products such as 'Magic Mop' (floor cleaning); '3M Polarizing Task Light' (technology that reduces glare and provides effective illumination); and 'Filtrete Ultra Clean Air Purifier'. ■

Pattern VII In this case, a foreign affiliate first develops a location-bound FSA, typically to cater to the host country market requirements for national responsiveness, as in Pattern IV, but then upgrades this FSA to make it internationally transferable, again guided by the home country corporate headquarters. The recombination capability is co-located in the home and the host country, as in Pattern VI.

Such a pattern can be found in the historical cases of 3M Canada and Citibank (now the retail and corporate banking arm of Citigroup, the largest financial services company in the world). 3M Canada developed distinct marketing strategies, which eventually led to earning a North American mandate; Citibank honed its capability to respond to financial crises during the Latin American crisis and the Mexican peso crisis and later transferred this locally created knowledge to its Asian operations, allowing it to more effectively address the Asian crisis.

Case example Established in the United States in 1981, the animal health care business at 3M expanded to Canada in 1984, to market a flea-control insecticide to Canadian customers.

In the United States, the product was sold through distributors. However, the Canadian business manager preferred direct sales to veterinarians through 3M representatives, believing that such a channel choice 'would provide greater control and a better understanding of the market'.[114]

Through the late 1980s and early 1990s, the insecticide product held around 50 per cent market share in Canada, but only about 10 per cent in the United States. This discrepancy 'was felt to be a function of the different distribution systems'.[115]

The 1993 reorganization of the animal health care business established a distinct insecticides division. When the US and Canadian managers joined the business team of this new insecticides division, both the team leader and the marketing representative were Canadians. This shifted the business management and marketing activities of the insecticides division largely to Canada, allowing the division to change its distribution system across North America. ■

Case example As another historical case example, US-based Citibank suffered losses as a result of the Latin American debt crisis of the 1980s and the Mexican peso crisis of 1994/1995. As a result of these crises, both the corporate executives at the headquarters and senior managers in Latin America learned to take preventive measures in the face of potential financial crises: techniques included removing weak customers, applying stricter accounting standards, and shunning certain business sectors.

When Mexico experienced severe financial problems in 1994, Citibank, like many other investors, started to investigate whether such a crisis could occur in Asia. Two weeks after the Mexican peso crisis in 1994, Citibank sent Alex Erskine, an economist in Citibank Australia, to Asia to find out which Asian countries were economically similar to Mexico. In 1996, Citibank Vice Chairman William Rhodes chaired a conference to evaluate the firm's risk, followed in 1997 by two similar conferences on its Asian operations.

Citibank made sure that many of its senior Asian personnel had first-hand experience of the Latin American crisis. The corporate banking unit for all emerging markets, emerging market retail banking, the North Asia division, and the South Asia division were all headed by veterans of the Latin American crisis, who had been relocated to these positions in the early 1990s. Also, many senior executives in Thailand, Indonesia, South Korea, and the Philippines had lived through the Latin American crisis. For example, Dennis Martin, an Argentine and head of corporate banking for all emerging markets, spent seventeen years with Citibank in Latin America; Michael Contreras, who led the Southeast Asia Division in 1996, had spent twenty years with Citibank in its Central American Division.

As a result, Citibank was able to interpret correctly the early signs of the Asian crisis in 1997/1998. Even before the Asian crisis emerged, Citibank took several preventive measures. By mid-1996, when the first signs of a crisis materialized in Asian financial markets, its senior executives deployed strategies they had learned in Latin America. For example, Michael Contreras started to cut Citibank's lending volume in Thailand and Indonesia by about half; Citibank in Asian countries also strengthened its scrutiny when lending money to conglomerates by investigating the health of the entire company rather than just that of the division receiving the money. Ultimately, the knowledge transfers, embedded in the managers operating in Asia, helped Citibank not only to avoid disastrous losses in Asia, but even to achieve some earnings growth in 1997.[116] ■

Pattern VIII Several affiliates, located in different countries, develop an internationally transferable FSA together. Some may contribute upstream knowledge (e.g., in the technological sphere), whereas others may contribute downstream knowledge (e.g., in the marketing and distribution sphere). In this case, the recombination capability is co-located in all the participating affiliates, without central guidance from home country corporate headquarters.

Case example As a historical case example, the development of a so-called 'technology transfer toolbox' at HP involved engineers, scientists, and managers working in several countries. An HP scientist, dissatisfied with the impact of the main research centres on HP businesses, took the initiative to build a project toolbox for scientists and project managers, recruiting team members in research centres in England, the United States, and Italy. These team members then in turn identified key new members. Ultimately, the team consisted of scientists, engineers, and managers who continued to work in their separate countries.

Lacking a common vision, the project did not start well, but after the team members held a two-day face-to-face discussion on the project's objectives it proceeded smoothly, with team members communicating by email, video, or telephone.

The team's work resulted in the 'technology transfer toolbox', based on internet technologies and packaged in a process reference documentation template. By 2003, this template was considered 'a de facto standard internal to HP for capturing best practices'.[117] ■

Pattern IX Again, a set of affiliates develops an internationally transferable FSA, as in Pattern VIII. In this case, however, location-bound knowledge is added in the various countries involved, thereby allowing national responsiveness, similar to Pattern III.

This pattern is reflected in the organization of Citibank in the late 1980s and early 1990s, as well as in the development of the cleansing cloth at Procter & Gamble (P&G).

Case example As a historical case example, from the very beginning of its international expansion, Citibank operated through autonomous national subsidiaries. In the 1980s and 1990s, however, it slowly changed its decentralized structure in Europe into a network-based structure.

In 1985, Citibank's European regional management started 'the European Bank' initiative. This initiative created informal regional product and customer units. Normally, an executive from a large affiliate would head each unit, and would be responsible for identifying opportunities and challenges facing the subsidiaries in the region. However, the regional units did not actually develop any specific strategic responses, and national subsidiaries kept their autonomy to respond as they deemed fit in each market.

Further regional coordination continued with 'the Unique European Bank' initiative, announced in 1988, and a global reorganization in 1990. Still retaining its geography-based national structure, Citibank structured linkages 'across affiliates to leverage dispersed resources'[118] through specialized product- and customer-focused units. Thus, the specialized units and the local affiliates became jointly responsible for local activities, through 'shared management'[119] of these activities.

Citibank in Europe continued to pursue such regional integration strategies in the early 1990s. By 1994, it had transitioned to a truly network-based structure. ■

Case example As another classic case example, in the late 1990s, consumer researchers at US-based consumer goods MNE Procter & Gamble (P&G) found that women in the United States, Europe, and Japan were not satisfied with their facial cleansing products. In the United States, bar soaps left the skin dry; in Europe, cleansing milk did not clean the skin very well; and in Japan, foaming facial cleansers did not leave the skin sufficiently moisturized.

In response, P&G set up a technology team in Cincinnati (United States) to apply technologies from all over the world to design a product suitable to satisfy consumers' needs internationally. For example, the team drew on Japanese technologists for their knowledge of cleansing processes. Using input from experts around the world, the team developed a cleansing cloth truly effective at both cleaning and moisturizing the skin.

This impregnated cloth technology became the 'chassis', based upon which subsidiaries engaged in further adaptations, adding location-bound knowledge specific to their own geographic markets. For example, a Japanese technology team impregnated the cleansing cloth with a cleanser specific to the Japanese market.

At the same time, a US marketing team developed the one-step routine concept for the US market, and a marketing team in Japan emphasized the cloth's ability to increase skin circulation 'through a massage while bossing skin clarity due to the micro fibers' ability to clean pores and trap dirt'.[120]

Thus, '[I]n the end, each market ended up with a distinct product built on a common technology platform'.[121] ■

Pattern X As with the previous pattern, a set of affiliates works together. Here, they first jointly develop a location-bound FSA geared towards one specific host country market. When successful, this FSA is then upgraded into an internationally transferable FSA, under the guidance of the MNE corporate headquarters. This pattern is often observed in strategic management consulting, whereby international expert teams provide solutions to specific problems in a specific country and, if particularly successful, then turn their approach into a company best practice with wide geographic application potential. The case of TRW Automotive illustrates this pattern.

Case example As a historical case example, TRW Automotive (purchased by The Blackstone Group in 2002; sold to the German firm ZF Friedrichshafen in 2015; and renamed as ZF TRW Automotive Holdings) is a large supplier of automobile components. In 1993, Nissan, one of TRW's customers, complained about the high defect rate and high cost structure of the steering assemblies manufactured by TRW-UK. An internal investigation at TRW-UK found that employees responsible for engineering, product design, and process design had poor communications with one another and were also particularly weak at execution.

To solve this problem, TRW established the Nissan Global Team. For each of the three regions (the United States, Japan, and the United Kingdom), TRW chose the individuals considered the best engineer and best customer support professional. These six members together 'represented TRW's best capabilities in lean principles as they applied to product and process engineering and design, manufacturing, shop floor issues, and customer service'.[122] Within less than two years, TRW-UK became one of the most efficient and high-quality operations inside TRW.

TRW did not stop there. As of 1996, the Nissan Global Team was still in operation, applying what it had learned to other parts of TRW's operations.[123] ∎

The ten above patterns of FSA development may not be an exhaustive set, but each can be observed regularly in international business practice. An MNE's overall recombination capability can be described, roughly, as its mastering a variety of FSA development patterns. The firm's recombination capability will evolve over time, particularly as foreign affiliates develop their own recombination strengths.

Complementary Resources of External Actors

Having discussed value creation through recombination, *let us turn now to the fifth concept of the unifying framework: complementary resources of external actors*. In many cases, MNEs need complementary resources of external actors (technology providers, licensees, local distributors, joint venture partners, etc.) to be successful abroad. The firm's domestically successful stand-alone FSAs, its routines, and even its recombination capabilities may be insufficient or inappropriate to operate successfully in host countries and regions, because of the cultural, economic, institutional, and spatial 'distance' from the home country or home region. In other words, some success ingredients may be missing, and these can then be provided by external actors, if at least two conditions are fulfilled. First, internal development of the required strengths is expected to bring a lower net value than relying upon external actors. Second, the need to rely on external actors can be satisfied in practice, and does not jeopardize the specific expansion project considered.

Case example As a historical example, the experience in the United States of the Italian MNE Montedison, active in chemicals until 1990 (thereafter an energy company renamed as Edison and acquired by Electricité de France in 2012), helps to illuminate the importance of complementary resources of external actors. Montedison tried to re-enter the United States in the early 1980s, a few years after it failed in that same market with a wholly owned subsidiary.

Montedison held about 17 per cent of the European capacity in polypropylene production, but it was weak in the United States. Although it had experienced success in Europe and had even developed an advanced new processing technology for the production of polypropylene, venturing into the unfamiliar US market on its own appeared too risky, especially given its earlier failure.

Montedison decided to team up with Hercules, the leading polypropylene producer in the US market. Hercules had FSAs in marketing and product applications, but was weak in process technology. Thus, the two companies felt they could achieve synergies through collaboration.

In 1983, the two companies established a fifty-fifty equity joint venture, incorporating the successful marketing strategies from Hercules and the process technologies from Montedison. This joint venture grew into the world leader in polypropylene.[124] ■

Case example As another historical case example, EnCana, Canada's largest natural gas producer, and ConocoPhillips, the US oil major, agreed in October 2006 to form a joint venture and to invest more than US $10 billion over the next decade to expand the joint venture's production. The joint venture would include two new companies, one in upstream activities and one in downstream activities. The upstream company would own two EnCana oil sands projects at Foster Creek and Christina Lake in Alberta, Canada. The downstream company would own two ConocoPhillips refineries in Roxana, Illinois, and Borger, Texas, both in the United States. Today, as part of a split transaction in 2009, EnCana's joint operations have been transferred to Cenovus Energy, EnCana's integrated oil company.

EnCana contributed unique strengths in underground oil sands operations. EnCana CEO Randy Eresman told reporters at a news conference in Calgary, Alberta, in 2006 that EnCana, compared with other players in the oil sands business, had been particularly effective in extracting oil from oil sands. However, EnCana did not have sufficient expertise in above-ground processes, such as processing the heavy tar extracted from rock and sand. Moreover, building a refinery in Alberta was not perceived as a cost-effective solution. Construction costs in Alberta had soared because oil sands development had created a labour and materials shortage.

For its part, ConocoPhillips contributed expertise in heavy oil refining. However, strong competition had made it difficult for ConocoPhillips to access stable and secure oil supplies. With crude output from Alberta's oil sands expected to triple to 3 million barrels a day by 2015, ConocoPhillips was eager to become a significant player in the oil sands game.

Thus, the partnership had something to offer to both companies. It strengthened ConocoPhillips' presence in North America by 'repositioning 10 per cent of its US downstream business to access a large upstream resource base'.[125] EnCana immediately became involved in the North American refining industry and had the opportunity for future upgrader development.[126] ∎

Bounded Rationality

Having discussed value creation through complementary resources, *let us turn now to the sixth concept of the unifying framework: bounded rationality*. Bounded rationality reflects 'scarcity of mind', meaning that the managers responsible for making decisions and engaging in purposive action in the firm always face information problems.[127]

Access to information sufficient in quality and quantity to guide decision making and managerial action is the first problem. However, even in the presence of all required information, managers have a second problem as well: a limited capability to process complex information bundles. Let us look at these information problems in more detail.

The first problem: any information about the environment relevant to the MNE's functioning and performance, especially about the future state of the environment, is necessarily partial and incomplete, given the complexity and uncertainty characterizing the environment and its evolution.

Incomplete information about environmental complexity may impede successful international expansion, as documented by hundreds of international business case studies, and as observed on an almost daily basis in the media. However, we should also recognize, paradoxically, that newly acquired foreign market knowledge may in some cases alleviate bounded rationality constraints at home.

Case example As a historical case example, in 1997, the US-based ice cream company Häagen-Dazs launched the 'dulce de leche' flavour – a flavour similar to caramel – in Argentina, as the company realized that this flavour of ice cream accounted for about 30 per cent of the Argentinian market. This locally developed product proved to be a big hit in Argentina.

At training seminars, 'North American executives who had tried dulce de leche at a brand conference in 1997 realized it might fit with the company's recent move to target Latinos in the US'.[128] The dulce de leche flavour ice cream was introduced in the United States in 1998, at first only in heavily Hispanic areas. The product did better than expected: sales in the United States grew by about 27 per cent per month in 1998, and by 2001 it became the company's sixth-best-selling flavour in the United States (out of thirty-four flavours).[129] 'It's remarkable and unusual to have a new flavour do so well,' said Vivian P. Godfrey, former Häagen-Dazs Vice President for North America.[130] The product's success in Argentina had given the company information relevant to its home market. ∎

The second problem: even if critical information is abundant and rather accurate, senior MNE management faces a problem of processing this information, especially in determining its relevance to the firm and its implications for strategy.

Case example   As another historical case example, consider the use of newspaper inserts by Walmart, the world's largest retailer, in Japan in 2004 and 2005:

> [Walmart] has made several changes in its use of newspapers' inserts, for instance, first eliminating them, then bringing them back when sales suffered. But it still hasn't made the inserts attractive enough … [During 2005, Walmart planned to] make more use of the inserts to highlight products centred on traditional Japanese holidays and events such as cherry blossom viewing.[131]

Newspaper inserts may be viewed as a minor, almost trivial managerial issue, but even for this seemingly trivial matter, it is interesting to observe that mighty Walmart – with an experienced management team and a great deal of information about the Japanese consumer – could not easily and rapidly process this information to find the optimal insert template for Japan. ▪

These two bounded rationality problems – incomplete information and difficulty with processing information – are compounded when operating in multiple geographic environments simultaneously, each with different levels of complexity and uncertainty, and therefore different implications for international business strategy.

Let us look at an example of bounded rationality that is particularly relevant to senior managers in MNEs. When contemplating international expansion, and reflecting on transferring FSAs abroad, senior management in MNEs try to choose the optimal entry mode: for example, FDI (whereby FSAs covering the entire value chain are transferred to foreign affiliates) versus licensing (whereby typically technology-based and manufacturing FSAs are transferred to a foreign licensee) versus original equipment manufacturing (OEM, whereby typically only technology-based FSAs are transferred, to be combined with the manufacturing capability of a foreign producer). Which entry mode will likely lead to the highest value creation and the greatest satisfaction of stakeholder needs? Four problems arise in this enormously complex decision. The first problem is one of property rights: if outside actors such as licensees and OEM suppliers can capture the MNE's FSAs, even within the realm of what is legally permitted, this may reduce the value of these FSAs to the MNE. Second, outside contracting partners may not fully respect the quality standards normally upheld by the MNE; these actors may thereby create negative spillover effects for the MNE, such as negative responses by customers and shareholders. Third, in the case of FDI, the MNE has to cope with a new institutional regime and usually foreign employees and work practices. Here, the question arises whether the MNE will be able to reach home country or pre-set productivity standards, and perhaps more generally, whether home country routines in the workplace and established best practices can actually be deployed successfully. Even past experience abroad, in a number of foreign environments that has led to new routines on how to operate in host markets, may be of little use in new host environments that are 'distant' from the originally penetrated markets. Finally, to the extent that international expansion implies recombination of resources, the use of outside actors versus complete internalization will have an impact on the development trajectory of the MNE's recombination capability.

Case example The unique benefits attainable through global alliance formation, and the substantial costs involved in the establishment of their own worldwide service networks, pushed many intercontinental passenger carriers to offer global services through international alliances, even when they had free access to host countries without institutional restrictions. In this case, the bounded rationality problem consisted of figuring out how to combine extant intercontinental services with local services in a multitude of host countries, and also how to combine these extant intercontinental services with other intercontinental services so as to achieve a seamless, worldwide network service. No single airline in the world has figured out how to achieve this on its own. By July 2020, the three global alliances, namely Oneworld, SkyTeam, and Star Alliance, accounted for more than 50 per cent of realized revenue passenger kilometres in scheduled traffic.[132]

From a customer perspective, a fully integrated service across regions is more convenient than separate offerings from a number of independently operating airlines. For example, suppose that a passenger needs to travel from a spoke station (e.g., Pittsburgh) in the United States to a spoke station (e.g., Lyon) in Europe. Without a global alliance, the passenger has to buy three flights from three airlines separately: a flight from the US spoke to a US hub (e.g., New York), a second flight from the US hub to a European hub (e.g., Paris), and a third flight from the European hub to the European spoke. With a global alliance, by contrast, the passenger only has to buy flight services from a single airline. Through this type of seamless service, a global alliance may provide more convenience and better coordination of schedules than independent, non-allied airlines.

Global alliances offer cost advantages to the member carriers. It is expensive (and institutionally perhaps impossible) for carriers to establish an independent marketing base and obtain strategic landing slots in host countries; it is usually cheaper to provide such services via alliance partners.

In addition to cost savings, global airline alliance groupings also give their members increased traffic volumes across the combined networks, operational bases, brand names, computer reservation systems, and FSAs in external relations. For example, a member carrier increases its foreign partners' existing market through extra traffic generated by the feed to the foreign partners, and it also expands its own market through extra traffic by the feed from foreign partners; joint advertising across markets increases demand and the number of passengers in the global alliance group; and frequent-flyer programmes allow passengers to collect air miles even if they fly with a partner airline, and to spend air-mile points on flights of all member carriers, thereby offering more opportunities for passengers to earn air-mile points and use rewards.[133] ■

A second noteworthy example of bounded rationality, commonly encountered by senior managers of MNEs, is the phenomenon that senior managers in the home country and senior managers in the host country may adopt different decision-making approaches. Senior managers in the home country, especially those at the corporate level, and managers in foreign subsidiaries may select different information facets as relevant to strategy, given the multifacetedness of the relevant information. Multifaceted information is not the same as complex information; rather, multifacetedness refers to the variety of types of accessible information, and to the phenomenon that decision makers will select only some of these types as relevant to strategic decisions, based upon elements such as personal or institutional experience. Furthermore, even if corporate and subsidiary managers agree that the same information facets are relevant, the two groups of managers may interpret those facets differently in terms of their implications for strategy. Such divergence in judgement, which leads to alternative predictions of the future in a context of high uncertainty, again results from elements such as differences in experience between the corporate level and the firm's subsidiaries.

Why would subsidiary managers view opportunities for value creation differently from corporate-level management in the home country? First, subsidiary managers receive information directly from the local, external environment (local clients, suppliers, newspapers, etc.): this information is typically optimistic and framed in the form of very broad opportunities (new customer demands, supplier suggestions, macro-economic trends, etc.). Second, acting on this information, the subsidiary managers then engage in their own framing efforts: they reconstruct the outside information in the form of demand forecasts, growth scenarios, and so on. Such reconstruction leads to the creation of an 'inside view'. The inside view is typically an optimistic perspective on the future. This optimism is grounded in three forms of subsidiary manager confidence: confidence in the subsidiary unit as the source of success; confidence in the probable state of the future environment, especially the local environment; and confidence in the subsidiary's ability to control events. By contrast, projected scenarios that come from home country managers are typically more pessimistic and conservative.

Case example As a well-known, historical case example, such a divergence of judgement occurred at Xerox when its Japanese affiliate, Fuji Xerox, wanted to develop compact copiers. As an insider in the Japanese market, Fuji Xerox viewed this as a good business opportunity, while the Xerox group in the United States thought differently.

63

Fuji Xerox was established in 1962 as a joint venture between the US document management company Xerox and the Japanese photographic company Fuji Photo. Fuji Xerox gradually expanded its mandate from merely marketing xerographic products to developing its own products, as well as modifying Xerox designs to local demands. In the late 1960s and early 1970s, some Japanese competitors (e.g., Ricoh) started to produce high-quality, low-cost copiers. Competing with these local Japanese rivals, Fuji Xerox experienced these market changes intimately and foresaw increasing demand for compact, high-quality copiers.

However, at the same time, the central management at Xerox was more concerned with IBM and Eastman Kodak entering the copier industry in the United States. These two new entrants targeted the mid- and high-volume segments of the US market, which were the key businesses and lucrative market segments for Xerox. From the Xerox perspective, the low-volume segment was a minor part of its business.

Fuji Xerox in Japan and Xerox in the United States had very different perceptions about future market development, and they also assessed the technical knowledge at Fuji Xerox quite differently. By the late 1960s, Fuji Xerox had already developed experimental inexpensive compact copiers. However, from Xerox's perspective, such technical capabilities were not comparable to those of IBM or Kodak, and Fuji Xerox was perceived as little more than a faraway unit in a tiny market. Fuji Xerox tried to convince Xerox to develop compact machines, but different perceptions between Fuji Xerox and Xerox on future market developments made this task very difficult. As explained by Tony Kobayashi, the former President of Fuji Xerox, 'we had been insisting that the Xerox Group needed to develop small copiers as an integral part of its worldwide strategy. However, Xerox's attitude was that the low end of the market was not a priority ... On the other hand, we were seeing rising demand for small copiers in Japan'.[134]

The senior managers at Fuji Xerox persisted and successfully developed small copiers for the Japanese market. Later, in 1979, Fuji Xerox even started to export such compact copiers to Xerox in the United States, and Fuji Xerox literally rescued Xerox when Xerox failed to mount an effective response to the rise of Japanese competitors, which took away Xerox's market in the United States.[135] ∎

Bounded Reliability

Having discussed bounded rationality, *let us turn now to the seventh and final concept of the unifying framework: bounded reliability*. Bounded reliability reflects the 'scarcity of effort to make good on open-ended promises': agents do not always carry through on their expressed intentions to try to achieve a particular outcome or performance level. This is why firms introduce safeguards or enforcement mechanisms to heighten detection of, and provide punishment for, reneging.

A *first source* of bounded reliability is opportunism, which involves *ex ante* false promises and/or *ex post* reneging on promises, either by external contracting parties or by employees inside the firm. Opportunism is self-interest-seeking behaviour with guile. Here, an intentional effort to cheat/shirk prevails, which benefits the cheating/shirking party.[136]

A *second source* of bounded reliability is benevolent preference reversal, in which an actor's initial promise is made in good faith, but the actor's preferences then change over time, though not with the intent to harm the party to which the promise was made. For senior managers in MNEs, there are two key types of benevolent preference reversal: 'good faith local prioritization' and 'scaling back on over-commitments'.

In the realm of reprioritization, a common case involves overseas actors initially making a promise in good faith, but, over time, diverting their effort (and resources under their control) to the pursuit of local preferences, at the expense of organizational/global preferences. For example, at the level of foreign affiliates, the subsidiary manager may typically promise to try to carry out specific investment projects determined by corporate headquarters, and commit to specific performance requirements. However, the manager may change his/her preferences for several reasons, including: a substantial distance in time from any punishment for non-achievement; a substantial distance in space from the headquarters' monitoring apparatus; and the relative proximity and intrinsic satisfaction derived from focusing on autonomous, locally driven investment opportunities that give immediate local rewards to the subsidiary (such as an improvement of relationships with local stakeholders).

Scaling back on over-commitment typically implies that the actor who made an initial promise was overconfident in his/her capacity to deliver. This overestimation may have various sources, including: a dysfunctional impulsivity when making a promise; fallacious planning, meaning the consideration from past experience of only 'best case' rather than 'average case' implementation scenarios; excessive discounting of known risks; exaggerating the extent to which the environment can be controlled, etc.

A *third source* of bounded reliability relates to 'identity-based discordance'. This concept means that individuals fail to make good on commitments because they are personally attached to an identity that conflicts with the promise. Identity-based discordance can also take two forms. First, 'regression' often occurs when MNEs engage in organizational change. In this instance, managers (and by extension any economic actor) may abandon new commitments made in good faith, because they favour the managerial practices and routines that prevailed before the change. Either they really believe that 'the old ways were better' (lack of willingness to change), or they are simply incapable of adjusting. Second, 'divided engagement' refers to multi-actor situations whereby individuals, in spite of their promises, may ultimately identify with goals that conflict with the promises they made. These conflicting goals are typically at a level different from the organizational goals. Such conflicting goals may be the ones prevailing at the department/unit/subsidiary level, thereby potentially setting up conflicts with other departments/units/subsidiaries, or even with the corporate head office. In some cases, the conflicting goals can be unrelated to a specific unit inside the organization. Such goals may reflect views prevailing in another organization with which one identifies more (as often found in the context of international alliances), or they may reflect ideologies on how the organization should function in society, thereby negatively affecting purposive action that serves organizational goals. Divided engagement typically leads individuals and groups to start working against one another (though without guile) in a way that undermines overall MNE goal achievement, even though the undermining individuals may actually be convinced, because of their identity, that they are doing the right thing for the organization as a whole.[137]

These bounded reliability problems cannot be simply reduced to bounded rationality issues, because they are not caused by a lack of information or an inability to process information. In the case of opportunism, the individual may possess all the relevant information, and in fact may process it perfectly. The problem with opportunism lies with the individual's self-centred desires and effort. In the case of benevolent preference reversal, the problem is not with the individual's assessment of how the world is or will be. It is about making the same mistakes over and over again, even if the outcomes of these mistakes are predictable. Bounded reliability not only occurs at the subsidiary level, but can also be characteristic of head office behaviour, for example, when specific promises for resource allocation are made to particular affiliates and then reversed at a later stage. *Bounded rationality is about the imperfect assessment of a present or future state of affairs, thereby leading to incorrect beliefs; bounded reliability is about imperfect effort towards pre-specified goal achievement, thereby leading to incomplete fulfilment of promises.*

A single individual can engage in both benevolent preference reversal or identity-based discordance and opportunism. For example, suppose that an individual has engaged in good faith local prioritization: good faith promises were made to corporate headquarters, but efforts to make good on those promises have been replaced by the pursuit of local goals. As the time for performance appraisal approaches, this individual may wilfully and opportunistically engage in incomplete and inaccurate reporting of the performance gap.

It is also worth pointing out that individuals can perform as expected in the short term, yet also have underlying tendencies towards good faith local prioritization – tendencies that have not yet affected their behaviour (perhaps they are 'doing the right things for the wrong reasons'). Such individuals especially may produce long-term conflicts between the subsidiary and corporate headquarters (and perhaps the remainder of the MNE network).

It is important to recognize that bounded reliability at the level of the individual may translate into behaviour of teams, entire units within the MNE, and even the MNE as a whole. When transactions are conducted with external actors, bounded reliability challenges emanating from both the MNE and from these external actors should be assessed. Irrespective of the sources of bounded reliability, it should be emphasized that a particular level of unreliability in the MNE can be eliminated by a number of governance mechanisms. These include, *inter alia*: (1) contractual safeguards (such as sufficient monitoring and proper incentives) to align interests, thereby curbing opportunism; (2) joint goal development, goal segmentation (setting milestones), and frequent communication to align expectations and to sustain cognitive proximity, thereby reducing reprioritization; and (3) routines such as multi-level and multi-stage decision-making processes to reduce the impact of individual evaluation biases and impulsivity, thereby reducing the occurrence of over-commitments and the subsequent need to scale back on such over-commitments.[138]

Implications of International Business Strategy for MNE Performance

MNE managers can use the seven core elements of the international business framework described in this chapter, at various levels: the level of a single expansion project, the level of a divisional/business unit's growth strategy, or the level of the firm's overall international business strategy. It is critical for managers to reflect on the MNE's strengths (relative to rival companies) and its ability to match its distinct resource base with the challenges and opportunities found in the international environment, thereby creating value and satisfying shareholder needs.

The question then arises whether an international expansion programme is likely to improve MNE performance. A vast international business literature attempts to answer the question whether international expansion and the related increase of international diversification (e.g., the share of foreign investment to total investment, foreign sales to total sales, or foreign production to total production) is likely to have positive effects on the MNE's return and risk. The answer is: it depends on several factors.

First, at the project level, the MNE should compare the expected net present value per invested monetary unit in foreign expansion with that of domestic expansion, taking into account a variety of risk factors. MNEs should undertake foreign expansion projects only if these make more economic sense than domestic projects. MNEs should expand internationally until, at the margin, the next domestic and foreign expansion projects are equally attractive.

Second, the international transfer of FSAs, whether embodied in final products (leading to scale economies), intermediate products such as R&D and marketing knowledge (leading to scope economies, as benefits are gained from transferring and sharing valuable knowledge across borders), or coordinating skills (leading to benefits of exploiting national differences), is not costless. In most cases, even internationally transferable FSAs need to be complemented by additional, location-bound FSAs in host countries. In more general terms, even with a strong recombination capability (entailing entrepreneurial dynamism, available excess resources, and access to new resources in host environments) international success requires substantial investments, learning, and legitimacy creation over time.

Third, even if the necessary investments in location-bound knowledge have been made, and both learning and legitimacy-building have occurred in host nations, the MNE's growth will not necessarily lead to improved economic performance. Substantial adaptation to host country environments will increase the costs of internal governance. Central headquarters, faced with increased bounded rationality and bounded reliability problems, will find it more difficult to select particular investment trajectories and to choose among alternative international expansion patterns, each favouring specific subunits in the organization located in different countries.

The framework outlined in Figures 1.1 and 1.2 suggests that expanding internationally may have important effects on the firm in terms of where and how it creates value. However, the keys to successful international business strategy – and thus the MNE's performance – are its FSAs relative to rivals, and its effectiveness and efficiency in deploying and augmenting these FSAs across borders.[139]

Strategic Challenges in the New Economy

Richard Dobbs, *Tim Koller* and *Sree Ramaswamy* contrast the drivers of many developed economy MNEs' long-term competitive success in the post-World War II era, with the present, *new economy* demands for continued growth and profitability.[140] Their analysis highlights the importance of the seven concepts underlying this book's analytical framework, as discussed earlier in the chapter.

The largest North American, European, and Japanese MNEs enjoyed a long period of growth in global demand, and rising industry profitability in the post-World War II era. Among many underlying drivers that strengthened the location advantages of host nations, two elements stand out. The first driver was 'deregulation and privatization' around the world.[141] Private-sector competition was introduced in many infrastructure-related industries, such as telecom, transportation, and utilities, all with a strong legacy of state ownership, and often linked with a heritage of easily remediable inefficiencies under new governance conditions. The second driver was 'urbanization and industrialization', which was taking place in many emerging markets.[142] This particular driver contributed substantially to the growth of a global consumer class with purchasing power to access a wide variety of products, ranging from the good-enough market to luxury goods with worldwide appeal.

Many developed economy MNEs expanded rapidly as a response to these favourable environmental conditions. The widespread, improved location advantages in many emerging economies allowed these MNEs to increase their international footprint, building upon three types of FSAs. *First*, especially larger MNEs with scale advantages in production were able to increase profitability further because of low marginal costs per unit when entering foreign markets (e.g., Nippon Steel, becoming the world's largest steel firm). They thereby implemented the typical strategies conventionally associated with centralized exporters, and with commanding non-location-bound FSAs embodied in exported products. This strategy very much reflected Pattern I of capability building discussed earlier in this chapter (Figure 1.7).

Second, MNEs with knowledge-based resource reservoirs could engage in geographic diversification on the strength of these non-location-bound FSAs being transferred to foreign subsidiaries, as would be expected from the international projector archetype. In addition to faster growth, entry into host countries with business cycles different from the home country also conferred more stable economic returns. Other benefits included learning in host environments and further reductions in unit costs because of newly created, location-bound FSAs, as would conventionally be expected in multi-centred MNEs (e.g., General Electric's global presence worldwide, generating 70 per cent of total revenues outside the United States in 2018[143]). This largely represents Pattern III of capability building in the MNE, as we described earlier in the chapter.

Third, MNEs also engaged in novel resource combinations, skilfully complementing their tangible, intangible, and human-capital-related FSAs with easily accessible resources (location advantages) in host nations, as exemplified by the rapid growth of offshored production and offshored outsourcing of manufacturing assembly activities in countries such as China and India. Importantly, in many of these cases of resource recombination, non-location-bound FSAs were created, in line with the strategy of international coordinators. Here again, we see a specific version arising of Pattern III of capability building, as discussed earlier in the chapter.

Unfortunately, according to Dobbs and his co-authors, the above three approaches to relatively easy international expansion no longer hold, because of two major changes in the global economy. *First*, many emerging country MNEs (or EMNEs) have entered international markets, building more on home country institutional features than on conventional non-location-bound FSAs in R&D, marketing, or production quality and efficiency. Even with these initial deficits, successful international expansion does require at least a threshold level of non-location-bound FSAs (as we explained earlier in this chapter), including sound entrepreneurial judgement, to assess which expansion moves make most economic sense. In addition, many EMNEs are agile, i.e., they appear to have the ability to respond rapidly to the market, thereby recombining pre-existing technologies and focusing on cost cutting. But home country location advantages such as the deep financial pockets from government controlled economic actors and other institutional support mechanisms (e.g., trade and investment barriers discriminating against foreign firms; country-to-country, diplomatic relationship building efforts from the home-country government) can go a long way to creating favourable platforms for international expansion. Such institutional features also make continued international growth of developed economy incumbents more challenging. This special version of Pattern I from Figure 1.7 implies that targeted home-country location advantages, especially those related to government support for domestic firms, gain extra weight and translate directly into non-location-bound FSAs.

Second, recent advances in technology have created another new source of competition for developed economy MNEs, especially in the form of the 'Internet of threats'. For example, the marginal cost of processing big data is very low for firms equipped with digital platforms that enable them to reach 'hyperscale' in terms of potential customer base (e.g., Amazon, Netflix, Expedia). Digital economy firms often maintain tight control over their businesses through keeping private ownership in their early stages of development. This control through private ownership, rather than having their shares publicly traded, allows them to adopt a long-term focus on growth instead of short-term profitability (e.g., Amazon, Twitter, Yelp); in addition, a large set of small, entrepreneurial tech firms now competes against much larger counterparts by utilizing global e-commerce platforms provided by these digital MNEs (e.g., Amazon, Alibaba, Airbnb). Small, tech-based companies have also been combining different types of FSAs and location advantages as compared to those utilized by developed economy MNEs to catch up with them. Digital assets alone in many cases do not guarantee competitive success, as they often require complementary resources that are location specific. Even Uber's international expansion, building upon this US firm's digital platforms that support ride sharing, has required conforming to local regulatory pressures and taking into account the vehicle fleet and quality of drivers available locally. However, established MNEs that insufficiently recombine extant asset reservoirs with new assets in the digital and broader ICT spheres are almost bound to fail, as they will forego industry-level efficiencies and fail to attract a new customer base expecting state-of-the-art digital features of the products and services they purchase. In conceptual terms, the point made here is that the presence of digital assets can make resource recombination processes, along the lines of Pattern III in Figure 1.7, more demanding than before.

In general terms, the great difficulty for established MNEs is to respond effectively to the dual challenges of new entrants (especially EMNEs) expanding into global markets, and digital and related ICT technologies being rapidly introduced in industry. Traditional 'brick and mortar' firms are particularly at risk of being affected if they rely solely on traditional types of FSAs such as large physical asset bases, but lag behind in accumulating digital and ICT-related, complementary assets. This risk is exemplified by the demise of some large retail chains that suffered from the rise in internet sales and did not respond rapidly themselves to this new trend.

To help incumbent MNEs survive and prosper, given the challenges outlined above, the authors formulate five guidelines for effective FSA development, especially for those developed economy MNEs that face increased competition from EMNEs built around new technologies.[144]

1. *Unrelenting diligence to gather and act upon competitive intelligence.*[145] This proposed unrelenting diligence that should guide senior managers from developed economy MNEs is viewed as inevitable: EMNEs will often deploy entirely new success recipes in an industry, in the form of novel business models and resource combinations that may not be fully understood by incumbents who have been in business for many decades with more traditional FSAs. These incumbents face a bounded rationality problem that takes the form of 'uncertain imitability': they would like to emulate EMNE capabilities, but encounter significant *ex ante* uncertainty as to the likely outcome of such efforts. It is often indeed unclear whether the intended capabilities to match those of EMNEs, as they might materialize *ex post*, would actually enable the MNE to counter effectively these new entrants. Making great efforts to reduce this bounded rationality problem and to understand at a deep level EMNE FSAs is thus essential.[146] New recipes are typically informed by early successes in the EMNE's home base, and can have a critical technological component. For example, South Africa's MTN (Mobile Telephone Networks) and Kenya's Safaricom both provide mobile financial services to millions of customers without relying on client bank accounts or credit records, thereby rendering obsolete traditional delivery models for financial services.

2. *New focus on mobilizing patient capital.*[147] Perhaps paradoxically, new entrants in industry increase volatility, uncertainty, complexity, and ambiguity for incumbent companies, but also unintentionally provide an opportunity for senior management and boards of directors of developed economy firms to adopt longer-term strategies, in collaboration with investors willing to adopt a long-term view on firm-level growth and financial returns. New entrants in industry, whether EMNEs or new technology firms, are likely to remain relevant in the longer run. Short-term adjustments to these new entrants' strategies, taking the form of price changes, cost reductions, or marginal changes in product features – some of the typical responses to

satisfy short-term oriented shareholders – are therefore unlikely to be a sufficient response to maintain competitiveness. Taking firms private and using private equity to replace broad, public equity ownership is one recipe to achieve a longer-term orientation.

3. ***Purposeful resource reallocation.***[148] In line with the previous point, incumbent firms that are able to reallocate capital and other critical resources towards new products and markets, rather than relying primarily on the status quo in response to changing conditions, are more likely to build relevant FSAs with the potential to generate sustained growth rates and returns to shareholders in the longer term.

4. ***Investment in knowledge-based and relational FSAs.***[149] Even more than in past decades, it is intellectual capital that now represents the core FSA for most companies, even those outside of conventional, knowledge-intensive businesses. Some companies build their intellectual assets by creating communities (or ecosystems) of users, suppliers, and innovators. Especially ecosystems in the innovation sphere that involve ongoing relationships with a large number of external actors are typically more complex to develop for MNEs than for domestic companies, at least if some of these ecosystems must be built abroad. Here, the first challenge is to become an insider in foreign communities, which is not always easy (see Chapter 6 on the difficulties of becoming an insider in foreign innovation centres). In this regard, EMNEs have been aggressively working on cross-border mergers and acquisitions as a means to acquire necessary intellectual assets abroad (e.g., the Indian firm Sun Pharmaceutical Industries has engaged in a series of acquisitions since the 1990s in the realm of strategic asset-seeking FDI).

5. ***Investment in internationally deployable human capital.***[150] Recruiting ambitious managers, as well as scientific and technical staff members, who have a global mindset (geared towards achieving integration across borders and overall company goals), while respecting the needs for local responsiveness, constitutes a major challenge for most MNEs (see, e.g., Chapter 10 on 'Managing Managers in the Multinational Enterprise'). It is well understood that MNEs must try to access the best available and affordable natural resources, production technologies, managerial practices, sustainability routines, etc., but hiring the best talent can be particularly difficult, because such talent may be accessible only in distant locations and must often be displaced from its own home base and redeployed in a completely different firm-level context. For instance, Ms Angela Ahrendts (born in Indiana, United States) built a professional career in the American fashion and apparel industry. She moved to Burberry (United Kingdom) as CEO and revitalized this MNE by introducing this conservative fashion house to e-commerce and new in-store technologies. She subsequently moved to Apple (United States) as head of

retail in 2014, and applied her prior knowledge from the fashion industry to this electronics company, e.g., by making Apple customers experience luxury shopping at its stores and by providing them with both digital and brick-and-mortar shopping options. In February 2019, Apple announced that Ms Ahrendts would leave the company.[151] She continued to serve on the Board of a number of large MNEs.

In short, MNEs need to review and evaluate continuously the FSA reservoirs they command, as well as the location advantages they can access and build upon. The importance of this value creation process with MNEs continuously recombining resources was well captured in the late Alan Rugman's perspective that any successful internationalization typically requires the MNE to command strong, non-location-bound FSAs and to have access to strong, host-country-specific advantages – as well as related complementary resources – with the latter elements typically being exogenous to the MNE.[152] Hillemann and Gestrin (2016) extended this bundling approach. They argued that one should not just answer the question whether the FSAs an MNE commands and the location advantages it wishes to benefit from are 'strong'. One should also investigate whether the underlying resources inside the firm and the requisite complementary resources external to the firm can be contracted for in efficient markets. If MNE FSAs cannot easily be transacted in efficient markets, for example, because a licensee could simply steal the knowledge involved such as the blueprints of a product, the firm will engage in FDI to protect and exploit its FSAs. If, in addition, the coveted complementary resources in the host country can easily be purchased on open markets, wholly owned FDI will be the result. This might even entail an acquisition, if there is an efficient market for purchasing host country firms. If, on the contrary, the external complementary resources are difficult to access in open markets (e.g., monopolistic distribution networks to reach the consumer), then FDI through cooperative ventures with local partners will ensue.[153] In instances where both MNE FSAs (e.g., stand-alone, patented knowledge) and complementary resources can easily be contracted for in efficient markets, a variety of market contracts will likely be negotiated. Finally, in case the complementary resources in host countries are not easily accessible in efficient markets, but the MNE's FSAs are, this could lead host country businesses to engage in technology purchasing from the MNE.

One key challenge not explicitly considered by Dobbs and his co-authors is the presence of bounded rationality and bounded reliability when trying to implement their five guidelines. The guideline to focus on gathering competitive intelligence is somewhat problematic in terms of potentially triggering unreliability. The suggestion to collect and process diligently as much information as possible on new and potential rivals is good advice. The problem with being too relentless about this is that it may demotivate managers of existing businesses who are responsible for the bulk of the firm's past and present cash flows. In addition, as we noted already, observing the success of new entrants does not mean that incumbents can easily imitate their recipes, especially if these new entrants' home country location advantages played an important role in such success. Reducing bounded rationality problems through gaining knowledge on what rivals do is not the same as gaining sufficient knowledge to emulate their success.

The guideline on seeking patient capital would appear consistent with the 'going concern' philosophy prevailing in most established companies, but it is difficult to ascertain *ex ante* whether shareholder promises to be patient are truthful, and how long such patience would last in the face of disappointing company performance. Supposedly patient shareholders, including private equity owners, can be unreliable too, as can senior managers of an incumbent firm when trying to convince potential investors about the longer-term prospects of their company.

The 'purposeful reallocation of resources' guideline again sounds reasonable, but especially for large MNEs with multiple product and geographic divisions, senior management at the head office may lack requisite information to make the right resource reallocation decisions. This is the case especially when mainly external consultants or head office staff members give advice to senior management, at the expense of individuals in the firm's divisions with deep knowledge of value-generating routines, i.e., the processes of moving from initial idea generation to ultimate product delivery to the customer. Some economic actors inside the firm may also be opportunistic, namely when proposing self-disruption initiatives that would benefit them personally, for example, if these initiatives would allow growing their own units inside the firm at the expense of other units.

The recommendation to build new knowledge-based FSAs is almost self-evident in industries characterized by fast-paced innovation, but the key issue is how much to invest in specific intellectual assets, in particular locations, and through utilizing particular entry modes. Here again, there is no shortage of bounded rationality and bounded reliability challenges. For example, foreign acquisition targets may overplay the value of their pipeline of innovations, and such overestimation may be difficult for the acquirer to identify, especially if the acquisition represents a strategic move into unrelated diversification (new technologies; new markets). Here, the acquiring MNE will be comparatively ignorant on the value of the coveted intellectual assets. In addition, foreign acquisitions may be difficult for acquirers to 'digest', as discussed in greater detail in Chapter 13 on international mergers and acquisitions.

Finally, a focus on human capital sounds good at a superficial level, but as is the case with any resource acquisition, a key question is how this resource can be productively recombined with other resources inside the firm. The ability to integrate 'talent' into broader resource bundles and to deploy these bundles productively through managerial practices such as innovation routines, is as important as the intrinsic quality of the talent itself, but because of bounded rationality, integration difficulties may be underestimated. As regards bounded reliability, it should be remembered that the value of supposed talent is difficult to estimate *ex ante*, divorced from a firm's reservoir of FSAs, and many firms tend to overpay at least some of the time for talent that ultimately proves disappointing (e.g., as demonstrated by high-cost purchases of players in major league sport clubs around the world).

International Business Strategy During Globally Disruptive Events

We have defined the MNE as a firm conducting economic transactions across national borders. This is done through both trading relationships (exports, imports, licensing agreements, production contracts, distribution agreements, and a wide variety of partnerships) and FDI. Foreign operations resulting from FDI include both greenfield subsidiaries – wholly owned or taking the form of equity joint ventures – and acquisitions (full or partial). The entirety of the MNE's market-based relationships with external network actors, together with its domestic and foreign operations, allow integrating a large number of spatially dispersed milieus in the world economy.

The question arises whether globally disruptive events such as the 2020 COVID-19 pandemic and its aftermath can fundamentally affect MNEs and their functioning across borders. The pandemic represented an extreme and unpredictable disruption of the global economy. This particular environmental shock did affect all seven components of the unifying framework developed in this chapter that describes MNE functioning. At the same time, reflecting on how the pandemic has had an impact on these seven elements should support MNE managers in their efforts to operate successfully in any 'new normal'.

Influential voices have suggested that the new normal arising out of the pandemic has fundamentally altered MNE functioning, somewhat similar to the expression that 'old customs crumble and instability rules'.[154] Time will tell, as researchers in international business strategy study the pandemic as a quasi-natural experiment and MNE executives cope with its aftermath in the real world of management and business leadership. Yet, as we explain below in the context of the pandemic, the prediction that a globally disruptive event will radically change everything in MNE functioning is unlikely to materialize.

First, and most importantly, a critical question is whether MNEs can retain their pre-pandemic ability to deploy and exploit *non-location-bound FSAs* in foreign markets. This ability could be affected by sudden increases in 'distance' between countries, especially the administrative or institutional component of distance (discussed in more detail in Chapter 4). The pandemic has highlighted the vulnerabilities of national economies in the realm of their capacity to procure medical equipment, pharmaceutical products, and a variety of other products supplied from abroad and it has led to calls for more national control over a wide range of 'sensitive' industries from a health and national security perspective in many countries. In theory, this new protectionism favouring domestic production and domestic firms could make it more difficult for the MNE to deploy its FSAs abroad, and to manage both its external market-based relationships and foreign subsidiary networks. However, the counterargument to this scenario is that only MNEs command FSAs in international network governance, meaning that they can reassess at any point in time both the nature of ownership and control of any and all of their activities in the global value chains they command, as well as the location thereof. What new barriers to international trade and investment do achieve is that the relative importance of the various types of non-location-bound FSAs in the MNE's capabilities reservoir, as well as the ways in which these are deployed, may shift. For example, reliable network relationships with foreign alliance partners may become more important relative to other FSAs, so as to access more easily contextual intelligence on foreign government regulations and market conditions. Another example is the potential for developing new subsidiary-specific advantages in foreign operations via subsidiary initiatives, if government regulations hamper the design and functioning of global value chains operated by MNEs. Here, governance-related FSAs supporting 'intelligence' and 'business model diversification' may – on a relative scale – gain in importance vis-à-vis more conventional FSAs, such as those in R&D and marketing, as we describe further in Chapter 2.

Second, the pandemic, in exacerbating global institutional fractures and giving more credence to anti-globalization movements around the planet, has not only led to a relative shift in importance among various categories of non-location-bound FSAs. It has also highlighted the need to focus more on relational and corporate-diplomacy-related *location-bound FSAs*. Anti-globalization forces are driven by two parallel, albeit entirely contradictory, ideological agendas: the 'country first' agenda, focused on promoting home-grown firms (including MNEs); and the 'anti-MNE' agenda, with the latter constructed around the myth that MNEs are more than any other economic actor responsible for societal problems such as environmental pollution, climate change impacts, income disparities, social injustices, etc.[155] In the aftermath of the pandemic, those MNEs capable of developing new location-bound FSAs based on relationship building with local providers of complementary assets and on stronger subsidiary embeddedness in host country milieus will be the most likely to thrive. We discuss key issues in this realm, such as redefining subsidiary roles and evaluating subsidiary severability, in more detail in Chapter 5.

Third, the meaning of *location advantages* and the MNE's ease of access to requisite location advantages in various host country milieus will also be affected. In this realm, senior MNE managers (and corporate Boards of Directors) should pay close attention to new government policies at various institutional levels that might affect trade-offs in location choices. Elements such as the role of the MNE as a national 'diamond connector' and senior management's assessment of the potential for reshoring, nearshoring, or even simply relocating specific activities in a new normal, are touched upon in Chapters 3 and 4. One element that has become more important because of the pandemic is the value attached to 'geo-redundancy', meaning that economic activities should be conducted in a larger number of locations (whether in MNE subsidiaries or by network partners) than would be the case if only static cost efficiencies were considered. Geographic milieus that allow MNEs to reduce the risk of supply chain interruptions may therefore gain strength in terms of their location advantages.

Fourth, the future of large MNEs in general is bright in our view, given these firms' unique expertise in creating value through distinct *resource recombination*. Their ability to cut resources that are no longer needed, and to develop – or otherwise access – resources that have become more important (e.g., in the realm of digital governance tools and cyber security) reflects a much-needed type of flexibility in the post-pandemic world that non-MNEs typically lack. Critical elements in this regard include the 'micro-modularization' of international value chains and MNEs' strategic agility in governing their micro-modularized activities, as we discuss in Chapter 5.

Fifth, as already noted above, *complementary resources* held by external actors in host countries may become more important than ever. Here, MNEs may need to consider alternative forms of governance, especially in the realm of alliance formation with external partners, whereby sophisticated micro-level relationships can to some extent substitute for multilateral cooperation among governments. We touch upon this issue in Chapter 3.

Finally, a radical disruption such as the pandemic increases substantially the *bounded rationality* problems facing MNEs, given the new uncertainties created on multiple fronts: supply chain interruptions at the input side; disturbances during the production process itself because of the unavailability of requisite financial, human, and service-related resources; difficulties to assess what the demand will be for the firm's products in the post-pandemic new normal; etc. A major disruption can also trigger opportunistic behaviour and other forms of *unreliability* from the MNE's partners, who may be fighting for their own survival in the new normal. National governments at home and abroad may also become more unreliable as they put health and national security considerations – and more broadly national economic independence for a wide variety of sensitive goods and services – ahead of respecting private property rights and the efficient functioning of free markets. We explore in more detail strategic elements such as investing in intelligence, adequately protecting proprietary knowledge, and continuously reassessing the ownership, control, and location of vulnerable activities in Chapters 2 and 3.

Takeaway Messages for Managers: The Seven Key Questions in International Business Strategy

The above analysis suggests that managers should answer the following seven basic questions in international strategy formation:

1. What is our distinct resource base, including elements of our administrative heritage, that provides internationally transferable FSAs?
2. Which value-added activities in which foreign location(s) will permit us to exploit and augment to the fullest our distinct resource base?
3. What are the expected costs and difficulties we will face when transferring this distinct resource base?
4. What specific resource recombination (associated with each alternative foreign entry and operating mode) will be required so as to make the proposed international value-added activities successful?
5. Do we have the required resource recombination capability in-house?
6. What are the costs and benefits of using complementary resources of external actors to fill resource gaps?
7. What are the main bounded rationality and bounded reliability problems we will face when extending the geographic scope of our firm's activities, given the changed boundaries of the firm, the changed linkages with outside stakeholders, and the changes in our internal functioning?

2

The Critical Role of Firm-Specific Advantages

Five Learning Objectives

1. To describe the four characteristics of core competencies, which are the higher-order firm-specific advantages (FSAs) of the firm.
2. To explain the importance of the corporation's 'strategic architecture' in the context of core competencies.
3. To develop an understanding of MNEs' business model diversification, whereby the FSAs deployed in each business model, though at least different in part, should also mutually reinforce one another to drive growth and profitability.
4. To identify the bounded rationality and bounded reliability problems associated with MNEs outsourcing their R&D, if they want to maintain or build core competencies in innovation.
5. Based on the conceptual framework in Chapter 1, to analyze the managerial implications of an ill-conceived, sole focus on core competencies.

This chapter explores Prahalad and Hamel's idea that 'core competencies' constitute the most important source of an MNE's success. Core competencies are really any company's most important FSAs: its vital routines and recombination abilities. According to Prahalad and Hamel, the company's main strategy should be to build or acquire core competencies. This idea will be examined and then critiqued using the framework presented in Chapter 1.

Significance

C. K. Prahalad and Gary Hamel have provided the clearest exposition of the importance of higher-order FSAs in their path-breaking *HBR* article 'The core competence of the corporation', published in 1990.[1]

Prahalad and Hamel suggest that senior managers need to rethink the very concept of the large, diversified firm seeking worldwide leadership. This type of firm is more than a group of independently managed strategic business units (SBUs), or in the case of MNEs, more than a set of independent subsidiaries or subsidiary-groupings (e.g., in geographic or product divisions) in various countries. Senior managers should view their firm as a portfolio of 'core competencies', which are its higher-order FSAs, namely, the firm's routines and recombination capabilities. These higher-order FSAs include the company's shared knowledge (organized into routines), its ability to integrate multiple technologies (reflecting the recombination of internal resources), and the routines/recombination abilities carried by key employees (the so-called competence carriers) that can be deployed across business units. In the authors' words: 'In the long run, competitiveness derives from an ability to build, at lower cost and more speedily than competitors, the core competencies that spawn unanticipated products. The real sources of advantage are to be found in management's ability to consolidate corporate-wide technologies and production skills into competencies that empower individual businesses to adapt quickly to changing opportunities.'[2] According to Prahalad and Hamel, core competencies are more important than stand-alone FSAs.

What do these core competencies do? They produce the physical, tangible things that the authors call 'core products'. Core products represent areas of technological leadership in the form of key *components* from which end products are developed and created (e.g., highly reliable engines in automobiles, or sophisticated data drives and lasers in compact audio disc systems).

The third and final level in the hierarchy of sources of competitiveness (in addition to core competencies and core products) is the level of 'end products'. End products are finished goods. Core products are integrated into these finished goods, establishing a visible corporate brand presence with end users.

To summarize: according to Prahalad and Hamel, *core competencies*, meaning the firm's routines and recombination capabilities, produce components called *core products*, which are put together to create *end products*.

The authors cite several examples to illustrate core competencies. Honda, for example, has developed a core competence around designing and building a versatile core product: compact engines. Honda is good at 'exploiting what it ha [s] learned from motorcycles – how to make high-revving, smooth-running, lightweight engines'[3] and then applying and extending these routines to make end products in a range of related businesses, including automobiles, lawn mowers, and electric generators. Sony's core competence of recombination in electronics miniaturization has allowed it to anticipate and pioneer a wide range of new features (i.e., core products) in consumer electronics goods.

Identifying core competencies and differentiating them from other FSAs is an intricate process. Stand-alone FSAs such as technological know-how and strengths derived from vertical integration are not core competencies. In practice, core competencies in the form of routines and recombination capabilities involve collective learning, communicating, harmonizing multiple streams of technology, and organizing value-creation skills across departmental boundaries. Prahalad and Hamel outline three characteristics to help managers identify core competencies. A core competence should:

- be difficult for competitors to imitate in terms of achieving the required internal coordination and learning (which points to the distinctiveness of the firm's routines and recombination abilities);
- provide potential access to a wide variety of markets (which points to the capability's contribution towards combining or recombining resources for success in new environments, as discussed in Chapter 1); and
- make a significant contribution to the perceived customer benefits of the end product (which points to satisfying the needs of customers, a key stakeholder group).

To these three characteristics we should add a fourth, assumed implicitly in Prahalad and Hamel's analysis, and especially important for a large MNE: the loss of a core competence would have an important negative effect on the firm's present and future performance, in terms of value creation and satisfying stakeholder objectives. This last criterion is essential. If senior corporate-level managers do not apply this fourth criterion, then every SBU, every functional area in the firm – and every foreign affiliate – could claim it is the home of a number of core competencies. This would divert senior management's attention from the elements that are truly critical to the firm's performance, and might lead to ineffective resource allocation to support the exploitation, further development, and deployment throughout the firm of alleged core competencies.

According to Prahalad and Hamel, the primary role of senior management should be to develop the 'strategic architecture' to guide the corporation in building and acquiring core competencies, either through internal resources or external acquisitions and alliances. The strategic architecture is a 'road map of the future that identifies which core competencies to build and their constituent technologies'.[4] Such a strategic architecture is necessary to overcome the challenge of decentralized units acting in their own self-interest, which is a critical intra-organizational bounded reliability problem. In the long term, a strategic architecture will also help foster company-wide innovation, competitiveness, and success. In the international context, this vision of the ideal corporation obviously implies a rejection of the multi-centred approach to foreign operations, as well as a deep suspicion of firms that operate with powerful product and geographic divisions.

Prahalad and Hamel argue that the firm's resource allocation process and incentive systems should support the firm's strategic architecture. For example, corporate-level senior management should reallocate the individuals who carry core competencies, namely, have deep knowledge of routines and can be instrumental to resource recombination across functional and business units so as to yield the highest return for the firm as a whole. Lower-level units such as divisions or subsidiaries should be made to justify the continued location of competence carriers in their operations in the same way that they need to justify new capital spending. In addition, the incentive system should be designed to reward divisional or subsidiary managers for acting in the interest of the firm rather than their own unit, thereby reducing bounded reliability problems. For example, unit managers should be rewarded for volunteering competence carriers – often their most valuable employees – to a central pool for reallocation.

Finally, the authors address the issue of acquiring FSAs through external strategic alliances rather than through internal, organic development. In this case, the firm intends to internalize the knowledge and skills of the alliance partner(s), thus furthering the creation of the company's own technological and process-related FSAs. However, the authors caution against two dangers. First, the company must have a clear understanding of the FSAs it is trying to build through the partnership, and those it is seeking to protect from being transferred to potential competitors. Second, outsourcing strategies for key components, as a shortcut to increased short-term profitability, may lead to the loss of FSAs. Outsourcing often means that no more FSA development occurs in the outsourced areas, thereby leading to the atrophy of knowledge and skills embodied in the firm's employees and, in a broader sense, the firm's routines and recombination capabilities in the outsourced areas.

Context and Complementary Perspectives

Prahalad and Hamel's work was published in 1990, a time when much attention was devoted to the unbridled success of Japanese companies (more than to the Japanese economy as a whole) with their strong focus on scale and scope economies in product development and marketing. Many Asian MNEs were on the rise, while those in North America and Europe seemed to be declining in terms of innovation and world market share in a variety of industries.

Consistent with this setting, many of the positive examples cited in their work are derived from the small sample of the most successful Japanese companies, such as NEC, Canon, Sony, Honda, and Matsushita. These are contrasted with lower-achieving competitors from the United States and Europe, such as GTE, Xerox, Chrysler, and Philips. The authors focus almost exclusively on consumer manufacturing industries such as computers, photocopiers, automobiles, and electronics (TVs, VCRs, etc.), where the redeployment potential of technology from one set of products to another plays a key role in long-term success and a global approach to product development and marketing, typical for **centralized exporters** and **international projectors**, is well suited.

Paolo Aversa, **Stefan Haefliger** and **Danielle Giuliana Reza** wrote an article in *SMR* complementing Prahalad and Hamel's path-breaking *HBR* work, where they argue that a focus on overarching core competencies may not be the way to achieve international corporate success.[5] Many large firms now combine several different business models in their portfolio, which amounts to 'business model diversification'.[6] A business model can be defined simply as a set of purposively crafted routines (or managerial practices) meant to: (1) create value out of assembling and combining resources; (2) deliver this value to customers; and (3) capture (at least part of) this value in the form of profitable growth. Business model diversification means that firms use at least two clearly distinct sets of such routines (higher-order FSAs) to create, deliver, and capture value. As one example, US-based Netflix creates, delivers, and captures value through a digital subscription streaming model. This approach permits the online screening of existing movies. But it also operates a separate business model to create original digital content for movies.

When deploying multiple business models, each building on specific resource bundles and routines that amount to higher-order FSAs, the key to success is not so much to try to develop a single core competence or overarching FSA, but rather to craft complementarities among the different business models, so as to create synergies. Complementarities arise if the value delivery systems used in each business model cater largely to the same customer base; or partly use the same underlying resource base (e.g., capital, human resources, etc.); or share some activities such as customer ordering, distribution, etc. These complementarities all point to the presence of a 'strategic fit' between FSAs used in a successful, existing (or initial) business model, and the FSAs deployed in the added business model, when the firm diversifies.[7]

One danger of business model diversification is 'cannibalization' or 'resource dilution': adding a new business model may make firms 'de-focus' resources from their existing, core activities.[8] For example, when a computer firm such as Hewlett-Packard adds a direct-sales business model to its existing ways of competing, in order to challenge Dell Computer, this might negatively affect its relationships with conventional distributors and retailers who work out of brick-and-mortar stores. In this particular instance, challenges of divided engagement – as an expression of the bounded reliability of the MNE itself – may arise in terms of how it manages its external partnerships. Even if senior management thinks that the firm will likely benefit from complementarities between business models, the possible negative effects from the business model diversification should therefore also be carefully considered.

Whether business model diversification makes economic sense for an MNE is not always easy to ascertain. Adding a new business model almost by definition brings more complexity, and the expected benefits of this new model therefore need to be assessed carefully vis-à-vis the expected costs. For example, a new operating mode may be contemplated when expanding into a distant foreign market. A firm may decide to use external distributors to boost its exports (as compared to its prior model of managing fully all export sales), or it may opt for an international joint venture (as compared to its prior model of working only with wholly owned operations). Working with various operating modes and operating mixed modes in foreign nations can quickly add costs to the MNE's business model portfolio and can make the MNE's governance particularly complex.

As such, a few key questions to be answered when deploying multiple business models include: (1) which novel resource combinations are required to make a newly added business model work successfully?; (2) which (potential) new business model has the strongest complementarities with the existing model(s)?; and (3) does the firm need to adjust its arsenal of performance measures and other governance tools, so as to accommodate the new business model in its business portfolio, with a special focus on potential challenges of divided engagement?

In addition to answering the aforementioned key questions, it should be noted that managing a portfolio with multiple business models is a dynamic process, and as a result, managers need to be ready for divesting from a new business model if it does not produce anticipated synergies. Therefore, when various business models are being operated simultaneously, it is important to assess regularly the viability and performance impacts of each model, both in their own right, and by taking into account complementarities (or substitution effects) with the other models. Special attention needs to be devoted to the added complexities these models may bring to effective MNE governance.

Markus C. Becker and *Francesco Zirpoli* have provided a second perspective complementary to Prahalad and Hamel's.[9] Their *CMR* article focuses on core competencies in the realm of R&D, which are the main source of competitive advantages for many knowledge-driven MNEs. As noted by Prahalad and Hamel in their *HBR* paper discussed earlier, firms sometimes grow by depending increasingly on external production. They reap benefits from outsourcing, such as cost-efficiencies, financial risk reduction, and access to complementary resources, as compared to what can be achieved in-house. In the realm of R&D, the development of many modern technologies is often becoming more complex in nature, meaning that firms can benefit from sharing risks with other companies and accessing external specialists' knowledge and capacity to innovate. Outsourcing often goes hand in hand with offshoring, in order to achieve cost efficiencies in low-cost foreign locations, whereby the firm pursuing outsourcing and offshoring becomes an MNE.

However, the benefits from R&D outsourcing are also accompanied by new challenges in terms of the MNE retaining its capacity to develop and exploit core competencies. The danger of becoming too dependent on external sources of innovation is that it can deprive the MNE of 'learning-by-doing for developing R&D competences', especially when tacit knowledge is involved.[10] For example, R&D outsourcing can prevent firms from building 'component-specific know-how', when they operate as system integrators. Component-specific know-how can only be accumulated in – and maintained by – firms when learning-by-doing occurs internally.[11] The question therefore arises how the MNE can earn the main benefits from outsourcing, while at the same time retaining its capacity of 'learning by doing', especially in the R&D sphere.

Since the 1990s, the Italian automobile manufacturer Fiat has aggressively worked on R&D outsourcing for up to 85 per cent (in terms of value) of new car model components. In a first stage, this led to negative outcomes for the firm, because Fiat lost its ability to learn about the tacit knowledge embedded in the components:

> Fiat's problem was the result of assuming that the product architecture was more modular than it was in reality; relying, in turn, too much on the coordination properties of standard interfaces among components and systems; missing exposure to learning about components and systems development tasks due to their complete outsourcing to suppliers; and, as a consequence, gradually losing component-specific knowledge.[12]

Even with these negative outcomes, Fiat could not consider a full 'back-sourcing' of R&D and performing it in-house again, because it lacked the requisite financial resources and time needed to re-learn.[13] Instead, senior management at Fiat decided to become more strategic about which component-related R&D activities could reasonably be outsourced, building on two criteria: (1) the level of interdependencies between the component considered and the remainder of the car; and (2) the component's impact on what customers value highly as to the car's performance.[14]

The strategic guideline for components with high scores on both criteria (interdependence and value attributed by the customers) became to develop and produce such components in-house (e.g., suspension/handling). This approach reduced bounded rationality problems, especially in terms of allowing the MNE to retain knowledge on the relevant interdependencies. It also reduced bounded reliability challenges from suppliers by making sure that the MNE would retain control over those components that customers value most. For components with a high score on interdependency, but a low score on the value attributed to them by the customers, the guideline became to co-design these components (e.g., safety systems) with specialized suppliers. Here, the danger of supplier opportunism is low, but the MNE keeps reducing its own bounded rationality challenges by retaining full access to all relevant information and the co-design permits the MNE's ongoing learning process, especially as regards control over the interdependencies involved. For components with a low score on the interdependency criterion, meaning that they are basically stand-alone components, but with a high score on how the customers perceive their importance (e.g., braking systems), the guideline became to outsource them, but with detailed specifications. Finally, for components with low scores on both criteria (e.g., air conditioning systems), the strategic guideline became to outsource these components, with providing only broad specifications to suppliers.

In addition to the above analysis at the component level, Fiat also made a distinction at the higher level of the automobiles themselves, between 'template' car models and subsequent 'derivative' ones.[15] For template models, the guideline was to design and engineer all key components and systems in-house, and to use these subsequently 'as a template to design and engineer derivative products'.[16] For the derivative models, the guideline became to outsource the 'complete development of entire vehicles' to specialized suppliers.[17] The above, hybrid approach enabled Fiat to maintain ample opportunities for learning-by-doing with its template models, while gaining benefits from R&D outsourcing in the realm of derivative models.

Becker and Zirpoli formulate four takeaways from the case of Fiat's R&D outsourcing:

1. R&D-related activities critical to maintaining or building core competencies should be kept in-house.
2. Over time, some activities may become less critical as to their overall contribution to the firm's competencies (in terms of technical interdependencies and value to the customers), and these activities can then be outsourced to suppliers (sometimes even involving an entire 'derivative' car model).
3. The allocation of R&D activities to in-house units versus outside suppliers does not change the MNE's vertical scope: the MNE still performs all activities across the entire value chain, but within each vertical segment, R&D activities for components unrelated or weakly related to core competencies can be outsourced.
4. Given the above, the decision on which R&D activities to outsource becomes more than just the conventional make-or-buy decision that would be focused solely on reducing production costs, and perhaps taking into account first-order financial and supply-chain interruption risks.[18] The most important question is always related to the impacts of outsourcing on the MNE's core competencies in the longer run.

Becker and Zirpoli's analysis provides a useful complement to Prahalad and Hamel's view that a firm's strategy should focus on core competencies. In fact, Becker and Zirpoli provide clear guidelines on how to implement this focus in the context of R&D activities:

1. They highlight the importance of innovation and R&D-related capabilities as one of the MNE's highest-order FSAs: it can only be developed and

maintained further through the MNE's 'learning-by-doing' and resource recombination involving in-house R&D personnel.[19]

2. They also highlight the importance of the firm's strategic architecture in terms of maintaining 'component-specific know-how',[20] even if they operate as system integrators, for example, when they develop 'template' models.[21]

3. Finally, they validate the often-made comment on the dangers of outsourcing activities that embody the firm's core competencies. They provide practical guidelines to use when firms determine what R&D tasks and even products can be outsourced or should be kept in-house.

Overall, Becker and Zirpoli's work confirms the relevance of the main conceptual framework introduced in Chapter 1. For example, being able to manage the interdependencies between a component and the remainder of the vehicle represents an automaker's accumulated knowledge in a specialized technical area of resource recombination. It is a higher-order FSA typically held by capable system integrators. In addition, the value attached by customers to specific components may be location-dependent: a high demand in a particular country (i.e., demand-side LAs) may only be satisfied by a foreign MNE if this firm properly caters to these location dependencies, through building new, location-bound FSAs in-house, in host country environments. Their analysis also focuses on the importance of the time dimension in deciding between in-house production and outsourcing. Here, new resource recombination involving outside suppliers may sometimes become warranted as a component becomes less critical, but the opposite situation is possible, too, if a component becomes more interdependent with other ones and if customers start attaching more value to the interdependent component (e.g., some electronics features in vehicles).

Applying the concepts developed in Chapter 1, we see that Prahalad and Hamel's notion of core competencies is largely equivalent to the higher-order FSA concept, with a strong focus on routines and recombination capabilities. Recombination capabilities are especially critical for Prahalad and Hamel, but, as they correctly point out, these can be difficult to define exactly or to deconstruct. These FSAs are also affected by the administrative infrastructure or heritage that has evolved over the life of the company. However, the key ingredients are similar to the ones described in Chapter 1: an **entrepreneurial attitude** of senior corporate-level managers and competence carriers, critical to identifying and pursuing new **market opportunities** and to uncovering **resources that are not yet fully utilized** and can be deployed in other markets, and an **organizational ability** to **meld extant and new resources** in novel ways.

In terms of the patterns of FSA development discussed in Chapter 1, the authors paradoxically focus largely on Pattern I (see Figure 1.7 in Chapter 1), with core competencies typically developed in the home country (guided by corporate-level senior management) and then diffused to the rest of the firm. Here, the firm has been very effective in recombination at home, across product lines and units, but there is little need for further recombination abroad. The authors assume that North American and European firms are less effective than Asian companies in implementing Pattern I. As the authors see it, internationally transferable FSAs are typically developed in the home country, but their exploitation is, unfortunately, usually bounded to one unit, rather than shared across the company. The authors advocate that North American and European firms shift their strategic focus to align with that of Japanese MNEs, but observe that North American and European firms are hampered by an administrative heritage of 'bounded innovation'. Bounded innovation means that innovation activities and resulting resource recombinations are guided by decentralized unit goals rather than corporate goals, and innovation outcomes remain within the unit, rather than being deployed throughout the firm. The authors also criticize the presence of imprisoned resources, whereby the different units fully control specific individuals and technologies underlying core competencies. The authors thereby point to extensive bounded rationality problems in Western firms, since corporate-level senior management lacks the insight to engage in corrective action.

To some extent, this corporate structure also produces a bounded reliability problem, because individual units have sufficient power to block the transfer of knowledge from other units inside the firm (this is an expression of the 'not invented here' syndrome: whatever innovation comes from outside the unit must be bad or irrelevant). In addition, SBUs often refuse to cooperate with other units on joint innovation, and jealously guard their own resources, including valuable employees, so as to preclude these resources from helping other units. In other words, the unit's commitment to the pursuit of corporate goals is diverted towards the pursuit of local goals. In the authors' view, the resource allocation process should therefore not just limit itself to capital, but should also include the key, competence-carrying individuals. Corporate-level senior management should have the power to reallocate these individuals to serve corporate goals.

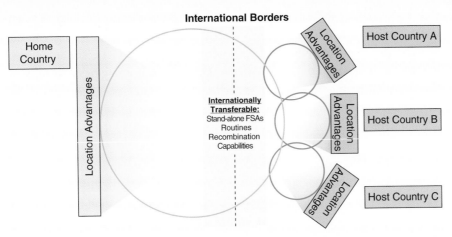

International Borders

Home Country

Location Advantages

Internationally Transferable: Stand-alone FSAs Routines Recombination Capabilities

Location Advantages

Location Advantages

Location Advantages

Host Country A

Host Country B

Host Country C

Figure 2.1
Non-location-bound (or internationally transferable) FSAs as drivers of economies of scope across markets and products

The shading of the NLB FSA area in the circle of the home country and the blank area of the rest of the home country circle indicate the emphasis on NLB FSAs and the assumed irrelevance of home country LAs and LB FSAs in Prahalad and Hamel's model. The circles of the home country and host countries intersect as a result of the NLB FSAs that the MNE has transferred to its foreign operations, and which are now shared by all these geographic milieus. The blank areas of LB FSAs in the middle section of each host country triangle on the right reflect the lack of development of new LB FSAs. Extant NLB FSAs suffice to be successful globally, and to access – and benefit from – LAs across the world, in terms of the demand for the MNE's products.

Figure 2.1 illustrates how Prahalad and Hamel's argument relates to the conceptual framework outlined in Chapter 1.

The circle on the left of Figure 2.1 represents the domestic milieu of a firm that normally relies on three forms of resources simultaneously to be competitive, namely, a foundation of location advantages (LAs), upon which location-bound FSAs and internationally transferable FSAs are built. However, Prahalad and Hamel really emphasize the internationally transferable component. The authors also suggest that competitiveness in the global economy requires a focus on higher-order FSAs. Specifically, firms need to expand continuously their resource base by developing new overarching technologies that are shareable across product lines and that are supported by a variety of managerial routines, thereby permitting economies of scope across markets. When expanding across markets, the only relevant FSAs are the internationally transferable ones in their model. Prahalad and Hamel's view is reflected in the set of non-location-bound FSAs transferred to the right-hand side, and exploited in each distinct host country market.

The three circles on the right of Figure 2.1 show the host country milieus where the MNE's non-location-bound FSAs are deployed. These circles are interlinked, which means here that the same core competencies are shared across global geographic space, and are possibly continuously strengthened through interactions among operations in the different markets. The blank spaces in the host country triangles show the absence of location-bound FSAs. The authors do not think it necessary for the MNE to develop additional strengths in the form of new, location-bound FSAs to access the location advantages of host nations, in particular the demand in these markets.

On a critical note, the conceptual framework in Chapter 1 helps to identify five main weaknesses in Prahalad and Hamel's analysis.

First, they do not explicitly touch on the issue of location advantages (general or firm-specific) and geographic determinants of FSAs, nor do they consider the feasibility and cost in practice of transferring non-location-bound FSAs to other locations. They suggest that developing a firm's higher-order FSAs can be proactively planned and moulded by senior management through what they call a strategic architecture. However, their underlying assumption is that FSAs are non-location-bound and can be seamlessly transferred and exploited internationally, which is often not the case in practice.

Second, the authors overlook the importance of the geographical embeddedness of competence carriers, namely, the individuals and groups with a deep knowledge of the company routines and the ability to drive resource recombination. Prahalad and Hamel go as far as to suggest that managers in decentralized units should be made to compete for the allocation of this talent carrying core competencies. This intra-firm competition should occur irrespective of where the competence carriers are located, similar to the way business units compete for capital resources in an annual budgeting process. In reality, however, individuals and even teams designated as competence carriers are embedded in specific locations, and their geographic reassignment may lead to the loss of this embeddedness, in turn causing the loss of the (often routinized) mutually enriching exchange of knowledge between the individual or team inside the firm and specific complementary actors, both in the affiliate itself and in the local, external environment. Co-location matters! Losing this exchange of knowledge can lead to a loss of value for the firm as a whole. From an international perspective, the authors thus neglect the link between location advantages and the more intricate internal processes of FSA creation, crafted as the result of the unique external environment in which each business unit operates and its own internal functioning.

Third, the authors overlook the (sometimes critical) role of subsidiary-level capabilities for MNE competitiveness and the problems associated with transferring these to other units in the MNE. Prahalad and Hamel suggest that decentralized units often develop unique competencies over time, which they should not be allowed to keep for themselves at the expense of value creation for the firm as a whole. The difficulties in the relationship between corporate-level senior management and decentralized unit management in general are similar to those prevailing in the relationship between the MNE's central headquarters and its foreign subsidiaries. Here, the concept of SBU or decentralized unit evolution over time mirrors that of developing autonomous subsidiary initiatives in host country subsidiaries. While Prahalad and Hamel mention the advantages of transferring one unit's competencies to other units, once again there is no discussion of the difficulties involved in this transfer.

Fourth, the authors overlook important bounded rationality and bounded reliability problems. In terms of hierarchical control within the corporation, Prahalad and Hamel implicitly suggest that strongly centralized decision making by corporate-level senior management is preferred over decentralizing to independent units. However, there are reasons why most large MNEs are organized into multiple divisions with relative autonomy and only limited, selective intervention from central headquarters. One important reason is that extensive intervention by central headquarters will face important bounded rationality and bounded reliability problems when trying to identify a set of competence carriers, assert control over these competence carriers, and then reallocate them according to the perceived contribution they can make in each location.

The sheer volume of information used by a large MNE also produces bounded rationality and bounded reliability problems for Prahalad and Hamel's highly centralized MNE. While it is true that economies of scope can often be gained by interactions among decentralized units, it is also true that inter-unit communication, coordination, and FSA sharing must remain limited: companies are divided into divisions precisely as a governance mechanism to reduce bounded rationality and bounded reliability problems caused by information overload.

Fifth, the authors fail to distinguish between the back-end and customer-end segments of the value chain. It makes sense to build on core competencies at the back end of the value chain (i.e., all activities where no direct interface is required with customers, such as sourcing, the manufacturing of intermediate goods, and logistics). At the back end, the MNE should attempt to streamline operations and to earn economies of scope by sharing knowledge across borders as much as possible, much in line with Prahalad and Hamel's recommendations. Here, overall efficiency considerations should in many cases trump individual subsidiary preferences. However, this does not hold for the customer end of the value chain, where a strong focus on national or regional responsiveness is often critical to exploit profitably core competencies. Here, the firm has to make sure that its home-grown core competencies do not turn into core rigidities – namely, barriers to necessary adaptation and profitable expansion in foreign markets.

Strategic Challenges in the New Economy

Ramon Casadesus-Masanell and *Jorge Tarziján* provide a *new economy extension* of Prahalad and Hamel's path-breaking perspective on core competencies.[22] They analyze the key success factors underlying the competitiveness of LAN Airlines, a Chilean carrier (now a part of LATAM Airlines, managed by LATAM Airlines Group since 2016), with a focus on this firm's business models. As noted earlier, a business model as a set of routines or managerial practices is a manifestation of idiosyncratic resource bundling and resulting FSAs accumulated in a company. One would normally expect any firm to deploy a single business model, in order to guarantee corporate cohesion and related internal efficiencies (e.g., through a single, well-understood approach to pricing its products). However, many firms, including LAN Airlines, deploy multiple business models, whereby each model represents a distinct, creative combination of resource bundles, and thus a variation in the FSAs actually deployed in the marketplace.

Successful MNEs, responding to the demands of distinct customer segments, must often operate different business models simultaneously. Recognizing that 'one model does not fit all' is consistent with our analysis in Chapter 1. Expanding into any new country typically requires at least some novel recombination of resources as compared to domestic operations. Acknowledging the need for adaptation, and moving away from proven domestic approaches, is a common precondition to avoid failure in international markets, especially if domestically deployed resource bundles and resulting FSAs are location-bound.

However, international markets themselves may well require deploying different resource combinations for distinct customer segments. Commercial success abroad then hinges on three conditions being met. *First*, differentiating the international approach from the domestic one is a starting point, as described in Chapter 1. *Second*, the crafting of different resource combinations, and the resulting unique FSAs, for each international customer segment can also be critical. Deploying different resource bundles for each customer segment may be effective, but such variation is typically also costly as compared to uniformity. *Third*, and most importantly, in order to keep the costs of deploying different business models under control, firms must identify complementarities between the resource bundles and related ways of doing things, deployed in each market segment. More specifically, if the different customer segments share at least some common resources and especially routines, synergies might be achieved between segments. This way of thinking is aligned with Prahalad and Hamel's thinking on the core competence of the corporation. But in this case, the core competence (or higher-order FSA) need not necessarily result from a technology shared among distinct customer segments. The core competence allowing the firm to deploy distinct business models simultaneously, at an acceptable cost, can result from sharing any type of asset or bundle of resources, or managerial practice among customer segments in international markets.

As one example of this core competence approach, LAN Airlines first differentiated its international passenger operations from domestic operations. The latter represented a 'no-frills passenger model', but for international travel, the firm deployed a 'full-service international passenger-airline business model'.[23] At the same time, the firm diversified into international air cargo transport. Rather than operating the cargo business independently from the international passenger travel, it sought to develop commonalities underlying the two business models for international markets, despite the obvious fact that goods transport is a very different business from passenger transport.

In the international passenger business, LAN served major destinations in the Americas and Europe, using hubs and alliances as a member of the Oneworld airline alliance, similar to what many other international airlines do. As to the international freight business, LAN 'transported salmon from Chile, asparagus from Peru, fresh flowers from Ecuador, and other such perishables to the US and Europe while flying high-value-to-weight merchandise such as computers, mobile phones, and small car parts from the US and Europe to Latin America'.[24] Importantly, LAN transported the cargo in the same wide-bodied planes as used for the passengers, with the two businesses sharing at least partly the same cities of origin and destination.

LAN's resource sharing between the two businesses was both creative and unique as compared to other major airlines:

> A LAN flight from Miami arrives in Santiago, Chile, at 5:00AM. It continues to another Latin American city, say Bogota, Lima, or Buenos Aires, to deliver cargo from the US. Then it returns to Santiago to fly customers back to Miami or New York, because passenger flights to the US from South America are at night. Meanwhile, competitors with no cargo operation are forced to park their aircraft at Santiago's airport for most of the day.[25]

This example suggests the sharing of multiple key resources between the two businesses, including route planning services, airline personnel, aircraft, and foreign entry/exit cities. This approach led to high growth and profitability of LAN for the 1993–2010 period.[26]

LAN's senior management correctly identified the strong complementarities between its international passenger and air-cargo businesses. It developed the ability to operate effectively and profitably two distinct business models, which catered to very different market segments. It did so by seeking complementarities and crafting opportunities for sharing resources between both businesses, thereby reinforcing the competitiveness of each, and the firm in its entirety. In practical terms, this systemic resource sharing across businesses was associated with several benefits, including an improved capacity utilization of the aircraft fleet and a lower 'break-even load factor (BELF)', as well as a new reputation as a 'one-stop shop for cargo in Latin America'.[27] More broadly, the complementarities between the two businesses led to risk reduction by having better diversified revenue sources, while at the same time creating mobility and entry barriers for other airlines.

Deploying two distinct business models, but with a focus on shared resources, comes with a unique set of challenges. On the positive side, other airlines faced substantial ambiguity in terms of understanding properly how the integrated model worked. On the side of new challenges, LAN itself needed to craft novel managerial routines with high information demands, themselves requiring added skills and flexibility from employees. Importantly, only through such sophisticated shared routines in the realm of *new economy* functioning, namely, effective usage of information and communications technology, activity-based accounting systems, etc., can effective and low-cost interfaces between distinct businesses be achieved.

More generally, even with state-of-the-art technologies at their disposal to reduce bounded rationality challenges, a key strategy question facing MNE managers is to identify where resources might be usefully shared across businesses, with a particular focus on sharing those resource bundles that are at the heart of the firm's international strategy. In LAN's case, these resources included managerial practices (e.g., route planning), physical assets (e.g., wide-bodied airplanes), human resources (e.g., flexible employees with dedication), and the foreign flight destinations (e.g., shared origin/destination cities for both passengers and cargo) themselves, with each destination point associated with location advantages for running the two businesses simultaneously.

This 'Strategic challenges in the new economy' article demonstrates that core competencies do not simply arise from pre-existing technologies to be shared subsequently across businesses, in contrast to what Prahalad and Hamel suggested. Rather, such core competencies are crafted over time and may build upon resources spread across downstream value chain activities. When these resources are productively shared between different businesses, they can create a variety of potential synergistic effects. Prahalad and Hamel neglected the possibility of such a broader FSA recombination in resource sharing, for which home and host country location advantages can also be a key ingredient.

International Business Strategy During Globally Disruptive Events

As we noted in Chapter 1, the COVID-19 pandemic as a global disruptive event forced many MNEs to respond to a new normal across their entire spectrum of economic activities, including sourcing, production, logistics and coordination, marketing, distribution, etc. The closing of some international markets, as well as restrictions on the mobility of physical and human resources, led to a variety of direct, negative effects. But what also became clear very quickly was the resilience of many MNEs as to the agile redeployment of their resource base, except in sectors where government restrictions completely shut down their activities, as was the case with cruise-line operators.

The following elements in the realm of core competencies as discussed in this chapter would appear especially important to MNE managers. These are some lessons learned from the pandemic: the critical role of 'intelligence capabilities' as key FSAs; the potential benefits of business model diversification; and a renewed focus on protecting core competencies in the realm of innovation.

First, MNE investments in intelligence helped reduce bounded rationality and bounded reliability problems.[28] For example, at Samsung (the largest South Korean MNE conglomerate), 'early and decisive action' was instrumental in preventing 'any meaningful production disruptions'.[29] This included, *inter alia*, providing production support to suppliers of personal protective equipment (PPE), flying components between factories when facing land border closures, and securing permissions from a number of national governments to send engineers to factories across the world in the middle of the lockdown.[30] As noted by the head of Samsung's coronavirus response task force: '[From] four to eight weeks ahead of the massive outbreak in Europe and the United States, we already had our factories abroad ready for the virus'.[31] As the pandemic unfolded, Samsung ensured access to local information across its sites and put in new routines to prevent commitment failures.

Second, the pandemic was an opportunity to diversify the MNE's geographic or product scope, and to increase dynamic efficiencies across its value chain.[32] For example, Wizz Air sought 'opportunities to expand its route network into new countries as other, weaker airlines were forced to cut back by the crisis', with 'several new routes and three new bases in Europe'.[33] Similarly, the French luxury goods company LVMH was quick to pivot from 'producing perfume to making hand sanitizer, a lead that was swiftly followed by many small distilleries'.[34] In the realm of efficiency improvements, many firms rapidly moved to 'streamline production – through the use of remote-work and automating technologies, for example – potentially reducing labour demand down the road'.[35] The examples above reflect MNEs' agile management of resources and capabilities in the direction of diversification, multi-business models, and even organizational restructuring.

Third, many MNEs placed a renewed focus on how to protect their core competencies, especially with the rise of the virtual workplace. For example, workers at Apple could not 'access crucial internal systems from home due to strict security policies meant to fend off outsiders'.[36] These types of issues can become even more critical when MNEs are involved in R&D abroad, and innovation-related activities involve other companies. Here, new security-driven routines must be introduced that include the external value chain partners and that reflect a careful trade-off between information sharing (reducing bounded rationality problems) and protecting adequately proprietary knowledge (reducing bounded reliability challenges).

Five Management Takeaways

1. Identify and nurture your company's core competencies, and differentiate their treatment from that given to less critical FSAs.
2. Develop a 'strategic architecture' to guide your company in building and acquiring core competencies.
3. Understand the economic potential and drawbacks of acquiring FSAs through external strategic alliances.
4. Do not overestimate the transferability of your FSAs across borders, and understand the costs of successful resource recombination.
5. Reflect on the potential opportunities and drawbacks of strategies such as outsourcing and business model diversification when expanding internationally and investing abroad, using a core competencies lens, and do take into account expected dynamic effects unfolding over time.

3

The Nature of Home Country
Location Advantages

Five Learning Objectives

1. To describe the relationship between a firm's strengths relative to international rivals and the competitiveness of its home country.
2. To explain 'Porter's diamond' and the interaction among the four diamond attributes.
3. To develop an understanding of how innovative firms can benefit from location advantages in a home cluster.
4. To identify the role of MNEs as 'diamond connectors' in the context of location advantages held by different countries.
5. To discuss the managerial relevance of a 'national diamond-based' analysis on the competitive advantage of nations.

This chapter explores Porter's idea that the most important aspect of international business strategy is four key home country location advantages, often simply referred to as 'Porter's diamond'. Porter's idea is that, ultimately, an MNE's long-term competitiveness results from vigorous domestic pressure in its home base, forcing it to innovate and improve productivity. This idea will be examined and then critiqued using the framework presented in Chapter 1.

Significance

In the early 1990s, **Michael Porter's** now classic *HBR* article, 'The competitive advantage of nations' (and the identically named book), created substantial debate on the sources of international competitiveness.[1]

Porter argues that any company's ability to compete in the international arena is based mainly on an interrelated set of location advantages in its home country. A high level of pressure in its home base pushes the firm to innovate and to upgrade systematically, resulting in FSA creation. These FSAs are then instrumental to expansion in foreign markets. According to Porter, 'a nation's competitiveness depends on the capacity of its industry to innovate and upgrade. Companies gain advantage against the world's best competitors because of pressure and challenge. They benefit from having strong domestic rivals, aggressive home-based suppliers, and demanding local customers.'[2]

According to Porter, FSAs are primarily developed not because firms have a strong, internal entrepreneurial drive, or because they can easily access external resources, but because they face external pressure. Companies should therefore not rely on 'natural' factor endowments such as an abundance of raw materials, low labour costs, a large domestic market, or favourable exchange rates provided by their home base, nor on playing a national champion role in their protected home market. This type of thinking leads firms to rely on short-term advantages. Such advantages are short-lived because replication by rival firms is usually easy to achieve, simply by accessing these natural advantages (e.g., by acquiring the sources of coveted raw materials). Alternatively, in the case of sheltered markets, these advantages depend on precarious political circumstances and priorities of public policy makers, who are themselves faced with enormous bounded rationality problems – for example, when attempting to select national champions. Building mainly upon natural factor endowments or a protected market environment is usually detrimental to innovation and growth; the firm then has an incentive to become complacent and interested mainly in the status quo.

In contrast, long-term competitiveness results from innovation and firm-level productivity improvements. Here, it is the interplay among various home market attributes (especially those pressuring firms to innovate and improve productivity) which acts as the key location advantage for firms embedded in this home base, and is instrumental to long-term competitiveness. Porter visualized the four key sets of country attributes as the points of a 'diamond of national competitive advantage'. Note that 'Porter's diamond' therefore refers to the four-sided geometric figure representing one of the four suits in a deck of playing cards in addition to spades, hearts, and clubs, rather than the very hard native crystalline carbon valued as a gem. Porter's diamond consists of:

1. Factor conditions: these include not only factors of production in the home base such as natural resources, but also, and more importantly, created factor conditions such as skilled labour, scientific knowledge, and infrastructure. These are particularly valuable if they are specialized, meaning customized towards effective deployment in very specific economic activities and companies.
2. Demand conditions: here, the focus is not on domestic market size alone, but also on domestic buyer sophistication.
3. Related and supporting industries: high-quality, internationally competitive home-based suppliers, as well as companies in related industries, are critical to the firm's international competitiveness.

4. Firm strategy, industry structure, and rivalry: a highly competitive, home-based industry with efficient macro-level governance and several domestic rivals may help the firms in that industry become internationally competitive.

According to Porter, it is the synergetic interactions among these four attributes, along with two external variables – government and 'chance' – that determine the competitiveness of specific industries in the international marketplace. 'Chance' includes stumbling upon a new commercial application for an existing resource, or being lucky in an innovation process and coincidentally creating a valuable new product technology or process knowledge. The interaction among the four diamond attributes causes an industry-wide recombination capability not attributable to the actions of the individual firms in that industry.

Here, *factor conditions* accessible by domestic firms need to be continuously upgraded through the development of skills and the creation of new knowledge, not simply inherited from the country's natural endowments. Porter makes the point that, even where a country's natural endowments are limited, disadvantages can be turned into advantages when they spur creativity and ingenuity to overcome deficiencies. For example, in the case of Japan, firms in several industries such as steel, shipbuilding, and automobiles developed technological and design expertise to overcome a lack of natural resources, and the just-in-time production process was pioneered in response to a lack of affordable warehousing space.

The presence of sophisticated *demand conditions* at home also incites companies to be innovative. Companies must respond to new customer demands by pushing the envelope of existing technology and design features. As a result, they gain early insights into the future needs of customers across borders, and thereby build the potential to achieve first-mover advantages on a global scale.

Highly competitive firms in *related and supporting industries* at home, especially suppliers, are crucial to enhancing innovation through more efficient inputs, the ongoing exchange of ideas, timely feedback, and short lines of communication between sequential and parallel activities in the vertical chain.

Lastly, vigorous *domestic rivalry* is instrumental to international competitiveness. Such rivalry forces companies to develop unique FSAs, beyond the generally available location advantages in their home base. Firms then become motivated to enter international markets as an outlet for exploiting these FSAs.

While each of the four attributes of the diamond model can have a stand-alone impact on the competitiveness of a specific industry, their joint impact is even more important. The four determinants operate as an interdependent system, with each element affecting and stimulating the other ones, often in a small geographic space where most firms in the industry are concentrated, thereby forming a cluster.

According to Porter, a home country diamond cannot be identified for a national or regional economy as a whole, across industries. The diamond of competitive advantage will be different for each specific industry considered. Porter is adamant that ***industry-specific*** pressures, associated with particular interactions among diamond determinants, lead to innovation and productivity improvements, and thereby to international competitiveness. An MNE's FSAs are thus strengthened, not simply through easy access to favourable generic location advantages in the firm's home base, but rather through absorbing or building upon the complementary resources arising out of its industry context. Such complementary resources are provided by sophisticated individuals (whether skilled workers or demanding customers), other firms, and a variety of industry-specific institutions, ranging from accepted rules of competition to educational facilities training specialized workers.

Porter's findings resulted from a four-year study of over 100 industry groups in ten nations, including Denmark, Germany, Italy, Japan, Korea, Singapore, Sweden, Switzerland, the United Kingdom, and the United States. In each of the sample nations, industries were chosen based on their domestic importance and international competitive success as measured by substantial and sustained exports, as well as outward FDI, arising from advantages created in the home country. Examples include automobiles and chemicals in Germany, semiconductors and electronics in Japan, banking and pharmaceuticals in Switzerland, footwear and textiles in Italy, aircraft and motion pictures in the United States, TVs and VCRs in South Korea, and health care in Denmark. We should note, however, that Porter developed his diamond concept prior to directing the empirical work. The empirical work was aimed mainly at validating the diamond framework, rather than augmenting it further or refining it in a substantive fashion.

Context and Complementary Perspectives

Porter worked on the diamond-based approach to international competitiveness throughout the late 1980s when many academics, managers, and policy makers were reflecting on the sources of sustainable competitive advantage at the macro-level. How could a resource-poor nation like Japan achieve astounding competitive success while the mighty economic engine of the United States sputtered? During this time, a fascination developed about Japanese business practices and the question was raised whether these practices were built upon a superior management system, a starting point similar to that adopted by Prahalad and Hamel in their work on core competencies, discussed in Chapter 2. Porter argued against this trend in thinking, stating that 'no one managerial system is universally appropriate – notwithstanding the current fascination with Japanese management'.[3]

Another important contextual element was the ongoing debate as to how the United States should respond to the alleged threat of declining competitiveness. One option being considered at that time was increased protectionism through trade barriers in an attempt to shelter US companies in the domestic market and keep out foreign competition. In Porter's view, that was not the solution to the problem. According to Porter, sources of competitive advantage do not lie in conventional comparative advantage, nor in specific management styles or trade barriers, but rather are achieved through the promotion of domestic rivalry. Vigorous rivalry leads to long-term innovation and productivity improvements. Here, the home country diamond represents a fertile basis for FSA development, much of it of the recombination type, since individual firms systematically interact with other actors in this diamond, thereby absorbing and benefiting from complementary resources that strengthen their own FSAs.

Porter focused primarily on the rise of industries at the national level, and less on firm-specific challenges and knowledge exchange among cluster participants. As a result, his work provides relatively little practical guidance to the managers or owners of firms, in terms of what they should know about locating in a cluster at the sub-national level. **Willy C. Shih** and **Sen Chai**, in their 2015 *SMR* article, describe how firms benefit from being located in a cluster, especially in the realm of innovation.[4]

They argue that firms located inside a cluster can more easily hire capable workers commanding sophisticated knowledge and skills than if they operate outside of the cluster. Proximity to carriers of innovativeness in a cluster facilitates spillovers of tacit knowledge that is embedded and sticky, namely, that has location-bound dimensions. In practical terms, it is strong labour mobility within a cluster, meaning the ease for employees to move from one organization to the next, that drives knowledge transfers across cluster participants. The paradoxical effect of higher labour mobility inside a cluster is that it allows easy access to external knowledge, but at the same time any knowledge-based firm also faces greater difficulties in keeping its own knowledge reservoir proprietary vis-à-vis other competing firms in the same cluster.

As one example, Denmark is home to a number of biotechnology R&D centres, operating within a vibrant life-sciences cluster in Copenhagen. The prosperity of this cluster results from local labour mobility confined to the cluster, because of the rather sticky nature of the knowledge involved. This has resulted in 'shared resources' within the cluster, among independent firms located in close proximity of one another.[5] Foreign MNEs, through participating in the cluster, can use their local presence to pursue novel resource combinations by exploiting their access to the shared resources in proximity, and can thereby augment their FSAs.

An important characteristic of the Danish biotech cluster is that proprietary know-how does not just move between direct competitors: local knowledge-sharing also occurs through cross-sectoral labour mobility. As one example, Shih and Chai observed that 'among 89 individuals employed at Novo Nordisk A/S who specified expertise in fermentation, 56 previously worked at industrial enzyme specialist Novozymes A/S, 28 at contract manufacturer CMC Biologics, 27 at food ingredient specialist Chr. Hansen A/S, 84 at medical devices company Coloplast A/S, and 9 at Carlsberg A/S.'[6]

It is remarkable that most changes of employers by these workers occurred within the life-sciences cluster, confirming the prevalence of localized rather than geographically dispersed knowledge sharing. The cross-sectoral mobility of local employees commanding tacit organizational knowledge gained from their prior employers also helped the firms in the biotech cluster address the challenge of radical technological shifts:

> Novo Nordisk got their start extracting insulin from pigs and cattle, exploiting their proximity to the Danish agricultural sector. In the late 1970s, when Genentech offered to share its method for producing human insulin using recombinant DNA (rDNA) technology . . . Novo declined. (At the time, there was much wariness about the production or use of rDNA products.) When the company changed its mind, it didn't have to look far . . . as it could recruit extensively from the University of Copenhagen and could draw heavily on other local businesses . . . Today, Novo Nordisk is the global market leader in recombinant insulin, producing 50% of the world's supply.[7]

Shih and Chai (2015, p. 11) suggest various factors that can help the success of firms inside a cluster. These include a strong physical presence of firms and social ties among them inside the cluster: 'Companies can capture returns from investment in public goods if they have a geographic presence and are tied to the right subcommunities.'[8] In addition, the presence of (knowledge) resources that span multiple sectors can support exploratory innovation in firms. Here, a requisite balance must be achieved between firms having access to knowledge resources possessed by other cluster participants, while allowing reasonable access by others to their own knowledge resources.

Shih and Chai highlight two preconditions for a Porterian, home-based cluster to function as a source of competitive advantages for the firms operating inside the cluster. The first precondition is the possibility of movement of human resources from one organization to another inside the cluster, whereby knowledge spillovers can be achieved, but without unduly endangering the proprietary knowledge base of the various cluster participants. The second precondition is to accommodate a relatively diverse set of cluster participants willing and able to cross diverse sectors. Such diversity allows cross-sectoral collaboration and knowledge exchange among the cluster participants, and it can help them avoid the danger of becoming stuck in an over-specialized cluster, incapable of conducting exploratory innovation and creating new FSAs. The presence of foreign MNEs in a cluster can be helpful to achieving such diversity.

David Teece provides a second complementary perspective to Porter's. Teece published an article in *CMR* focused on inward FDI in Silicon Valley, one of the world's best-known technological clusters.[9] The location advantages provided by the Silicon Valley cluster in the San Francisco Bay Area are well known to MNEs from around the world, but should not be viewed in static terms, and in isolation of evolving foreign MNE strategies. Teece focused primarily on the rationale for Japanese FDI in this cluster and its effects. His analysis suggests two things. First, Porter-type single diamond thinking breaks down when foreign investors can provide complementary resources not provided by the domestic diamond itself, but instrumental to domestic, firm-level sustainability and expansion (see also the critical analysis below). Second, foreign MNE activity through inward FDI can act as a bridge between the location advantages provided by two very different nations, in this case the United States and Japan.

Japanese investors entering Silicon Valley through mergers, acquisitions, alliances, and venture capital vehicles bring to local, high-technology firms a set of FSAs these firms cannot develop themselves by simply building upon the location advantages embedded in the US diamond. These FSAs, injected by Japanese companies into Silicon Valley, result themselves from the location advantages provided by the Japanese diamond: 'patient capital, engineering talent, manufacturing excellence, and access to the Japanese market'.[10] From Porter's perspective, some of these resources provided by Japanese companies could be interpreted as reflecting inadequacies of the US diamond. For example, a lack of patient capital means the US diamond fails to provide the proper capital market conditions conducive to success in long-gestation sub-sectors of biotechnology, computers, and semiconductors. However, the real story is not one of failure. Japanese FDI in Silicon Valley leads to substantial benefits to the US firms and to the Japanese actors involved: 'With technological competence and capabilities put centre stage, Japanese companies are free to focus on the long run, and to imagine constellations of future products deriving from technological capabilities.'[11]

The Japanese companies benefit from these arrangements in many ways. Silicon Valley provides Japanese companies with unique access to US entrepreneurial capabilities, early-stage technology developments in innovation-driven sectors, and a more general window on new trends in these sectors – location advantages sorely missing in Japan. In addition, conducting these types of entrepreneurial activities in Japan itself would be problematic. Managers who engage in initiatives characterized by substantial ignorance about future industry conditions would be ostracized, and the initiatives would probably fail. In contrast, experimenting in Silicon Valley is much more legitimate, and carries the promise of diffusion to Japan of any successful new technologies, and the further development thereof in Japan itself. Finally, Japanese companies can sometimes gain privileged access to US distribution channels and other stakeholders – location advantages embedded in the US diamond – through investing in these Silicon Valley ventures.

However, the effective melding of location advantages provided by the US and Japanese diamonds through Japanese FDI in Silicon Valley is not easy to achieve in practice. It requires long-term efforts to develop personal relationships between the Japanese and US actors with the intent to overcome potential challenges of identity-based discordance between managers from distant cultures (as a source of bounded reliability), and to achieve international technology exchange and absorption. Importantly, it is not the higher cost of capital in the United States that explains Japanese FDI, but rather differences in governance mechanisms: Japanese firms are much less interested in short-term profits, dividends, and stock buybacks, and much more interested in long-term capability development. Here, the Japanese MNEs perform the role of diamond connectors: they act as a conduit for injecting Japanese-style governance mechanisms into Silicon Valley companies, while aiming for knowledge transfer to their Japanese operations.

MANAGEMENT INSIGHTS

Turning now to the framework developed in Chapter 1, it is clear that Porter holds a rather narrow view about how FSAs are created. According to Porter, the home country national diamond attributes determine a firm's innovation capabilities and related productivity improvements. Any company's FSAs thus systematically result from location advantages found in its home base. This home base is the location where the firm retains effective strategic, creative, and technical control of its operations. This is usually the firm's original home country, unless it decides to move this home base to a more attractive foreign diamond for specific business units. Porter thereby makes a sharp distinction for each business unit between the home base, as the primary source of location advantages critical to innovation and productivity improvements, and other nations, which are selectively tapped into for certain diamond attributes, but are primarily a channel for exploiting or incrementally extending FSAs developed at home. The MNE is thus either a **centralized exporter** or an **international projector**. Given his focus on a single home base per business unit, Porter implicitly rejects the relevance of a **multi-centred MNE** or an **international coordinator**.

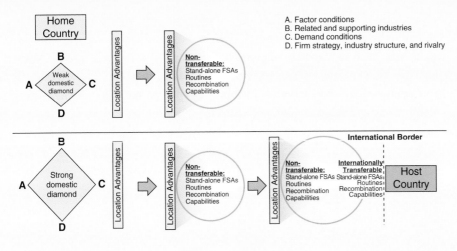

A. Factor conditions
B. Related and supporting industries
C. Demand conditions
D. Firm strategy, industry structure, and rivalry

Figure 3.1
Domestic 'diamond'
determinants as
drivers of home-base
location advantages,
and subsequent FSAs

Where the domestic diamond is strong (represented here as the large diamond in the bottom part of the figure), this model predicts that after the creation of LB FSAs, the development of NLB FSAs will also be stimulated, whereas this will not occur where the diamond is weak (represented here as the small diamond in the top part of the figure).

Figure 3.1 shows Porter's interpretation of international business strategy in terms of the general framework outlined in Chapter 1. For Porter, location advantages in the home base are the key source of location-bound FSAs, including a company's stand-alone FSAs such as its technical knowledge, as well as its routines and recombination capabilities. The latter precisely derive from the interplay among the various diamond determinants in the home base.

In the case of a weak diamond, as shown at the top of Figure 3.1, the firm is unable to develop non-location-bound FSAs, and thereby unable to expand internationally. In contrast, at the bottom of Figure 3.1, the pressures arising from the strong home country diamond lead to innovation and productivity improvements, and ultimately to non-location-bound FSAs that can be exploited internationally, whether embodied in final products (exports), or transferred as an intermediate product and then exploited by host country subsidiaries. As regards the patterns of FSA development from this book's framework, Porter focuses mainly on Pattern II, in which location-bound FSAs are developed in the home base and then upgraded to become internationally transferable; see Figure 1.7 in Chapter 1.

An implicit normative message for managers is that they should cherish their domestic home base and reflect on what they can do themselves to improve diamond conditions in their industry beyond what would be immediately beneficial to their own firm.

Porter's analysis, while intuitively plausible, especially for technology-driven industries in large economies such as the United States, unfortunately suffers from five main weaknesses.

First, Porter's perspective does not address fully the complexities of international management, especially for MNEs based in smaller countries with large neighbours, such as Canada, Belgium, or New Zealand. In such cases, a 'single diamond' approach fails to recognize the significant impacts on a country and its firms exercised by the diamond attributes of one or several – often larger – neighbouring countries or trading partners.

Figure 3.2
Porter's single diamond model and the double diamond model

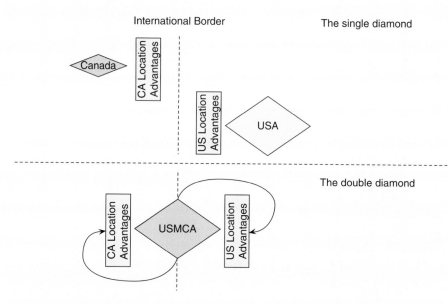

With the single diamond model, the home country LAs determine whatever FSAs a company may develop. With the double diamond model, firms also draw on LAs of other nations than the home country to strengthen their own FSAs. Trade and investment liberalization (as with the USMCA) institutionalizes this possibility of freely accessing and drawing on the resources present in a host country diamond to strengthen FSAs. This is why the rectangles representing Canadian and US location advantages are shown as being similar in size, though the USMCA obviously does not eliminate completely country borders.

Take Canada as an example. The US economy is ten times larger than the Canadian one. A single diamond approach would predict little good for Canadian-based firms, having to compete with US-based ones; see Figure 3.2 (top part). However, firms in Canada benefit from unlimited market access and national treatment in the United States through the North American Free Trade Agreement (NAFTA) and its successor (as of 2020), the United States–Mexico–Canada Agreement (USMCA). For these reasons, Canadian firms are often forced from their inception to work with – and react to – the various national diamond determinants present in both Canada and the United States (as well as Mexico, which we do not discuss here for simplicity), or they risk missing out on key strategic signals and pressures in an increasingly integrated regional market.

Canadian companies often consider the United States as a 'natural' component of their output market, and in many industries face largely the same demand pressures and consumer sophistication as US firms. Since industries such as the automotive sector are organized at the North American continental level, sector-based rivalry in many cases is also almost identical, with the exception of some protected sectors such as those related to maritime transport or Canadian health care (and save the problem of the so-called fair trade laws, including countervail and anti-dumping regulations, which can still be applied against the other country's firms, as has occurred in the softwood lumber industry). Finally, Canadian firms have the same access as US firms to most production factors and inputs from related and supporting industries in the United States. One could even argue that Canadian firms will not be hindered by any ineffective intra-US diamond interactions inherited from the past, but will selectively access US diamond determinants to satisfy present, urgent FSA development needs. In other words, they will take from the US diamond any elements not provided fully by their Canadian diamond; see Figure 3.2 (bottom part).

The same is also true for countries within the European Union, where a firm's home base may not provide all of the necessary ingredients to develop the FSA bundles a company's top management wishes to control. The MNE must therefore remain attuned to conditions in the other, closely linked national markets. In this case, the close linkages among nations result from the single EU market, which constitutes a much more integrated economic system than the USMCA.

The European Union and USMCA cases suggest a 'double diamond' (or 'multiple diamond') model, in which the attributes of two or more countries are critically important to the FSA development process. This contrasts sharply with Porter's view. Porter states that 'relying on foreign activities that supplant domestic capabilities is always a second-best solution',[12] and '[u]ltimately, competitive advantage is created at home'.[13]

The double diamond model has important managerial and policy implications. For example, in his 1990 book on the competitive advantage of nations, Porter describes in detail both the Singaporean and Korean diamonds.[14] His conclusions on the Korean diamond across industries are largely favourable, whereas he is less impressed by the Singaporean diamond. In reality, Singapore's GDP per capita has consistently been much higher than Korea's (it was approximately double that of Korea's in 2018). This implies that Singapore has a stronger economy than Korea. If we abandon Porter's model and apply double diamond thinking instead, we can see why Singapore has done better than Korea. Singapore's outward FDI has allowed it to access inputs (such as natural resources) from other countries. In addition, inward FDI by foreign MNEs (enticed by Singapore's attractive geographic location and its well-run institutions) has allowed Singapore's domestic economy to access foreign MNEs' knowledge bases.

Second, in line with the above point about the need for double diamond thinking, inward FDI as a force for upgrading a local economy, as described by Teece in his *CMR* piece, is not given the attention it deserves. Though Porter acknowledges that foreign-owned firms could in principle be part of a domestic cluster, at least if the domestic operation can function independently from the foreign parent, he focuses on home-grown firms, with domestic suppliers and buyers, using the home country diamond as a lever for subsequent international success. He thereby largely neglects the important issue of a country's location advantages being instrumental to inward FDI (rather than only outward FDI), and therefore to economic growth and prosperity. When adopting Porter's mindset, large-scale inward FDI in an industry is obviously not entirely healthy, as it can be interpreted as a failure to develop successful, home-grown firms in the same industry; namely, it results from a national diamond with intrinsic weaknesses.

However, developing advanced new knowledge within a robust national diamond does not necessarily create more wealth for a country's citizens than exploiting and further augmenting such knowledge through inward FDI. The latter case also adds value, benefiting workers and consumers in the host country as much as it may benefit the firm's shareholders in its home base. In addition, the knowledge complementarities and exchanges with other economic actors in a host country may be as intensive as in the home country, even if these complementarities and exchanges are likely to occur to a larger extent in downstream value chain activities. For example, if the United States experiences substantial inward FDI in the automotive industry, this does not simply reflect the relative failure of domestic firms to remain competitive or hold on to their market share. It also signals that the United States is perceived by foreign producers as an attractive location to engage in value creation. What counts is how consumers and other stakeholders, especially skilled workers, in the United States benefit from this inward FDI. Foreign firms such as the Japanese automotive companies also benefit, because they gain proximity to large numbers of consumers, unchained from past loyalties, and willing to try new products and services. The consumers' willingness to explore new products may well be one of the United States' greatest location advantages across industries.

Third, Porter ignores the need for location-bound FSAs in host countries. Porter's model assumes that FSA development depends initially on domestic market factors, but can then be decoupled from the home location, when the FSAs are transferred for exploitation in host countries. This is in line with Ray Vernon's international product life cycle thinking.[15] As noted above, this approach is represented by Pattern II in Figure 1.7 in Chapter 1, whereby location-bound FSAs are created in the home base, and subsequently transformed into internationally transferable FSAs. This diffusion process can take the form of exports or transfers of intermediate outputs, such as technological knowledge or brand names, to subsidiaries. As outlined in Chapter 1, however, even strong FSAs crafted in the home country may need to be complemented with location-bound FSAs in every country where the firm operates in order to achieve a balance between integration and local responsiveness. Porter neglects this necessary process of linking existing knowledge bundles with new knowledge in host countries and regions.

Fourth, Porter's framework is fundamentally tautological. Porter argues that selective factor disadvantages may actually drive domestic innovation and upgrading, as long as the disadvantages send signals to innovate to domestic companies (e.g., given a lack of natural resources at home, domestic firms may need to focus on developing brand-named products) and the other diamond determinants are strong. Unfortunately, this point fundamentally undermines the value added (and explanatory and predictive power) of the single diamond approach. It implies that, *ex post*, any domestic industry's international success in terms of exports or outward FDI can always be explained by Porter's diamond determinants. If one of the four diamond determinants shows an obvious weakness, this weakness can be simply reinterpreted as a driver for domestic firms to upgrade and to increase productivity. The diamond framework is thus fundamentally tautological, as there is no way to disprove it. *Ex post*, success follows from strong home country determinants, unless some of these determinants happen to be weak, in which case they are interpreted as selective factor disadvantages that have pushed domestic firms to overcome this weakness through innovation.[16]

Fifth, Porter places too much emphasis on **the country** as the appropriate geographic level of analysis. Consider a manager trying to operationalize Porter's diamond. It is actually feasible to operationalize the diamond, while overcoming the problems outlined above.[17] For each of the diamond determinants, managers should compile a list of all the parameters that can affect a firm's competitiveness (assuming that a diamond-driven analysis is conducted at the level of a firm, rather than an entire domestic industry). For example, within the determinant *factor conditions*, and the sub-factor *human resources*, a distinction could be made among scientists with R&D knowledge, skilled blue-collar workers, multilingual managers with advanced marketing, organizational and financial knowledge, etc. The question then arises as to the relevant geographic area where the firm can access each relevant type of personnel.

As noted above, Porter's work focuses primarily on the national level, and on the distinction between home country and host countries. The present book also makes a similar distinction, but without assuming that, in terms of access to location advantages, an MNE is constrained to whatever the home country diamond has to offer, with access to the strengths of host country diamonds largely off-limits. Porter's work simply misses one of the most basic points in international business: firms expand abroad only if they can establish a match between their FSAs and the location advantages of the host environments they penetrate, whether input markets or output markets. If international expansion involves more than the pure exploitation of extant FSAs, namely, some form of resource recombination, the firm can actually improve on its existing strengths.

Conceptually, it is helpful to distinguish between the local level, the state/provincial level, the domestic national level, the regional level of one or more foreign nations (e.g., NAFTA or the European Union), and the global level, as the relevant geographic spaces where parameters may be accessed by the MNE. Consider the case of a petrochemical firm located in Rotterdam, the Netherlands. Its highly skilled technical workers may be available largely as a result of educational facilities at the local and provincial levels. The relevant competitors producing similar chemicals may operate primarily out of Germany. The suppliers used by the MNE may be scattered around the European Union. Finally, demand for the products may be global, namely, the firm's products can in principle be sold around the world.

Figure 3.3
A multilevel analysis of the diamond determinants

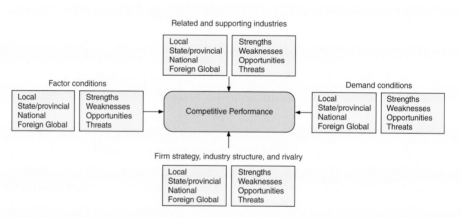

Some of the above parameters, ***at each geographic level***, can be interpreted as either a strength or a weakness, namely if the firm can directly influence the parameter (e.g., quality control systems adopted by suppliers). Similarly, other parameters can be viewed as either an opportunity or a threat, to the extent that these parameters are largely exogenous to the firm (e.g., domestic taxation regimes or global energy prices). Figure 3.3 shows a stylized version of this approach, in which Porter's original diamond model has been transformed into a tool to classify in an intuitively appealing fashion a variety of environmental parameters that can affect a firm's international competitiveness. This classification can then be supplemented with an analysis of dynamics, namely, the interactions among various critical parameters, leading to virtuous cycles of making the firm stronger or vicious cycles of downgrading.

Strategic Challenges in the New Economy

William Kerr, in an *HBR* paper, describes the importance of sub-national location advantages in the new-economy context of continuous innovation and the related need for firms to attract top talent from hot spots.[18] The main challenge for many firms operating outside of innovation clusters or 'talent hubs' is that relocating core activities to an urban centre at the heart of such a hub can be prohibitively expensive and also be associated with negative externalities (for instance, the high crime rates and urban violence in large US cities). He observes three alternative strategies that firms can pursue in this realm.

The *first* strategy is to relocate core operations such as the head office to a talent hub.[19] For example, many firms such as McDonald's, Motorola Solutions, Kraft Heinz, etc. have moved their head offices to downtown Chicago, one of the main talent hubs in the United States. The easy access to advanced talent pools granted from the headquarters relocation can be very significant as a location advantage, if a large number of college-educated and highly skilled young people are available in the vicinity, subject to being given the opportunity to work in the urban centre. A head office and its employees can typically also be effectively shielded from negative externalities in the urban centre, for example, by massive investments in security and selecting safe locations for the head office and employee housing. However, a full relocation of core activities can be very expensive, and may require the firm to develop completely new, location-bound FSAs from scratch (e.g., local customer relations and political connections). In addition, the mirror image of better access to talented employees to drive innovation is that these employees might easily move to rivals if offered better working conditions or a more competitive remuneration, thereby triggering unwanted knowledge dissipation to the rivals in proximity.

The *second* strategy is to keep most core operations outside of a coveted innovation cluster, and to deploy only smaller, less expensive, and more easily reversible innovation teams in that talent hub, as the US retailer Walmart did in 2011, when opening Walmart labs in Silicon Valley.[20] The physical presence of an innovation outpost in a talent hub can then help firms benefit from tacit knowledge spillovers from other participants in the cluster. In addition, establishing corporate outposts in talent hubs is much less expensive than moving broader bundles of core activities to such hubs, and can even occur through acquiring a capable local firm in the hub.

Despite substantially lower costs due to a smaller footprint, *inter alia* in terms of the size of the firm's outpost site and the limited number of employees to be dispatched in the new urban centre, the benefits of locating outposts in knowledge hubs may be disappointing. For example, gaining knowledge spillovers from cluster participants requires close proximity, as well as a critical mass of interactions with them, both of which the outpost may lack. In addition, local entrepreneurs and innovators in the talent hub may not be particularly inclined to cooperate with a small-sized outpost. Furthermore, the small size of the outpost, which implies the absence of slack resources, may prevent newly developed or acquired local knowledge from flowing back to the firm's core internal operations systematically. The above problems will likely be exacerbated when an outpost is established in a foreign hub, where the MNE is unlikely to enjoy the same reputation as in the home market. The MNE establishing an outpost, rather than a fully fledged operation in a knowledge hub in a foreign country, thus faces severe resource recombination challenges, meaning that the development of new location-bound FSAs is either incomplete or problematic in the foreign location.

The *third* strategy is one whereby firms encourage their executives to make short trips to talent hubs on a regular basis, so as to keep them informed about innovations in these hubs, and updated on the evolving knowledge frontiers.[21] This approach may be cost-effective, but its overall impact in the innovation space may be disappointing. The main problem with the third approach is the shallow nature of most visits to knowledge clusters. There is often insufficient time available to develop sticky social ties with local participants or to benefit from tacit spillovers they may generate, especially in remote foreign countries. Executives may thus end up returning home from their visits with partial and insufficient information that cannot be transformed into actionable FSAs afterwards, and that may even provide erroneous insights, because of an imperfect understanding of the innovations observed in the knowledge clusters.

Kerr's article confirms some of the weaknesses of Porter's single diamond model. The key issue for a firm is not always to look inside its existing configuration of national or local diamond conditions, but rather to reflect on how it can tap into other diamonds, possibly across national borders. In Kerr's narrative, these diamonds take the form of knowledge hubs, wherein an innovative and creative pool of talent is deeply embedded. For example, MNEs commonly attempt to tap into the location-specific advantages of host regions, by establishing regional head offices in talent hubs. They also set up R&D subsidiaries or innovation labs in foreign markets, as a form of strategic asset-seeking FDI, with top talent being one of the strategic assets targeted using the FDI. Other types of resource recombination than the ones Kerr acknowledges (he focuses on those based on having core operations in hubs; or establishing outposts; or making visits by executives) are also possible. One example is the hiring of experienced local executives in talent hubs, who possess extensive networks of their own in the cluster and a deep knowledge of local innovations therein. These executives can serve as a conduit for accessing, absorbing, and transferring local knowledge to the entire MNE network internally. All the cases above illustrate the importance for firms to tap into foreign diamonds, and more specifically talent hot spots in host countries, so as to access knowledge embedded in these foreign innovation clusters.

Aditya Pande, in his *HBR* article, provides a second strategic challenge to Porter's view in the new economy. He discusses firms' cost-driven decisions to relocate activities in information technology (IT) services, towards off-shoring and onshoring sites. Each represents a distinct strategic option, but both can be pursued simultaneously to achieve cost reductions.[22] On the one hand, firms can choose to 'offshore' information technology work to foreign countries (and emerging economies in particular) with very low wages.[23] Here, double diamond thinking prevails. On the other hand, they can also 'onshore' some of their prior offshored work to low-cost sites in highly developed economies, for example, in North America and Europe.[24] Here, it is not the home national diamond that matters most, but specific low-cost locations within the home country.

A variety of elements may influence the location-specific advantages of offshoring versus onshoring sites. First, highly specialized IT work requiring technicians with advanced skills will often be onshored and located in the firm's home country. Home-country governments typically also require some types of data processing activities to be performed within the country's borders, for example, activities related to financial, health, and national security data. They thus impose locational restrictions on the firms involved and their site selection process. Home-country governments (sometimes at both central and local levels) may also provide incentive packages to IT firms to stimulate their onshoring activities. Second, cost-driven IT onshoring may mean that most of the core operations will be conducted outside of an innovation cluster, namely by establishing smaller, less expensive, and more easily reversible innovation teams in the heart of talent hubs within their home country, as the US retailer Walmart did in 2011, when opening Walmart labs in Silicon Valley. The physical presence of an innovation outpost in a talent hub can then help firms benefit from tacit knowledge spillovers generated by other participants in the cluster. In addition, establishing a corporate outpost in a talent hub is much less expensive than moving broader bundles of core activities to such a hub, and it can even be implemented at lower costs through acquiring an already-existing capable local firm in the hub. Pande provides the following example of such onshoring: '. . . one global company opened a midwestern U.S. facility with more than 1,000 IT service employees. Wages at the facility are 35% lower than at headquarters, and the company received $50 million in government incentives'.[25]

However, it should be noted that the location-specific advantages benefiting firms that establish information technology centres in low-cost onshoring sites can change over time, especially for those sites in relative proximity to the head office of firms in a high-cost hub. For example, the location advantages of low-cost, secondary municipalities and venues in developed countries can become weaker as more firms are attracted to locate in the same cities, particularly because these firms will compete for a limited pool of highly skilled local talent, thereby driving up wages and also triggering other cost increases in the form of 'congestion' costs related to real estate and transportation. Firms should therefore carefully assess the evolving nature of location advantages of supposedly low-cost, onshore locations.

Pande's analysis suggests that countries do not simply have a single, uniform set of national diamond characteristics. There is much diversity within countries, *inter alia* in terms of the cost advantages of specific, within-country locations. Particular FSAs that can best be exploited in low-cost locations may sometimes be leveraged better out of onshore sites domestically, rather than through offshoring and accessing low-cost production factors in host nation diamonds.

For example, exploiting and further developing higher-order FSAs, such as the firm's most sophisticated IT services that contain advanced proprietary knowledge, can often best be combined with well-trained and skilled employees in information technology services, to be accessed through onshoring activities in mid-sized university campus towns in the home country. In contrast, activities employing lower-order FSAs, including tele-marketing or tele-customer services, can often best be offshored to ultra-low-wage host countries. However, the location advantages of low-cost onshore cites should not be taken as a given. Over time, especially in case of rising competition for specialized local labour, and the mushrooming of 'congestion' costs, the MNE may be incentivized to consider other sites, including offshoring options, in order to remain competitive.

International Business Strategy During Globally Disruptive Events

Globally disruptive events do not affect all firms and all locations in the same way. For example, the spread and impacts of the COVID-19 pandemic were uneven across geographic space. It 'hit earlier in the rich, developed countries of the northern and western hemispheres (Western Europe, the US) and later arrived [in] less globalized areas like central Asia, South America or Africa'.[26] The responses of governments to a spectrum of pandemic challenges (e.g., health-care spending, economic welfare reductions, lockdowns and quarantines, mobility restrictions) also varied across nations and over time. *The Economist* pointed out that '[m]any poor and middle-income countries face a balance-of-payments crisis and a collapse in government revenues'. And whereas 'rich countries can borrow cheaply in a crisis as investors flock to safety, poor countries see their borrowing costs soar'.[27]

At the micro-level, MNEs faced a variety of new, location-related challenges. Perhaps most importantly, the pandemic exacerbated trends towards stronger nationalism and protectionism.[28] It also added fuel to trade wars, leading to a further decoupling of the US and Chinese economic systems.[29][30] *The Economist* noted that '. . . [a] new era of economic self-reliance has begun . . . European Union officials talk of "strategic autonomy" and are creating a fund to buy stakes in firms. America is urging Intel to build plants at home.'[31] These types of narratives do suggest a revival of the importance of Porter's single diamond model, or alternatively a more regional as opposed to global approach to optimal location. However, stronger self-reliance could become self-defeating if one or more of the four home diamond determinants were negatively affected by the pandemic. For example, on the supply side, the pandemic showed the inherent dangers of Indian firms' overdependence on domestic factor conditions: 'The world's diamond sector has ground to a halt because of the exodus of 200,000 migrant workers from Surat in India – the global hub of diamond manufacturing – to their rural hometowns. India processes 90 per cent of the world's stones.'[32] Given that any home country diamond might have strong vulnerabilities to global disruptions such as the pandemic, MNEs reshoring activities back to their home country, as observed by Pande in his *HBR* article, is unlikely to be the optimal response in all circumstances to achieve secure, crisis-proof operations.

What, then, is the best way forward for an MNE to overcome location-specific disturbances associated with a global disruption? Our view is that the MNE should nurture its strong connections across national borders when any large external shock disrupts the global economy.[33] A global crisis amplifies the relevance of Teece's argument on the role of MNEs as 'diamond connectors'. For example, in the context of the pandemic – given the observed institutional fracturing and the related breakdown of the multilateral trade and investment regime that was originally established to reduce barriers to international economic exchange – MNEs reduced the impact of ensuing disruptions of their value chains by amplifying micro-level relational contracting with key partners in their multinational networks.[34]

Global disruptions raise awareness within MNEs that they need to reassess on a continuous basis whether they have activities that should be relocated or have their status changed as an internalized activity versus an outsourced one. This needed ongoing reflection on location and ownership is visualized in Figure 3.4. An MNE that structurally and systematically reflects on needed change – through dedicated decision-making routines at the level of the top management committee or the Board of Directors – and makes the required changes, can be viewed as an agile or flexible firm. Here, no MNE activity (nor any individual involved with an activity) should escape scrutiny as to whether it is actually performed in the optimal location and with an optimal ownership and control structure.

On the vertical axis of Figure 3.4, existing locations may become more or less attractive for particular activities. For instance, if the home-country government, and possibly a number of host country governments, set up new barriers to international trade and investment, the domestic market may be more attractive in relative terms than before. However, if the hurdles imposed by host country governments include mainly import barriers and not barriers to FDI, MNEs that operated as centralized exporters may be incentivized to set up new operations abroad. In the above cases, the answer to the question on optimal location is likely that some locational change may be required, and thus that for a number of activities a move should occur towards the top of Figure 3.4 (namely quadrants 1 and 3).

On the horizontal axis, a breakdown of multilateral and bilateral agreements at the macro-level may drive MNEs to attach more importance to relational contracting with external partners, while at the same time avoiding heavily dedicated investments abroad that could be expropriated or otherwise discriminated against. In Figure 3.4, this means a push towards the right-hand side (quadrants 3 and 4). There are, of course, many variations on the above themes, but the main point is that in the new normal arising after a global disruption, quadrant 3 in Figure 3.4 may become the most pertinent quadrant for many of the firm's activities, even those activities whose location and ownership status had not been challenged before.

Figure 3.4
MNE ownership and location decisions per separable economic activity

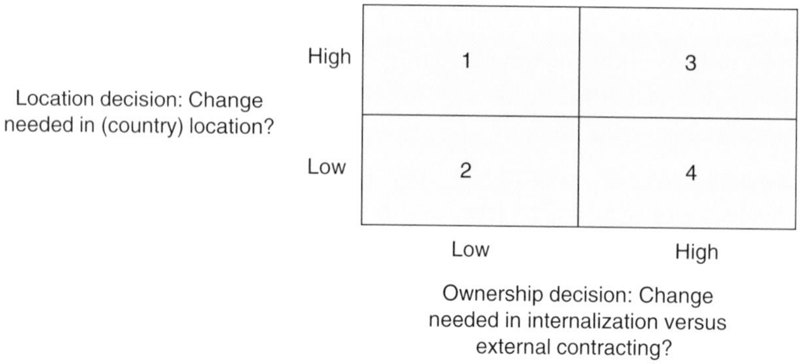

Location decision: Change needed in (country) location?

High — 1 — 3
Low — 2 — 4

Low — High

Ownership decision: Change needed in internalization versus external contracting?

Five Management Takeaways

1. Apply the 'diamond' framework to evaluate the sectorial strengths and weaknesses of your domestic industry.
2. Reflect on the relevance of national diamond characteristics to explain – at least partly – the short- and long-term competitiveness of your own firm.
3. Define industry-specific pressures that can strengthen your FSAs through absorbing – or building upon – the complementary resources present in your industry environment.
4. Analyze the economic potential of foreign diamonds, namely, foreign input markets for providing resources to your firm, and foreign output markets for absorbing its end products.
5. Assess the suitability of the diamond framework for analyzing your industry and adjust/add determinants and sub-factors according to your firm-specific needs.

4

The Problem with Host Country Location Advantages

Five Learning Objectives

1. To describe the four main dimensions of 'distance' (cultural, administrative, geographic, and economic) in the context of host country location advantages.
2. To link these various dimensions of 'distance' to bounded rationality problems faced by MNEs.
3. To develop an understanding of the alternative perspective of 'distance' as an opportunity, rather than a problem.
4. To highlight the importance of paying sufficient attention to the attractiveness and opportunities associated with some high-distance markets, for example, developed economy MNEs targeting rural markets in comparatively less wealthy countries.
5. To identify the managerial implications of 'distance' on the international transferability of FSAs.

This chapter explores Ghemawat's idea that, even in the contemporary era of advanced communications technology (especially digital tools) and enormous international trade, senior managers still need to take into account 'distance' when assessing host country location advantages and making decisions about global expansion. As Ghemawat uses the term, the 'distance' between two countries includes differences in culture, societal institutions, physical location, and economic status. According to Ghemawat, senior managers often overestimate the attractiveness of foreign markets because they fail to take into account the risks and costs associated with distance. Ghemawat concludes that higher inter-country distances correspond with lower inter-country trade levels, implying a lower probability of success. This idea will be examined and then critiqued using the framework presented in Chapter 1.

Significance

In 2001, **Pankaj Ghemawat** wrote an insightful *HBR* article, 'Distance still matters: the hard reality of global expansion', demonstrating that distance still matters: 'Technology may indeed be making the world a smaller place, but it is not eliminating the very real – and often very high – costs of distance.'[1]

Ghemawat convincingly demonstrates that companies often overestimate the attractiveness of foreign markets, focusing solely on macro-level measures of market size and growth, while neglecting to address the risks and additional costs associated with entering a new market. These risks and additional costs arise from what he calls 'distance':

> Much has been made of the death of distance in recent years. It's been argued that information technologies and, in particular, global communications and digital networks are shrinking the world, turning it into a small and relatively homogenous place. But when it comes to business, that's not only an incorrect assumption, it's a dangerous one. Distance still matters, and companies must explicitly and thoroughly account for it when they make decisions about global expansion. Traditional country portfolio analysis needs to be tempered by a clear-eyed evaluation of the many dimensions of distance and their probable impact on opportunities in foreign markets.[2]

Ghemawat's term 'distance' encompasses various components, which he organizes into four basic categories:

1. **Cultural distance**: this distance component results from differences in national cultural attributes such as language, religious beliefs, social norms, and race.
2. **Administrative (or institutional) distance**: this distance component reflects differences in societal institutions. This distance can be low (or lowered) if two or more countries share a common history (including colonial relationships), have political ties, have engaged in efforts towards economic and monetary integration or preferential trading arrangements, and synchronize government policies.
3. **Geographic (or spatial) distance**: this distance component represents the physical distance between countries, taking into account the ease of transport between the countries. Having a common border or easy access via river and ocean waterways may keep this distance low. Differences in topography or climate may make this distance higher. Human intervention, such as the creation of efficient transportation and communication links, can reduce this distance.
4. **Economic distance**: this distance component represents differences in consumer wealth, income level and distribution, infrastructure characteristics, the cost and quality of natural, financial, and human resources, and prevailing business practices.

Ghemawat's general conclusion is that higher distances correspond with lower inter-country trade levels, implying a lower probability of success.

Ghemawat describes in some detail these four dimensions of distance and outlines how they can affect different industries in different ways.[3]

While some aspects of **cultural distance** may be readily apparent, such as differing languages, Ghemawat suggests that other aspects may be more difficult to discover. He offers two examples of how prevailing attitudes in China create a high cultural distance for Western firms doing business there. The first is the failure of media mogul Rupert Murdoch's Star TV, which rebroadcast English language programming directly by satellite in an effort to overcome geographic distance constraints. Star TV underestimated the market's preference for locally produced, Chinese language content. The second is the tolerance for copyright infringements, which contrasts sharply with the protection of intellectual property rights in Europe and North America. The underlying causes for the prevailing Chinese attitude reside not only in the country's recent communist ideology in the second part of the twentieth century (the People's Republic of China was established in 1949), but also in deeply rooted social norms from 'a precept of Confucius teaching that encourages replication of the results of past intellectual endeavours'.[4] In general, 'soft' consumer goods such as food items, selected on the basis of personal tastes and cultural identity, are more sensitive to cultural distance than 'hard' items such as industrial machinery and bulk commodities.

Along with cultural distance, Ghemawat also argues that businesses often overlook **administrative (or institutional) distance**. He demonstrates that common historical and political ties significantly increase trade levels: 'Colony-colonizer links between countries, for example, boost trade by 900% . . . Preferential trading arrangements, common currency, and political union can also increase trade by more than 300% each.'[5]

He points out that governments can be very effective at creating administrative distance. In order to protect domestic industries, host countries raise barriers through trade tariffs, quotas, restrictions on foreign-owned companies, and preferential treatment of domestic firms. A firm's home country can create distance through unilateral measures, such as US policies prohibiting US-based firms from trading with Cuba, or from engaging in bribery anywhere in the world, irrespective of host country laws. Lastly, 'institutional infrastructure' characteristics such as corruption and systemic social upheaval have an important impact on administrative distance. According to Ghemawat, the firms most affected by administrative distance are large employers (including national champion companies), are vital to national security, produce essential goods and services, or exploit the country's key natural resources.

The third attribute, **geographic (or spatial) distance**, involves more than just physical proximity. Geographic distance also encompasses other aspects affecting the separation of countries in space (and therefore in time), including man-made elements such as transportation networks and communication infrastructure. Ghemawat argues that products with 'low value-to-weight' ratios (such as steel and cement) and highly perishable items incur the greatest cost increases as transportation distances increase.[6] Surprisingly, his research shows that trade in services and investment capital are also negatively correlated with greater geographic distance, largely because of diminished levels of information infrastructure.

The fourth and final dimension of distance, **economic distance**, relates to differences in wealth, income, and standard of living between consumers in different countries. In his discussion of economic distance, he identifies two broad approaches to expanding abroad: replicating existing competitive advantages, building upon scale and scope economies, and exploiting differences in input costs or prices between markets through 'economic arbitrage'.[7] If a firm focuses on scale or scope economies, typical for **centralized exporters** and **international projectors**, this strategy is likely to be more effective if the economic distance between home and host countries is small. Both scale and scope economies require standardization, meaning that there is no requirement to adapt to host country requirements. In contrast, if a firm focuses on economic arbitrage, typical for **international coordinators**, the firm embraces economic distance because it possesses FSAs that allow it to exploit and link the diverse location advantages of high-distance countries. This is the strategy adopted by, for example, vertically integrated MNEs in resource industries.

Ghemawat's methodology is based on a thorough analysis of economic data concerning international trade. To reach the conclusion that increased distance generally corresponds with reduced inter-country trade, his research team 'regressed trade between every possible pair of countries in the world in each of 70 industries on each dimension of distance'.[8] To demonstrate how his distance framework can improve a firm's analysis of foreign market potential, Ghemawat provides a case study of US-based Tricon Restaurants International, the parent company of fast-food chains such as Pizza Hut, Taco Bell, Habit Burger Grill,[9] and KFC. (Tricon Restaurants changed its name to YUM! Brands, Inc. in 2002. YUM! Brands is headquartered in Louisville, Kentucky.) When the four dimensions of distance are factored in to complement traditional country portfolio analysis, a revised and more accurate picture of the opportunities and risks becomes clear. Countries with lower-distance factors vis-à-vis the United States, such as Mexico and Canada, become obvious top choices; countries that are seemingly attractive in terms of market size and growth, such as Japan and Germany, become less so when their higher levels of distance are taken into consideration. According to Ghemawat, 'The results confirm the importance of distinguishing between the various components of distance in assessing foreign market opportunities.'[10] Each distance component compounds the bounded rationality problem faced by the MNE's senior management: the problem of uncertainty increases, as does the problem of imperfect processing of information.

Context and Complementary Perspectives

Ghemawat's article demonstrates that the extent of globalization has been vastly exaggerated. The dot-com boom – namely, the speculative stock market bubble built upon growth in the internet sector between 1996 and 2001 – was supposed to signal the end of distance. The possibility of Web-based sales, instant communication within and between firms, and technology-supported, seamless, global supply chains was supposed to eliminate former barriers of time and space. A truly global marketplace would materialize thanks to information technology, with unlimited potential for firms to expand into foreign markets, develop centres of global excellence, and experiment with cross-border structures of management and reporting. Ghemawat's article acts as a wake-up call, dismissing the belief that distance has finally been conquered. Cultural, administrative, geographic, and economic (CAGE) differences between countries are here to stay, and will present continuing barriers to international business.

Till Vestring, *Ted Rouse* and *Uwe Reinert*, three partners with the consulting company Bain & Co., wrote a complementary perspective in *SMR*.[11] Their message is that MNEs intending to be cost leaders in their industry should establish portfolios of low-cost countries to which selected activities can be outsourced. They observed that many cost leaders in industries ranging from automotive and chemicals to consumer products and technology do not simply outsource to a few high-profile, low-cost destinations such as China and India, but attempt to reduce risk by including a broader set of countries in their offshoring strategy. Though the authors also caution against undisciplined fragmentation of offshoring activities, they focus on the benefits of accessing multiple 'high-distance' input markets.

Note the contrast with Ghemawat: whereas Ghemawat focuses on the risk of penetrating too many high-distance output markets, Vestring, Rouse, and Reinert focus on the risk of using too few high-distance input markets. For Ghemawat, distance is fundamentally a barrier; for Vestring, Rouse, and Reinert, distance is fundamentally an opportunity.

Vestring, Rouse, and Reinert argue that a large MNE would be insufficiently diversified if it outsourced all of its inputs to, for example, China. Whereas China's factory labour cost of US $5.78 per hour (2019)[12] still represents a global cost leadership position, China has more political uncertainty than several offshoring alternatives (such as a number of Eastern European nations) with higher labour costs. In addition, if transport costs and time-to-market are factored into the equation, and these cost components are more important than labour costs for particular products, many offshoring locations with substantially higher labour costs than China may become more attractive. Vestring, Rouse, and Reinert conclude that large MNEs should create a portfolio of offshoring countries based upon the particular bundle of location advantages offered by each country, often a function of the specialized skills offered:

> The Boeing Co., for instance, has a centre that does design and technical work in Russia, a country with deep aerospace engineering skills. Procter & Gamble Co. has its taxes done in Costa Rica, which has a strong cadre of workers with accounting skills. General Electric Co. has built an R&D centre in India with more than 4,000 employees, many of whom are locals with doctorates.[13]

Vestring, Rouse, and Reinert argue that large MNEs should develop a particular recombination capability: an FSA in offshoring. In practical terms, that means that strategic offshoring decisions are not left to individual business units, but are handled in a centralized fashion, so as to create cost advantages across business units by pooling resources, jointly developing new suppliers, or expanding economies of scale in low-cost countries.[14]

However, in spite of advocating expansion into high-distance locations, the authors implicitly take on board Ghemawat's cautionary suggestions about the risks of distance. They argue that MNEs must be well informed on all relevant cost categories and other relevant country characteristics such as the availability of specialized skills, both now and in the future, before selecting particular offshoring locations. In addition, firms must make substantial investments in location-bound FSAs – including local logistics, engineering, and manufacturing capabilities – before starting local production.

Fabio Ancarani, *Judy K. Frels*, *Joanne Miller*, *Chiara Saibene* and *Massimo Barberio* provide a second complementary perspective to Ghemawat's analysis, using fifteen examples of MNEs that have been particularly successful in high-distance environments. Their *CMR* article focuses specifically on the (perhaps unexpected) attractiveness of rural markets in comparatively less wealthy economies, and provides guidance to developed economy MNEs when entering sub-national regions within such economies.[15]

On the surface, the location-specific advantages of such rural markets would appear compelling, as illustrated by the following statement: 'In India, 53% of fast-moving consumer goods demand and 59% of consumer durable demand comes from rural markets and overall, rural markets generate between 56–60% of GDP.'[16] But the question for foreign MNEs, especially those from advanced economies, is how to build on host-country-specific advantages that are supposedly present, even in poorer, sub-national regions. These advantages are related to the potentially high demand in final product markets, but tapping into them often requires novel and creative resource combinations, much in line with how ***multi-centred MNEs*** function. Rural markets in less wealthy economies may be very different from the conventional national markets served by MNEs, whether for fast-moving or durable consumer goods. These differences will typically be related to Ghemawat's CAGE distance components. The authors identify a number of creative resource recombination approaches that have led to MNE success in rural areas of emerging markets.

First, MNEs should *rethink their products* and possibly develop new ones for poorer, rural contexts: '. . . most successful companies rework products from their existing product portfolio. However, in parallel, they are also likely to have new products for these markets under development, to incorporate knowledge they glean about the market as they gain experience there.'[17] As one example, the German automobile company Volkswagen served the Eastern European markets with a locally designed and locally manufactured Skoda car. The firm's product offering had several features tailored to the rural setting. These included a so-called 'rough road option' to address the harsh road conditions in several Eastern European markets.[18] Recombination of resources in rural markets can also lead to new, non-location-bound FSAs, as illustrated by the following example of a Finnish phone manufacturer: 'Nokia used India as a source of innovation ideas for its worldwide markets . . . Rather than developing phones with longer battery life just for rural markets . . . Nokia fed the request into the global R&D effort as a potential future feature for all handsets.'[19]

Second, MNEs should also *rethink distribution strategies and co-opt local partners* to deliver their products to rural customers efficiently and effectively: 'Channel partners were used more often than they might be in urban or developed areas because in rural emerging markets, partners are often a more economical solution that provides greater flexibility.'[20] For example, the American soft drinks MNE Coca-Cola's distribution strategy in Africa focused on engaging local businesses, and allowed for creative resource combinations. For instance, the 'micro distribution centre (MDC) model' allowed Coca-Cola to solve the problem of selling deep into rural areas:

> This system sets up small businesses that have the objective to cover the last leg of delivery: in urban areas where trucks may be blocked from entering narrow alleys and side streets and in rural areas, where roads, paths, and terrain are not amenable to trucks. These 'last kilometers' are covered by the business owner using whatever means is most appropriate in that environment: pushcarts, donkey-carts, bicycles, or even carried by hand . . . Coca-Cola does not require the distributors to partner exclusively with Coca-Cola but allows them to leverage the value of their operation by performing, for example, small parcel delivery along with Coca-Cola's products.[21]

As another example, Unilever, the British-Dutch consumer goods MNE, utilized local partners in India, in order to respond appropriately to the unique tastes, norms, and culture of local buyers. Its 'Shakti' project empowered local individuals to engage in effective door-to-door selling:

> Unilever's Shakti project . . . covers over 100,000 villages through a network of 45,000 Shakti Ammas (empowered mothers) or Shaktimaans (male members of the initiative) across 15 states reaching 3 million homes. These entrepreneurs are selected and then trained to sell Hindustan Unilever Limited products to local villagers . . . Unilever assigns to each entrepreneur a given area, creating a sense of ownership and responsibility . . . A final objective is to develop partnerships with non-competitive companies so that the Shakti entrepreneurs can sell a wider range of products.[22]

Third, a *locally tailored service strategy* is essential. For instance, Volkswagen in Eastern Europe developed the capacity to provide instant service when a vehicle would experience failure in rural areas: 'All services covered under warranty were properly budgeted and tracked, and spare parts stocks were kept at levels needed to ensure timely repair in all areas of the region.'[23]

Fourth, *creative financing solutions* may be required for rural markets, such as micro-financing organizations making loans available to local partners (e.g., in distribution) or to final customers. As one example related to India: 'Nokia partnered with microfinance institutions so that they could provide customers a phone up-front at no cost, but with payments spread over 25 weeks.'[24]

Fifth, *new human resources and talent management strategies* may also be needed for the reality of rural markets. Tailoring human resources management systems to match local requirements can include incentive systems that work best for employees in these rural markets. Beyond their direct functionality, non-monetary incentives such as flexible hours, training programmes, and equal pay and promotion opportunities for women, are sometimes viewed by employees in rural contexts as status elements, especially as compared to what domestic firms offer to their employees, and this can enhance motivation and performance. In addition, firms such as Unilever have their 'employees worldwide take on special assignments of six months or even longer in rural emerging markets to provide first-hand experiences of the challenges there. This can help develop future leaders with more global and rural exposure and with an appreciation for the challenges faced in markets that hold the key to their firm's future.'[25] This is a variation on Pattern VII in the set of ten patterns of FSA development that we described in Chapter 1. In this instance, MNE human resources are being sent to a foreign operation and become enriched through host-environment experiences. They thereby gain in strength as non-location-bound FSAs to benefit the entire MNE internal network.

The CAGE distance dimensions described by Ghemawat are likely to be greater when MNEs from developed economies target rural areas in less wealthy markets. The customer base in relatively isolated rural areas of such markets may have its own sub-culture, partly due to underdeveloped transportation and communication infrastructure, meaning that cultural distance experienced by a foreign MNE may actually be much higher than suggested by national indicators. Local government agencies, NGOs, and other non-market interest groups active in rural areas may affect the rules of the game and the norms adhered to by businesses and consumers. As a result, the administrative distance can also be substantially higher than suggested by nation-based parameters. Finally, economic systems and behaviour in rural areas, for example, in the financing, logistics, marketing, distribution, and after-sales service spheres, can be very different from what is prevailing in urban areas, thereby imposing a much stronger burden on MNEs to develop location-bound FSAs dedicated to rural area characteristics. The notion of **multi-centred MNEs** thereby becomes more encompassing, because multi-centricity now potentially extends to a variety of different markets within a single nation.

Ancarani *et al.* provide MNEs with a variety of actionable suggestions to overcome the added CAGE distance challenges in large rural markets located in comparatively poorer economies. All these challenges amount to sharp increases in bounded rationality, when MNEs seek to engage in far-reaching resource recombination to be successful. These MNEs also need to be attentive to new bounded reliability challenges as they engage with local partners, who may be more used to informal contracting than to formal agreements, thereby potentially creating identity-based discordance issues. Here, fine-grained analysis is important for those novel resource combinations that lead to actual MNE success in rural markets.

The most important connection between Ghemawat's work and the framework developed in Chapter 1 is the limits on the transferability, deployability, and exploitation of FSAs across borders. Ghemawat cautions against the assumption that FSAs developed in the home country can be easily exploited in other markets regardless of distance. When firms try to transfer, deploy, and exploit abroad their home-grown FSAs or create new FSAs and engage in resource recombination, they face additional barriers and complexities not faced by local competitors in the host country. While Ghemawat does not explicitly discuss the distinction between location-bound and internationally transferable FSAs, he emphasizes that the international exploitation potential of FSAs depends critically upon the type and level of distance among countries. Here, because of bounded rationality, managers often overestimate the international profit potential of their companies' FSAs, and underestimate the efforts required to create location-bound FSAs in high-distance host countries, as a precondition for accessing those countries' location advantages. Figures 4.1 and 4.2 illustrate the

MANAGEMENT INSIGHTS

point, highlighting the diminishing effectiveness of transferring, deploying, and exploiting FSAs to foreign markets, and the increasing requirements for new FSAs, as the various distance components grow between the firm's domestic base and the host location considered.

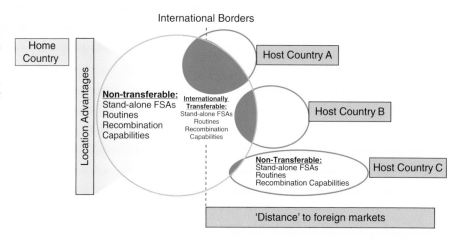

Greater 'distance' leads to weaker transferability, and weaker deployment and exploitation potential of NLB FSAs, as illustrated by the smaller sections in the NLB-FSAs circle from the home country available for successful transfer to – and deployment and exploitation in – host countries.

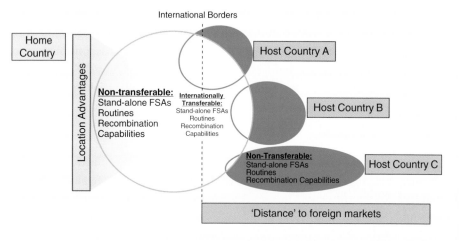

Greater 'distance' leads to higher investment requirements in LB FSAs, as illustrated by the larger size of the LB FSA spaces that need to be filled, in the host countries, meaning new entrepreneurial resource combinations, as a complement to the NLB FSAs available from the home country (see Figure 4.1).

Ghemawat's perspective initially appears similar to Pattern III of this book's framework (see Figure 4.3) insofar as allegedly internationally transferable FSAs developed in the home country are susceptible to difficulties when operating abroad because of the distance between the home and host countries.

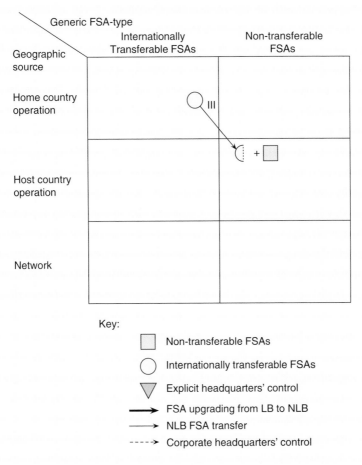

Figure 4.3
Ghemawat's perspective of FSA development in MNEs

Key:

▢   Non-transferable FSAs

◯   Internationally transferable FSAs

▽   Explicit headquarters' control

⟶   FSA upgrading from LB to NLB

→   NLB FSA transfer

---->   Corporate headquarters' control

However, rather than arguing that firms should follow Pattern III and develop additional, location-bound FSAs in foreign markets in line with the conventional 'think global – act local' perspective, Ghemawat advocates that firms should reduce their geographic scope and focus on those countries where low distance will allow the easy transfer, deployment, and profitable exploitation of the firm's main FSAs. The firms contemplated by Ghemawat include primarily **centralized exporters** and **international projectors**, focusing on scale economies and scope economies respectively, and engaging in market-seeking foreign expansion.

Ghemawat's perspective on distance recognizes the enormous bounded rationality problems faced by MNE senior managers. Host markets that are attractive in terms of macro-level parameters such as absolute wealth and industry growth cannot simply be accessed at will.

In spite of its valuable insights, the paper has five limitations.

First, macro-level distance may be an important explanation for lack of success in a foreign market, but this observation itself only reflects a macro-level reality, which is not necessarily relevant to individual firms. In other words, the distance for a particular firm may be much less than the distance for the home country as a whole. Consider a US-based consumer goods company contemplating an expansion into Taiwan. A Ghemawat-type analysis would likely conclude that this makes little sense, as the cultural, administrative, geographic, and economic distance components between the United States and Taiwan are enormous. It is a safe prediction that countries such as Canada, Mexico, and several EU countries would be more attractive options when performing a country portfolio analysis, corrected for distance. However, now imagine that several members of the US firm's senior management have Taiwanese roots. They were born and raised in Taiwan, earned their first university degree there, and have maintained close contacts with a wide social network in their mother country. In this case, the firm may already command the necessary location-bound FSAs (meaning here limited to Taiwan) to access successfully the attractive Taiwanese market. In more general terms, the investments required to develop location-bound FSAs to access a foreign market will be different for each company, because each will be equipped with a different recombination ability, and any analysis limited to macro-level parameters, whether or not corrected for macro-level distance components, neglects firm specificity.

Second, similar to the suggestion made by Vestring, Rouse, and Reinert, companies can develop their recombination capabilities, improving their ability to overcome distance barriers. Simply abandoning the playing field and restricting the firm's geographic scope to low-distance locations is not the only appropriate strategy. For example, increasing the diversity in the senior management's (cultural and experiential) background lets the firm benefit from multiple cognitive and skills bases. In addition, a higher functional diversity of senior management may allow a better estimation of the challenges likely to occur in each functional area when penetrating a host country. A larger senior management team, with some managers developing or sustaining expertise in specific geographic areas, may also be useful. In general, if a firm is on a trajectory of international expansion, it should build into its human resources base and key decision-making routines a deep knowledge of foreign markets, including cultural affinity and experience-based business knowledge. For firms that do this, some of the location-bound knowledge required to penetrate a new host market will already be available in-house. In this context, we should also mention that international experience in foreign markets, sometimes built over many decades, may eliminate the macro-level distance problem altogether if a newly entered country has a low overall distance vis-à-vis the firm's existing network of operations. Here, it is not necessarily the distance from the home country that counts, but rather the distance between the host country and the MNE's affiliate most closely resembling that host country.[26]

Third, the impact of macro-level distance may be very different in the different parts of the value chain: Ghemawat's conclusions are less persuasive at the upstream end than they are at the downstream end. Most MNEs indeed show a sales distribution oriented towards low-distance countries, for example, Europe-based companies focusing on other European nations, Canadian companies focusing on the United States, and Japanese companies focusing on Asia. However, these same MNEs appear relatively unconstrained in the geographic location of upstream activities such as sourcing and sometimes even production.[27]

Consider, for example, the upstream and downstream activities of the US-based clothing company Levi Strauss. The North American region accounted for US $3.1 billion of Levi Strauss' US $5.8 billion in total sales in 2019,[28] showing a strong concentration of sales in the home region. However, by 2004, Levi Strauss had shut down all its manufacturing factories in North America and moved these comparatively high-cost, upstream activities to Latin American, Middle Eastern, and Asia-Pacific countries.[29] In this example, high distance does not appear to hinder relocating all upstream activities. In recent years, many MNEs have relocated entire upstream activity bundles, as described extensively in the popular business press.

What is the reason for this asymmetry between upstream and downstream activities? In the case of market-seeking FDI (see Chapter 1), the MNE commits resources and creates location-bound FSAs to link its existing FSAs with location advantages, in this case the presence of a large market, in the high-distance host country. Unfortunately, the resource commitments made to attract potential foreign customers are completely one-sided, coming only from the MNE. Thus, effective resource recombination is difficult. This contrasts with, for example, strategic resource-seeking FDI, in which the MNE also engages in location-specific linking investments in the high-distance host country. In this case, however, the resource commitments are made to acquire knowledge or reputational resources and are made by all the relevant parties: foreign suppliers, workers, and acquired companies them-selves engage in reciprocal commitments to make these investments worth-while. With this input from host country actors, resource recombination is much easier. This analysis suggests that resource recombination is generally harder for downstream activities than for upstream ones. Ghemawat's analy-sis may thus be particularly appropriate for *centralized exporters* and *inter-national projectors*, focused on expansion in foreign output markets, but less so for *international coordinators*, attempting to access and coordinate mul-tiple input and intermediate output markets.

Fourth, Ghemawat assumes that FSAs are developed in the home country and subsequently exploited in other markets. He does not address the role of host countries, including high-distance ones, in fostering FSA development. Ghemawat's conclusions are useful for companies looking to transfer and exploit their bundles of internationally transferable FSAs in foreign markets, and facing restricted access to the location advantages of high-distance host countries. However, they are less useful for companies seeking to enter foreign markets to cultivate new FSAs within the host location environment. For example, in the case of strategic resource-seeking investment, a high-distance location, though creating high costs for the firm, may also be instrumental to learning opportunities unavailable in low-distance locations. (This is ultimately the strategy adopted by the *international coordinator* archetype discussed in Chapter 1. The *international coordinator* combines the location advantages provided by a variety of locations, including high-distance ones, and ultimately benefits from recombining these geographically dispersed resources.)

Unfortunately, Ghemawat's model relies heavily on macro-level trade statistics, which show only that – *lumping together all motivations for investing abroad* – higher distance attributes correlate with lower inter-country trade levels, and therefore seem to imply a lower probability of success. However, this approach overlooks the differences among foreign entry motivations. The managerial prescription of reduced geographic scope at the firm level is not valid for all foreign entry motivations: the required resource recombination may be easier to achieve with some entry motivations than with others.

Fifth, Ghemawat's model does not address how cooperative entry modes, such as strategic alliances and joint ventures with host country firms, can affect, and perhaps soften, the impact of high distance. Very often, such arrangements are set up precisely to overcome the various macro-level distance components when the MNE does not have the resource recombination capability to address the distance challenge on its own. Here, the partner firm's complementary resources may reduce distance. Micro-level distance may remain, however, especially cultural differences with host country partners, and this raises the question whether the reduction in macro-level distance achieved is sufficient to overcome the micro-level distance associated with a cooperative entry mode. Do cooperative entry modes alleviate or compound the challenges posed by high distance? Ghemawat's model assumes that companies enter foreign markets on their own, primarily to exploit FSAs developed in the home market. The model does not address how cooperative entry modes can facilitate foreign entry.

Strategic Challenges in the New Economy

Marcel Corstjens and *Rajiv Lal*, in an *HBR* paper on the internationalization of the grocery retail industry, convincingly show the limits to the non-location-boundedness of most MNEs' FSAs in this sector.[30] The authors observe that 'globalization is no panacea'.[31] They also argue that supposed globalization in the form of a worldwide successful distribution of operations may be a non-starter for most successful MNEs in the sector.

There are many reasons for retailers to attempt international expansion in the new economy that is characterized by low overall growth for grocery retail products in the most developed markets; the presence of highly digitized supply chains; and the relative ease and speed with which supplies at the input side can be procured from all over the world: (1) tapping into high-growth foreign markets because of low margins in the domestic retailing industry (e.g., in the United States); (2) earning additional economies of scale and scope; (3) gaining risk-diversification benefits, from non-synchronized business cycles across geographic space; (4) accessing valuable human resources in foreign locations; and (5) overcoming regulatory constraints by being a full, local player.

One key problem appears to be the lack of preparedness of MNEs in the retail sector when entering high-distance markets. For example, the possibility of an acquisition in a high-distance market may seem attractive at first sight, but senior management teams in MNEs always need to think through carefully the sometimes complex, resource recombination challenges that will ensue after completing the acquisition. Here, the focus must be on understanding the limits of the acquiring firm's supposed non-location-bound FSAs that will be deployed in the acquired target. Due diligence efforts are also required to ascertain which investments will be needed to develop new location-bound FSAs in the host market, or to meld extant FSAs from the acquired company with the MNE's existing FSA reservoir.

The authors observe that no single, large retailing MNE (e.g., US-based Walmart or France-based Carrefour) is actually operating successfully in terms of market share and profitability across all of the key triad markets of North America, Europe, and Asia. Many large retail MNEs have experienced failures in some foreign markets. In most countries, local retailers, not MNEs, have been holding a dominant market share in their home market. Attempts by MNEs at standardizing, meaning a sole reliance on deploying FSAs wrongly assumed to be non-location-bound, have often led to disappointing results: '. . . standard globalization strategies haven't worked in retail'.[32] As noted by the authors: 'Retailers face many barriers to entry in foreign markets.'[33] The CAGE distance components appear to be particularly detrimental in the retail sector, and include *inter alia* difficulties in finding good acquisition targets and suitable greenfield sites for retail operations, as well as reliable business partners (economic distance); responding in a satisfactory way to local shoppers' tastes and perceptions (cultural distance); and addressing legal/regulatory constraints (administrative distance) across national borders.

Corstjens and Lal formulate a variety of suggestions to increase the likelihood of success in distant markets. One suggestion is to think carefully about which non-location-bound FSAs could actually be deployed in the host country. For example, the key to the German supermarket chain Aldi's international success has been the 'simplicity of its business model, with a focus on lowering operating costs'.[34] In parallel, empowering the local operations with substantial flexibility and autonomy to develop and deploy location-bound FSAs tailored to host country needs has also been important.

In sum, Corstjens and Lal's analysis of grocery retailing confirms the importance of the CAGE (i.e., cultural, administrative, geographic and economic) distance dimensions suggested by Ghemawat. The distance dimensions may play out even more strongly in the grocery retail sector than in other industries, because the retail sector in every country typically has strong incumbents, who exploit well-accepted templates across the value chains, and they tend to have long-lasting and relatively loyal customers and reliable suppliers. In addition, economic and cultural distances are not easy to separate here, because consumer preferences and business models for grocery delivery tend to be closely intertwined. Because of the nature of the business, successful grocery retailers must also draw upon numerous highly regulated supply chains following host country norms (e.g., for dairy products, meats, alcohol, cleaning products, natural supplements, etc.), which will tend to exacerbate the challenges of melding extant non-location-bound FSAs with newly accessed or newly developed ones.

This article is also reminiscent of Rugman and Verbeke's (2004) path-breaking work on regional MNEs, which highlighted the importance of regional strategies rather than global ones, even among the world's largest firms.[35] The inter-regional liability of foreignness (e.g., an American firm's operating supermarkets in Europe) is typically much greater than the equivalent, intra-regional one. Here, the totality of the CAGE distance dimensions, including geographic distance, contributes to a compounded liability of foreignness in host regions. As a result, MNE senior managers often try to prioritize entering nearby foreign countries within their home region. This type of international expansion can provide MNEs with a (profitable) balance between gaining easy scope economies from transferring extant FSAs to foreign countries, and minimizing the impact of the CAGE distance dimensions through developing or accessing rather easily the resources instrumental to new location-bound FSAs within the home region.

International Business Strategy During Globally Disruptive Events

Global disruptions typically trigger changes in government intervention that can affect MNE functioning. For example, we already noted implicitly in earlier chapters that pandemic-induced public policies in many cases altered the CAGE distance characteristics of foreign nations vis-à-vis the home country. Especially, the 'A' component (administrative distance) led to new uncertainties for MNE senior management. Here, MNEs' managers need to pay particular attention to safeguarding the secure, international transfer and exploitation of key FSAs in a geopolitical context where governments may prioritize national interests to the detriment of efficiently functioning global value chains led by foreign MNEs. These firms may want to relocate activities when faced with new, disruption-induced, host country location disadvantages.

For instance, Poland sought 'to gain market share from India, where the chaotic coronavirus lockdown left many outsourcers scrambling to avoid outages as they switched to remote working'.[36] Essentially, Poland presented itself as a low-distance location for European-based MNEs with greater stability and only marginally higher costs than India.[37] China was especially affected by MNE relocation decisions, in large measure because of the fear that it would be increasingly operating as a 'rule of rulers' country, rather than a 'rule of law' country:[38]

> Evidence of the shifting tide can [also] be found in surveys of senior executives of big companies from America, China and north Asia (e.g., Japan and South Korea), conducted by UBS, a Swiss bank. Among its 1,000-plus respondents, 76% of American companies, 85% of north Asian ones and even 60% of Chinese firms said that they had already moved or were planning to move some production away from China. Keith Parker of UBS estimates that companies might shift between 20–30% of their Chinese manufacturing capacity. The relocations will not happen overnight but they will slowly chip away at China's dominance in manufacturing.[39]

Japan 'devoted a $2.2bn chunk of its coronavirus stimulus package to help companies move production out of China'.[40] India and Taiwan offered loans, inexpensive plant location sites, and incentives to lure companies from China.[41]

Increased administrative distance also became apparent in the sphere of international mergers and acquisitions. Governments increased scrutiny (e.g., the United States,[42] the United Kingdom,[43] Europe,[44] and India[45]) in order to prevent hostile takeovers by foreign acquirers of prominent and budding national companies with depressed share prices, especially from companies with extensive ties to governments pursuing foreign intellectual property.[46] In more general terms, the pandemic increased the distance among various countries, especially in the administrative and economic spheres, and affected MNE location strategies.

Facing a global disruption, MNEs are likely to consider seriously more home-region-oriented relocation strategies rather than global ones and prioritize nearby foreign countries for their own production (even though some MNEs may also move towards a more multi-centred approach and allow for more autonomy in high-distance subsidiaries, as we explain in Chapter 5). The reason is that the inter-regional CAGE distances are typically much higher than the equivalent, intra-regional ones. For instance, in the context of the pandemic: 'central and eastern Europe could benefit from "nearshoring" (moves by China-wary western European manufacturers to bring production closer to home)'.[47] Such relocations to lower-distance countries can also have macro-level effects. For example, again as a result of the pandemic, 'Central Europe could benefit from its dependence on Germany, which is expected to recover quickly. It is by far the biggest trading partner of the Visegrad countries (the Czech Republic, Slovakia, Hungary and Poland)'.[48]

Five Management Takeaways

1. Pay attention to the four key dimensions of 'distance' when evaluating the attractiveness of foreign markets.
2. Analyze your company's position in the realm of cost leadership and thereby your potential (or need) to develop an FSA in offshoring, especially if this means moves to high-distance countries.
3. Consider the right products, the right partnerships, the right service requirements, etc. when entering high-potential, rural areas in high-distance markets: be multi-centric, even within single countries.
4. Reflect on the transferability, deployability, and profitable exploitation of your FSAs across borders, as well as on the need to create new FSAs, and on the possibilities of resource recombination. Do not overestimate the profit potential abroad of FSAs that worked well at home.
5. Before making a final decision about entry in potential host markets, do assess several firm and host-country-specific characteristics which amount to 'distance': evaluate whether strong but hypothetical profit potential in foreign markets can actually be achieved in practice, given the presence of distance. Do this even when commanding sophisticated, proven routines and digital assets, and functioning with flexible, international supply chains.

5

Combining Firm-Specific Advantages and Location Advantages in a Multinational Network

Five Learning Objectives

1. To describe the challenges associated with centralizing strategic decision making and control in MNEs, and to highlight the possible ineffectiveness thereof.
2. To develop a framework for classifying MNE subsidiaries as a function of the location advantages they can access and the unique bundles of FSAs they command inside the firm, but with due consideration to the value chain activities involved.
3. To foster reflection on the 'procedural justice' concept and to highlight the impact thereof on decision making and organizational effectiveness.
4. To explain MNEs' strategic agility in terms of balancing the tensions between head office priorities and local priorities in high-distance markets.
5. To highlight the managerial implications of assigning differentiated roles to MNE subsidiaries.

This chapter explores Bartlett and Ghoshal's idea that large MNEs are making a mistake when they adopt the two simplifying strategies of homogenization (treating all their subsidiaries the same) and centralization (making all their strategic decisions at central headquarters). According to Bartlett and Ghoshal, this is poor strategy: by selectively decentralizing elements of strategic decision making and control, these companies could instead optimize the deployment and exploitation of their present FSAs and support the development of new FSAs in their multinational subsidiary network. Bartlett and Ghoshal offer a model that helps senior corporate managers differentiate among their subsidiaries and decide which subsidiaries should do more than merely implement centrally determined strategy. These ideas will be examined and then critiqued using the framework presented in Chapter 1.

Significance

In 1986, **Chris Bartlett** and **Sumantra Ghoshal** wrote an important article in *HBR* on how MNEs should manage their subsidiary network.[1] The substance of this paper was included three years later in their now classic book on the so-called 'transnational solution'.[2] The paper discussed here is actually the most important part of the book, as it contains a practical tool for senior managers to allocate specific roles to subsidiaries.

The authors suggest that many MNEs mistakenly view host country subsidiaries simply as recipients and distributors of company knowledge and products. These MNEs do not recognize their subsidiaries' potential to develop unique strengths in their own right and to augment further the MNE's existing FSA bundles. For these centralized MNEs, strategic decision making and control reside solely in the home country corporate headquarters, which can become isolated and oblivious to changing conditions in key international markets. This can lead to enormous bounded rationality and bounded reliability challenges (the latter in the sense of senior managers not making sufficient efforts to increase the subsidiaries' potential value). Bartlett and Ghoshal argue that by selectively decentralizing elements of strategic decision making and control, companies can optimize the deployment and exploitation of their present FSAs and support the development of new FSAs in their multinational subsidiary network.

In their study of twenty-one MNEs based in the United States, Europe, and Japan, Bartlett and Ghoshal found that senior management frequently adopted two simplifying strategies. The first strategy is what the authors call the 'United Nations model' of multinational management. MNEs adopting this approach treat each subsidiary in a similar manner in terms of the roles and responsibilities these units will have, and the coordination and control systems they will be subjected to, regardless of these subsidiaries' specialized resources or the strategic importance of the host market in which they are located. Usually, this homogenized approach involves either complete subsidiary independence (as found in **multi-centred MNEs**) or complete dependence (as found in **centralized exporters** or **international projectors**). For **centralized exporters** and **international projectors**, this simplifying strategy is often adopted to offset the increasing complexity of managing large-scale international operations, even though '[as] a company reaches for the benefits of global integration . . . there is little need for uniformity and symmetry among units'.[3]

The second assumption is what the authors term the 'headquarters hierarchy syndrome'. Here, senior management views the organization as consisting of two distinct levels – one dominant and one subordinate. The dominant central corporate headquarters control key decision-making processes and overall company resources in order to implement a consistent global strategy. In contrast, all the national subsidiaries are subordinate and merely 'act as implementers and adapters of the global strategy in their localities'.[4]

These two simplifying strategies – homogenization and centralization – cause tensions between headquarters and subsidiaries, as corporate headquarters attempt to maintain control of the subsidiary network, while entrepreneurial subsidiary managers fight for more independence and freedom of action in their local markets.

Bartlett and Ghoshal conclude that these two simplifying strategies have other dysfunctional effects on the MNE as well. As a result of the first strategy, important markets and subsidiaries are treated in the same way as unimportant ones, and therefore the opportunities they provide are not optimally exploited. As a result of the second strategy, subsidiaries with a distinct, specialized resource base are unable to escape from an implementer role and unleash their entrepreneurial abilities. In other words, Bartlett and Ghoshal acknowledge that the corporate headquarters of a large MNE face serious bounded rationality problems, but they argue that responding to these problems by adopting these two simplifying strategies will trigger bounded reliability challenges (as senior managers in central headquarters do not make sufficient efforts to maximize the potential value of each subsidiary, and senior managers in the subsidiaries attempt to deviate from their prescribed role).

In response to the above problems, the authors observe that a number of MNEs have moved towards 'an organizational model of differentiated rather than homogenous subsidiary roles and of dispersed rather than concentrated responsibilities'.[5] The authors offer two examples – one negative and the other positive – to illustrate the point. The first is the case of the UK-based firm EMI and its development of the CAT scanner. Although this technology revolutionized the medical industry, earned a Nobel Prize (awarded to the EMI scientist Godfrey Hounsfield), and established EMI as the market leader in this business, the company was unable to sustain its position over time and eventually was forced to sell the business. According to Bartlett and Ghoshal, the core problem resided in an ineffective and overly centralized organizational structure and related decision-making processes. Senior management in the UK headquarters maintained centralized control, and their strategy was overly focused on domestic market needs, at the expense of key foreign markets such as the United States. For example, the firm filled all backlogged orders worldwide in the order they had been received, rather than giving priority to key customers or markets (e.g., important US customers). Corporate headquarters also refused to allow subsidiaries to engage in local sourcing to alleviate bottlenecks in production, and focused product-development efforts on British demands for improved image resolution rather than US demands for lower times per scan. As a result of these decisions, EMI was unresponsive to changing needs outside its home market, was unaware of emerging competitive threats in the United States, and left its national managers without the resources to address these growing threats.

The second example is US-based Procter & Gamble's (P&G) innovative approach to creating 'Eurobrand' teams. Earlier efforts to launch a Europe-wide campaign controlled by regional headquarters in Brussels had failed. The failure was caused by neglecting the specialized resources – especially local market knowledge – held by the subsidiaries, and by demotivating local managers. For its new effort, P&G instead identified the most successful national subsidiary for each product and put that subsidiary's managers in charge of the pan-European team for that product. The goal was to move beyond P&G's traditional multi-centred approach – whereby countries operated independently of one another – in order to capitalize on greater scale efficiencies and effectiveness in promotional campaigns and product development. By delegating responsibility and authority for specific products at the pan-European level to specific lead countries, the head office created a new system of interdependence and reciprocal cooperation among the network of national subsidiaries. As a result, P&G 'captured the knowledge, the expertise, and most important, the commitment of managers closest to the market'.[6] The key point of this example is that P&G rejected both a global and a local/national approach to strategy. A global approach dictated out of the United States would have been unworkable, given the bounded rationality constraints facing senior management at corporate headquarters. This bounded rationality challenge resulted from the substantial cultural, economic, institutional, and spatial distance separating the United States and Europe, whereby inappropriate, centrally made decisions would also have been a source of new bounded reliability challenges, with subsidiaries opposing centralized decision making. At the same time, a local/national approach to strategy would have prevented the firm from earning scale and scope economies at the regional level. In this case, the potential to earn scope economies – benefits from sharing the knowledge base of successful lead subsidiaries – was critical. Senior managers of lead subsidiaries at the regional level faced far fewer bounded rationality challenges when setting strategy for their region, and their proximity to national subsidiary managers also reduced bounded reliability.

Bartlett and Ghoshal offer a simple normative model to help senior management assign differentiated subsidiary roles. First, senior corporate management should assess each market according to its strategic importance (e.g., its market size, demand sophistication, or technological innovation). Next, senior corporate management should rate each subsidiary's resource base in terms of sales and marketing achievements, production capabilities, R&D, or any other strength contributing to competitiveness. The result is a simple subsidiary classification system (see Figure 5.1), which distinguishes among four subsidiary types.

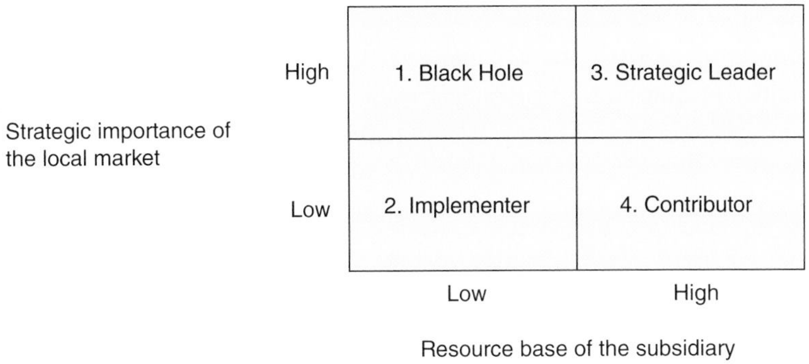

Figure 5.1
A classification of
subsidiary roles in
the MNE

1. **Black Hole:** this is a rather weak unit in terms of specialized resources, but it is located in a strategically important market. The MNE can use this unit to maintain a presence in a key market in order to keep abreast of new innovations or strategic moves by competitors, despite a lack of specialized resources or even profitability in the local subsidiary unit itself. The black hole status does reflect, however, an undesirable competitive position in a key market. In the longer run, MNEs may want to commit more resources to such markets in order to build up their subsidiary, or they may want to engage in acquisitions or strategic alliances in order to access complementary resources and improve market success.
2. **Implementer:** this is a subsidiary with weaker (or absent) specialized resources, and located in a market of lesser importance with regard to the MNE's long-term survival, profitability, and growth. The authors suggest that most MNE subsidiaries are in this category. Implementers are often key to a firm's overall success, however, because they may generate a steady stream of cash flow, and may help build competitive advantage by contributing to company-wide scale and scope economies.
3. **Strategic Leader:** this is a highly competent local subsidiary in a strategically important market. The role of this type of business unit is to assist corporate headquarters in identifying industry trends and developing new FSAs in response to emerging opportunities and threats.
4. **Contributor:** this is again a highly competent national subsidiary, but one located in a less important market. This subsidiary type has typically developed new FSAs, often as the result of an entrepreneurial host country management team. Its subsidiary-specific, specialized resource base might then benefit other units in the firm if corporate headquarters understands its potential economic value to the entire MNE.

Keeping these four subsidiary categories in mind, senior management at corporate headquarters must provide a clear sense of overall strategic direction, and allocate appropriate roles and responsibilities to the different subsidiaries in the

MNE network, as a function of the specialized resources they command and the importance of the market in which they are located. This includes providing sufficient autonomy to strategic leader subsidiaries in order to stimulate their entrepreneurial and innovation potential.

Context and Complementary Perspectives

Bartlett and Ghoshal's article saves its harshest criticism for the homogenized, unidimensional approaches to subsidiary management commonly used by *centralized exporters*, *international projectors*, and to some extent *multi-centred MNEs* expanding in the post-World War II period up to the mid-1980s. While the Iron Curtain was still in place across Eastern Europe and communist countries such as China remained essentially closed to foreign MNEs, many firms continued to grow their international operations. Their expansion into foreign markets typically followed the blueprints and conventional 'cookie cutter' patterns of FSA development and exploitation that had been set by the founders of the firm or its senior management in the early stages of its international growth.

A first complementary perspective to Bartlett and Ghoshal was provided by **W. Chan Kim** and **Renée Mauborgne**, two INSEAD-based scholars. Their important article on making global strategies work, published in *SMR*, is only one of several influential articles these authors have published on the topic of due process in MNEs.[7] 'Due process' here refers to the way strategic decisions are made, irrespective of their outcome. Kim and Mauborgne start from an observation similar to Bartlett and Ghoshal's: senior managers at MNE corporate headquarters, faced with the need to make difficult, company-wide strategic management decisions, including resource allocation decisions, often centralize the decision-making process, presenting subsidiary managers with a demotivating *fait accompli*. This strategy is especially problematic if the host country unit has grown very large relative to the home country operations and has accumulated substantial specialized resources. Destroying the entrepreneurial spirit and motivation in such subsidiaries is especially detrimental to the firm if those units are supposed to contribute to knowledge transfers and inter-subsidiary learning inside the MNE network. In such cases, the bounded reliability problem faced by senior managers at corporate headquarters becomes worse because they can no longer take for granted the commitment of subsidiary managers to pursue company goals, nor these subsidiary managers' willingness to implement company strategy wholeheartedly. Consistent with the above observation of subsidiary network growth, Kim and Mauborgne also noticed a more limited ability of corporate headquarters to evaluate appropriately each unit, to exert hierarchical power, and to establish a common corporate culture. Problems of bounded rationality and bounded reliability arise, requiring new managerial and organizational solutions.

However, rather than focusing on treating subsidiaries differently as a function of their specialized resources and the strategic importance of their location, as advocated by Bartlett and Ghoshal, Kim and Mauborgne propose a different solution. They note that subsidiary managers attach substantial importance to due process and will usually accept an allocation of MNE resources that does not benefit their unit if they believe that due process was observed in making that strategic decision.

Due process (also called 'procedural justice') implies that decision making respects five simple principles:

1. Corporate headquarters' familiarity with the local situation at the subsidiary level: this implies that senior managers at corporate headquarters understand – or at least appear to understand – all the implications of specific decisions for the subsidiaries affected.
2. Effective two-way communication between corporate headquarters and subsidiaries: in particular, the bottom-up part of this two-way communication signals that senior managers at corporate headquarters take subsidiary managers' views seriously and are willing to engage in a dialogue with these subsidiary managers.
3. Consistency in decision making across subsidiaries: consistency – in the sense of adopting clear and transparent criteria and routines to make decisions across the entire subsidiary network – prevents perceptions of politicized decision making and favouritism advantaging one subsidiary over another.
4. Possibility for subsidiary managers to challenge the dominant perspective at corporate headquarters: this signals to subsidiary managers that senior management at corporate headquarters – even if confident in its perspective – is nonetheless willing to hear its assumptions and conclusions challenged by individuals in the trenches, knowledgeable about the local situation in host countries.
5. A transparent explanation of final decisions made by corporate headquarters: here, senior management at corporate headquarters makes a serious effort to explain in depth the rationale for the decisions made, thereby pre-empting any second-guessing or rumours on the substantive reasoning behind these decisions.

Kim and Mauborgne explain why adhering to the above principles of due process is so important. First, following due process can reduce *bounded rationality* problems in the MNE. For example, by actively seeking input from host countries (through an investment of time and resources), senior management at corporate headquarters can make fundamentally better-informed decisions. Good relations with subsidiary management will also create new (informal) channels to access critical, bottom-up information from foreign units in the future.

Furthermore, following due process can also reduce *bounded reliability* problems in the MNE:

> ... those managers who believed that due process was exercised in their firms' global strategy-making process were the same executives who trusted their head offices significantly, who were highly committed to their organizations, who felt a sense of comradeship or unity with the corporate centre, and who were motivated to execute not only the letter but also the spirit of the decisions.[8]

These subsidiary managers behave this way because they feel that they have been treated with fairness and respect. Such treatment tends to reduce challenges in the sphere of identity-based discordance. Furthermore, by receiving full disclosure of the reasons for specific decisions affecting subsidiaries, these subsidiary managers become better informed on the views of corporate headquarters, and are more likely to align their own decisions with corporate headquarters' views.

Kim and Mauborgne tested their ideas on a sample of 119 subsidiary top managers in nineteen MNEs. Their main conclusion: procedural justice has a tangible positive impact on reducing bounded reliability. Reducing bounded rationality (better information obtained and processed by senior managers at headquarters, and better information disseminated more effectively to subsidiary managers) was undoubtedly instrumental to reducing bounded reliability. As procedural justice increases, the 'losers' in the corporate resource allocation process (i.e., those subsidiaries that do not receive the resources they request) refrain from dysfunctional behaviour in the form of divided engagement. Increased procedural justice, Kim and Mauborgne found, reduces the negative impact of unfavourable resource allocation decisions on (1) commitment, (2) 'trust', and (3) subsidiary managers' willingness to execute centrally made decisions (whether such execution was compulsory or voluntary). This beneficial effect of procedural justice on bounded reliability was systematically larger for disfavoured subsidiaries than for subsidiaries that had experienced favourable resource allocation decisions, except for the voluntary execution parameter (see Figure 5.2). In other words, with a higher level of procedural justice, it does not matter whether subsidiaries are winners or losers: in both cases, managers will try to go beyond the call of duty to implement voluntary strategic decisions.

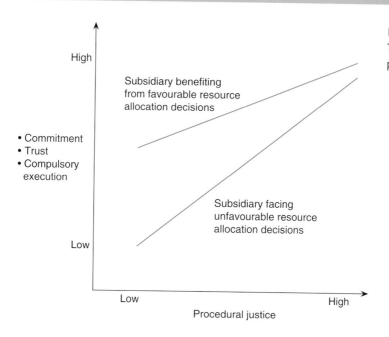

Figure 5.2
The impact of
procedural justice

Sebastian P. L. Fourné, Justin J. P. Jansen and ***Tom J. M. Mom*** wrote an
article in *CMR* that discusses the organizational complexities of MNEs beyond
the subsidiary roles recognized in Bartlett and Ghoshal's study.[9] This complementary perspective, on the concept of strategic agility, is somewhat similar to
the discussion of MNEs' working with multiple business models, as explained in
Chapter 2. However, in this instance, the need for applying different business
models results directly from operating in a set of high-distance environments, as
discussed in Chapter 4.

Strategic agility refers to creating and capturing value from local entrepreneurial opportunities in markets that are distant from one another, while at the
same time developing overarching, firm-level complementarities across all operations. As MNEs try to be agile, they will typically need to balance tensions
between head office priorities and local priorities in foreign operations, which
work with distinct business models.

The authors discuss the development of location-bound FSAs in high-distance
markets and propose three possible approaches. A *first* line of attack is for the
MNE to 'create local presence and maintain strong ties with local partners', as
the Dutch electronics MNE Philips did with its 'Design in and for' approach.[10]
A *second* and complementary line of attack is to 'assess new opportunities by
applying tailor-made metrics for evaluating and rewarding initiatives from
emerging markets'.[11] In this realm, Philips has used 'growth' and 'speed' as the
basis for a differentiated incentive and reward system in emerging markets.
A *third* line of attack is for the MNE's head office to 'champion local initiatives

by flexibly managing the interface between local subsidiary managers and senior executives'.[12] As one example, Siemens' 'SMART-strategy' entailed subsidiaries developing, testing, and pilot-selling products without initially informing headquarters, much in line with a subsidiary's autonomous capability development process described in Chapter 1.

As a follow-up to these three approaches supporting local entrepreneurial initiatives that amount to developing location-bound FSAs to create value, the MNE, as a relative outsider (as compared to domestic companies), must also secure capturing a fair share of this value. For example, it can try to 'build legitimacy in local power networks'.[13] One example is the German automobile manufacturer Volkswagen's community outreach to help local children and to protect the local environment in Mexico. It may also want to 'create dynamic barriers to imitation'.[14] For example, BMW and Volkswagen broke up value chain activities and located them across different countries, so as to make sure that local partners could not simply replicate the entire production process and capture the fruits of these MNEs' proprietary knowledge.

But within a single MNE, creating and capturing value thanks to new location-bound FSAs in distant markets only makes sense if this can be combined with developing and deploying new non-location-bound FSAs spanning the entire MNE. Such FSAs are meant to reduce the proliferation of intra-firm bounded rationality and bounded reliability challenges associated with the simultaneous creation of multiple new sets of location-bound FSAs in foreign operations. This approach is reminiscent especially of what the **International Coordinator** MNE archetype does best (see Chapter 1), but with the qualification that new FSAs can actually originate anywhere in the network, including in foreign subsidiaries.

Fourné *et al.* refer to the process of creating these new, overarching FSAs as 'enacting global complementarities'.[15] A first approach is to create *centres of excellence* commanding FSAs that can benefit the entire firm. Here, one foreign subsidiary is given the worldwide mandate to develop specialized, non-location-bound FSAs that will be diffused throughout the MNE. In other words, among different, specialized operations with sometimes competing sets of FSAs, one is chosen as the strategic leader. For example, Philips assigned specific local R&D centres to assume worldwide strategic leadership for cross-market applications. The MNE's agility arises from its willingness to select the best site, rather than simply a 'comfortable' home country or home region site to be the firm's strategic leader in a particular type of activity.

A second, common approach is for the MNE to 'coordinate cross-market operations and tasks'.[16] For example, Volkswagen has pursued an integrated cross-market production strategy with several plants producing for both local and global markets. In other words, subsidiaries are supposed to coordinate and align their activities, following new, higher-order routines.

A third essential approach is for the MNE to 'leverage resources and best practices' across all of the markets where it operates, again without necessarily favouring home country or home region operations.[17] For example, BMW has used sites in emerging markets as test facilities for novel car features that allow operating vehicles under extreme circumstances.

Creating centres of excellence, coordinating international activities, and leveraging throughout the MNE sets of distinct resources and best practices that might originate anywhere, all reflect management crafting new, non-location-bound FSAs in the MNE's primary value chain activities, based on available resources. This must be complemented with parallel design changes in the firm's governance structure and systems. Three governance design elements can be particularly useful here.

First, an increase of *modular elements* in the organizational structure is essential, meaning that the MNE unbundles its organizational structure into somewhat independent pieces, but with standardized interfaces among them. This is, of course, typical for multidivisional structures with quasi-autonomous divisions, each working with their own business models, but then being subject to largely standardized systems in the realm of accounting and finance, head office monitoring, resource allocation rules, etc.

Second, such modular structures should be complemented with senior executives at the head office who can act as *integrative thinkers* and must craft creative solutions to potential tensions among different units of the MNE, for example, when engaging in resource allocation decisions. Their roles are very much related to establishing procedural justice as discussed earlier in this chapter, and to the concept of competence carriers, discussed in Chapter 2. They eliminate expressions of identity-based discordance, especially in the realm of divided engagement, and make the organization more reliable.

Third, high-performance human resources systems are also critical to alleviate tensions among different units within the firm.[18] MNEs need to fill key positions throughout the managerial hierarchy with a balanced mix of expatriates from the head office and managers from foreign operations. This is the subject matter we expand upon in Chapter 10.

This article usefully discusses the organizational complexities faced by MNEs *after* having assigned initial roles to their portfolio of subsidiaries. It appears that there is much more to MNE functioning than assigning roles to international operations. Especially when entrepreneurial, strategic-leader subsidiaries work according to their own business models in order to be successful in foreign markets, the head office must deploy governance tools that allow requisite integration among international operations. Strategic agility means empowering some subsidiaries to sense and act upon market opportunities in high-distance environments, while not ending up with an anarchy.

In terms of the conceptual framework outlined in Chapter 1, strategic agility simply represents the ability to engage in novel resource combinations in multiple foreign markets, and then to make sure that each individual resource recombination process and outcome (which can amount to a distinct business model with its own underlying FSAs) is properly aligned with the MNE's overarching operations and governance approach. However, the over-arching governance system cannot simply be imposed by the head office: it must co-evolve in real time with the new resource combinations, as these flourish in subsidiaries in distant environments. Intra-firm bounded rationality and bounded reliability challenges arising at both the head office and subsidiaries must be properly addressed, especially as regards divided engagement. Various strategic leader subsidiaries are supposed to act entrepreneurially, but it only makes sense to have them perform their activities inside a single MNE, if complementarities can be achieved with what occurs elsewhere in the firm.

In short, each operation in the MNE's portfolio of foreign subsidiaries should work to develop new location-bound FSAs, some of which can then be upgraded into internationally transferable FSAs across all markets under a shared governance framework, for the MNE to continue to remain competitive in global markets.

MANAGEMENT INSIGHTS

In their *HBR* article, Bartlett and Ghoshal caution against homogenization and centralization and provide a model that helps senior corporate managers differentiate among their subsidiaries. The authors thereby provide a useful perspective on FSA development, particularly by noting the dispersed nature of FSA development and the roles of both host country location advantages and specialized subsidiary resources in this process (see Figure 5.3). In Figure 5.3, the size of each subsidiary's base of location advantages, location-bound FSAs, and internationally transferable FSAs is different, which determines the subsidiary's type in the typology. Bartlett and Ghoshal suggest that firms need to move beyond the conventional ***centralized exporter***, ***international projector***, and ***multi-centred MNE*** models (interestingly, they neglect the very existence of the ***international coordinator*** model). With the first two approaches, internationally transferable FSAs are developed in the home country and subsequently diffused to foreign markets, either embodied in exported goods (***centralized exporters***) or as intermediate goods, typically technological and marketing know-how (***international projectors***). This reflects Pattern I in this book's framework, as shown in Figure 5.4. The authors also reject the pure *multi-centred MNE* approach, with its exclusive focus on Pattern IV – location-bound FSAs developed by individual foreign subsidiaries for their particular host country markets.

Instead, Bartlett and Ghoshal advocate a mix of FSA development processes, including Patterns I and IV, but with an additional focus on Pattern III, whereby internationally transferable FSAs are recombined with a location-bound component. Bartlett and Ghoshal also draw attention to a rather narrow version of Pattern VI, whereby some subsidiaries – especially strategic leader subsidiaries – are given a mandate to contribute to developing new, internationally transferable FSAs. This remains a narrow version of Pattern VI, however, because for Bartlett and Ghoshal even the strategic leader subsidiaries are not supposed to develop truly autonomous initiatives outside the realm of the MNE's 'dominant logic' (i.e., the prevailing mindset in the company regarding the core businesses the firm should compete in and the required resource allocation processes to support those businesses). Resource recombination roles are still allocated by corporate headquarters and do not result from subsidiary initiatives.

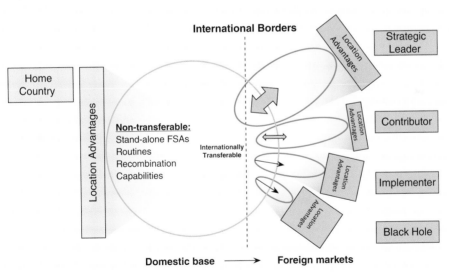

Figure 5.3
MNE resource base – subsidiaries as driving factor

Each type of subsidiary builds on a different configuration and level of LAs, LB FSAs, and NLB FSAs, as reflected by the different sizes of the oval segments that overlap with each triangle. The double-headed arrows reflect cases where the flow of NLB FSAs is two-way. Here, subsidiaries can play a key role in driving international FSA transfers (which could also occur between the subsidiaries themselves).

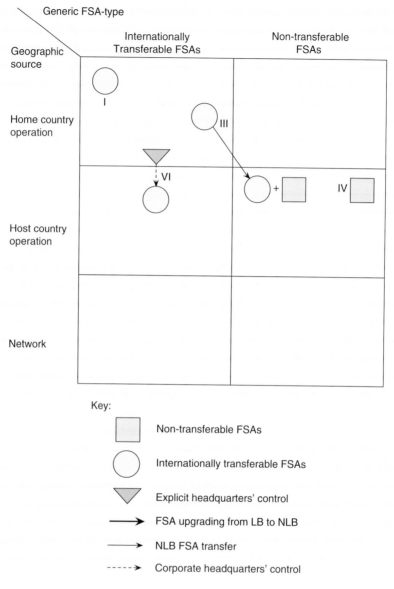

Figure 5.4 Bartlett and Ghoshal's perspective on FSA development in MNEs

In general, Bartlett and Ghoshal's work has four main limitations.[19]

First, senior managers at corporate headquarters need to recognize that good ideas can come from anywhere. In line with the observation above – that their version of Pattern VI is too narrow – Bartlett and Ghoshal assume that subsidiary roles and resources should be simply allocated to individual subsidiaries, as a function of the host market attractiveness/importance and the specialized resources held by the subsidiary. In reality, however, valuable subsidiary initiatives often arise in spite of a particular, narrow charter given to a subsidiary. The key challenge for senior management at corporate headquarters is usually not to classify subsidiaries into four categories, but rather to craft a set of routines allowing valuable initiatives to arise from the bottom up and to provide support for such initiatives. Unfortunately, senior management at corporate headquarters faces substantial bounded rationality problems, in terms of its limited ability to assess appropriately new ideas and projects, especially if they come from the periphery, namely, subsidiaries that have neither 'strategic leader' nor 'contributor' status. Thus, the problem is not simply to select those subsidiaries that should or should not contribute to FSA development. The challenge is to identify and then act on what constitutes potentially valuable knowledge, irrespective of its origin. Fortunately, several best practices have been identified to increase the likelihood that such subsidiary initiatives will contribute to FSA development.[20] These include the following mechanisms:

1. **Giving seed money to new initiatives**. Here, MNEs need to find a balance between focusing on short-term profitability expectations and allowing subsidiary managers the flexibility to pursue local new initiatives.

2. **Formally requesting proposals** (including proposals from the periphery) for projects that corporate headquarters wants to see implemented. Here, subsidiaries compete for funding through a process similar to the selection of arm's length, outside service providers.

3. **Using subsidiaries as incubators**. Here, subsidiaries are allowed to develop new products or services outside of the direct observation and control by corporate headquarters or by the senior management of core businesses. The lack of visibility keeps new initiatives safe from the so-called 'corporate immune system' (the set of forces that come into play inside the firm when new initiatives are perceived as threatening the company's prevailing dominant logic). The corporate immune system is valuable because senior management in a diversified firm can effectively manage only a limited number of distinct businesses at any given time. However, the corporate immune system can also destroy potentially valuable future businesses if the businesses are not protected from it in their early stages of development.

4. **Creating internal subsidiary networks** as the organizational centrepiece of the MNE's recombination capabilities. MNEs continually need to build formal and informal networks across foreign units. These networks are crucial for cross-pollinating ideas and providing a wider scope of connections from which innovators at the periphery can draw support. Such networking can be stimulated through multiple short-term overseas assignments and the use of idea brokers. Idea brokers are individuals who link innovators with the people who allocate resources (in this context, 'resources' include everything that is required to implement a subsidiary initiative – typically, financial or organizational support).

Second, Bartlett and Ghoshal's simple divisions into 'low' and 'high' are insufficiently fine-grained. They correctly recognize that the appropriate subsidiary role depends on both the strategic importance of the local market and the subsidiary competencies, but they fail to take that realization far enough. These variables should be measured as matters of degree, not just placed into the categories 'low' or 'high'. For example, if the local market has *extremely* high labour costs and taxes (suggesting very low strategic importance on the input side), then even if the subsidiary's competencies are high, senior management must ask whether the subsidiary's competencies are high *enough* to justify a role of 'contributor' (versus being closed down, moved, integrated, or sold).

Third, another limitation of the Bartlett and Ghoshal typology is that it mixes the importance of host country environments as input markets versus output markets; this crucial difference often leads to very different resource recombination challenges.[21] It is no coincidence that the examples provided in the *HBR* article (EMI and Procter & Gamble) address primarily the output market. Little attention is devoted to the input market – for example, the local environment for specialized labour or R&D knowledge. When an MNE specifically wants to access foreign input markets, the subsidiary must play a different role: it contributes resources and capabilities at the upstream end (e.g., labour, technology, sourcing). When assessing a subsidiary's role, it is thus important to investigate the strategic importance of the local environment at both the input market and final products market side, as well as the subsidiary's capabilities at the upstream and downstream ends, with actual manufacturing activities potentially linked to either end. The strategic motivation/purpose of any FDI decision that leads to the creation or expansion of a subsidiary usually focuses on either the input or the output market in any given country, and either the upstream or downstream FSAs of the subsidiary. Senior managers need to recognize that many subsidiary roles will be defined primarily by the host country's input market rather than its output market, and by upstream FSAs rather than downstream ones. The Bartlett and Ghoshal model, shown in Figure 5.1, must thus be unbundled, as shown in Figure 5.5. Note that this creates a separate, previously overlooked Figure 5.5A, which will now be discussed quadrant by quadrant.

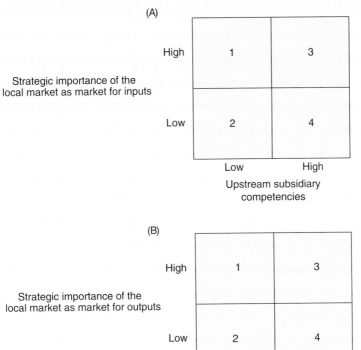

(A)

Strategic importance of the
local market as market for inputs

High | 1 | 3

Low | 2 | 4

Low High
Upstream subsidiary
competencies

(B)

Strategic importance of the
local market as market for outputs

High | 1 | 3

Low | 2 | 4

Low High
Downstream subsidiary
competencies

Figure 5.5
Unbundling
subsidiary roles in
Bartlett and
Ghoshal (1986)

Quadrant 1 of Figure 5.5A contains subsidiaries with weak back-end com-petencies in a strategically important input market. Examples include subsid-iaries unable to benefit fully from low-cost services in Eastern Europe or China because of poor relational networks, as well as subsidiaries that cannot acquire important technological expertise in key triad markets such as the United States. A classic example is that of the European semiconductor manufacturer SGS-Thomson (which changed its name to STMicroelectronics in 1998) when it opened its Shenzhen factory, its first operation in China, in 1996.[22] The lower salaries at this plant compared to the salaries received by the workers when they were trained in Malaysia led to a strike, which embarrassed the local government. To settle the strike, the plant eventually had to agree to house and feed its 600 workers, as well as raise its salaries. Expecting to benefit from lower wages, SGS-Thomson instead found that 'the unit cost for chips out of the Shenzhen plant was about 10% higher than the cost at its Malaysian counter-part',[23] even though the costs arguably should have been much less (in nearby Guangdong province, costs were 40 per cent less than in Malaysia).[24] This is an example of a firm-level failure to benefit from a generally available input-side location advantage (low wages) in a host country (China) due to a poor upstream recombination competence (poor management of local relational networks).

A subsidiary will also be in quadrant 1 of Figure 5.5A if weak upstream competencies preclude it from acquiring valuable knowledge in strategically important locations. As a classic example, in the 1980s, the Swiss pharmaceutical giant Roche had poor success in biotech in the United States, even though it operated biotech labs in New Jersey.[25] Thus, Roche's US operations in the 1980s were located in quadrant 1 of Figure 5.5A, characterized by weak upstream capabilities in the biotech industry's lead country.[26] Incidentally, Roche's weak position in biotech in the United States led it to purchase, in 1990, a major share in Genentech, the leading US biotech firm. Roche decided that, given its relative upstream weakness, acquiring US biotech firms was 'the cheapest way . . . to catch up'.[27]

Quadrant 2 of Figure 5.5A describes subsidiaries operating in input markets viewed as relatively unimportant to MNE competitiveness, and where the subsidiaries' upstream competencies are too weak to compensate for such deficiencies. A classic example is that of UK-based HSBC Banking Group's logistics, technology support, and data centres in Great Britain. Despite the United Kingdom's strategic importance as an output market, it is strategically unimportant as an input market in these areas. When HSBC transferred these functions to India and mainland China, it reduced its overall service costs and improved the competitiveness of these back-end activities.

Quadrant 3 is the most desirable quadrant in Figure 5.5A. This position is achieved by finding input markets that contribute substantially to competitive advantage and then establishing (or acquiring) subsidiaries with strong upstream FSAs there. Many manufacturing subsidiaries in low-cost countries such as China and India are located in this quadrant, but this quadrant also includes R&D centres in the most highly developed input markets, such as Silicon Valley for technological knowledge. For instance, as noted earlier, Logitech – the world's largest mouse manufacturer – closed its factories in Ireland and the United States, consolidating manufacturing facilities in its Suzhou plant in China in 1994.[28] This showed both the confidence of the firm in the competencies of the Suzhou plant and the strategic importance of China as an input market. Logitech expanded its manufacturing base in Suzhou by launching a new factory in 2005, with products from the Suzhou facilities contributing close to half of its global production.[29] In early 2020, nearly half of its employees were employed in the Suzhou manufacturing facilities.[30]

As another example, the world's largest chemical producer BASF[31] opened its first plant in Nanjing, China in 1992.[32] One of BASF's non-location-bound FSAs is its 'Verbund' approach to manufacturing. In a Verbund site, value chain ingredients ranging from R&D activities, production plants, infrastructure, logistics operations, and customer demand are integrated, thereby improving efficiencies in resource usage. Producing fine chemicals in China can be done at 40 per cent of European and US cost levels.[33] In 2005, after having built up substantial experience in China, BASF launched its first integrated Verbund site in Nanjing (it was also its sixth Verbund site worldwide), in cooperation with the Chinese petroleum and chemicals company Sinopec. This site represented BASF's largest single investment at that point in time.[34] In 2018, BASF planned an additional $10 billion investment to build a Verbund chemical production site in Zhanjiang, a coastal city in South China's Guangdong province, again being its largest investment to date.[35] By the end of 2019, BASF had established twenty-nine production sites in China, employing more than 9,000 people.[36] In parallel, in 2012, BASF established one of its largest R&D sites outside of Germany in Shanghai, which is considered a world-class hub for technological innovation.[37]

In contrast, many MNE activities in North America are located in quadrant 4 of Figure 5.5A: the input market does not contribute to MNE competitiveness, but the local upstream subsidiary compensates for this deficiency through highly efficient manufacturing operations. This quadrant includes, for instance, the major Japanese automakers' North American subsidiaries such as Toyota and Honda. Japanese car makers captured approximately 40 per cent of the US market in 2017. Although North America does not complement these companies' FSAs with distinct location advantages at the input side, the subsidiaries have still been able to stay competitive through the (partial) transfer to the United States of the Japanese keiretsu-style management and modular production methods, as well as the use of transplanted Japanese suppliers.[38]

This last example also illustrates the importance of analyzing subsidiary roles using both Figure 5.5A and Figure 5.5B. The Japanese subsidiaries in the United States span both Figure 5.5A and Figure 5.5B, in terms of value activities performed, but on the input side – Figure 5.5A – they are largely 'contributors' (quadrant 4) rather than 'strategic leaders' (quadrant 3). They benefit from the transfer of upstream competencies developed in Japan, and may further develop those, but they operate in an environment with the relative location disadvantage of sourcing in the United States rather than Japan. However, on the output side – Figure 5.5B – they are strategic leaders (quadrant 3). It is critically important to produce and market automobiles in the huge US market, and to be an insider there, because outsiders face the danger of rising trade protectionism. Thus, in this case a strategically unimportant input market is combined with a strategically important output market, and the subsidiary has both strong upstream and downstream FSAs. The point is that subsidiaries must be evaluated using both Figure 5.5A and Figure 5.5B. If a subsidiary's input and output side cannot be completely separated – as they cannot in the case of sourcing, building, and selling automobiles in the United States – then managers should take into account the results of both evaluations when assigning a role to that subsidiary.

Fourth, Bartlett and Ghoshal do not address fully the issue of subsidiary role dynamics. In reality, the situation is much more complicated than central headquarters simply deciding which role to assign which subsidiary. Subsidiaries often compete among themselves for roles, and central headquarters can also choose to restructure or reorganize, perhaps eliminating a subsidiary completely.

To illustrate some complexities of subsidiary role dynamics, let us examine the consequences of regional integration, one of the key drivers of external change throughout the triad markets of Europe, North America, and Asia. Two variables stand out in determining the impact of regional integration on subsidiary role dynamics: the **extent of regional unification** of national environments as a market for inputs/outputs, and the **commodification of upstream/downstream subsidiary competencies** in terms of resource recombination. The first variable refers to the overlap among the markets served by national subsidiaries. The second variable reflects the extent to which subsidiaries have similar strengths. High levels of regional market unification and competence commodification – see Figure 5.6 – both increase the internal competition among subsidiaries and provoke parent-driven rationalization programmes.

Figure 5.6
The impact of regional integration on subsidiary dynamics

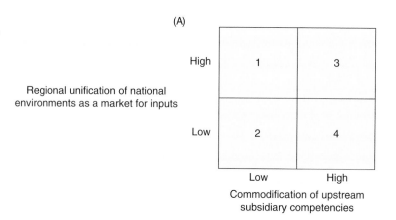

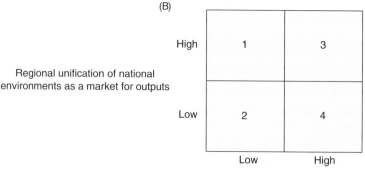

Let us look at a concrete example. In order to serve foreign markets, *international projectors* have historically engaged in market-seeking FDI in each individual host country so as to overcome tariffs, with each national subsidiary typically designed as a replica of the parent firm. As a result, subsidiaries in different countries tended to have similar internal resources. However, once regional integration occurs, the subsidiaries find themselves in either quadrant 1 or quadrant 3 of Figure 5.6, depending on whether the subsidiaries have different strengths (i.e., depending on whether commodification is low or high). In either case, the dispersion of similar resources across different countries in the same region becomes unnecessary, and reduces the potential to earn scale economies. Typically, central headquarters then implements a rationalization programme, closing some subsidiaries and giving others extended charters, based on their respective strengths.

As discussed earlier, it is important to decouple Bartlett and Ghoshal's framework into upstream and downstream competencies. For example, sales of branded consumer goods usually require proximity to the customer, because there are almost invariably differences among nations' consumers. In this industry, therefore, even if regional unification is high on the input side, it is likely to be low on the output side. The MNE that recognizes this difference between its input and output markets is unlikely to rationalize its operations.

In any case, a regionally unified market resulting from regional integration becomes a new geographic level relevant to multinational strategic management, in addition to the global and national levels.

As a final note, the essence of Bartlett and Ghoshal's message remains pertinent. They state: 'an international company enjoys a big advantage over a national one: it is exposed to a wider and more diverse range of environmental stimuli' in terms of customer preferences, competitive behaviours, government demands, and sources of technological innovation and learning.[39] Their view contrasts sharply with Ghemawat's in Chapter 4. Ghemawat cautioned against rapid international diversification, since MNEs with a broad geographic scope face various distance barriers as compared to domestic firms and MNEs with a narrower geographic scope. Ghemawat emphasized that the MNE's strengths in recombination should not be overestimated. Bartlett and Ghoshal, however, contend that an MNE can improve its FSA bundles by tapping into – and leveraging – the competencies found in its subsidiary network. In other words, an international presence and international experience through foreign subsidiaries may strengthen the MNE's recombination capability, if MNE senior management makes proper use of its internal network.

Strategic Challenges in the New Economy

Organizational structure represents the governance hardware deployed by MNEs to transfer their FSAs abroad and to reduce bounded rationality and bounded reliability challenges when trying to access resources in host environments and engaging in various forms of novel resource combinations. This hardware (such as a multidivisional structure with formal monitoring and a specific reward system for employees) can be interpreted as a higher-order, non-location-bound FSA. But this hardware is not deployed in isolation from other MNE resources, especially its key FSAs in technology, marketing, relationships, etc. As the MNE internationalizes into more geographically remote and unfamiliar foreign environments, the challenges associated with this type of resource deployment increase, as explained in Chapter 4.

Importantly, as explained by **Erin Meyer** in her *HBR* paper on organizational culture, namely, what can be considered a firm's governance software, MNEs typically hire at least some foreign executives and other employees to work in their subsidiaries, and these individuals join the company with their own preconceived values and norms guiding their behaviour.[40] The challenge is that these individuals' values and behavioural norms may be very different from those prevailing in the MNE's home country and at the head office. Their views on what constitutes appropriate communication, decision making, and purposive action may differ strongly from the prevailing views in the MNE's head office. A shared organizational culture matters, but the author argues that a 'cultural disintegration' may occur as the MNE expands its geographic scope, thereby sharply increasing challenges of bounded rationality and unreliability (especially in the realm of divided engagement as an expression of identity-based discordance).[41] This situation materializes if the MNE's organizational culture, which may have been built up over decades, is at odds with the cultural values in host country operations, thereby potentially triggering massive cultural conflicts inside the MNE.

In order to prevent cultural disintegration, MNEs often try to impose routines that encourage employees to 'recap' and 'repeat' key messages in both their oral and written communication, so as to prevent miscues. However, relying mainly on formal routines can make MNEs bureaucratic and slow in internal communication, and it neglects the unspoken cues and non-formalized language in the workplace as the following example illustrates: 'For example, at Louis Vuitton . . . a lot of work is done in this implicit way without anyone's taking note . . . The more we wipe out ambiguity between what was meant and what was heard, the further we wander from that essential mysterious ingredient in our corporate culture that has led to our success.'[42]

The focus on formal routines to guide communication among individuals dispersed across distant locations, can be at the expense of informal knowledge transfers. Employees in overseas operations may then create their own 'overseas cocoons', isolated from their head office colleagues, and impeding conversations between operations in different locations.[43] Ultimately, MNEs must find ways to anticipate and mitigate conflicts between the dominant corporate culture and various local cultures inside the firm. Meyer proposes five governance tools to reduce the incidence and impact of internal cultural conflict inside the multinational organization. This is important especially in the new social and economic era when employees may be strongly influenced by social media or state-run media, or by highly biased heritage media in their own country, and when these media systematically convey nationalistic or xenophobic messages about foreign-owned or foreign-controlled MNEs, or simply advocate in favour of different types of 'justice' (e.g., economic justice, gender justice, racial justice, environmental justice, etc.) and exhibiting pride in local cultural values and norms.

First, MNE senior management should try to identify the *underlying dimensions* of organizational culture that may trigger intra-firm conflicts.[44] These dimensions could be related to elements such as decision-making style (e.g., directive versus consensus-seeking leadership, focus on meeting deadlines versus allowing flexibility, etc.). This identification process should be the basis of fine-tuning the firm's routines, whereby varying approaches can be allowed for particular dimensions, subject to the condition that such variety will not, in the big picture, negatively affect organizational performance.

Second, each cultural group in the multinational organization should be given the *opportunity to be heard* in meetings and multi-level interactions, for example, by being invited systematically to participate in conference calls and conversations, and to provide input and feedback during group conversations.[45]

Third, irrespective of their idiosyncratic culture and whether this culture is aligned or conflicts with the head office culture, the MNE's *most creative units should be protected*.[46] As MNEs expand internationally, senior management needs to make a distinction between key units that build upon creativity, openness, and flexibility, and implementer units whose efficiency hinges on formalization, routines, and timeliness (e.g., manufacturing operations in emerging economies that produce according to pre-set specifications). In other words, there is always a trade-off between the benefits of imposing standardized approaches and the benefits of giving innovative units in organizations the flexibility they need.

Fourth, all units in the organization need to *conform to a baseline of values and norms* that constitute the MNE's organizational culture and identity, meaning that all employees and executives should be trained to accept this baseline as a precondition to be able to work from a common work platform.[47]

Fifth, assuming the presence of the above, baseline platform, MNEs can likely *build bridges of cultural understanding* by promoting diversity, for example, in terms of the age, gender, citizenship, and racial distribution of their workforce, so as to fight dysfunctional conformity to stereotypes.

Using the lens of organizational culture, Meyer compellingly explains how large MNEs can avoid making the mistakes of excessive homogenization and centralization, as described by Bartlett and Ghoshal. A balance must be struck between the costs of cultural disintegration and the benefits from embracing local cultural norms and practices to strengthen the MNE, *inter alia* because of the easier, novel resource combinations that would ensue. Respecting and nurturing local voices are especially important in creative units inside the MNE, typically strategic leader and contributor units. But all units need to build upon a common platform of routines that articulate the MNE's organizational culture, as a minimum baseline for effective organizational functioning. The challenge is thus to find the right mix between foreign subsidiaries adhering to this requisite baseline and allowing them to express their cultural specificities, especially in the realm of informal organizational functioning in the MNE. Such a mix will go a long way towards anticipating and mitigating instances of divided engagement and regression, namely, bounded reliability.

Nirmalya Kumar and **Phanish Puranam**, in their *HBR* article, attempt to provide some guidance on how firms from developed economies should adjust their organizational structure when entering large, emerging economies such as China and India.[48]

Many MNEs have long been working with 'back end – front end' structures.[49] Here, the choice is made to keep highly competent, back-end employees and activities such as R&D, centralized in the home country and other prime locations. At the same time, front-end activities requiring close proximity to customers are geographically dispersed and decentralized with the related cross-border transfer of competent employees and downstream FSAs, for example, in the realm of marketing and distribution.

The authors point to several mistakes that some developed economy MNEs make in terms of organization. *First*, they point to a 'passion gap', suggesting some bounded reliability from developed country expatriates, who often lack a strong commitment to develop emerging markets.[50] In other words, they are not the ideal individuals to meld extant non-location-bound knowledge with requisite location-bound knowledge that must be accessed externally or developed internally. *Second*, the authors identify an 'ambition gap', meaning that the expatriate intrapreneurs managing the subsidiaries are sometimes unlikely to pursue aggressive annual growth targets (e.g., 25 per cent), in contrast to such high growth rates being viewed as normal by local entrepreneurs in emerging economies.[51] This ambition gap could again be viewed as an expression of bounded reliability, with insufficient motivation to achieve superior growth performance from the expatriate subsidiary managers. *Third*, the authors describe a 'value-proposition gap', whereby Western MNEs appear unable to develop the unique business models required by local conditions, especially at the downstream end: bounded rationality problems prevent them from recognizing the needed resource combinations to be successful in the local market.[52] *Fourth*, and related to the previous point, there is often a 'product line gap' at the downstream end: standardization benefits are typically preferred as an initial strategy over the requisite level of local responsiveness, again largely as an interplay between bounded rationality and bounded reliability challenges.[53]

In order to address the above challenges, and building upon the 'back end – front end' distinction, the authors see two opposite pressures on MNEs.[54] At the downstream, customer side, MNEs need to address the pressures for achieving national responsiveness by localizing their front-end operations. In contrast, at the upstream end, involving R&D and production, MNEs must address the pressures for achieving economic integration, and locate R&D, manufacturing, and other scale-dependent activities in those places where they can be conducted most effectively and efficiently. What we see here is largely the MNE archetype of international coordinators (see Chapter 1) coming to life. The authors suggest the generic solution of a 'T'-shaped organizational structure.[55] Here, the horizontal '—' component describes the importance of back-end, scale-efficient operations that must subsequently be integrated across the MNE through intra-MNE linkages with other centres of excellence. In contrast, the vertical '|' component represents the depth of MNE operations in each country, illustrating the importance of decentralized strategic actions and localized resource deployment and recombination.

With some of the horizontal activities in the T-shaped structures moving to centres of excellence in emerging economies, it means that a number of head-office functions may need to be moved there too. Local managers should be recruited for these functions in emerging economies such as China and India, as they will likely be more effective in melding non-location-bound and location-bound FSAs, and in accessing host country-specific advantages where useful. At the same time, the vertical legs in the T-shaped organization should allow radical business model rethinking to cater to local needs and preferences.

The proposed T-shaped organizational structure goes beyond Bartlett and Ghoshal's classification of MNE operations in four categories of subsidiaries. The analysis suggests that the notion of strategic leader subsidiary may be more complex than originally envisioned. Great depth and strength in the vertical component of the T-shaped structure may reflect 'strategic leader' status of some subsidiaries at the *front end* of the value chain. But great strength on the horizontal dimension may simultaneously reflect strategic leadership benefiting the MNE at the *back end*, instrumental to future-generation, non-location-bound knowledge creation. At this *back end*, both the head office and potentially all subsidiaries could be the beneficiaries of creating and sharing new core knowledge, as is typically the case with, for example, digital platforms.

International Business Strategy During Globally Disruptive Events

The COVID-19 pandemic uncovered hidden risks for MNE foreign subsidiaries that conducted value chain activities built on the assumption of a stable international environment. As noted by Beata Javorcik, Chief Economist at the European Bank for Reconstruction and Development, a singular focus on cost reductions 'left many companies without a plan B. Businesses will be forced to rethink their global value chains . . . the disadvantages of a system that requires all of its elements to work like clockwork have now been exposed'.[56] At a lower level than that of global value chains, even the foundations of regional integration were affected. Wojciech Bedyński from the University of Warsaw in Poland observed the fragility of the 'four pillars or "freedoms" of the European Union: mobility of goods, services, capital and labor'. These four pillars were literally discarded a few days after the pandemic started, for example, when national governments blocked all foreigners from entering their respective countries via intra-European flights.[57]

On a global scale, *The Economist* warned that '[t]he new coronavirus could have a lasting impact on global supply chains'.[58] The pandemic-induced disruptions of supply and demand in many markets significantly increased bounded rationality and bounded reliability challenges facing MNEs and their foreign subsidiaries. Fourné's *et al.* insights are instructive here as to the appropriate responses. Their analysis suggests that MNE managers should focus on modularizing further their foreign subsidiary activities to prepare for future global disruptions. MNE managers should also create geo-redundancies across their modularized activities and rethink subsidiary roles.

First, MNE managers need to identify and isolate narrow activity sets performed by foreign subsidiaries (as well as external network partners), and 'micro-modularize' their value chains.[59] This should result in geo-redundancy, namely, having options for the rapid and easy substitution of micro-modules when external shocks occur, and for mitigating the disruptions that any individual module could have on the MNE's overall network.[60]

Second, by modularizing foreign subsidiary activities, MNEs develop a greater strategic agility to respond to exogenous shocks in foreign locations.[61] Strategic agility can help MNEs balance the evolving tensions between head office priorities and local priorities during and after a global disruption. On the one hand, it becomes easier for subsidiary operations to adapt to the demand and supply conditions of local contexts. On the other hand, the head office is able to make swift decisions and restructure its value chains by reconfiguring the portfolio of modules at its disposal.[62] Managing modules in an agile fashion does not necessarily mean eliminating from value chains particular subsidiaries located in countries that are hard-hit by a global disruption. It may simply mean that different value chain modules are allowed to work under different business models, and that these models can themselves be altered by foreign subsidiaries in crisis situations.

Third, by focusing on the modularizing of value chain activities and on strategic agility, MNEs may want to redefine the unique roles of their foreign subsidiaries. Here, Bartlett and Ghoshal's insights may still be instructive. Their classification of MNE subsidiaries was based on the strength of the host country location advantages that the subsidiary can access and on the unique FSA bundles it commands inside the MNE. These two elements can now be augmented with a third parameter: the extent to which the subsidiary's activities can be modularized for flexible – and if needed independent – functioning, or in other words, the extent to which 'severability' can be applied. Can the subsidiary quickly and effectively start functioning differently and more independently in instances where the international value chains of which they are part break down? Subsidiaries that earn high scores on the severability criterion could be called 'super' strategic leaders, 'super' contributors, and 'super' implementers respectively. Higher severability can be fostered if the MNE is more diversified, more tolerant towards local subsidiary entrepreneurship, and more competent in its functioning with multiple business models, some of these led by subsidiaries.

MNEs with higher degrees of modularizing, more strategic agility, and more severability in subsidiary operations will typically be able to reallocate resources more swiftly and effectively across their foreign subsidiary network in response to major shocks in their environment. For example, the US-based water technology giant Xylem Inc. was able to redirect resources rapidly as a response to the pandemic-induced drop in demand for pumps and other equipment when 'industrial and commercial customers as mining and construction projects shut down'.[63] Instead, Xylem prioritized investments in software for 'utility customers that provide drinking water and wastewater services [and] wanted to operate their systems remotely'.[64]

As a final note, global disruptions highlight the futility of some MNE goals pursued through the international growth of their portfolios of foreign subsidiaries and external partnerships. Such goals include market share leadership and global dominance at the expense of crafting agile, carefully modularized networks that can largely insulate the firm from macro-level shocks.

Five Management Takeaways

1. Assess the current organizational structure and decision-making processes in your firm and reflect on the different roles performed by your subsidiaries.
2. Classify your portfolio of subsidiaries as a function of the strategic importance of each market where they operate and the resource base they command.
3. Respect the five components of due process in each corporate head office decision that will affect subsidiaries.
4. Review current tensions between head office priorities and local priorities in your firm and reflect on how to address mismatches, so as to avoid cultural disintegration.
5. Analyze best practices (inside your firm and in industry) for FSA development in subsidiaries and reflect on the key drivers of subsidiary roles and dynamics.

PART II

FUNCTIONAL ISSUES

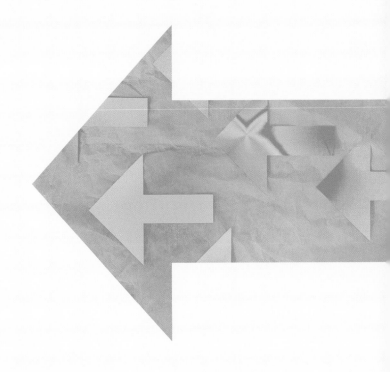

6

International Innovation

Five Learning Objectives

1. To explain the reasons for the trend towards R&D decentralization and to describe the difference between 'home-base-exploiting' and 'home-base-augmenting' innovation sites inside the MNE.
2. To highlight the key stages in the development of foreign R&D units.
3. To explain the role of subsidiary initiatives in the innovation sphere and the functioning of the 'corporate immune system', geared towards destroying such initiatives.
4. To foster understanding on how clusters of innovation (COIs) contribute to MNEs' new upstream FSA development, and function as cross-border ecosystems.
5. To examine the potential conflicts between host country research sites and the corporate office.

This chapter examines Kuemmerle's idea that many MNEs, particularly international projectors, are wisely decentralizing their R&D by building worldwide networks of R&D labs. He examines R&D labs in host countries, dividing them into two types: (1) home-base-exploiting sites, which primarily receive information from the central lab in the home country and adapt products to local demand; and (2) home-base-augmenting sites, which primarily access local knowledge and send valuable information back to the central lab. Kuemmerle gives practical advice about how those two different roles imply different needs and requirements, including different location and management requirements. Kuemmerle strongly recommends that both types of labs should interact regularly with the firm's other R&D units. These ideas will be examined and then critiqued using the framework presented in Chapter 1.

Significance

In his *HBR* article, 'Building effective R&D capabilities abroad', **Walter Kuemmerle** shows that many MNEs are changing their strategic approach to R&D. In particular, **international projectors** are decentralizing their R&D: instead of keeping all their R&D activities in their home country, they are building international networks in which foreign R&D laboratories fulfil specific roles within the firm.[1]

There are two main reasons for this trend. First, many MNEs feel they need to be present in various knowledge and innovation clusters scattered around the world. Often, a host country presence is essential in order to monitor and absorb new developments – typically, complementary resources from foreign input providers such as competitors, host country universities, and scientific communities. Second, given the commercial requirement of moving quickly from innovation to market, MNEs must integrate their R&D facilities more closely with host country manufacturing operations, so as to support complex production tasks. This often involves complementing existing, internationally transferable FSAs in the upstream, technological knowledge sphere with a set of location-bound FSAs in host countries.

Kuemmerle studied thirty-two MNEs in the pharmaceutical (thirteen) and electronics (nineteen) industries – two manufacturing sectors with substantial product innovation and a high technological R&D intensity. The MNEs' home countries/regions were the United States (ten), Japan (twelve), and Europe (ten). The location of these firms' R&D labs initially reflected a triad-based, home-region approach, with most of the fundamental innovation activity conducted in the home country. Kuemmerle analyzed the development trajectories of these companies' international R&D networks, eventually involving 238 labs with nearly two-thirds (156) located in host countries.[2]

Kuemmerle observed the internationalization of the R&D function over time. Building on the 'home base' concept developed by Michael Porter,[3] discussed in Chapter 3 of this book, Kuemmerle identified two distinct types of host country R&D facilities based on their primary strategic role inside the MNE: home-base-exploiting sites and home-base-augmenting sites.

Home-base-exploiting sites 'support manufacturing facilities in foreign countries or . . . adapt standard products to the demand there'. '[I]nformation flows *to* the foreign laboratory *from* the central lab at home'.[4] In contrast, home-base-augmenting sites act as the firm's eyes and ears in host countries, and access knowledge from rivals and research institutions there. With these labs, information generally flows '*from* the foreign laboratory *to* the central lab at home'.[5]

Building on the above, Kuemmerle outlined three key stages in the development of foreign R&D units: first, the selection of decision makers; second, the set of decisions and actions that strengthen the facility's initial capabilities; and third, the decisions and actions designed to maximize the lab's contributions to the MNE's overall corporate strategic goals.

First, the MNE selects the decision makers. Most MNEs set up a technology steering committee, usually consisting of five to eight members, with extensive technical and organizational expertise, and representing a broad variety of educational backgrounds. The technology steering committee typically reports directly to the CEO. This approach reduces the bounded rationality problems faced by the MNE, by reducing the uncertainty involved in assessing alternative, high-distance locations.

Second, when trying to strengthen the lab's initial capabilities, senior management should bear in mind that home-base-exploiting and home-base-augmenting lab types have different needs and require different skills. *Home-base-exploiting labs* should be located close to key markets and the MNE's own foreign manufacturing units so that the firm's technological innovations can be rapidly adapted to host country requirements if needed and absorbed by host country manufacturing operations. This is an example of how adapting to key markets sometimes requires building new, location-bound FSAs in host countries (in this case, produced by the home-base-exploiting lab) to link the MNE's internationally transferable FSAs more effectively with the location advantages of the host country's output markets. The initial leadership of such labs should be placed in the hands of 'highly regarded managers from within the company – managers who are intimately familiar with the company's culture and systems . . . to forge close ties between the new lab's engineers and the foreign community's manufacturing and marketing facilities'.[6] One of the key bounded rationality problems facing the MNE is to reduce the 'distance' (see Chapter 4) between home country R&D operations and host country manufacturing operations; a home-base-exploiting R&D operation – particularly if led by managers selected from within the company – will reduce this distance.

In contrast, *home-base-augmenting labs* should be located in critical knowledge clusters relevant to the MNE's businesses, where they will be well positioned to tap into new sources of innovations. The initial senior managers selected to guide this type of lab through the capability-strengthening stage 'should be prominent local scientists . . . to nurture ties between the new site and the local scientific community'.[7] Here, the MNE's main problem is that it cannot access knowledge resources available in foreign locations without becoming an insider there.

Third, to maximize the lab's contributions to the MNE's strategic goals, each lab, especially the home-base-exploiting ones, should interact regularly with the other R&D units, as well as with the firm's manufacturing and marketing operations. The home-base-augmenting labs should, in addition, remain focused on strengthening their insider status in their host country scientific communities.

As regards the internal knowledge sharing required from all labs so as to maximize their impact on the firm as a whole, senior managers must ensure, in this third stage, that contributions complement the MNE's existing FSA base, including applications relevant to manufacturing operations. This goal cannot be achieved if the labs work as islands, isolated from the rest of the company. For effective knowledge recombination to occur, each lab must become integrated as quickly and seamlessly as possible with the other parts of the MNE. This entails substantial interaction, both with home country R&D managers in the central lab(s) and directly with other units in the company research network. In this context, Kuemmerle offers the following description of the ideal profile of R&D unit leaders, who will be instrumental to the necessary knowledge recombination:

> The best candidates for both home-base-augmenting and home-base-exploiting sites share four qualities: they are at once respected scientists or engineers and skilled managers; they are able to integrate the new site into the company's existing R&D network; they have a comprehensive understanding of technology trends; and they are able to overcome formal barriers when they seek access to new ideas in local universities and scientific communities.[8]

In short, senior R&D lab managers must be able to marshal the resources necessary for the lab to be successful in meeting its objectives, including new FSA development. The managers do this by connecting the lab with other resources inside the firm and, especially in the case of home-base-augmenting labs, effectively tapping the external environment in host markets for new knowledge.

Throughout his article, Kuemmerle describes real-world examples to illustrate his insights. In the case of US-based document services company Xerox, senior management decided to establish a home-base-augmenting site in continental Europe as it believed that the unique opportunities for new research and knowledge extraction in that area warranted a second lab to complement an existing one in the United Kingdom. Given the lab's proposed knowledge-augmenting role, the company decided to locate the lab in Grenoble, France, viewed as an established centre of scientific excellence. Xerox hired a renowned French scientist to head up the unit and integrate it within the local scientific community. This manager was instrumental in recombining the firm's existing FSAs with complementary resources in the French environment. Xerox also had new staff visit other company R&D centres in order to expedite the lab's integration into the firm's internal R&D network. This facilitated the transfer of non-location-bound FSAs across borders.

In another example, the US-based pharmaceutical firm Eli Lilly set out to increase sales in Asia by more effectively exploiting its research capabilities and adapting its portfolio of pharmaceutical products to meet needs in that region. The company decided to open a home-base-exploiting lab in the region and selected Kobe, Japan, for its proximity to existing MNE operations, as well as key markets in Japan and Southeast Asia. To integrate the new lab as quickly as possible with the rest of the company, a senior research manager with extensive knowledge of both production and marketing activities was selected to lead the new unit. In addition, the firm implemented a staff transfer programme in which veteran R&D scientists were assigned to the new location, and new staff visited other labs to enhance the exchange of information. This approach to transferring the MNE's non-location-bound FSAs from the home base using a location-bound FSA was successful as the lab quickly passed through the capability-strengthening stage and began effectively commercializing R&D capabilities for the Asian market in a relatively short time period.

As a third example, Japan-based electronics giant Matsushita has set up an effective, international R&D knowledge network consisting of both home-base-exploiting and home-base-augmenting labs. Units can communicate directly with one another, formally and informally, rather than using a central R&D office as an intermediary. This process of direct communication increases the level of knowledge transfer and resource recombination within the company. Furthermore, R&D managers meet on a regular basis to discuss their current scope of technological capabilities and also participate in planning sessions with manufacturing and marketing managers to develop a more accurate sense of the types of R&D innovations that could be valuable in the future. Here, the focus is on the international transfer of non-location-bound FSAs in multiple directions.

These three examples illustrate Kuemmerle's view that MNEs have been increasingly adopting an interlinked network of host country facilities to improve their R&D efforts, rather than relying on a centralized approach with all core R&D performed in the firm's home market. In addition, the labs can play different roles, depending on whether their primary purpose is to exploit knowledge or augment knowledge.

Context and Complementary Perspectives

When Kuemmerle published 'Building effective R&D capabilities abroad' in 1997, the prior decade had witnessed a proliferation of innovations in communications technology that changed how R&D could be performed. The emergence of the Internet and the adoption of email, wireless communications, electronic data transmission protocols, and robust database management systems all significantly affected the R&D process, allowing researchers to communicate remotely and near-seamlessly across borders in new ways that removed previously existing barriers.[9] As a result, companies no longer had to rely on physical proximity within a centralized location in order to obtain the efficient communication necessary for effective R&D.

However, at the same time that advances in communications technology made physical proximity less important, new knowledge clusters sprung up around the world, and physical proximity to these clusters remained as important as ever (see Chapter 1). The benefits of spatial clustering in cases of abundant localized markets for specialized resources (e.g., specialized labour, local government support), as well as localized knowledge spillovers, caused MNEs to place knowledge-generating activities inside these foreign clusters in order to access these resources.

This combination of international transferability of FSAs and international accessibility of some resources with the need to have value-added operations physically embedded in specific locations to reap the full benefits of clusters is the 'sticky places in slippery space' paradox.[10] This phenomenon can also be interpreted as an expression of the double diamond model described in Chapter 3: site location matters, but the location advantages of several countries/regions may need to be combined to gain competitive advantage on an international scale. This points to the key strengths of the ***international coordinator*** archetype: coordination skills allowing the continuous recombination of internationally dispersed resources.

Overall, this change in thinking on how R&D should be approached mirrored a change in international business strategy in general, in particular the evolution of conventional ***international projectors***. These MNEs realized that their value-generating activities, including R&D, should include tapping into host country input markets as new suppliers of valuable resources. They also understood the need for more adaptation in order to meet host market demand requirements.

Julian Birkinshaw and ***Nick Fry*** provide a first piece complementing Kuemmerle's analysis.[11] Their 1998 *SMR* article on subsidiary initiatives in MNEs focuses primarily on the drivers of new development activities in large, established MNEs, and it addresses one of the critical limitations in Kuemmerle's study, namely that Kuemmerle overlooks subsidiary role dynamics. The reality of international innovation, especially in large MNEs with large portfolios of foreign subsidiaries, is that corporate headquarters in the home country does not simply choose locations and assign roles to foreign sites in terms of R&D charters. In many cases, entrepreneurial managers in MNEs assume extended roles inconsistent with their unit's formal charter (which might specify whether the unit is to be home-base-augmenting, or merely home-base-exploiting).

Entrepreneurial subsidiary managers, especially in a well-established foreign affiliate, will often pursue a subsidiary initiative, defined as: 'the proactive and deliberate pursuit of a new business opportunity by a subsidiary company, undertaken with a view to expand the subsidiary's scope of responsibility, in a manner consistent with the MNC's strategic goals'.[12]

Birkinshaw and Fry make a key distinction between 'internal' and 'external' subsidiary initiatives. In the context of R&D, ***internal*** subsidiary initiatives reflect attempts by subsidiary managers to become the chosen location for new corporate R&D investments. Here, it is not simply the corporate steering committee that selects an 'optimal' location. Rather, subsidiary managers attempt to influence this decision through a process of internal competition. Subsidiary managers use their wide-ranging arsenal of formal and informal linkages with headquarters, including personal contacts, to sell their unit as the best place for the firm to invest. Subsidiary managers may thereby reduce significantly the bounded rationality problems faced by senior management in the home country, as those senior managers will be thoroughly updated about the foreign units' innovation potential and broader capabilities.

In contrast, **external** subsidiary initiatives result from foreign subsidiary managers identifying an opportunity in their business environment. Often, this results from interactions with customers, suppliers, or competitors. To the extent that subsidiaries benefit from high autonomy, some slack resources, and discretion in resource allocation, they may fund pilot projects themselves, sheltered from corporate headquarters. After some initial positive results have been achieved – for example, in the form of customer buy-in or a successful technical prototype – they may go to corporate headquarters with a strong case for funding and for formal acknowledgement of the de facto upgrading of their original corporate charter.

Both internal and external initiatives reflect attempts to earn home-base-augmenting innovation charters. Such attempts will likely become even more important in the future given the rise of internal benchmarking in many MNEs, whereby corporate headquarters allocates resources based on the subsidiary initiatives' potential to contribute to internal network optimization or to external market expansion. Chapter 5 discussed several best practices that corporate headquarters can use to increase the likelihood that subsidiary initiatives fulfil their potential (i.e., giving seed money to new initiatives, formally requesting proposals, using subsidiaries as incubators, and creating internal subsidiary networks).

The corporate immune system is a key problem facing entrepreneurial subsidiary managers interested in pursuing creative resource recombinations. This resistance to subsidiary initiatives is largely due to bounded rationality problems facing senior managers at corporate headquarters. Here, the lack of proper understanding of subsidiary initiatives by headquarters leads to false attributions of empire building or opportunistic sub-goal pursuit by subsidiaries. In addition, individuals at corporate headquarters and other MNE units may actually engage in opportunistic behaviour themselves: because every subsidiary initiative ultimately reflects a reallocation of resources away from present priorities, perverse incentives may exist, even for senior managers, to kill valuable initiatives.[13] The corporate immune system, designed to protect merely the MNE's dominant logic (so as to avoid, for example, excessive diversification), becomes instead an instrument of powerful stakeholders inside the firm, who do not want to see their existing charter and responsibilities challenged by foreign subsidiaries, especially if those subsidiaries are located in peripheral countries and lack an established reputation for work similar to the new initiative. In such cases, the major bounded reliability problem inside the MNE is not subsidiary empire building whereby subsidiary managers pursue their own goals at the expense of overall MNE goals. Rather, the major bounded reliability problem is that individuals and groups outside of the subsidiary and driven by their own interests falsely portray the initiative as detrimental to overall MNE goals. The great challenge for the MNE is then to create an environment empowering subsidiaries to go forward with innovative and valuable initiatives while maintaining an appropriate level of initiative scrutiny to economize on bounded reliability problems, including empire-building attempts by subsidiaries and more benevolent forms of 'scarcity of effort to make good on open-ended promises'.[14]

Jerome S. Engel provides a second complementary perspective to Kuemmerle's analysis.[15] Engel's *CMR* paper focuses on clusters of innovation (COIs), and more specifically on the functioning of these clusters as ecosystems. His emphasis is not on the single MNE, but on how COIs operate on the basis of evolving connections among their constituent parts, somewhat similar to the analysis by Furr and Shipilov in their *SMR* paper, which we will discuss later in this chapter under 'Strategic challenges in the new economy'.[16] As noted, Engel's main focus is not on the lead firm as the driver of an ecosystem of innovations, but rather on what actually happens in the locations where innovations abound, in other words the unfolding resource recombination processes. This insight is important for MNEs, especially when they establish foreign home-base augmenting labs.

Engel views a COI as having two main key characteristics that set it apart from other clusters. First, it is an entrepreneurial ecosystem of multiple actors, who are engaging themselves with rapidly developing new technologies. Such engagement can lead to new business models, new firms, and even new industries, whereby requisite inputs such as financial resources, talent, and tacit knowledge are increasingly mobile across firms. Second, the COI concept also takes into account the cross-sectoral movement of these mobile resources across industries; this fluidity explains the rise of software, biotechnology, and social media start-ups in the semiconductor cluster of Silicon Valley, much in line with Shih and Chai's (2015) analysis of clusters, discussed in Chapter 3.

According to Engel, the following elements were drivers of COI development in Silicon Valley:

1. *Universities* conducting an open-innovation type of collaboration with private firms, for example, Stanford Research Park that set up partnerships with well-known American manufacturing firms such as GE, IBM, Eastman Kodak, Lockheed, Varian, and HP.[17]

2. *Government policies, inter alia* in the realm of fostering innovation-related, intellectual property rights, such as the 'Bayh-Dole Act that allowed universities' ownership of their innovation and patents'.[18]

3. *Entrepreneurs* with easy access to abundant external financing, which helps explain the rise of technology-based firms in the region, such as Apple, Google, and Facebook.[19]

4. *Venture capitalists* who encourage a virtuous cycle of start-up creation, rapid scale-up, and early buyouts.

5. *Mature corporations* that understand the benefits of collaboration with start-up firms in the realm of innovation.

6. *A diverse set of research centres*, including public research labs funded by government agencies, corporate R&D centres, and R&D spin-offs from universities.

7. *An abundance of professional management and specialized services providers*, offering expertise to firms in such diverse areas as customized R&D, accounting, finance, human resources management, legal services, marketing, product design, and development.

The above elements could be viewed as the bundle of infrastructural location advantages underlying the ecosystem of innovation in Silicon Valley. Building on these driving forces, the following five key behaviours then describe the actual functioning inside the Silicon Valley ecosystem:

1. **Mobility of resources**:[20] New ventures go through a virtuous cycle of creative founding, rapid growth, and successful exit. As such, venture financing, employees, and knowledge/technology also become highly mobile and fluid along the dynamic cycle. For example, venture capitalists take part in staged financing with limited lifetimes of funds; many employees change jobs every three to five years and move their knowledge and experience with them; etc.

2. **Entrepreneurial orientation**:[21] Under flexible and team-based leadership, entrepreneurial firms keep exploring opportunities for innovation, focus on the rapid commercialization of new innovations, and engage in continuous experimentation with new business models.

3. **Cross-border strategic perspective**:[22] Start-ups are eager to gain access to new markets for inputs and outputs that can support innovative activities, irrespective of where in the world these markets are located.

4. **Alignment of interests and incentives**:[23] In order to encourage significant early success of start-ups, and the profitable and easy exit out of them, venture capitalists provide incentive structures geared towards aligning the interests of diverse stakeholders towards big wins.

5. **Cross-border ties:**[24] International linkages evolve from 'weak ties' to more 'durable bonds' and even 'covalent bonds' (referring to distant locations structurally sharing common resources) via the role of immigrant entrepreneurs, making it possible for geographically distant COIs to exhibit features of a single, integrated cluster.[25] One example is the Silicon Valley (United States)–Israel high-tech cluster, with immigrant entrepreneurs performing the role of diamond connectors in the innovation space, as also discussed more broadly in Chapter 3.

An important question is whether the insight into the functioning of the Silicon Valley COI leads to any generalizable conclusions as to the success factors to make such an ecosystem of innovation work in other locations. On the business side, there is a strong consensus that entrepreneurial firms are at the heart of any innovation cluster. On the broader level, a strong institutional foundation, including a transparent legal system to protect contractual and intellectual rights, well-developed infrastructure, and social stability, appears to play a critical role, too. But local context does matter. For example, some Chinese innovation clusters appear to be much more governed by public policy targets than is the case in many market-driven economies.[26]

A COI should be built on the existing reservoir of local resources and capabilities in a region, especially in terms of its pool of entrepreneurs and (cross-) sectoral specialization.[27] Any government's attempts to stimulate COI development that neglects these two elements is bound to fail, except in a command-and-control economy. Even though the whole point of a COI may be to develop new industries, effective resource recombination does require a threshold level of similarity and melding potential among resources. It is therefore important to observe which entrepreneurial initiatives to innovate are present or can reasonably be fostered at the bottom, rather than to deploy a heavy-handed government approach from the top.[28] Government agencies in market-driven economies can typically perform a facilitating and coordinating role, and should also monitor unintended consequences of COI development[29] (e.g., new demand for talent and the mobility of talent can have labour market implications for incumbent firms).

Engel studied a number of COIs and it would appear that a few other sets of actors than the entrepreneurs themselves and government can play an important role.

First, educational research institutions can perform a number of roles in building a COI, for example through commercializing scientific knowledge and creating spin-off firms; signalling via teaching and research that entrepreneurship is a valuable career path to pursue; encouraging creative and entrepreneurial experiments with acceptance of business failure; and disseminating best entrepreneurial practices to the local community.[30]

Second, interpersonal networks can be a driving force in ecosystem development, such as cross-industry horizontal networks with peers in Silicon Valley, the networks of Quanxi in China, and army-service based teams of tech-trained talents in Israel.[31]

Third, actors involved in international trade can connect value-added activities occurring in distant clusters[32] (e.g., US-based MNEs manufacturing in Taiwan, as a complement to product development and marketing in Silicon Valley).

Fourth, large MNEs can provide collaboration opportunities to start-ups, leading to business model innovation, access to a variety of services, and the scaling-up and commercialization of R&D.[33]

Fifth, even for innovative firms located in the heart of a COI and benefiting from the rich resources and connections inside the cluster, international connections with distant innovation partners through 'covalent bonds' can be important to success.[34] These cross-border collaborations may involve both MNEs and new ventures.

Engel's analysis in *CMR* complements Kuemmerle's exposé on MNEs pursuing the spatial distribution of R&D inside their own network. Three additional insights appear to be critical here. *First*, in the context of COIs, MNEs can perform the role of flagship firms, which take on the strategic leadership of a business network involving a variety of ecosystem partners: key (entrepreneurial) suppliers, key customers, selected competitors, and the non-business infrastructure such as universities and research institutions. *Second*, Engel's focus on the importance of deep international ties for successful COI development is fully consistent with the double diamond framework described in Chapter 3, but in this instance with a focus on innovation. *Third*, the possible role of government highlighted in this article needs to be evaluated carefully in terms of 'symmetrical' versus 'asymmetrical' clusters. An asymmetrical cluster is built around one large (and typically internationally operating) company that acts as the main orchestrator in the cluster.[35] The role of government can be limited and may even be unnecessary for cluster development in such an asymmetrical COI, because the large orchestrator and its network partners organically complement each other.[36] In contrast, if the COI is a symmetrical cluster, consisting mainly of smaller companies of similar size and scope, a larger coordinating role of government may be warranted to reduce bounded rationality problems. Government can support building the symmetrical COI by, for instance, bringing together economic actors, facilitating requisite training, coordinating export development, etc., and showing the symmetric cluster participants that there is more to the cluster than fierce internal rivalry.[37] Through such support, government can contribute to reducing bounded rationality challenges facing cluster participants, and to developing patterns of reliable behaviour and related reputational FSAs (e.g., by having a variety of participants working jointly on successful export promotion) that may in turn foster deeper forms of cooperation.

Kuemmerle's work usefully describes the changes characterizing two of the key parameters set out in the conceptual framework in Chapter 1, namely location advantages and internationally transferable FSAs. The old model, according to Kuemmerle, is that of the ***international projector***, with unidirectional flows of knowledge from the home country to host countries, building on the location advantages of the home country. In Kuemmerle's new model, the old approach is complemented by knowledge transfer the other way: home-base-augmenting sites in the host countries also create internationally transferable FSAs, building on the (input side) location advantages of their host countries. As Kuemmerle puts it, 'companies must establish a presence at an increasing number of locations to access new knowledge and to absorb new research results from foreign universities and competitors into their own organization'.[38] The underlying assumption is that some knowledge bundles are embedded in specific locations and can only be accessed through being physically present in these locations. However, when such knowledge is combined with the MNE's extant resources, firm-level learning and new FSA development may occur, with these new FSAs being fully transferable to a central lab in the home country or to other affiliates.

Even Kuemmerle's home-base-exploiting sites are more than just recipients of parent company knowledge. These sites act as the vehicle through which companies transfer FSAs to foreign markets, but they must develop new (location-bound) FSAs in order to adapt the firm's goods and services to host country customers. Here, it is important to differentiate between stand-alone technical knowledge, which may be easy to transfer between R&D centres, and the related routines and recombination capabilities developed by the various centres, which may be more difficult to diffuse. Figure 6.1 displays the old and new approaches to R&D operations in MNEs.

The traditional approach of R&D activities centralized in the home base reflects Pattern I in this book's capability development model, whereby internationally transferable FSAs are developed in the home country and subsequently diffused internationally with the purpose of straightforward exploitation by subsidiaries in host markets.

The two types of labs Kuemmerle identifies reflect the growing trend towards additional, distinct patterns of FSA development. Home-base-augmenting research centres reflect Pattern VI in this book's framework (see Figure 6.2). Here, internationally transferable FSAs in the form of upstream, technological knowledge are generated by R&D operations in host countries, but are closely linked to – and guided by – corporate headquarters. Close communication between the parent and subsidiary organization (or lab) is maintained – in fact, this communication is identified by Kuemmerle as a crucial component to ensuring that the lab is meaningfully integrated into the company's network. In contrast, home-base-exploiting R&D sites are more representative of Pattern III, whereby internationally transferable FSAs are developed in the home base, but their diffusion to host country subsidiaries is accompanied by regional modifications or enhancements in response to local market needs. Finally, Kuemmerle stresses the importance of the various host labs working directly together to create new FSAs without channelling through the home office: 'Reducing the instances in which the central lab must act as mediator means that existing knowledge travels more quickly through the company and new ideas percolate more easily.'[39] This scenario reflects Pattern VIII and Pattern IX, whereby internationally transferable FSAs are jointly created by a network of MNE affiliates, and then exploited internationally, either with or without the addition of location-bound FSAs for specific countries or markets.

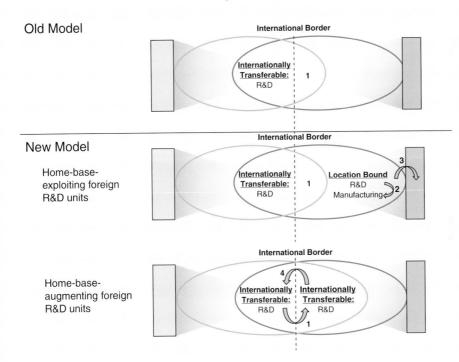

Figure 6.1
Home-base-exploiting and augmenting foreign R&D units

1. NLB FSAs related to R&D, transferred from home to host countries.
2. Internal links between host country R&D and local manufacturing.
3. External links between host country R&D and local output market.
4. Reverse transfer of new NLB FSAs related to R&D, from host country operation to home.

Kuemmerle's analysis has three main limitations. First, he does not thoroughly examine the critical issue of ongoing tension between host country labs and central headquarters in terms of setting the research agenda.[40] Should the research agenda include only projects induced by corporate headquarters and consistent with the MNE's dominant logic, or should it include external initiatives driven by opportunities identified in host country subsidiaries, and to what extent? Who gets to set the research agenda? This tension mirrors the more general tensions between subsidiary managers and central headquarters across value chain activities, as described by Birkinshaw and Fry.[41] As noted above, senior managers in the central lab must determine whether subsidiary R&D initiatives are compatible with overall corporate strategy. Here, bounded rationality constraints facing these managers may lead to false attributions of severe bounded reliability problems to foreign labs, and thus a dysfunctional application of the corporate immune system. In fact, such dysfunctionality limits the MNE's recombination capabilities.

Figure 6.2
Patterns of FSA development in home-base-exploiting and augmenting research centres in MNEs

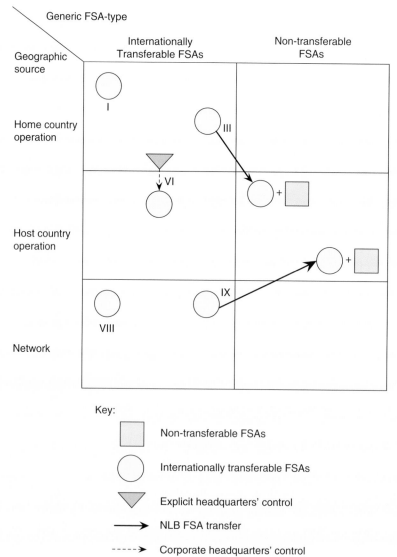

As a second limitation, Kuemmerle fails to discuss the role of joint ventures, strategic alliances, and ecosystems of cluster participants in reshaping how MNEs conduct R&D internationally. In fact, such cooperative arrangements, both formal and informal, are contributing to changes in how MNEs engage in R&D and organize their international research network.

Indeed, what the conventional MNE (engaged in strategic resource-seeking investments) lacks, when attempting to become an insider in foreign knowledge clusters through a home-base-augmenting R&D lab, is often access to a social network or broader ecosystem. The MNE may be unable to access autonomously and utilize effectively this host country location advantage through market-based supplier contracts or acquisitions. This is especially troublesome when the MNE needs long-term, multilateral linkages (rather than static, bilateral linkages) with members of host country clusters in order to create reputational FSAs. In these cases, the MNE cannot just purchase resources or acquire activities from specific actors in order to reap the expected benefits of clustering. The R&D subsidiaries of US MNEs in Japan have often encountered this problem.[42] Primarily because of their inability to hire and retain top scientists, these subsidiaries have often been locked out of Japanese clusters. The US MNEs' inability was itself the result of insufficient understanding of the complex linkages prevailing in Japan among institutions such as universities and firms that hire scientific personnel. For example, professors from lead universities in Japan systematically 'allocated' graduates to a small set of leading domestic companies. In its most extreme form, a professor would send one letter of reference for a Master's student to a single firm, and this firm would then hire the graduate based on the one recommendation it received. Foreign firms hoping to tap into this pool of young scientists had to emulate the human resources management practices of the large domestic companies, including long-term employment commitments, large R&D expenditures and well-funded labs, and the building of networking relationships with leading universities.

In the context of requisite network development, the Chinese MNE Huawei adopted a new approach to gain access to foreign knowledge clusters. Schaefer (2020) suggests that this MNE systematically goes out to employ in its foreign R&D labs specialized and highly experienced offshore experts. These individuals may be local cluster participants who were being 'phased out' because of retirement or because of having been laid-off, and who have therefore recently become available as 'experts for hire'. These individuals are able to generate innovation inputs directly to Huawei, in order to develop new, state-of-the-art products.[43]

This direct form of learning via the hiring of independent experts highlights another reason not to simply acquire R&D labs. Such acquisitions sometimes eliminate the opportunity for learning by destroying the complementary cognitive specialization and idiosyncratic resource bundles of the firms acquired. This happens if the MNE attaches too much importance to institutionalizing its own routines at the expense of using its recombination capabilities. In this context, a poor reputation for making good on promises, such as respecting acquired firms' knowledge bundles, may also negatively affect the MNE's ability to become an insider in host country clusters.

A third weakness of Kuemmerle's classic article on MNEs building R&D activities abroad is that his normative guidance on what to do remains limited to high-level, generic prescriptions. **Keeley Wilson** and **Yves Doz**, in their *HBR* article, complemented this work by providing more detailed practical advice about what MNEs should do to manage global innovation projects successfully.[44]

As business organizations conducting operations across national borders, MNEs are often faced with a dilemma of where to generate new knowledge, namely, innovation in a single location versus innovation across dispersed multiple sites. Innovation concentrated in a single location confers a variety of immediate integration benefits to MNEs. First, the team members who work together on innovation projects can meet face to face on a daily basis. They can more easily craft a common vision, norms of behaviour, and managerial practices than if they were operating in geographically dispersed locations. Second, and related to the previous point, team members can more easily exchange tacit knowledge that is critical to the innovation process. Third, senior management is available on-site in case quick decisions need to be made and can provide both strategic guidance and requisite support for the innovation process.

However, an important trade-off needs to be considered here. If useful knowledge, talent, and other resources relevant to the innovation outcome are geographically dispersed, and are to some extent immobile, MNEs should try to gain access to these resources, even in remote locations, by conducting their innovation activities in multiple places, much in line with Engel's analysis described above. This means that MNEs can gain new FSAs from decentralized innovation by tapping into scarce knowledge resources available in multiple dispersed locations. Here, the following ten practical guidelines may be helpful when MNEs attempt to move towards internal network innovation that involves multiple locations:

1. **Start Small.**[45] Teams engaged in international innovation processes should try to build internal strengths in collaborating and recombining knowledge across borders, by starting with relatively small-scale projects, involving only a few locations. For example, STI (a joint venture between Schneider Electric from France and Toshiba from Japan) initiated a series of small joint projects, which subsequently became a solid foundation for complex international initiatives.

2. **Provide a Stable Organizational Context.**[46] MNEs should make sure to avoid perceptions that innovation team members in particular locations

might lose their jobs as a result of the evolving international dispersion of their firm's innovation activities. For instance, in the electronics industry, it may be critical to retain key engineers in R&D when the MNE undergoes restructuring processes, for example, as a result of foreign acquisitions.

3. ***Assign Oversight and Support Responsibility to a Senior Manager.***[47] It is important to designate particular senior executives as having formal oversight and managerial support roles when conducting dispersed innovation. In the absence of such clear role assignment, anarchy and chaos in the dispersed innovation processes could easily take over. For example, when Essilor (a global corrective lens manufacturer headquartered in France) developed photochromic lenses, one executive was put in charge of the entire project. This unity of command resulted in a disciplined time-to-market management of the resulting products from a geographically dispersed innovation process.

4. ***Use Rigorous Project Management and Seasoned Project Leaders.***[48] Routinized managerial practices are essential to bring innovation projects spanning multiple locations to fruition. For example, Siemens, a German industrial manufacturing MNE, adopted rigorous quality management programmes called 'Design for Six Sigma' in its international innovation projects.

5. ***Appoint a Lead Site.***[49] MNEs typically need to select a single innovation site that will act as the leader for the dispersed innovation efforts, again in order to reap benefits from unity in command. It is this selected lead site that will be responsible for implementing the international innovation projects under its command, especially in terms of respecting time and budgetary constraints. For example, in the STI project mentioned above, the French site was assigned the leadership role, and charged with defining the new product requirements in the innovation.

6. ***Invest Time Defining the Innovation.*** Given the expected complexity of undertaking an innovation project across national borders, MNEs should devote enough time and resources to carefully defining the project upfront. It should be clear from the outset to all team members involved what the project is about, and what it attempts to achieve, thereby avoiding subsequent bounded reliability problems in collaborating and recombining knowledge across innovation sites. For example, in the case of the French MNE Essilor's photochromic lens, the innovation team invested the first nine months of a two-year time frame foreseen for the project to define the modules and multiple interfaces among geographically dispersed innovation units and specialists.

7. ***Allocate Resources on the Basis of Capability, not Availability.*** MNEs should assign innovation tasks among multiple sites, and allow the related, needed resources to be used in the innovation process, based on each site's

capabilities. It is not because specific sites have a high volume of basic, slack resources at their disposal, such as an available pool of idle engineers, that this alone should give them a lead position in the innovation process.

8. ***Build Enough Knowledge Overlap for Collaboration.*** As a follow-up to guidelines 1, 4, and 5, MNEs should try to build up a threshold level of common knowledge, shared among all sites, to be used as a platform for further cross-border collaboration in the innovation process. For example, the German MNE Siemens' virtual, cross-functional innovation teams are supposed to ensure the development and maintainance of adequate knowledge overlaps within the MNE's dispersed units.

9. ***Limit the Number of Subcontractors and Partners.*** Given the high internal complexity of the international innovation process, MNEs need to economize on bounded rationality by being particularly selective when engaging external subcontractors and partners in the innovation process, so as to keep the project feasible and manageable. As one example of excessive complexity from having too many partners involved, the American MNE Boeing's 787 Dreamliner project with fifty plus partners across the United States, Europe, and East Asia made the MNE lose orders to its rival, the Airbus A350, because coordinating so many key partners required the MNE to continuously modify its integration process, ultimately leading to a three-year delay in delivering its final product. This example illustrates the difficulty of operating with external networks or 'ecosystems', when (too) many partners are involved in the innovation process.

10. ***Don't Rely Solely on Technology for Communication.*** MNEs should try to emulate the rich and deep communication channels available to spatially concentrated teams, by using as much as possible face-to-face tools such as site visits, team meetings, and short-term transfers of key employees. For example, the Indian MNE Tata allocates travel budgets to foster face-to-face interactions among international innovation team members, in addition to investing heavily in ICT-based communication, much in line with Patterns VIII and IX of MNE subsidiary development, as discussed in Chapter 1.

As highlighted in the beginning of this chapter, Kuemmerle examined MNEs' international innovation activities by making the critical distinction between innovation in home-base-exploiting sites and home-base-augmenting sites. Wilson and Doz usefully expand on this analysis by considering cases (which remain rather uncommon) where multiple sites may be involved in a single innovation project. This approach is much in line with the strategy of ***international coordinators*** discussed in Chapter 1, but focused here on the innovation function only.

The ten guidelines are also very useful to *international projectors*, for example, by recognizing that the oversight role given to a senior executive and the leader role assigned to a specific unit need not be placed in the home country, but could well be located in a distant nation where strong, requisite innovation capabilities are present. The prescribed, common platform of knowledge overlaps among the multiple R&D sites enhancing further collaboration is very much aligned with the concept of multiple units contributing jointly to MNE capability building. On the other hand, the ten guidelines also usefully suggest how *multi-centred MNEs* (with subsidiary independence and autonomy in generating new knowledge) could improve their innovation outputs worldwide. Such MNEs' dispersed talents and knowledge assets in host countries could be more closely aligned with the MNEs' overall vision for successfully developing and commercializing outputs from international innovation projects. For both *international projectors* and *multi-centred MNEs*, the ten guidelines suggest a significant departure from the original, archetypal behaviours characterizing these firms.

Strategic Challenges in the New Economy

In their *SMR* article, **Nathan Furr** and **Andrew Shipilov** argue that companies often need to collaborate with partner firms in the innovation sphere to generate new products and services.[50] The question then arises what form of collaboration, or 'ecosystem', is likely to be the most effective.[51]

A *centralized ecosystem* reflects a traditional hub-and-spoke structure whereby a 'broker company' builds connections with familiar partners who are complementary to the broker's existing business, but who do not interact much among themselves with the purpose to innovate.[52] In contrast, an *adaptive ecosystem* represents a seamless network structure whereby an 'orchestrator company' builds connections with unfamiliar partners, who can then bring new opportunities to the orchestrator as a result of cooperative interactions among themselves.[53] Within a stable environment and with a well-defined problem to address, a centralized ecosystem may be optimal. However, when operating in a dynamic environment and facing the threats of disruptive new technologies and new competitors, building an adaptive ecosystem may be more effective to develop new FSAs against rivals.

As one example of the value brought by an adaptive ecosystem of innovation, Samsung Electronics (a South Korean MNE active in consumer electronics manufacturing) developed a personal-health-monitoring business through intensive collaboration. It partnered with twenty plus start-ups and academic researchers in the fields of blood pressure, hydration, and nutrition. The MNE developed the 'Voice of the Body' platform whereby the various partners, who were mostly unfamiliar to one another, worked as a team to innovate in the sphere of personal medical care and clinically proven food products.[54]

As a second example, Mastercard International (an American MNE in financial services) developed creative digital payment options linked to other non-financial services, through an adaptive ecosystem based in London. In addition to enlisting well-known partners such as banks and merchants, it also added uncommon partners to the network, such as Transport for London, Cubic Transportation Systems, and consumer goods retailers. Using this adaptive ecosystem of innovation: 'it could offer commuters discounts at coffee shops and other businesses if they opted not to use transportation systems during certain times of day'.[55]

Furr and Shipilov formulate six general guidelines to make adaptive ecosystems of innovation work:

1. ***Define the 'battlefield'.***[56] Ecosystem orchestrators need to creatively imagine the contours of new solutions in rapidly changing and uncertain environments. For example, Mastercard collaborated with Pizza Hut and Softbank to explore an application of artificial intelligence (AI) for its business. This resulted in the development of 'a new mobile customer interface using Pepper, Softbank's humanoid robot, as a diner's assistant in some Pizza Hut restaurants'.[57]

2. ***Use 'bat signals' to attract partners.***[58] Ecosystem orchestrators should first engage in experiments to attract unconventional but highly useful partners. For example, Lowe's (i.e., an American firm active in home improvement) partnered with a 3-D designer, a 3-D printing company, and a sensor manufacturer to explore innovations in the 3-D printing market, 'hoping that the right set of partners would come together',[59] thereby taking a clear risk, since hope is not a strategy.

3. ***Connect uncommon partners.***[60] Ecosystem orchestrators need to search for opportunities of 'cross-fertilization'.[61] They should bring together and orchestrate the activities of unfamiliar business partners. For example, Cisco (an American networking hardware MNE) partnered with firms from different fields to explore creating a new digital supply chain business. The partners included DHL (a German courier and express mail service firm), Caterpillar (a US-based construction machinery and equipment firm), and Airbus (a European large civil aircraft manufacturer).

4. ***Glue the partners together.***[62] Ecosystem orchestrators need to cultivate new types of bonds to hold together their uncommon partners from different fields, so as to sustain collaborative interactions over time. For example, when Samsung Electronics developed its personal-health-monitoring business, the technology-based glue that held the MNE's various partners

together was 'the hardware and software that integrates the sensors and analytics to create an individualized and dynamic picture of a person's health'.[63]

5. *'Leverage opportunities to transform from the inside out'.*[64] Ecosystem orchestrators need to use their adaptive ecosystem and outside partners to transform their intra-firm functioning. For example, Galeries Lafayette (a high-end department store chain from France) collaborated with independent start-ups to 'disrupt its traditional brick-and-mortar business' and to 'create digital solutions to enhance the retail experience'.[65]

6. *Make contracts flexible.*[66] Ecosystem orchestrators must understand that adaptive systems of innovation, needed in instances of great uncertainty, disruptive emerging technologies, and new rivalry, cannot be governed through conventional contracts. An adaptive ecosystem of innovation cannot build on the *ex ante* design of fully contingent and detailed agreements with uncommon partners in diverse domains. Partnership agreements entered into, in this sphere of high bounded rationality and unclear reliability, should have ample room for substantial further adaptation and *ex post* governance, as innovation activities and their outcomes unfold over time.

Furr and Shipilov suggest vastly extended options for MNE innovation activities beyond establishing Kuemmerle's home-base-exploiting and home-base-augmenting foreign R&D subsidiaries. Adaptive ecosystems of innovation go far beyond the internal organization of core innovation activities. The key challenge for adaptive ecosystems of innovation is to engage in new types of resource combination across very different partners that can lead to novel value creation. In the international business sphere, the role of the MNE as network orchestrator can be viewed as an extension of its role in orchestrating geographically dispersed subsidiaries, and pursuing several distinct capability development processes, as outlined in Chapter 1.

This article also reinforces the importance of two key concepts introduced in this book's unifying framework in Chapter 1. MNEs should preferably build and/or accumulate strong FSAs in the technology and governance spheres before going abroad to build adaptive networks for innovation, because these FSAs will be the initial glue to connect and hold together multiple uncommon partners engaged in new value creation. When attempting to attract uncommon partners using 'bat signals', it should be noted that with these experiments, MNEs are still subject to the dual challenges of bounded rationality and bounded reliability. The ensuing problems with external partners may ultimately reduce the contributions of an adaptive ecosystem of innovation to the network-orchestrating MNEs.

Five Management Takeaways

1. Analyze your firm's portfolio of international R&D facilities, and categorize these according to their home-base-exploiting versus home-base-augmenting status.

2. Assess whether your knowledge-generating activities are located in the best possible knowledge clusters with optimal access to specialized resources.

3. When exploring the drivers of innovation inside your firm, examine the potential contribution of subsidiary initiatives.

4. Reflect on the potential to partner in alliances, so as to absorb new knowledge in your industry, and on the roles the firm could play in external networks that function as ecosystems.

5. Align your R&D initiatives in host country sites with the firm's overall corporate goals and consider alternative avenues for acquiring new knowledge (e.g., strategic alliances, acquisitions, adaptive ecosystems, etc.), thereby also reflecting on practical guidelines to achieve effective distributed innovation.

7

International Sourcing and Production

Five Learning Objectives

1. To describe the changes in the international business environment leading to new roles assigned to international factories.
2. To explain the two key parameters underlying the roles of foreign manufacturing plants and to highlight the six generic factory roles.
3. To explain the benefits and challenges of reshoring as a source of new firm-specific advantages for MNEs, as they bring offshored production activities back to their home country.
4. To develop an understanding of the locational impacts of technological advances, such as additive manufacturing (AM) or 3-D printing, on MNEs' international sourcing and production activities.
5. To identify the limitations of a strategy aimed at upgrading foreign manufacturing plants.

This chapter examines Kasra Ferdows' idea that senior MNE managers should try to upgrade their host country factories to give them the ability to develop FSAs. For Ferdows, a factory's ability to develop FSAs is at least as important as low costs. In general, he argues, this will require that senior managers invest in each factory for the long term, and not move production based on changes in exchange rates, costs, or government incentives. These ideas will be examined and then critiqued using the framework presented in Chapter 1.

Significance

In an *HBR* piece entitled 'Making the most of foreign factories', **Kasra Ferdows** provides a detailed argument in support of the market-seeking and strategic resource-seeking arguments for FDI in the context of international manufacturing.[1]

Chapter 5 has already described how MNEs can tap their foreign subsidiaries as sources of competitive advantage, selectively giving certain subsidiaries increased control and decision-making power. Chapter 6 then extended this analysis, with a focus on foreign R&D centres. These centres can develop new knowledge that exploits or even augments the knowledge developed in the home country. This chapter will extend this analysis further, looking at how MNEs can tap their foreign factories.

Ferdows bases his research on a wide variety of sources, including his own consulting work with a dozen large manufacturing MNEs, a four-year study conducted with ten large MNEs (Apple, Digital Equipment, Electrolux, Ford, HP, Hydro Aluminum, IBM, Olivetti, Philips, and Sony), industry surveys of companies (pharmaceuticals, food processing, and paper machinery), and the Global Manufacturing Futures Surveys project, studying the practices of nearly 600 manufacturers operating in the triad regions of North America, Europe, and Japan.

Ferdows attempts to answer one key question: 'How can a factory located outside of a company's home country be used as a competitive weapon not only in the market that it directly serves but also in every market served by the company?'[2] The answer depends largely on the mindset of home country senior managers: what do they think is the proper role of foreign factories?

Senior managers who view their factories merely as sources of efficient, low-cost production typically don't allocate their factories many resources, and these managers get only what they expect: efficient, low-cost production. In contrast, senior managers with higher performance expectations from their foreign factories require innovation and customer service as well: these managers 'generally expect their foreign factories to be highly productive and innovative, to achieve low costs, and to provide exemplary service to customers throughout the world'.[3] These managers allocate their factories more resources and get more in return.

In his study, Ferdows observes that the most successful manufacturing MNEs view their foreign factories as sources of FSAs beyond the ability to save costs as with conventional offshoring plants. Ferdows therefore concludes that, beyond the traditional motives such as 'tariff and trade concessions, cheap labour, capital subsidies, and reduced logistics costs', MNEs should leverage their foreign factories 'to get closer to . . . customers and suppliers, to attract skilled and talented employees, and to create centres of expertise for the entire company'.[4]

Ferdows describes three changes in the international business environment driving the assignment of these new foreign factory roles. First, international trade tariffs declined substantially in the second half of the twentieth century, reducing the need to establish foreign plants merely to overcome trade barriers. Second, modern manufacturing is increasingly technologically sophisticated (meaning capital-intensive) and has complex supply-chain requirements. As a result, MNEs seldom select manufacturing locations based simply on the lowest possible wages. Rather, the emphasis is on the overall productivity level, which is determined by several factors, including the available levels of infrastructure, technology, worker education, and skills. Third, the time frame available to move from development to actual manufacturing and marketing has become shorter. As a result, MNEs increasingly co-locate development and manufacturing activities in highly specialized plants, which then receive broad geographic mandates within their areas of expertise.

These changes are consistent with the argument developed in Chapter 6, that the successful penetration of foreign markets requires more than merely transferring non-location-bound knowledge from the home country to the host country. MNEs are increasingly attempting to augment conventional, host country production with at least some local R&D activities, rather than centralizing such activities in the home country and then deploying this non-location-bound knowledge to host countries as the basis of foreign manufacturing. A subsidiary located in a specialized foreign knowledge cluster, as described in Chapter 3, must become the company's specialist for those knowledge areas in which the cluster has core strengths. In other words, the subsidiary must develop, in its own right, internationally transferable FSAs, building on the location advantages of the host country cluster.

The article distinguishes among six possible roles for foreign manufacturing facilities, based on two parameters. First, the strategic purpose of the plant, which is intimately related to the host country location advantages the MNE wants to access (e.g., proximity to market, access to low-cost production, and access to knowledge and skills). Second, the level of distinct FSAs held by the plant (weak or strong). Here, the level of distinct FSAs refers to the additional strengths added by the plant itself, augmenting the FSAs transferred from the home country. Note also that this includes the plant's higher-order FSAs, such as the ability to generate new knowledge and new FSAs. As regards purpose, it was noted in Chapter 5 that a distinction should be made between the subsidiary's role in accessing host country input markets (e.g., for skilled labour) versus output markets (i.e., for selling the company's products). Ferdows makes a similar distinction in the context of manufacturing activities. His 'proximity to market' purpose reflects the importance of output markets for selling the MNE's products (output-market-seeking investments). His second purpose, 'access to low-cost production', reflects the factory's need to access input markets. Finally, his third purpose, 'access to knowledge and skills', is often closely tied to both input and output markets. By definition, it encompasses some need to tap into input markets, especially for sophisticated production factors, but in many cases the ultimate goal is to serve (output) markets with innovative products.

The two parameters above allow Ferdows to distinguish among six specific factory roles (see Figure 7.1):

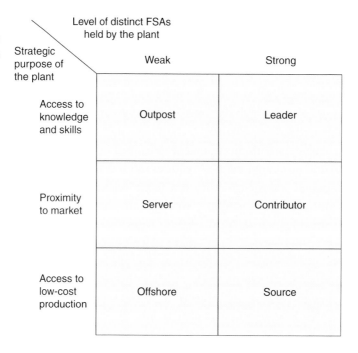

Figure 7.1
Six roles of foreign
manufacturing plants

Level of distinct FSAs
held by the plant

Strategic
purpose of
the plant

	Weak	Strong
Access to knowledge and skills	Outpost	Leader
Proximity to market	Server	Contributor
Access to low-cost production	Offshore	Source

1. **Offshore factory:** this factory's primary purpose is simply to access low-cost production factors as an implementer on the input side. The plant's manufacturing output, typically predetermined by senior management in the home country, is then exported. This factory type typically does not develop new FSAs and receives minimum autonomy.

2. **Server factory:** this factory's primary purpose is to manufacture goods and to supply a predefined, proximate national or regional output market. Market imperfections such as trade barriers, logistics costs, and foreign exchange exposure usually explain the establishment of such factories in specific host countries. A server factory may engage in some FSA development, but it ultimately has a narrow charter with relatively little autonomy or specialized capabilities.

3. **Outpost factory:** similar to the 'black hole' type subsidiaries discussed in Chapter 5, the primary purpose of this factory is to gather valuable information from advanced host country clusters, mainly on the input side. On the actual manufacturing side, this role is usually combined with that of an offshore (input-market-driven) or server (output-market-driven) factory.

4. **Source factory:** this factory's primary purpose is to gain access to low-cost production factors on the input side, similar to an offshore factory. However, it also receives resources to engage in resource recombination and to develop FSAs that will turn it into a 'best practice' plant in the MNE's network for the assigned product range. It therefore has more autonomy in terms of logistics, product customization, redesign, etc. The MNE sets up source factories in

locations with good infrastructure and a skilled workforce. This type of factory may be a strategic leader on the input side of the value chain, but nonetheless has a narrow charter.

5. **Contributor factory:** this factory type is oriented primarily towards the host country or host region output market, similar to a server factory, but it commands stronger capabilities than a server factory. More at the upstream end of the value chain, it is responsible for resource recombination in the form of process improvements, new product development, customizations, etc.

6. **Leader factory:** this factory type is the most important one in terms of resource recombination and new FSA development. It accesses valuable inputs from the local cluster where it is embedded and plays a key role in localized manufacturing innovation. It is also closely connected with both the key players on the input side (such as research labs) and the end users on the output side.

Overall, says Ferdows, the MNE should aim to upgrade its offshore, server, and outpost factories so that they gain the ability to develop FSAs as source, contributor, and leader factories. However, this upgrading process requires a high level of commitment, as it 'entails a substantial investment of time and resources, as well as changes in a factory's culture and management style'.[5]

Upgrading, according to Ferdows, involves substantial resource recombination spread over three stages: enhancing internal performance (e.g., through employee training and education, self-managed teams, and adopting just-in-time manufacturing (JIT)), accessing and developing external resources (e.g., strengthening the plant's supplier network and improving the logistics integration with distributors), and developing new knowledge that can benefit the overall MNE network. As the MNE guides its foreign factories towards taking on upgraded, FSA-developing roles, it tends to place greater emphasis on intangible internal strengths and location advantages rather than tangible ones such as lower costs, taxes, or the benefit of avoiding trade barriers. Intangible strengths include the factories' recombination capabilities, especially their capacity to absorb host country knowledge, to learn from customers, suppliers, and rivals, and to attract new talent. The end result of the upgrading process is a 'robust network'[6] of factories with FSA-developing roles, able to adapt swiftly to changes in the marketplace. According to Ferdows, such a network is conducive to stability and security of internal MNE functioning over the long term, even if many plants are located in so-called 'high-cost' locations. This 'robust network' view of the MNE is in sharp contrast with the popular view that many MNEs should operate a so-called 'footloose' set of plants. Footloose operations imply low exit barriers, as well as the capability to relocate manufacturing operations and redeploy resources across geographic space rapidly in response to changing cost conditions.

According to Ferdows, MNE strategic manufacturing planning should focus on specializing foreign factories, with each plant taking on a leadership role in a specific area, and avoiding the duplication of R&D efforts: 'The solution lies in specialization. Whenever feasible, a foreign factory's ultimate mission should include developing a world-class specialty.'[7]

A number of examples illustrate this point. In the late 1970s, the US-based technology company NCR (set up in 1884 as the National Cash Register Company, acquired by AT&T in 1991, and re-established as a separate company in 1996) had closed down five factories in the area of Dundee, Scotland, and had one remaining, a server factory that was fighting for its survival. Building on a structural change inside NCR that included a new focus on business units, the subsidiary management decided to refocus this factory, specializing in auto-mated teller machines (ATMs) for the banking industry. The upgrading efforts included improving performance and speeding up product development cycle times. 'By 1990, Dundee had become NCR's leader plant for ATMs, with primary responsibility for developing and manufacturing the products that the billion-dollar business needed.'[8]

During the same period, Sony built a new plant in Wales (United Kingdom), initially intended as a server factory to overcome European trade barriers against outsiders. Over fifteen years, however, the factory pioneered new quality control processes, both internally and with local suppliers, and eventually took on responsibility for R&D to customize television product designs for the European market. 'Since 1988, the plant has designed and developed most of the products it has produced . . . It continues to be a strong and valuable contributor plant in Sony's global network.'[9]

In closing, Ferdows cautions managers about four common obstacles that may prevent the upgrading of foreign factories: fear of relying on foreign operations for critical skills, treating overseas factories like cash cows and neglecting long-term investment, creating instability by shifting production in reaction to fluctuating exchange rates and costs, and the enticement of government relocation incentives to move factories to new locations that possess minimal potential for upgrading.

Context and Complementary Perspectives

Ferdows' article appeared in the same 1997 edition of the *HBR* as Kuemmerle's 'Building effective R&D capabilities abroad', discussed in Chapter 6. At that point in time, as noted above, it had become necessary for many firms to improve linkages between host country manufacturing and actual knowledge development activities, so as to command the required location-bound FSAs to function effectively in host country environments.

In addition, senior MNE managers perceived the need to gain access to geographically dispersed innovation clusters as the basis for new resource recombinations, culminating in new, internationally transferable FSAs. For these two reasons, many MNEs created R&D labs in host countries, often in conjunction with host country factories.

The potential of host country subsidiaries as a source of both location-bound and internationally transferable knowledge provided the impetus for companies to review their international operations. Freer trade in the form of lower tariffs and non-tariff barriers alike resulting from institutions and agreements such as GATT (and its successor WTO), NAFTA, and the European Union had dramatically changed the landscape of international business. Companies were no longer forced to establish factories in local areas simply to overcome unnatural market imperfections imposed by governments. At the same time, fiscal instability, dramatic devaluations of currencies, and political uncertainty in developing countries in Latin America, Asia, and Eastern Europe created new bounded rationality problems for MNEs trying to reconfigure their dispersed subsidiary networks. The latter part of the 1990s also saw a halt in the seemingly endless boom of several Far East economies, as Japan and the developing Asian Tigers became mired in a prolonged recession. Senior MNE managers were thus forced to rethink the bigger picture when planning the location of their factory networks to achieve optimal efficiency and effectiveness. As Ferdows suggests, companies were beginning to realize that across-the-board relocation of activities to low-wage, offshore production areas was not necessarily the panacea to achieve higher overall productivity, lower manufacturing costs, and better access to customers.

A first complementary perspective is provided by **Willy C. Shih**, a professor of management practice at Harvard Business School, as well as a director of Flextronics International Ltd, in an *SMR* piece entitled 'What it takes to reshore manufacturing successfully'.[10] The author, in his *SMR* article, argues that after a wave of advanced economy MNEs' offshoring manufacturing activities to China and other emerging economies, the reverse has occurred. Rising costs of labour and utilities, logistics challenges, etc. in foreign locations have prompted many firms to reshore activities back to their home country.[11] For example, in the American context, Walmart has been pushing its vendors to produce in the United States and Google has partnered with Flextronics, the Singapore-based contract manufacturer, to assemble a smartphone in Fort Worth, Texas. The benefits that MNEs expect from reshoring include reductions in their inventory levels, shorter delivery times and ordering cycles, and nimbler responses to changes in market demands. However, reshoring is not always an easy process, and MNE managers should prepare carefully for the following six challenges in the reshoring process.

As the *first challenge*, MNEs reshoring their production operations means that these firms will need to hire employees with requisite skills in the newly established plants in the home country. Newly hired workers will need to be trained adequately to conform to the requirements of state-of-the-art manufacturing, which may be very different from what prevailed in the old, pre-offshoring production facilities. In addition, new human resources management practices, such as 'skills promotion paths' for workers upgrading their skills to conform to technological changes, may need to be introduced in the new plants. MNEs may also want to collaborate with local colleges to attract and train students, thereby building a localized industrial commons for reshoring.

The *second challenge* is that an insufficient number of high-level production engineers and production managers may be available in the home country after a few decades of offshoring. As one example, Flextronics had to assemble a team of 150 manufacturing engineers for Fort Worth from all over the world, and also had to retain five highly experienced managers to establish the plant. After an initial plant set-up is complete and the experienced engineers leave the reshored assembly operations, leadership challenges still remain to run the plant efficiently; for example, the plant manager at Fort Worth explained that 'the United States has abandoned that part of the industry with all of the offshoring, and we will need to rebuild this base for electronic manufacturing if we want it to come back'.[12]

The *third challenge* is to rethink the capital/labour ratio. Advanced economy MNEs often pursued offshoring to take advantage of cheap labour, but then later on simply assume that they can use more automation as they reshore. However, this assumption often turns out to be wrong: for example, as the author observes: 'If you want to have five million new smartphones on hand to sell on the first weekend after a new phone model launches, you will need a lot of people, not automation.'[13] Finding the right balance between manual and automated processing is thus a critical but difficult decision for MNEs to make, especially because higher automation typically implies higher capital costs and dedicated (non-redeployable) physical assets, whereas having a larger workforce and lower automation typically allows for the more flexible redeployment of human assets as a function of changing economic circumstances.

The *fourth challenge* is that MNEs engaged in reshoring may face a 'hollowed-out supply base'.[14] This means that the offshoring of manufacturing often went hand in hand with entire supply chains being removed from the home country. A long-term commitment to a more proximate supply base can be a critical component of reshoring. For this purpose, proximate 'co-innovation' may be required between a manufacturer and its suppliers through deep levels of mutual information sharing and collaboration efforts.[15]

The *fifth challenge* for MNEs is to enlist customers in their reshoring efforts. Especially in the business-to-business sphere, corporate customers typically will not want to pay more for 'made-in-the-home-country' products from reshoring. However, a more proximate supply chain may also benefit them, and they can help reshored manufacturers by sharing early signals on demand changes and by making reciprocal commitments to improve efficiency through open and transparent communications.

Finally, the *sixth challenge* is to link the reshored production with R&D activities, much in line with the analysis in Chapter 6 on the potential benefits of co-locating R&D and production. Reshoring production operations close to home-based R&D can lead to benefits such as a faster adaptation of products and shorter lead times between innovation and manufacturing. In the Flextronics case mentioned above, managers in Fort Worth argued that 'incremental innovations most often come when teams get their hands dirty in the production environment'.[16]

The key conclusion from Shih's analysis is that MNEs reshoring their production can potentially realign their manufacturing activities with downstream markets, with suppliers, and with proximate, upstream R&D, thereby creating a more compact and manageable supply chain ecosystem in the home country or home region. Reshoring could thus be a source of new firm-specific advantages for MNEs as they overcome the six challenges above.

Starting from the six roles of foreign manufacturing plants suggested by Ferdows, this article provides an alternative development path for foreign plants lacking distinct capabilities, namely, the offshore, server, and outpost factories. Rather than focusing on upgrading these plants and contemplating an expansion of their mandates, so that they would ultimately command stronger FSAs in their foreign locations, the alternative is to close them and to reshore the relevant activities to the home country or home region. This relocation strategy in the form of reshoring makes a lot of sense if host country plants with weak FSAs face rising costs and uncertainties, especially on the input side, but also on the demand side (for server factories). However, manufacturing plants that have developed subsidiary-specific advantages and whose main purpose may include escaping from trade barriers, or from foreign exchange exposure, etc., may not be good candidates for reshoring. And even when there are good reasons to close offshored facilities in their foreign locations, the question should be answered whether an MNE from a highly developed country can reasonably address the six challenges associated with reshoring as described above.

Avner Ben-Ner and *Enno Siemsen* provide a second complementary perspective with their *CMR* piece on the locational impacts of additive manufacturing (AM) or 3-D printing.[17] This technology was developed in the early 1980s and is increasingly being applied to manufacture components and even finished goods using a 3-D printer. Additive manufacturing works as follows: 'A 3D printer emits materials from one or more spouts that add layer upon layer to generate a product; the process is guided by computer-aided design or manufacturing software.'[18] This approach has two main characteristics: it exploits benefits from intensive automation (such as the precision to produce according to specifications) and it enables flexible manufacturing at low cost.

The objective of traditional manufacturing (TM) was often to achieve economies of scale, thereby also resulting in industry concentration and the rise of large firms, especially MNEs.[19] In contrast, AM has five features that make it very different from TM:

1. AM does not require large investments and, as a result, there are no substantial fixed costs to recoup, nor are there any major barriers to exit.
2. With AM, unit costs do not decline as in TM. Instead, unit costs remain constant, independently of the scale of production. This feature allows small firms to compete against larger incumbents in the market.
3. AM depends less on suppliers of intermediate inputs, due to the sharply reduced usage of externally sourced parts as compared to TM. Its main inputs consist of materials, which can be flexibly transformed into a wide range of products.
4. AM flourishes in industries where customers possess very heterogeneous preferences and customization needs, and where product life cycles are short, and where timely delivery linked to proximity is critical.
5. AM drives the localization of product development, production, sales, and consumption, thereby reducing the complexity and geographic scope of international supply chains.

Here are a few examples of AM in real-world production contexts:

1. *In the medical sphere*: 'Prosthetics for children must be customized, and a new prosthetic is required every few months as the child grows. In 2011, Ivan Owen, a puppet artist . . . developed first finger prosthetics, and eventually a whole hand, using a 3D printer . . . This open-source development of a physical product involved rapid feedback cycles . . . These efforts yielded a 3D printed hand that can now be printed for $50 and assembled within two hours. The nearest substitute produced by TM has a price tag of more than $1,000.'[20]
2. *In the spare parts inventory sphere*: 'Appliance manufacturers are actively exploring the opportunity of replacing their spare parts warehouses with 3D printers attached to the cars of each service technician. Some stores have introduced 3D printers to supply outdated parts . . . The technology thus enables outsourcing the whole spare parts and post-purchase maintenance aspect of a business to third-party service, logistics and manufacturing providers . . . .'[21]

3. *In the sphere of textiles*: Buyers can visit an online fashion store with various pieces of clothing displayed and put on this clothing, virtually, using a 3-D scan. The buyers then purchase online a right to print the chosen clothing, which will subsequently be printed at a proximate, local printing shop and delivered to the buyers. Some of the benefits include: (1) absence of inventory costs for the clothing; (2) immediate access by customers to new clothing designs; (3) customization of clothing, reflecting buyers' tastes; and (4) lean showroom stores (with no space for inventory) established in city centres with a high number of customer contacts.

4. *In the sphere of automobiles (US example)*: 'Local Motors – which operates four AM microfactories that make cars, trikes, furniture, and more – is producing a minicar with about 50 parts.'[22] The complexity of this industry, however, as compared to textiles, is partly in the area of safety concerns, with much higher scrutiny imposed by regulators (e.g., in terms of the requisite technical features of the product and legal restrictions to purchase the product).

The industries most likely to be disrupted by AM (e.g., hearing aids and spare parts) often have the following characteristics: usage of abundantly available and easily accessible base materials for production; small-batch size of production; high product differentiation and variety; heterogeneous customization; need for local adaptation and responsiveness; and short lead time from innovation to market. In contrast, industries unlikely to be disrupted by AM (e.g., pharmaceuticals, semiconductors, and most services) have very different features, such as using key ingredients or outputs that cannot simply be printed (e.g., organic materials, agricultural outputs, services that need to be performed physically and instantly). Standardized products with high volumes and related scale economies are also poor candidates for AM.

The main consequence of AM is that in some sectors a number of large industrial firms and MNEs may be replaced by smaller-sized, specialized companies engaged in local production. However, large MNEs may unexpectedly still play a key role in industries with high potential for AM, especially if AM requires substantial complementary resources not amenable to 3-D printing. These complementary resources, both upstream and downstream from the actual AM production, may play a key role in determining the competitiveness of specialized AM-based firms versus large MNEs. Such complementary resources include, *inter alia*: costly R&D; a sophisticated supply chain to move materials to localized production units with 3-D printers; the need for massive marketing campaigns to reach the customer base; a large after-sales service component; and the need for large-scale, continuous investment to deal with regulators and a variety of other stakeholders who give firms their licence to operate. None of these elements is likely to reverse the trend towards localized (rather than globalized) production where AM can be efficient. However, these elements do suggest that in many instances, large MNEs will keep control of production, and will not simply be replaced by an army of small, independent producers.

Advances in AM technology will undoubtedly affect the business landscape of manufacturing MNEs, but as noted above the role of MNEs will not necessarily be reduced. The main impact will be some decentralization of production closer to local customers, thereby not necessarily affecting negatively MNE competitive strengths. Ultimately, FSA reservoirs do matter, and a manufacturing MNE commands many other FSAs than just strengths in production. For example, the two key features of AM, namely more intensive automation and flexible manufacturing, can often easily be absorbed by MNE plants with strong capabilities (i.e., leaders, contributors, and source factories) as described by Ferdows. These plants may actually become more valuable than before if they themselves also control some 3-D operations that can be localized across geographic space.

In other words, local production does not mean local ownership and control of this production by small independent manufacturers. Well-prepared MNEs will leverage the distinct capabilities embedded in each manufacturing plant to take advantage of the AM opportunity in an entrepreneurial fashion. Here, AM technology may strengthen further the 'robustness' of the multi-centred plant network structure of MNEs advocated by Ferdows.

MANAGEMENT INSIGHTS

Ferdows' *HBR* piece focuses on the key issues of location advantages, the transferability of home country FSAs, and the creation of FSAs in host country factories. The key assumption is that factories located in various host markets offer new bases from which to acquire and develop FSAs: 'Why spread these specialized units around the globe? Why not keep them in one location or close to one another? Why not keep them in the home country? Because a company would miss opportunities to collect and digest the expertise that other regions have to offer.'[23]

As we have done with previous authors in previous chapters, we can classify Ferdows' recommendations as advice for senior managers to follow certain patterns of FSA development over others. His recommendation to upgrade offshore, server, and outpost facilities – established to access and exploit respectively low-cost production factors, proximity to markets, and available skills and knowledge – ultimately reflects a shift from the top part of Figure 7.2 (FSAs developed at home), towards its middle part (FSAs developed in a host country) and bottom part (FSAs developed by the internal network).

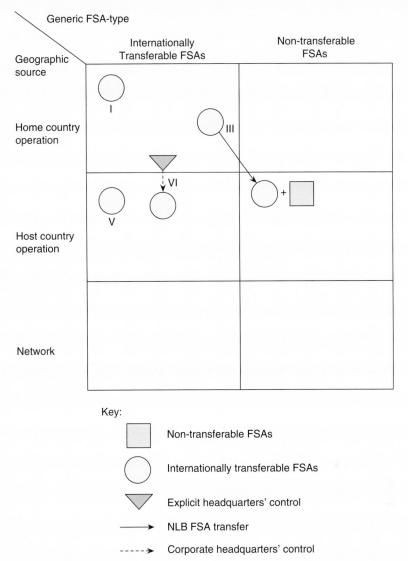

Figure 7.2
Ferdows' analysis of
FSA development
in MNEs

Overall, the FSAs held by the weaker foreign factories (i.e., offshore, server, and outpost plants) are primarily the non-location-bound FSAs transferred from the home country, with little if any distinct knowledge added. This is consistent with Pattern I in this book's conceptual framework, the behaviour of the *international projector*.

In contrast, the upgraded plants (i.e., source, contributor, and leader factories) reflect other patterns in this book's framework. Contributor factories, which customize products to suit the host market, fit Pattern III: internationally transferable FSAs developed in the home country and diffused to host country plants are accompanied by regional modifications or enhancements in response to local market needs.

Finally, consider source and leader factories, both of which exploit valuable (input side) production factors present in host countries (with leader plants having a broader mandate). These types of host country factories are supposed to develop into centres of excellence with world-class competencies in specific product areas. These factories follow Patterns V and VI, whereby non-location-bound FSAs are generated through operations in host countries, either autonomously (Pattern V) or under close direction and guidance of head office (Pattern VI).

Ferdows' analysis has three main limitations. First, Ferdows ultimately believes that senior managers should try to upgrade *all* their factories. This homogenizing strategy flies in the face of what was suggested in Chapter 5 on giving subsidiaries different roles. Ferdows most definitely does not view the MNE as a portfolio of operations, with some of these acting as 'implementers' indefinitely. Even though he is correct that an internal MNE network of plants is a dynamic system, and that plants' roles can change, it would be somewhat naïve to assume, especially for large manufacturing firms, that all plants should be candidates for upgrading in the sense of becoming specialized centres of excellence with a distinct knowledge base inside the MNE. Here, the economies of scale and scope resulting from an approach with little plant upgrading obviously need to be weighed against the benefits of allowing plants to become increasingly embedded in host locations and to deviate substantially from adopting and applying the MNE's key routines. This trade-off must be assessed for each plant in the MNE network, and there is no guarantee that every single plant should be upgraded. In fact, most large MNEs operate with a number of 'strategic leader' plants (using the terminology from Chapter 5), positioned on the upper part of Figure 7.1, but usually also have many 'implementer' plants, consistent with the various roles described by Ferdows on the lower part of Figure 7.1.

The key differences among the six plant types identified by Ferdows are visualized in Figure 7.3.

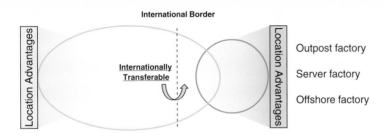

Figure 7.3
Key differences
among the six
plant types

Outpost factory

Server factory

Offshore factory

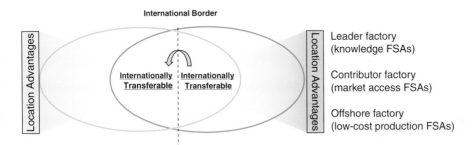

Leader factory
(knowledge FSAs)

Contributor factory
(market access FSAs)

Offshore factory
(low-cost production FSAs)

The bottom, host country triangle covers a larger area than the top one, because of greater LB FSA development in these types of factories. The bold, curved arrow out of the bottom host country triangle, pointing to the left, means the NLB FSAs developed in the host country can be transferred back to the home country or to other affiliates in the MNE network.

As a second limitation, Ferdows' article does not discuss the changing nature of production in terms of outsourcing and the increased use of long-term, relational contracting with external suppliers. Especially within the sampled industries of technology-based companies, many of the market leaders at the time of writing have long pursued an outsourcing strategy.[24] For these companies, manufacturing generally occurred in the host country, emerging economies by dedicated contract manufacturers or original equipment manu-facturers (OEMs) such as Flextronics, Solectron (acquired by Flextronics in 2007),[25] and Sanmina-SCI (changed its name to Sanmina in 2012),[26] in exchange for long-term, exclusive contracts to manufacture products designed by the MNE. These large MNEs focus instead on the control of R&D on the upstream side and investments in branding on the downstream side.

A significant driver of outsourcing is the use of information and communi-cations technology (ICT) to monitor and coordinate with outside suppliers. Here, the MNE can easily and inexpensively identify poor quality, cost inefficien-cies, delays in the logistics chain, etc. The result is increasingly blurred organiza-tional boundaries between in-house product development and manufacturing and similar activities performed by manufacturing partners. This new division of labour may give the MNE full access to attractive production factors, including knowledge and skills in host environments, without the need to upgrade its own manufacturing facilities. The possibility of long-term, relational contracting adds a new trade-off to be considered when reflecting upon the upgrading of factories abroad: a 'robust network' may include 'robust' relationships with external contracting parties, rather than solely a set of upgraded factories.[27]

The third limitation of Ferdows' analysis is that he underestimates the value of having low-cost, highly efficient factories in host countries, especially emerging markets that simply adopt and exploit both stand-alone technological knowledge from the parent as well as its key routines. On the one hand, this allows MNEs to improve their margins in their home country and other highly developed economies – markets where large and powerful distributors may try to squeeze the manufacturers' prices, and there may be strong competition and low growth rates. On the other hand, low-cost, highly efficient production may in some cases be the most practical tool to penetrate emerging, host countries – markets characterized by lower income levels and local low-cost manufacturers with lesser quality products (see also Chapter 14).

Strategic Challenges in the New Economy

Marco Iansiti and *Karim R. Lakhani*, in their *HBR* article on the new economics of digital-based production, observe that a small number of hub firms operate at the heart of a very large number of connections in international networks.[28] These firms are playing an increasingly dominant role in several industries. On the positive side, they can create real value for end users, while fostering a more participative and democratic business ecosystem.[29] But on the negative side, they sometimes capture a major portion of the value created in their networks by creating monopoly-type, quasi-markets benefiting mainly themselves as the digital platform hubs connecting all other participants.[30] In such cases, and absent regulation and other countervailing forces, their economic performance may result not only from FSAs that are efficiency-based, but also from market power.

It should be noted that hub firms can diversify into a number of industries. They can utilize their scale-based advantages in their base network to enter new sectors, thereby reshaping the latter from being 'product-driven' to becoming 'network-driven'.[31] They can thereby also attempt to control these more diversified networks by being at the heart of all transactions and connections. As one example related to the Chinese multinational technology firm, Alibaba: 'The Alibaba spin-off Ant Financial builds on data from Alibaba's already vast user base to commoditize traditional financial services and reorganize a good chunk of the Chinese financial sector around the Ant Financial platform.'[32]

The emergence of hub firms in the digital economy is due to three principles of network functioning that work in concert. *First*, the principle of exponential increases in the power of data processing (i.e., Moore's law) has led to a rapid rise in digitalization (or the potential thereof), in a number of sectors. *Second*, the principle that having a greater number of connected users in a network increases the network's value to all in the network (i.e., Metcalfe's law) has led to the rapid growth of networks in a number of sectors. *Third*, the two above elements have facilitated highly connected hub firms in one sector to generate new connections more easily in other sectors and to earn hub status in those newly entered sectors: this is called the 'digital domino' principle.[33] For example:

> With the introduction of iOS and Android, the (cell phone) industry began to tip away from its hardware centricity to network structures centered on these multisided platforms . . . Each new app makes the platform it sits on more valuable, creating a powerful network effect that in turn creates a more daunting barrier to entry for new players . . . Google and Apple are extracting the lion's share of the sector's value.[34]

How does the digital domino principle reshape conventional industries, such as the automotive sector? Cars used to be mainly hardware products. They are now starting to provide new sources of value to their buyers (i.e., drivers), for example, with the advent of self-driving vehicles, because drivers can then spend the time in their car using Apple or Google apps during their commuting. Such new types of value creation may redefine and reshape car manufacturers' future business models, because at present the software and networks valued highly by car drivers are outside of the car manufacturers' direct control. One example is the 'Connected-Car Ecosystem' for integrating smartphone functionality into vehicles: it connects insurance companies, auto service providers, regulators, and commercial businesses to drivers, using software platforms controlled by hub companies (e.g., Android Auto, Apple CarPlay, and OpenCar).[35] Rival auto-makers therefore need to collaborate with one another to counteract the hub power of firms such as Google and Apple, at least if they want to retain control of their core businesses. As one example: 'Here Technologies . . . acquired by a consortium of Volkswagen, BMW, and Daimler . . . provides third-party devel-opers with sophisticated tools and APIs [Application Programming Interfaces] for creating location-based ads and other services.'[36]

In traditional product and service businesses, there are limits to scale econ-omies. Adding new purchasers or users does not automatically lead to higher profitability. A variety of costs may actually increase more than proportionally when firms attempt to become larger and more diversified, including: the governance costs of inter-unit coordination; the added costs of increased product differentiation; the marketing and advertising costs needed to lure customers away from rivals; etc. These limits to scale economies allow multiple competitors to co-exist in the same market. In the international sphere, there are also limits to the non-location-boundedness of FSAs, which may curb the geographic reach and market power of large MNEs. In contrast, for hub firms using digital technologies and benefiting from network effects, increasing returns to scale are not subject to the same boundary conditions, at least in theory: adding new users to a network almost automatically confers enhanced economic benefits to the hub firm, without disproportionally rising costs. This feature can generate skewed advantages favouring the firm that commands the largest network.

Fortunately, a variety of responses from the market do place limits on the market power of hub firms. *First*, traditional brick-and-mortar companies can become hub firms themselves – see, for example, the US-based multinational conglomerate GE's 'investment in the Predix platform and the creation of GE Digital'.[37]

Second, especially because of barriers to international competition, firms from different countries and regions in the world may be investing simultaneously to become hubs, thus leading to the presence of multiple hubs in one sector. For example, 'Deutsche Telekom is partnering with Microsoft Azure (rather than Amazon Web Services) for cloud computing in Central Europe'.[38]

Third, the rise of hub power can be countered by purchasers and users on the demand side engaging in 'multihoming'.[39] This concept means that they can switch purchasing from one hub to another, as a function of their situational context, and are therefore not completely dependent on – or loyal to – one network. For example: 'Drivers and passengers routinely multihome across different ride-sharing platforms, often checking prices on Uber, Lyft, and Fasten.'[40]

Fourth, countervailing collective action can reduce the occurrence – and mitigate the effects – of supposed monopolies. One example of this situation is: 'The Linux operating system to compete against Microsoft Windows . . . actively supported by traditional players such as IBM and Hewlett-Packard and reinforced later by Google and Facebook.'[41]

Finally, and this is more a speculative point rather than one that has yet been clearly demonstrated, there may also be a self-restraining force at work, at least if hub firms want to retain their licence to operate sustainably. Here, 'value sharing' rather than maximizing 'value capture' might be critical to the long-term viability of hub-based networks, and of the hub firms controlling these networks.[42]

Ferdows suggested six roles of foreign manufacturing plants by combining the 'strategic purpose of the plant' and the 'level of distinct FSAs held by the plant'. According to Iansiti and Lakhani, who focus more on the firm's network connections in the new digital economy, rather than on its internal functioning, traditional manufacturing MNEs should attempt to neutralize the rising power of network hub firms. MNEs can achieve this by building on the leader roles of some of their foreign plants.

Leader factories are important instruments for MNEs pursuing resource recombination and new FSA development in the digital economy. Their mandates can be extended to include digitalization, network-driven services, and software functions, added to traditional hardware-type manufacturing. Importantly, these leader factories are also closely connected with key players on the input side and end users on the output side. As such, they should try to emulate the behaviour of network hub firms, and create their own ecosystems in the host countries where they are embedded. Precisely as a result of their extensive brick-and-mortar presence, they may be much more capable than digital network hub firms, to create viable, adaptive ecosystems of innovation, as described in Chapter 6, built around their product- and technology-specific FSAs.

Five Management Takeaways

1. View each of your foreign manufacturing plants as performing primarily one of six generic roles in your firm's portfolio of affiliates.
2. Consider the potential of 'upgrading' the existing, market-seeking, and resource-seeking roles of individual foreign factories.
3. Re-evaluate your portfolio of international operations by recognizing changes in initial drivers for expansion and assess whether and how this portfolio could be improved further.
4. Consider the potential of reshoring production activities in an increasingly complex world, especially when weaker foreign factories without distinct capabilities are involved, but also do take into account the costs needed for successful reshoring.
5. Take on board the realities of the new digital economy, including phenomena such as 3-D printing and the rise of hub-based digital networks, thereby reassessing how your foreign factory network can best be used to maintain and strengthen your competitiveness.

8 ➡

International Finance

Five Learning Objectives

1. To define economic exposure and its strategic significance for the MNE.
2. To describe the various approaches to manage and minimize economic exposure.
3. To explain the added complexities surrounding economic exposure when MNEs operate multiple business models, following from a high level of diversification.
4. To introduce a new-economy financing tool, namely, crowdfunding, that could be used by resource-constrained MNEs to raise financial resources and to manage potential economic exposure across national borders.
5. To explain the linkages between the MNE's administrative heritage and its organization of the risk exposure management function, thereby also paying attention to the advent of digital assets.

This chapter examines Lessard and Lightstone's recommendations for how MNEs should deal with economic exposure. Economic exposure (also known as operating exposure) is the impact (i.e., the effect on the net present value of the MNE's future income streams) of changes in real exchange rates relative to the MNE's competitors. To minimize this impact, Lessard and Lightstone recommend that senior managers strive to: (1) have a flexible sourcing structure (i.e., be able to shift production from one country to another quickly and efficiently); and (2) attain the capability to engage in exchange rate pass through (i.e., the capability to raise prices in response to exchange rate fluctuations without losing sales volume). To obtain this second capability, senior managers should try to obtain a market leadership position with highly differentiated products. According to Lessard and Lightstone, senior managers at MNEs should take economic exposure into account when determining their international business strategy (e.g., the likelihood of negative currency fluctuation should be taken into account when assessing location advantages). Lessard and Lightstone also present other specific strategies that senior managers at MNEs can use to minimize their economic exposure. These ideas will be examined and then critiqued using the framework presented in Chapter 1.

Significance

D. R. Lessard and **J. B. Lightstone's** classic *HBR* article on the risk created by volatile exchange rates adds useful aspects of international finance to the discussion of MNE strategies.[1] Though this article was written several decades ago, its substance remains important for multinational strategic management today. In essence, the authors observe that fluctuations in foreign exchange rates create the risk of net present value reduction of the firm's future income streams. This potential value reduction is called economic exposure. It is different from the more conventional transaction exposure (reflecting the risk of financial losses resulting from outstanding but unfulfilled contractual commitments, such as sales contracts in a foreign currency to be fulfilled at a later date; here, the relevant income streams are known, and can often be secured fully in the home country currency through simple hedging instruments) and translation exposure (reflecting the risk of losses resulting from the translation of accounting statements expressed in foreign currencies into the home country currency at consolidation date).

In strategy terms, economic exposure refers to the possible negative effects of largely unexpected changes in exchange rates on a firm's competitiveness relative to rivals. A firm's economic exposure is affected by the geographic configuration of its input and output markets: 'The measurement of [economic] exposure requires an understanding of the structure of the markets in which the company and its competitors obtain labor and materials and sell their products and also of the degree of their flexibility to change markets, product mix, sourcing, and technology.'[2]

Here, the issue is not simply to understand how fluctuating foreign exchange rates directly affect a company's income stream through immediate price changes, but rather to gain insights into the longer-term relative impacts of these fluctuations on the income streams of the various firms competing in an industry. If two firms have the same structure in terms of sourcing production inputs from a foreign country and command a similar position in the market in terms of market share, product differentiation, flexibility to shift production, etc., then any changes in the corresponding exchange rates will impact both firms equally and advantage neither firm relative to the other. If, however, one of these firms or a third competitor sources its inputs from a different country, or is very differently positioned in terms of market share, product differentiation, flexibility to shift production, etc., then fluctuating exchange rates will affect the firms differently. Here, the firm with the strongest market position, most differentiated products, and greatest flexibility to shift production will incur the lowest negative impact on the net present value of its future income stream. It is important to note that even purely domestic firms without foreign operations or production imports can incur economic exposure if their market rivals include MNEs whose competitive position is positively affected by exchange rates for internationally sourced inputs.

When assessing economic exposure, it is important to distinguish between 'real' versus 'nominal' exchange rates. Nominal rates refer to the direct exchange ratio between currencies – for example, how many euros or yen one US dollar will buy – while real exchange rates refer to 'changes in the nominal exchange rate minus the difference in inflation rates' between two countries. So, for example, a nominal rate change of 4 per cent with an inflation difference of 3 per cent implies a 1 per cent change in the real exchange rate. Here, the country faced with the higher inflation should experience an equivalent drop in the value of its currency, mirroring the fact that a unit of this currency can now only purchase a lower volume of goods and services.[3]

The distinction between changes in nominal and real exchange rates is important, as it is changes in real exchange rates that affect the level of economic exposure for firms. If, in the very long run, purchasing power parity holds, then (starting from an equilibrium situation) differences in inflation rates and resulting price levels between countries should be precisely offset by corresponding changes in their nominal exchange rates. In that case, changes in real exchange rates would be negligible or close to zero. However, casual empiricism teaches that differences do persist in the medium term (sometimes spanning several years), and it is these real exchange rate fluctuations that create economic exposure risk for companies: 'In the short run of six months to several years, however, exchange rates are volatile and greatly influence the competitiveness of companies selling to the same market but getting materials and labor from different countries.'[4]

For example, a US manufacturer of durable consumer goods that sources, sells, and finances its operations entirely domestically would not be considered exposed to contractual foreign exchange risk in the form of transaction exposure, nor to translation exposure. However, if its main competitors in the market are Japanese, centralized exporters sourcing from Asia, the company is actually exposed to economic risk through the US dollar to yen exchange rate. While the Japanese firms price and sell their products in US dollars, their underlying competitiveness may be largely dependent on yen-based costs. As a result, if the US dollar depreciates against the yen in real terms, then the US manufacturer will enjoy an improved competitive position vis-à-vis its Japanese competitors. But if the dollar's real exchange rate increases, the company's position will be weakened through higher relative costs, and its economic exposure will become visible in the form of a negative impact on its income streams.

Only in cases (again starting from an equilibrium situation) whereby the nominal exchange rate changes between the dollar and yen correspond exactly with differences in inflation rates between the United States and Japan, is purchasing power parity maintained. In this (unlikely) scenario, the companies do not experience any change in their competitive positions due to exchange rate changes, since the real exchange rate does not change and no negative impact on the income stream occurs during that period.

The authors observe, *inter alia*, that economic exposure depends not only on decision making inside the individual firm, but also on choices made by rivals in terms of the geographic configuration of their investments and their sourcing policies. As noted above, a substantial economic exposure may thus result entirely from the international sourcing patterns and foreign production operations of rivals, irrespective of whether the particular firm in question itself engages in any international sourcing and/or has foreign production operations.

In terms of this book's framework, three elements are important. First, economic exposure should be viewed as a parameter that adds uncertainty to the value of a firm's location advantages. It implies that even unfettered, privileged access to location advantages in a desirable geographic area may not lead to long-term competitive advantage if the economic value attributed to these location advantages depends on the evolution of macro-level parameters, such as currency exchange rates. Second, the economic exposure concept also implies that the location advantages benefiting an MNE should be considered not solely in a positive sense and on a country-by-country basis, but also as a portfolio of potential risks for future cash flows. Third, MNEs can choose to develop specific FSAs allowing risk mitigation in the foreign currency area by 'immunizing' their products to economic exposure, thereby allowing full 'exchange rate pass through' (see below).

Companies occupying a market leadership position with highly differentiated products will generally be best positioned to engage in exchange rate pass through, meaning that they can adjust their pricing if necessary to offset any increased costs arising from economic exposure without incurring a loss in sales volume. For such firms, economic exposure is minimal. In the case of an MNE with a geographically dispersed subsidiary network, each subsidiary may face a unique level of economic exposure depending on the industry and geographic market in which it operates, its sourcing policies, and the market power it commands.

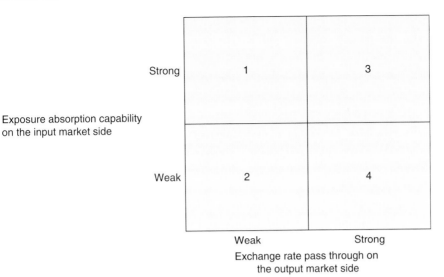

Figure 8.1
A classification of
operating exposure
at the
subsidiary level

Exposure absorption capability
on the input market side

Strong

Weak

1

3

2

4

Weak

Strong

Exchange rate pass through on
the output market side

Figure 8.1, inspired by the Lessard and Lightstone paper, describes the situation faced by each MNE unit in terms of two parameters.

First, there is each unit's capability relative to rivals to adjust its sourcing structure, and thus its cost position, to a potential new exchange rate reality. This is weak or strong exposure absorption capability on the input market side, measured on the vertical axis. It is important to realize that the value of the unit's exposure absorption capability needs to be assessed relative to competitors: even if the unit's sourcing structure is relatively inflexible, its absorption capability would still be 'strong' if its rivals are faced with the same situation of having to import materials from the same input markets, characterized by real exchange rate increases.

Second, there is each unit's capability to 'pass through' changes in real exchange rates: is the subsidiary in a position to pass any price changes on to its customers, without a loss of volume and thus income? This is weak or strong exchange rate pass-through capability on the output market side, measured on the horizontal axis.

Quadrant 3 describes the most desirable situation, where economic exposure effects are absent. The MNE unit is able to make the necessary adjustments on the input market side relative to rivals to reduce the effect of real exchange rate changes. At the same time, its market position is sufficiently strong that any cost increases can be translated into price increases for customers without a loss of business.

Quadrant 2 is clearly the least favourable (1 and 4 being intermediate cases), since the MNE unit lacks any exposure reduction capability in its supply chain. MNEs in this quadrant typically sell commodity-type products, the sales of which can be greatly affected by even a small price increase (i.e., there is high price elasticity of demand). This is typical for subsidiaries that import products from the parent company home base (e.g., in retail) and that lack a strong market position in the host country (e.g., are faced with other, larger providers of a similar product). If the home country real exchange rate increases and the subsidiary is fully dependent on supplies from the home country, whereas rivals in the host country source domestically, then economic exposure may substantially affect the subsidiary's profitability and growth, since any price increase imposed on customers will lead to a substantial drop in sales volume. Hence, the subsidiary will need to engage in a difficult trade-off between reduced profitability and lower sales.

The authors provide the example of Laker Airways, a UK-based airline that was instrumental in creating a commodity-type market for air travel in the early 1980s. Because it targeted primarily UK-based customers, its income was primarily in UK currency, namely, in British pounds. When the real exchange rate of the pound decreased vis-à-vis the US dollar, Laker Airways' income, expressed in British pounds, did not increase substantially (given the relative lack of US-based travellers using the airline). However, its costs expressed in British pounds did, because it had purchased aircraft with fixed payments to be made in US dollars. This asymmetry between its rising costs in US dollars, leading to much higher payments expressed in British pounds, and the impossibility of passing on these rising costs to its low-budget, UK-based travellers, led to the firm's bankruptcy.

What are the implications of the above for MNE strategy, apart from the rather simple observation that differentiated products are more likely to allow exchange rate pass through, and thus immunization against economic exposure? The authors conclude that: 'In the long run, managers should consider [economic] exposure when setting strategy and worldwide product planning.'[5] Companies that hedge their transaction exposure, but fail to take economic exposure into account may be actually raising their total exposure.[6]

From their research, they suggest that companies typically manage economic exposure through one of three approaches, which tend to be more strategic in nature than the more administratively oriented, currency-hedging instruments available for managing contractual exposure.

In the first approach, each business unit is assessed individually, and each unit therefore configures its own operations in such a way as to reduce its specific economic exposure. This strategy entails a trade-off between increased production costs and lowered risks (e.g., a higher number of operating plants can be established in various countries or regions at the expense of gaining economies of scale).

The second approach reflects a company-wide perspective, whereby a portfolio of businesses and operational structures is selected with offsetting exposures, which balance one another (similar to investment management principles underlying the creation of diversified mutual funds). The result of such diversification is a lower total rate of exposure across the company, even though individual units may continue to have higher levels of risk on their own.

The third and final approach incorporates flexibility in operational planning. Here, the company exploits fluctuating exchange rates by switching production between factories. Here, again, a trade-off is necessary between the increased costs of carrying excess capacity (so as to allow production transfers) on the one hand, and reduced economic exposure risks on the other.

As a final note, the authors suggest that managers who cannot set company policy on economic exposure should not be held responsible for the economic exposure effects of volatile exchange rates. When assessing the performance of these managers, senior management should reduce their own bounded rationality problem by adjusting either performance indicators or goal-based expectations to eliminate the economic-exposure effects on performance of fluctuations in real exchange rates. The authors note, however, that these types of administrative adjustments will be insufficient, and that real bounded rationality reduction will require substantial investment in communication: 'Highly reliable models and hence correct performance or budget adjustments will probably be impossible. This uncertainty underscores the need for open and continuing communication between top executives and operating managers to improve understanding of these exposures and also to anticipate responses to possible exchange rate scenarios.'[7]

Context and Complementary Perspectives

As noted above, Lessard and Lightstone's article was written more than thirty years ago. At that time, floating exchange rates were becoming more volatile than they had been in previous decades when many currencies in developing countries were pegged to benchmarks such as the US dollar. There was currency instability in Latin America and Asia, and several countries – including Mexico, Argentina, and Thailand – experienced acute financial crises and sudden devaluations of their currencies.

The demise of the Soviet empire in the early 1990s also brought new volatility to the currencies of Eastern Europe and Central Asia, which had previously been pegged to the Russian rouble under a centrally planned communist system. Lessard and Lightstone also observed that countries were increasingly following divergent monetary policies in managing their own domestic economies. One significant exception to this trend emerged in the decade following the publication of their article, when several member states of the European Union decided to link their currencies and national monetary policies more closely together through the European Monetary Union and the introduction of the Euro, though this currency itself has been under fire as of 2011, thereby increasing volatility of European financial markets.

The authors also noted the move away from American hegemony, and the rise of triad power: 'The United States no longer has a 70% or 80% world market share in key industries but shares markets more equally with Europe and Japan.'[8] This statement is still valid today, except that China has replaced Japan as the main Asian economic power, and is now the largest manufacturing centre in the world. In the present, triad-based regional system with large MNEs from Asia, Europe, and North America competing internationally in the same industries, fluctuations in the currencies of both traditional powerhouse economies and newly emerging low-cost production regions continue to impact the operating profits and exposure risks of MNEs around the globe.

A first complementary perspective on this issue of international financial management is provided in the *SMR* piece 'A new playbook for diversified companies', co-authored by **Ulrich Pidun**, **Ansgar Richter**, **Monika Schommer** and **Amit Karna**.[9] In this article, the authors provide a fresh perspective on the issue of diversification, which typically takes the form of producing more distinct product lines or serving a higher number of distinct markets.

Higher diversification is often intuitively perceived as having an inverted U-shaped association with firm-level performance. At low levels of diversification, an increase thereof leads to knowledge sharing across products and markets, and to the wider distribution of overhead and other sunk costs (e.g., the R&D expenditures and marketing costs needed to build FSAs). However, higher levels of diversification after a certain threshold is reached are expected to undermine firms' value creation and performance, especially when they diversify into unrelated businesses. Senior management may be tempted to diversify beyond this threshold for efficient governance, in order to gain higher compensation and to reduce takeover risks. But in the longer run, this will typically have a negative effect on performance. As a result, many large diversified firms have divested out of some of their non-core businesses. As a few examples, US-based Kraft Foods spun off its North American grocery operations, while Hewlett-Packard separated its activities in services and software from the manufacturing of printers and personal computers. The German MNE Siemens spun off its division specialized in medical technology.[10]

Nevertheless, many large firms do not appear to suffer from the supposed curse of high diversification. For example: '[the US MNE conglomerate] Alphabet and [the Indian MNE conglomerate] Mahindra Group are thriving in multiple lines of businesses'.[11] In addition, in financial markets that are efficient, or moving towards greater efficiency, over-diversified firms will tend to disappear, so that the average returns to properly governed diversified companies in countries with well-functioning financial markets may actually increase. The authors meta-analyzed all scholarly studies published in the

1962–2016 period, and showed that: (1) although the effect of unrelated diversification on performance was negative, this negative effect was much lower at the end of the period; and (2) the effect of related diversification on performance was positive throughout the period. Apart from the fact that many national financial markets have become more efficient over time, through higher transparency and disclosure (and thus less bounded rationality) and better external monitoring (meaning less bounded reliability), the important question that should be raised at the micro-level is: 'How can multi-business companies manage their portfolios for success?'[12]

The authors provide a three-step guidance for successfully managing highly diversified companies. The *first step* they recommend is to 'limit the number of business models in the portfolio and support each one with a strong, cohesive operating model'.[13] Successful companies, including MNEs especially, diversify using their dominant business model(s), not by just adding new products or markets with each of these requiring a completely separate business model. Importantly, 'successful diversified companies tend to have a dominant logic governing their portfolio that allows them to leverage expertise and experience across a wide range of businesses'.[14] For example, London- (UK-) based EasyGroup, established in 1995, successfully diversified from EasyJet (a low-cost airline), into EasyBus, EasyCar, EasyHotel, EasyCoffee, EasyGym, and EasyMoney because it shared the same higher-order capabilities across product lines and markets, in this instance, the FSAs of low-cost, no-frills service offerings.

The recommended *second step* for successful diversification is to 'tailor the corporate parenting strategy to the portfolio'.[15] Corporate parents must share effectively with their diversified units, a variety of FSAs, such as financial resources, expertise in strategy formation, avenues to achieve cost advantages, as well as operational and human resources management skills. In the case of an MNE, these would include especially the company's non-location-bound FSAs. However, as explained in Chapter 1, each firm must develop its own patterns of capability building. For example, in terms of governance, the firm must balance in its portfolio strategy the requisite level of centralization (with strong involvement from the head office) and the needs for decentralization towards the units (with supposedly weaker head office involvement). On the FSA sharing and development front, there is also the need to balance the needs of subsidiaries to access – and exploit – company-wide capabilities (especially in highly regulated environments), with the needs of these same subsidiaries for maintaining autonomy and for exploring autonomous initiatives, in the sense of crafting novel resource combinations (especially in highly dynamic industries with dispersed innovation).

The recommended *third step* is to 'allocate resources based on clear portfolio roles'.[16] 'Disciplined capital allocation' is viewed as the most important and effective internal mechanism by which corporate parents, including MNEs, can implement a coherent strategy involving all their subsidiaries that are dispersed across product and geographic space.[17] Such disciplined capital allocation should be at least partly based on the specific roles of subsidiaries in the overall portfolio, much in line with Bartlett and Ghoshal's analysis of subsidiary roles,[18] as described in Chapter 5.

The above steps highlight the added complexities faced by diversified MNEs when trying to address a variety of finance challenges. Lessard and Lightstone's classic *HBR* paper discussed the challenges of economic exposure, which can be solved through: (1) a flexible sourcing structure on the input side; and (2) exchange rate pass through on the output side. In practice, the above three steps require extensive collaboration between the corporate head office and subsidiaries, especially in **international coordinators** and **multi-centred MNEs**.

Pidun *et al.*'s article points to the added complexities surrounding economic exposure and many other financial management sub-functions, when the MNE has a higher level of diversification, whether in product or market terms, or both. *First*, there cannot be a wide variety of ways in which financial management is conducted in the MNE to accommodate the needs of the diversified portfolio of subsidiaries. One dominant logic (admittedly with some allowance for variation) must prevail to maintain coherence, and to economize on bounded rationality and bounded reliability. *Second*, company-wide FSAs in financial governance must be shared and utilized across the diversified portfolio, and reasonably tailored to subsidiary-level needs, especially as a function of industry- and country-level requirements. *Third*, in line with the subsidiary roles identified in Chapter 5, the head office of the highly diversified MNE must pursue the disciplined allocation of resources among its subsidiaries, based on their assigned (and sometimes assumed) roles. Subsidiaries are not all created equal, and whether in the context of managing economic exposure, capital budgeting, or other financial sub-functions, some units' voices will be heard more loudly and carry more weight because of proven past reliability than other ones. If the disciplined capital allocation does not fit some units at all, divestment is an option.

Gary Dushnitsky, Massimiliano Guerini, Evila Piva and *Cristina Rossi-Lamastra* provide a second complementary perspective on the issue of international financial management in their *CMR* piece. The complexity of international financing deals has grown exponentially in the past decades, often with many, highly technical contractual clauses benefiting the financial intermediaries involved (e.g., imposed safeguards that amount to providing core FSAs as collateral, or *ex ante* programmed debt-to-equity conversions). Paradoxically, this has sometimes led entrepreneurial firms to turn directly to financial markets instead of intermediaries – for example, by accessing a new-economy financing tool, namely crowdfunding.[19] Crowdfunding can be defined as: 'The practice of funding a project or a venture by raising many small amounts of money from a large number of people, typically via the Internet.'[20] There are different types of crowdfunding models, with two of these being especially relevant in the sphere of international business. First, the *lending model*, whereby crowdfunders, as debt holders, receive interest on the funds they have provided. Second, the *equity model*, whereby crowdfunders de facto gain equity through their invested funds, and subsequently dividends and voting rights. This new funding approach became popular among resource-constrained entrepreneurial start-ups, especially during and after the financial crisis in 2008, when other sources of funds sometimes became difficult to access for small and young companies.

Dushnitsky and his colleagues conclude that for now: 'National boundaries play a significant role in shaping the creation of crowdfunding platforms.'[21] They argue that such platforms are 'associated not only with economic and entrepreneurial activity, but also with the existence of supportive legal environments as well as certain culture traits'.[22] In other words, the success of crowdfunding transactions much depends on national location advantages.[23] Importantly, in the context of the platform operators themselves, the authors argue that the practice may increasingly attract incumbent firms as operators and potentially larger firms as fund seekers.

Dushnitsky *et al.* also report that more than 60 per cent of crowdfunding platforms are still domestically oriented. As these platforms internationalize themselves or become accessible to firms operating across national borders, however, crowdfunding is likely to become a new source of funding for resource-constrained internationalizers. Crowdfunding could thereby become an effective vehicle for small, innovative internationalizers to reduce or diversify foreign exchange rate risks, by utilizing geographically dispersed crowdfunders for specific projects.

In the long run, crowdfunding platforms providing international services could develop non-location-bound FSAs in their own right, mirroring the situation of 'crowdsourcing'. With crowdsourcing, firms aim 'to gather global ideas and solutions to address the latent needs of foreign customers'. A number of technology start-ups have utilized successfully crowdsourcing for the rapid internationalization of their entrepreneurial business from inception.[24] For example, 360Cities, a publishing platform of photos founded in Prague, Czech Republic, in 2007, used crowdsourcing to access millions of panoramic photographs of worldwide locations from professional photographers all over the world.[25] The firm 99designers, an online marketplace for graphic designs founded in Melbourne, Australia, in 2008, utilized crowdsourcing to enable small businesses in need of logos, websites, mobile apps, etc. to work with artists, graphic designers, web designers, and advertisement designers from global communities at affordable prices.[26] Threadless, a T-shirt company established in Chicago, United States, in 2000, crowdsourced customizing novel T-shirt designs to an online community of artists, graphic designers, and even the general public across national borders.[27] The main challenge facing technology start-ups using crowdsourcing is to attract 'good crowds' from all over the world that will not only provide necessary expertise and ideas to the start-ups, but also purchase the start-ups' products.[28] Assuming that crowdfunding as a financing tool were to follow a pathway to international development similar to that of crowdsourcing, the platform operators could bring together innovative internationalizers with crowdfunders specifically interested in their business, and who could potentially purchase some of the international new ventures' outputs, in addition to providing financial resources.

This new way of sourcing financial capital internationally, and circumventing conventional financial intermediaries, might also be helpful in alleviating any economic exposure challenges these entrepreneurial firms may face, especially at the input side, as highlighted by Lessard and Lightstone. Foreign suppliers of funds could easily be compensated in the same currency they provided, if these funds were used to set up local operations and generate at least some sales in the relevant currency. The potential use of crowdfunding by internationally operating firms is in line with Rugman's (1979) argument that these companies can gain from some form of international-risk diversification by going abroad, in this case by accessing financial resources through new vehicles that are geographically dispersed across countries and regions, thereby possibly also smoothing out exchange exposure risks.[29]

MANAGEMENT INSIGHTS

Lessard and Lightstone's analysis should be considered not simply as the study of one specific, functional area in international business. Rather, it sheds additional light on the nature of location advantages: any configuration of location advantages, whether in input or output markets, carries risks, in this case the risk of unexpected exchange rate fluctuations affecting future cash flows. In response, MNEs should aim to develop, as an FSA, a central routine that integrates economic-exposure information into the capital budgeting evaluation of large investment projects. This is especially relevant in the context of large-scale foreign expansion. The development of this type of FSA reflects Pattern I in this book's framework (see Figure 8.2). However, especially for large subsidiaries, it may be useful to combine this internationally transferable knowledge with local capabilities in the particular affiliates, following Pattern III. Obviously, especially in the absence of a central economic exposure policy, one would also expect Pattern IV to occur, whereby individual affiliates learn how to protect themselves against the hazards of economic exposure.

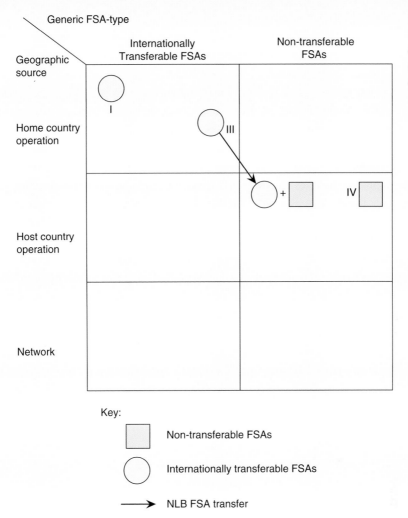

Figure 8.2
Patterns of FSA
development from
managing operating
exposure in MNEs

This last pattern allows us to identify a first limitation of Lessard and Lightstone's story line, namely the suggestion that operations managers lacking responsibility for setting economic-exposure policy should not be held account-able for performance differentials resulting from such exposure. The problem is that many large MNE subsidiaries, operating without strict firm-wide economic-exposure policies or guidelines, have substantial autonomy in their supply chain management processes and targeting of markets – actions that create economic exposure. Chapters 5, 6, and 7 addressed precisely this issue of strategic leader-type subsidiaries benefiting from substantial autonomy and in some cases developing their own knowledge bases. Why should the managers of such subsidiaries be exempted from the risks resulting from economic exposure?

How is this different from any other type of external risk facing the entrepreneurial MNE subsidiary, such as unexpected new restrictions on business imposed by government agencies, or technological changes making existing product lines obsolete?

The reality is that subsidiary managers who can influence the supply chain management of their own operations, as well as the geographic markets where they will operate, should be held responsible for the economic exposure they have created. The key managerial challenge is not to exempt individuals who have somehow been forced to accept the economic-exposure policies of the MNE corporate headquarters from being accountable for the consequences thereof. On the contrary, the much more common challenge, arising in the absence of a strictly imposed firm-level economic-exposure policy, is to make subsidiary managers responsible for the economic exposure they create themselves through their own decision making at the affiliate level. This averts a bounded reliability problem whereby these subsidiary managers could argue that poor results are the outcome of unfortunate external circumstances.

A second limitation of Lessard and Lightstone's *HBR* piece, much in line with mainstream scholarly thinking in international business strategy on the linkages between strategy and the finance function,[30] is that the way to address economic exposure – and how to link it with strategy – will depend critically on the MNE's administrative heritage. Here, the nature of the MNE's FSAs, its internal organization, and its historical trajectory of location decisions will largely determine the content and process of international financial management decisions.

In the case of a **centralized exporter** (e.g., a Japanese firm exporting to the United States), shown in Figure 8.3, the main economic exposure at the firm level results from all production occurring in the home country. Two questions then arise. First: on the input market side, is the firm's supply chain, often managed primarily through contracting with external parties, sufficiently flexible that the firm can change suppliers rapidly and effectively in case of high economic exposure? This is usually not the case if the main part of the cost structure is incurred at home, in the home country currency. Second, and usually more important: on the output market side, are the exchange rate pass-through problems (caused by a high price elasticity of demand) sufficiently threatening to support moving production into a particular host country, thereby creating a more decentralized production system?

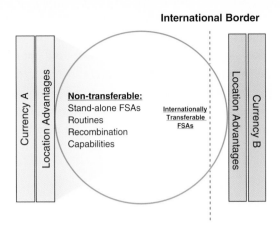

Figure 8.3
Centralized exporter:
Operating exposure
from changes in the
real exchange rate
between the
currencies of
countries A and B

The central circle out of the home country triangle, tangent to the host country's LAs, means that the firm's NLB FSAs allow for a strong exchange rate pass-through capability in the output market: unfavourable changes in exchange rates, leading to price increases in the host country's currency, are simply passed on to host country customers without loss in exported sales volume. The areas on the extreme left and right, named Currency A and Currency B, reflect macro-level location characteristics affecting the real exchange rate between the currencies of countries A and B.

Case example American film producers typically operate as centralized exporters. One classic instance of the currency exposure they face unfolded in 1999 and 2000 when the Euro plunged against the US dollar. The Euro slumped from US $1.17 on 1 January 1999 to US $1.07 in mid-1999, and then to US $0.89 in mid-2000. This was bad for American film producers, as Europe was an important market for them. They usually pre-sell the foreign rights before a film goes into production, and presales to major continental European distributors often account for nearly a third of the movie's total revenues.

The international movie business is almost exclusively priced in US dollars. The rise in the value of the dollar made American movies too expensive for European distributors. As a result, American producers found it hard to pre-sell the foreign rights.

In response, both American producers and European distributors tried to look for ways to deal with exchange rate fluctuations. European distributors sought creative financing, such as stretching out payments or setting a floor price with additional payments for future currency appreciation; American producers talked about lowering prices or switching to contracts in euros for their foreign rights.[31] ∎

In the case of a ***multi-centred MNE***, shown in Figure 8.4, the economic exposure challenge is really the opposite of the one characterizing the ***centralized exporter***: here, the firm's overall economic exposure results from the individual exposures of all the foreign affiliates. In a conventional firm of this type, there is no powerful, centralized treasury function because all host country subsidiaries have substantial autonomy. Here, economic-exposure challenges will usually be addressed at the subsidiary level, and solutions are more likely to involve changing international suppliers on the input market side rather than making changes on the output market side. A change in this decentralized approach is likely to occur only as one ingredient of a much larger move towards more balance between the centre and the subsidiaries. Here, location-bound FSAs become increasingly complemented by an infusion of non-location-bound capabilities where useful; a centralized exposure management tool may be part of such a move.

Figure 8.4
Multi-centred MNE:
Overall exposure
from the individual
exposures of all
foreign affiliates

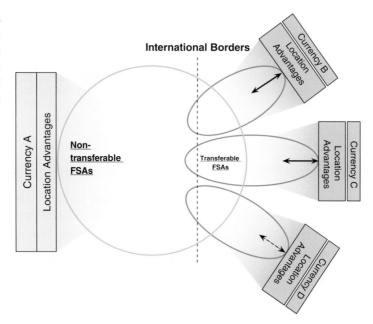

Each subsidiary commands its own exchange rate pass-through capability (weak or strong) when serving its host country market, as shown by the three double-headed arrows in the host market space. The bold arrows for country B and country C represent a strong exchange rate pass-through capability in these countries, whereas the dotted arrow for country D suggests a weak exchange rate pass-through capability in that country. Currency A versus Currency B, Currency A versus Currency C, and Currency A versus Currency D as shown here reflect macro-level location characteristics affecting the real exchange rates between the currencies of countries A and B, A and C, and A and D, respectively.

Case example As discussed in Chapter 1, the French MNE Lafarge (merged with Swiss cement company Holcim to form LafargeHolcim) is a typical multi-centred MNE. One of the world's largest manufacturers of building materials, Lafarge historically managed exposure using both its central treasury department and its subsidiaries. Due to the local nature of its business, in most cases operating costs and revenues were in the same currency. When purchase and sale transactions were performed in currencies other than this prevailing functional currency (usually the domestic currency) at the subsidiary level, the subsidiary managers themselves were allowed to address elements of economic exposure. Lafarge also expected each subsidiary to borrow and invest excess cash in its functional currency. At the same time, the corporate treasury department attempted to reduce the overall exposure by netting purchases and sales in each currency on a global basis when possible.[32] Even in 2018, subsidiaries in the merged entity still faced the same industry circumstances, with substantial decentralization of currency management decisions.[33] ∎

The growth of **international projectors** (shown in Figure 8.5) can produce substantial new economic-exposure problems. This occurs when new subsidiaries replicate not only home country production patterns, but also home country supply chain strategies (with contracts in foreign currencies from the perspective of the host country subsidiary). This may create economic-exposure challenges if the subsidiaries' exchange rate pass-through capabilities are weaker than those in the home country, especially if the subsidiaries' market position is much weaker than in the home country. The upshot is that it may be easier to introduce a centralized economic-exposure management system in these companies than in **multi-centred MNEs.**

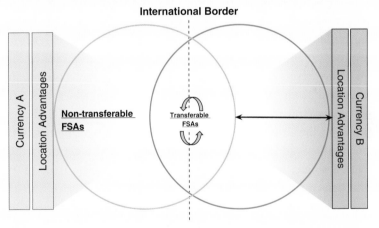

International Border

Non-transferable FSAs

Transferable FSAs

Currency A — Location Advantages

Location Advantages — Currency B

Figure 8.5
International projector:
Centralized exposure management

The firm operates a centralized exposure management system, meant to reduce overall operating exposure risks faced by the firm, but the unique currency exposure position of each subsidiary co-determines the functioning of this central system (shown by the curved arrows in the middle, connecting the two triangles across home and host countries). The exchange rate pass-through capability of each subsidiary depends on the specific inputs it is mandated to access in the host country and/or the specific outputs it must sell in the host country (shown by the bold double-headed arrow in the triangle of the host country). Currency A and Currency B as shown here reflect macro-level location characteristics affecting the real exchange rate between the currencies of countries A and B.

Case example As a classic case, before 1994, Goodyear mostly imported supplies for its Mexican plant and then sold the plant's output to local Mexican customers. However, in December 1994, the crash of the peso dramatically decreased the domestic demand for Goodyear tyres by more than 20 per cent, or 3,500 units a day. Goodyear managers had only two options: to downsize or to look for new export markets. The headquarters and the Mexican subsidiary managers worked together to export the Mexican production, mostly to the United States, but also to Europe and South America.[34] ▪

Case example General Motors' (GM's) centralized treasury team has historically dealt with the hedging of currency risks. GM's overall foreign exchange (FX) risk management approach was designed to meet three primary objectives: '(1) reduce cash flow and earnings volatility, (2) minimize the management time and costs dedicated to global FX management, and (3) align FX management in a manner consistent with how GM operates its automotive business.' One commonly used managerial practice shared within the company that resulted from this general philosophy was to hedge 50 per cent of all commercial (operating) exposures, and deviations from this were viewed as special situations.[35] ▪

Finally, for ***international coordinators***, shown in Figure 8.6, managing economic exposure is usually completely integrated into their overall strategy. This MNE type's main strength is precisely the coordination of internationally dispersed operations, with substantial product and knowledge flows that may be traded internally and externally in a variety of currencies and may be exposed to a broad spectrum of external risks. In the case of commodities, as in many resource-based industries, the main protection against economic exposure is to add value that makes the products more differentiated (a common strategy in the petrochemical and chemical industries), so as to improve the firm's exchange rate pass-through capabilities. Of course, if no such value is added and the products remain commodities (in the extreme case with a single, world market price), then there is no issue of exposure pass-through capability. The firm has to accept the world price, and its only defence against economic exposure (assuming its cost structure is not incurred in the same currency as the world price) is the use of financial instruments such as currency swap agreements.

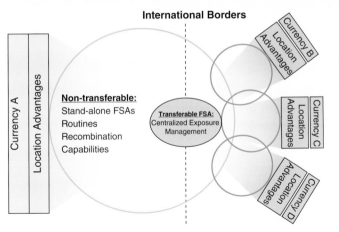

Figure 8.6
International
coordinator:
Network
optimization

The firm's centralized exposure management system acts as an FSA to optimize results for the network as a whole (shown by the core circle across international borders). Impacts of this central system on individual subsidiaries are considered secondary. Currency A, Currency B, Currency C, and Currency D as shown here reflect macro-level characteristics affecting real exchange rates, and can influence the complex network linkages that exist among subsidiaries in countries A, B, C, and D.

Case example Statoil (subsequently StatoilHydro, and renamed as Equinor in 2018), is a Norwegian energy company and one of the largest oil firms in the world.[36] It does business in all the vertically related activities associated with petroleum and petrochemical products, such as exploration, production, processing, transport, sales and trading of crude oil, natural gas, and refined products.

The firm's petroleum and petroleum products are priced on world markets, and primarily in US dollars. However, costs and cash disbursements are to a large extent denominated in Norwegian kroner. Thus, fluctuations in exchange rates could have significant effects on the firm's operating results. To manage its exchange risk, it utilizes different types of foreign exchange contracts such as hedges, forward foreign exchange contracts, and non-functional currency swaps. At the same time, the firm also enters into commodity-based derivative contracts (e.g., futures, over-the-counter forward contracts, market swaps).[37] ■

A third limitation is that Lessard and Lightstone detail the benefits of a flexible sourcing structure without also addressing its costs. They are correct that a flexible sourcing structure (the capability to quickly shift production from one country to another) yields a strong exposure absorption capability on the input market side, with all the benefits they discuss.

However, exposure absorption capability is not the only legitimate goal of international business strategy. As we saw in Chapter 7, Ferdows would strenuously object to Lessard and Lightstone's view, pointing out that at least some factories should be considered long-term investments. A factory that is no longer the low-cost producer due to exchange rate fluctuations can still make contributions in other ways. For example, it can be the company specialist in a knowledge area, develop best practices in a product area, innovate, or develop new FSAs. Realizing these benefits typically requires long-term commitment. Thus, there is a trade-off between the benefits of a flexible sourcing structure and the benefits of long-term commitment. This trade-off must be assessed for each plant in the MNE network.

Strategic Challenges in the New Economy

Vijay Govindarajan, *Shivaram Rajgopal* and *Anup Srivastava*, in their new-economy contribution published in the *HBR*, observe that large companies must publicly disclose their business operations in their financial statements, following the Generally Accepted Accounting Principles (GAAP).[38] The problem is that GAAP-approved financial statements do not necessarily provide investors with relevant and valuable information about the main value drivers of modern digital companies. Bounded rationality challenges loom large. As one example about a well-known American digital company: 'Facebook announced its quarterly performance . . . that exceeded analysts' forecasts, but it lost market capitalization of more than $100 billion in just two hours, because it failed to meet its revenue and subscriber growth targets.'[39] To address these types of concerns, the authors of this article propose a new blueprint for financial reporting of digital companies.

The *first component* of this blueprint builds on the observation that digital companies often generate revenues in ways that are not well understood, due to their unique business model. Again, using Facebook's example, this digital company's primary customers are its daily subscribers and users; however, Facebook generates revenues from its secondary customers, namely companies that post advertisements on its digital platform. It is the primary customer base that determines revenues earned from the secondary customer base, so insight on the primary customers is essential.

The authors therefore suggest that digital companies should disclose how the following value-driving metrics translate into actual revenues. These are especially important for MNEs, so as to determine the main drivers of both existing and potential growth in *revenues* in the domestic versus international markets, thereby reducing bounded rationality challenges:

1. Number of active, primary users;
2. Active users' geographical distribution;
3. Retention rates of active users;

4. Where applicable, average time spent by active customers using platform services of the digital company (or average number of times that platform services are used within a given period);
5. Growth or decline in any of the above metrics.

The *second component* of the blueprint is related to the *cost* side. In digital companies, capital investments (such as investments in digital equipment, servers, and hardware) are often necessary to maintain short-term competitive advantage. All amounts spent on supporting current operations should therefore be treated as ordinary expenses in calculating operating profits, irrespective of whether these items relate to soft or hard assets. In addition, substantive outlays for more future-oriented investments with much higher uncertainty should always be reported separately. Investors can then determine themselves whether these investment expenditures should actually be interpreted as normal capital investments, or should instead be treated as expenditures to be deducted from operating revenues, depending on the perceived reliability of the firm and stakeholders involved. Investors should also be provided with information on one-time or exceptional cost items, so that they can again decide whether or not these items should be treated as operating expenses.

In addition to the above components, the authors suggest that digital companies should carefully define their 'asset units' that are the basis of present and future revenues, for instance 'one new, frequent user of Facebook'; 'one new car joining the Uber fleet'; or 'one new rental unit added to Airbnb'.[40] Senior management should then evaluate the 'lifetime value' of these asset units, which would allow rewarding appropriately the firm's downstream, sales, and marketing activities that have succeeded in acquiring such units.[41]

Digital companies should add all the above information to their normal financial disclosures, as it is this type of information that will reflect the real value-creation potential of their FSAs. There are, of course, limits as to which information firms can disclose. Some of this information goes to the heart of the firms' business model, and thus reflects their underlying FSAs, about which much causal ambiguity may exist, especially when evaluated by rivals (rather than the investors in the firm). Here, bounded reliability problems, and especially opportunism, must be anticipated and prevented, when sharing proprietary business model information with external parties.

According to the classic *HBR* article by Lessard and Lightstone, MNEs should develop capabilities to adjust their current sourcing structure flexibly, and also to pass through changes in real exchange rates when facing economic exposure. The main point from an international business strategy perspective is that MNEs need to tailor their internal financial system to the requirements of the firms' strategy, and this is also the case for digital MNEs.

From the perspective of Govindarajan *et al.*, the main value drivers in modern (digital) MNEs should be correctly understood and monitored by senior managers, as well as by existing and potential investors. Just as the dangers and the outcomes of economic exposure typically do not appear in financial statements required by regulators (at least not transparently), so can the underlying FSAs of digital companies not necessarily be linked directly to the main sources of revenues or capital outlays. Given that the initial international expansion of digital MNEs often follows an ***international projector*** model, the question arises to what extent the intangible and to some extent invisible FSAs of these digital companies are non-location-bound. Neither the underlying FSAs – nor the underlying risks – of domestically successful digital firms expanding abroad through future-oriented projects can be fully understood from conventional financial statements, as, for example, US companies such as Google and Amazon have experienced when venturing outside of their home region, and trying to operate in high-distance environments such as China; in those cases, stronger bounded reliability problems arose than expected, and were triggered by a variety of host country institutions.

Five Management Takeaways

1. Analyze how your company can reduce its economic exposure and achieve the lowest possible negative impact on the net present value of its future income stream.
2. Assess your operating exposure at the level of each subsidiary with regard to the possibility of making adjustments at the input as well as the output market side.
3. Consider the impacts of having multiple business models as is often the case in a diversified firm, on economic exposure management, and more broadly on the firm's international financial management.
4. Discuss the degree of responsibility for economic exposure and financial management, to be held at the subsidiary level, and define clear guidelines on what the head office versus the subsidiaries are responsible for.
5. Examine the impacts of new financing tools such as crowdfunding and new-economy-type business models, on international business opportunities and financial risks.

9

International Marketing

Five Learning Objectives

1. To define the term 'global standardization' and to understand the intellectual arguments in favour of global standardization.
2. To describe a variety of features of national responsiveness for attracting consumers in foreign markets, even when using the Internet in international operations.
3. To explain the new types of location-bound FSAs catering to the specific preferences of host country customers, for success in digital industries.
4. To examine the potential and the constraints of global account management.
5. To identify the managerial challenges associated with simplistic views on the globalization of markets.

This chapter examines Levitt's idea that MNEs should not worry very much about customizing to cultural preferences. According to Levitt, technology has largely homogenized consumer preferences – most consumers simply want quality, reliability, and low price. Therefore, MNEs should focus on offering such products and services. MNEs should standardize their products and services worldwide in order to achieve economies of scale, and should implement global strategies across all markets. These ideas will be examined and then critiqued using the framework presented in Chapter 1.

Significance

'The world's needs and desires have been irrevocably homogenized. This makes the multinational corporation obsolete and the global corporation absolute.'[1] This statement sums up *Theodore Levitt's* bold assertions in his well-written, landmark *HBR* article, 'The globalization of markets'.[2]

In terms of this book's framework, Levitt sees the ***multi-centred MNEs*** being gradually replaced by ***centralized exporters*** and ***international projectors***. He argues that advances in technology, communications, and travel have revolutionized commerce and trade in all parts of the globe, basically conferring additional value to non-location-bound FSAs, and strengthening the MNE's ability to deploy and exploit such non-location-bound FSAs, irrespective of cultural, economic, institutional, or spatial distance.

Customers throughout the world are thirsty for new products that can now be made available universally. While MNEs have traditionally customized their products to cater to perceived cultural differences across countries and regions, these preferences are converging as technology brings the world closer together into one global market. According to Levitt, the majority of the world's consumers want the same thing: high-quality, reliable products at low prices. They are often willing to accept globally standardized products without expensive customization or modifications for cultural preferences if the three above attributes of quality, reliability, and low price are present. Companies that grasp this new 'global' reality, and that can inject these attributes into simplified products coming out of scale-efficient manufacturing processes, will win the competitive battles against those rivals that continue to pursue a polycentric approach of customizing products for different markets, thereby incurring higher costs simply to cater to what are in Levitt's view superficial local preferences.

Levitt's argument in favour of global standardization rests on two foundations. The first is that cultures and national societal tastes are not fixed, but subject to continuous change, with technology guiding such change towards homogenization. According to Levitt: 'technology drives consumers relentlessly towards the same common goals – alleviation of life's burdens and the expansion of discretionary time and spending power'.[3] The force of technology and the allure of modern goods create converging global preferences, and overpower traditional differences rooted in national cultures and historic customs. As a result, cultural preferences follow one of two paths: they eventually lose relevance to economic decision making, or they diffuse to other groups and become the substance of global trends. This is true not only for commodities and high-tech products, but also for 'high touch' goods and services, which are gaining popularity with large consumer groups. ('High touch' refers to items where personal interactions among individuals remain critical, either at the moment of purchase or later, during consumption/usage.) Levitt offers examples such as the worldwide diffusion and gain in popularity of certain ethnic foods (pizza, pita bread, Chinese food), music (jazz, country, and western), and product brands (Coke and Pepsi soft drinks, McDonald's fast food, Sony TVs, Levi jeans).

Levitt's second point builds on the first. Converging tastes now allow companies to offer globally standardized products, harnessing economies of scale to deliver high-quality, dependable goods at low cost. According to Levitt, high quality and low cost are not mutually exclusive objectives: they represent complementary goals achievable through innovation and efficiency. The key is standardized products that allow for economies of scale in production, as well as in downstream activities such as distribution and marketing and in management activities in general. Scale efficiencies translate into lower prices, which are a powerful draw for consumers everywhere. Levitt gives the example of Japanese firms who, despite commanding limited domestic resources, suffering from a high cultural distance vis-à-vis Europe and North America, and lacking traditional marketing departments or market research, have nevertheless 'cracked the code of Western markets', meaning they have found a way to cater to the above-mentioned demand for high-quality, reliable, aggressively priced goods, and have beaten rivals on their own home region turf.

No matter how small or niched a product area may be, there are always equivalent segments in other markets worldwide that allow for a global approach satisfying the above three criteria (quality, reliability, and low price). As a result, neither MNEs nor local firms can continue to rely on their domestic markets as safe havens from global competition.

As an example, Levitt discusses the European strategy of US-based Hoover, a manufacturer of vacuum and laundry machines. The company conducted research on national markets in Europe and identified a number of differences in consumer preferences among countries. Accommodating these preferences through product customizations resulted in shorter production runs and higher costs than if one standardized machine had been produced for the whole region. In contrast, Italian competitors offered lower-cost machines with far fewer of the allegedly preferred features, yet still managed to gain market share, even in high-end markets such as Germany. Levitt concludes that: 'Two things clearly influenced customers to buy: low price regardless of feature preferences and heavy promotion regardless of price.'[4] To Levitt, this example demonstrates that companies need to avoid conforming in a slavish fashion to the different cultural preferences expressed by consumers in various markets.

In fairness to Levitt, he does not in fact 'advocate the systematic disregard of local or national differences'.[5] Nor does he propose that customization based upon fundamental differences such as language or regulatory systems be ignored. Some customization may thus still be required, if all efforts to achieve acceptance of standardized products and to change local preferences have been exhausted.

Finally, despite his uncompromising assertions regarding the need for a global approach to strategy, Levitt concedes that administrative heritage and corporate culture play a large role in determining the success or failure of a firm's managerial efforts: 'There is no one reliably right answer – no one formula . . . What works well for one company or one place may fail for another in precisely the same place, depending on the capabilities, histories, reputations, resources, and even the cultures of both.'[6] This warning acts as a reminder that even when adopting a global approach to marketing, it is effective organization and implementation – namely, the MNE's routines and recombination capabilities – that count.

Context and Complementary Perspectives

'The globalization of markets' was published in 1983, when computers were in their infancy and mobile phones had not yet taken the world by storm. Trade barriers between most countries were still significant, reinforcing national borders and hindering the development of a truly global marketplace. As discussed in earlier chapters, exchange rate volatility and environmental uncertainty were increasing. One could interpret such environmental conditions as conducive to an increased focus on national responsiveness through developing location-bound FSAs. Yet, Japanese firms had proved successful in pioneering a 'global' approach in a variety of industries, including steel, automobiles, and home electronics. Here, export-based strategies (using standardized goods) and international-projector-type strategies appeared to be sure-fire recipes for rapid international expansion.

Levitt, not surprisingly, draws heavily on such Japanese examples, but also outlines successful 'imitators' from all over the world, including even the United States and Western Europe. From his perspective, these successes substantiate his theory that: 'If a company forces costs and prices down and pushes quality and reliability up – while maintaining reasonable concern for suitability – customers will prefer its world-standardized products.'[7]

Given the above classic analysis, a first complementary perspective is provided by **Shu Li**, **François Candelon** and **Martin Reeves** in an *SMR* paper focused on China, as a rapidly growing and potentially attractive market for firms in digital industries.[8] At the time of writing this *SMR* piece in 2018, there were more than 700 million internet users in China. The country was the home-base for half of the ten largest internet companies in the world. And Chinese companies accounted for one-third of the world's start-ups with values of over US $1 billion, most of these being active in online businesses in digital markets.

Despite the economic potential of the Chinese digital market, Western MNEs in the digital sphere have not performed well there. As a few examples, American firms that once had a large or even dominant market position in China, such as eBay, Amazon, Microsoft, Uber, and Airbnb, all saw their market shares collapse and all were outperformed by home-grown Chinese rivals. The poor performance of Western MNEs in China's digital market was in part due to their misunderstandings about the specificities of China's digital market.

The most important specificity was China's weak economic and business infrastructure at the beginning of the digital era, for example, in the retail and information and telecommunications spheres. As a result, digital technology itself became instrumental to supporting the country's baseline economic and business infrastructure. For example, China did not have a modern, nationwide brick-and-mortar retail system, even in the 1990s. E-commerce in China thus created a completely novel shopping option for the rising middle-class consumers, rather than functioning as a complement to existing brick-and-mortar retail, as typically found in developed economies. Chinese digital companies were quick to respond to this opportunity, and focused specifically on domestic customers. As a few examples of this: 'Alibaba's Taobao, the most prominent Chinese e-commerce platform, reached half of the nation's online customers in nine years . . . Alipay, the largest mobile payments provider, hit 50% penetration in China in four years.'[9]

The question then arises what foreign MNEs should do to be successful in the Chinese digital market. The authors have four suggestions in this regard. The *first* suggestion is what they call 'localization', which amounts to the appropriate development of location-bound FSAs, to cater to Chinese customers.[10] This can be achieved in part by empowering local employees to be innovative.

The *second* suggestion is related to 'speed'.[11] The authors argue that the main source of competitive advantage of digital firms in China is fast decision making, not scale, due to low entry barriers in developing online products and services. Fast decision making, when responding to local opportunities, could again be viewed as a location-bound FSA in China, requiring substantial subsidiary autonomy.

The *third* suggestion is 'online and offline integration', which means that foreign digital firms must complement their digital offerings with sufficient 'brick-and-mortar' presence in China.[12] Resource recombination appears very difficult to achieve when relying solely on digital infrastructure. Accessing local resources in China and leveraging digital assets require non-digital assets on the ground.

Finally, the *fourth* suggestion is to engage in 'local ecosystem development', whereby foreign MNEs collaborate with local Chinese partners to become insiders in the country.[13] We discuss the issue of international strategic alliances in greater depth in Chapter 12, but the essence of partnerships around local ecosystem development is often that foreign MNEs meld their non-location-bound FSAs in the digital sphere, with location-bound, customer-oriented FSAs from host country partners.

China's home-grown digital MNEs are likely to pursue increasingly overseas market opportunities themselves, building on their main, non-location-bound FSAs. According to the authors, these FSAs could include fast-decision-making routines in the sphere of technology applications (somewhat similar to the strategic agility concept discussed in Chapter 5) to fulfil unmet market demand. As one example: '. . . in addition to its mobile payment platform, Alipay has launched a range of innovative applications in more than 10 vertical industries, ranging from online outpatient services to car insurance services. [US-based] PayPal Inc. has not followed suit.'[14] In addition, Chinese digital companies' FSAs could also include their willingness to engage in deep collaboration with other partners, in the form of an ecosystem-based approach, to build location-bound FSAs. As an example:

> The strong payment and social network ecosystems of Tencent and Alibaba . . . have helped drive the success of Didi. Riders can both hail and pay for a ride through Tencent's WeChat Pay and Alibaba's Alipay, and then seamlessly share their experience through social channels, such as WeChat and Alibaba's DingTalk . . . Uber's failure to do so is one of the main reasons why it was unable to crack the Chinese market.[15]

But the above example may actually simply reflect location-bound FSAs that allowed these Chinese firms to outperform foreign rivals in China. It is unclear whether fast decision making and the willingness to partner with other firms that command complementary resources actually constitute non-location-bound FSAs for Chinese MNEs. Similar FSAs would commonly be held by digital MNEs in their own home countries. The significant point, however, is that Chinese MNEs are likely to become credible competitors for developed economy digital MNEs in emerging markets. Perhaps the real lesson to remember for Chinese and non-Chinese digital MNEs alike is that superior technology alone will not guarantee success in any host country market.

Li *et al.*'s article, using the context of China's digital market, highlights the limitations of Levitt's prediction that many consumer products businesses would globalize. Levitt's key argument was that technology would steer customer preferences towards homogenization. As a result, MNEs were advised to focus on standardization and gaining economies of scale as a precondition to capture a global leadership position.

But the failure of leading digital companies from developed economies, with the most advanced technologies available, to succeed in China, shows that even in digital industries, features of national responsiveness, and the related need to build location-bound FSAs at the customer end, still do matter. The recommended strategies for MNEs when entering host markets are therefore different from Levitt's. First, MNEs should cater to the specific preferences of host country customers, building on location-bound FSAs. For this purpose, MNEs should empower local employees towards being innovative, especially at the customer end of the value chain. Second, especially in digital industries, strategic agility in the form of fast adaptation to changes in host country markets may be critical to success.

David Arnold**, **Julian Birkinshaw and ***Omar Toulan*** provide a second complementary perspective to Levitt's on the globalization of markets. Their *CMR* article discusses the potential and the limits of global account management.[16]

Global account management can be defined as dedicating specialized resources, typically involving non-location-bound routines, to serve internationally operating customers in an integrated fashion. This implies a move towards standardized supply contracts with these customers, as well as a consistent international platform of predetermined service content and processes. In many cases, this may mean host country subsidiaries lose their ability to alter the marketing mix when serving local operations of international customers with global account status (much in line with Levitt's approach discussed above). Host country subsidiaries must be willing to give up this control: 'Global account relationships cannot work unless both partners are committed to global marketing . . . [I]t is important that there is a compelling demand for a consistent global platform for the agreement.'[17]

On the positive side, global account management, with its focus on standardization, can be interpreted as a logical reaction to the internationalization of large customers eager to gain a tighter grip on their supply chain. From the supplier's perspective, this practice is also in line with the strategy of crafting a stronger customer orientation across borders.

However, Arnold *et al.*, building on research conducted with sixteen large companies, conclude that there are two main pitfalls to effective implementation of global account management. First, if the customer/potential global account is more internationally coordinated than the supplier, then the main effect of global account management may be price squeezes, with little benefit accruing to the supplier except perhaps more certainty about future sales volumes. In this case, the customer has more knowledge than the supplier about pricing in the various international markets. The customer will automatically demand that the lowest price be applied across the board, and may ask for additional volume discounts. The authors observed several instances of this unfortunate outcome for the supplier.

Only if the supplier engages in international coordination to the same level can this type of bounded rationality problem (i.e., the supplier incorrectly predicting the customer's response to a global account management value proposition) be avoided. If the supplier engages sufficiently in international coordination, then price reduction requests by the global account customer can be appropriately anticipated and resisted. Here, the focus of negotiations on the substance of the global account agreement can be redirected from mere cost considerations to strategic issues such as additional value-added services that could be provided by the supplier, including a more streamlined and transparent supply chain, customized services, and help in new product development. This strategic approach to global account management usually only makes sense if the vendor is one of the customer's main suppliers for a specific product range, and the customer is a 'lead user' of the vendor's products.

Second, important internal problems of bounded rationality and reliability occur if the supplier pays insufficient attention to implementation details. Global accounts should be assigned to experienced executives with a long-term vision, rather than to mere salespeople interested in maximizing short-term sales irrespective of profit margins and without an interest in building lasting relationships with the customer.

It is equally critical to recognize that the supplier's local marketing and sales organizations in host countries will often remain active in fulfilling specific contracts with local affiliates of the global account (e.g., distribution and after-sales servicing). In fact, when serving a global account in a specific host country, it may be impossible to separate precisely the value added by the supplier's global account management team from the value added by the local marketing and sales organizations. This is a typical intra-organizational bounded rationality problem that may cause, as a dysfunctional outcome, more bounded reliability challenges at the local level. If local marketing teams feel that the global account management team is just taking business away from them, they may experience severe alienation and may not commit themselves to the accounts. To counter such bounded reliability problems, senior MNE management must communicate clearly to their local marketing organizations what role the global account managers will play, including their interaction routines with the local marketing and sales organizations. Senior MNE management must also provide adequate administrative support at corporate headquarters for their global account managers, who are often physically located close to their assigned customer's international headquarters, in the customer's home country. Finally, senior MNE management must spend sufficient time and energy to enlist the commitment from local marketing and sales organizations in host countries to the principles of global account management, especially through adopting the common best (though expensive) practice of allocating sales commissions to both global account management teams and local marketing and sales organizations (formalized incentive splitting).

In a related and highly actionable *CMR* article, **Noel Capon** and **Christoph Senn** also focus their attention on the business-to-business challenge facing many MNEs, namely the increasing globalization of their (downstream) customers.[18] According to these authors, customer globalization typically has two implications for MNEs acting as suppliers to other MNEs. *First*, their business customers may develop a strong preference for global procurement, meaning procurement that no longer occurs on a country-by-country basis. *Second*, multinational customers may want to engage in a substantial reduction of the number of their suppliers, so as to gain efficiencies, and reduce bounded rationality and bounded reliability challenges in contracting for worldwide operations. Case studies show that 'globalizing procurement often leads to severe supplier reduction . . . Motorola (10,000 to 3,000); Xerox (5,000 to 500); Lucent (3,000 to 1,500); Volkswagen (2,000 to 200); Boeing (30,000 to 10,000); Airbus (3,000 to 500); Barclay's Bank (2,000 to 180); and BAA airports (11,500 to 3,000)'.[19] If an MNE wants to remain a supplier to such global customers, it should engage in carefully designed global customer management (GCM), a concept similar to Arnold *et al.*'s (2001) global account management.

Traditionally, supplying MNEs have served their downstream business customers country by country, with service variability and price differences across different countries. However, as multinational customers move towards global procurement, they aim to achieve uniform global pricing for equivalent goods and services across borders. They can thereby gain a variety of efficiencies in their transactions with suppliers, streamline internal procurement processes, and reduce overall supply costs on a global basis.

GCM is supposed to address this challenge of managing globalizing customers by switching from a country perspective to a customer perspective. As examples of one UK-based and one US-based supplying MNE: 'Over 50% of Rolls-Royce's total revenues come from just two multinational firms – Airbus and Boeing. Procter & Gamble has a revenue stream well diversified by product and geography, yet 30 percent of revenues come from just 10 customers, including 15 percent from the globalizing Wal-Mart.'[20]

GCM programmes have two dimensions. *First* is the 'program size, specifically the number of global accounts and their percent of total firm revenues'.[21] *Second* is the organizational commitment: it includes 'the number of global account managers (GAMs), GAM job assignments (part-time versus full-time), training and development spending, information technology (IT) investment, and senior executive support'.[22] By combining these two dimensions, GCM programmes typically fit into one of the following profiles.

1. The 'limited scope, limited commitment' profile, which could be considered a first stage 'pilot', preparing the supplier MNE for a larger experiment.[23]
2. The 'broad scope, limited commitment' profile, which is typically ineffective in the longer run, for lack of requisite resources and therefore leads to a 'dead-end'.[24]
3. The 'limited scope, deep commitment' profile, whereby MNEs are very selective to give a limited number of customers a 'global purchaser' status and develop appropriate systems to deal with these key customers. Potentially, this is a 'springboard' on the way to achieving broad scope profile.[25]
4. The 'broad scope, deep commitment profile', whereby a GCM programme is a priority in the MNE and becomes 'embedded' in the organization.[26]

Given the four profiles above, three evolutionary patterns of GCM have been observed in company transitions over time.

1. After having adopted a 'pilot' profile, supplying MNEs typically move to either a 'dead-end' or a 'springboard' profile.
2. When firms move to the 'dead-end' profile, they may want to return to the 'pilot' profile and rethink their GCM strategy.
3. After successfully establishing a 'springboard' profile, MNEs can more easily move to the 'embedded' profile.

The authors identified two separate evolutionary paths at IBM and Xerox. IBM followed the sequence of pilot, springboard, and embedded profiles. With each transition, IBM increased its resource commitments and the number of global business customers involved using multiple tiers: 'By 2000 . . . IBM reduced first-tier GCM accounts from 150 to around 60 . . . [However] the second tier consisted of about 4,000 large customers . . . Account team resources for the 60 first-tier accounts increased significantly.'[27] In contrast, Xerox went through a transition path starting with the pilot profile (with six accounts in 1989), unsuccessful dead-end (with an increase to sixty-five accounts by the mid-1990s, and to 125 accounts in the late 1990s), back to pilot using a two-tier structure (with fifteen main accounts in 2003), spring-board (increasing to 35 main accounts in 2005), and then partly to the embedded profile (placing vice-president-level executives in charge of the top seven accounts in 2006). MNEs adopting a GCM programme may spend three to five years with a particular profile, meaning that it could take ten to fifteen years before reaching an embedded profile, assuming this is the desirable endpoint.

Successful GCM strategies usually entail appointing a global account director in the supplying MNE. This manager must design the GCM pro-gramme and interact with the affected geographic managers (e.g., at the national and subsidiary levels) and product managers, with the latter now also needing to focus on the requirements of global accounts. In order to make GCM programmes successful, these should be viewed as long-term investments, leading to new, non-location-bound FSAs for the supplying MNE. Here, both intra-functional and cross-functional collaborations within the MNE are indispensable to reduce bounded rationality challenges (e.g., making sure that all actors involved know about a global customer's needs) and bounded reliability problems (e.g., making sure that GCM routines are meticulously followed by foreign subsidiaries, even when these could benefit from sticking with proven sales practices, as they serve a customer included in the GCM programme). Supplying MNEs should also have strategic agility and adapt swiftly to the evolving needs of their MNE customers included in their GCM programme.

Levitt's work advertised the 'global' approach to international business strategy for MNEs, with centralized exporting and international projection taking on a worldwide scale. This approach builds on a key assumption regarding MNE FSAs: the key FSAs of relevance are non-location-bound ones, predominantly developed in the firm's home market. Figure 9.1 illustrates the concept as it relates to this book's framework. Recall that in earlier figures the three elements on the left-hand side of the figure represent the conventional triad of location advantages, location-bound FSAs, and non-location-bound FSAs in the home country. Figure 9.1 shows Levitt's perspective: non-location-bound FSAs (the core circle in the middle connecting home country and triangles in host countries), embodied in globally standardized products, largely if not exclusively determine the MNE's competitiveness. This is very similar to the Prahalad and Hamel model on the core competence of the corporation discussed in Chapter 2. The difference between the two approaches is that Levitt focuses on high-quality, low-cost, reliable products, whereas Prahalad and Hamel emphasize the knowledge bundles underlying these products.

MANAGEMENT
INSIGHTS

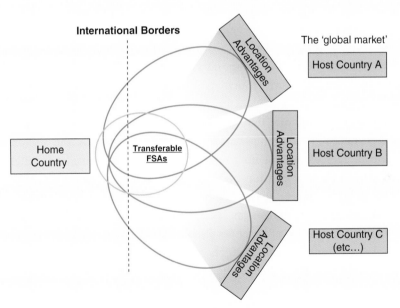

Figure 9.1
Product standardization as the driver of global competitiveness

Absence of LA and LB FSA segments in the home country section on the left-hand side reflects the model's exclusive emphasis on NLB FSAs as drivers of MNE competitiveness. The similar sizes of the host country triangles and their weak separation (shown as these countries being connected through strongly overlapping ovals) reflect the model's emphasis on treating all host countries in a similar fashion using standardized products to serve the 'global market'.

According to Levitt, successful global companies 'sell in all national markets the same kind of products sold at home or in their largest export market'.[28] This perspective mirrors Pattern I from this book's framework, whereby internationally transferable FSAs are developed in the home country and subsequently diffused to national subsidiaries for exploitation in foreign host markets (as with **international projectors**) or embodied in final products exported to the rest of the world (as with **centralized exporters**) (see Figure 9.2). Levitt explicitly contrasts this with the polycentric approach represented by Pattern IV, the pattern most representative of the **multi-centred MNEs**. Levitt views this last pattern of international expansion, whereby location-bound FSAs are developed to cater systematically to host country preferences, as a relic of the past.

These characteristics of Levitt's model allow us to identify its five main limitations. First, Levitt pays relatively little attention to the role of either home country location advantages or host country location advantages in the development of new FSAs. However, as we have explored extensively in earlier chapters, the MNE's presence in particular locations often plays a key role in the company's FSA development processes, and its resulting international competitiveness.

Second, Levitt argues that firms should implement a global strategy across all markets rather than respond excessively to distinct customer preferences in host countries. Even though he does not completely dismiss customization, he views it as a sign of weakness that increases costs, rather than as a strength. However, companies that go too far in implementing a top-down standardized decision-making process risk overlooking both the unique location advantages of various host markets by curtailing subsidiary initiatives, and the need for new location-bound FSAs as a precondition for value creation in those host markets. It is, of course, a question of balance between standardization and customization, as Levitt recognizes, but his suggestion that existing customer preferences in host markets can often be altered to conform to standardized products perhaps oversimplifies the time and effort required to achieve such a change.

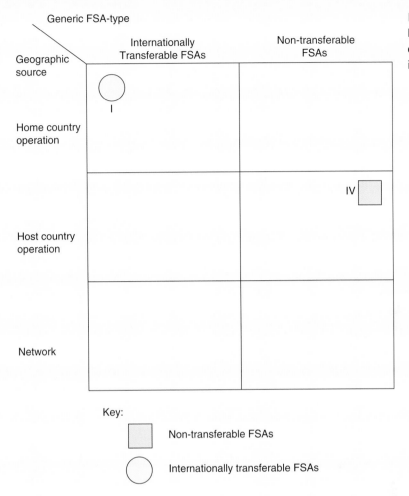

Figure 9.2
Levitt's perspective
of FSA development
in MNEs

Third, and related to the two previous points, when adopting Levitt's mindset, a serious bounded rationality problem may be created: senior managers may well become overoptimistic about the international transferability, deployment, and exploitation potential of their FSA bundles. These bundles may actually contain unnoticed location-bound components, and thus may have a much more limited international deployability and exploitation potential than anticipated.

Fourth, Levitt's perspective on the substance of scale economies appears relatively simplistic. In most industries, there is a minimum efficient size of production, but this minimum efficient size may represent only a small fraction of the world market for a product. In other words, the minimum efficient size and the lowest marginal cost per unit may often be achieved in a single, large economy such as the United States, or in an economic region such as the European Union or the USMCA zone. In these cases, increasing the scale by 'going global' will not decrease the marginal cost per unit. There may also be vastly differing scale economies in the different value chain activities, with upstream activities typically providing the greatest potential for scale economies. Finally, scale can evolve from being the expression of a key FSA to a potential liability or core rigidity, especially in industries where a very high capacity utilization is required to make profits. Here, customizing the MNE's product offering across geographic markets can stabilize sales volumes and profitability.

Fifth, Levitt identifies and contrasts only two types of corporations: 'multinational' ones, engaged in excessive national responsiveness, and global ones, striving to maximize scale economies. However, in reality there are many shades of grey, in the sense of more complex strategies available to MNEs, such as international strategies focused more on scope economies (through international knowledge transfers) than scale economies, and strategies building upon the exploitation of national differences, as found in *international coordinators*.

In this context, it is important to mention that Levitt's suggestion of technology forcing convergence and global commonality is only partly correct: in many sectors, technology has enabled the customization of services and products, through computer-aided design and computer-aided manufacturing (CAD/CAM), 3-D printing, and sophisticated logistics (see Chapter 7), and has reduced the importance of conventional scale economies. Levitt, however, dismisses the benefits of such customization, arguing that the large-scale production of standardized goods is systematically cheaper than smaller-scale production runs. Here, he neglects the fact that in many industries, customization – building on tools such as CAD/CAM and 3-D printing – is actually demanded and highly valued by customers.

In the business-to-business sphere, Arnold *et al.* and Capon and Senn show the need to complement global standardization with strong customization. These authors adopt the vantage point of MNEs supplying goods and services to other MNEs. If an MNE's key customers develop preferences for global procurement, the supplying MNE should follow suit, at least if it wants to remain a preferred supplier over the longer term. It should therefore establish a GCM programme, typically following a number of stages. In such cases, paradoxically, customization becomes a precondition for globalization.

Strategic Challenges in the New Economy

Frank van den Driest, *Stan Sthanunathan* and *Keith Weed* in their *HBR* article make the bold suggestion that large MNEs selling consumer products, such as the Dutch MNE Unilever, need an 'insights engine' to connect better with their customers.[29] They define an insights engine as the 'ability to transform data into insights about consumers' motivations and to turn those insights into strategy'.[30] An effective insights engine ultimately reflects a downstream FSA in the form of superior customer intelligence. It builds on big data related to customer needs, shopping behaviours, preferences for particular products and brands, cultural identity and lifestyle, etc. This 'customer centricity' then becomes a driver of strategy.[31] Ultimately, the insights engine is a tool to reduce bounded rationality challenges related to consumer behaviour.

The authors describe the case of Unilever's insights engine and identify ten features that make it an FSA, and a superior strategy tool of the MNE.

1. **'Data synthesis'**: [32] Integrating and connecting diverse sets of data are viewed as more critical than the size of the data, as a precondition for delivering true insight on consumer behaviour. For example, at Unilever, such data allowed the insight that at least three weeks of consumption are needed for consumers to develop any loyalty to a product. This implies that marketing campaigns should keep such time-related considerations in mind.

2. **'Independence'**: [33] A superior insights engine group should be assembled as an autonomous unit, and be independent from the marketing function, in order to reduce bounded reliability. One common source of unreliability is divided engagement among different functional areas, thereby creating inertia. The insights engine group should be linked directly to senior management, and help other functions achieve their business goals. As one example at Unilever, a dedicated insights engine group at this MNE engaged in new-economy-type 'advertising pretesting'.[34] The dedicated team 'implemented a disciplined (advertising) testing program; using consumer surveys and software that reads facial expressions, the . . . team can now see if people find the ads authentic, relevant, and conversation-worthy – before they are aired'.[35]

3. **'Integrated planning'**: [36] The insights engine group should be involved in all critical stages of the firm's planning cycle, including strategy formation, finance, marketing, sales, etc. At Unilever, the insights engine group participated in the MNE's planning cycle using two software tools. *First*, 'Growth Scout' is to guide the MNE in choosing 'where to play?' by 'mining millions of data points on consumer demand across demographies, regions, and countries to quantify the potential value of deeper category or brand penetration'.[37] *Second*, 'Growth Cockpit' is to help the MNE in formulating 'how to win?' by 'providing a one-screen overview of a brand's performance in a market relative to the category'.[38]

4. **'Collaboration'**: [39] An effective insights engine group should collaborate closely with other functions and with customers, so as to gain the best possible information to be used in the MNE's planning cycle. For example, at Unilever, this group collaborates extensively with IT to establish information-sharing platforms, with marketing to allow effective communications with customers, as well as with other functions relevant to the MNE's planning cycle.

5. **'Experimentation'**: [40] A culture of experimentation, asking for proposals and allowing for errors, is often an important feature of highly performing,

innovative firms. This is similar to the discussion in Chapter 6 on how to promote autonomous initiatives from foreign subsidiaries.

6. *'Forward-looking orientation'*: [41] Many firms selling consumer products have been successful in using internet-based tools to capture present consumers' tastes and preferences online. But a more sophisticated approach should try to predict and influence customers' future behaviours. The insights engine group at Unilever has worked towards achieving this goal with Google. As one example: 'Using a custom tool to analyze hair-related Google searches, the program identifies styling trends and rapidly creates how-to videos featuring Unilever products on a YouTube channel called All Things Hair.'[42]

7. *'Affinity for action'*:[43] An effective insights engine group should participate in strategic decision making with an action-orientation. At Unilever, the goal of this group is 'to inspire and provoke to enable transformational action'.[44] For example, when trying to help the marketing function with market development, the group 'helped break the challenge into three parts – generating more product users, more usage, and more benefits for users. . . . In the area of more usage, the [insights engine] suggested that promoting nighttime use of toothbrushes and toothpaste could boost business growth.'[45]

8. *'Whole-brain mindset'*:[46] An insights engine group should be ambidextrous in using both analytics (i.e., left-brain skills) and holistic thinking (i.e., right-brain skills). One easy tool to promote this ambidexterity in a firm, is through organizing cross-functional workshops: at Unilever, the insights engine group brought together employees from R&D, marketing, etc. 'to brainstorm ways to boost hair-conditioner sales in Southeast Asia'.[47]

9. *'Business focus'*:[48] An effective insights engine group and its action-oriented recommendations should always be business-focused. For example, Unilever tries to '. . . reinforce the connection between insights and growth, [and] staff bonuses are linked to the wider business unit performance. This creates shared accountability with other functions, encourages [insights engine] teams to take responsibility for growth, and motivates them to go the extra mile.'[49]

10. *'Storytelling'*:[50] An insights engine group should hone its skills at delivering their key messages throughout the MNE, using storytelling narratives. At Unilever: 'Although data has its place, the [insights engine] has moved away from charts and tables and toward provocative storytelling, embracing an ethos of "Show, don't tell." Increasingly, the [insights engine] is making its points with memorable TED [technology, entertainment, and design]-style talks and other experiential approaches.'[51]

Levitt's classic argument for the globalization of markets highlighted the supposedly global trend towards homogenized customer preferences, and MNEs' need to earn integration benefits from standardization and economies of scale. The main focus was on non-location-bound FSAs, developed centrally, in close proximity to the MNE's head office.

One key problem with Levitt's argument is that it assumes away bounded rationality challenges at the head office, and bounded reliability problems residing in the conventional functional areas of MNEs. The customer-centric insights engine could be viewed as the equivalent of the R&D function in terms of expected innovative outputs, but at the downstream end of the value chain, instead of the upstream end. Even though the authors do not emphasize the requisite, geographically dispersed nature of the insights engine's activities, in practice many of these activities will be related to foreign customers and host markets. The great paradox in this new world of marketing is that usage of big data and sophisticated tools of intelligence gathering and analysis permit improved customization. Or to put it differently, the insights engine, as a non-location-bound FSA, represents a higher-order capability that facilitates creating novel location-bound FSAs in host countries in support of national responsiveness. As was the case with Capon and Senn's analysis of global customer management in the B2B context, successful globalization requires extreme attention to customization.

The above analysis may be particularly useful to *multi-centred MNEs* that can empower their subsidiaries by making available to them insight engines at the interface between the firm and its heterogeneous foreign customers. But struggling *centralized exporters* and *international projectors*, namely, firms that typically overestimate the non-location-boundedness of their existing FSA reservoirs (see also Chapter 4), may also benefit from this improved customer orientation through establishing insights engines.

Five Management Takeaways

1. Study your firm's product portfolio and assess its potential for global standardization.
2. Examine the potential of the Internet and digital assets to increase your revenues and reduce your costs in international markets.
3. Assess the extent to which digital assets must be complemented with host country brick-and-mortar assets, as well as local partnerships, to be successful against home-grown rivals.
4. Determine the potential and limitations of global customer management in your firm.
5. Reflect on your own industry and firm-level context (e.g., administrative heritage, internationalization strategy) to determine how standardization routines can be usefully combined with extreme customization, whether in the B2B or B2C sphere.

10

Managing Managers in the Multinational Enterprise

Five Learning Objectives

1. To identify best practices in managing expatriates and to outline the roles of these managers in FSA development and transfer processes.
2. To examine the main pitfalls when managing expatriates.
3. To describe how to craft effective organizational change in the MNE through following a rigorous eight-step process.
4. To explain how modern human resources management (HRM) practices in a digital MNE can be nurtured, building on a global community of employees and contributors.
5. To show how successful MNEs can improve their organization-wide capacity to integrate interdependent international operations through 'managing managers'.

This chapter focuses on expatriate managers and examines Black and Gregersen's idea that, when it comes to successfully managing expatriate managers, there are three best practices: '[Successful companies] focus on creating knowledge and developing global leadership skills; they make sure that candidates have cross-cultural skills to match their technical abilities; and they prepare people to make the transition back to their home offices'. In theory, expatriation is supposed to, *inter alia*, produce managers who have an in-depth knowledge of the MNE, understand the pressures leading to benevolent preference reversal in subsidiaries, and can integrate geographically dispersed operations. These ideas will be examined and then critiqued using the framework presented in Chapter 1.

Significance

MNEs must develop managers with a broad mental map covering the entirety of the MNE's geographically dispersed operations. This is critical to the

MNE's long-term profitability and growth, especially in an era when foreign markets are becoming increasingly important contributors to innovation and cost reduction at the upstream end of the value chain, and to overall sales performance at the downstream end. In fact, managers commanding deep knowledge of internal MNE functioning – including the challenges of simultaneously addressing legitimate business objectives/interests at multiple geographic levels within the firm – represent the MNE's key resource to facilitate international expansion and to coordinate geographically dispersed, established operations. Such managers are best positioned to: (1) engage in the international transfer of non-location-bound FSAs from the home nation; (2) identify the need for new FSA development in host countries and facilitate such development; and (3) meld both location-bound and non-location-bound FSAs. These managers are especially valuable when transferring the MNE's routines across borders if those routines include a substantial tacit component. Often, these managers are also the physical carriers of the MNE's recombination capabilities.

Expatriation is the most direct and rigorous way to give managers this in-depth knowledge of the MNE's internal network, as well as the abilities to transfer routines abroad and be a catalyst for recombining resources. Furthermore, expatriate experience gives managers valuable experiential knowledge of the pressures for good faith local prioritization and other types of benevolent preference reversal in affiliates. Consequently, managers with extensive expatriate experience are often the best equipped to reduce bounded rationality problems in headquarters–subsidiary relations, and to anticipate bounded reliability problems arising in host country affiliates.

Unfortunately, while many MNEs incur high costs from sending managers abroad as expatriates, few reap the expected returns because of poor expatriate management practices. These are the main findings presented by **J. S. Black** and **H. B. Gregersen** in their compelling, evergreen *HBR* article on the management of expatriates.[1]

The authors studied the expatriate management practices of nearly 750 US, European, and Japanese firms over a decade. Their data gathering included feedback from the expatriates themselves and from the executives who sent them overseas. The research covered a range of subject areas, with a focus on selection and training, perceived value of the assignment, post-assignment return, and integration back into the organization.

Overall, the authors consider their findings 'alarming'. They note that nearly 80 per cent of all mid- to large-sized MNEs send managers abroad, at a significant cost to the company. With full packages costing two to three times the average equivalent position at home, expatriation is 'probably the single largest expenditure most companies make on any one individual except for the CEO'.[2]

What is the return on such investments? Black and Gregersen's research shows that 10 to 20 per cent of US expatriates actually came back home early because of dissatisfaction or disillusionment with their new position and difficulties adjusting to a new foreign culture. The performance during the assignment of more than 30 per cent of those who stayed did not meet senior management expectations. Of those who completed their assignment, 25 per cent ended up leaving the company within a year of their return – double the average turnover rate in the companies studied.

Often, returning expatriates did not find suitable jobs awaiting them after repatriation. More than 30 per cent were still in temporary positions three months after returning home. Of those who came back to a permanent position, over 75 per cent experienced their position at home as a step down, often associated with substantially less independence than they had become accustomed to during their assignment abroad.

Finally, over 60 per cent of recent expatriates felt that there was little or no opportunity to leverage and productively apply the knowledge gained from their foreign experience once they were back in the home office.

Black and Gregersen attribute these unfavourable outcomes to four common problems in how firms manage their expatriates. First, senior managers in the home country often underestimate the impact of cultural distance on organizational functioning and, as a result, do not invest sufficiently in programmes to select and train properly potential candidates. Second, responsibility for expatriates is often assigned to human resources managers, very few of whom (only 11 per cent according to the authors' research) have any international experience themselves. Most human resources managers thus have little insight into the problems faced by expatriates and the ways to remedy them. Third, senior management in many MNEs view expatriates as being well paid and well looked after, and therefore as having little to complain about. Fourth, in many MNEs, a common misconception persists that expatriates do not need help readjusting after having returned home, despite the fact that changes will likely have occurred during their absence (e.g., company reorganization, appointment of new staff and decision makers, shifts in office politics and corporate culture, and changes to the expatriates' own family and personal life).

Black and Gregersen did identify a few firms with superior expatriate management practices, in terms of job satisfaction, performance, and retention. This group includes MNEs of various sizes, in a variety of industries, but all tend to adopt three best practices in managing expatriates:

> Companies that manage their expats successfully follow the three practices that make the assignments work from beginning to end. They focus on creating knowledge and developing global leadership skills; they make sure that candidates have cross-cultural skills to match their technical abilities; and they prepare people to make the transition back to their home offices.[3]

A key component of the first best practice (creating knowledge and developing global leadership skills) is that both senior management in the expatriate's home country and the individual sent abroad share a clear understanding of the expatriation's purpose and related expectations. What types of knowledge should be acquired or disseminated by the expatriate and what areas of leadership skills should be honed? Black and Gregersen note that careful planning on these issues yields far more long-term benefits to both the company and the employees than expatriate assignments geared simply towards filling an immediate staffing shortage or business need abroad, rewarding successful staff, or shipping unwanted employees to peripheral host country affiliates.

The authors identify Nokia as a best-practice example. At Nokia, the Finnish telecommunications MNE with an internationally decentralized R&D function, creating knowledge (meaning recombining resources) instrumental to new product development is made an explicit objective of expatriate R&D assignments. This helps explain Nokia's success in bringing innovative ideas to market.

The second best practice involves selecting appropriate candidates whose 'technical skills are matched or exceeded by their cross-cultural abilities'.[4] Cross-cultural abilities are often overlooked, as companies tend to send people who are 'capable but culturally illiterate'.[5] In other words, effective resource recombination requires a mix of technical and social skills.

The third best practice involves devoting substantial attention to reintegrating expatriates into their home country after their assignment. Here, successful MNEs 'end expatriate assignments with a deliberate repatriation process'.[6] Such a process allows effective absorption of the former expatriate into the home country's professional and personal environment.

The authors suggest it is the simultaneous adoption of all three practices above that leads to successful expatriate management; adopting only one or two of these practices does not suffice to achieve successful assignments.

Honda of America Manufacturing is cited as 'perhaps one of the best examples of a company that implements all three practices'.[7] Its expatriation approach systematically includes clearly stated expatriate assignment objectives, personal strengths/weaknesses surveys completed by the individuals selected for expatriate assignments, a repatriation job-matching programme triggered six months before the end of the assignment, and a debriefing interview after the expatriate's return to capture what can be learned from the expatriate's experience. Honda's approach has resulted in consistently successful assignments that meet or surpass objectives and expectations, with a turnover rate of less than 5 per cent.

In addition to outlining the appropriate way to manage expatriate employees, Black and Gregersen also discuss the required personal characteristics for employees to be high-potential expatriate prospects. Successful companies look for five characteristics: a drive to communicate, broad-based sociability, cultural flexibility, a cosmopolitan orientation, and a collaborative negotiation style.[8]

Through describing a few real-world examples, the article outlines three different successful approaches MNEs can use to select the most suitable candidates for expatriation. First, the authors give the example of a large, privately held chemicals company that utilizes an informal but efficient selection process. Here, a senior executive personally observes the actions, reactions, and instincts of employees in various cultural settings, especially when they accompany the executive on international business trips. The information resulting from such direct observation is then used to determine whether a particular employee has the potential to become an expatriate.

Second, at the other end of the formality spectrum, LG Group, a large South Korean conglomerate (set up in 1947 as Lucky GoldStar), employs a much more formal approach. The firm uses an extensive survey early in the employee's career to assess individual preparedness for expatriate assignments. It then organizes discussions between potential candidates and senior managers to identify how personalized development and training plans might contribute further to honing the individual's strengths and shoring up weaknesses. This long-term approach to developing individuals ready for expatriation is costly and time intensive, but has led to a 97 per cent success rate in overseas assignments.

Third, Colgate-Palmolive, a US-based company established in 1928 as the result of a merger between Colgate and Palmolive-Peet, looks for prior international experience in new hires, thereby leveraging the investments and training in international management provided by previous employers. Colgate-Palmolive then sends prospects for expatriation on shorter-term, foreign training assignments (six to eighteen months). These training assignments are devoid of the costly perks and compensation packages normally provided to expatriates. Only after completion of such assignments are prospects given longer-term expatriate positions.

Black and Gregersen suggest that any MNE's expatriate selection process entails a trade-off between accuracy and cost. Here, a thorough assessment process in the form of carefully crafted routines – like those used by LG Group and Colgate-Palmolive – is costly upfront, but also very accurate in terms of selecting the right individuals for expatriation. This approach reduces the risk of subsequent costs resulting from failed expatriate assignments. In the end, 'the key to success is having a systematic way of assessing the cross-cultural aptitudes of people you may want to send abroad'.[9]

Context and Complementary Perspectives

Published in 1999, Black and Gregersen's *HBR* piece pre-dates the 11 September 2001 terrorist attack on the World Trade Center twin towers in New York. Thus, the article did not address the stress associated with the perceived and actual security risks of travelling and living abroad for expatriates, especially employees from US- and UK-based firms in Muslim regions of the world (and more generally in many developing countries). This event has increased further the importance of properly selecting, training, and managing expatriates along the lines suggested by Black and Gregersen. Many MNEs have indeed responded to heightened security concerns by improving their candidate selection processes and training programmes.

Other insights in Black and Gregersen's article are not necessarily new, but rather serve as a reminder of the importance of considering cultural distance challenges inherent in international business (discussed in detail in the classic works of researchers such as Geert Hofstede, dating back to 1984).[10]

C. K. Prahalad and **Yves Doz** provide a first complementary perspective on the management of managers in MNEs with a set of two related pieces published in SMR,[11] where they propose a new approach to strategic control in MNEs (i.e., who actually determines the MNE's expansion and restructuring path), which has also become a timeless piece of managerial insight. Their articles do not focus on human resources management in the narrow sense, but rather on the creation of an appropriate 'organizational context'. In cases where senior management lacks what the authors call 'conventional substantive control', the authors recommend that senior management instead implement change by gradually and collaboratively changing the organizational context.

'Organizational context', discussed in detail below, refers to 'a blending of organizational structure, information systems, measurement and reward systems, and career planning and a fostering of common organizational culture'.[12]

By contrast, conventional substantive control typically uses centralized financial resource allocation, and is often associated with unidirectional knowledge flows from the home country to foreign affiliates.[13] Furthermore, conventional substantive control is usually immediate rather than gradual, and hierarchical rather than collaborative.

One way that corporate senior management might lack conventional substantive control is if foreign subsidiaries have become too powerful. Prahalad and Doz describe the interesting paradox whereby higher effectiveness in home country FSA transfers to foreign affiliates, especially as regards technology and management capabilities, simultaneously makes foreign affiliates less dependent on the home country and corporate headquarters. This holds true especially if these affiliates grow in size and relative importance of their sales and assets vis-à-vis the rest of the company thanks to the initial FSA transfers. In fact, Prahalad and Doz describe the possibility of an unintended and almost accidental transformation over time from an **international projector** into a **multi-centred MNE**.

Other ways that corporate senior management might lack conventional substantive control include situations of high bounded reliability among subsidiaries, mistrust of corporate headquarters, and warring factions with different strategic visions.

In these cases, what should senior management do when change is required? For example, suppose that increased international competition and an industry-wide focus on cost cutting impose rationalization of the internal MNE network. To continue to be profitable, the company needs to rationalize product lines at the level of an entire region (e.g., the European Union) by closing down product lines, reallocating product lines among affiliates, and bringing cost levels in line with those of other MNEs. Yet, corporate headquarters is unable to impose such rationalization, because they lack conventional substantive control over key resources. In such cases, a 'control gap' exists, which Prahalad and Doz suggest can be closed through creating an adequate organizational context. This can be achieved, they argue, only by following a particular sequence of steps.

Before discussing these steps, it is necessary to first explain how complex organizations such as MNEs can be described in terms of four orientations. Successful change requires changing all four orientations.

First, the *cognitive orientation* is the perception by managers of what constitutes the relevant business environment and the main competitive forces in this environment. Managers in different functional areas or operating at different hierarchical levels may not share the same perception of these parameters. Importantly, substantial differences may exist between senior management in the home country and managers in foreign affiliates on the substance of present and future environmental changes, and on the appropriate way for the MNE to respond to such changes.

Any successful change process in the MNE network needs to focus first on creating a shared cognitive orientation between senior management at corporate headquarters and subsidiary management.

Second, the *strategic orientation* is the managers' interpretation of the changes occurring in the relevant external environment – specifically, in terms of recognizing the business threats that need to be answered in a particular way and the business opportunities that can be exploited.

Here, successful change processes require senior management at corporate headquarters and subsidiary management to find common ground. A precondition for achieving a common strategic orientation is the prior development of a shared cognitive orientation, and both are required for major change.

Third, the *administrative orientation* refers primarily to the information management system within the MNE, particularly the management of accounting data and personnel-performance-related data.

A proposed change such as closing down specific product lines and expanding other ones may require, for empirical support, a new administrative orientation in the form of detailed data on performance differentials. In turn, agreeing on the correctness and significance of specific analytical tools (such as internal accounting measures) and the resulting, actual performance data will contribute to commonality in strategic orientation. Thus, a new administrative orientation can bring about a new strategic orientation.

Fourth, the **power orientation** refers to who in the firm has the power to do what.

To effect change, it is not enough to simply have **unanimous adoption of new cognitive, strategic, and administrative orientations** (as discussed above). The senior manager(s) responsible for – and capable of – reallocating resources (financial, human, etc.) must ultimately change the power orientation in the MNE. This means changing who gets to decide what. In the cases examined by Prahalad and Doz, this typically involves taking away decision-making power from subsidiaries in cases where they have benefited from extreme decentralization.

Prahalad and Doz studied actual change processes in several large firms where corporate headquarters lacked formal resource allocation power. In each case, these MNEs were suddenly faced with the need to rationalize specific businesses, driven by competitive pressures such as the penetration by other MNEs of their subsidiaries' markets. Prahalad and Doz found that each successful change process focused on altering the organizational context and, ultimately, the four orientations discussed above.

Each successful change process included the same sequence of eight steps in the same order. First, each process started with the appointment of a new key executive, formally assigned the task of effecting change. The substantive purpose of the change process, from the perspective of the newly appointed key executive, typically included increased inter-subsidiary coordination, accompanied by substantial rationalization in manufacturing to reduce costs and gain scale economies.

Second, though external pressures in the form of increased competition typically legitimized the executive's appointment and role as change agent, this executive spent considerable time trying to alter the cognitive orientations of subsidiary managers. Here, the executive typically employed relatively 'soft' conflict resolution mechanisms, such as coordination committees and task forces involving senior subsidiary managers to achieve the required changes in cognitive orientation and to plant the first seeds in the subsidiary managers' minds for a subsequent shift in strategic orientation.

Third, after the second stage, and precisely thanks to that stage, the executive explicitly stated the consequences of new environmental threats for firm strategy. For example, an increase of low-cost foreign exports by Asian firms to Europe might imply that the highly autonomous subsidiaries in Europe of an American manufacturer must now engage in pan-European consolidation of manufacturing, namely, must concentrate product lines in specific countries so as to serve the entire European market with scale-efficient production. In other words, the executive laid out the new strategic orientation.

Fourth, when supported by adequate data-management tools, generating credible comparative cost and performance data, it became possible to have a productive dialogue on specific changes in responsibilities held – and activities performed – by the different affiliates, thereby legitimizing minor reallocations of authority. Here, it was critical that the data systems provided sufficient accuracy and allowed appropriate differentiation among product lines and businesses, not all of which required the same level of inter-subsidiary coordination or rationalization. Often, new data-management tools had to be introduced (i.e., a new administrative orientation adopted) and applied selectively – namely, applied to those product lines and businesses in need of international rationalization, but not to the lines and businesses where a multi-centred approach was still appropriate. The resulting data on costs and productivity also had to be so clear and credible as to leave no room for alternative judgements on their implications for organizational restructuring (e.g., in the case of product interdependencies and related inaccurate cost allocations).

Fifth, on the basis of the above cognitive, strategic, and administrative shifts, multiple minor reallocations of authority (i.e., changes in the firm's power orientation) became possible, often directly benefiting the affected subsidiaries, such as centralized export coordination or international knowledge transfer coordination.

Sixth, the cumulative effect of the multiple reallocations of authority established the key executive as a powerful actor in the change process.

Seventh, building on the new position of power, the key executive was then able to engage in more drastic changes that typically included changes in the status and career paths of specific managers, new approaches to incentive systems, etc., thereby altering more fundamentally the MNE's power orientation.

Eighth, the key executive systematically supported and validated the newly created cognitive, strategic, and power orientations using finely tuned data-management tools, including performance measurement systems, resource allocation procedures, and budgeting procedures (i.e., using the new administrative orientation).

The above led Prahalad and Doz to conclude that '[w]hat can be accomplished organizationally sets limits on what is feasible as a strategy'.[14] If an organization's control mechanisms are dysfunctional, then attempting to exert 'brute force' conventional substantive control over subsidiary managers using immediate, hierarchical decision making will be unsuccessful. Instead, senior managers should use a gradual, sophisticated, eight-step approach that takes into account the organizational context and the firm's cognitive, strategic, administrative, and power orientations.

A second complementary perspective is by *Homa Bahrami*, and was published in *CMR*.[15] In this piece, the author describes modern human resources management (HRM) practices in a digital MNE, namely, Mozilla Corporation. In 1998, the now defunct American firm Netscape initiated the Mozilla project (with the name derived from Mosaic and Godzilla, or killer). The project was meant to create a global community that would develop innovative web browser programs, using an open source ecosystem.

Mozilla is a unique software company, built on four pillars: (1) developing 'open source' software; (2) operating with only a minimum number of workers with formal employee contracts; (3) working with millions of volunteering 'contributors'; and (4) embracing the global dispersion of employees, contributors, and software products.[16] Mozilla's main internet-based products have included Firefox, Firefox OS, Marketplace, Persona, Thunderbird, and Webmaker. At the time of writing this *CMR* piece, Bahrami noted the firm's impressive 'usage share' of over 20 per cent in the web browsers market using its main product, Firefox, competing with the software giant Microsoft's Internet Explorer and the search engine giant Google's Chrome.[17] Bahrami's article describes the key initiatives developed by Debbie Cohen, at that time Mozilla's 'Chief of People' and Vice President.[18]

Given its 'open source environment' and 'open community participation', a firm such as Mozilla needs to build a unique talent base that could ultimately constitute one of the company's key FSAs, at least if it is managed effectively.[19] On the one hand, being an internet-based software company, Mozilla's critical human resources need to include employees with advanced technology- and engineering-related skills, which are really basic ingredients for a non-location-bound FSA. On the other hand, Mozilla functions with a 'geo-distributed structure', whereby employees are hired and contributors attracted from all over the world, and software products distributed globally.[20] As a result, there is a need for sufficient polycentricity – meaning in this instance, attempts to foster locational responsiveness around specialized human resources in a variety of distinct host environments. But what actually matters most is non-location-bound routines to serve these polycentric purposes and to permit rapid absorption of new human resources into the MNE's overall resource pool. This absorption reflects reduced bounded rationality challenges; it will make newly selected human resources productive more quickly, and it will 'unlock their potential'.[21] As such, rather than adopting and deploying from the outset a top-down, centralized set of rather ethnocentric, human resources management practices, typical for an ***international projector***, Debbie Cohen adopted a more participative approach, asking for substantial bottom-up inputs before deciding on the substance of the firm's human resources management infrastructure.[22]

Starting with the *onboarding* stage, when employees and contributors begin working for the company, one of the key bounded rationality reducing components at this stage was to make sure that new recruits would be empowered rapidly to 'understand the whole system, all the moving parts, and how to affect them', rather than to expect them to 'go figure it out'.[23] A formal onboarding process template was therefore necessary to help new 'Mozillians' develop familiarity with the company and its people, even before embarking on their actual work.[24] But given the global nature of the organization and the large number of contributors recruited from all over the world, the onboarding tool needed to accommodate the specific needs of all these individuals, including the fact that many of them did not master the English language. In addition to addressing this language issue, the onboarding tool was also customized for different communities of contributors.[25]

Beyond the onboarding stage, Mozilla developed a culture of *distributed knowledge* based largely on informal knowledge sharing and mentoring, rather than on developing and diffusing knowledge out of a formal 'learning and development department'.[26] Here, scalability, allowing the involvement of all geographically dispersed employees and contributors, but then having the ability to move towards crafting company-wide products, was viewed as critical. To accommodate this cultural feature at Mozilla, *leadership training* did not focus primarily on developing specialized skills. Instead, each employee or contributor was in principle given the opportunity to become a 'self-generated leader' using a peer-to-peer leadership development initiative.[27] And as to formal training, one of its components, called 'Big Picture', 'focused on getting the leaders to lift their chins up and focus on the entire ecosystem, and to understand the meaning of strategy'.[28] Other components emphasized individuals' own gap analyses as to their leadership skills and profiles, and the view that leadership should be instrumental to organizational change.

Ultimately, all the actions above were meant to reduce bounded reliability challenges, and to promote 'global connectedness' among all individuals working for or at Mozilla, thereby combining geographically distributed, innovative talent and ideas with cross-border routines. This combination, in turn, allowed the scalability of product innovations and the easy global diffusion thereof.[29]

This article expands Black and Gregersen's analysis, which focused on traditional MNE expatriate management. Bahrami describes the HRM practices in a 'born digital' MNE, whereby staff and open source contributors are globally dispersed. Here, the emphasis is on both formal routines and the often simultaneous, informal socialization of individuals across national borders, so that they would adopt the values of the organization, thereby fostering voluntary, informal knowledge sharing and absorption. Digital MNEs like Mozilla operating in an 'open source environment' and building on 'open community participation' from globally dispersed talent must strike a delicate balance between centralized control of product quality and product delivery and tailored talent development strategies. The firm's products will cater to a global customer base expecting high reliability, but at the same time there is the need for bottom-up, decentralized innovation to create these products.[30]

In many contemporary MNEs, the upstream and back-office activities are largely centralized (consistent with the first pattern of capability development outlined in Chapter 1), while the downstream and customer-end activities are locally responsive (consistent with the fourth pattern of multi-centred, capability development). But in this digital MNE, the knowledge creation and dissemination process itself has features of the multi-centred archetype. Here, the more informal requirements of bottom-up knowledge creation and sharing by highly specialized human resources – including the semi-independent contributors dispersed across geographic locations – must necessarily be fused with the requisite, subsequent crafting and scaling-up of global products. This mix can be instrumental to outperforming competitors operating a centralized innovation function, and is consistent with the network patterns of FSA development outlined in Chapter 1: it combines key features from both *international projector MNEs* and *multi-centred MNEs*, but with the multiple centres engaged in dispersed innovation activities, the results of which must then be shared with the other parts of the multinational ecosystem following commonly understood and respected routines.

MANAGEMENT INSIGHTS

The most relevant element in Black and Gregersen's *HBR* article, in terms of this book's framework, is that using expatriate managers is a key channel through which MNEs – especially *international projectors*, *multi-centred MNEs*, and *international coordinators* – can diffuse their FSAs from the home country to host country affiliates and among internationally operating affiliates in general. Of course, in each of the MNE archetypes, the purpose and scope of expatriates is different (see Figures 10.1, 10.2, and 10.3).

With *international projectors*, the purpose of expatriates is to transfer knowledge, especially technical knowledge and routines, from the home country to host country affiliates, but the human resources reservoir held by each subsidiary will co-determine how the role of expatriates plays out in practice. With *multi-centred MNEs*, expatriates constitute part of the minimal glue to hold the internal MNE network together through fostering the sharing of core values and acting as reliable communication channels between corporate headquarters and the foreign affiliates. In the case of *international coordinators*, expatriates are the most important: they are instrumental to creating effective international value chains, linking economic activities across borders. They thereby constitute an integral part of the MNE's recombination capability. Black and Gregersen described the source of this capability as the MNE's 'focus on knowledge creation and global leadership development',[31] the first of their three recipes for successful expatriate management. Here, the emphasis is clearly on new FSA development and the use of the expatriates themselves as key resources to meld internationally transferable FSAs with location-bound FSAs in host locations. Expatriate managers thus: (1) facilitate the process of transferring existing FSA bundles across borders; (2) improve the exploitation potential of such FSAs in host country environments by augmenting them with

locally developed FSAs; and (3) engage in the appropriate melding of internationally transferable FSAs and location-bound FSAs into effective value-
added activities and products.

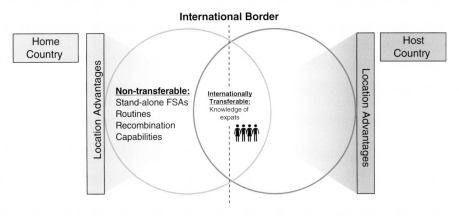

Figure 10.1
International
projector: Expatriates
as knowledge
carriers

The small 'people' icons in the middle represent the role of expatriates in facilitating the transfer of home country NLB FSAs to the host country. The firm operates a centrally designed, resources management system for expatriates, but the unique human resources reservoir held by each subsidiary co-determines the actual functioning of this central system, as visualized by the two main circles.

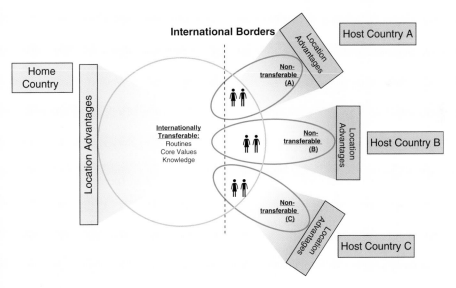

Figure 10.2
Multi-centred MNEs:
Expatriates as
carriers of core
values and as
reliable
communication
channels

The small 'people' icons represent the role of expatriates, both in facilitating the transfer of home country routines to the host countries, and in acting as conduits for cross-border communication. The multiple, large ovals represent this dual role of expatriates sent to host countries A, B, and C: they typically foster the sharing of core values and knowledge from the home country and act as reliable communication channels between corporate headquarters and the foreign affiliates.

In addition to these roles of transferring and implementing FSAs, high-quality, experienced expatriates constitute a non-location-bound FSA in their own right. They can be deployed anywhere in the network to – as discussed above – transfer and implement other FSAs, foster the sharing of core company values, help communication between subsidiaries and central headquarters, facilitate the management of the MNE's internal network, and integrate geographically dispersed operations.

It is important to note that the FSA diffusion processes facilitated by expatriates are multidirectional. Expatriates not only facilitate the process of disseminating FSAs from the home office (or other high-competence units) to host country subsidiaries, but they also acquire new knowledge and international experience abroad that can be redeployed to other units inside the MNE. This latter process is largely an emerging phenomenon, which cannot be exactly predefined in the form of detailed expatriation objectives, but is largely crafted through many interactions with other employees in a variety of affiliates.

Figure 10.3
International
coordinator:
Expatriates as key
resources to link
internationally
transferable FSAs
and location
advantages of host
nations

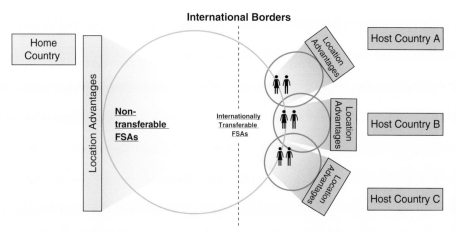

The small 'people' icons represent the roles of expatriates in facilitating the transfer of specific bundles of home country NLB FSAs to each host country. Each of the small circles in the host country spaces represents the expatriates' role in facilitating the alignment between the firm's NLB FSAs and the LAs sought in each host country. The firm's centralized expatriate management system acts as an FSA to optimize results for the network as a whole: it represents the overall coordination of expatriates, guided by the head office in countries A, B, and C being connected to create effective international value chains.

This leads to the first of the five major limitations of Black and Gregersen's piece. As noted by Bartlett and Ghoshal in their analysis of the Dutch MNE Philips, expatriation can be a permanent way of life for managers, analogous to the diplomatic service in government, whereby a career trajectory is essentially a series of foreign assignments. In Black and Gregersen's article, expatriation ends with reintegration of the expatriate back into the home country, but this neglects the point that extended (if not permanent) expatriation is critical in creating executives with a widely dispersed informal social network, very high cross-cultural skills, and a profound understanding of the multiple perspectives in the MNE's geographically dispersed operations.

The second limitation is related to Black and Gregersen's observation that the process of knowledge creation and dissemination by expatriates may not always proceed as smoothly as planned. Black and Gregersen observed that a substantial number of expatriates either return home early or perceive only limited opportunities to leverage their overseas knowledge when returning to their home country environment. However, in addition to the reasons presented by the authors, this lacklustre record of expatriation may be indicative of the inherent friction in home country–host country relationships. Established foreign affiliates may be reluctant to accept guidance from the head office through expatriate managers, especially when procedural justice is perceived to be lacking (see Chapter 5). Senior subsidiary managers may also be unwilling to share freely with the rest of the company, via expatriates, the specialized knowledge and processes developed by the subsidiary if they do not expect a fair return for such diffusion or at least proper recognition of their contributions. Similarly, attitudes and prejudices within the home office may limit the flow of information back to the top after an expatriate returns home. In each of these cases, the end result is missed opportunities in terms of new FSA diffusion and exploitation across the MNE's internal network. Here, the prior creation of a receptive organizational context may contribute to the success of subsequent expatriate management.

As a third limitation, Black and Gregersen do not discuss 'external' expatriation. In addition to expatriate assignments internal to the organization, joint ventures and strategic alliances give rise to another form of expatriate placement, as managers are seconded abroad to partner firms or international joint venture projects. In such cases, the best practices outlined by Black and Gregersen are likely to remain valid, but the requirement to outline clear objectives for knowledge creating may need to be augmented so as to prevent the unintended leakage of FSAs to partner firms, who may be competitors in particular market or industry areas (see also Chapter 12).

A fourth limitation is that expatriates, if they do their job 'too well' in terms of transferring knowledge, might actually transform subsidiaries into knowledge centres developing subsidiary-specific advantages in their own right. There is nothing inherently negative in such transformation over time, but the head office and the expatriates themselves need to remain attentive to unintended and dynamic spillover effects of tacit knowledge transfers by expatriates. These may include subsidiary role changes in the MNE and also knowledge leakage by local actors, who may act opportunistically as an expression of bounded reliability or simply move to rival firms and deploy their acquired knowledge to benefit these companies.

Finally, the fifth limitation is that Black and Gregersen, at the time of writing their article, could not possibly anticipate the potential of modern information and communications technology, permitting strategic trade-offs between deploying expatriates versus using digital knowledge management and transfer tools to support foreign operations and even outside partners. Bahrami describes some of the latter tools in the Mozilla context (see above). This does not imply that expatriation represents a human resources management tool of the past, but that the functions of expatriation need to be carefully unbundled, with its comparative value assessed vis-à-vis that provided by digital tools for each of these functions (e.g., intelligence gathering, knowledge development, knowledge transfer, specialized management skills deployment, general management skills deployment, foreign employees' socialization, stakeholder negotiations and management, etc.).

Strategic Challenges in the New Economy

N. Anand and **Jean-Louis Barsoux**, in their *HBR* article on modern change management, argue that corporate transformation is increasingly a way of life in large firms, given rapid changes in both internal and external environments.[32] The conventional trade-off that senior management should supposedly make is between 'improving efficiency' (meaning lower costs) and 'reinvesting in growth'.[33] In reality, this is now often a false dichotomy and both goals are mostly complementary. As a result, firms should not focus too narrowly on just one of these two goals. Especially MNEs need to understand that there is more to corporate transformation than targeting lower costs versus higher growth. The authors argue that firms need to reflect on five possible goals of change processes that go to the essence of corporate transformation. The goals to be considered are: '(1) global presence, (2) customer focus, (3) nimbleness, (4) innovation, and (5) sustainability'.[34] As one example, where sustainability appeared the most critical goal:

> The [Finnish-Swedish] paper giant, Stora Enso . . . concluded that pursuing nimbleness, global presence, or customer focus would merely yield more market share in a declining industry. Innovation would not solve the main issue either. But the company had developed some breakthrough green offerings, including environmentally friendly packaging for the expanding e-commerce delivery market. Its greatest opportunity lay in shifting the whole axis of the business to specialize in offerings made with renewable and bio-based materials.[35]

Corporate transformation, especially in large MNEs, requires a credible leader as a change agent to alter the cognitive and strategic orientation of managers, and to execute on the goals to be pursued. For example:

Jouko Karvinen, the CEO of Stora Enso until July 2014 . . . set up a parallel 'Pathfinders' leadership team – a dozen managers from various parts of the organization – and gave them a mandate to identify sustainability opportunities that were falling between silos and, more broadly, to challenge the old ways of doing business. Each year the organization replaces its Pathfinders with a new cohort of up to 16 members.[36]

Firms should also recognize that deficiencies in leaders' capabilities – given particular corporate transformation goals selected – will lead to disappointing outcomes. Let us consider the example of two computer manufacturing MNEs aiming to achieve a greater global presence, starting in 2008.[37] Taiwan-based computer manufacturer Acer subsequently reduced the number of foreigners on the top management team, whereas Lenovo did the opposite. By 2015, Lenovo had become the global market leader, whereas Acer had moved down to sixth place.

More generally, three corporate transformation traps are common and can lead to failure in firms' change management. *First,* firms need to link the goals of the attempted transformation with their strategy execution.[38] If an MNE pursues a stronger global presence, but does not adjust the top management team accordingly, as in the Acer example above, it will not achieve a successful corporate transformation. *Second,* the temptation may exist in firms to mimic what rivals do in terms of corporate transformation, but they may not possess the requisite resource base and FSAs to achieve the same goals as competitors.[39] *Third,* given the five possible goals mentioned above, firms sometimes take on too many of these transformational targets at once.[40] This may require more and different resources than the firms actually command and it may also lead to unnecessary confusion within the firms on what should be prioritized as they execute on the targeted goal(s) in corporate transformation.

According to Black and Gregersen, expatriate managers are expected to perform the key roles of developing and transferring FSAs, and recombining old and newly accessed resources into novel FSAs at the interface between MNEs and foreign customers. These authors view it as critical for MNEs to invest in development programmes whereby they can select, train, and nurture expatriate managers with appropriate qualifications. Anand and Barsoux's analysis comple- ments Black and Gregersen's view, by suggesting implicitly that the capability of 'change management' is one of the key qualifications expatriate managers need to have in instances of intended corporate transformation.[41]

More specifically, the roles of expatriate managers should not be confined to just addressing 'how to develop', 'how to transfer', or 'how to recombine' extant resource bundles. What may matter more, especially in instances of crisis, is how to nurture capable change managers. This goes far beyond the mere technically oriented recombination of resources (even if this were to involve sophisticated relational contracting with stakeholders). Developing expatriate leaders with the capability of change management may be critical as MNEs change their generic approach to governance, for example, when transforming from the **international projector** archetype to include more features of **multi-centred MNEs** (e.g., 'customer focus', or location-bound 'nimbleness' and 'sustainability' as transformational goals).

Erin Meyer, in her **HBR** article, develops a simple framework for senior managers in MNEs to address cultural distance.[42] Her framework certainly does not do justice to the rich scholarly literature on the meaning of cultural distance and the impact thereof on international business, but it does provide a few useful and simple rules of thumb on how senior MNE leaders in general, and top expatriate managers in particular, can think about exercising authority and managing decision-making processes, as they shape leadership styles in culturally distant foreign subsidiaries.

As explained in detail in Chapter 4, MNEs face limits to the non-location-boundedness of their FSAs when they venture abroad, *inter alia*, due to the cultural distance between their home country and host countries. Cultural distance has long been discussed in international business studies, especially after Hofstede's (1980; 1983) seminal contributions, and Kogut and Singh (1988)[43] utilizing a composite index built from country scores for Hofstede's (1980) original four dimensions of national culture, namely: (1) individualism vs. collectivism; (2) uncertainty avoidance; (3) power distance; and (4) masculinity vs. femininity.[44] The original conceptualization of cultural distance has evolved over five decades. It now includes a wider variety of dimensions,[45] including on the one hand individuals' perceptions/cognition of – and personal values/attitudes towards – different cultures,[46] and societal values and institutional characteristics in interpreting different cultures on the other.[47]

It is worth mentioning three emerging trends in recent scholarly research on cultural distance in the sphere of international business and MNE functioning. *First*, it may be erroneous to try to understand the cultural distance challenges the MNE faces by adopting a mere national perspective, because country does not always coincide with culture.[48] There are often unique sub-national local cultures, in turn affected by the growing diversity of the workforce due to immigration, and by firm-level behaviour itself (e.g., the creation of top management and employee teams with diverse multicultural backgrounds and profiles, concentrated in hub-cities). *Second*, and related to the first point, the 'distance' component in cultural distance used to be closely associated with geographic distance between the physical locations of the MNE's operations: however, it now also needs to take into account the unfolding of contextual change that will affect the MNE expanding abroad.[49] *Third*, cultural distance issues facing MNEs can no longer be assessed from a mere static perspective because initial effects of cultural distance at the time of foreign entry, especially in terms of magnitude, are expected to change over time: the MNE's foreign operations will mature and its network may grow in scale and geographic scope.[50]

All of the above suggests that the MNE will (or will need to) become more flexible and adaptable to foreign contexts as it engages in continuous learning from managing overseas operations. Here, it is critical for MNE senior executives and top expatriate managers to interpret cultural challenges in terms of the specific contexts and processes characterizing foreign subsidiary locations.[51]

What then remains of national culture that MNE managers should still systematically address? Meyer argues that two important dimensions of national 'leadership culture' deserve the attention of MNE senior managers, namely, how authority is exercised and how decision-making processes unfold. For example, in the realm of authority, Japanese team members are supposedly treated in a less egalitarian fashion than American ones. In the area of decision making, Japanese leaders and team members tend to be more consensus-oriented than American employees. Meyer describes the Japanese leadership culture as follows:

> . . . the management structure is hierarchical [low egalitarianism], but decisions are most often made by group consensus [high consensus building] . . . Two words define this consensual process, so common in Japanese companies. The first is *nemawashi* – the practice of speaking with each individual stakeholder before a meeting in order to shape the group decision and develop agreement in advance. The second is *ringi*, which involves passing a proposal around level by level, starting at the bottom and then working through the layers of middle and senior management before arriving at the top.[52]

Meyer suggests that senior managers should adapt to – or at least understand – the unique leadership culture of each foreign country, in terms of the two above dimensions, namely, authority and decision-making processes.

First, attitudes towards authority, in terms of the level of egalitarianism, reflect the answer to the question: 'How much attention do we pay to the rank or status of a person, and how much respect and deference do we pay to that status?'[53] There are two alternative expressions of authority in terms of how team members are treated: high or low egalitarianism. Second, attitudes towards decision making reflect the answer to the questions: 'Who calls the shots, and how? Does the boss decide, or does the team decide collectively?'[54] There are thus two types of decision-making processes: high or low consensus building. Low consensus building typically means quick and flexible decisions made by the team leader. In contrast, high consensus building involves a larger number of team members (and perhaps other stakeholders) involved in reaching convergence on decisions, over a longer time period and along a series of layers within the organization.

The two attitudes considered together lead to four types of national cultural attitudes in leadership:

1. *High consensus building in process and high egalitarianism in how team members are treated.* It takes longer to make decisions in this process, and the leader is not the final decision maker, but rather a facilitator trying to craft convergence of views. This is supposedly the dominant cultural leadership style in countries such as Denmark, the Netherlands, Norway, and Sweden.[55]

2. *High consensus building in process, but low egalitarianism in treatment of team members.* Here, the leader is actually expected to make final decisions, but will also invite substantial input and participation in the decision-making process from the team before making these decisions. This is the dominant cultural leadership style in countries such as Belgium, Germany, and Japan.[56]

3. *Low consensus building in process, but high egalitarianism in treatment of team members.* Team members are treated as equals in the sense that they are supposed to provide input in a free-wheeling fashion, without much importance attached to their status in the hierarchy and with their initiatives welcomed. But team members are then expected to show loyalty to the decisions once these are made by the leader, even without consensus. However, these decisions are typically not cast in stone and may subsequently be revisited for further change as circumstances dictate. This is the dominant cultural leadership style in countries such as Australia, Canada, the United Kingdom, and the United States.[57]

4. *Low consensus building in process and low egalitarianism in treatment of team members.* Here, any leader's words are viewed as a decision ready to be executed, and the leader therefore needs to be very explicit and clear about expectations from employees. This is the dominant cultural leadership style in countries such as Brazil, China, France, India, Indonesia, Mexico, Russia, and Saudi Arabia.[58]

It should be mentioned, however, that the 'scores' of countries, even when positioned in the same quadrant of Figure 10.4, may still differ significantly.

Figure 10.4
A classification of leadership cultures

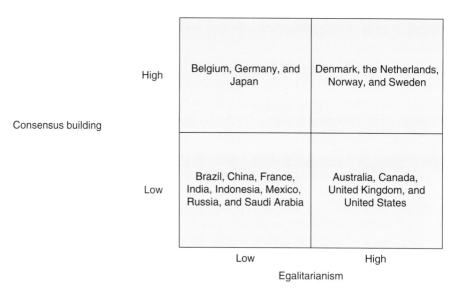

Note: Based on "Mapping Leadership Cultures" on p. 75 in Meyer (2017).

Whether Meyer's classification and positioning of countries as a function of dominant, cultural leadership style are 'correct' is open to debate. Identifying dominant national styles clearly does not do justice to enormous intra-country variation among firms and inter-firm heterogeneity within a country, but the main point is that within a single MNE, senior managers and expatriates need to adopt flexible and adaptable cultural leadership approaches depending on the country in which they operate. And having this cultural leadership agility can go a long way towards effective resource recombination across national borders.

Black and Gregersen suggest three best practices to manage expatriates, whose 'leadership skills' and 'cross-cultural skills' are critical to operating successfully across national borders. Meyer's article complements Black and Gregersen on two fronts. *First*, it highlights the cultural leadership-related FSAs embedded in top expatriate managers of foreign subsidiaries (somewhat reminiscent of the competence carrier concept discussed in Chapter 2). *Second*, it provides a simple classification of national, cultural leadership styles, thereby reflecting the possible gap between the home-country-driven 'baseline' of an expatriate's cultural leadership style, and the host country expectation of a particular leadership approach. Attitudes about 'authority' (treating team members with high or low egalitarianism), and the 'decision-making' process (being high or low on consensus building) help define the dominant, national cultural leadership. If the gap is large between an expatriate's cultural leadership style and the expectations about such leadership in a foreign subsidiary, this may jeopardize successful FSA transfer and novel resource recombination. Ideally, prospective subsidiary leaders should have the ability to adapt their cultural leadership style to the dominant cultural leadership specificities in foreign countries. As a minimum, understanding expectations on how authority should be exercised and how decision-making processes should unfold in host countries can go a long way towards successful expatriate assignments.

Five Management Takeaways

1. Learn about common problems and best practices to manage expatriates, including experiences from competitors.
2. Given your firm's administrative heritage, explore the various possible purposes and forms of expatriation (e.g., 'external' expatriation, overseas knowledge transfers, extended/permanent expatriation).
3. Focus strategic change processes on fine-tuning the MNE's organizational context, and follow a sequence of eight implementation steps that have proven successful in many firms, whereby expatriates could function as change agents.

4. Train your managers to integrate successfully the activities of interdependent but geographically dispersed international operations: here, the value of expatriation should be assessed for each of its functions, against the value of alternative human resources management tools, including digitally supported ones.

5. Understand that senior MNE managers and especially expatriates must exhibit agility when faced with varying, dominant cultural leadership styles in different countries.

PART III

DYNAMICS OF GLOBAL STRATEGY

11

Entry Mode Dynamics 1: Foreign Distributors

Five Learning Objectives

1. To explain the reasons why MNEs establish long-term relationships with local distributors, even when they also command a wholly owned distribution network.
2. To foster an understanding of the role foreign distributors can play in the FSA development process.
3. To provide concrete guidelines to MNEs on how to manage supply chains in their entirety (from sourcing to distribution), in international environments characterized by great uncertainty and volatility.
4. To describe the need for adaptive governance of supply chains and related investments in logistics-related technologies.
5. To highlight the benefits of mapping the MNE's supply chain network with a focus on those points in the network that could trigger major negative impacts if a large-scale disturbance occurred.

This chapter examines Arnold's idea that, when selling in foreign markets, MNEs should maintain relationships with local distributors over the long term even after establishing their own local network to handle major clients. In theory, local distributors provide insight into the local market, knowledge of local regulations and business practices, existing major customers at low cost, and the ability to hire appropriate staff and develop relationships with potential new customers. Selecting and managing distributors is difficult, though, and Arnold provides a list of seven best practices. These ideas will be examined and then critiqued using the framework presented in Chapter 1.

Significance

In an important *HBR* article, **David Arnold** studied the role of external actors, specifically foreign distributors, in international strategy.[1] Arnold focused on the evolving role of local distributors when MNEs first establish themselves in new markets and then try to grow in these markets. He observes that many MNEs initially establish relationships with local distributors in order to reduce costs and minimize risks. In other words, the local distributor's complementary capabilities (e.g., knowledge of local regulations and business practices, ability to hire appropriate staff and relationships with potential customers) substitute for developing new, location-bound FSAs required to access the host country market, in cases where market success is highly uncertain. Unfortunately, however, after enjoying some early market penetration, sales often flatten and may even start declining. Typically, the MNE then responds by calling into question the effectiveness of the local partner and its ability to make good on performance commitments and expectations. The MNE's reflex may even be to take control of local operations by buying out the distributor or by reacquiring the distribution rights in order to build a self-owned, dedicated distribution network. The resulting transition period is often difficult, disruptive, and costly – problems that could be avoided, according to Arnold, through better strategic planning of distributor selection and governance of the relationships with local distributors.

Arnold's research included a two-year field study of the international distribution strategies of eight MNEs active in the consumer, industrial, and service sectors as they entered nearly 250 new host country markets. Arnold observed, perhaps surprisingly, that MNEs often select new countries for market-seeking purposes in a largely unplanned or reactive way. This approach typically begins with a positive response to unsolicited proposals from local distributors, advertising the location advantages of the host country in which they operate and their own capabilities to help the MNE serve that market.

The MNE then aligns itself with an independent local distributor in order to minimize upfront risk and to tap existing knowledge about the local market and potential major customers at low cost. Here, the distributor is supposed to add complementary capabilities to the MNE's internationally transferable FSAs, which are embodied in the products it wishes to export.

Typically, the MNE invests very little in marketing and business development, as it assumes that the local distributor will take care of these areas critical to foreign market penetration. But in doing so, 'companies cede control of strategic marketing decisions to the local partners, much more control than they would cede in home markets'.[2] Arnold calls this minimal, low-risk, low-investment strategy the 'beachhead strategy'. The MNE's attitude is to wait and see what can be achieved with such minimal commitment.

Behind this hands-off 'beachhead' approach may be the MNE's longer-term intent to eventually take direct control of local operations and to integrate these into the MNE's existing international network after some initial market penetration has been achieved. Arnold notes that 'for many multinationals, it's a foregone conclusion that local distributors have merely been vehicles for market entry, temporary partners incapable of sustaining growth in the long term'.[3] Observing this past behaviour by MNEs, many local distributors conclude, quite reasonably, that the relationship will only be temporary. In such cases, the local partners may be unwilling to make the significant investments in strategic marketing and business development that are necessary to grow the business over the longer term. Thus, a vicious cycle of increasing bounded reliability challenges is set in motion: the distributor's expectation of MNE unreliability (to provide adequate long-term support) in turn creates distributor unreliability (to invest for the growth of the business).

If sales growth falters, once the initial 'low-hanging fruit' (selling the MNE's core products to the distributor's existing customer base) has been captured, each side may embark on a path of blaming the other for the disappointing results. Typically, the MNE laments that the local distributor 'didn't know how to grow the market . . . didn't invest in business growth . . . [and] just wasn't ambitious enough',[4] whereas the local partner counters that the MNE did not provide enough support to match its overly high expectations.

In reality, both parties may share responsibility for the relative failure of the distribution agreement. Arnold's research shows that 'the same themes repeatedly emerge: neither party – the multinational nor the distributor – invests sufficiently in strategic marketing or in aggressive business development'.[5]

However, according to Arnold, senior MNE managers usually deserve the main burden of responsibility, as they should realize that 'distributors are implementers of marketing strategy, rather than marketing departments in the country-market'.[6] Arnold's point is that MNEs often delegate too much of their strategic marketing planning activities and the control thereof to local distributors when first entering new markets without providing proper direction and resources. In addition, the local market's life cycle stage typically changes after entry, but the MNE often fails to adjust its market strategy or market commitments to reflect the evolution from early penetration to rapid growth. Instead, the MNE sticks with its initial market-entry strategy (i.e., the beachhead strategy) for too long.

What is the solution to these common problems between MNEs and their international distributors, especially in developing countries? According to

Arnold: 'The key to solving the problems of international distribution in developing countries is to recognize that the phases are predictable and that multinationals can plan for them from the start in a way that is less disruptive and costly than the doomed beachhead strategy.'[7]

Interestingly, Arnold finds that companies usually have success when they evolve from a beachhead strategy to a mix of direct distribution by the MNE itself and long-term relationships with local distributors. This mixed strategy often lets the MNE retain control of distribution where feasible, while relying on the complementary capabilities of distributors where necessary: 'It seems probable that some national distributors will become part of a mixed distribution system, in which the multinational corporation will manage major customers directly, while other, independent, distributors will focus on discrete segments of national markets or smaller accounts . . . independent local distributors often provide the best means of serving local small and medium accounts.'[8]

In other words, MNEs are advised to maintain relationships with independent local partners for distribution activities over the long term even after establishing their own local network to handle major clients. The key for the MNE is to find the correct balance between three competing objectives: strategic control over important customers, benefits from the local partner's market knowledge and market access, and risk reduction when faced with high demand uncertainty in the new market.

Arnold's research also contains recommendations for local distributors who want to continue to work with the MNE as it gains market share. Arnold's research shows that, in the cases where distributors successfully maintained their relationship with an MNE over the longer term, these local partners shared a number of characteristics: they did not distribute competing product lines from rivals, they shared market information with the MNE, they initiated new projects, and they collaborated with other distributors in adjacent markets. They also invested in areas such as training, ICT, and promotion to grow the business.[9]

The article concludes by offering a list of seven guidelines for MNEs when dealing with local distributors. These guidelines should help MNEs avoid the commonly observed pattern of local market underperformance as a result of underinvestment and over-reliance on distributors, followed by an over-correction in the form of complete internalization of all distribution activities:

1. *Proactively select locations and only then suitable distributors.* The MNE should identify for itself the countries it wants to enter, in relation to its strategic objectives (and the related country-level location advantages), and then suitable partners in those countries, rather than expanding internationally to particular locations in response to unsolicited proposals from local

distributors (e.g., in the context of trade fairs). The best partners are not necessarily the largest distributors, as the latter may already have contracts with (competing) MNEs for similar product lines, and may thus have an interest in dividing the existing local market among MNE rivals, rather than rapidly building the market for one firm.

2. *Focus on distributors' market development capabilities.* It is critical to find the best 'company fit' in terms of strategy, culture, willingness to invest and to train staff, etc., rather than merely a 'market fit' with those distributors already serving key target customers with related products.

3. *Manage distributors as long-term partners.* This approach, which may include incentives related to actual sales performance, will make distributors willing to invest more in strategic marketing and long-term development. Using distributors for short-term market penetration purposes only, and making this clear through distribution rights buy-back clauses in the contract, takes away the incentive for distributor investment in market development and may even increase bounded reliability problems. For example, if the buy-back price depends on sales volumes, irrespective of profit margins achieved, the distributor may attempt to position the MNE's product as a commodity, rather than extract the highest possible price from customers. The distributor may thereby harm the product's future positioning in the local market.

4. *Provide resources (managerial, financial, and knowledge-based) to support distributors for market development purposes.* Arnold's research indicates that MNEs rarely withdraw fully from a new export market. Committing more resources earlier may therefore foster better relationships with local partners, as well as higher performance. The resources provided may include skilled support staff, minority equity participations (e.g., to co-fund investments), and knowledge sharing (e.g., to augment simple equipment selling with related service provision to customers).

5. *Do not delegate marketing strategy to distributors.* While distributors should be able to adapt the MNE's strategy to the needs of local markets, it is up to the MNE to provide clear leadership in terms of the choice of products to be marketed, the positioning of these products, and the size and use of marketing budgets.

6. *Secure shared access to the distributors' critical market and financial intelligence.* In many cases, local distribution partners may be the only economic actors holding such valuable information in the host country, and their willingness to share this information signals their commitment to becoming a solid, long-term partner. At the same time, the distributors reduce the MNE's bounded rationality problems by improving its limited understanding of the idiosyncrasies of the local market.

7. *Link national distributors with one another, especially at the regional level (spanning several countries).* Such linkages, in the form of regional headquarters to coordinate distribution efforts, or autonomous distributor councils, may lead to the diffusion of best practices inside the distributors' network, and act as an internal monitoring mechanism, stimulating more consistent strategy implementation throughout the region.

Context and Complementary Perspectives

Arnold's work can be interpreted as a complement to Bartlett and Ghoshal's perspective, discussed in Chapter 5, which addressed the MNE's need to tap its foreign subsidiaries as new sources of competitive advantage. It is also consistent with Kuemmerle's view on innovation, discussed in Chapter 6, that foreign R&D centres are key to acquiring new sources of advanced knowledge, and Ferdows' assessment, discussed in Chapter 7, that successful manufacturers should develop their foreign factories into sources of new FSAs.

Whereas Bartlett and Ghoshal's, Kuemmerle's, and Ferdows' views are applicable in principle to all MNE types, but especially to the **international projector**, Arnold's article is especially relevant to the **centralized exporter**. For the latter MNE category, neither simple market contracts with foreign distributors nor the full internalization of international distribution operations may be the optimal way to bring exported products to the overseas customer. In cases where the key to success in a host market is continued, long-term access to the (not generally available) market knowledge and management expertise of local partners to reach customers, strategic partnerships with distributors may be the optimal entry mode.

Arnold's 'seven rules of international distribution' are in line with a key theme in international business thinking throughout the past thirty years, namely that companies may benefit from strengthening their international linkages with external parties that command complementary FSAs, rather than trying to develop such FSAs within the company, especially if such FSAs would take a long time to develop internally and cannot be simply purchased in the host country market.

Laurent Chevreux, **Michael Hu** and **Suketu Gandhi** provide a first complementary perspective on international distribution in a 2018 *SMR* article, arguing that many manufacturing and logistics firms now face dual challenges.[10] *First*, they must adapt rapidly to unexpected changes in demand. *Second*, they must have the technological capability, often in the digital realm, to support governance focused on fast responses.

As regards the ability to respond fast, the authors focus on the need to 'sense and pivot'.[11] Companies can become 'organizationally adaptable', when they make manufacturing, distribution, and logistics flexible in the face of demand volatility. As one example of what 'sense and pivot' would look like in practice, the authors argue that: 'Some logistics companies . . . are exploring more flexible yet reliable ways of making the countless trade-off decisions required to effectively respond to volatility through a combination of new processes, rules, and analytics.'[12]

Here, *new decision processes* could imply much shorter time lags between intelligence gathering (sensing) and actual managerial decisions (pivoting), with these decisions also relying on a higher and more diverse number of intelligence sources. *New rules* could imply more weight given to a variety of uncertainties about the future (sensing) and contractual clauses allowing renegotiations (pivoting) with a variety of parties on commitments made (suppliers, distributors, etc.), when changing demand conditions require this. Finally, *new analytics* could refer to the sensing tools providing detailed, accurate data on the sources and magnitude of demand volatility (e.g., forecasting tools), thereby providing the substantive basis for pivoting.

The focus on sensing and pivoting as described above, when facing extreme uncertainty and volatility coming from the outside world, is important but may not be sufficient to reduce internal disruptions. Firms must also make major investments in 'digitizing and automating' their supply chains.[13] This amounts to developing a technological capability that will provide the underlying asset base to support sensing and pivoting. Digital and automated assets should reduce frictions between sequential or interdependent stages in the supply chain, and drive cost-efficiencies. For example, the authors note: 'Major shipping and logistics companies are making massive capability investments in automation, robotics, and other technologies to speed warehouse throughput, truck utilization, and overall operations.'[14]

Ultimately, both an improved sensing and pivoting ability in the realm of *adaptive governance* and higher capital expenditures in digital and automation-related assets leading to a *technology-based* FSA, but not in the realm of conventional R&D outputs, are needed to address deep uncertainties and volatility coming from the external environment.

Arnold described local distributors' changing roles when MNEs try to grow their business in foreign markets, and he suggested seven guidelines for MNEs to manage their local distributors. Chevreux *et al.* provide useful extensions to some of these guidelines, when facing extreme demand uncertainty and volatility. For example, MNEs are supposed to help local distributors develop their own marketing capabilities. Here, it is important that local distributors also become more organizationally adaptable themselves by developing the ability to 'sense and pivot' in the face of uncertainty and volatility in local demand.[15]

Selecting local distributors keen to augment their sensing and pivoting abilities, which will then become complementary to the MNE's own FSAs in adaptive governance, is key to achieve this goal. MNEs should also help local distributors' capacity to act on intelligence on local market demand fluctuations, possibly through joint investments in 'digitizing and automating', so as to make them 'technologically capable'.[16] Again, selecting and supporting local distributors who are serious about augmenting their FSAs in areas such as data analytics and digitization is becoming increasingly critical.

Hau L. Lee provides a second complementary perspective in an insightful *CMR* paper on how manufacturing companies should manage uncertainty on both the input market and output market sides of the supply chain.[17]

Obviously, both demand- and supply-side uncertainties are detrimental to the firm's ability to serve customers effectively and efficiently. For example, even if demand were predictable, the **bullwhip effect**, meaning 'the amplification of order variability as one goes upstream along a supply chain',[18] could occur if there is poor planning or execution by the foreign distributor. Only if sufficient information on demand is shared – and replenishment/distribution planning and execution aligned – with the MNE's supply chain management, can this effect be avoided, and distributor-driven demand uncertainty removed.

Lee notes that another way to manage demand uncertainty is to adopt a postponement strategy, whereby some production activities are performed at the end of the production process, thereby maximizing this process's flexibility. In this way, customization of end products is done as late as possible, in line with changing customer demand. For example, Benetton, the Italian clothing retailer, delays dying its sweaters with particular colours until very late in the production process. In the international business sphere, the optimal location for postponed activities such as final assembly, testing, and packaging is often a distribution centre close to the final customer, for example, European Distribution Centres (EDCs) in the European Union.

On the supply side, the MNE must also attempt to eliminate unnecessary uncertainty. Here, risk hedging is critical, for example, by setting up inventory pools at the regional level, close to the customer, to mitigate supply interruptions and to stabilize order fulfilment.

Lee's main point is that much of the uncertainty on the input and output market sides can be reduced or avoided by effective supply chain management. Here, vertical integration need not substitute for strategic partnerships with a variety of actors on the input market side (suppliers) or output market side (distributors). However, the management of such uncertainties requires substantial efforts in information sharing, joint coordination, and planning with suppliers and distributors. Here, the MNE can develop a new, non-location-bound FSA in the form of an 'agile supply chain', common among **international coordinators**. For example, Cisco Systems, a US-based supplier of networking equipment and network management for the Internet, created an 'e-Hub' that uses 'intelligent planning software' allowing 'the identification of potential supply and demand problems early, with proper warning given to the appropriate parties and resolution actions taken promptly via the Internet'.[19]

Even though the argument in Lee's paper addresses only specific types of uncertainty, Lee's recommendations and his conceptual analysis have broad applicability to all manufacturing firms. His recommendations are particularly relevant in the context of MNE supply chain challenges when penetrating foreign markets, because such penetration has enormous uncertainty surrounding both demand and the optimal supply chain to link sourcing, production, and distribution.

In the case of penetrating foreign markets, demand uncertainty on the output market side is not primarily the consequence of innovative product characteristics (in contrast to Lee's paper). Rather, demand uncertainty results from the MNE's limited capability to understand beforehand what set of new location-bound FSAs in the distribution sphere will need to be developed to penetrate the new market, as a complement to its internationally transferable FSA bundle, embodied in its exported products.

Supply uncertainty on the input market side, in the context of MNE management, is not primarily the consequence of a lack of maturity and stability of the supply chain in a technological sense (as it is in Lee's paper). Rather, uncertainty in the supply chain, starting on the input market side, results from bounded rationality challenges faced by senior MNE managers in their quest to optimize logistics when a new country needs to be linked to the existing supply chain.

Whereas Arnold's *HBR* piece addressed the broad, strategic challenges in MNE–distributor relationships, Lee's *CMR* piece usefully proposes adopting an agile supply chain in cases of high demand and supply uncertainties. With an agile supply chain, the MNE and its suppliers and distributors can all benefit from concerted action to reduce such uncertainties. Furthermore, Lee agrees with Arnold that vertical integration (i.e., ownership of the entire supply chain) is not necessary to manage uncertainty – with effective information sharing, joint coordination, and planning, the MNE can effectively manage uncertainty together with (external) suppliers and distributors. Lee's analysis is fully consistent with Chevreux *et al.*'s perspective that both the MNE and its supply chain partners must learn to 'sense and pivot', and engage in technology-based investments to address rapid environmental changes.

One of Arnold's main points in his *HBR* piece on foreign distribution is that, when penetrating a host country, MNEs should develop location-bound FSAs. Arnold's research essentially reveals that in the early stages of an MNE's entrance into a new market, FSA development is usually neither the main focus

MANAGEMENT INSIGHTS

of the MNE's strategy, nor of its local distribution partner. Rather, the MNE's primary goal is typically to reap the benefits of its bundle of existing, internationally transferable FSAs, embodied in its exported products, while minimizing costs and investment risks associated with foreign market penetration. This is made possible by using the existing, location-bound FSAs of distributors that allow easier market access.

As Arnold points out, however, MNEs thereby often cede strategic decision-making control to the local partner, assuming that this partner will handle critical areas of marketing and business development. The local distributor, however, often remains focused on short-term sales growth, knowing that this is the MNE's primary interest. The local distributor assumes (often correctly) that little MNE support or long-term commitment will be forthcoming to improve the outcome of the distribution arrangement, and that great market success might actually lead to MNE attempts to internalize the distribution activity, especially in cases whereby both parties would need to invest heavily in proprietary knowledge (e.g., brand name development) to sustain and further strengthen such success. The development of new FSAs suffers because of this lack of credible, mutual commitments.

By contrast, in the few examples Arnold provides of successful, long-term distribution partnerships and in his recommendations for properly building such partnerships, both sides place greater importance on new FSA development, even in the short run, especially in terms of effectively linking the MNE's and the distributor's knowledge base. Distributors who have managed to remain successful over the long run have contributed to MNE competitiveness by sharing market intelligence and helping to build new FSAs, for example, by initiating new projects and working collaboratively with other distributors in neighbouring markets. Such distributor commitments have been associated with similar commitments from the MNE, in terms of managerial, financial, and knowledge-based resources to develop the market.

Such credible, mutual commitments only make sense, according to Arnold, if there is an overall 'company fit' between the MNE and its local distributor; namely, they must be willing and able to work together as partners in building new FSAs, rather than focusing solely on the immediate 'market fit' when linking the MNE's products (and thus the MNE's underlying, internationally transferable FSAs) with the distributor's existing customer base (and thus its location-bound FSAs, providing local market access). The linking of internationally transferable FSAs held by the MNE and location-bound FSAs held by the distributor should thus not be assessed merely in static terms, at the time of the agreement. Rather, such linkages must be crafted over time, and initial similarities between the MNE and the distributor (e.g., in terms of corporate culture, incentive systems, or supply chain routines) can greatly facilitate this crafting process.

This idea of distributors – actors external to the MNE – contributing to the generation of FSAs provides an interesting extension of this book's main framework for analyzing patterns of FSA development. In earlier chapters, we assessed whether FSA development took place through the parent organization in the home country or through subsidiaries in host markets. Arnold's article adds another level to the analysis by assessing whether, and to what extent, FSA development in foreign host markets should take place internally, through wholly owned subsidiaries, or externally, through partnerships with local distributors. This view is also aligned with Becker and Zirpoli's (2017) analysis in Chapter 2 on making trade-offs between outsourcing and back-sourcing. Furr and Shipilov's (2018) analysis of adaptative ecosystems of innovation, discussed in Chapter 6, dealt with similar managerial challenges in the realm of upstream innovation activities. In each of these cases, the most important, generic conclusion is perhaps that bounded rationality and bounded reliability obstacles to efficient management driven by external uncertainties do not require vertical integration of all affected economic activities. Instead, what matters is the judicious management of partnerships with a variety of actors who hold FSAs better managed outside the MNE than within its internal network.

Arnold's prescription for the long term is to adopt a mix of the two governance mechanisms in distribution: establishing subsidiaries to control the company's international marketing strategy, especially in the context of serving key global customers, while also retaining external distributors as partners to service optimally smaller, local customers. The normative conclusion is thus clearly to establish long-term strategic alliances with external partners, in this case local distributors, to benefit from their FSAs – a concept covered in greater depth in Chapter 12.

Following Arnold's advice – adopting a mix of 'internal' and 'external' distribution operations – would allow an MNE to pursue a mix of strategies of FSA development, which can be analyzed using our framework of FSA development patterns. According to Arnold, the subsidiary should play to its strengths (i.e., transferable FSAs) and adhere to a more standardized approach focusing on large international accounts. By contrast, the local distribution partner should play to its strengths (i.e., location-bound FSAs) and should be nationally responsive in providing service coverage that is unique and adapted to each host market. These strategies correspond to Patterns I and IV of our framework, respectively (see Figure 11.1).

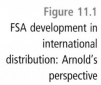

Figure 11.1
FSA development in
international
distribution: Arnold's
perspective

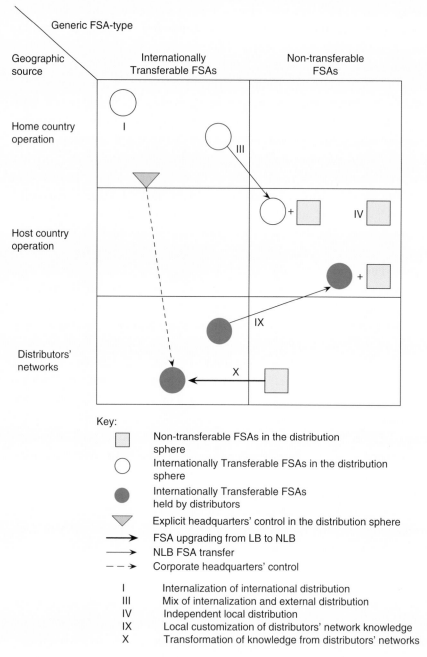

Key:

☐   Non-transferable FSAs in the distribution sphere

○   Internationally Transferable FSAs in the distribution sphere

●   Internationally Transferable FSAs held by distributors

▽   Explicit headquarters' control in the distribution sphere

⟶   FSA upgrading from LB to NLB

⟶   NLB FSA transfer

– – ➤   Corporate headquarters' control

I	Internalization of international distribution
III	Mix of internalization and external distribution
IV	Independent local distribution
IX	Local customization of distributors' network knowledge
X	Transformation of knowledge from distributors' networks

Pattern I builds on standard, internationally transferable FSAs in the realm of distribution that the MNE can deploy in its foreign subsidiaries around the world to manage large global clients (this is really the equivalent of global account management, discussed in Chapter 9). In contrast, Pattern IV here involves external distributors, who are supposed to provide unique, location-bound FSAs to satisfy the requirements of smaller, local customers, but with their exploitation potential largely confined to the specific host country market.

Arnold's fifth guideline for MNEs, that they should maintain control over strategic decision making, is a warning against domination of international distribution by Pattern IV, with independent local distributors afforded such a high level of autonomy and control that each country operates independently of the others, with market success determined by each national distributor's FSAs. This outcome would reduce the MNE's potential to reap economies of scope by sharing valuable knowledge across borders.

If the MNE relies solely on independent, foreign distributors – and if strategic control exerted by central headquarters remains weak – FSA development is unlikely to occur through Pattern V or VIII, even in the longer run, since the independent distributors will have little incentive to act as entrepreneurs and to generate new FSAs either autonomously (Pattern V) or collectively (Pattern VIII), to be shared subsequently with other MNE distribution partners or MNE subsidiaries. In this case, the independent distributors will not generate and share such FSAs because they know they will receive no benefit from successes achieved outside of their local markets.

If the MNE subsidiary cooperates with the local distributor, FSA development in the broad sense may end up resembling Pattern III, with the MNE introducing internationally transferable FSAs to the market and the local distributor adding unique location-bound FSAs to optimize sales and distribution within the country.

Arnold's seventh guideline, recommending the crafting of linkages between national distributors at the regional level, is a pitch for Patterns IX and X. Here, subsidiaries and local distributors work together as a network to create new FSA bundles that can then be customized with location-bound additions for each host market, in the case of Pattern IX, or transformed into internationally transferable FSAs and exploited internationally under the guidance of central headquarters, as in Pattern X.

In spite of its useful managerial prescriptions, Arnold's work has two major limitations. First, Arnold mistakenly recommends internalizing some customers and outsourcing others based primarily on the customer's size. According to Arnold, larger (and thus presumably more important) customers should be served by the MNE itself. In reality, however, parameters other than size may be more strategically important. The key question is whether a customer requires extensive interaction and customization, and expects continuous product adaptation. These customers should be dealt with internally, because such attention requires substantial resources, and because continuous product adaptation will probably be easier and more efficient if carried out directly by the MNE subsidiary rather than the distributor. (The subsidiary will have a closer and more direct relationship to the production facilities than the distributor will.) On the other hand, if a customer just purchases large quantities without any need for customization or continuous technical improvements, the use of an external distributor with strong location-bound FSAs may be the optimal solution.

Figure 11.2 incorporates this modification of Arnold's work. The figure shows two parameters critical to deciding the optimal governance of international distribution.

Figure 11.2
Optimal governance
of international
distribution

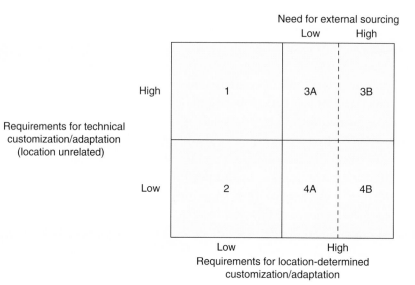

The vertical axis measures the final customer's needs for technical customization/adaptation of the product offering (low or high). Note that the word 'technical' is used here to indicate that these customer requirements are intrinsically unrelated to the customer's location. In other words, the MNE's success in meeting technical customer requirements depends on its proprietary technical capabilities, which are in principle non-location-bound. In contrast, the horizontal axis measures the level of customer requirements that are location-determined (low or high), for example, so as to meet prevailing health and safety standards considered normal in the host country. A high level of location-determined customer requirements on the right-hand side of Figure 11.2 implies that the necessary customization/adaptation cannot be performed simply by recombining and deploying internationally transferable knowledge, but necessitates deep knowledge of the local situation. The right-hand side of the horizontal axis is further subdivided into two segments, which address the need for external sourcing to develop the required location-bound knowledge (versus the ability to develop it internally). The latter need is again expressed as being low or high.[20]

In cell 2 of Figure 11.2, exports can occur without major governance complications, perhaps using simple market contracts with distributors if these can operate with low costs, since the customer imposes no requirements to alter the product offering. In cell 1, substantial technical customization/adaptation to customer requirements is necessary, thus providing an incentive for the internalization of distribution to facilitate smooth adaptation. In cells 3A and 4A, there is an additional need to satisfy location-determined customization/adaptation, and this need can be met internally by the MNE, namely, by developing new, location-bound FSAs inside the company. Note that in cell 3A, the MNE has exceptional recombination capabilities: it can develop further and recombine both technical knowledge (internationally transferable) and location-bound knowledge. Finally, in cells 3B and 4B, only external parties can satisfy the need for location-determined customization/adaptation. Cell 3B represents perhaps the most intriguing case: here, the MNE can customize/adapt its product offering to purely technical customer requirements, but it must also meet location-determined requirements for customization/adaptation which cannot be met internally. This is likely to lead to complex distribution arrangements, perhaps in the form of equity joint ventures, since both the MNE and its distributor need to engage in customization/adaptation processes to satisfy customer requirements.

Second, Arnold's sole focus on distribution leads to a relative neglect of the remainder of the supply chain, especially the input market side and the need for an integrative approach to the various supply chain components. Figure 11.3 displays such an integrative approach: here, the value chain consists of three main components – the left-hand side describes the input market, whereby external actors provide at least some inputs to the MNE. The middle section describes the upstream and downstream activities performed by the MNE itself. Finally, the right-hand side describes the output market, where distributors may play a key role, as discussed above.

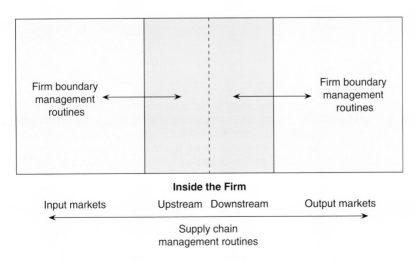

Figure 11.3
An integrative approach to coordinate various components of the supply chain

For reasons of simplicity, Figure 11.3 does not show explicitly the dispersed geography that may characterize this supply chain. However, dispersed geography imposes additional needs for recombination capabilities to coordinate the various components of the supply chain.

To increase efficiency, the MNE will typically try to adopt similar routines on the input market and output market sides. For example, if JIT systems are adopted on the input market side, a similar system will probably be used on the output market side. If production coordination occurs to a large extent through the use of sophisticated ICT systems, then sophisticated ICT will probably be used at the boundaries with suppliers and distributors. The point is simply that understanding a relationship with a foreign distributor, in terms of why and how it was set up, and how it should be managed in the future, may require an understanding of the MNE's entire supply chain set-up, rather than simply an understanding of the distributor and the MNE's distribution needs. Figure 11.4 illustrates the case of routine-type FSAs (which may span the entire supply chain) being transferred to host countries, where these are then augmented with complementary resources of distributors.

Figure 11.4
Managing foreign
distribution

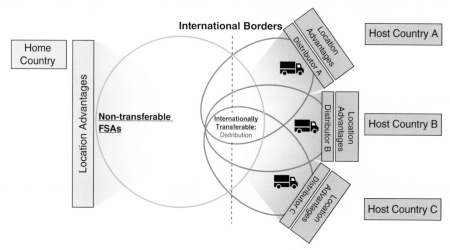

The NLB FSAs relevant to distribution and transferred to foreign operations in different host countries are indicated by small truck icons in host countries A, B, and C. The complementary resources provided by distributors in each of these host countries to meet local requirements are indicated by Distributor A, Distributor B, and Distributor C. In this particular visual, the host country ovals overlap, suggesting that the MNE may coordinate its export distribution strategy across a number of host countries.

Strategic Challenges in the New Economy

David Simchi-Levi, *William Schmidt* and *Yehua Wei* argue in their *HBR* article that conventional tools to anticipate and manage supply chain disruptions will not work properly when large-scale, unpredictable interruptions must be addressed.[21] The authors focus on suppliers, but their analysis is also largely valid for the distribution side of the supply chain.

When predictable and ordinary disruptions are considered, supply chain managers can calculate both the probability of such an event's occurrence and the magnitude of the expected (negative) impact on the firm from the event. This approach typically builds on a firm's historical data to quantify the risk from potential disruptions. The focus is then on anticipating and mitigating potential problems involving the most important supply chain partners.

But some supply chain disruptions are rare and unpredictable, and could lead to significant losses if they occurred. Examples include the Hurricane Katrina disaster (in United States) in 2005 and the Fukushima earthquake (in Japan) in 2011. In these instances, there were no historical data to prepare for such events or to quantify either the risk of occurrence or the magnitude of the impact. Importantly, even disruptions at the level of small suppliers, in terms of the volume of purchases involved, could cascade throughout the entire supply chain and lead to major disruptions for the MNEs involved.

The authors propose new guidelines that focus 'on the impact of potential failures at points along the supply chain rather than [on] the cause of the disruption'.[22] These guidelines include the following steps:

- *Step 1*: For each node in the supply chain, calculate the time to recovery (TTR) needed for the node to be fully restored after a disruption.[23]
- *Step 2*: Construct a complete supply chain network map, using the TTR data and other firm information to identify any hidden dependencies.[24]
- *Step 3*: Assess the performance impact (PI) of each node, by hypothetically removing it from the network for the length of its TTR.[25]
- *Step 4*: Assign a risk exposure index (REI) of 1.0 to the node with the highest PI, and relative scores between 0 and 1.0 to all other nodes.[26]

The above step-wise approach can help firms 'identify hidden exposures . . . [and] avoid the need for predictions about rare events . . . [and] reveal supply chain dependencies and bottlenecks . . . [and] promote discussion and learning'.[27]

The four-stage approach allows firms to bring risks to the surface that would have remained hidden when using conventional risk assessment approaches. Obvious high risks include large suppliers in terms of the monetary amounts spent on purchases, and that have a high performance impact on the MNE. These suppliers could be incentivized to diversify operations (and thereby risks) across multiple manufacturing sites in different countries and regions, or the MNE could engage in supplier diversification itself. However, many hidden risks that now become visible are related to suppliers from whom much smaller purchases are made, but still have a high performance impact. Mitigation strategies associated with these hidden risks can include adding flexibilities in the supply chain, for example, by making substitution of particular inputs from specific supplier sources easier through the use of standardized components rather than components specific to a single supplier, or by having alternative supply options readily available.

Arnold described local distributors' changing roles when MNEs try to grow in foreign markets, and he suggested seven guidelines for MNEs' managing local distributors. Simchi-Levi *et al.* complement Arnold by focusing on the supply chain at the input side. The guidelines they propose to predict and mitigate the impact of unexpected disruptions of supply chains at the input side are also largely valid at the distribution side. The potential 'time to recovery' and 'performance impact' on the entire supply chain after a disruption can be assessed for each supplier and distributor. Importantly, Arnold's view that dedicated distributors should be viewed as strategic partners holds for suppliers as well. In fact, a predicted high performance impact of a disturbance with any supply chain actor should, in many cases, lead to a dialogue with this actor, so as to work jointly on solutions for possible future disturbances. Both the MNE and this supply chain actor can benefit from joint efforts to anticipate supply chain inter-ruptions that could materialize, thereby reducing bounded rationality and the likelihood that either of the two partners would behave opportunistic-ally post-interruption.

The proposed network mapping should be especially useful to help MNEs prepare for low-probability but high-impact supplier and distributor risks, with impacts cascading throughout the entire supply chain. The paradoxical conclusion is that higher expected performance impacts from a disruption at one actor's site do not necessarily imply more unilateral attempts at diversifi-cation by the MNE (so as to allow circumventing the high-impact supplier or distributor). If treated as long-term strategic partners, reliable suppliers and distributors may well be willing to engage in joint risk impact-mitigation efforts with the MNE.

Five Management Takeaways

1. Review your international distribution strategy and portfolio of relationships with local distributors.
2. Follow the seven guidelines for MNEs when using local distributors in international expansion.
3. Assess in a comparative fashion the uncertainty in your input and output markets in your supply chain.
4. Apply an integrative approach to coordinate your entire supply chain, whereby outside economic actors should often be regarded as partners in an adaptive governance system.
5. Conduct detailed network mapping to identify accurately the locus and potential impacts of unpredictable supply chain disruptions, and work with supply chain partners to reduce the magnitude of potential negative impacts.

12

Entry Mode Dynamics 2: Strategic Alliance Partners

Five Learning Objectives

1. To describe the meaning of 'strategic alliances' and their main benefits.
2. To explain the concept of 'dependency spiral' and the ways to avoid it when outsourcing.
3. To develop an understanding of the risks of dependence, exploitation, and abuse in strategic alliances.
4. To support a reflection on the meaning of the 'learning race' and 'learning asymmetry' concepts in the alliance context.
5. To illustrate how MNEs select wholly owned affiliates versus alliances in the emerging economy context.

This chapter examines Hamel *et al.*'s idea that, when pursuing strategic alliances with partners who are also rivals, firms should try to learn as much as possible from their partners while giving away as few of their FSAs as possible. In theory, strategic alliances have three main benefits: they allow firms to share risks and costs (particularly R&D costs), they allow firms to benefit from their partner's complementary resources, and they allow the quicker development of capabilities to deliver products and services valued by the output market. Hamel *et al.* provide other advice on carrying out strategic alliances, including the advice to keep developing FSAs independently and to avoid a vicious cycle of dependency on the partner. These ideas will be examined and then critiqued using the framework presented in Chapter 1.

Significance

In 1989, **Gary Hamel**, **Yves Doz** and **C. K. Prahalad** wrote an influential *HBR* article on the dynamics of international strategic alliances.[1] They focused on the phenomenon whereby large MNEs form strategic alliances with equally large foreign firms that are also rivals in the international marketplace.

Such 'competitive collaboration' occurs because MNEs find it increasingly difficult to bear alone the enormous R&D costs – and singlehandedly gain easy access to the scarce resources required – to launch new products. These problems are amplified in the context of the compressed time frames necessary to stay ahead of rivals. Hamel *et al.* attempt to explain why some MNEs benefit greatly from these partnerships, in terms of new FSA development, while others do not.

Hamel *et al.*'s methodology involved a five-year study of fifteen international strategic alliances at various levels within the organizations involved, covering industries such as automotive manufacturing, semiconductors, computers, and electronics. The sampling reflected a triad-based approach with a mix of cross-region alliances, including: seven US–Japanese cases, four US–European ones, two European–Japanese ones, and two intra-European ones. Wherever possible, both partners in the alliance were carefully investigated to uncover the role of strategic alliances in corporate strategy and competitive positioning, as well as the factors affecting the company either gaining or losing relative advantage by collaborating with a rival.

The benchmark adopted for evaluating alliance success was not how long the alliance lasted, which the authors claim is a commonly used, but misguided, performance parameter. Rather, they focused on the change in each partner's competitive strength: 'We focused on how companies use competitive collaboration to enhance their internal skills and technologies while they guard against transferring competitive advantages to ambitious partners.'[2] The authors focused on how to win the so-called 'learning race' – namely, how to learn more from your partner than your partner learns from you.

The authors identified four key principles that successful companies adhere to when forming strategic alliances:

1. Collaboration is competition in a different form . . .
2. Harmony is not the most important measure of success . . .
3. Cooperation has limits. Companies must defend against competitive compromise . . .
4. Learning from partners is paramount . . .[3]

Their study revealed that, overall, Japanese MNEs – and Asian firms more generally – benefited the most from their strategic alliances with MNEs from other areas of the world. Hamel *et al.* provided four reasons why Asian MNEs tended to win the learning race. First, Asian firms tended to be intrinsically more receptive and more willing to put effort into learning from their alliance partners. This aspect is rooted in cultural and historical differences; the authors suggest that: 'Western companies won't realize the full benefits of competitive collaboration until they overcome an arrogance born of decades of leadership.'[4]

Second, the Asian MNEs viewed alliances as an opportunity to develop new FSAs, and not primarily as a convenient tool to reduce investment costs and risks, (usually) on the upstream, technology development, and manufacturing side, in contrast to several Western firms.

Third, Asian MNEs usually defined clear learning objectives regarding what they wanted to achieve from a partnership, and focused their efforts on acquiring new knowledge and observing their partners' practices in order to support such learning.

Fourth, the Asian MNEs' contribution to alliances often involved complex, tacit process knowledge that is not easily imitated or transferable, whereas the Western partners' contribution often involved easily transferable, codified product and marketing knowledge.

While some companies gain competitive strength from alliances, others fall behind as their FSAs are transferred to – and absorbed by – the alliance partner. For example, the authors noted that Western companies in particular often fall behind when they form alliances with Asian MNEs that are largely outsourcing arrangements, whereby manufacturing and technology development become the responsibility of the Asian partners, who essentially act as original equipment manufacturers (OEMs). This can cause a dangerous ratchet effect, since outsourcing to an OEM leads to lower investments in R&D (and in product and process design) by the Western firm until eventually not only manufacturing, but all the upstream, FSA-developing activities have been transferred to the Asian partner. The risk is that the Asian partner firm can then enter markets on its own and compete outside the realm of the alliance agreement because of what it has learned inside the alliance.

The authors also observed that companies positioned as 'troubled laggards' often pair up with 'surging latecomers' to the market.[5] The lagging companies are trying to find a quick fix for their own deficiencies, especially in terms of their inadequate innovation capabilities (e.g., their lack of 'manufacturing excellence' routines, such as appropriate total quality control systems), whereas the newcomers are seeking to fill specific capability gaps, often in the realm of stand-alone knowledge (e.g., product or market knowledge) that can more easily be absorbed. With this starting position, the weaker firms (in practice, usually the 'troubled laggards') may become trapped in a 'dependency spiral'. Here, their attention may shift from continuously reassessing the merits of the alliance vis-à-vis strategic alternatives (such as a wholly owned subsidiary or market-based contracting), towards trying to keep the present partner satisfied with the relationship, which may become increasingly critical to the survival of the dependent company.

When outsourcing, senior MNE managers should respect four principles in order to avoid a vicious cycle of increasing dependency on a partner, and to maintain a focus on developing the FSAs required for competing in the international marketplace. First, outsourcing to provide a competitive product cannot replace the need to build FSAs over the long term. Second, senior managers should consider the negative consequences of outsourcing in terms of capability losses, and not just the short-term beneficial cost effects of de-internalizing key value-creating activities. Third, senior managers should be aware of the cumulative effects that individual outsourcing decisions can have, in terms of creating a vicious cycle of deepening dependence on outside actors. Fourth, if FSAs do dissipate towards a partner in an outsourcing relationship, they must be rejuvenated and strengthened as quickly as possible.[6] Hamel *et al.* note that, while ending up with a winner and a loser in an alliance is a common scenario, it is nonetheless possible for both MNEs to benefit from working together. The key condition here is each MNE's willingness and ability to learn from its partner, so as to allow new capability development, while avoiding excessive transfer and diffusion of its own proprietary knowledge. Moreover, the new knowledge obtained from the external partners must be effectively disseminated internally: 'Knowledge acquired from a competitor-partner is only valuable after it is diffused through the organization.'[7]

In order for both MNEs to benefit from the alliance, each must share some but not all of its knowledge and skills. Each partner must acquire new knowledge and skills and foster new FSAs without transferring its proprietary strengths:

> The challenge is to share enough skills to create advantage vis-à-vis companies outside the alliance while preventing a wholesale transfer of core skills to the partner. This is a very thin line to walk. Companies must carefully select what skills and technologies they pass to their partners. They must develop safeguards against unintended, informal transfers of information. The goal is to limit the transparency of their operations.[8]

The nature of the FSAs contributed by an MNE to an international alliance affects how easily these FSAs will diffuse to a partner. One important variable here is called 'mobility'. Mobility refers to the ease of moving the complete physical instructions of how to duplicate an FSA. For example, if FSAs in the realm of technical knowledge can be represented in their entirety in easily understandable technical drawings and manuals, these FSAs are highly mobile. The more mobile the FSA, the more easily it may diffuse. A second relevant variable is called 'embeddedness'. An FSA is embedded if it cannot easily be shared through communication with actors outside the firm, without problems of interpretation or absorption across cultures. For example, stand-alone knowledge is usually less embedded than integrated skills or processes. The more embedded the FSA, the less easily it may diffuse.

Hamel *et al.* advise companies to take steps to limit the easy replicability and unintended diffusion of FSAs to their alliance partners. Such steps might include limiting the formal scope of the alliance to a well-defined learning area. They might also include carefully considering where the alliance should be physically located, with a preference for a location away from the MNE headquarters, so as to avoid providing the alliance partner with a window on all the MNE's key FSAs (e.g., critical technologies), even those unrelated to the alliance's scope of activity.

Still another step may entail establishing incremental, performance-related checkpoints, whereby specific knowledge bundles valuable to alliance functioning are shared only within the alliance context, and only when the alliance has achieved some pre-set performance benchmarks.

A last step consists of empowering company 'gatekeepers' to control and moderate informal information transfers at lower operational levels to the partner. Here, easy access to key people and facilities must be prohibited, employee discipline and loyalty must be stimulated, and cultural differences that affect information flows must be carefully assessed. For example, as regards the last point on cultural differences, Western engineers often like to share information on their technical achievements, driven by their enthusiasm and professional pride. Their Japanese counterparts, on the other hand, are generally more likely to keep their company's proprietary knowledge confidential.

Context and Complementary Perspectives

Hamel *et al.* published their *HBR* article in 1989, one year before Prahalad and Hamel's classic *HBR* piece 'The core competence of the corporation', which we discussed in Chapter 2. The context for these two articles is similar in terms of the level of attention devoted in the academic literature at that time to the competitive strengths of Japanese (and more generally Asian) manufacturers, relative to US and European MNEs. As in the other *HBR* article, many of the examples cited in the article on strategic alliances were drawn from manufacturing industries such as automobiles, semiconductors, computers, and electronics, where strong international competition prevails, and where the potential of reaping cost efficiencies through incremental innovation, as well as scale and scope economies, is compelling. In these industries, however, it is difficult to access the required volume and span of the diverse resources needed to achieve such benefits. Therefore, risk mitigation is critical. Here, strategic alliances may provide a way rapidly and efficiently to access the required resources, as compared to the other governance alternatives available to MNEs, such as internal development of the relevant FSAs or purchase of the required knowledge through market-based contracts.

During the thirty years since this article was written, the trend towards collaborative partnerships among large, international firms vis-à-vis other governance alternatives has persisted, motivated by the same three factors identified by Hamel *et al.* First, alliances allow partners to share high R&D costs and the risks thereof. Second, alliances allow each partner to benefit from complementarities in scarce talent and related capabilities brought to the table by the other partner. Third, with shortened time frames to bring new products to the market, alliances may also reduce the risk of being too late to develop the capabilities to deliver products and services valued by the output market.

At the same time, concerns about unintended knowledge dissipation as a result of alliances have become even more severe over the past twenty-five years, given the proliferation of internet and cellular communication technologies, which make information easier to transport and disseminate (i.e., more mobile).

Erin Anderson and **Sandy Jap** provide a first complementary perspective to Hamel *et al.*'s piece on strategic alliances. Anderson and Jap's *SMR* article addresses the so-called 'dark side' of alliances: dependence, exploitation, and abuse.[9]

Recall that Hamel *et al.*'s *HBR* piece explicitly noted that a superficially harmonious relationship may not be a good indicator for alliance success, as surface harmony may hide deep dysfunction, such as one partner becoming overly dependent on the other, or dissipating too much proprietary knowledge to its alliance partner.

Anderson and Jap take this perspective a step further. On the basis of a number of large-scale research studies, they argue that the best relationships on the surface – namely, the most stable and long-lasting ones, with excellent personal ties among alliance partner managers – are often the *most* vulnerable to problems of bounded reliability. If one partner engages in continuous, strong alliance-specific investments, whereas the other does not, then the incentive for the latter partner to start abusing the relationship grows stronger. This observation is similar to the one made in Chapter 11, which discussed the problem of manufacturers becoming too dependent on mega-distributors. In that case, once the dependency relationship is established, mega-distributors increasingly squeeze the manufacturer to reduce prices, even when the manufacturer cannot realistically make the necessary productivity improvements. Anderson and Jap's perspective provides a useful antidote to the somewhat naïve view, often promulgated in business schools, that longer-term relationships usually lead to trust and therefore better alliance performance through improved knowledge transfer and joint FSA development processes. The reality may be quite the opposite: high levels of trust make a relationship more vulnerable to bounded reliability, whether in the form of benevolent preference reversal or opportunism, unless safeguards are introduced to prevent it.

Anderson and Jap advocate the use of six types of safeguards to avoid the dark side of close relationships from creeping into alliance functioning:[10]

1. *Regular re-evaluation of the alliance relationship.* One particularly effective way to re-evaluate the relationship is to bring in new evaluators. The rotation

of employees and managers, similar to the rotation observed in many countries' diplomatic services, may contribute greatly to avoiding – and mitigating the effects of – bounded reliability problems. This is because bounded reliability can be a problem not only on the partner's side (e.g., the partner purposely overbilling for contributions to the alliance), but also inside the firm itself (e.g., a manager misguidedly trusting the partner's cost estimates for contributions to the alliance based on a harmonious relationship with an associate in the partner firm).

2. *Continued focus on profitability rather than volume.* Especially in supply-chain relationships, senior managers often attach great importance to the absolute and relative size of their relationship with particular suppliers and distributors. However, relationship size can be a poor indicator of the relationship's contribution to profitability, especially when it is abused by the partner (e.g., when the promise of loyalty by a customer or distributor is accompanied by unreasonable demands for volume discounts, thereby negatively affecting the firm's profitability).

3. *Continued attention to alternatives ('back-ups').* By focusing on realistic alternatives (and even moderately investing in such alternatives), which can be tapped into if the relationship sours, managers can avoid becoming too dependent on one specific alliance partner, thereby reducing the possibility of sustained abuse by that partner. This is a form of risk minimization, equivalent to assessing the possible loss that could occur in case the alliance fails to perform, and then making sure such potential losses are minimized by ensuring access to non-alliance alternatives.

4. *Swapping hostages.* This means that both partners should invest resources that cannot easily be redeployed outside of the alliance without significant loss of value. Irreversible, alliance-specific investments create an incentive for each partner to make the alliance a success. However, such investments must be made by both partners. If only one partner provides a 'hostage', and the other does not, then the failure of the alliance would have less serious economic consequences for the latter partner. This gives the latter partner undue leverage, which can cause bounded reliability problems. In the ideal case, the hostage provided by each firm constitutes a credible safeguard for the other.

5. *Setting and reassessing common goals.* Strategic alliances typically face substantial uncertainty about the future, sometimes more so than when a firm expands alone, because the value of the resources contributed by the partner is difficult to estimate in advance. This value will depend to a large extent on the firm's evolving ability to recombine the partner's resources with those already present in the firm itself. Setting clear goals and re-evaluating these goals based on actual alliance performance is critical, especially after the dust

has settled over the initial unrealistic expectations regarding the economic potential of resource recombination within the scope of the alliance.

6. *Avoiding vicious cycles of suspicion and the resulting build-up of bounded reliability.* If one firm in the alliance suspects that its partner will not make good on its promises and systematically interprets its partner's moves as attempts to abuse the partnership, or as signs that the partner is no longer committed to the alliance, this may lead to the alliance's breakdown. A breakdown is especially likely if such suspicion leads to signals that the alliance is not functioning properly and if the partner reacts negatively to such signals (e.g., new company policies to withhold technical information from the alliance upsets the alliance partner, who then retaliates by introducing a similar policy). Transparency of all available information (especially in the realm of cost accounting) and open communication, together with the first five guidelines above, are critical to avoiding such vicious cycles of suspicion.

Although Anderson and Jap do not focus specifically on international alliances, their study of the dark side of alliances is particularly useful in the international context, especially in the context of expansion to high-distance countries (e.g., alliances among North American and Asian MNEs), for three reasons. First, the goals of the alliance partners, and the time frame adopted by managers from high-distance countries, are likely to differ more than in the case of a single-country partnership, because of greater cultural, economic, institutional, and spatial differences than would be found within a single nation. Hence, extra attention must be devoted to joint goal setting and the regular reassessment thereof, so as to bridge the additional bounded rationality problems (especially information-processing issues). Second, higher distance is likely to be a driver of suspicion, especially when alliance performance problems occur that are (erroneously) attributed to the alliance partner's different country culture (as in 'firms from country X cannot be trusted to respect intellectual property rights'). Third, higher distance between partners may also have important effects in the realm of resource combination. The impact of various distance components may be underestimated when transferring and melding FSAs from different companies, especially when a large tacit component is involved, as well as routines that are affected by cultural, institutional, and economic norms prevailing in the different countries. When the alliance is between high-distance countries, the firms need to make special efforts to recognize such potential problems beforehand, and to continuously monitor these areas so as to identify any problems early.

Prashant Kale and *Jaideep Anand* provide a second complementary perspective to the Hamel *et al.* piece. Building on Hamel *et al.*'s insights, Kale and Anand describe in their *CMR* article the problems associated with establishing alliances, typically in the form of joint ventures (JVs) set up for market-seeking purposes in emerging economies such as India.[11]

Kale and Anand observe that such JVs are often set up when they are the foreign MNE's only penetration option, given a restrictive regulatory regime preventing wholly owned operations. Deploying and exploiting the MNE's FSAs then requires the use of a local partner, whose main substantive contribution may result from FSAs in government relations (especially if the local venture partner is state-owned) and from other location-bound FSAs allowing national responsiveness (e.g., reputational resources). If the MNE is trying to learn from a local partner without giving away too many of its own FSAs, building on the advice of Hamel *et al.*, which kind of partner should the MNE select? Kale and Anand suggest that, in the short term, the MNE can learn more from a privately owned local partner than from a state-owned partner, because with a state-owned partner, the MNE's learning efforts will be diverted by its overriding need to maintain a harmonious relationship simply to secure continued access to the local market. Because of its government connections, a state-owned partner will typically have more leverage in this area than a privately owned partner. In the long term, however, this state-owned partner may still be the better option, because an ambitious, privately owned partner may face stronger incentives to enter into a competitive learning race with the MNE, and to try to absorb the MNE's proprietary knowledge in order to upgrade its own FSA bundles. Senior managers must thus balance these short- and long-term concerns when choosing alliance partners.

In 1991, when the rigid regulatory system restricting FDI in India was liberalized, Kale and Anand observed five important changes in a majority of the JVs, based on their study of sixty-nine cases in India, in a variety of manufacturing industries, including chemicals, pharmaceuticals, engineering, information technology, and consumer goods:[12] stronger MNE involvement in strategy setting, an increased MNE equity stake (which had previously been restricted), greater MNE control over JV operations, an increase in MNE board representation, and the replacement of the local CEO by an expatriate.

Importantly, with ongoing liberalization, the incentive to form alliances with a local Indian partner in many cases disappeared, except in special cases of strong resource complementarity. In those cases where there remained an incentive to form an alliance, Kale and Anand found that the MNEs usually appeared much better equipped to win the 'learning race' against the local partner. The reasons for this better learning performance included three key elements: first, a systematically stronger MNE intent to learn from the partner; second, the better preparedness of the MNE to identify valuable learning opportunities on the basis of prior experiences with local partners elsewhere; and, third, the existence of learning routines underlying the MNE's learning capability. Such routines included, *inter alia*: (1) explicitly assigning specific individuals or units to manage the learning function within the alliance, for example, through formal working teams with the partner firm's managers and employees; (2) rotating managers and employees between the MNE and the JV, so as to facilitate knowledge flows into the MNE network; and (3) fostering systematic interactions between alliance personnel and personnel in the MNE parent and other MNE affiliates to diffuse knowledge gained in the JV.

Kale and Anand make the important observation that this learning asymmetry between the MNE and its local partner creates an inherent instability in the JV. Once the MNE learns what it needs to learn, this often eliminates the very resource complementarity that may have existed at the outset. Thus, there will be a growing incentive to transform the JV into a wholly owned subsidiary, especially for MNEs that operate as *international projectors* or *international coordinators*. Such firms may want to improve operational efficiency by changing the role of their affiliates and rationalizing international operations. Such changes may be more difficult to achieve when a JV partner is involved, namely when reassigning roles leads to perceived losses of activity bundles previously performed by the JV. There may also be discrepancies in the alliance partners' interests, for example, when the MNE engages in transfer pricing to maximize overall profitability, or when it attempts to transfer internal best practices across borders.

The instability of the JV may thus lead to its termination, possibly through the forced exit of the local partner. This dynamic – and the MNE's strong bargaining position – is the opposite of the one observed in the conventional international business literature, whereby the MNE faces the problem of 'obsolescing bargaining', meaning a rapid decline of its bargaining power once it has engaged in irreversible investments (in this case, investments that are location-specific and cannot be redeployed elsewhere without a large loss in value). This has been typical in the past for MNE investments in resource-based industries (e.g., mining and petroleum), whereby governments of developing countries (rather than local companies themselves) often reneged on agreements concluded with the MNE once the latter had engaged in large, irreversible investments. However, in many contemporary cases, much of the MNE's value added may reside in internationally transferable, intangible FSAs, which can easily be redeployed across borders without loss of productive value.

MANAGEMENT INSIGHTS

The Hamel *et al. HBR* article focuses on the process by which firms align themselves with their competitors to develop jointly new FSAs, but with each firm driven by the ulterior motive to appropriate for itself the largest possible part of the benefits arising from the alliance. In this process, each partner attempts to absorb as much knowledge as possible from the other, while protecting against the diffusion of its own FSAs. As the authors point out, an MNE's strategic goal in entering an alliance must always stay focused on new FSA creation – by definition, strengths specific to the firm itself – while guarding against FSA dissipation benefiting the partner. It is a challenge to stay focused on such long-term goals, as many senior managers have an incentive to pursue short-term cost reductions through the alliance (e.g., through outsourcing activities), even if those activities have FSAs embedded in them.

Importantly, the authors observe that some FSAs by their nature are more readily transferable to alliance partners than other ones, depending on how easily they can be transported, interpreted, and absorbed across cultures. Different FSAs have different levels of mobility and embeddedness. In the examples provided, complex skills and processes such as Japanese systems of manufacturing tend to be much more embedded, and thus more difficult to absorb, than the discrete, stand-alone FSAs held by Western MNEs. This analysis is displayed visually in Figure 12.1.

At the top (Figure 12.1A), we see two MNEs, one on each side of the conventional border line. The actual alliance is shown simply as a set of FSA bundles around the border line, because the essence of the alliance's dynamic functioning lies in the knowledge transfer processes among the MNEs involved and the alliance they have set up, irrespective of which specific international market(s) is to be served with the knowledge involved. The firm on the right-hand-side triangle in Figure 12.1A is the typical Asian company in Hamel *et al.*'s analysis. It is supposed to contribute routines, such as knowledge about total quality control processes, to the alliance. The firm on the left-hand-side triangle is the typical Western firm, providing stand-alone technical knowledge to the alliance. The alliance, shown in the figure between these two MNEs, benefits from the knowledge provided by each partner (see the curved arrows), and engages in recombination. Within the alliance, recombination occurs among the various types of knowledge involved, possibly taking into account location advantages of the geographic area where the alliance is physically placed. However, the thick arrow pointing upwards to the Asian MNE suggests substantial knowledge transfer from the alliance to that company, whereas the dotted arrow pointing downwards to the Western MNE suggests only limited knowledge transfer to that company. Once the Asian firm has absorbed all the knowledge it needs from the Western one, we can see the new situation visualized in Figure 12.1B. The Asian firm can exit from the alliance, possibly leading to the alliance's closure, having achieved its learning goals, as shown on the right-hand-side of Figure 12.1B. This firm has a vastly augmented reservoir of location-bound and non-location-bound knowledge, with the latter transferable across national borders. In contrast, the Western firm on the left-hand side is now left with a depleted reservoir of internationally transferable FSA bundles, because the alliance distracted it from pursuing independent FSA development, and because part of its relevant knowledge base is now in the hands of its previous partner, a major international rival.

Figure 12.1A
Dissipation of FSA bundles to alliance partners: The process

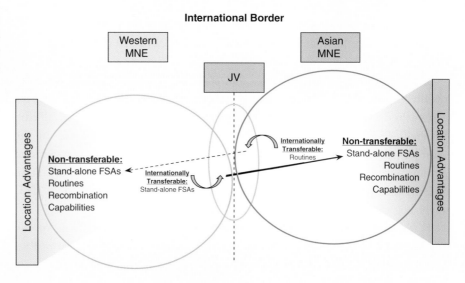

The two curved arrows pointing to the oval in the middle represent the JV, indicating that the Western MNE contributes stand-alone FSAs and the Asian MNE contributes routines to the JV. The thick arrow pointing right and the dotted arrow pointing left indicate that more of the JV's contribution to knowledge can be captured by the Asian MNE as compared to the Western one.

Figure 12.1B
Dissipation of FSA bundles to alliance partners: The outcomes after JV dissolution

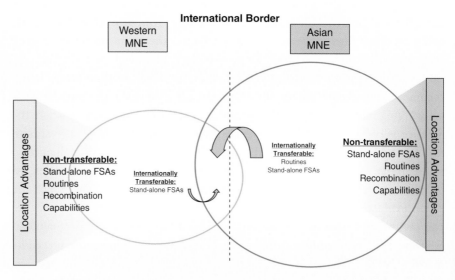

The NLB FSAs of the Asian MNE have expanded due to the absorption of its partner's stand-alone FSAs. The newly gained NLB FSAs of the Asian firm are represented by the thick arrow from the right, and by the expanded surface of its NLB-FSAs circle. In contrast, the Western MNE's stand-alone FSAs have not strengthened and may even have shrunk in relative terms, due to the dissipation of its knowledge base to the Asian MNE. This asymmetry with the Asian firm is represented by the much smaller arrow and the smaller surface of the NLB-FSAs circle.

Given the two different kinds of FSAs contributed, should the Western MNE have rejected such an alliance in the first place? This question is difficult to answer. On the one hand, the Western firm clearly came out second-best relative to the Asian firm. On the other hand, it nonetheless was able to access the Asian firm's complementary resources for the duration of the alliance. If it had been possible to replicate easily the Asian firm's complementary resources inside the Western MNE or to acquire them in the external market through simple contracting, there would have been no need for the MNE to engage in the international alliance. International alliances are formed when an MNE is unable to replicate the same or equivalent FSAs as those provided by a foreign alliance partner within an accept-able time frame or cost structure. Therefore, given these benefits, the alliance may have been good for the Western firm in an absolute sense as measured by profits, revenues, etc., compared to what would have happened if the alliance had not been formed. That is the appropriate standard. The answer as to whether the alliance was a good idea will depend on the specific case.

Once firms have decided to cooperate, they can choose among a range of different strategic alliance types, and the possibility of a merger or acquisition, as will be discussed in Chapter 13. Alliances will be preferred over mergers and acquisitions (M&As) when two conditions are satisfied. First, each firm needs only a subset of the resources/FSAs held by the partner. Second, it is difficult to dispose of the prospective partner's unusable resources because those resources are firm-specific. Thus, the advantage of strategic alliances is to have access to precisely those resource/FSA bundles that are really needed. In addition, strategic alliances may be preferred if the synergistic potential of the human and organizational resources is likely to be eliminated or diminished under the new identity in the case of a complete merger or takeover. Of course, greenfield investments and M&As may be legally prohibited in the first place, as a result of anti-trust policy, restrictions on foreign ownership, etc. In such cases, firms form alliances as a second-best solution.

Kale and Anand's *CMR* story line on alliances in emerging economies describes a conceptually similar challenge for the MNE. If the MNE faces a competence gap when operating internationally, and is unsuccessful in linking its FSAs with location advantages in host countries, the question arises whether this problem can be solved through cooperating with local firms that do have the resources required to establish such a link. Here, cooperation is a valid strategy, especially for customer-end activities, if the required resources cannot be acquired in the market and replicated within an acceptable time frame and cost structure. More specific-ally, strategic alliances can lead to rapid local embeddedness and access to social network ties in ways that are not possible by acting alone.

Alliances can help link the MNE's FSAs with location advantages abroad or other coveted resources in two ways (see Figures 12.2 and 12.3). First, the alliance can facilitate access to the **location-bound FSAs** of the local partner, similar to Kale and Anand's story line described above, as shown in Figure 12.2. Cooperation lets the MNE avoid high-cost location-specific adaptation investments. Second, the alliance facilitates the combination of the MNE's non-location-bound resources and existing FSAs with the equivalent resources of the partner (who may be another MNE) to create new *non-location-bound FSAs*, for example in the realm of technological innovation, as shown in Figure 12.3A. To the extent that strategic alliances reduce the needed resource commitments from a single MNE, they enable the MNE to obtain broader geographic coverage with the same resources.

Figure 12.2
Alliance in emerging economies: Foreign MNE accesses the partner's LB FSAs

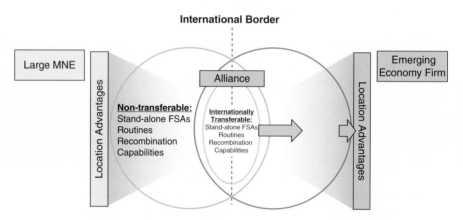

In a typical alliance in an emerging economy, represented by the oval in the middle of the figure, the foreign MNE transfers NLB FSAs to the alliance, whereas a local partner in the host country contributes LB FSAs. The NLB-FSAs bundle thereby indirectly becomes part of the local partner's FSA reservoir. Together, these FSA bundles deployed through the alliance allow accessing and benefiting from the coveted LAs in the host country, as indicated by the two thick arrows on the right.

Figure 12.3A
Alliance in emerging economies: Both partners access each other's NLB FSAs

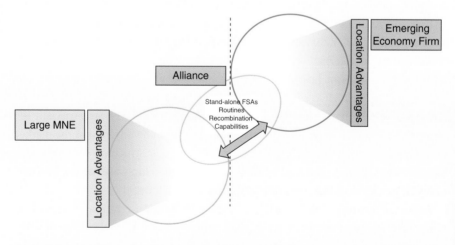

As equal partners, both the foreign MNE and the emerging economy MNE contribute NLB FSAs to the alliance in the emerging economy (represented by the diagonal oval in the middle of the figure).

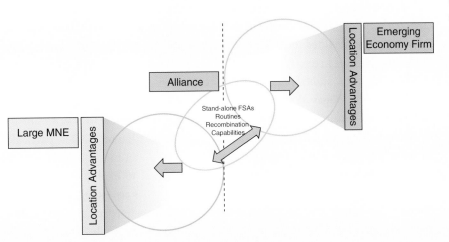

Figure 12.3B
Alliance in emerging
economies: Learning
as an outcome

The outcome of this emerging economy alliance is that both the foreign MNE and the emerging economy MNE have been able to strengthen their NLB FSA base by learning from their partner through the alliance activity. This learning has two parts: first, the absorption of the existing knowledge of the partner (represented by the short one-way thick arrows in each triangle); second, new knowledge creation arising from the alliance activity (represented by the longer, two-way thick arrow in the diagonal oval).

The benefits of cooperative agreements must always be weighed against the two significant costs. First, the MNE's FSAs could be appropriated by the alliance partner, which means that the MNE must introduce sufficient safeguards against such dissipation, as explained in this chapter by Hamel *et al.*

Second, an alliance may reduce coherence within the MNE, if the MNE becomes biased towards maintaining its initial arrangements with the alliance partner at the expense of long-term profit or cost considerations. Fortunately, steps can be taken to ensure that profit goals are not subordinated to other considerations, and that strategic alliances are not maintained without effective monitoring of their value added, as explained in this chapter by Anderson and Jap.

The partners' objectives have important implications for the alliance's stability. If each partner simply aims to extract resources from the other partner, alliances result in a learning race, as described above. The partner who first acquires the desired resources may dissolve the alliance even if the other partner has not completed its learning. If, however, the main purpose of the alliance is to create value by combining the resources of both firms, the resulting synergies can take the form of new FSAs that can be exploited globally, but are not necessarily amenable to being captured fully by individual alliance members (e.g., if the FSAs require the sustained infusion of resources from each partner).

This analysis suggests that we introduce the concept of alliance-specific advantages (ASAs), which cannot be classified using the old distinction between endogenous FSAs (originating inside the firm) and exogenous location advantages (originating outside the firm). ASAs have international exploitation potential, but are embedded in alliances and cannot be simply transferred to the individual partner firms.

ASAs are thus somewhat similar to subsidiary-specific advantages (SSAs), which are advantages that have international exploitation potential, but are embedded in subsidiaries and cannot be simply transferred to the rest of the MNE network. (As Bartlett and Ghoshal noted in Chapter 5, if a particular subsidiary has this kind of special expertise, it is sometimes wisest to let that subsidiary expand beyond its initial, assigned market to exploit its advantages internationally.) In contrast to SSAs, conventional FSAs are either non-location-bound FSAs (easily transferable and deployable across borders in foreign affiliates, and providing benefits of global exploitation, typically through scope economies) or location-bound FSAs (difficult to transfer to other affiliates across geographic space, but providing benefits of national responsiveness).

Like SSAs, ASAs can be exploited globally, for example, through world product mandates given to the alliance, but they cannot be simply diffused within the partner firms because of alliance-specific isolating mechanisms. Isolating mechanisms or mobility barriers exist, *inter alia*, because knowledge is tacit (difficult to codify), context-specific (each individual alliance partner's contribution may actually be locally embedded and these individual contributions may depend on the alliance's own technological and organizational trajectories), and dispersed across several individuals within the alliance (embedded in teams with members belonging to the different partner companies).

We now see that the concept of a 'transferable' advantage is more complicated than we thought. To this point, it has meant that the advantage can be transferred to another **economic actor** in another **location**. We now see that we must treat these two elements separately. While conventional transferable FSAs are transferable to other economic actors in other locations, ASAs and SSAs are transferable to other locations, but are not transferable to other economic actors.

ASAs enhance an alliance's stability. With an ASA, the advantage depends on the synergies gained by combining, in an evolutionary process, the partners' resources. These advantages would be lost to the individual firms if they left the alliance or if the alliance were dissolved. As ASAs grow stronger, the partner companies have greater incentives to stay in the alliance.

Turning to our framework of FSA development patterns, alliance formation takes various forms, consistent with a number of patterns from our framework. The difference between alliance formation as an entry mode to penetrate foreign markets and going in alone is shown in Figure 12.4.

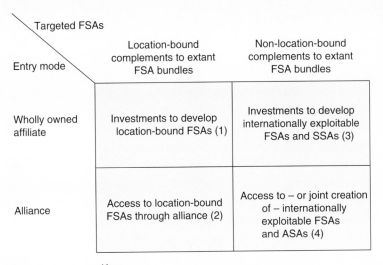

Figure 12.4
MNE foreign market penetration via wholly owned affiliates versus alliances

Quadrants 2 and 4 are the quadrants relevant to alliance formation. Quadrant 2 reflects the main case described in Kale and Anand's *CMR* article, whereby an MNE partners with a local firm in an emerging economy, largely driven by government restrictions on entry mode choice and other regulations of MNE activities. However, from a dynamic perspective, the MNE may soon learn all that is required to operate independently in the foreign market. Therefore, if FDI is liberalized, the MNE may shift its longer-run entry mode to quadrant 1, thus making the alliance only an intermediate market penetration option.

Quadrant 4 reflects the content of Hamel *et al.*'s *HBR* article, whereby two firms may engage in a learning race, with one of them coming out as the winner and having little incentive to continue with the alliance. However, if ASAs have been created, for example, within multi-partner global airline alliances such as Oneworld and Star Alliance, partners in the alliance cannot simply exit from the alliance and take their learning with them, as several sources of competitive advantage are embedded in the alliance itself. For example, in the case of the global airline alliances, the MNEs involved share brand names, operational bases, computer reservation systems, and external relationships across markets. These ASAs resulting from the pooling and recombination of the FSAs of the individual companies simply cannot be replicated by individual companies that have left an alliance.

Hamel *et al.*'s prescription to learn more from your partner than your partner learns from you has three major limitations. First, senior managers who pay too much attention to that goal may overlook the important goal of creating ASAs. ASAs are simply not the sort of things that either partner can learn from the other.

Second, attempts to win such a learning race may cause dysfunctionalities: if each partner attempts to learn as much as possible through the alliance, while contributing as little as possible, the intent to limit knowledge sharing may itself be instrumental to a vicious cycle of ever-increasing bounded reliability problems.

For example, individuals and subunits may engage in resource commitments to the alliance and then be told by dedicated gatekeepers that they are out of line, and that what was promised to the alliance would jeopardize the firm's competitiveness. The problem for gatekeepers assigned to regulate knowledge flows is to identify the fine line between information that is critical to the alliance's success and information that is not required to achieve such success, but simply makes the partner/rival stronger. An aggressive gatekeeper may thereby hinder valuable recombination of resources coming from the two partners and thus reduce the learning capability of the alliance itself, ultimately reducing its value to both partners. Gatekeepers who limit knowledge transfer without knowing all the relevant information (e.g., facing bounded rationality problems caused by geographical distance from the alliance activity centre) may trigger a vicious cycle of suspicion, as described in Anderson and Jap's *SMR* article. This vicious cycle can then produce bounded reliability problems (including opportunistic behaviour), which would not otherwise have occurred.

A third and related limitation of Hamel *et al.*'s *HBR* article is that it insufficiently addresses the impact of culture on alliance dynamics. Their article observes, for example, that Japanese firms often appear to be the winners in international alliances, at the expense of their Western partners. However, it is not entirely clear what role culture plays in this superior learning performance, nor how cultural differences leading to learning performance differentials should be addressed.

One simplistic interpretation could be that MNEs from some cultures are more inclined to engage in opportunistic behaviour than those of other cultures, thus implying that the latter should avoid engaging in alliance formation with the former, irrespective of the economic and technical complementarity of FSAs. A second, equally simplistic interpretation is that some cultures are simply not conducive to competent cooperative behaviour in business, and should for that reason try to abstain from alliance formation. A third, more sophisticated view of the impact of culture is that some countries may have developed, at the macro-level, a superior ability to successfully manage alliances, because of a variety of historical events, such as a multi-decade-long tradition of absorbing and adopting foreign knowledge bundles (e.g., through licensing, as the Japanese did after World War II).

Finally, the question arises whether country-level culture is necessarily relevant to alliance success or failure, as compared to the corporate cultures of the respective firms engaged in alliance formation. Here, a corporate culture suggesting that alliance functioning is little more than a learning race and advocating the protection of proprietary knowledge against diffusion to alliance partners, especially those of a high-distance culture, may jeopardize alliance success. This is especially the case if the alliance is established in a context whereby opportunistic behaviour (cheating) by the partner is expected: culturally determined, false attributions of cheating may lead to genuine attempts to cheat, as the result of a vicious cycle of suspicion build-up.

Strategic Challenges in the New Economy

Herman Vantrappen and *Daniel Deneffe* argue in their *HBR* article that, in the modern economy, the size of capital investments for physical assets has risen considerably in recent years (illustrative examples from their 2016 article include requisite capital expenditures of US $600 million for an oil rig; $200 million for a container ship; $500 million for a biopharmaceutical facility; $25 billion for nuclear reactor designs).[13] These rising capital investments create a dilemma for companies that must make immediate investments in physical assets to remain on par with (global) rivals, but worry about the irreversible nature of some of these investments, and the impossibility of alternative deployment in case market demand sours on their intended purpose. In the international sphere, a key additional challenge may be the political risk foreign companies incur (e.g., the 2007 nationalizations of foreign-owned assets in Venezuela).

The authors therefore propose considering a broad spectrum 'of alternative asset ownership and operation models' that move away from full ownership and control, and allow sharing risks with partners.[14] They propose seven alternative models when engaging in large-scale physical asset investments, whereby for our purposes Company A and Company B below can be firms from different countries involved in a cross-border partnership.

- *'Model 1: Virtual operator'*.[15] Company A (an operator company that could be a foreign MNE) rents asset capacity from Company B (an integrated owner in a host country).
- *'Model 2: Asset capacity pooling'*.[16] Company A and Company B increase the capacity utilization of their respective assets by making a sharing agreement involving these assets.
- *'Model 3: Joint venture involving similar assets'*.[17] Company A and Company B establish a joint venture, and selectively transfer similar assets to the joint venture (e.g., a joint venture between two MNEs from different countries to build a new production plant).
- *'Model 4: Joint venture involving complementary assets'*.[18] Company A and Company B establish a joint venture and transfer complementary assets to this

joint venture (e.g., technology-rich assets from Company A and production-related assets from Company B).

- *'Model 5: Dual asymmetrical joint venture'.*[19] Company A (a financial investor) and Company B (an industrial operator) establish two joint ventures, one that owns the asset and the other that operates the asset, with an agreed-upon, negotiated ownership structure of each venture.
- *'Model 6: Co-funding of a third-party asset'.*[20] Company A and Company B co-fund Company C, which will build an asset for subsequent joint exploitation.
- *'Model 7: Joint takeover of an asset'.*[21] Company A and Company B invest together in the takeover of an asset that can only be purchased at a high cost.

In each of the above cases, an MNE might avoid the risk of 'missing the boat' on requisite large-scale investments in physical assets.[22] At the same time, each of these 'shared risk' cases paradoxically carries some risk of sharing proprietary, extant resource bundles and FSAs that can ultimately lead to a new or stronger rival,[23] or to domestic political actors feeling emboldened to take over fully the physical assets from the foreign-owned MNE without adequate compensation. The main message is that strategic alliances can come with a variety of governance structures, which makes a comparison with wholly owned operations more complex.

Under the heading of 'competitive collaboration', Hamel *et al.* analyzed both the potential and the risks of international strategic alliances with foreign competitors to launch innovative products resulting from high investments in R&D. These alliances were specifically driven by the desire to reduce upfront investment costs and related risks thereof. Vantrappen and Deneffe's analysis is aligned with Hamel *et al.*'s perspective, but is focused on investments in physical assets rather than R&D. It discusses seven alternative asset ownership and operation models that supposedly make it unnecessary for firms to maintain full ownership and control over expensive and non-redeployable physical assets.

MNEs often utilize these types of alternative investment models in international settings. The potential benefits can be significant. For example, airlines around the world have successfully adopted international asset pooling (Model 2). International joint ventures (Models 3, 4, and 5) have been used extensively as MNEs share similar or complementary resources with actors in foreign countries in the pursuit of common goals. Finally, MNEs often work in consortia to acquire or develop and exploit foreign assets (Model 7) that are very expensive and are associated with substantial risks (e.g., in natural resources industries).

But all of these alternative governance models come with their own bounded rationality and bounded reliability challenges that should not be underestimated, especially in cross-border settings. Hamel *et al.*, although not expanding on the different governance options available to MNEs, correctly pointed out that learning by different partners may occur at a different pace, and that some firms therefore structurally benefit more from partnerships than others. Differential learning trajectories of partners may pose less of a problem in the context of investing in large-scale physical assets, but the challenge of properly anticipating and mitigating *ex post* governance costs remains largely the same.

Five Management Takeaways

1. Remember the four key principles of how to establish successful international partnerships and how to prevent excessive dependency on an alliance partner.
2. Limit the unintended diffusion of FSAs by assessing their 'mobility' and 'embeddedness'.
3. Examine whether sufficient safeguards have been established in your alliance agreements.
4. Consider the impact of your own strategic decisions on the quality of your relationship with your alliance partners.
5. Evaluate the entire spectrum of governance options within the alliance category, thereby assessing risk reduction impacts of each option, and taking into account possible impacts of differential learning by the firm and its alliance partner(s).

13

Entry Mode Dynamics 3: Mergers and Acquisitions

Five Learning Objectives

1. To develop an understanding of international mergers and acquisitions (M&As) as instruments to create economic value for the firm.
2. To explain the challenge of 'management biases' when contemplating M&As, and the possibility of pursuing potentially superior alternatives that focus on developing and profitably exploiting FSAs.
3. To describe the challenges of effective governance in the post-acquisition process.
4. To support a reflection on the barriers to success and the common mistakes in M&A implementation processes.
5. To describe the process of integrating extant FSAs of the acquirer with the FSAs of the acquired company in international M&As.

This chapter examines Ghemawat and Ghadar's idea that global M&A transactions usually do not make economic sense. The authors note several management biases that lead to inefficient M&As, and they recommend several alternative strategies as potentially superior to global M&As. These ideas will be examined and then critiqued using the framework presented in Chapter 1.

Significance

Pankaj Ghemawat and *Fariborz Ghadar* wrote a classic *HBR* article in 2000, criticizing the observed trend towards international M&As, especially those among large MNEs from different regions of the world (the so-called 'global mega-mergers'). Such M&As typically aim to create a company with a much wider geographic reach than that commanded by each partner individually.[1]

Ghemawat and Ghadar ask whether such large-scale M&A transactions between MNEs, attempting to create firms with inter-regional or even worldwide market coverage, make economic sense. According to the authors, a general belief persists in many industries that increasing internationalization, in the sense of growing interdependence of markets in the world economy, will ultimately lead to industry consolidations whereby only a few large firms, commanding impressive scale economies, will survive. The obvious implication for senior managers is to get big in order to survive. This view is exemplified by the main strategy rule introduced at General Electric by former CEO Jack Welch. This rule, which still prevails in this highly diversified, US-based MNE, states that the firm should be active only in businesses where it can be the number one or two in the world in terms of size, and should divest businesses in which it cannot achieve that goal.

Ghemawat and Ghadar argue that this approach is inappropriate, since the underlying conceptual rationale for it is weak, and the predicted consolidation is, in many industries, simply not happening. Their empirical research reveals that several industries characterized by increasing internationalization have actually also witnessed *de*creasing levels of market share concentration over the past half century. In light of this observation, they argue that MNEs should contemplate alternatives to strategies of increased geographic reach through large-scale, international M&As.

Their *HBR* article starts by briefly discussing some of the economic theories underlying the perceived link between internationalization and industry concentration. The conventional theory of comparative advantage argues that specific production activities will become concentrated in those countries that possess advantages relative to other countries. But, as the authors correctly point out, this theory 'simply predicts the geographic concentration of production, not concentration of the number of companies in an industry'.[2]

While the conventional theory of comparative advantage does not account for economies of scale, which is a key factor in the trend towards global consolidation, other mainstream economic models, such as the theory of monopolistic competition, do. However, application of the latter models usually does not lead to the conclusion that increased internationalization triggers extreme consolidation. The exception consists of some rare (mainly theoretical) cases of industries characterized by very large R&D expenditures, whereby a few firms are expected to win the learning race and drive out their less successful rivals (as occurred in the 1960s with US-based Kodak and Japan-based Fuji, who won the innovation race in colour photo technology).

Ghemawat and Ghadar's methodology involved examining data relating to the worldwide market share of companies in over twenty industries, going back several decades as of the time of writing their article, to the 1950s. From this work, they computed a so-called 'modified Herfindahl index' for each industry, based on data from the ten largest companies in each industry (rather than including all the companies in each industry). A Herfindahl index is a measure of market share concentration. The index is smaller than – or equal to – the number 1.00. In this particular case, a modified Herfindahl index was calculated for each industry, as the sum of the squares of the market share of the ten largest companies. A higher number reflects a higher degree of market share consolidation (the extreme case being the hypothetical scenario of one firm commanding 100 per cent market share, meaning the index would take the value 1.00), while a lower number implies a lower level of concentration. If there were only ten competitors, each with an identical market share, the index would be 0.1. If there were many more competitors, again with the largest firm(s) holding 10 per cent of the market, but the smallest of the ten firms included in the index commanding much less than 10 per cent market share, the index could be substantially lower than 0.1.

The article presents a sample of the results by industry. For example, calculations for oil production and refining show an increasing number of companies and decreasing market concentration since the 1950s, rather than a consolidation of companies into a few global energy giants, as is commonly perceived. The only exception to the trend is the observation, in the late 1990s, of a number of mega-M&As that created some of today's largest oil majors (e.g., BP Amoco, now BP, formed in 1998 by UK-based British Petroleum and US-based Amoco). The modified Herfindahl index calculated for the oil industry in 1997 stood below 0.05, implying the equivalent of more than twenty significant rivals in terms of market share. Such industry structure is far removed from a conventional monopoly or oligopoly with a small number of dominant firms.

Other natural resource industries such as zinc, bauxite, copper, and aluminium also showed a similar increase in the number of international competitors and a decrease in market concentration over the same time period. The automobile industry displayed a trend similar to that of oil, with decreasing market concentration for decades, with the exception of the years characterized by a few mega-M&A consolidations in the 1990s (e.g., the now defunct merger of Daimler-Benz of Germany with US-based Chrysler Corporation to form DaimlerChrysler in 1998).

Even in high-tech industries, the examples of computer hardware, software, and telephony also suggest a decrease in the market share of the largest firms during the 1990s.

As an aside, the authors do concede that their concentration measure does not include other forms of inter-company concentration such as strategic alliances, but they argue, in line with the 'competitive collaboration' discussion in Chapter 12, that such partnerships often fail or otherwise dissolve over the long term, and are therefore not indicative of a sustained consolidation trend.

Of course, not all industries exhibit this decrease in concentration. In those industries, Ghemawat and Ghadar argue that even if some level of consolidation is observed, and this results mainly from M&As rather than from organic growth, there is not necessarily a sound economic rationale for it. Ultimately, the aim of consolidation must always be to create value. 'To profit from dominating in a concentrating industry, a company needs to extract value by pushing certain economic levers – for example, reducing production costs, reducing risk, or increasing volume.'[3]

Creating value through consolidation, however, is often harder to accomplish successfully than might be expected by senior managers contemplating an M&A. In fact, consolidation often *reduces* value because of the pre-integration (negoti-ation) challenges, purchase price premiums, and post-integration barriers asso-ciated with M&As.

Having reached these anti-M&A conclusions, Ghemawat and Ghadar then attempt to discover why some industries have an ineffective and inefficient tendency to consolidate through international M&As:

> Why are cross-border consolidations pursued even when they destroy economic value? It seems there is often a pathology involved. Management appears to suffer from one or more of several motivational and cognitive biases towards mega-mergers, which can lead to irrational decision making and large-scale destruction of value.[4]

The authors provide a list of six senior management biases, which can all be interpreted as reflections of bounded rationality and, in some cases, also bounded reliability:[5]

1. *'Top Line Obsession'*. This occurs when senior managers focus too much on growing revenues (the top line of an accounting statement) rather than profits (the bottom line of an accounting statement) because corporate goals for growth are formulated in terms of revenue, and performance incentives are tied to achieving such top line goals. The bounded reliability problem is that, given these ill-conceived incentives, managers neither pursue share-holder interests, nor the interests of consumers or workers, but solely their own interests.

2. *'Stock Price Exploitation'*. Senior managers are likely to engage in M&A activity if the firm has an overvalued stock price that makes it more afford-able to engage in large M&A transactions, or if the managers are looking to maintain an elevated share price based on the promise of operational (cost-reducing) synergies, even if few of these synergies will actually materialize over time. To the extent that senior managers know that the promise of substantial synergies is unlikely to occur and provide false information to relevant stakeholders, there is again a problem of bounded reliability, in this case akin to opportunistic behaviour.

3. **'Grooved Thinking'**. Senior managers will often follow the traditional mindset within an industry even if it has become obsolete (e.g., the focus of conventional telecoms on maximizing the number of telephone lines under their control, even in the age of the new communication possibilities provided by the Internet).
4. **'Herd Behaviour'**. Senior managers tend to follow and imitate the actions of their main competitors, especially in oligopolistic industries (e.g., M&A activity in the European banking industry). Herd behaviour can also reduce managers' individual risk of underperforming rival firms. This is another example of bounded reliability, whereby senior managers engage primarily in self-serving behaviour.
5. **'Personal Commitments'**. Individual senior managers may hold fast to their own personal views in favour of M&As even in the face of evidence that M&As in their industry systematically lead to underperformance.
6. **'Trust in Interested Parties'**. Outside parties such as investment bankers and consultants can influence companies to engage in M&As, thereby furthering their own interests in earning commissions and fees. Here, the source of bounded reliability problems resides with the external parties to the transaction; these parties have an incentive to further their own interests, rather than act in the best interest of the firm that hired them.

As an alternative to pursuing international M&A deals, the authors offer a host of alternative strategies that senior managers can pursue. As a general point, they caution that companies must remain focused on developing and profitably exploiting FSAs, rather than on attaining a particular scale as measured by revenues:[6]

1. **'Pick Up the Scraps'**. Spin-offs and divestments that arise from the mega-M&As of other companies can offer profitable growth opportunities for the firms that refrained from engaging in large-scale M&As themselves, if the assets are complementary to the buyer.
2. **'Stay Home'**. Many companies have ample opportunity to improve their competitive position locally or in their home region, rather than pursuing large-scale, inter-regional M&As to expand their geographic reach.
3. **'Keep Your Eye on the Ball'**. Companies can improve their competitive position by remaining focused on developing and exploiting their key FSAs, while their competitors become consumed with pursuing M&A deals and struggle with post-M&A integration.
4. **'Make Friends'**. Strategic alliances offer an alternative expansion trajectory, often with less resistance internally and from external parties such as government regulators. See Chapter 12 for a discussion of the relative merits of alliances versus M&As.
5. **'Appeal to the Referee'**. Short of a real strategy, assuming a company cannot, or will not, pursue a mega-M&A itself, it may be able to slow those of its competitors by calling on regulators to review anti-trust implications.

6. **'Stalk Your Target'**. In industries where first-mover advantages associated with international market expansion, especially outside the home region, are dubious, it may be best to wait and observe as others test the waters, rather than trying quickly to increase the MNE's geographic reach through M&As.

7. **'Sell Out'**. If consolidation is economically justified, it may prove more profitable to be the seller rather than the buyer, given purchase price premiums, integration difficulties, etc.

Context and Complementary Perspectives

The timing of Ghemawat and Ghadar's article is highly significant: it was published in 2000 at the height of the 'dot-com' boom. The implausible escalation of technology and internet-related share prices through the latter part of the 1990s had temporarily turned some industries upside down, with new entrants commanding enormous market capitalization overnight. Many of these firms leveraged their overvalued stock to fuel buyout sprees of other companies in a frenzy of M&A activity that focused primarily on size and revenue growth rather than profitability. The authors' reference to America Online's huge acquisition of Time Warner helps recall the context of the era: 'Some think AOL will eventually recover what it paid, but others believe this may be the deal that brings some rationality to the valuation of Internet stocks.'[7] Although the dot-com bubble was indeed about to burst, the epic events in the e-business world had spillover effects in other industries, creating a desire to pursue similar blockbuster-type M&As in order to compete for the attention of investors' heightened expectations. In an environment where companies were pressured to produce double-digit annual growth percentages, even in mature industries, many larger firms turned to mega-M&As, especially on an inter-regional scale, in order to meet otherwise unattainable targets.

By way of additional context, it should be noted that the large-scale inter-regional M&As of the 1990s were possible only because the previous two decades witnessed a trend towards freer trade and investment. These M&As would have been infeasible in an era of high, protectionist trade and investment barriers.

In an *SMR* article, **James K. Sebenius** provides a first complementary perspective to Ghemawat and Ghadar's article.[8] Rather than criticizing the rise of large-scale, inter-regional M&As, Sebenius focuses on the success story of the Italian copper producer Società Metallurgica Italiana (SMI, operating under the name KME Group since 2006), which grew rapidly and profitably during the 1990s as a result of cross-border acquisitions throughout Europe (involving France, Spain, and Germany), and was able to solve most of the pre- and post-acquisition problems observed by Ghemawat and Ghadar.

There were two reasons for SMI's sustained acquisition success. First, for every transaction contemplated, senior management was always 'very clear about the industrial and strategic logic behind [the] proposed acquisition and the genuine value it will create'.[9] SMI carefully scrutinized outstanding acquisition targets, and pursued only related rather than unrelated diversification, thus reducing bounded rationality problems. SMI also had the patience to wait on purchasing these targets until several of the target's relevant stakeholders were predisposed towards shedding assets.

Second, senior executives engaged in careful stakeholder management. They adopted this approach long before starting negotiations. In those early stages, they attempted to develop good personal relationships with relevant actors working for the acquisition target and tried to understand salient governance issues in the macro-level context and at the level of the target, for example, governance rules that could block the acquisition. Astute stakeholder management was even more critical during and after the acquisition negotiations. A target was never defined simply as a set of complementary FSAs, with the potential of synergies and value creation, and therefore commanding a particular, appropriate price. A target was also, and foremost, a set of diverse stakeholder groups, covering an entire spectrum of attitudes towards being an acquisition target, from great enthusiasm to strong dismay. A key to success at SMI was its ability to craft acquisition transactions in such a way as to shift the negotiation focus from the economic valuation principles (i.e., the price of the targeted firm), from which SMI was unwilling to depart anyway, towards clauses allowing even the most critical stakeholder groups to see value in the acquisition for themselves. Such stakeholder-specific crafting of transaction clauses, representing attempts to develop a shared vision with each stakeholder group, sometimes included commitments towards senior staff, for example, the promise of continued autonomy of the entity to be acquired, in the sense of respecting the value of its location-bound FSAs or involving it in new non-location-bound FSA creation, such as technology development. It sometimes involved commitments towards the selling firm's shareholders, for example, by allowing the seller to remain a minority partner in the acquired entity and by involving the seller in setting pan-European strategy. In politically sensitive situations, as in the case of a French acquisition, the design of an industrial plan with specifics on the benefits of cross-border integration of fragmented, inefficient firms rather than the threat of plant closures, increased legitimacy vis-à-vis political stakeholders. Mostly, the crafting of a shared vision with the various stakeholder groups meant that agreement was reached about broad restructuring principles rather than detailed operational measures, with the latter being designed later, as part of the post-acquisition integration process.

As regards this post-acquisition process, effective governance meant on the one hand cross-border integration of operations through international product-type divisions with clear leadership, and cross-border, horizontal coordination of functions such as ICT, finance, and administration on the other. This dual integration approach, with the most competent individuals in charge of divisions and intra-functional coordination across borders (including human resources from the acquired units) was superimposed on the conventional, national subsidiary structure kept for legal and tax reasons.

Andrew C. Inkpen, *Anant K. Sundaram* and *Kristin Rockwood* give a second complementary perspective in a *CMR* piece[10] addressing less successful cases than those discussed by Sebenius in his *SMR* article. Specifically, Inkpen *et al.* studied European acquisitions of technology-based firms in California. They observed, in the cases they studied, that usually the only winners of such transactions were the shareholders of the acquired entities, commanding stock price gains of more than 43 per cent (as compared to the stock price one month before the acquisition announcement), versus gains of only 14 per cent when the acquirer was a US firm.

In contrast, the European acquirer, typically a large MNE, usually ended up with negative value creation. Importantly, the staff and management of the acquired firm were often also negatively affected by the transaction (e.g., because the prevailing stock option packages for staff were cancelled).

Inkpen *et al.* described in some depth the various barriers that made these acquisitions so unsuccessful. These barriers were largely related to the difference between the general entrepreneurial culture, corporate governance practices, and related routines prevailing in Silicon Valley versus those characterizing the large European MNEs engaged in strategic resource-seeking investments. For example, the European acquirers typically restricted the autonomy of the smaller firms they purchased and had little if any experience with stock option compensation packages for employees, thus alienating key personnel, often the carriers of the acquired firms' main FSAs (the so-called 'assets that walk out of the door every evening', with no guarantee that they will show up the next day), with ample opportunity to move to other companies in the same geographical area. One of the problems facing European MNEs was of course that allowing 'option package' type compensation in US-based, acquired operations could lead to demands elsewhere in the MNE network for the generalized introduction of such packages. This would disrupt prevailing compensation routines with proven, past effectiveness, as well as potentially drive up labour costs.

Given this overall difference in environmental and governance context, Inkpen *et al.* usefully discuss four ways that the European MNE displayed inappropriately slow integration and rigid decision making.

First, European MNEs typically adopted time-consuming consensus-building strategies before making a decision on changes to be effected in the acquired unit. This contrasted sharply with the rule of thumb adopted by some US firms to complete integration within 100 days (sometimes using formal integration teams). Senior management of European MNEs also made excessive use of supposedly hard data (e.g., formal marketing plans instead of intuition about market opportunities) to guide decision making.

Second, the European MNEs involved typically neglected to convey quickly to the new staff a clear and credible picture of the future of the acquired entity, thus leading to high turnover rates. A much faster dissemination of a vision for the future would have been required to avoid such turnover, given the hot Silicon Valley labour market.

Third, the expatriates sent by the new European parent typically socialized only among themselves, rather than attempting to become insiders in Silicon Valley social networks, a key source of information about business and technology trends.

Fourth, immediately after acquisition, confusion often arose about who was actually at the helm of the acquired entity and had responsibility for strategic decision making. Parent company managers typically just visited the acquired entity for short time periods without engaging in fundamental restructuring, another expression of slow post-acquisition integration.

Note that, in contrast to SMI's excellent job of managing all the stakeholders in the acquired company, these European MNEs did a poor job of managing one important stakeholder group: the employees of the acquired company.

Ghemawat and Ghadar's *HBR* piece focuses on the issue of whether firms actually improve their strategic position and truly acquire new FSAs through large-scale, international mega-mergers. The authors reject the widely held assumption that FSAs can be created solely through larger size and economies of scale, with a few MNEs eventually dominating all other firms in an industry at the global level. Ghemawat and Ghadar's research shows that many industries have actually experienced decreasing levels of concentration over recent decades, but this empirical result, describing a historical trend, obviously does not answer the question of when M&As are appropriate. What the article does describe very well is the challenges posed by bounded rationality (and bounded reliability) constraints – both at the individual manager's level and more generally, at the broader organizational level – that come into effect when considering mega-mergers.

As the authors correctly point out, firms must stay focused on developing and exploiting their FSAs, and not just on growing larger. On the one hand, it is true that FSA development can sometimes be strengthened through acquiring complementary capabilities of competitors. Complementary capabilities can, *inter alia*, broaden the scope of innovation, thereby minimizing the risk of falling behind competitors in terms of new FSA development. On the other hand, the melding of the FSAs of both companies may require hard work to make the new

MANAGEMENT INSIGHTS

post-merger organization effective and efficient. Many earlier chapters in this book have made the point that senior MNE managers often overestimate the international transferability and profitable international deployment of the MNE's FSAs, even within the firm itself. In the present case of international mega-mergers, the key challenge is not really the large-scale transfer of FSAs across borders, but rather that FSAs of two MNEs must be combined and some key FSAs, such as overall routines, diffused throughout the merged entity. This challenge is shown in Figure 13.1.

Figure 13.1A
M&A partners: Envisioning the new entity

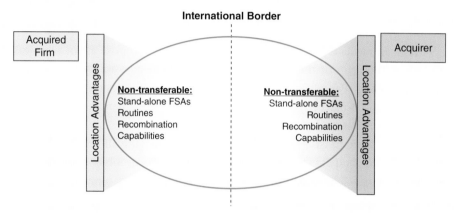

The oval encompasses the assets and resource bundles the merged entity hopes to integrate.

Figure 13.1B
M&A partners: The new entity after M&A completion

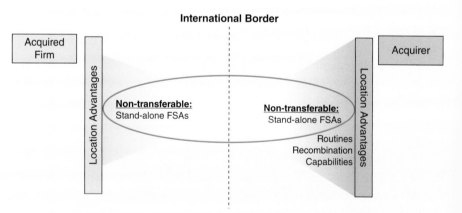

The flattened oval reflects the acquisition being completed, with the acquired firm having only a fraction of its initial resource base being retained. The LB and NLB FSA segments of the acquired firm's triangle 'shrink' due to conflicts when attempting to integrate this firm's routines and recombination FSAs into the merged entity's dominant routines and recombination FSAs, which are mostly inherited from the acquirer.

The top part, Figure 13.1A, shows the acquired and acquiring firms, respectively left and right of the country border, with their idiosyncratic structure of location advantages, location-bound FSAs, and internationally transferable FSAs. When a merger or acquisition occurs, the FSA bundles are supposed to be melded, but this is difficult to achieve for two reasons. First, the FSA bundles found in each firm are often to some extent location-bound, grown out of location advantages and a unique company strategy building on access to those location advantages. Severe post-M&A integration problems can therefore be expected when the distance between locations is large (as is usually the case with inter-regional as opposed to intra-regional M&As). Second, there can be problems even around completely transferable FSAs. Even though synergies may be created by combining resources held by each firm, it is particularly unlikely that all of the two firms' routines and recombination capabilities will be able to reinforce each other, or even to co-exist: there cannot be 'the two ways we do things in this firm'. Here, integrating an acquisition may be somewhat easier to achieve than integrating two entities in a merger, because specific resources and FSAs considered inconsistent with the acquirer's overall dominant logic can be legitimately shed, and the acquirer's own routines legitimately imposed on the acquired entity. Figure 13.1B shows the problem of integrating the non-location-bound routines and recombination capabilities; here, at least partial incompatibility can be expected.

It should also be noted that the integration of stand-alone FSAs is much easier to achieve in the case of related (rather than unrelated) diversification, because the carriers of these FSAs (ranging from groups of research scientists to marketing managers) will face much less difficulty creating shared cognitive and strategic orientations (see Chapter 10) and outlining a joint way forward.

On a somewhat more critical note, and moving back to Ghemawat and Ghadar's lucid *HBR* piece, three limitations of this work are worth noting.

First, in spite of the valid criticism voiced against 'global' M&As (in the sense of M&As with partners outside the home region), this type of expansion may actually be a realistic and worthwhile strategic option for large MNEs. Sometimes a global M&A is the right choice, picked for the right reasons. While Ghemawat and Ghadar are right that many senior MNE managers overestimate the potential for cost cutting and synergies, and underestimate the integration difficulties, not all senior MNE managers are blinded by the thrill of the chase. Some correctly view an M&A as the best choice out of a number of imperfect, real-world alternatives (which may include other market entry mode choices, such as setting up wholly owned subsidiaries, licensing agreements, and alliances).

This is especially true for MNEs that already command a dominant position in a highly competitive, slow-growth industry in their home region, whereby any further attempts to grow with the present product lines may lead to price wars.

The M&A transaction may then act as a trigger for implementing cost-cutting/ synergy-seeking initiatives that might otherwise be foregone, given the preference for the status quo and the presence of vested interests typically found in any large organization.

There is an important general point here for senior managers to recognize: the benefits of a large-scale M&A do not derive solely from the FSA complementarity between the partners, though such complementarity constitutes an efficiency and effectiveness-related precondition for the M&A to occur in the first place. An additional key source of benefits is the legitimatization of deep, structural change throughout the entire MNE(s) involved. For example, an M&A may provide the only context within which shareholders and other stakeholders can be persuaded that the firm needs to contract.

Another important point to keep in mind is that it may be unfair to compare the stock market prices of the firms involved just before and after the M&A. The more important question is what would have occurred to the stock market prices (over both the short and long term) in the absence of an M&A? A small short-term dip is better than a large long-term decline.

Second, Ghemawat and Ghadar argue that the international consolidation of industry is often vastly exaggerated. However, if national markets are indeed increasingly interrelated, then data on low consolidation levels in industry may paradoxically provide a strong rationale for M&As. Through M&As, it becomes possible for MNEs that previously dominated national and home region markets to continue being a major player in the industry. Intending to remain a major player in industry may be driven by efficiency and effectiveness considerations such as being able to have a voice in industry standard setting, preventing other MNEs from tying up suppliers and distribution channels, and broadening the scope of innovation to reduce the risk of falling behind in terms of new FSA creation. Note that these reasons are distinct from the more conventional scale economy rationale, in this case not in terms of single plant scale economies, but rather in terms of the new, larger firm's ability to spread R&D costs across larger production volumes.

Third, when a merger or acquisition is disappointing in terms of value creation, this does not imply that another entry mode would have been better. As Ghemawat and Ghadar note, a decision to engage in a large-scale, international M&A is often driven by information that underestimates the impact of distance. However, this is often a general bounded rationality problem that might have occurred irrespective of the entry mode chosen.

Some bounded rationality problems are common to every collaborative entry mode, like the correct identification and valuation of the partner's FSAs in the intangible asset sphere such as R&D resources, brand names, and reputational resources, and in the organizational capability sphere (managerial strengths, employee loyalty, etc.). This difficulty is amplified by the fact that it is not the other firm's resources per se that should be assessed, but rather the value-creating potential of combining the two firms' complementary resources. On the other hand, as this book has noted, other bounded rationality problems await if the firm tries to enter a foreign market alone, particularly a high-distance market. Therefore, when an M&A is unsuccessful, senior management should sometimes be criticized for venturing outside of their home country or region at all, rather than for choosing an M&A per se.

Strategic Challenges in the New Economy

Much has been written about the impact of the new economy on MNE globalization, with one perspective arguing that the presence of digital-assets-based FSAs will make it easier for 'winner-takes-all' strategies to be implemented by dominant companies. These firms can supposedly also use their digital assets to control more easily an ecosystem of partners. Extending this thinking, one could argue that digitalization is likely to facilitate global M&As, because of easier resource recombination and routinization in the newly formed entity, thereby vastly reducing bounded rationality problems. But the digital economy also creates new challenges for acquiring firms.

Chirantan Chatterjee and **D. Daniel Sokol**, in an *HBR* article, describe the new economy danger of acquiring a firm that misrepresents its true state of affairs in terms of digital integrity, meaning that it is actually a 'data lemon'.[11] A 'data lemon' is a bundle of 'compromised' assets and activities that can endanger the economic value of the entire company to be formed (i.e., both the acquirer and the acquired firm in an M&A).

The problem for acquirers is that they may face significant bounded rationality problems in the sense of being completely unaware of data lemon issues, for example, that there has been a serious cyber security or quality control problem involving an acquisition target. Cyber security breaches, and more generally quality control problems and related risks, are not necessarily highlighted in conventional financial statements or audit documents and can often be kept hidden from the acquirers, thereby creating a major bounded reliability problem. The acquisition target's owners and senior managers face perverse incentives to keep compromised data security and information of defective quality hidden until the acquisition deal has been closed, so as to keep the acquisition price as high as possible. Such expression of bounded reliability (opportunism) can ultimately do a significant amount of harm to the overall company, including damage to the company's brand. In some cases, the owners and management of the acquisition target may, of course, have been unaware of cyber security breaches or quality issues.

One example is US-based Marriott (multinational hospitality company) acquiring Starwood (hotel chain) in 2016, without knowing that the latter had been subject to a cyberattack in 2014.[12] Another example is US-based Verizon (wireless communications firm) purchasing Yahoo in 2017, with Yahoo's data breach exposures revealed only after the acquisition.[13] A global business example is Japan-based Daiichi Sankyo's (multinational pharmaceutical company) acquiring India-based Ranbaxy, with the latter firm's owners misrepresenting to the acquirer significant security compliance information critical to the US Food and Drug Administration (FDA), which ultimately led to a sell-off and retreat by Daiichi Sankyo from the Indian market.[14]

The authors propose three options to address a data lemon problem. The first option is really a non-starter: it suggests completing the acquisition of a data lemon as long as the expected benefits are greater than the risks arising from the deal. This option should, almost as rule, not be selected, because the entire challenge of dealing with a data lemon is that accurate and full information on the risks incurred is missing. The second option proposed is to discount the original valuation of the M&A deal with a data lemon, thereby reflecting the risk factors associated with data security, but here again it must be (wrongly) assumed that the potential costs of, for example, a data breach can be correctly assessed. The third and only valid option is to engage in 'due diligence' on data security and transparency in the target selection process and subsequent negotiations, so as to prevent the purchase of data lemons that will negatively affect the entire new entity to be formed.[15]

The authors propose five due diligence actions in the realm of data security:

1. 'Investigate target's past data breaches using prior data-related audits.'[16]
2. 'Conduct a full review of target's information security processes and procedures.'[17]
3. 'Evaluate target's compliance with cyber security standards.'[18]
4. 'Conduct a review of data privacy requirements with third-party contracts.'[19]
5. 'Be aware of risks for "information spillage" – the unintended release of private data – during the M&A due diligence process.'[20]

If, in spite of these due diligence actions being applied, the acquirer still ends up with a data lemon, it then becomes critical to establish an 'incident response strategy' to address data-related risks.[21] Implementation should be quick and decisive, with a competent, multi-disciplinary action team to fix the problems and with the Board being involved.

In their classic *HBR* article, Ghemawat and Ghadar criticized the pursuit of 'global' M&A transactions from different regions. Such M&As typically aim to create a mega-company with a much wider geographic reach than manageable by each partner firm individually. The ensuing problems can be largely interpreted as bounded rationality and bounded reliability challenges. Inter-regional M&As exacerbate information problems as well as challenges to assess properly partner reliability, both at the partner selection stage and when trying to negotiate a deal. For example, pieces of detrimental financial information can be hidden more easily so as to extract a higher price from the partner. Chatterjee and Sokol complement this classic article by introducing the novel idea that the target firm could be a 'data lemon', and thereby an important liability in the new economy setting.

They view the absence of knowledge on the quality of data security of an M&A target as a serious bounded rationality issue. These problems are severe especially in instances when the M&A target is not sufficiently cyber-secured or does not have the requisite data-gathering and disclosure mechanisms on the quality of its products and processes. As a result of the former problem, information from customers around the globe could get compromised. The latter problem can endanger the quality of the entire, newly formed company, especially if some products or processes from the acquired company pose health, security, or environmental risks.

Especially when purchasing digital companies or companies with digital assets, sufficient due diligence needs to be applied to anticipate data breaches and threats to cyber security.[22] As such, data lemons constitute new economy risks of cross-border M&As: when integrating the ICT systems of two companies in an M&A deal, the entire newly formed entity (i.e., the acquirer and acquired firm) might become vulnerable to unforeseen data security issues. In the worst-case scenario, an incident response strategy must be deployed to minimize data-related risks.[23] This may be more difficult to achieve in the international context across distant regions than within a proximate region.

Five Management Takeaways

1. Do not *over*estimate the potential of international M&As for value creation and do not *under*estimate their potential for value destruction.
2. Do not fall into the trap of typical senior management biases when deciding on possible M&A deals, and trade off the benefits and costs of international M&As vis-à-vis alternative uses of resources for expansion.
3. When assessing merger and takeover targets, always focus on the 'industrial logic' of the proposed M&A, and engage in comprehensive stakeholder management from the outset.
4. Try to understand how to benefit as much as possible from the complementary capabilities of acquired parties and focus on effective post-merger integration.
5. Exercise due diligence in the realm of new economy, 'data lemon' challenges linked to M&A targets.

14

The Role of Emerging Economies

Five Learning Objectives

1. To describe the complexities facing MNEs when operating in emerging economies because of 'institutional voids'.
2. To explain how to create a map of an emerging economy's institutional context and its implications for strategy.
3. To outline four possible strategies that MNEs can use when they engage with local start-ups to reduce distance factors in emerging economies.
4. To make clear how emerging economies can develop a circular economy (CE) that typically involves the input of foreign MNEs.
5. To throw light on the emerging economy's specificities affecting bounded rationality and bounded reliability facing the MNE.

This chapter examines Khanna and his colleagues' idea that emerging economies are primarily characterized by important institutional voids (i.e., a lack of both local intermediary firms and broader macro-level institutions such as contract-enforcing governmental institutions), and that the primary challenge for MNEs operating in emerging economies is to understand and deal with these voids. According to these authors, an emerging economy's institutional voids are even more important than traditional metrics (e.g., GDP analysis). Building on their theory, the authors supply a list of institution-related questions that senior managers should ask in order to assess whether and how to penetrate an emerging economy. These ideas will be examined and then critiqued using the framework presented in Chapter 1.

Significance

Emerging economies are playing an increasingly important role in both the world economy and MNE strategic activity. Since the early 1990s, emerging economies have provided the world's fastest growing markets for most products and services.[1] MNEs are attracted to these countries as they offer potential cost and innovation advantages, and represent new output markets. First, the availability of relatively inexpensive skilled labour and trained managers in emerging economies offers MNEs lower manufacturing and service costs. Second, these economies can also give MNEs access to a different genre of innovation than can be found in mature markets. The foundation of such innovation often resides in the creativity of individuals driven to find original solutions to meet basic needs of large but poor segments of the emerging economy's population. Finally, from a purely sales-related perspective, MNEs from North America, Europe, and Japan need to enter emerging economies as a counter-strategy to the increasing expansion of emerging economy MNEs into the world's developed markets.[2]

Historically, these countries were called 'less developed' countries, 'newly industrializing' countries, or 'third world' countries, but the rising interest in – and belief in – their growth potential has shifted perceptions such that, in economic contexts, they are now generally called 'emerging markets' or 'emerging economies'.[3] While the importance of emerging economies is increasing, there is still no definitive definition as to what constitutes an emerging economy. There are, however, three common aspects of a country's economy that underlie various definitions of 'emerging economy': first, the absolute level of economic development (e.g., GDP per capita); second, the pace of economic development (e.g., GDP growth rate); and, third, the extent and degree of stability of the 'free market' system features.[4]

In a 1997 *HBR* article, **Tarun Khanna** and **Krishna Palepu** took a different approach, arguing that the most important criterion in defining emerging economies is the presence of **institutional voids**.[5] Institutional voids are forms of market failure. For example, in the absence of efficient, external capital market institutions, large firms must finance themselves and establish internal capital markets for resource allocation.

In 2005, **Khanna** and **Palepu**, together with **Jayant Sinha**, wrote an *HBR* article that extended the analysis of institutional voids, elaborating on how these voids affect MNE strategic decisions.[6] The authors suggest that MNEs face difficulties in emerging economies due to the unavailability of two kinds of institutions that can facilitate business: efficient local intermediary firms; and certain broader macro-level institutions (e.g., contract-enforcing governmental institutions). In the (developed) home country, these would be considered generally available location advantages, and often taken for granted. In the emerging economy, they are absent, and MNEs would do well to notice their absence and adapt accordingly.

The authors propose that MNE success in emerging economies depends on managers understanding the institutional context of the local economy, identifying the institutional voids and developing strategies to work around or fill such voids. Senior managers must not assume they can do business in emerging economies the same way they do in developed nations.

Consider the effects of the absence of intermediary firms. In advanced economies, intermediary firms provide a valuable source of location-bound, complementary resources allowing MNEs to deploy and successfully exploit their non-location-bound FSAs. For example, the strong retailing networks found in advanced economies offer MNEs some confidence that their products will be effectively and efficiently distributed, an assumption that typically cannot be made in emerging economies. Other examples of 'market intermediary' institutional voids include a lack of skilled market research firms to inform MNEs about customer preferences, few end-to-end logistics providers to assist in distribution, and a lack of human resources management firms to help screen potential employees.[7]

The authors recommend that MNEs customize their approaches to fit each nation's specific institutional context (i.e., to reduce the institutional distance).

Put another way: institutional voids in emerging economies require MNEs to engage in substantial investments to create compensating location-bound FSAs, instrumental to the successful exploitation of the MNE's extant, internationally transferable FSAs.

However, the difficulty of doing this makes many MNEs simply avoid such markets. For example, in 2002, American corporations had only 2.5 per cent of their US $6.9 trillion worth of assets in emerging economies such as Brazil, Russia, India, and China (BRIC).[8] As a more recent example but on the output market side, in 2017, American MNEs' foreign affiliates realized only 3.59 per cent of their US $1.4 trillion worth of overall net income in what were for them key emerging economies, including the BRIC countries.[9]

As described in Chapter 1 of this book, MNE cross-border expansion should have well-defined motives, such as natural resource seeking, market seeking, strategic resource seeking, or efficiency seeking. Furthermore, the choice of a particular host country should take into account that host country's location advantages vis-à-vis potential alternative locations. Khanna *et al.* note that senior managers generally do try their best to assess the potential for successful FSA transfer and resource recombination in alternative locations, but the managers are usually subject to severe bounded rationality constraints. Therefore, senior managers' actual selection of a target country may be based on their personal experiences, family ties, gut feelings, anecdotal evidence, a rival's entry strategy, or simple biases.[10]

Khanna *et al.* argue that, when choosing host countries, senior managers' priorities are almost completely backwards. The authors argue that understanding institutional distance should rule location decisions,[11] yet empirical evidence from a McKinsey Global Survey of business executives indicated that 61 per cent place market size as the priority in entering a new country, 17 per cent rank political and economic stability as the most important factor, and only 13 per cent indicate that structural conditions, or the institutional context, is the most important factor.[12]

A key bounded rationality problem facing MNE managers is that many analyses of host country location advantages do not account for the unique institutional make-up of individual emerging economies. In fact, Khanna *et al.* argue that traditional analyses of emerging economies may conceal more than they reveal. These traditional approaches include country portfolio analysis, political risk assessment, GDP analysis, per capita income growth rates, population composition, exchange rate analysis, purchasing power parity, a nation's standing in the World Economic Forum's Global Competitiveness Index, and Transparency International's corruption ratings.[13] Unfortunately, such tools often leave out information about the country's institutional characteristics, and therefore about the institutional distance to be overcome by MNEs.

To illustrate the difficulty with traditional rankings for emerging economies, the authors compare Russia, China, India, and Brazil on six traditional indices (competitiveness in terms of growth; competitiveness of business; governance quality indicators; corruption perceptions; composite country risk; and overall weight in emerging markets).[14]

When Khanna *et al.* (2005) published their article, these four emerging economies obtained rather similar scores on most indices, yet their location characteristics in terms of parameters relevant to MNEs – namely, relevant to (1) the transfer, deployment, and exploitation of extant, non-location-bound FSAs and (2) the need to develop new, location-bound FSAs – varied widely. For example, while multinational retail chains had been able to penetrate China and Russia, Brazil only had a few global chains in key urban centres, and India prohibited FDI in retailing until February 2005.[15] Thus, MNEs considering entering any or all of these emerging economies must design a unique distribution strategy for each. In each case, the combination of extant non-location-bound FSAs with newly developed, location-bound FSAs will be idiosyncratic.

To facilitate the understanding of differences among emerging economies, the authors provide a conceptual device for mapping a country's institutional context. They isolate the five components of the institutional context they consider most relevant to MNEs: macro-level political and social context, macro-level openness of the economy, product markets, labour markets, and capital markets.

So, in the case of Chile, for example, the authors looked closely at that country's macro-level political and social context, capital markets, and labour markets. Chile's political milieu had allowed for liberal economic policies that in turn led to vibrant capital markets. At the same time, however, the political system had constrained trade unions, which in turn left the country's labour markets underdeveloped and inefficient. Efficient labour markets require at least some level of power in the hands of the suppliers of labour. If this is not the case, and wages of unskilled and skilled labour alike can be suppressed at will by powerful employers, there is no incentive for upgrading the labour supply pool. In Chile, there was little such incentive. Similar effects could be observed in China, where workers also could not form independent trade unions.

In the case of South Africa, the authors examined its macro-level political and social context and capital markets. In South Africa, institutional support for the transfer of assets to historically disenfranchised indigenous Africans had hindered the development of capital markets. For MNEs, the underdeveloped South African capital markets had made it difficult to value potential South African acquisitions or partners.[16]

Khanna *et al.* flesh out these five components of the institutional context they consider most relevant – macro-level political and social context, macro-level openness of the economy, product markets, labour markets, and capital markets – by providing a series of questions for each component. These questions are tools for MNE senior managers to create a map of a country's institutional context and gauge the extent to which the MNE would need to invest in location-bound FSAs in each context. (The authors do not focus on conventional industry analysis, as they suggest this is useful only *after* understanding the country's institutional context.[17])

First, as regards the analysis of the macro-level political and social context, senior managers should identify a country's power centres and assess whether there are checks and balances in place. To understand this first of the five components, important questions to be answered include: What form of private property rights protection exists? How independent are the media? How accountable are the politicians? Can strangers be trusted to honour contracts?

As an illustration, the US and EU systems are characterized by vibrant democracies with checks and balances. MNEs can count on the rule of law. The media and NGOs within the United States and the European Union also provide further checks on corporate activity. In contrast, while Brazil and India have vibrant democracies with a dynamic press, these countries also have rampant bureaucracy and moderate levels of corruption. The emerging economy of Russia is characterized by stifling bureaucracy and corruption at most levels of government, and the media is largely controlled by the government. Finally, in China, the Communist Party has a monopoly on political power and the media and NGOs have little influence.

Second, senior managers should determine the country's openness. Openness refers to the extent that the country welcomes FDI, but it also includes openness to ideas and openness to travel (e.g., are MNE managers free to travel inside and outside the host country?).

The level of openness in a country affects the markets directly relevant to firms. For example, open economies are more likely to attract global intermediaries, thus supporting MNE operations by offering both local and global intermediary services. Khanna *et al.* also note, however, that highly open countries may also reduce the strength of the MNE's FSAs relative to host country firms. For example, local firms in open economies are as likely as foreign MNEs to have access to the international capital markets. To assist in assessing the openness of emerging economies, useful questions include: Are the government, the media, and the population at large receptive to foreign investment? Can a company make greenfield investments and acquire local companies? Are foreign intermediaries allowed (e.g., advertising firms, retailers, auditing firms)? Can executives leave and enter the country freely? Can citizens travel abroad?

For example, the developed economies of the United States and the European Union are largely open to all forms of FDI except where monopoly or national security concerns prevail. The emerging economies of Russia and Brazil allow greenfield investments and acquisitions, but MNEs often partner with local firms to get access to needed local expertise in Brazil and access to government and local inputs in Russia. Joint ventures in India, on the other hand, are the only entry mode for MNEs in some sectors of the economy, as there are certain restrictions on greenfield investments. Finally, China appeared open in 2005, allowing both greenfield investments and acquisitions in many sectors at the time, but MNEs had to be aware that many acquisition targets used to be state-owned, and could have hidden liabilities. In addition, freedom of movement for employees and MNE managers could be somewhat restricted in China.

Third, as regards product markets in emerging economies, these are becoming increasingly attractive, but MNEs still struggle to get reliable information about the consumers in such markets. From the consumer's perspective, emerging economies tend to lack consumer courts or advocacy groups, thus creating consumer distrust of large MNEs. In assessing emerging economies' product markets, MNE managers should assess such areas as intellectual property rights, brand perceptions, and brand management. Managers will also need to gauge the availability and quality of intermediaries such as suppliers, logistics providers, and retail chains. Questions to facilitate such assessments include: What is the availability of data on customer tastes and purchasing behaviour? Are there cultural barriers to market research? Can consumers obtain unbiased information? Can companies access raw materials of good quality?

The EU and US product markets are characterized by sophisticated design capabilities, national and international suppliers, mature markets with a profusion of brands, and governments that enforce and protect trademarks. The emerging economies vary on most of these aspects of the product market. For example, focusing on intellectual property rights (IPR) reveals that while Brazil and India have some IPR problems with the United States, Russia exhibits an ambivalent attitude towards IPR and China struggles with severe problems of imitation and piracy.

Fourth, in the labour market sphere, emerging economies are often characterized by large labour pools, but these countries often lack both managerial and skilled workers. Part of the complication with emerging economy labour markets is the difficulty in assessing the quality of talent available. MNEs encounter this problem because of a lack of recruiting agencies to screen potential employees, as well as a lack of organizations that rate the quality of the training provided by various training institutions and business schools in emerging economies.

In assessing emerging economy labour markets, MNE managers should gauge the education infrastructure, particularly technical and management training, as well as the availability of data to sort out the quality of the educational institutions. Other useful questions include: What is the language of business? Are there large post-recruitment training needs? Can employees move easily from one company to another?

Applying a labour market analysis suggests that the United States and the European Union have a large and varied pool of management talent, and India also possesses a large pool of English-speaking management. Brazil and Russia have large pools of managers with varying degrees of English proficiency, while China has a comparatively smaller market for managers.

Fifth, emerging economies' capital markets are typically not entirely efficient and may lack specialized intermediaries in areas such as credit rating, investment analysis, banking services, venture capital, and auditing. Here, it may be difficult for the MNE to raise capital, evaluate the creditworthiness of other economic actors, and enforce contracts.

MNE senior managers should therefore assess the capital market's inefficiencies in a wide variety of areas, including barriers to raising capital, weaknesses in corporate governance (especially as regards investor protection), absence of financial intermediaries, inefficiencies in regulating the financial services sector, poor accounting standards, and inadequate procedures surrounding financial distress.

Whereas the US and EU financial markets are largely efficient, and do not suffer much from all the problems described above, the emerging economies' capital markets are not as advanced. The emerging economies of India and Brazil have reasonably developed banking and equity markets, while China is not as highly developed on this measure. Russia has a strong banking system, but it is largely dominated by state-owned banks.

Khanna *et al.* propose that, after determining these five components of an emerging economy's institutional context, MNE managers need to choose among three options. The first option is for the MNE to adapt its business model to the host country while keeping its core dominant logic constant. In its simplest form, this option was described in Chapter 1 of this book as Pattern III of FSA development, whereby the MNE melds non-location-bound FSAs from the home country with newly developed location-bound FSAs in the host emerging economy. The MNE adapts its business model to the unique context of each emerging economy, paying special attention to filling the key institutional voids that make 'business as usual' a non-starter.

A second option available to MNEs is to change the emerging economy's institutional context (e.g., to create more efficient markets). Obviously, this option is only available to a limited number of large MNEs. For example, when Japan's Suzuki entered India, it forced local suppliers to raise their quality standards, and this had significant positive spillover effects on quality management in a number of other industries.[18] Here, resource recombination not only benefits the MNE, but also has important societal spillovers.

A third option available to MNEs is simply to stay out of emerging economies where the requirements for new FSA development are too high. For example, Home Depot's business model builds upon the US transportation system and sophisticated logistical management systems to reduce inventory. The company also utilizes employee stock ownership to motivate employees. In emerging economies, however, a lack of transport infrastructure combined with certain institutional voids – namely, a lack of logistics intermediaries and a lack of sophisticated capital and labour markets – make it difficult for Home Depot to realize its value proposition of low prices, great service, and good quality. This became apparent with Home Depot's unsuccessful attempt to enter Chile and Argentina, where operations had to be sold at a loss only a few years after being established.[19] Similarly, Home Depot opened twelve stores in China by acquiring a Chinese home retailer, The Home Way, in 2006, but they all had to be shut down only six years later in 2012.[20]

Context and Complementary Perspectives

The new framework for analyzing emerging economies described above was published in *HBR* in 2005. As noted above, this piece extended Khanna and Palepu's earlier 1997 *HBR* article, which first discussed the important issue of institutional voids in emerging economies.[21] The 1997 article argued that focused strategies are usually appropriate in highly developed economies. Here, large firms limit their activities to where they have true FSAs compared to what is available in the external markets. In contrast, in emerging economies, highly diversified conglomerates may have more success because they can fill the institutional voids themselves. Conglomerates can control or produce internally all the inputs and intermediate goods not provided effectively and efficiently by external markets.

Building on the 1997 article, Khanna *et al.*'s 2005 piece focused much of its analysis on the emerging economies of Brazil, China, India, and Russia. These countries illustrated how traditional tools of analysis fail to reveal many of the unique and critically important institutional features of emerging economies. Because understanding a particular country's institutional voids is so important to the MNE's success, senior managers need to use more than just these traditional tools of analysis. While the four large emerging economies provided much of the context for the article, the conclusions are applicable to emerging economies in general.

Shameen Prashantham and **George S. Yip**'s 2017 *SMR* article, 'Engaging with startups in emerging markets', usefully complements the 2005 Khanna *et al.* piece by expanding on the challenges faced by MNEs when internationalizing into emerging markets.[22] The typical distance factors – cultural, administrative, geographic, and economic – still hold, as described in Chapter 4. In order to reduce the possible negative impacts of high distance related to each of these four dimensions, MNEs can partner with external actors in emerging markets to access needed complementary resources therein, as we also discussed in Chapters 11 to 13.

However, when trying to engage in innovative activities, technology-intensive MNEs entering emerging markets are subject to a specific problem of bounded rationality, which is tied to the macro-level conditions of these economies. This problem is especially acute when MNEs operating out of established markets are trying to find entrepreneurial start-ups as partners in emerging economies to grow their business. The authors suggest four possible strategies for MNEs engaging with start-ups in emerging markets such as China, India, and South Africa.

The *first strategy* is to 'compensate for the immaturity of the entrepreneurial ecosystem', namely, weak location advantages due to institutional voids such as 'poor access to reliable information, weak property rights, and unsound governance in the entrepreneurial ecosystem'.[23] To overcome such host-country-specific disadvantages in emerging markets, MNEs may choose to support upgrading efforts by 'bearing a greater burden to compensate for deficiencies'.[24] One example is Microsoft's BizSpark programme in South Africa. Through this programme, Microsoft provided mentoring services to start-ups in the country, aligned with their stage of development.

The *second strategy* is to 'commit resources to tapping the entrepreneurial energy in emerging markets'.[25] As one example, Microsoft Ventures' #CoInnovate programme in India focused on three critical ingredients for engaging with start-ups, namely: (1) selecting high-potential start-ups to participate in the #CoInnovate programme; (2) involving key Microsoft customers; and (3) facilitating go-to-market strategies for these start-ups, targeting key Microsoft clients.

The *third strategy* is to 'work with local groups to overcome the limitations of outsider status'.[26] Outsider status is common for MNEs from advanced markets and such status is shaped by 'the deficits in their knowledge base and the multiplicity of stakeholders that Western MNEs face in emerging markets'.[27]

In order to address this issue, MNEs are advised to 'use existing actors to build a bridge between themselves and local startups'.[28]

As one example, Amazon Web Services Inc.'s partnership with Dream T incubator in China led Amazon to provide start-ups in the Dream T incubator with Amazon cloud technologies, business services, and training opportunities. In return, the Dream T incubator was supposed to provide Amazon with access to necessary local infrastructure. This initiative was also aligned with the Chinese government's priority to support entrepreneurship in the Chinese market. This type of initiative boils down to an exchange of technology-based FSAs for access to location advantages via an 'intermediary'. The question of course arises, as discussed in Chapters 12 and 13, whether the advantages exchanged are ultimately equivalent and can be maintained by each party. Technology, once acquired, cannot easily be taken away, but market access, to the extent it is granted by powerful host country actors, especially those supported by government, can be retracted more easily. The role of the intermediary as a possible source of bounded reliability in the future should also be carefully scrutinized.

The *fourth strategy*, and probably the most promising one, because of the clear 'win-win' goals targeted from the outset, is to 'co-innovate with startups to access novel technologies'.[29] According to the authors, co-innovation may be particularly promising in the realm of 'frugal innovation', whereby products and services are created to serve an emerging economy's customers, with the requirement that pricing must ultimately be commensurate with market conditions, which typically means a focus on low costs.[30] For example, Germany-based SAP SE, an enterprise application software company, established co-innovation labs in China and India with local partners.

When MNEs enter emerging markets to innovate, and engage with local start-ups to access host country location advantages and complementary FSAs, they do this to overcome their outsider status. But as noted above, each emerging economy has unique characteristics that may impose specific requirements for partner selection, given the specific community priorities and restrictions, and the baseline of start-ups at hand. For example, in terms of priorities, promoting mass entrepreneurship is important in China, but fostering black empowerment is critical in South Africa. In terms of restrictions, China imposes constraints on foreign digital companies that may be unique to this country's preference to control information flows tightly. As to the baseline of start-ups, China and India have a critical mass of start-ups, but this is not the case in South Africa.

Khanna *et al.* highlighted the challenge of institutional voids, namely, host-country-specific disadvantages facing MNEs when entering emerging economies. Prashantham and Yip complement Khanna *et al.*'s insights by suggesting four strategies helpful to fill these institutional voids.

The *first strategy* is aligned with Khanna *et al.*'s option of changing the emerging economy's institutional context. It is typically restricted to large

MNEs, because upgrading weak host-country-specific advantages through pro-viding training and mentoring opportunities for local start-ups requires substan-tial slack resources, available upfront for investment.

With the *second strategy*, MNEs are supposed to combine their non-location-bound technology resources with start-ups' entrepreneurial capacity in emerging markets, thereby giving these start-ups a platform from which to operate suc-cessfully. Such resource recombination also requires substantial upfront MNE investment, and it typically has uncertain outcomes.

The *third* and *fourth strategies* highlight the roles of external actors who are equipped from the outset with complementary resources to support foreign MNE activities, but only the latter strategy, involving co-innovation with start-ups, would appear to represent a real win-win situation with credible, reciprocal commitments from the outset that would reduce subsequent bounded reliability challenges.

A second complementary perspective to Khanna *et al.*'s piece is provided in a 2018 *CMR* article by **John A. Mathews**, **Hao Tan** and **Mei-Chih Hu**. Mathews *et al.* focus on how to develop a circular economy (CE), with an application to China that involves the input of foreign MNEs.[31]

The authors argue that as a fast-growing, emerging economy: 'A distinctive feature of China's CE development is to leverage its supply chain advantages in the large number of industrial parks using the formation of closed loops of resource flows among firms in the regional industrial agglomerations at a large scale.'[32] These closed loops entail waste from one economic activity becoming a productive input for another activity, thereby creating a CE (as opposed to a linear economy). CE principles revolve around making maximum use of inputs, and recovering and regenerating materials throughout the production process and the entire life cycle of a product (rather than simply viewing waste from one process as having no other potential usage, and viewing products at the end of their useful life as mere waste).

A circular economy approach can typically not be made actionable by a single firm. Without incentives, no individual firm may even be interested to become a circular economy player. The Chinese strategy, initiated by various levels of govern-ments, was therefore to develop joint programmes of action, using companies' prior inter-firm relationships and cooperative linkages in industrial parks. Mathews *et al.* argue: 'Hence, we pose the systematic solution being sought in China, starting with an introduction of innovative forms of network governance that enable firms to find ways to cooperate and overcome opportunistic firm behavior that blocks industrial symbiosis . . . to create closed loops of resource flows.'[33]

China embarked on a CE strategy from the early 2000s. For example, initiatives were taken to transform existing industrial parks into eco-industrial parks (EIPs) by attracting 'activities that would plug gaps in industrial value chains',[34] and the transformation was achieved 'mainly through closed-loop materials flow'.[35] In addition, new CE-oriented industrial parks were established using projects focused on '"loop-linking" activities that either link or extend existing industrial chains and that facilitate utilization of byproducts'.[36] Finally, the above was complemented with an eco-city initiative 'by the introduction of a citywide circular system'.[37] The authors describe in detail three circular economy examples, involving both domestic actors and foreign MNEs.

As an example of an *existing industrial park* being transformed, the Nanjing Chemical Industrial Park (NJCIP) was selected as a pilot eco-industrial park (EIP) project at the provincial level in 2005 and at the national level in 2011. It involved more than 100 chemical firms around value chains for petrochemical products and carbon products. As noted by the authors:

> The park administration set the goal of finding uses for these materials (turning outputs into inputs) and to that end attracted the U.K. chemicals giant INEOS to enter a joint venture (JV) with the Sinopec Yangzi Petrochemical company in 2014. The project aims to make use of the products of benzene, propylene, and hydrogen from upstream enterprises in the Park, and to produce phenol and acetone as main inputs for downstream polycarbonate manufacturers; in this way, the problem of dealing with hazardous wastes is solved while new businesses are established on the basis of the former outputs now turned into inputs.[38]

The NJCIP is an example of closed-loop eco-industrial transformation, which extended value chains by creating new activities, using waste products within the Park.

As an example of a *new park*, the Suzhou New District (SND) was selected as one of thirteen National Circular Economy Pilot Projects in 2005, and approved as one of the three National Eco-Industrial Park Demonstration sites in 2008, with more than 16,000 firms involved by the end of 2013. The authors highlighted the following example of SND functioning:

> [In] the example of urban mining of copper for use by printed circuit board (PCB) manufacturers . . . firms utilize flows of waste copper as source for new PCBs . . . The other kind [of flow] captures aspects of a 'circular loop' that involves the recycling of copper in waste etching solution, waste copper foil, and sludge for the use of other firms in SND . . . This second type of value chain is one based on closed-loop linkages or circularity; it effectively involves 'mining' the flows of copper as alternative to mining copper as virgin resource . . . while also providing solutions to the problems of waste copper disposal . . . in the SND.[39]

The authors also noted the role of the SND park administration in attracting the input of foreign MNEs: 'For example, to attract Dowa Metal from Japan with advanced metal recovering technologies, the SND EDGC [Economic Development Group Corp.] formed a JV with the Japanese company to establish an advanced metal resource recycling business in SND in 2003. The new enterprise became the first Japanese-invested e-waste recovery and recycling business in China.'[40]

As an example of a *city-level circular economy*, the Sino-Singapore Tianjin Eco-City (SSTEC) was initiated in 2007 by China and Singapore, extending the principles of CE parks to include a mix of industrial and residential development. The project was successful initially in attracting many foreign MNEs, including Cisco, Siemens, and Hitachi, to the city. In a later stage, this was complemented by cross-border strategic alliances to promote CE initiatives: 'The [green building energy management alliance] brings together leading Singaporean firms with Chinese counterparts in such sectors as solar cells production. In this way, the SSTEC master company can draw on the best available international technology to promote green building practices, which will both save on energy costs and promote interfirm linkages.'[41]

In each of the three above cases, establishing a 'supra-firm administrative institution' in this rather centrally controlled economy was instrumental to identify business opportunities that would close loops along value chains, with waste outputs turned into productive inputs, and with network governance – sometimes involving foreign MNEs – playing a pivotal role.[42]

In their classic *HBR* article, Khanna *et al.* highlighted the existence of institutional voids as the greatest challenge (i.e., host-country-specific disadvantages) to MNEs operating in emerging economies. Mathews *et al.* introduce one way for MNEs actually to utilize such host-country-specific disadvantages to their benefit, namely by participating in the transformation process towards a circular economy in fast-developing, emerging markets. Closed-loop value-chain activities, reflecting circular economy principles, with the waste of one activity becoming the productive input for another, often require sophisticated technologies. In some of the Chinese cases, foreign MNEs were attracted to form an international joint venture with Chinese partners. This resulted in new value creation, with ample business opportunities for the MNEs involved to make productive use of the waste created within the relevant ecosystems. Here, MNEs had to recombine their extant non-location-bound FSAs with location-bound supply chain strengths provided by the local partner firms. These recombination processes were strongly supported by host-country public agencies at both the national levels and the regional levels in China.

Access to informal and private network relationships (the 'Guanxi') is critical for foreign MNEs to operate successfully in China. These MNEs must therefore tap into the network governance of the country's CE development. They must act as 'closed-loop generators', influencing resource flows among firms in regional industrial ecosystems. For technologically sophisticated MNEs, the role of 'closed-loop generators' can represent a pathway to success in an otherwise difficult market. The Chinese situation is just one example of an emerging economy where foreign MNEs commanding FSAs related to advanced green technologies can enter the market and operate successfully. But success in the market depends not only on the MNEs' technological superiority per se, but also on their direct contributions to serving host-country societal goals, in this case through helping create closed loops for the circular economy.

Khanna *et al.* contend that emerging economies are characterized by institutional voids and that MNEs must understand and work around these voids to be successful in such markets. Further, the authors suggest that each emerging economy is likely to have its own unique set of institutional voids to be filled. Thus, the MNE's recombination capabilities are critical to success in emerging economies. Substantial bundles of location-bound FSAs will likely have to be developed for each country.

MNE adaptation to the local context of emerging economies can involve various FSA development patterns.

Figure 14.1
Patterns of FSA development by MNEs in an emerging economy

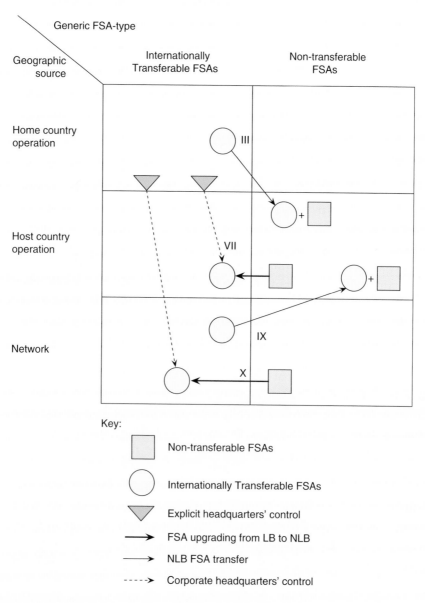

Key:

▢ Non-transferable FSAs

◯ Internationally Transferable FSAs

▽ Explicit headquarters' control

⟶ FSA upgrading from LB to NLB

⟶ NLB FSA transfer

----▸ Corporate headquarters' control

As Figure 14.1 illustrates, Patterns III and IX represent the most common FSA development patterns in the emerging economy context. With both patterns, extant, non-location-bound FSAs are combined with new, location-bound strengths developed in the emerging economy. The resulting recombination is specific to the unique emerging economy context. It should be noted that Pattern IX, a network-based source of FSAs, captures cases whereby MNEs source ideas from multiple, emerging economy operations to address common challenges posed by these various contexts.

Patterns VII and X are also included in Figure 14.1 to capture the possibility of FSAs developed in emerging economies being transferred to other emerging economy locations or even to developed economies. These two patterns will occur when adaptations to the unique emerging economy context create FSAs deployable in MNE operations in other locations and contexts. However, it is likely that any international transfer of FSAs will need to be associated with developing additional, location-bound FSAs in the various recipient countries.

Sustained FSA development in emerging economies may also enhance the location advantages of these host economies. The filling of similar institutional voids by several MNEs at the same time may lead to new intermediaries being set up by entrepreneurs sensing a business opportunity. For example, if several MNEs are forced to organize their own logistics operations in-house, even though they are not very good at this, this creates an incentive for new third-party logistics providers to enter the market, thereby allowing these activities to be outsourced. Also, having several MNEs address institutional voids may also drive a variety of stakeholders to push for changes in the existing institutional system (e.g., in terms of providing better property rights protection, training for workers, deregulation of capital markets – see Chapter 3). This impact of MNEs should not be underestimated by readers familiar only with developed economies: MNEs will cause more institutional spillover effects in emerging economies than they would in developed economies, as suggested by the double, bold arrows in the compressed circle in Figure 14.2A, whereby MNEs attempt to fill significant institutional voids. The enlarged LA areas in Figure 14.2B represent the enhancement of the host country's location advantages, associated with extensive investment in location-bound FSA development by MNEs in emerging economies.

Figure 14.2A
MNE operations in
emerging economies:
The challenge of
institutional voids

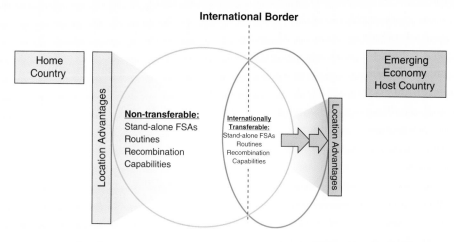

The compressed circle on the emerging economy side reflects a host-environment milieu with substantial institutional voids, as well as the close alignment, in the form of LB FSAs, that the MNE's emerging economy operations must develop in this milieu as a conduit between the MNE's NLB FSAs and the host country's LAs. The double bold arrows between the LB FSA and LA segments of the emerging economy's triangle represent an 'enhancement in progress' of these LAs. Such enhancement becomes possible because of the MNE's investments in LB FSAs related to filling institutional voids, represented by the first bold arrow in the compressed circle. The second bold arrow, pointing to the LAs, reflects the positive spillover effects on the emerging economy's LAs.

Figure 14.2B
MNE operations in
emerging economies:
The outcome of
filling
institutional voids

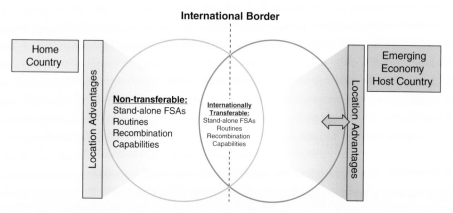

As a result of multiple MNE investments in the emerging economy, and the related efforts to fill institutional voids, the emerging economy's LAs and its milieu for business greatly improve as shown by the larger area they cover in the figure.

Market seeking is not the only motivation that can cause MNEs to develop emerging economies and enhance their location advantages – natural resource seeking and strategic resource seeking can have similar effects. For example, upstream MNE activity in the realm of R&D, as discussed in Chapter 6, can play an important role in upgrading the location advantages of emerging economies through technology and capital transfers and formal human resources training. Furthermore, bringing in new activities such as JIT logistics and sophisticated internal accounting introduces best practices to emerging economies.

In spite of the business potential provided by emerging economies, senior MNE managers face important bounded rationality and bounded reliability challenges. For example, institutional voids in capital, labour, and product markets make it difficult to assess potential partner firms, employees, and customers. This lack of information exacerbates the bounded rationality challenges.

A similar challenge exists with regard to bounded reliability, in terms of both benevolent preference reversal and opportunism. The mix of high cultural, institutional, economic, and spatial distances between the MNE's home base and most emerging economies increases the danger of benevolent preference reversal, namely, subsidiary employees in the emerging economy foregoing the pursuit of corporate-wide goals in favour of local goals, in line with routines prevailing in host country firms. The lack of transparency in these economies (e.g., in terms of reputational assessment) also hinders the proper evaluation of business partners' efforts to fulfil commitments. Deficiencies in the rule of law and lax protection of intellectual property rights also increase the likelihood of opportunistic behaviour by limiting the MNE's recourse in the face of failed commitments.

These increased problems of bounded rationality and bounded reliability imply that operating in emerging economies requires investments of resources to both prevent and remediate these problems. Khanna *et al.* do not discuss how to do this, which represents the first of three limitations of their article. Khanna *et al.* do identify the problems posed by institutional voids when MNEs work with partners to secure services normally associated with simple, arm's-length contracting in developed economies (e.g., transportation services). Khanna *et al.* make the important observation that institutional voids reduce the MNE's access to critical information and its ability to enforce contracts. Limited analysis is provided, however, on what the MNE can actually do to prevent and remediate the hazards of bounded rationality and bounded reliability when working with partners. For example, there is limited analysis of how to obtain credible commitments from partners.

A second limitation of Khanna *et al.*'s study is the lack of analysis regarding the unique characteristics that the MNE brings to the MNE–emerging economy relationship. The institutional context of emerging economies is undoubtedly an important parameter in MNE strategy, but equally important are the MNE's administrative heritage (***centralized exporter, international projector, international coordinator, or multi-centred MNE***) and motivation for international expansion (market seeking, natural resource seeking, strategic resource seeking, or efficiency seeking). A thorough understanding of both the MNE and the emerging economy context will help senior managers decide which markets to enter, with which FSAs, with what entry mode, and with which requirements for further resource recombination.

The third limitation of Khanna *et al.*'s piece is related to partner selection: when to use partners and how to choose them. The authors suggest that partner selection be based on relational competencies, but do not elaborate on mechanisms for assessing when to use a partner and how to choose this partner. This problem is magnified in emerging economies, precisely because partnering appears so attractive there. The need for local partnering stems from both local regulations requiring domestic partnering and the need to overcome market unfamiliarity and severe bounded rationality problems. On the other hand, the potential bounded rationality and reliability hazards posed by partnering may be much higher, given the deficiencies in partner selection and enforcement. Partnering strategies are called for if (1) internal FSA development is expected to bring a lower net value than reliance upon external actors, (2) external actors are available in practice (not tied up by competitors) for partnering, and (3) the use of external actors does not jeopardize the specific expansion project considered (e.g., because of goal divergence). As regards this last point, MNEs may wish to internalize services provided by emerging economy partners when only one or a few local suppliers of these services exist and new service suppliers are prohibited from entering the market.

To conclude, emerging economies provide increasingly attractive locations for MNE expansion. The difficulties in selecting specific countries and operating in those countries, however, remain substantial. To meet these challenges, senior MNE managers should carefully scrutinize the institutional context of these markets and assess whether and how the MNE's FSAs can be augmented so as to allow successful operation in these idiosyncratic environments.

Strategic Challenges in the New Economy

Richard Florida and **Ian Hathaway** argue in their *HBR* article that much commercial innovation activity and the related establishing of technology-driven start-up companies are now concentrated in a small number of global cities and their surrounding regions.[43] This rising phenomenon means that the country level is decreasing in importance for attracting or developing new technology companies. The sharp distinction between advanced and emerging economies may therefore also need to be revisited.

For example, in the United States, these hub areas include Silicon Valley in California, Route 128 in Boston, the triangle area of Durham, Raleigh, and

Chapel Hill in North Carolina, Seattle in Washington, and New York City in New York. Outside of the United States, global innovation hubs can be found in many countries, including Shanghai and Beijing in China, Mumbai and Bangalore in India, London in the United Kingdom, Berlin in Germany, Stockholm in Sweden, Toronto in Canada, and Tel Aviv in Israel, among others.

The authors analyzed more than 100,000 venture deals across more than 300 global city regions in sixty countries between 2005 and 2017. They reported an enormous concentration of venture capital investment. For example, the top ten global city areas, four of which are located in emerging economies, accounted for $100+ billion in venture capital investment each year, which represents around 60 per cent of the total venture capital allocated, and even within these global cities, a small number of 'postal codes' appeared to represent the bulk of venture capital investment, thereby indicating strong geographic concentration. During the 2015–2017 period, San Francisco attracted the largest annual venture capital investment volumes among the top ten global cities, with US $27.3 billion. It was followed by Beijing with $24.3 billion, New York with $11.3 billion, San Jose with $8.3 billion, Boston with $8.2 billion, Shanghai with $7.9 billion, Los Angeles with $5.8 billion, London with $5.2 billion, Hangzhou with $3.8 billion, and Bangalore with $3.5 billion.[44]

The concentration of innovation in a limited number of global city clusters has been facilitated by three elements: the rise of digital-technology-related business opportunities; the increasing global demand for digital products and services; and the fact that many governments are trying to improve the local educational, scientific, and institutional infrastructure to attract capable foreign investors and entrepreneurs, who embody FSAs that can be the foundation for new ventures.

Global cities have strong location advantages for establishing new ventures due to the presence of large reservoirs of complementary resources within their confines or in close proximity (e.g., public digital infrastructure, a pool of skilled and talented employees – including immigrants, specialized financial and insurance services, high-quality suppliers and distributors, etc.). Technology entrepreneurs and venture capitalists can therefore shop for their ideal global city location around the world and select the city region with the most desirable reservoir of complementary resources, including options in emerging economies.

In their classic *HBR* article, Khanna *et al.* highlighted institutional voids as the greatest challenge (i.e., host-country-specific disadvantages) for MNEs contemplating entry into emerging economies. Florida and Hathaway, however, paint a different picture. Emerging economies as countries may be deficient in many areas, but they may be the home of pockets of excellence for new technology ventures in their core cities, such as Shanghai and Beijing in China and Mumbai and Bangalore in India. These global cities may be as attractive to clusters of start-ups as equivalent cities in highly developed nations.

The above represents a new economy facet of location: 'global cities', rather than nations, matter for technology ventures, with three Chinese cities and Bangalore in the global top ten. As such, the concept of location (dis)advantages may need to be revisited to account for city-based ecosystems as platforms for the growth of new ventures. An emerging economy may have severe institutional voids at the national level, but these may be largely absent in its global cities.

Five Management Takeaways

1. Reflect on the key institutional context dimensions of each newly entered emerging economy and create a 'map' of this institutional context to determine the required investments in location-bound FSAs, thereby taking into account sub-national specificities, such as the presence of city regions not subject to the critical institutional voids problems at the national level.

2. Decide, when contemplating entry into an emerging economy, whether you are: (1) willing to adapt your business model to this host country; (2) capable of changing this emerging economy's institutional context; or (3) ultimately unwilling to take the risk of investing in this emerging economy, therefore staying out because of the challenging institutional context.

3. Revisit your partnering strategies with entrepreneurial local start-ups when entering an emerging economy, and assess carefully when to use local partners and how to choose them.

4. Focus sufficiently on scrutinizing how your advanced green technologies can contribute to an emerging economy pursing circular economy (CE) initiatives, and more generally on how your FSAs can be instrumental to serving societal goals, thereby potentially strengthening your social licence to operate.

5. Carefully envision the various possible patterns of capability building specific to expansion in a particular emerging economy as compared to a more developed economy, including the impact of the 'relational component' of contracting.

15

Emerging Economy Multinational Enterprises

Five Learning Objectives

1. To predict when developed economy MNEs versus emerging economy MNEs will end up as winners or losers in competitive battles in international markets.
2. To describe the growth and international expansion trajectories of MNEs from emerging economies.
3. To explain the specific challenges facing MNEs from emerging economies, given their particular location advantages and FSAs.
4. To highlight the significance of 'good-enough' market strategies in the emerging economy context.
5. To provide a classification of international expansion strategies pursued by MNEs as a function of their R&D and marketing FSAs.

This chapter builds on **Pankaj Ghemawat** and **Thomas Hout**'s view expressed in the *HBR* that it is unclear at the outset whether developed economy versus emerging economy MNEs will end up as the future 'global giants', namely, the undisputed international market leaders in their industry.[1] Much will depend on: (1) how these two sets of firms will react and flexibly adapt to the underlying FSAs and location advantages of their counterparts; and (2) how effectively each set of MNEs will be able to emulate and deploy FSAs similar or equivalent to those held by the counterpart companies in the various locations where they compete with one another. The authors focus primarily on firms operating in China and India, both foreign MNEs and the firms that are the subject of the present chapter, namely emerging economy MNEs (EMNEs). The authors describe the different parameters that will ultimately determine which firms will end up as the winners in the international marketplace. As is the case in the other chapters, the ideas presented by Ghemawat and Hout will be assessed in terms of their managerial relevance, using the framework presented in Chapter 1 as the frame of reference.

Significance

There has been a sharp rise in the number and relative importance of EMNEs in recent years. A general observation has been that companies from emerging economies are successful primarily in industries with a low level of technology and advertising intensity. In most cases, initial success comes from effectively using low-cost labour and materials in the context of large-scale manufacturing plants, and then combining these production efficiencies with equally efficient inbound and outbound logistics. Privileged network ties with local stakeholders, especially regulatory authorities that can make life difficult for foreign MNEs, further amplify and sustain these production-cost-driven advantages over longer periods of time. However, Ghemawat and Hout focus on several contemporary cases whereby MNEs from the developed world have attempted to emulate the FSAs of their rivals in emerging economies, and on cases whereby firms from emerging economies have tried to develop or acquire technology-based or marketing-based FSAs. In other words, both sets of firms are de facto trying to disprove the idea that 'industry is destiny'. These firms attempt to engage in new forms of resource recombination. EMNE success appears to result largely from a mix of experimenting with 'upgrading' and a 'coopetition' mindset whereby these firms try to emulate the FSAs of rivals, and engage in various forms of cooperative behaviour (alliance formation, M&As) to access the desired knowledge if they cannot develop this internally at a reasonable cost and risk, and within an acceptable time frame.

For example, the authors discuss how Google and eBay started as industry leaders in China, but were then beaten at their own game by firms such as Baidu and Taobao respectively. These Chinese firms were perhaps not able to provide the same level of global content or quality assurance respectively, but were better equipped to understand local customer preferences and address regulatory requirements, for example, in the realm of self-censoring content viewed as inappropriate by the government, thereby capturing dominant market shares in the Chinese market. As one example from India, the wind power firm Suzlon was better able than international rivals to provide one-stop shopping for wind energy solutions, addressing such issues as gaining government permits to establish wind farms, doing the maintenance thereof, and selling the power generated.

In the above cases, competitive success of local Chinese and Indian companies domestically against large, foreign MNEs resulted from FSAs in low-cost production, combined with a deep understanding of evolving local customer needs and stronger network ties with regulatory authorities.

However, initial FSA bundles are not static, but evolve over time. This explains why Procter & Gamble (P&G) was able to gain a dominant position in China in multiple market segments (e.g., the high-end economy, and low-end segments) for many consumer products: it creatively combined its extant superior technology with access to low-cost products and factors in China and with knowledge about local customer preferences. Resource recombination was achieved in various ways. P&G sent local product developers from China to its international technical centres, where the developers would meet product specialists with extensive international expertise. Second, it learned how to adapt to social networks in emerging economies, thereby overcoming various instances of cultural and institutional distance. Alliances and acquisitions were critical here.

The EMNE can react in four different ways to developed economy MNE entry and resource recombination efforts in its home country. *First*, the EMNE can continue specializing in cost-efficient, mass-scale manufacturing at home, as an OEM supplier to large MNEs from developed economies, with the latter increasingly focused on two sets of FSAs, namely back-end platforms (i.e., routinized business processes) and customer-end strengths in marketing and sales. Here, learning by the emerging economy MNE may then still entail extending its value chain scope over time, but at an incremental pace.

Second, the EMNE can try to perpetuate its initial cost advantages by spreading its own value chain across borders, acknowledging that other countries may become more cost efficient as locations for various activities in the value chain, especially if home country labour costs are rising rapidly, as has been the case in the Indian software development industry.

Third, the EMNE can attempt to increase its own value added by moving up the value chain in the form of technology development or creating brand names. However, internal FSA creation on the technology or branding side may take too much time or may simply not be feasible because of insufficient knowledge resources in these areas inside the firm. Both acquisitions and alliances may then speed up the knowledge-accessing process. For example, Ghemawat and Hout describe the case of the Chinese company Wanxiang taking over poorly functioning US manufacturers of auto parts in the Midwest of the United States, restructuring these companies and gaining access to these companies' knowledge-based FSAs.

Fourth, the EMNE may decide to specialize in narrow segments of the value chain, namely those segments where it is most competitive and can command high value. The authors give the example of India-based Bharti Airtel, specialized in mobile telephone services. This company outsourced much of its value chain to companies such as IBM (for IT services) and Ericsson, Nokia, and Siemens (for network management). Bharti Airtel itself decided to focus on developing FSAs in customer care and relationships with regulatory authorities.

The main challenges for EMNEs, as they grow and expand internationally, ultimately become very similar to those faced by incumbents from developed economies: managing an internationally dispersed network of operations is very difficult, and engaging in resource recombinations whereby initial FSAs are complemented with location-bound ones in new host countries can be very challenging, as explained throughout this book, especially if what binds the different parts of the firm together, namely, what is non-location-bound, is neither in the technology area, nor in the brand name sphere. As stated by Ghemawat and Hout: '[EMNEs'] biggest vulnerability . . . is inexperience in coordination and conflict management across borders and a lack of depth in global customer and channel knowledge'.[2] The likely outcome could then be that 'as emerging players grow, they soon face the same problems established [MNEs] do: international coordination, diminishing usefulness of the [centre] for delivering products or services, loss of product uniqueness, and the need to tap more pools of talent around the world'.[3]

The main point made in Ghemawat and Hout's paper is simply that EMNEs should not take for granted that their initial FSAs in low-cost, mass-scale production, deep knowledge of local customers, and their privileged network ties (e.g., with home country regulatory authorities) will remain unchallenged. Foreign MNEs, including developed economy companies, will try to emulate these FSAs or engage in new resource recombinations to improve their own competitive position. Sustained competitive success of EMNEs requires continued resource recombination for new capability development. Here, expanded size and internal network development across borders quickly leads to new management challenges very similar to those faced by incumbents from the developed world.

Context and Complementary Perspectives

Ghemawat and Hout's 2008 article provides a welcome alternative perspective to the mainstream view that EMNEs will continue to dominate cost-driven manufacturing and services industries in the decades to come, whereas sectors and sector-segments characterized by advanced technology development as well as strong brand name recognition will remain largely out of reach. Ultimately, competitive success results from the ability to recombine resources in such a way that viable business opportunities are acted on. Here, the appropriate strategy is often a hybrid of the conventional, discrete choices between (1) low-cost leadership in production and logistics versus (2) differentiation on the technology or marketing side.

Orit Gadiesh and *Till Vestring*, in their 2008 *SMR* piece 'The consequences of China's rising global heavyweights', provide a somewhat different perspective on the role of EMNEs, as compared to Ghemawat and Hout's view.[4] The authors focus on the rise of Chinese MNEs, and argue that their success can be largely attributed to their focus on products of sufficient quality and sufficiently low price to gain market share in segments of the middle class and the business-to-business market. One example is Huawei Technologies, which has become a major player in the Chinese market for telecommunications networks. Huawei is a firm for which not industry, but strategy is destiny. This strategy has been built on three main pillars. The *first* pillar has been that of government support, which allowed the firm to increase market share in China. The *second* pillar has been to augment the company's initial FSAs in cost leadership with advanced technologies and brand names by engaging in partnerships with firms such as 3Com, a computer network infrastructure specialist (acquired by HP in 2010; an earlier attempt by Huawei at gaining a minority equity share in 3Com through an acquisition formerly conducted by Bain Capital was aborted due to resistance from US regulators). Huawei's *third* pillar has been to outsource some of the manufacturing to Chinese suppliers, while engaging itself in low-cost R&D and engineering. This approach is reminiscent of what developed economy MNEs have done with their own OEM suppliers.[5]

The outcome has been that in some industries such as TV sets and washing machines, the share of the *good-enough* products represents 80 per cent of the total market. One strategy of foreign MNEs to counter the efforts of Chinese firms to develop FSAs in technology and branding has been to engage in so-called *dual branding*, with products covering either the upscale portion of the market or the good-enough market. One example of dual branding is the one applied by the firm Gillette (a unit of P&G), which sells Duracell batteries in the (small) upscale segment of the market and Nanfu batteries in the much larger *good-enough* segment. The latter has been possible as the result of the 2003 acquisition of Fujian Nanping Nanfu Battery Co. by Gillette.[6]

In order to achieve success in the *good-enough* market, foreign MNEs have often been compelled to pursue joint ventures with – and acquisitions of – Chinese manufacturers. The outcome has been both broader product portfolios and newly acquired cost advantages. The longer-term result of acting on the opportunities provided by the Chinese *good-enough* market for both Chinese and foreign MNEs has been an increase in exports and in other forms of market involvement in developing economies characterized by the rapid growth of their own domestic *good-enough* market.

As was the case in Ghemawat and Hout's paper, the focus of the analysis is on the dynamics of competing in an emergent economy. Here, many Chinese firms may benefit from an initial FSA in providing low-cost products to *good-enough* markets, but foreign MNEs may then engage in a two-pronged approach, whereby they try to complement their initial FSAs in upscale market segments with new FSAs to be deployed in the potentially much larger, *good-enough* market.

A second complementary perspective to Ghemawat and Hout's paper was developed in a 2010 *CMR* article by **Huei-Ting Tsai** and **Andreas B. Eisingerich** on the internationalization strategies of emerging market firms.[7]

The authors looked at the international expansion strategies of firms from four emerging markets, namely South Korea, Taiwan, Hong Kong, and India. Given the conventional perspective discussed above that EMNEs are not supposed to have any particular initial strengths in R&D or branding, the authors investigated to what extent R&D and branding were actually present in EMNEs. They developed a simple framework that allows positioning any firm as a function of its relative focus on R&D and branding. This is represented in Figure 15.1, where the vertical axis reflects the presence of FSAs in R&D (low or high) and the horizontal axis represents FSAs in marketing (low or high).[8]

Figure 15.1
Six types of EMNEs

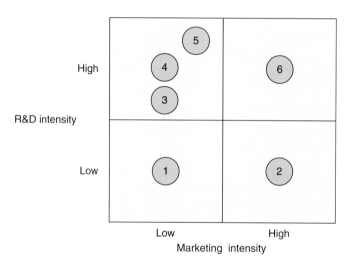

R&D intensity

High

Low

Low　　　　High
Marketing intensity

1. Regional exporters/importers.

2. Global exporters/importers.

3. Technology fast followers.

4. Technology leaders.

5. Global market niche players.

6. Multinational challengers.

As could be expected, many EMNEs were found to have low R&D intensity and limited strengths in marketing. These *first* category firms can be positioned in quadrant two of Figure 15.1. The authors classified these firms as *regional exporters/importers*. At the output side, these firms engage primarily in sales and distribution of their products in neighbouring countries. These countries are usually other developing economies, where limited competition can be expected from large, developed economy MNEs. This category of MNEs builds on cost-driven strengths in narrow product niches.

The *second* category of firms consists of *global exporters/importers*. These companies are positioned in quadrant four of Figure 15.1. These firms invest much more in sales and distribution than companies in the first category, but do not perform much R&D. Such companies focus on product quality and are supported by well-functioning, international supply chains and distribution arrangements.

Three more categories of firms can be found in quadrant one of Figure 15.1. The *third* category consists of *technology fast followers*, which are really contract manufacturers. These firms hardly invest in marketing, but do attach importance to technology, so as to be able to pursue original equipment manufacturing (OEM) or original design manufacturing (ODM) contracts with other large MNEs. A distinct *fourth* group of firms consists of *technology leaders* in the OEM sphere. These firms rely much more than the previous category on their in-house technological innovation, but do not attach much importance to sales and marketing. The *fifth* category of firms is represented by the *global market niche players*, which typically have both high R&D expenditures, but are also focused more on marketing than the two previous sets of companies. Their continued success depends on finding a narrow product niche where they can be successful in international markets.

Finally, the *sixth* category of firms is located in quadrant three of Figure 15.1. These *multinational challengers* are companies that invest heavily in R&D and in marketing, and as a result can engage in head-to-head competition with large MNEs from the developed world. Examples include South Korea-based LG and Samsung.

The dispersion of EMNEs across six categories, which can be positioned in the four quadrants of Figure 15.1, illustrates that MNEs from emerging economies are a very diverse set of companies, some of which are indeed attempting to move up the *smiling curve*, as shown in Figure 15.2. The smiling curve was first proposed by Stan Shih, the founder of Taiwanese computer manufacturer Acer, as a way to position his firm in industry. Ram Mudambi, a well-known inter-national management scholar, extended the smiling curve concept to position firms in knowledge-intensive industries.[9] The point is that not each activity in the value chain leads to similar value creation per unit produced. Some activities, especially knowledge-intensive ones, lead to more value being created than 'commodity-type' activities, which in the extreme case could be simply out-sourced to contract manufacturers.

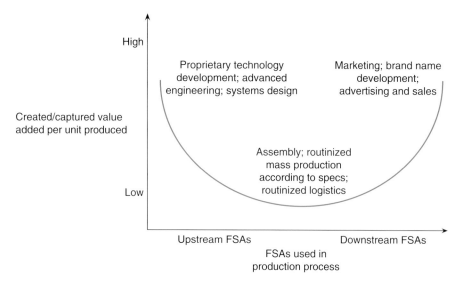

Figure 15.2
The 'smiling curve'

In Figure 15.2, the horizontal axis describes all the value chain activities that can be performed by a company, with upstream activities such as R&D on the left-hand side, assembly and manufacturing of products according to pre-set specifications in the middle, and downstream activities such as market research and branding on the right-hand side. The vertical axis measures the degree to which each activity creates value added per unit produced for the company. The smiling curve assumes that most EMNEs start as producers of commodity-type products and services, often resulting from OEM/ODM contracts with large MNEs from the developed world. In other words, these emerging economy firms tend in a first stage to assemble and manufacture according to the exact specifications of a powerful international client, who can request OEM contract bids from several suppliers, thereby making sure that supply costs are kept low. As time goes by, the OEM supplier from an emerging economy will typically attempt to perform more upstream activities in the form of technology development, and engage in marketing so as to increase revenue. If these strategic moves are successful, value will be added both at the upstream and downstream ends of the value chain, with the overall value added per unit produced increasing substantially, and the EMNE potentially becoming a rival of its original MNE client. The question obviously remains what party in international transactions will actually be able to capture the value and profits resulting from moves on the smiling curve.

Ghemawat and Hout's article complements Khanna *et al.*'s piece discussed in Chapter 14, which focused on the dynamics of filling institutional voids by creative resource recombination. The present paper focuses less on the MNE – host country linkages – and more on the dynamics of competition between EMNEs and their rivals from developed economies. The authors contend that industry is not destiny, but that both sets of MNEs face particular challenges in crafting resource recombinations leading to new FSAs.

MANAGEMENT
INSIGHTS

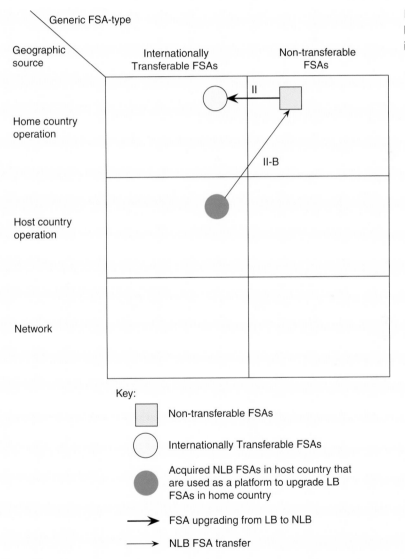

Figure 15.3
FSA development
in EMNEs

For EMNEs, the key challenge is really to upgrade their home-grown, location-bound FSAs into internationally transferable ones, somewhat as described by Pattern II in Figure 15.3. However, the unique feature of this pattern in the EMNE case is the proposed infusion of resources from *outside* the home country at the outset, whether in the form of upstream or downstream knowledge, to allow an upgrade of the firm's capabilities in the emerging economy to achieve non-location-bound FSA status. We have labelled this process as Pattern II-B in Figure 15.3.

In other words, the EMNE case is an excellent example of a situation whereby a multiple diamond approach to international competitiveness, as outlined in Chapter 3, is required to understand the resource-upgrading process inside the firm. Here, foreign direct investment supporting the upgrading process will typically be of the asset-seeking type. When entering developed economy markets through FDI to support such asset seeking, entry will typically occur through alliances or acquisitions to allow rapid access to the desired knowledge and subsequent absorption in the home country. Pattern II-B does acknowledge that the EMNE must have some initial, internationally transferable FSAs to engage in international activities, even if mainly consisting of entrepreneurial acumen and the charismatic personality of company founders and senior managers, and internalized strengths in low-cost production based on location advantages. However, it is then the newly acquired FSAs in host country environments that allow further upgrading of extant, location-bound FSAs in the EMNE's home environment.

When penetrating other emerging or developing economies, Pattern III in Figure 1.7 is often a common scenario. Here, home-based cost advantages and extant market knowledge can often relatively easily be transferred, deployed, and profitably exploited, for example, through exports, with only a limited need to develop additional location-bound FSAs. Obviously, all other patterns of FSA development described in Figure 1.7 in Chapter 1 could in principle be found in EMNEs, but Ghemawat and Hout's point is that many younger EMNEs simply do not command sufficient managerial resources (such as qualified managers for overseas assignments) or organizational routines to implement the patterns that draw substantially on FSA development activities in foreign operations.

It may be useful to highlight three limitations of Ghemawat and Hout's *HBR* paper on EMNE strategies. A *first* limitation is that the title of their article, which refers to 'global giants', is actually rather misleading. Indeed, the competition at the international level between EMNEs and developed economy MNEs is hardly discussed. Most of the analysis concentrates on the rivalry between these two sets of firms inside the EMNE home country (with a focus on China and India). An equally interesting analysis from a management perspective that would actually have done justice to the 'global giants' title would have been to focus on specific

EMNE success stories at the international level, and to have shown the dynamics of competition between EMNEs and developed economy MNEs in third countries, where both sets of firms face similar requirements to access complementary resources and adapt to local circumstances. Of course, the authors do predict that few EMNE success cases can be expected in the medium run given the relative lack of FSAs in management and organizational capabilities to run an international network.

A *second* limitation is that the scope and impact of government regulation in emerging economies are hardly touched on. For example, the fact that Chinese MNEs in the resources sector have often been used as conduits by the Chinese government to secure needed commodity supply from overseas has enormous ramifications for how these firms are managed and how resource recombination occurs in practice. An implicit assumption of the authors is that MNEs from developed economies will ultimately learn how to work optimally with emerging economy regulators, but this is a dangerous assumption, as greater success by foreign MNEs in the emerging economy may actually trigger negative policy responses of the emerging economy's government to protect domestic firms, as presently observed in China.[10] In such cases, regulatory dynamics may actually work against successful FSA recombination engineered by foreign MNEs. Several foreign MNEs experienced this in Venezuela, when starting in 2007, the late President Hugo Chavez engaged in efforts to nationalize local operations of foreign MNEs in the energy, cement, steel, glass manufacturing, and retail industries.

A *third* limitation is that Ghemawat and Hout do not distinguish between *value creation* and *value capture*, though this distinction should be at the heart of any discussion on the costs and benefits of moving away from OEM contractor status, and contemplating alternative strategies. The point is that there may actually be enormous economic value added created already by EMNEs supplying products to MNEs from developed countries, but without the possibility for these suppliers to command high prices for their products, because of weak property rights protection and low social embeddedness of the FSAs involved, and most importantly, a weak bargaining power vis-à-vis foreign MNE clients and other economic actors in the value chain. The real question, therefore, when contemplating strategy alternatives for these firms, is not simply how to rearrange a supply chain, nor how to lower costs further, nor how to enter into alliances with other companies, nor even how to specialize, but rather how to capture value and retain profits inside the firm. Doing more R&D and having more advertising expenditures, namely, moving up the smiling curve, sound like good ideas to escape from the 'industry as destiny' syndrome, but the reality is that both R&D and branding may require the allocation of large amounts of scarce resources without necessarily any guarantee of a positive return in terms of value capture at the level of the individual firm trying to move up the value chain, whether upstream or downstream. In other words, the real question is to know in which activities of the value chain FSAs can be developed and protected over the longer term, namely, cannot be emulated by rivals or substituted by other companies, while being associated with a bargaining position sufficiently strong to allow value capture by the firm. As the example of Flextronics – founded in Silicon Valley in 1969 and presently headquartered in Singapore – demonstrates, an MNE can achieve extraordinary success building on OEM status.

Strategic Challenges in the New Economy

Manuel Hensmans, in his *SMR* article, discusses the challenges facing EMNEs in the high-technology sphere when entering well-established, developed economy markets.[11] One Chinese, technology-based company that has been particularly successful in Europe by developing new, location-bound FSAs is Huawei Technologies. The EMNE achieved significant market penetration in several European countries based on three dimensions of its strategy, each supporting specific, innovation-driven partnerships in these host environments.

The *first dimension* of Huawei's strategy was to 'offer customized technologies that meet the practical needs and resource constraints of target customers'.[12] Huawei focused especially on identifying peripheral customers with urgent needs and provided these firms with superior customization. As one example, in 2004, Huawei supplied equipment to Telfort B.V., a no-frills mobile telecommunications provider in Amsterdam, the Netherlands.

As the author notes:

> Winning over customers such as Telfort was no easy feat. To do so, Huawei had to present a low-risk alternative to what the established vendors provided. It achieved this by offering free testing and technical support. The hardware itself was often priced significantly below that of established competitors. What's more, instead of limiting service to typical Monday through Friday business hours, Huawei promised service availability 24/7, with equipment transportation, installation, and maintenance at no extra charge.[13]

The *second dimension* of Huawei's strategy was to 'build customer loyalty by enhancing practical innovation with longer-term joint innovation partnerships'.[14] Huawei built high-quality partnerships with its customers by addressing pressing issues that other Western companies could apparently not solve, thereby engaging in joint innovation with their customers.

For example, in 2011, Huawei started to serve Telenor Group, a large Norwegian mobile telecommunications company:

> Telenor wanted to build a high-speed wireless base station in one of the most remote and frigid parts of Norway . . . Huawei demonstrated the flexibility and customer-centricity of

its engineers and its ability to perform under adverse conditions . . . Huawei formalized its relationships with Telenor by establishing joint innovation centers, which provide a collaborative environment for managing the customer–supplier relationship and remove some of the long-term uncertainties.[15]

As one other example, between 2006 and 2012, Huawei also partnered with Vodafone, a British MNE in telecommunications, by setting up six joint innovation centres, whereby the firms agreed that they would protect each other's intellectual property rights (IPRs), a critical issue for many European firms trying to protect their FSAs against potentially unreliable foreign partners.

The *third dimension* of Huawei's strategy was to 'enlist the support of governments, universities, and other industry stakeholders' by portraying itself as a reliable partner that European governments and industry players could work with closely.[16] Huawei achieved creating this image by proposing innovation projects that would result in new, highly skilled jobs in Europe, while also responding to national security concerns.

As the author notes: 'During the global financial crisis, Huawei maintained high levels of investment in R&D in Europe and became a champion for major innovation projects . . . In 2013, Huawei pledged to create 5,500 new jobs in Europe by 2019, which would increase its number of employees in the EU by more than 50%.'[17]

And he also observes that:

> In response to France's security concerns, Huawei in 2012 vowed to become more transparent: among other things, it promised to divulge its source codes to the French and European governments . . . Huawei France decided to forgo some of the tax benefits it might have claimed (from R&D credits and losses) . . . Huawei also made a commitment to invest $1.9 billion in R&D facilities in France by 2018, which was expected to generate about 2,000 new technical jobs.[18]

Despite the successful deployment of its strategy in Europe with the three dimensions described above, Huawei's market presence in other parts of the world has been limited, especially in North America. Hensmans argued in this context that alleged linkages with the Chinese government, and related security concerns, have been detrimental to the firm's expansion:

> In 2008, a U.S. government panel rejected Huawei's attempt to acquire 3Com Corp., a maker of internet router and networking equipment, citing concerns about national security. 3Com made antihacking computer software for the U.S. military, among other things, and Huawei is thought to have ties to the Chinese military. Similarly, Huawei was forced to abandon plans in 2011 to purchase 3Leaf Systems Inc., a U.S.-based company specializing in server virtualization solutions. Although Huawei executives including CEO Ren have consistently denied espionage allegations, saying that Huawei has no ties to the Chinese government and that it has never received a request from the Chinese government to spy on the United States, security concerns continue to limit Huawei's ability to sell network equipment to U.S. companies.[19]

According to Ghemawat and Hout, EMNEs' success will depend on a mix of 'upgrading' FSAs and a 'coopetition' mindset whereby these firms need to engage in new forms of 'resource recombination' and 'cooperative behaviour' in foreign markets. Hensmans confirms Ghemawat and Hout's insights, using the case study of Huawei's expansion in European markets.

Huawei first built FSAs in China by serving resource-constrained customers in peripheral and rural regions before going abroad, and then used this same strategy successfully in European markets. It identified similar customers with urgent and challenging needs, and engaged in superior customization, which European vendors were unwilling or incapable to provide. It thereby showcased the malleability of its non-location-bound FSAs by combining its underlying technologies with locally sensitive customer service. In addition, in the realm of resource recombination, Huawei invested in joint innovation centres with customers inside host countries, and engaged in elaborate stakeholder management with European governments and other industry players, thereby reducing societal concerns related to national security, fair taxation, etc.

Five Management Takeaways

1. Understand that FSAs from EMNEs evolve over time, and there may be a natural tendency for these firms to try to capture a greater share of value through new FSA development and sophisticated partnerships, thereby making them more of a competitive threat than would be suggested by a static industry analysis.
2. Consider that the Achilles heel of many EMNEs remains their lack of managerial and organizational capabilities to govern a multinational network. Therefore, platform capabilities in the form of well-oiled routines/business systems may be the best tool to keep EMNEs at bay.
3. Remember that building a successful business in emerging economies while competing with EMNEs may require a prime focus on the *good-enough* market. FSA development should therefore be carefully tailored to allow accessing that market.
4. Carefully classify EMNE rivals as a function of their relative strengths in R&D and branding. Each type of rival will require a different competitive response.
5. Keep the eye on *value capture* rather than on mere *value creation*. Moving up the *smiling curve* may be instrumental to value creation, but it does not guarantee value capture.

16

Multinational Entrepreneurship

Five Learning Objectives

1. To identify the different international expansion trajectories of newly established firms, namely, international new ventures (INVs).
2. To explain how entrepreneurs who establish INVs identify gaps in the present servicing of foreign markets and then exploit these gaps, *inter alia*, through usage of digital-assets-based business models.
3. To acknowledge that viable, 'sharing economy' business models can include the cross-border entrepreneurial initiatives of start-ups.
4. To consider how globally oriented entrepreneurs craft value chains that from the outset target access to requisite resources in distant environments.
5. To recognize that many of the normative recommendations made for INVs to be successful are subject to strong qualifications: the bounded rationality and bounded reliability challenges at play, in particular, should never be underestimated.

This chapter first builds on *Walter Kuemmerle*'s classic observations on the rapid international expansion of newly established firms.[1] Kuemmerle identifies three patterns of new firms' path to international expansion: (1) simple incremental accessing of a neighbouring country's input resources or output markets; (2) more aggressive exploiting of novel cross-border opportunities in output markets using home country resources; and (3) more aggressive tapping into foreign sources of inputs while maintaining operations and sales in the home country. However, Kuemmerle is generally sceptical about new firms' (overly) ambitious, wide-ranging searches for foreign market opportunities or resources at the early stages of these firms' development trajectories. We will reinterpret the key ideas presented by Kuemmerle in terms of their managerial relevance, using the framework presented in Chapter 1.

Significance

In a 2005 *SMR* piece on the entrepreneur's 'path to global expansion', **Walter Kuemmerle** provided core ideas on small and young firms' early internationalization.[2] His article was one of a few early studies with substantive, practice-oriented insight on a new breed of internationalizing firms (as compared to the more traditional focus on large, established MNEs).

Kuemmerle analyzed twenty-seven cases of international expansion by newly established firms. In many cases, these new firms started as responses to local opportunities (mostly driven by domestic demand), and built on local resources to achieve domestic success, much in line with Michael Porter's thinking on the importance of national diamond conditions (see Chapter 3). However, somewhat in contrast to Porter's perspective, early incremental internationalization often did occur, with even the initial business models foreseeing access, either to foreign input markets for valuable resources, or to foreign output markets for delivery of end products (e.g., as frequently observed in newly established software companies). This early internationalization usually entailed low-cost, low-risk experiments in neighbouring countries, whereby the firms' mix of critical internationally transferable knowledge and less important location-bound knowledge (needed abroad) required only incremental change.[3]

Importantly, Kuemmerle also identified two patterns of more aggressive international expansion, beyond the simple incremental accessing of a neighbouring country's input or output markets. In one set of cases, still consistent with Porter's perspective except for the early timing of internationalization, home country resources were used to exploit more substantial cross-border opportunities in output markets. This works well if the internationally transferable FSAs embodied in the product offering can immediately be used to access and satisfy demand in foreign markets, without the requirement of investing in location-bound FSAs (such as distribution channels or high-cost retail outlets) in these foreign markets.

In another set of cases, newly established firms tapped into foreign input markets to find (usually stand-alone) critical resources such as (venture) capital, while maintaining their operations and sales primarily in the home country. Here, foreign resources were instrumental to accelerated domestic expansion (and subsequent international expansion), demonstrating that there may be more to competitive success than domestic diamond conditions, even in the early stages of firm growth.

However, Kuemmerle generally cautioned against both these patterns of aggressive international expansion when undertaken too broadly (i.e., the ambitious search for foreign market opportunities or foreign resources at the early stages of a firm's development). Such expansion could reflect an overly optimistic view of the firm's internationally transferable FSAs, especially its recombination capabilities. It could also underestimate the magnitude of linking investments needed to access foreign location advantages or complementary resources of foreign business partners (such as suppliers or providers of management skills). This is a typical bounded rationality problem, with managers incapable of understanding properly the international logistics and broader contracting problems associated with rapid international expansion.

The effective coordination and control of multiple input and output markets is the key strength of the **international coordinator**, described in Chapter 1. However, developing the necessary recombination capabilities to coordinate and control activities in multiple input and output markets, as found in **international coordinators**, often requires extensive international experience. This experience can typically only be built up over time. Therefore, according to Kuemmerle, foreign input markets for resources and foreign output markets for end products need to be accessed and further developed in a selective and piecemeal fashion.

By recommending against broad-scope, aggressive international expansion for newly established companies, Kuemmerle generally accepts Porter's view that newly established companies will benefit from sustained exposure to vigorous domestic competition and should first focus on creating home-based FSAs by attempting to become major players in the domestic market. However, Kuemmerle also finds, somewhat in contrast to Porter, that newly established companies can often successfully expand internationally, especially if they engage in low-cost, low-risk, incremental entries in neighbouring countries.

Context and Complementary Perspectives

William Kerr, in his *SMR* article, contrasts conventional international expansion models, whereby the firm deploys its extant reservoir of FSAs across borders, with a more novel approach used by a number of international new ventures (INVs):[4] this novel approach consists of designing a digital-assets-based business model that can structurally co-opt external network partners across the world, so as to benefit the firm.[5] As one example, the US-based ride-sharing company Uber initially built its business model on bringing together in its network self-employed drivers and riders on a city-wide basis, and then replicated this model in a variety of foreign locations.[6] The firm subsequently provided a variety of services to riders who value its ride-sharing and adjacent services in overseas countries, including its Uber app that is available in select cities around the world.

Importantly, in most cases, some form of resource bundling with newly accessed resources in foreign markets is still required, in line with the need to overcome cultural, administrative, geographic, and economic (CAGE) distance barriers (see Chapter 4), even when using digital-assets-based business models. International new ventures constructed on the basis of such digital assets, operating as non-location-bound FSAs, should therefore still try to improve their 'contextual intelligence' and assess how they can develop or access requisite local resources to support their digital assets, in order to be successful abroad.[7] As one example, Germany-based Rocket Internet, headquartered in Berlin, specializes in building online start-ups. It assembles leadership teams for these start-ups that can apply advanced business models abroad by hiring international MBA graduates from leading business schools who plan to return to their home countries and have unmatched knowledge of these local contexts.[8]

In addition, alliances with external, local actors can also be important. One type of alliance to access requisite local resources can be formed with established, large players. For example, Planetary Power Inc. is a US venture based in Redmond, Washington, which manufactures power generators for telecom towers in less-developed economies. It 'leverages relationships with telecom-equipment providers that have existing relationships with target clients in developing countries'.[9] Another type of alliance involves cooperating with other fast-moving international ventures. For example, 'Seoul-based SK Telecom Co. Ltd., the largest mobile operator in South Korea . . . partnered with a Hong Kong-based mobile technology venture, Cherrypicks, whose founders had close connections with telecom operators throughout East and Southeast Asia that gave SK Telecom the ability to sell its products to new customers.'[10]

However, even international new ventures that use digital-assets-based business models and that pursue a broad international coverage of their activities are subject to the common problems of bounded rationality and bounded reliability, when establishing any alliances with external partners in foreign countries. As the number of foreign countries served increases, these challenges are amplified for resource bundling more generally. Kerr suggests implicitly that few international ventures can effectively serve more than five countries with a standardized business model that then needs to be complemented with the requisite resources identified through contextual intelligence. In practice, entering more countries typically requires an accumulation of changes to the initial business model: 'Figuring out how many countries the company should operate in can also help managers determine when significant changes to the business model are called for.'[11]

Kuemmerle's international expansion patterns of new ventures largely fit the conventional approach to internationalizing, based on FSA reservoirs that are successfully deployed at home, and based on (and matched with) home country location advantages. These reservoirs then need to be complemented with additional resources to build location-bound FSAs in host-country environments. Kerr's approach expands on this perspective by focusing on digital-assets-based new ventures. Such firms could in principle internationalize much more rapidly and broadly in geographic terms, based on their e-business models and on some key preconditions being satisfied to deploy successfully these business models abroad. These preconditions include carefully identifying gaps in terms of market segments that are not serviced or poorly serviced throughout the world, thereby providing the potential for global market penetration with the firm's e-business models based on digital assets.

In addition, Kerr's approach highlights international new ventures' active leveraging of the potential contributions from external network partners. From a theory perspective, however, there is, of course, nothing new here: digital-assets-based business models are simply supposed to confer a higher level of non-location-boundedness to FSAs and these business models should also increase the firms' capacity to co-opt more easily and more rapidly external partners who provide additional resources.

Yet, international new ventures are often actually confined to regional borders, or at least organized on a region-by-region basis because, as Kerr also highlighted: 'Regional platforms within global ventures can provide organizational benefits such as information sharing, faster decision making, and easier sales of assets.'[12] Usage of the word 'global' to characterize these ventures may therefore be misleading at best, because digital assets do not eliminate all problems of bounded rationality and bounded reliability. Resource bundling abroad and working with external partners remain challenging: how should governance agreements best be structured so as to gather, process, and utilize information critical to competitive success abroad? How can the most reliable partners abroad be selected, and how can they be kept reliable in ongoing alliances?

Pablo Muñoz and *Boyd Cohen* in their *CMR* article focus on the potential of the 'sharing economy',[13] defined as: 'A socio-economic system enabling an intermediated set of exchanges of goods and services between individuals and organizations which aim to increase efficiency and optimization of under-utilized resources in society.'[14] From a firm-level perspective, entrepreneurs can use the 'sharing economy' as the basis for new business models to be competitive with more traditional B2B (business-to-business) and B2C (business-to-consumer) models dominated by incumbents. The consultant PricewaterhouseCoopers (PWC) has actually predicted that: 'global revenues from sharing in five sectors of travel, car sharing, finance, staffing, and music/video streaming will increase from US $15 billion in 2015 to US $335 billion in 2025'.[15]

The most important feature of the sharing economy business models is, of course, the presence of shared resources, which can include new resources, used resources (e.g., when selling and purchasing through eBay), and, perhaps most importantly, underutilized resources. For example, '[o]ptimizing underutilized resources occurs with asset sharing models whether they be homes or parts of homes (e.g., Airbnb[16]), home goods (Peerby[17]), vehicles (BlaBlaCar[18]), or even medical equipment (Cohealo[19])'.[20]

The question arises which governance model will allow the most efficient exploitation and possible further development of underutilized resources, the supply of which is matched with demand by an intermediary company through some type of platform. The platform can be governed in a conventional, hierarchical fashion, for example, when an independent car rental company brings together car manufacturers with rental car users. But there is also the possibility of collaborative governance models that are closer to a joint venture, with different parties taking an equity stake. As one example, Peerby (a P2P or peer-to-peer rental platform) aims to provide immediate access to all the resources available in neighbourhoods: 'Peerby raised a funding round via crowdfunding with their own use community . . . reflective of collaborative governance, because the user community became partial co-owners in the platform as a result.'[21] Finally, there is the option of entirely cooperative governance models with the operations fully owned by individual suppliers (e.g., Green Taxi in Denver to compete against Uber).

In terms of goals pursued, sharing economy initiatives can vary from being fully market-oriented (focused on profitability and growth) to having an important commons-oriented mission. An example of the latter is Fairmondo. It is a 'member-owned platform cooperative designed to compete with eBay and others in the P2P marketplace arena, but with a particular focus on facilitating the exchange of ethical and environmentally responsible products'.[22] Combining market-oriented elements with a commons-oriented mission is also possible: 'BlaBlaCar offers a P2P ridesharing platform, connecting drivers with empty seats to passengers looking for a ride, with the aim of creating a people powered, city-to-city transport network . . . However, BlaBlaCar has a corporate governance model. Unlike Uber . . . BlaBlaCar does not allow drivers to convert their car into a business.'[23]

The important question arises to what extent the sharing economy business models are internationally deployable for firms that do pursue growth and profitability. The entrepreneurs themselves must realize that securing reliability from the members of the sharing community may be at least as important as the availability of technology-based FSAs, for example, when using P2P interactions. As noted by the authors: 'After all, Airbnb is not worth $30 billion because of its technology but rather for its proven ability to generate scalable revenue through the growing mass of users and listings on its platform.'[24] Here, the listings must deliver what they promise, and users must (in addition to paying for the services provided) respect the simple principle that the assets rented must be safeguarded for future use by others.

Perhaps most importantly, as compared to conventional business models, core FSAs for international growth and profitability may not reside in owning or even directly controlling the specific resources that are the subject of the transactions at hand, but in the ability to secure the reliable matching of suppliers and customers, and to streamline the information gathering and processing required for transactions to be conducted successfully.

Large MNEs with more conventional business models now often also try to become participants in the sharing economy. One example is that of a German car manufacturer allying itself with an another German MNE in the car rental business: 'BMW's Drive Now is a B2C carsharing business partnered with Sixt rental car company . . . one of the first to offer point-to-point carsharing. Exposure to their fleets through carsharing may breed brand awareness and loyalty if their younger users decide to buy a car in the future.'[25]

In instances where the community dimension matters, local stakeholders may need to be co-opted as requisite complementary resources, so as to highlight the intended positive benefits for local communities and to increase the likelihood of earning a social licence to operate, especially in sectors with large domestic incumbents.

In several economic sectors, INVs as well as established MNEs contemplating further international expansion must take into account the potential of the shared economy, especially when valuable, underutilized resources can be mobilized to cater to a large, latent demand across borders. In spite of the many bounded rationality and bounded reliability challenges that may materialize, especially if the suppliers of underutilized resources remain outside the firm's hierarchy, the international dimension of those sharing-economy opportunities that could span the world should be investigated thoroughly. Here, internationally operating firms may be in a good position to develop a sharing business model focused on exploiting the uneven spatial distribution of underutilized resources and the demand for these resources across multiple countries. The example of Airbnb is a case in point. Especially *international coordinators* and *multi-centred MNEs* are likely to have the capacity to identify geographic mismatches between supply and demand of underutilized resources on a global scale and generate scalable platforms to facilitate network functioning. Here, the entrepreneurial capacity of foreign subsidiaries in host countries may be important to gather and act on contextual intelligence. It should be noted that MNEs' creation of a unique sharing space could be expedited if equipped with FSAs such as state-of-the-art digital technologies and international network platforms. In addition, depending on the degree to which they should respond to corporate social responsibility issues, MNEs will need to make a strategy choice on the spectrum from full-profit to mission-driven business models, which will further determine the governance structure that will be set up for conducting shared economy transactions across national borders.

Kuemmerle presents compelling evidence of small and young firms' early internationalization. He identified various patterns whereby new firms engage in an international expansion path early after starting operations. Kuemmerle cautions, however, against new firms being overly ambitious when responding to foreign market opportunities and losing track of the often-considerable distance challenges at play.

The genesis of international entrepreneurship (IE) as an academic field dates back to 1994, when **Patricia McDougall** and **Benjamin Oviatt** published a seminal article on the infrequent but interesting phenomenon of rapidly internationalizing firms,[26] sometimes mistakenly characterized as 'born globals',[27] since most of these firms are just early exporters to a few adjacent countries outside of their home nation, meaning that they are really 'born regionals'. Oviatt and McDougall coined the term INV to describe the main actor pursuing IE. An INV is 'a business organization that, from inception, seeks to derive significant competitive advantage from the use of resources and the sale of outputs in multiple countries'.[28] They originally defined IE as 'new and innovative activities that have the goal of value creation and growth in business organizations across national borders'.[29] They subsequently expanded on the meaning of IE to include 'the discovery, enactment, evaluation, and exploitation of opportunities – across national borders – to create future goods and services',[30] in order to accommodate the internationalizing behaviours of small- and medium-sized firms and even corporate entrepreneurship in larger companies, as well as INVs. In reality, all international business expansion, including by the world's largest MNEs, reflects entrepreneurial actions, since such expansion almost by definition entails accessing complementary resources abroad and engaging in creative resource recombination and developing new FSAs, so as to compensate for the fact that some extant FSAs are inherently location-bound.

IE scholars have emphasized three aspects of INVs – newness, asset parsimony related to small size, and the critical role of the individual entrepreneur – as the academic foundation for explaining the phenomenon of small and young firms' internationalization. These three elements, they argue, make INVs very different from established, large MNEs. In reality, none of these elements is new, and in fact they are fully consistent with the conceptual framework we outlined in Chapter 1.

First, INVs are by definition *young firms* that enter foreign markets early, typically within three to six years from inception.[31] The early internationalization of firms has actually been frequently discussed subject matter in the field of international business strategy, and it does not at all reflect the presence of a new breed of firms requiring a separate theoretical foundation.[32] Many of the now established, large MNEs in the *Fortune Global 500* were early internationalizing companies too. To name a few examples, the US-based automaker Ford estab-lished a manufacturing subsidiary in Canada in 1905 within two years from its inception in 1903, and the German MNE Siemens opened its first overseas office in London (United Kingdom) in 1850, a mere three years after its inception.[33] As can be seen from the unifying framework introduced in Chapter 1 of this book, the (early) timing of a firm's internationalization is the outcome of the interplay among various elements, which include the early creation of a critical mass of non-location-bound firm-specific advantages (FSAs), combined with the presence of strong host country location advantages, and where required easy access to requisite complementary resources in these host environments.

Second, according to IE scholars, INVs are *small firms* with some specialized resources, but unlikely to have accumulated sufficient FSAs within their bound-aries before going abroad within just three to six years from their inception. This feature of 'asset parsimony' of INVs[34] makes them dependent on external network partners for mobilizing critical resources to support their rapid inter-nationalization.[35] However, the supposed 'asset parsimony' of INVs is actually consistent with the notions of heterogeneity and idiosyncrasy of any MNE's resource bundles and the necessary combination thereof into higher-level cap-abilities, as explained in Chapter 1.[36] In addition, the importance of external network partners holding complementary resources to the MNE's international success has also been the subject of much international business research over the past decades. Most MNEs require at least some resources that are held by network partners or are embedded in networks, regardless of firm size, especially in today's digital economy.[37] In addition to observing that most firms, small and large, need access to complementary resources in order to be successful abroad, we should also mention that not all INVs are actually resource-poor: many of them may be small firms employing only few people directly, but they may control both directly and indirectly large resource reservoirs via their networks. For example, Uber, a digital-assets-based car-sharing services provider, was established in the United States in 2010, and it had entered fifty-eight foreign countries by 2015.[38] Therefore, the essence of INV functioning is unrelated to the size of the firm's resource reservoir. What makes an INV unique is how it identifies and enacts entrepreneurial opportunities abroad, building on its loca-tion advantages and non-location-bound FSAs, and its ability to recombine resources across national borders, including complementary resources held by network partners.[39] This is exactly the approach adopted in the unifying frame-work introduced in Chapter 1 of this book.

Third, and related to the above two points, risk-taking *individual entrepreneurs* typically leave a lasting imprint of their values and vision on the companies they have founded.[40] There is a rich research tradition in international business strategy that has examined the roles of individuals in international entry and broader MNE functioning.[41] Key issues in this sphere include, *inter alia*, the composition and diversity of MNE top management teams, cross-border human resources management practices, the functioning of global leadership, the roles of expatriate managers in foreign markets, etc. International business strategy scholars have paid particular attention to issues of 'situational uncertainty' facing MNEs, and the related bounded rationality and bounded reliability challenges to be addressed by the key individuals involved (both within and outside the MNE). These behavioural elements are key components of the unifying framework introduced in Chapter 1.[42] The importance of individual entrepreneurial action is therefore not specific to INVs, though it is correct that older and larger MNEs may have routinized some of these behaviours. Imprinting by a founding entrepreneur ultimately refers to the transformation of this entrepreneur's values and vision for the company into managerial practices shared by all in the firm. These managerial practices reflect attitudes towards centralized decision-making, towards the importance attached to formal rules and processes, and towards to the role of socialization. The four MNE archetypes could be interpreted at least in part as the outcome of such imprinting by the founding entrepreneurs.

Given the above, it should be recognized that for some smaller and younger firms led by founding entrepreneurs with limited slack resources, rapid internationalization can be challenging, because transferring and deploying non-location-bound FSAs, as well as gathering and acting on contextual knowledge to achieve requisite resource recombination, is a difficult process. In the modern digital economy, INVs can try to scale up new business opportunities internationally in innovative ways as compared to incumbents and utilize novel combinations of digital assets and external network relationships to gain competitive advantage across national borders, leading to the patterns of FSA development described in Figure 16.1, which are somewhat similar to the Patterns IX and X in Figure 1.7 in Chapter 1. In the first case (equivalent of the original Pattern IX), geographically dispersed network partners work together with the INV to develop an internationally transferable FSA, after which location-bound knowledge may be added in the various countries where the network partners operate. For example, the Dutch start-up Peerby operates an online P2P rental platform with geographically dispersed owners of household items. This platform represents an internationally transferable FSA and it provides immediate access to all the location-bound household resources for which there is demand in local neighbourhoods in various countries.[43] In the second case (equivalent of the original Pattern X), geographically dispersed network partners work together with the INV to upgrade a jointly developed location-bound FSA, originally meant to cover only a narrow geographic area. For example, the online photo-publishing platform 360Cities (founded in Prague, Czech Republic, in 2007), with a geographic scope initially limited to Eastern European countries, subsequently morphed into a global publishing platform of photos via crowdsourcing millions of panoramic photographs from locations globally.[44] Guided by the INV's innovativeness, especially its creative use of digital assets that allow efficient network coordination (rather than hierarchical control), the original, location-bound strengths turned into an internationally transferrable FSA.

In either case, the question does arise how the INV, as network coordinator, will be able to capture a particular share of the value that was created jointly with its network partners. Sophisticated managerial practices, such as those described by Bahrami (2003) in the context of Mozilla (see Chapter 10), provide one avenue to achieve successful network coordination.

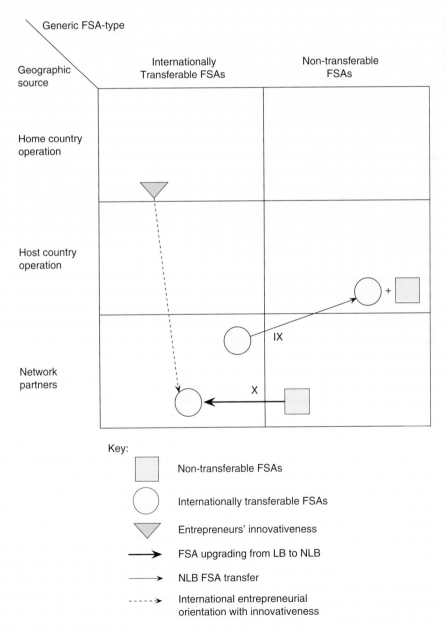

Figure 16.1
New patterns of FSA development in INVs that rely on external network partners

The external network partners can include providers of funds (e.g., development banks, venture capitalists, angel investors, etc.), knowledge co-creators, new-knowledge generators (e.g., universities, public and private R&D institutes, marketing agencies, etc.), 'crowd' consumers, local government agencies, other upstream and/or downstream firms willing to collaborate along the INV's value chain, and even foreign new ventures facing complementary resource needs. Therefore, INVs utilizing international network relationships in the value-creation process allows these firms to connect more easily with elements of foreign diamonds, such as valuable production factors, suppliers, market demand, etc. (see Figure 3.1 in Chapter 3).

Establishing new digital-assets-based business models, supported by online platforms and related, scalable network relationships, can indeed support the intensive use of external network partners. But INVs always need to keep in mind the challenges of bounded rationality and bounded reliability associated with governance involving external partners. Three technology start-ups introduced in Chapter 8 exemplify successful cases in the context of crowdsourcing. The above-mentioned 360Cities established a publishing platform for photos, allowing access to millions of panoramic photographs from all over the world.[45] The company 99designers (founded in Melbourne, Australia, in 2008) provided an online marketplace for small businesses to work with a wide variety of designers and artists from global communities, at affordable prices.[46] Threadless (founded in Chicago, United States, in 2000) represents an online community of artists who create new T-shirt designs that are put to a public vote on a weekly basis. Winning designs are then manufactured and sold globally via its online platform.[47] These INVs drew on ideas and solutions that could arise anywhere around the globe, to satisfy the unmet needs of customers across borders, and building heavily on online digital technologies. In recent years, INVs have also adopted sharing economy business models to expand internationally. As one example, Upwork Global Inc. (operating since 2015 and based in California, United States) is an online staffing company operating in the international contract labour market, and in 2017, it connected 12 million freelance contractors with 5 million registered clients across the world.[48]

There are instances of successful INVs utilizing digital technologies as the foundation for setting up foreign operations, but extant empirical research in IE has shown that INVs typically select exports as their primary entry mode when expanding early to foreign markets, namely, within three to six years after their birth.[49] In the rare cases involving the more complex entry mode of FDI, INVs are likely to set up sales subsidiaries or platforms to sustain foreign export sales. These features suggest that most INVs operate as **centralized exporters** or **international projectors** with market-seeking motivations, but then need to adopt some features of **international coordinators** or **multi-centred MNEs** as they start working with international network partners, who might be dispersed around the globe. In terms of INVs' geographic reach during their rapid internationalization process, it has been observed that foreign sales activities are often heavily concentrated in nearby, low-distance foreign countries, namely, they are *intra-regional*. As noted above, this means that most INVs are 'born regional' firms rather than 'born globals'.[50]

The above not only confirms much of Kuemmerle's insight, but also allows highlighting three limitations of his analysis on INVs. The *first* limitation is that the main sources of some INVs' non-location-bound FSAs can at least partly be found outside of their home base, whether in terms of input or output markets. From the outset, international entrepreneurs may engage in recombining resources across borders, utilizing especially international network relationships, much in line with the double diamond model discussed in Chapter 3.

The *second* limitation is that 'distance' in Kuemmerle's analysis is always viewed as a constraining factor, aligned with our analysis in Chapter 4. But in some cases, international entrepreneurs can try to utilize the distance component to their advantage, namely by 'endogenizing' distance through their external network relationships, thereby creating somewhat the same effect as when established MNEs engage in asset-seeking FDI (see Chapter 1), albeit in this case not through foreign subsidiaries, but through the resources provided by the external network partners in foreign countries.

The *third* limitation is that Kuemmerle did not anticipate fully the impact of the digital network economy. Digital-assets-based business models have helped some INVs to craft and scale up online platforms for trans-border transactions at low costs, thereby supporting their rapid internationalization process from inception. This trend is expected to continue in the years to come, as more INVs develop business models whereby digital assets can support, *inter alia*, the sales of high-quality products in global niches that entail low transportation costs, low communication costs, and little or no adaptation to specific host countries.[51]

Strategic Challenges in the New Economy

Daniel Isenberg, in his *HBR* article, focuses on the behaviour of entrepreneurs who want to expand their geographic scope rapidly in the modern economy.[52] What matters, in addition to the necessary presence of a reservoir of extant FSAs, and what supposedly distinguishes these INVs from other internationally operating firms, is the broad targeting from the outset of complementary resources in foreign markets. The author argues that 'global entrepreneurs' should nurture the following four process-related elements (thereby taking into account the qualification that the word 'global' typically refers more to the 'orientation' of the entrepreneurs than to proven INV performance in terms of geographic dispersion of assets, or sales, or any other value-adding activities).

First, these entrepreneurs should articulate a *global purpose*, meaning a clear rationale and direction for targeting a broad variety of complementary resources abroad from inception.[53]

Second, it may be necessary to engage in *alliance building* with larger MNEs, for example, to gain easy access to manufacturing or distribution capabilities abroad,[54] but severe problems of bounded rationality and bounded reliability may arise (as also noted earlier in this chapter), especially if these larger MNEs operate with a very different corporate culture.

Third, it is important to craft *supply chains* flexibly with the explicit purpose of accessing complementary resources available in very high-distance locations,[55] again taking into account the bounded rationality and bounded reliability constraints mentioned earlier.

Fourth, creative governance approaches must be developed that amplify the *shared value of 'reliability'* across each entire partnership, and that pay substantial attention to the *ex post governance* of agreements with what can possibly be a wide variety of partners. Here, the network partners should not only adhere to *ex ante* agreed-upon contracting clauses and formal rules, but also work through processes that address cultural and institutional differences, especially when much larger MNEs are involved.[56]

Globally oriented entrepreneurs can also focus on groups with whom they share ethnic linkages and make effective use of these diaspora networks, through gaining privileged access to them, thereby creating a new type of FSA.[57] Here, they should map diaspora networks in the communities and industries where they want to operate, and then tap into some of these networks' members, especially the 'influentials' in these communities, such as board members of relevant organizations.[58]

Kuemmerle identified various patterns of new firms' internationalization, but remained generally sceptical about broad and ambitious searches for foreign market opportunities or resources in the early stages of INVs. In contrast, Isenberg focuses on the entrepreneurs' *global orientation* and the design of supply chains and governance mechanisms that from the outset target accessing resources in distant markets, somewhat reminiscent of the **international coordinator** archetype discussed in Chapter 1. However, Isenberg may be underestimating the enormity of the challenges at hand for INVs. For example, building network alliances and managing supply chain partnerships across a wide spectrum of remote locations (suggested as being important in the minds of globally oriented entrepreneurs) can be expensive and may require substantial contextual intelligence and due diligence to identify reliable network partners, even for large and established MNEs, let alone for INVs. The magnitude of linking investments, especially in terms of requisite managerial effort, also needs to be considered when engaging in broad-scope international expansion. Here, experience-based FSAs are important and these typically only accumulate over time.

Five Management Takeaways

1. Carefully reflect on the rationale for your firm's early expansion into foreign countries, and assess whether it has the requisite FSAs to access effectively foreign resources in input markets, or to exploit novel cross-border opportunities in output markets, or to do both simultaneously.

2. Understand that digital-assets-based FSAs of INVs can indeed be instrumental to identifying and exploiting opportunities in foreign markets, but also that external local actors and their contextual intelligence, as a complementary resource, will often still be critical to overcoming cultural, administrative, geographic, and economic (CAGE) distance barriers.

3. Keep your eyes on opportunities to create FSAs in 'matching' the needs of your suppliers with those of your customers (e.g., by performing the role of platform), rather than simply focusing on owning and controlling resources, with a strict separation between actors in your firm's input markets versus output markets. Identifying underutilized resources that are redeployable internationally is a key foundation for new entrepreneurial business models in the sharing economy.

4. Remember that bounded rationality and bounded reliability challenges can overwhelm globally oriented entrepreneurs with overly ambitious international expansion plans. Increased international scope and coverage often require significant investments in location-bound FSAs such as contextual intelligence and due diligence in selecting and managing external network partners.

5. When embarking on rapid entrepreneurial internationalization, focus on nearby foreign countries within your home region that will be associated with low CAGE distance barriers. Many successful INVs turn out to be born-regional firms, not born-globals.

17A

International Strategies of Corporate Social Responsibility

Five Learning Objectives

1. To explain the significance of corporate social responsibility (CSR) in the MNE context.
2. To illustrate the linkages between strategy and CSR in contemporary MNE business practice.
3. To examine how CSR applied by MNEs can improve labour standards.
4. To develop an understanding of the trade-off between maximizing MNE profits in the short run and fulfilling obligations to society.
5. To clarify that there is no 'one size fits all' CSR approach across all types of economies (developed, emerging, and least-developed) and all types of MNE administrative heritage, and that there can be various patterns of CSR capability building.

This chapter examines Dunn and Yamashita's idea that MNEs truly can 'do well' and 'do good' at the same time. In other words, MNEs can engage in initiatives that not only benefit their stakeholders, but also fulfil the firms' 'corporate citizenship' obligations to society. Dunn and Yamashita detail the benefits that can accrue to the MNE from 'corporate citizenship' initiatives, including market growth, knowledge, contacts, and the development of international leaders. These ideas will be examined and then critiqued using the framework presented in Chapter 1.

Significance

CSR refers to good citizenship by the firm – namely, its obligations to society, particularly when society is affected by the firm's strategies and practices.[1] When expanding abroad, MNEs are expected to act as good local citizens in all the locations where they are active. Once considered merely a philanthropic option, good corporate citizenship is now increasingly imposed by the new economic reality of powerful NGOs, grassroots consumer networks, and rapid international information dissemination. While good citizenship can be viewed as the equivalent of a cost increase, it can also be an opportunity to develop FSAs and to improve performance.

In a 2003 *HBR* article, **Debra Dunn** and **Keith Yamashita** suggest that it is often possible for firms to **do well** and to **do good** simultaneously.[2] That is, profitable business models can go hand in hand with good citizenship and produce positive CSR outcomes. The authors focus on Hewlett-Packard's (HP) CSR efforts, particularly its i-community initiative in the Kuppam region of India.

According to HP, its international citizenship efforts are based on a simple framework: 'strong ethics and appropriately transparent governance form the platform of integrity on which all our policies and decisions must be based'.[3]

In practice, HP focuses its CSR in three areas. First is privacy, as demonstrated by HP advocating international data protection for consumers. Second is the environment, as demonstrated by HP designing products to minimize their ecological impact. Third is e-inclusion, in which HP uses technology to improve people's access to both social and economic opportunities.[4]

HP's citizenship efforts are closely aligned with its business strategy. HP establishes clear strategic objectives for each social issue that is addressed, and attempts to apply sound business practices to each project. Dunn and Yamashita detail seven such practices utilized by HP in its i-community initiative in Kuppam.

The first business practice applied in Kuppam is unearthing customer needs. HP's technology business operations demand the ability to 'divine the needs of their customers by probing at underlying problems and transferring that understanding to the innovation process'.[5] In the technology industry, products are rarely developed simply by asking customers what they want. Instead, customer problems must be uncovered (often with some effort) and technological solutions then developed to solve those problems. HP reports that most community development initiatives do not approach the problem with this type of underlying needs analysis.

In addressing social challenges, HP invests in a needs-finding process that takes the form of an iterative cycle. This resource recombination process, which HP refers to as its 'living lab methodology', involves uncovering a need and quickly developing a prototype solution. The prototype solution is then deployed on a limited basis, which allows for observation and solution modification. After modification, the cycle is started over again.

A second business practice applied to citizenship efforts is fielding a diversely talented team. MNEs often entrust community development initiatives to individuals with a background in philanthropy or development. Drawing on its business experience, HP sees the benefit of complementing those philanthropic and development skills with a broader range of knowledge, including line-management knowledge, expertise in government affairs, and a rich understanding of culture. In other words, citizenship efforts cannot be effective and perhaps even translate into FSAs without the involvement of (human and other) resources that are the core of the firm's more conventional FSAs.

A third business practice is adopting a systems approach. A systems approach does not attempt to optimize individual parts, but instead views these parts in a broader context and aims to optimize the whole. In HP's case, this approach suggests that development initiatives should do much more than provide technology. 'Community leaders must advocate for the solution, trusted individuals within the community must lend their reputations to the effort, Kuppam businesses must get involved, and other technology companies must integrate their technology into the solution.'[6] This third business practice shows the complexity involved in HP's efforts to combine its extant FSAs in technology with resources in the local environment.

Related to the above is the adoption of a fourth business practice, namely the creation of a leading platform. In the ICT industry, the concept of leading platform refers to a standardized, generally accepted configuration of hardware, as well as a specific operating system and other software, which allows the functioning of computers and computerized devices (e.g., personal digital assistants and cell phones), and which can be linked to other hardware or software. Working with all the partners involved, HP provides the main ICT infrastructure (both hardware and software), to which each partner can then add its own technologies and applications. HP's partners can thus add value by building on their own distinctive strengths.

In conjunction with creating a leading platform, a fifth business practice is building an ecosystem of partners. HP recognizes that most sustainable communities have many different stakeholders with a vested interest in a long-term solution. Thus, HP brings together government, local leadership, business people, health-care professionals, NGOs, informal networks within the community, and local and international technology partners. While it is not easy to align these interests in the short term, HP believes that the long-term alignment of strong interests from all these parties is the best path to sustainable solutions. The alignment of interests offers protection from hazards associated with each partner's bounded reliability. In short, HP does not attempt to drive all the value creation itself, but instead tries to create a healthy ecosystem of partners, all dedicated to solving problems and bringing their complementary resources to the initiative.

A sixth business practice applied by HP to community development initiatives is simply to set a deadline for the project. HP has found that deadlines create a sense of urgency, which keeps all participants in the partnership focused. Deadlines move the initiative to the action phase and encourage participants to find common ground quickly. Setting a deadline indicating the end of the MNE's active involvement also focuses the project on becoming self-sustaining after the MNE's direct involvement has ceased.

The seventh business practice used by HP in its community development initiatives is what the firm calls 'solving, stitching, and scaling'. This practice, derived from HP's experience in taking new products to market, initially customizes a solution for a single customer. This focus eliminates the bounded rationality challenge of trying to figure out all the possible forms the solution will eventually take. The single customer solution is also known as the lighthouse account because of its ability to point other customers towards the firm. Building on such experiences with single customers, managers can then begin to stitch a collection of solutions into a total solution that can be scaled.[7]

Dunn and Yamashita illustrate how HP has applied these seven business practices to its community development programme in Kuppam, India. Kuppam can be viewed as HP's first community development customer. The lessons learned and solutions developed in this region are scalable and transferable to other regions in need of community development.

Kuppam makes for a tough testing ground, as nearly half of its population lives below the poverty line. One-third of the population is illiterate, half has no electricity, and there is a high rate of HIV. HP sees value in this region, however, as regions that are very different from established markets and 'conventional customer thinking' may offer new potential for innovation.[8]

Within its three CSR areas noted above (privacy, the environment, and e-inclusion), HP centred its efforts in Kuppam on e-inclusion. E-inclusion means using technology to reduce economic and social divides. In this programme, 'the company creates public–private partnerships to accelerate economic development through the application of technology while simultaneously opening new markets and developing new products and services'.[9] One tangible expression of this community initiative is the Kuppam information centre, which allows people to make phone calls, photocopies, and faxes, and offers computers with access to the HP-built i-community portal. The centre not only offers the infrastructure for micro-enterprise development, but it is also itself owned by locals selected by an NGO. This ownership structure fits well with HP's 'ecosystem of partners' approach to community development. Kuppam's i-community now includes five community information centres where students, teachers, and parents can develop skills to access information via the Internet.

For the MNE manager, the business value of the project is the template or routine from which the project was developed. In this case, the template consists of four key phases of project development. The first phase, lasting approximately five months, is the 'quick start'. This phase attempts to establish credibility and momentum by achieving a few quick successes. Other elements in this phase include visioning exercises and the gaining of high-level alignment with partners in the public and private sectors. The second phase, lasting approximately eight months, is the 'ramp up'. This phase is characterized by gathering resources for prototyping, evaluating solutions, and training stakeholders so they can take ownership of the initiative. Key to the ramp-up phase is bringing the ecosystem of international and local partners into a true coalition. Third, running from the beginning of the second to the middle of the third year of the initiative is the 'consolidation' phase. In this phase, HP evaluates the intellectual property generated to date, helps local partners decide which solutions to deploy, and stops sub-projects unlikely to reach their goals. Fourth, overlapping with the consolidation phase is the 'transition' phase, which runs from the beginning of the second year to the end of the third year. Here, community leaders are identified, and power and knowledge are transferred to local participants.[10]

The benefits of the Kuppam initiative have extended to other communities. For example, HP transferred the lessons learned from the Kuppam i-community project and applied these to a project that tested new technology by providing portable solar-powered digital photography hardware to women entrepreneurs. These women were able to utilize the technological infrastructure to develop a solid business model. This approach gave them the confidence to seek a line of credit from a co-op bank, and the extra income offered the means to provide education for their children.

HP realized that its earlier philanthropic donations, though generating results, were actually suboptimal, and that much more could be accomplished if doing good and doing well could be made mutually reinforcing.[11] The benefits of the Kuppam initiative for HP have included market growth, leadership training, and technological development. HP emphasizes that projects such as Kuppam are not about short-term profits, but about the opportunity to achieve long-term growth and, in the process, improve the human condition in regions where the firm does business. Through the process, HP has also gained knowledge and contacts within new markets and these benefits have made HP a stronger competitor in those markets. These citizenship initiatives also help HP develop international leaders. In fact, the firm reports that more can be learned from living labs like Kuppam in three years than from virtually any leadership development programme or graduate course: 'Indeed, though it wasn't among the primary goals of the i-community, teaching leaders new ways to lead may be one of the largest competitive benefits of the initiative. Ultimately, it's the knowledge that these leaders and their teams gain in places like Kuppam that will allow HP to become a stronger competitor.'[12]

Context and Complementary Perspectives

In the years since Dunn and Yamashita's 2003 article, the pressure on MNEs to pursue good citizenship initiatives has intensified. Subsequently, movements such as the ***Make Poverty History*** campaign have put pressure on governments, banking institutions, and MNEs to help eradicate global poverty.[13] Thus, community development efforts such as HP's Kuppam project fit well with the current global context that demands CSR initiatives for less-developed communities.

Dunn and Yamashita's article focuses on efforts in India, an emerging economy. Dunn and Yamashita suggest that HP's i-communities initiative is scalable and transferable to other emerging economies. What about countries that are not emerging economies, such as the poorest regions of Africa? The question arises whether HP-type initiatives are transferable to these regions of extreme poverty and institutional voids. Unfortunately, it is unlikely that ***doing well*** and ***doing good*** could in fact mutually reinforce each other in the world's extremely poor regions. MNE activity cannot replace the role of a government in terms of providing public goods such as basic education, general infrastructure, and enforcement of the rule of law, which are really preconditions to be fulfilled for any HP-type initiative to come to fruition. Being forced to provide such public goods on a large scale might not only make many foreign investment opportunities prohibitively costly, but would also force the MNE into a role it is not meant to fulfil, and is unlikely to fulfil effectively and efficiently; enforcing the rule of law is the most obvious type of activity that should be performed primarily by government.

Good citizenship efforts in the least-developed countries may therefore still need to take the form of pure philanthropy until a minimum baseline of institutional infrastructure is developed. As the authors state in their *HBR* article, 'change is not possible until there is a capable network to support it'.[14] In other words, MNEs filling institutional voids may be instrumental to new FSA development and to the upgrading of a poor emerging economy (or region within that country), as discussed in Chapter 14, but MNEs cannot substitute for the lack of a baseline institutional infrastructure.

Beyond a renewed focus on poverty eradication, another movement since the publication of Dunn and Yamashita's article has been the heightened concern over climate change. This environmental concern has increased the pressure on MNEs to include environmental policies in their CSR initiatives. The role of the environment in MNE citizenship is not the focus of Dunn and Yamashita's article, and we cover this topic in Chapter 17B.

Richard Locke and ***Monica Romis*** provide a first complementary perspective to Dunn and Yamashita's *HBR* piece.[15] Their 2007 *SMR* article focuses on MNE

CSR efforts to improve labour standards. The authors argue that MNEs need to go beyond monitoring suppliers for compliance with labour codes of conduct and should instead collaborate closely with suppliers to attack problems of poor working conditions at their source.[16]

The extension of supply chains to developing countries, particularly by efficiency-seeking MNEs, has heightened the need for MNE senior managers to incorporate labour standards into their CSR policies, including their interactions with suppliers. Hazardous working conditions, poor wages, and child labour are problems that MNEs must address in sourcing from suppliers in countries where governments have a limited capacity or desire to introduce or enforce labour laws providing baseline protection to workers. Many MNEs and NGOs now monitor whether suppliers comply with codes of conduct in the realm of working conditions, but '[i]nformation is central to this model of private, voluntary regulation'.[17] The main problem in developing countries, however, is a bounded rationality challenge: does monitoring actually measure real workplace conditions, given the possibility for suppliers to hide relevant information from those performing the monitoring?

To further explore the utility of monitoring codes of conduct, Locke and Romis conducted a structured comparison of two Mexican firms that manufactured products for US-based Nike, the largest athletic shoe company in the world. Both factories had earned similar scores on Nike's principal monitoring tool, yet the two factories differed significantly in the type of working conditions found on the shop floor. For example, one supplier paid higher wages, capped overtime hours, and offered more worker empowerment than the other supplier.

Nike's monitoring of suppliers' compliance with codes of conduct began in 1992, when the MNE realized that substandard labour conditions in its suppliers' shops were damaging Nike's international brand image. It has even developed an FSA in this area: Nike now trains its suppliers to follow the code of conduct and has a team of ninety compliance staff based in twenty-one countries to monitor these suppliers. In 2002, Nike developed the management and working conditions audit ('M-Audit'), a tool that consolidates into a single score the performance on more than eighty items related to hiring practices, worker treatment, worker–management communications, and compensation.[18]

Such compliance tools represent the MNE's effort to reduce the problem of suppliers' bounded reliability by aligning these suppliers' interests with those of the MNE, particularly the MNE's CSR interests. Composite indices such as the M-Audit are also an attempt to overcome the bounded rationality problem associated with having to measure multidimensional labour conditions adopted by multiple suppliers in multiple countries. This bounded rationality problem is compounded by the difference between the management practices found in supplier firms and those prevailing within the MNE.

Locke and Romis found that composite measures of compliance with codes of conduct do not, however, lead to a complete understanding of the difference in working conditions among supplier factories, as illustrated by the case of the two Mexican suppliers. The authors found that the key variable influencing the working conditions in these facilities was the differing systems of work organization and human resources management.[19] The Mexican facility characterized by better working conditions provided greater worker autonomy, invested heavily in training, and organized workers into production cells. This facility also had more frequent visits with Nike management and participated in joint problem solving with the MNE. Such interactions reduced both the bounded rationality and bounded reliability problems associated with the MNE–supplier relationship.

Locke and Romis' 'findings suggest that interventions aimed at reorganizing work and empowering labour on the shop floor in global supply chain factories can lead to significant improvements in working conditions'.[20] These interventions should flow from increased communication and interaction between the supplier and the MNE in the context of a collaborative and transparent relationship. In alignment with these findings, Nike has created the 'Generation 3' compliance strategy. This strategy acknowledges that mere monitoring of suppliers should be supplemented with collaborative initiatives to transfer workplace and human resources management best practices among suppliers.[21] This development of supplier human resource practices under the guidance of the MNE is somewhat similar to Pattern VI of FSA development, described in Chapter 1. In this case, however, the MNE is supporting FSA development inside a supplier firm rather than inside a subsidiary. Ideally, this support enables the supplier to serve Nike in a sustained fashion with its key complementary resources (manufacturing excellence at very low cost), without this relationship being disturbed by external stakeholders. A possible positive spillover effect is that the supplier firm itself may in turn diffuse this FSA further through its global or local network.

Sushil Vachani and *N. Craig Smith*'s 2004 *CMR* article provides a second complementary perspective to Dunn and Yamashita's *HBR* piece. This article explores the MNE's CSR in the context of drug pricing in developing countries – a very timely topic, given civil society's focus on eradicating poverty and fighting AIDS in Africa. The article concludes that in order to make drugs affordable for customers in developing countries, the MNE must mobilize and recombine complementary resources provided by governments, multilateral institutions, and NGOs. Echoing Dunn and Yamashita on the necessity of an 'ecosystem of partners', Vachani and Smith conclude that all of these stakeholders must be involved in order for the initiative to be successful.[22]

Vachani and Smith suggest that pricing decisions are an interesting type of CSR because they typically present the MNE with a stark trade-off between maximizing profits in the short run and fulfilling obligations to society. In other words, socially responsible pricing affects the bottom line immediately and directly. The idea of socially responsible pricing can involve agreeing to pay higher prices for inputs, as seen with fair trade coffee. The concept of fair trade means that vulnerable producers are given prices for their production that will allow them a minimum level of economic security and sustained self-sufficiency, and will empower them as legitimate economic participants in international supply chains. Fair trade is particularly important in countries that lack sufficient institutional infrastructure to make markets work effectively and efficiently. In the absence of a fair trade approach adopted by MNEs from developed countries, vulnerable producers with virtually non-existent mobility to deploy their knowledge in other sectors or geographic locations, and lacking organizational competencies to counter power imbalances in multilayered logistics chains, often cannot even satisfy their families' most basic needs as human beings. The great benefit of a fair trade approach is that it recognizes the comparative, overall efficiency of international supply chains orchestrated by MNEs vis-à-vis alternative supply options. MNE-managed fair trade chains are characterized by the continued, productivity-enhancing recombination of resources by chain participants, but also by the presence of respect and related monetary compensation granted to the most vulnerable chain participants, mostly in the world's poorest countries. CSR expressed by support for fair trade can be viewed as a reputational resource for MNEs, often indicative of an FSA in stakeholder management.

On the output market side, most CSR pricing involves the MNE lowering prices, often by adopting differential pricing benefiting poorer customers less able to pay.[23]

Vachani and Smith highlight the case of AIDS drugs in developing countries to illustrate how drug-pricing policies can affect both the MNE and societal welfare. As much as 95 per cent of people with AIDS live in developing countries, yet despite price reductions on antiretroviral AIDS treatments, the annual cost for these medications remains above the annual per capita GDP of many of the least-developed countries.[24] Arguments can be made that local governments should pay for increased access to AIDS drugs, particularly when contrasts are made with health expenditures and spending on defence for some of these countries. Nonetheless, pharmaceutical MNEs face considerable pressure to increase access and affordability for these drugs. These companies are often viewed as insensitive and 'profit hungry' in their pricing policies in developing countries. However, pharmaceutical MNEs are often limited in their ability to drop prices without jeopardizing profits from developed countries. Vachani and Smith review three main approaches used by MNEs to improve access to drugs in developing countries: drug donation, out-licensing, and differential pricing.

First, the ***drug donation*** approach, as the name suggests, increases access to drugs in developing countries by offering the drugs free of charge. An example of this approach is Merck's development of a treatment for river blindness. Merck invested several million dollars to develop drugs to prevent this disease that are now administered to 25 million people annually through a free distribution programme. Drug donation gives the MNE tax benefits and gives the developing country social welfare benefits. One problem with this approach, however, is that host countries are often burdened with hidden costs such as drug distribution costs. In addition, this approach is not sustainable for diseases requiring extensive and long-term treatments, such as AIDS, because the MNE's ability to fund donation programmes depends on its own financial health, which may be highly uncertain over the long term.

Second, the ***out-licensing*** approach is consistent with an international projector strategy of licensing. A host country manufacturer produces the drugs under licence, though the MNE usually forgoes profits in the form of royalties. This approach has the advantage of offering the MNE distance from the lower price offered in the developing country. Distance from lower prices reduces the potential for ***price referencing***, in which downward pressure on prices in developed markets is caused by reference to the lower price charged in developing economies. Out-licensing has the further advantages of leading to favourable media attention for the MNE (a form of FSA development in the reputational sphere) and providing a commercially appealing response to competition from generic manufacturers.[25] A problem with this approach, however, is the limited complementary resource availability, as developing country manufacturers may not possess adequate quality control systems. In addition, drug access may still be limited as the price may not be low enough for a large portion of the population. Finally, the price referencing problem is unlikely to disappear completely.

Third, the most common approach to increasing drug accessibility is ***differential pricing***, which entails selling the same product at different prices in different markets. In conventional economics, price discrimination follows the consumer's willingness-to-pay, with the monopolistic producer reaping the consumer surplus.[26] Differential pricing is easily applicable in the drug industry, where non-location-bound FSAs, often in the form of patents, result from large and risky investments in R&D. These (usually stand-alone) FSAs can mostly be transferred easily as they are fully codified in the form of the products' patented formulas, and manufacturing costs are often a small fraction of total costs. Thus, MNEs can use their monopolistic position, as sole owners of patented knowledge, to sell in developing countries while covering only their manufacturing costs.[27]

While differential pricing arguably provides the flexibility to balance pharmaceutical MNE revenues and social welfare, this approach also has risks. As with drug donation and out-licensing, differential pricing has the risk of diversion. For example, if intermediaries such as wholesale distributors are unreliable, they may divert the product to other destinations. One example of such bounded reliability is the illegal resale in Germany and the Netherlands of low-priced drugs meant for African consumers. Such practices can only be stopped by government regulation in both developing and developed countries against product diversion.

As with out-licensing, differential pricing also has the risk of price referencing. Recent actions by Brazilian authorities illustrate the risk of price referencing when differential pricing is employed. In 2007, the president of Brazil authorized the country to bypass the patent on Efavirenz, an AIDS drug manufactured by Merck. The country will instead import a cheaper, generic Indian-made version of the drug. The decision came after talks between Brazil and the US MNE broke down. Merck offered Brazil almost a third off the cost – pricing the pills at US $1.10 instead of US $1.59. However, Brazil wanted its discount pegged at the same level as Thailand, which pays just US $0.65 per pill.[28] As shown in this example, price referencing develops in a context of bounded rationality, where governments (in this case from an emerging economy) are not interested in understanding the importance of recouping total R&D costs and have little patience for CSR-inspired MNE pricing structures. Governments simply want the lowest price charged elsewhere, and use this as a reference for an appropriate price in their country. From the MNE senior management's perspective, governments engaged in pricing negotiations are therefore unreliable (and in some cases opportunistic) actors who may have little respect for the protection of proprietary knowledge.

Beyond price referencing and product diversion risks, MNEs also encounter high administrative overhead costs from setting up, managing, policing, and fine-tuning differential price systems. These costs, while necessary to achieve CSR goals, may be difficult to justify in all countries. Setting a price correctly becomes particularly complicated if a country lacks infrastructure for drug delivery, or complementary resources from intermediaries and other contracting parties.

A further risk stemming from the lack of infrastructure is that the drugs may not be taken as prescribed, thus potentially leading to drug-resistant strains of the disease, strains which may spread to developed markets, thus reducing the value of the drug in those profitable markets. Vachani and Smith suggest that NGOs and governments must play a key role in developing the infrastructure necessary for efficient drug distribution.

Finally, differential pricing may have an unintended bounded reliability effect: MNE price reductions can reduce, *ex post*, host government (and donor) efforts to provide appropriate financial support for drug access.[29]

Vachani and Smith supplement their discussion of CSR and pricing with an analysis of AIDS drug pricing from 1999 to 2003. The authors found that 'having lost the support of developed country governments in the intellectual property rights battle, facing severe competition from generics, and with donors showing signs of substantially increasing assistance, multinationals cut prices significantly'.[30] While these price reductions have increased access substantially, it could be argued that such reductions should have occurred much earlier. Vachani and Smith's analysis suggests that MNEs could have accepted suboptimal earnings in developing countries that would have reduced their total profits by less than 1 per cent. The authors admit, however, that their analysis is made with the benefit of hindsight, a benefit that suppresses the a priori bounded rationality problem surrounding the potential risks of dropping prices.

In this context, Vachani and Smith make the normative claim that pharmaceutical firms are in a social contract, which gives the firms special treatment with regard to intellectual property. 'In return, society expects the profits from these activities to provide the incentive to develop new drugs, many of which may be life enhancing if not lifesaving.'[31] Arguably, this is another example where firms can do well by doing good: CSR initiatives by pharmaceutical firms support the social contract, thereby providing a normative rationale to retain a highly profitable business model.

MANAGEMENT INSIGHTS

Dunn and Yamashita's *HBR* piece highlights the crucial point that CSR initiatives should be aligned with MNE strategy and build on the company's FSAs if these initiatives are to be sustained in the longer run. The authors' description of doing well by doing good emphasizes that MNEs should apply their current FSAs to CSR initiatives. This was illustrated by HP's application of the living lab to the Kuppam community development initiative. The doing well by doing good approach also increases MNE competitiveness by allowing the firm to develop new FSAs through participating in CSR initiatives. This was illustrated by HP's ability to develop leaders and foster innovation through participation in community development projects. HP benefits by being able to transfer newly trained leaders and innovations to other international operations. This development of non-location-bound FSAs through participation in host country development programmes is captured by Pattern VII of FSA development, described in Chapter 1.

One important theme shared by all three articles is the importance of engaging and partnering with multiple stakeholders when pursuing CSR projects. Dunn and Yamashita described HP's use of an ecosystem of partners, in which many different players share a common interest in building a long-term solution. Locke and Romis argued for close partnering between MNEs and their local suppliers to improve working conditions. Vachani and Smith emphasized the importance of partnering with NGOs and governments to develop conditions conducive to lowering drug prices in developing countries. In each case, partnering with appropriate stakeholders may help reduce bounded rationality and bounded reliability challenges. Increased familiarity with one another and relationship building may help align the interests of the various stakeholders involved. Partnering also provides potential access to complementary resources instrumental to effectively deploying the MNE's FSAs in these high-distance host environments.

A first limitation of all three pieces reviewed in this chapter is their focus on CSR solely within the developing/emerging economy context. The *HBR* piece focused on community development in an emerging economy, the *SMR* piece centred on the working conditions in developing country manufacturing facilities, and the *CMR* piece explored MNE policies towards drug access in poor developing countries. A focus on developing/emerging economies for MNE CSR is appropriate given the particularly sensitive nature and importance of CSR issues in those countries. These countries suffer from substantial institutional voids (as discussed in Chapter 14) and extreme poverty. This focus is limited, however, as it neglects the role of CSR and CSR initiatives in developed economies.

It is worthwhile to widen the analysis and, with the help of Figure 17A.1, examine the potential of different forms of CSR in different country types.

In developed countries, CSR efforts can largely take the form of mandated CSR, as the institutional context in these countries usually establishes appropriate guidelines for good corporate citizenship. This institutional context is strongly affected by influential NGOs and the media, as well as the legal, tax, and educational systems. This institutional context provides fertile ground for pursuing CSR initiatives that may be very different from those pursued in countries lacking such context. MNE citizenship in developed economies is likely to centre on following the rule of law, paying taxes (including environmental taxes and multiple other taxes imposed on business based on externality or deep-pocket arguments), supporting the existing social and political system, and engaging in some targeted philanthropic initiatives. Building upon stakeholder-mandated CSR initiatives, firms may be able to develop internationally transferable FSAs, as suggested in Figure 17A.1.

Figure 17A.1
CSR and location
context

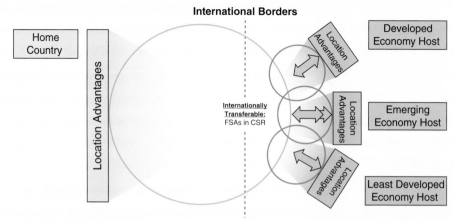

In the 'Home Country' triangle, the spearhead crossing international borders highlights the subset of the MNE's NLB FSAs related to CSR. In the 'Emerging Economy Host' triangle, the double head on the right end of the arrow reflects the extra effort that institutional voids impose on the MNE for it to access LAs through LB FSA development using CSR initiatives. The double-headed arrow on the right reflects CSR initiatives helping to fill institutional voids, thereby strengthening host country LAs.

In contrast, institutional voids – but also potentially lucrative markets – characterize emerging economies. The location advantages of emerging economies suggest the pursuit of CSR initiatives that are strategic (meaning here long-term performance-driven) from the outset. Here, increasing social welfare is aligned with the MNE's performance objectives: the firm can do well by doing good. As discussed in Chapter 14, and as indicated by the double arrow in Figure 17A.1, a CSR initiative may substantively improve the location advantages of an emerging economy (much more than it would improve the location advantages of a developed economy), but this also requires substantial investment by the MNE. Here, CSR initiatives and the development of more traditional business operations go hand in hand.

In the least-developed countries, and with the exception of fair-trade pricing, CSR initiatives usually focus on philanthropy. The least-developed countries possess neither the baseline institutional infrastructure to impose mandated CSR initiatives comparable to those prevailing in developed economies, nor the market potential of emerging economies to trigger strategic ('doing well by doing good') CSR initiatives. Examples of this form of CSR include the drug donation programmes described above. Philanthropic CSR initiatives may help the least-developed countries move towards an institutional and market baseline, at which point other forms of CSR initiatives could be implemented.

A further benefit of reflecting on the importance of location for MNE CSR initiatives is that MNEs need to select the best locations to pursue their CSR initiatives. In most cases, CSR initiatives will simply be deployed in countries where the MNE also wants to grow its business. However, sometimes the optimal location for business and the optimal location for CSR initiatives do not necessarily coincide. This is largely an issue of the time horizon adopted: CSR initiatives typically involve both the deployment of the MNE's internationally transferable FSAs in CSR and the creation of new location-bound FSAs in this area (represented by the top segment of the location-bound CSR FSA space on the right-hand side of Figure 17A.2). In specific emerging economies, this may lead to substantial societal spillover effects in the form of institutional voids being filled. However, the business opportunities in those countries may take a long time to materialize. The size of the CSR-related segment in the overall reservoir of newly created location-bound FSAs will depend on the MNE's evaluation of the host location's potential for initiatives that permit both 'doing good' (for society) and 'doing well' (for itself). A very small CSR section in the location-bound FSA space would indicate a discrepancy between the location advantages of a country for CSR initiatives versus those for traditional business initiatives. The two types of initiatives focus on different elements within the spectrum of a host country's location characteristics.

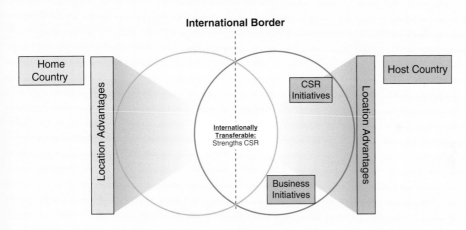

Figure 17A.2
Location advantages and MNE CSR

A smaller size of the upper segment of the location-bound FSA space for deploying CSR initiatives would illustrate the discrepancy between the LAs for CSR initiatives and those for traditional business initiatives: the host country may not be the optimal environment in which to deploy MNE resources related to CSR.

A second limitation of Dunn and Yamashita's piece is the lack of attention devoted to the different ways CSR initiatives can develop within the MNE. Figures 17A.1 and 17A.2 illustrate the simple case whereby the MNE transfers FSAs and other resources to the host environment, and starts pursuing CSR initiatives, thereby potentially creating new FSAs. Here, senior managers at the corporate headquarters may be the driving force behind these CSR initiatives.

Alternatively, such practices may be motivated by external pressures exerted by NGOs or government agencies.

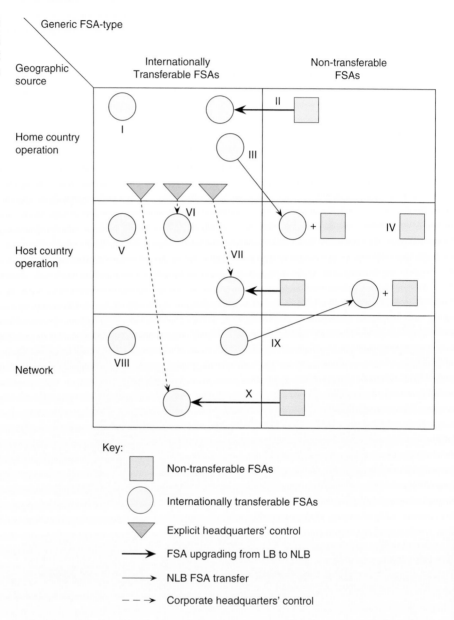

Figure 17A.3
Patterns of CSR development in MNEs

CSR initiatives may also develop autonomously within the host country, with the same drivers as above. Once developed, CSR initiatives can remain location-bound or they may become non-location-bound and transferred as best practices (routines) to other operations in the MNE network. Figure 17A.3 illustrates that the development of CSR initiatives can be associated with any of the ten major patterns of FSA development. Indeed, strategic and philanthropic CSR initiatives usually build on the MNE's existing FSAs, and strategic initiatives are generally expected to lead to new FSA development. Examples of CSR development patterns include HP's previously described CSR initiative, which followed development Pattern VII. We also previously described Nike's partnering efforts with suppliers as following development Pattern VI.

A third limitation of Dunn and Yamashita's *HBR* article is the lack of attention devoted to bounded reliability in CSR initiatives. The authors do highlight the need to align CSR initiatives with the MNE's business interests if the initiatives are going to be sustained over longer periods of time. Assuming such alignment exists, the question arises whether all the external partners will actually put forward their best efforts to support the initiative, or whether some of these actors will attempt to *free ride* (i.e., reap the initiative's benefits without exerting the *ex ante* expected or promised effort). The bounded reliability of Nike's suppliers and African AIDS drug distributors illustrates the importance of proper governance mechanisms to prevent or mitigate bounded reliability problems.

Strategic Challenges in the New Economy

Robert S. Kaplan, *George Serafeim* and *Eduardo Tugendhat*, in their *HBR* article, prescribe how to scale up initiatives aimed to 'do good' for society, while simultaneously achieving the firm's economic goals.[32] They focus on how to build 'inclusive ecosystems' in developing countries.

One guideline from the authors is that MNEs should initiate projects that generate both economic and social benefits for all key participants involved in these projects. In the realm of farming, a large MNE could help small farmers in a developing country integrate into international supply chains. Here, the MNE moves from a transactional perspective to a relational perspective, whereby these small farmers are treated as long-term partners in cooperative relationships which also include larger economic actors downstream in the value chain.

One example, initiated by US-based Carana (subsequently acquired by the Palladium Group), is the integration of small corn farmers in Uganda into:

> ... the mainstream regional economy [in Uganda]. This required deep engagement with multiple players, including Nile Breweries, grain traders, and the farmers themselves ... [After five years] Median crop yields had risen by 65% ... Annual household incomes had more than doubled ... Downstream in the new supply chain, annual sales of maize grits from the lead grain trader, AgroWays, to Nile Breweries had increased from 480 to 12,000 metric tons.[33]

Such focus on relational contracting in more integrated supply chains can lead to new FSAs that are difficult to imitate by outsiders.

In this realm, and strongly aligned with the relational contracting perspective, MNEs should try to partner with host-country organizations that command themselves sufficient expertise and have a stellar reputation for acting as catalysts for change. These first-tier partners can then engage other key participants from multiple sectors towards collaborating and sharing complementary resources. Some of these key partners (e.g., social enterprises, anchor corporations, impact investment funds, foundations of wealthy families, private equity groups, NGOs) can act as intermediaries, and be instrumental to sourcing seed capital and scale-up financing required, thereby making the coveted 'socially inclusive ecosystem' a reality.

Once an inclusive ecosystem is in place and scaled up, the MNE can largely let the partners run the project themselves. As noted by the authors: 'Once the new ecosystem in the Ugandan maize project was established, Carana could disengage as AgroWays, Nile Breweries, and other agribusiness companies made their own investments to reach a broader population of maize farmers.'[34]

Kaplan *et al.* conclude that 'to address persistent poverty and inequality, corporations must reach beyond their own capabilities and partner with other private-sector entities and with governments, communities, and nonprofits to create new ecosystems that will deliver value to all'.[35]

According to Dunn and Yamashita, MNEs can both 'do well' and 'do good', namely, achieving simultaneously their firm-level economic goals and broader societal objectives. Kaplan *et al.* confirm Dunn and Yamashita's case study of Hewlett-Packard in India, and formulate a generalizable script for doing well and doing good at the same time. In terms of our framework, this script includes the following:

First, the systemic search for multisectoral opportunities can build on foreign subsidiary entrepreneurial initiatives. MNEs' transfer of non-location-bound FSAs that are subsequently matched with host-country-specific business opportunities lies at the heart of the resource recombination process. This typically results in location-bound FSAs being created over time in subsidiaries in host countries. The difference with conventional recombination processes, which is highlighted here, is the move away from traditional, narrow value capture considerations towards focusing more on value distribution, benefiting the entire ecosystem of partners, including vulnerable actors.

Second, and related to the first point, is that entering unfamiliar foreign markets typically drives MNEs to identify and access complementary resources from external actors. Such complementary resources should help overcome the CAGE distance dimensions (see Chapter 4). In Kaplan *et al.*'s narrative, the complementary resources to be targeted include those that will support the inclusive ecosystem, rather than only the MNE's operations. The governance and managerial challenges of properly matching these complementary resources from different partners, so that they can create economic and social value, obviously remain the same. As a side note, the support provided by the MNE to the inclusive ecosystem may ultimately also help the MNE maintain its social licence to operate, both in the host environment and the home country.

Third, in its role of flagship company in regional business networks as analyzed by Rugman and D'Cruz in their 2000 book,[36] an MNE's self-financing of good causes should be supplemented with seed capital and scale-up financing from other partners in the public and private spheres in host countries that do have an explicit mission related to alleviating poverty, fostering more equality and inclusion, etc.

It should be noted that the balance between 'doing good' and 'doing well' is a dynamic one. For many MNEs, it now implies a move towards inclusive stakeholder capitalism, whereby especially larger firms implicitly or explicitly agree to social contracts with the societies in which they operate, beyond their ordinary business transactions. Here, the notion of environmental, social, governance, and data (ESGD) stewardship reflects the idea that international business strategy must integrate formally ESGD concerns in strategy formation, and that this must be done at the highest level, namely, that of the MNE's Board of Directors.[37] The main point is that new risks are on the rise for most MNEs in each of these four areas. Negative ESGD 'events' may actually emerge locally in any of the MNE's operations, but the fallout will often affect the firm in its entirety. As a few examples, a high carbon footprint of an MNE division (as an indicator of poor efforts towards climate change impact mitigation) can lead to boycotts from financial investors (E). Paying insufficient attention to human rights in the supply chain, or to employee safety, or to diversity and inclusion can negatively affect labour relations and thereby the firm's reputation globally (S). Having tax strategies that ignore where value added is actually created, and that systematically transfer profits to low tax jurisdictions, or turning a blind eye to subsidiary-level corruption in host countries in order to earn contracts, can again put the MNE at great risk in terms of litigation and possible reputational costs (G). Finally, paying insufficient attention to cyber security, with the potential for data breaches, illegal external access to sensitive business or personal data, and the subsequent dissemination of these data, could endanger the integrity of the firm's value chain, and ultimately the survival itself of the firm (D). But ESGD elements that are material to the effective implementation of the MNE's business strategy not only entail risks. They can also create opportunities for the MNE to build FSAs in these areas, especially if the firm can demonstrate high corporate reliability to societal stakeholders. Such reliability will ultimately help the MNE retain its social licence to operate, and therefore its long-term potential to create and capture value.

Five Management Takeaways

1. Determine the meaning of 'corporate citizenship' in each country where you operate and across all of the firm's international operations.
2. Assess each CSR initiative in terms of its joint contribution to 'doing well' and 'doing good', and evaluate the longer-term business opportunities that CSR activities can create for the firm in host countries.
3. Improve working conditions and labour standards at your factories and those of your suppliers by effectively implementing CSR activities.
4. Rethink your pricing decisions by trading off profit maximization against fulfilling obligations to society.
5. Align your CSR activities to your business objectives in the host country and to the host's socio-economic and institutional context. But also adopt formally a corporate-wide ESGD stewardship approach as part of your international business strategy to mitigate material risks for the firm as a whole and to capitalize on opportunities arising in the ESGD sphere.

17B

International Strategies of Corporate Environmental Sustainability

Five Learning Objectives

1. To assess the impact of environmental regulations as a created location advantage (or disadvantage) in the international business context.
2. To explain the impact of environmental regulations on firm-level innovation by MNEs.
3. To highlight the possibilities for new FSA development, resulting from environmental innovation and associated with an arsenal of MNE sustainability-oriented business practices.
4. To develop a classification scheme of alternative MNE environmental strategies.
5. To clarify that not all firms should try to develop environmental FSAs, since this may be a resource-intensive undertaking with uncertain outcomes.

This chapter examines Porter and van der Linde's idea that government-imposed environmental regulations can enhance competitiveness by pushing companies to come up with innovative ways to use resources more productively and potentially develop green FSAs. In this way, environmental regulations can actually benefit the firms being regulated. Porter and van der Linde recommend that senior managers respond to environmental regulations by adopting a resource productivity approach (embedding new environmental initiatives into the production system), rather than a pollution control approach (just dealing in new ways with whatever waste the production system generates). The authors note that raising resource productivity is good for both the firm and the environment. These ideas will be examined and then critiqued using the framework presented in Chapter 1.

Significance

In a classic 1995 *HBR* article, **Michael Porter** and **Claas van der Linde** argue that government-imposed environmental regulations can trigger innovative solutions to environmental problems, which may in turn lead to cost efficiencies or value enhancement.[1] These positive effects at the firm or industry level are often sufficiently high to offset any costs associated with these regulations for the companies involved.[2] The authors thus suggest that stringent environmental standards may lead to new FSAs.[3]

If environmental regulations can indeed benefit firms, then senior managers should stop reflexively opposing new environmental regulations or attempting to delay their implementation, as such behaviour benefits mainly lawyers and consultants thriving under an adversarial regulatory regime with a strong litigation orientation, while doing nothing to solve the environmental problems at hand.

Porter and van der Linde suggest a shift away from end-of-pipe and waste disposal solutions to a dynamic, **resource productivity** model of environmental regulation: 'The concept of resource productivity opens up a new way of looking at both the full systems costs and the value associated with any products. Resource inefficiencies are most obvious within a company in the form of incomplete material utilization and poor process controls, which result in unnecessary waste, defects, and stored materials.'[4] The authors point out that resource inefficiencies occur not only in the firm's production system, but also at the customer end of the value chain. Such inefficiencies include discarded packaging that has to be disposed of, pollution created when actually using the product (as is the case with automobiles), and costs of product disposal after its use by the customer has ended. Here, senior managers should adopt a systems approach to environmental strategy that takes into account all of the above resource costs over the products' life cycle, as well as the benefits from environmental innovation in the various value chain activities.

The systemic, resource productivity approach suggests that environmental initiatives should be embedded in the production system. This approach is very different from the more conventional pollution control approach whereby equipment is simply placed at the end of the production process, and attempts are made to dispose effectively of the waste that has been created. As a starting point, Porter and van der Linde suggest that companies inventory all their unused, emitted, or discarded resources. This waste requires solutions, not at the end-of-pipe, but at the source, through materials or equipment substitution and more generally through process innovations.

In conjunction with advocating a resource productivity approach, Porter and van der Linde also note the importance for companies to be proactive in redefining relationships with stakeholders such as environmentalists and regulators: 'How can companies argue shrilly that regulations harm competitiveness and then expect regulators and environmentalists to be flexible and trusting as those same companies request time to pursue innovative solutions?'[5] Stakeholder engagement offers MNEs an opportunity to seek innovative solutions to environmental problems – solutions that may lead to FSA development.

According to Porter and van der Linde, environmental regulation can trigger two broad forms of innovation. The first form of innovation involves technologies that reduce the costs of dealing with pollution. Some of the most creative innovations actually convert physical pollution into something of value. To illustrate this type of innovation, Porter and van der Linde describe the case of the French MNE Rhône-Poulenc's[6] plant that made a large investment to install new equipment for the recovery of previously discarded diacids (a by-product of making nylon). The recovered diacids were subsequently sold as additives for dyes and now generate substantial annual revenues.[7]

The second form of innovation addresses the root cause of pollution by improving resource productivity. Innovations of this second form lead to better utilization of inputs, better product yields, or simply better products. To illustrate this innovation type, Porter and van der Linde describe the case of US-based Dow Chemical's move to reduce its use of caustic soda. Dow traditionally used caustic soda to scrub hydrochloric gas in order to produce a variety of chemical products. The wastewater from this process was then stored in evaporation ponds. The company redesigned the process for creating these chemicals, substantially reducing the use of caustic soda. This US $250,000 process improvement not only reduced the need for caustic soda and subsequent wastewater storage, but also saved Dow US $2.4 million a year.[8]

The above examples illustrate how managers can turn environmental improvements into productive opportunities. The early adoption of advanced environmental management approaches may also produce a first-mover advantage for companies, and herein lies the article's relevance for international business strategy. The authors note that 'world demand is putting a higher value on resource efficient products. Many companies are using innovations to command price premiums for "green" products and to open up new market segments.'[9]

Porter and van der Linde illustrate this point by describing the case of German companies that have benefited from an international first-mover advantage by reducing the packaging intensity of their products. This advantage resulted directly from Germany's early adoption of recycling standards. In this case, environmental regulation conferred a location advantage on the firms subject to the regulation, which in turn led to FSA development.

This case highlights the fact that location advantages can be created by government regulation. Environmental regulation motivates, alerts, and educates companies to adopt environmental innovations and thus helps overcome bounded rationality challenges, especially the often-observed senior management's relative lack of knowledge about – and limited attention devoted to – environmental issues.

Porter and van der Linde describe five major features that, in their opinion, make for good environmental regulations. First, good environmental regulations 'create maximum opportunity for innovation by letting industries discover how to solve their own problems'.[10] The regulations should require that specific results be achieved, but should not specify the means. For example, the regulations should not force the adoption of specific so-called 'best practice' technologies. Second, in order for environmental regulations to encourage real behavioural change in industry through innovations, the regulations should be stringent rather than modest. Third, to reflect the realities of researching, developing, and adopting new technologies, the regulations should allow for a phasing-in period. Fourth, regulations should encourage environmental improvements as close as possible to the source of the pollution, namely, early in the value chain. In other words, the regulations should encourage a resource-productivity approach rather than a conventional pollution-control approach. Fifth, countries should ideally develop regulations before other countries, thereby allowing domestic industry to gain first-mover advantages on the international stage. This last recommendation is obviously subject to the condition that the general movement of environmental regulation on the international stage is correctly anticipated. Otherwise, a competitive disadvantage may result.

Porter and van der Linde offer some examples of regulations spurring environmental innovations that have been instrumental to success in the international marketplace. The US and Scandinavian pulp and paper industries are an illuminating example. In the 1970s, the United States imposed strict regulations with insufficient phase-in periods to allow the best technologies to surface. These regulations led US firms to adopt costly end-of-pipe solutions to meet the new regulations. In contrast, strict Scandinavian regulations were announced, but not immediately imposed. As a result, firms could act in anticipation of new regulations without being subject to impossible time limits. Given the extra time, firms could comply with the regulations by improving their production processes rather than adopting end-of-pipe solutions. The firms were able to incorporate environmental innovations into their normal capital replacement programmes. As a result, Scandinavian firms simultaneously met tough new emission requirements and lowered their operating costs. With the rise of the environmental movement worldwide, the superior Scandinavian technology resulted in price premiums for environmentally friendly products well into the 1990s.

The authors also point to the example of the Dutch flower industry. In response to concerns over pesticide, herbicide, and fertilizer contamination of soil and groundwater, the Dutch flower industry was forced to innovate. These innovations included developing a closed loop system, which used greenhouses to avoid soil and groundwater contamination. The industry also 'innovated at every step in the value chain, creating technology and highly specialized inputs that enhance resource productivity and offset the country's natural disadvantages'.[11] These responses to environmental concerns led to improved product quality and lower handling costs, and resulted in the Dutch flower industry commanding 65 per cent of cut-flower exports in the world.

Context and Complementary Perspectives

Environmental management is playing an increasingly important role in broader MNE corporate social responsibility (CSR) approaches. Recent concerns over global warming have put the environment at the forefront of consumer and non-governmental organization (NGO) advocacy efforts. MNEs are particularly scrutinized for their environmental footprint by a variety of stakeholders, as these firms tend to dominate pollution-intensive sectors such as the oil and gas, chemical, energy utility, and automotive industries.

Porter and van der Linde's article was published in 1995, before the development of the Kyoto protocol and the general rise of public concern over global warming. While the article does not speak specifically to climate change issues, the arguments in favour of environmental regulations that improve resource productivity – and potentially lead to FSAs – nonetheless apply. For example, carbon emissions can be reduced by using energy resources more efficiently (an example of increased resource productivity). These efforts will also reduce energy input costs, thus resulting in a more competitive firm. The company that makes this sort of change first may develop FSAs stemming from first-mover advantages.

Porter and van der Linde's arguments against end-of-pipe solutions also apply to the climate change context. Their arguments call into question many of the current climate change proposals involving carbon dioxide storage and sequestration, as well as many of the carbon trading schemes.

As an illustration of the article's relevance, one can think of US-based General Electric's (GE) adoption of 'ecomagination' initiatives, starting in 2005, to make the firm more environmentally friendly. Jeff Immelt, GE's CEO at that point in time, launched the company's large-scale investments in environmentally friendly technology and processes. He dubbed these investments 'ecomagination' after GE's slogan, 'imagination at work'. The strategy assumed that governments would, sooner or later, move to constrain the emissions of greenhouse gases. Immelt argued that GE could either assume the role of victim of new and forthcoming regulation by merely reacting to it, or alternatively turn the regulation into a business opportunity and use the changed scenario to its advantage by making it a key input for strategy. GE's environmental approach was a large-scale, international test case for the proposition that environmental sustainability can mean economic opportunity, not just financial burden. If Immelt were to succeed in substantially lowering operating costs and increasing value for customers by mitigating negative environmental effects and becoming a world leader in the adoption of green technologies, this might help redefine the corporate world's attitude towards capital investment in greening. Success looked probable for GE's initiative, as revenues from GE's eco-products and services had reached more than US $200 billion in 2015, an amount sixteen times higher than in 2006 and more than ten times higher than expected back then.[12] By 2019, GE's revenues from the renewable energy sector alone reached US $15.3 billion.[13] Unfortunately, GE's environmental progress has been hindered by a variety of wrong strategy bets, including, *inter alia* (and very paradoxically), the firm's large-scale investments in gas turbines and coal power plants. In September 2000, GE's stock was valued at around US $60 per share. In September 2020, it was valued at approximately $6 per share. This simple statistic suggests that high-profile CEOs such as Jeff Immelt, who ran this highly diversified MNE for sixteen years (until being retired by the Board in June 2017), trumpeting continuously the firm's environmental and social innovations, do not necessarily benefit overall value creation for shareholders. This example thus represents a cautionary tale for investors and stakeholders alike: larger-than-life figurehead CEOs will not always reliably deliver on open-ended promises about the firm 'doing good and doing well'.

David Kiron and his co-authors, in a 2017 article in *SMR*, provide a firm-level perspective complementing Porter and van der Linde's article. They discuss contemporary environmental strategies of large companies (including many MNEs) that are aligned with evolving societal views on the responsibility of business to operate sustainably.[14] The concept of sustainable development was popularized in 'Our Common Future' or 'Brundtland Report', published by the UN World Commission on Environment and Development in 1987.[15] Subsequently, the UN Global Compact was established by 9,000 companies in 2000 to help implement such a vision of sustainable development. Groups of countries and firms have actively worked together ever since to achieve 'sustainable business practices'.[16] This has resulted, *inter alia*, in the Paris Agreement among 195 countries in 2016, with target limits of greenhouse gas emissions.

The authors describe the rapidly rising importance of 'environment, social, and governance (ESG) metrics' that senior management teams, investors, and other stakeholders can use to improve firm-level sustainability performance.[17] We briefly touched on the ESG approach at the end of Chapter 17A, where we suggested that digitalization metrics (D) should be added to the new standard ESG performance measurements. The deployment of sustainability-oriented strategies and ESG metrics varies widely across geographies and industries, and it is also a function of firm size, with the largest companies being more likely to have a sustainability strategy. The authors note: 'For companies in chemicals, energy and utilities, industrial goods and services, and machinery, having a sustainability strategy is practically mandatory.'[18]

The authors formulate eight guidelines, mostly in the sphere of business processes and governance (thereby reducing bounded rationality and bounded reliability challenges), to help companies achieve a successful sustainability-oriented strategy:

1. *'Set your sustainability vision and ambition.'*[19] Senior management should announce a clear vision for sustainable business practices and integrate this vision into the firm's overall strategy. A focus on ESG factors can in some cases be instrumental to identifying sources of profitable business opportunities, rather than just highlighting constraints to be addressed. As one example of the Dutch MNE Unilever: '. . . executives realized that the company's future growth would come from emerging markets that had significant sustainability issues in areas like deforestation, poor sanitation, and water scarcity. The company subsequently analyzed its entire value chain across brands and countries and discovered that much of its footprint was at the consumer end, involving issues such as using more product than necessary or improper end-of-life disposal. This discovery gave the senior leadership team a purpose and a rationale for aligning its resources behind a strategic sustainability focus. In 2016, the company's Sustainable Living brands were growing 30% faster than its traditional brands.'[20]

2. *'Focus on material issues.'*[21] In order to 'walk the talk', senior managers should always investigate how a sustainability strategy can be incorporated into the firm's supply chain, and make a tangible difference. As one example, the US-based MNE Greif Inc., which manufactures industrial packaging products such as containers for transporting large steel drums, responded actively to some of its stakeholders interested in environmental issues: 'In the mid-2000s, more customers began asking Greif managers for environmental information, such as greenhouse gas emissions data. In response, the organization began lifecycle analysis (LCA) studies on its core products of steel, plastic, and fiber containers. The analyses showed that the most effective way to improve the environmental performance of its containers was to make the containers heavier, longer-lasting, and easier to reuse . . . Based on this discovery, Greif determined that its core business should strategically shift toward reconditioning containers and related services.'[22]

3. *'Set up the right [routines] to achieve your ambition.'*[23] As one example, Germany-based BASF, active in the chemical industry, introduced dedicated routines to achieve its sustainability goals: 'By 2014, the company had assessed 80% of its product portfolio – some 50,000 product applications – on a

sustainability scale that ranks whether a product is exceeding, meeting, or noncompliant with certain sustainability standards. At the top of the rankings are "accelerator" products . . . BASF has identified 13,500 accelerator solutions in its sales portfolio. "Performer" products meet basic market standards and are followed by "transitioners," which are products actively addressing sustainability issues. At the bottom of the list are "challenged" products that carry significant sustainability risks. Product teams develop plans to move their products up the ranks.'[24]

4. *'Explore business model innovation opportunities.'*[25] According to the authors, innovating for sustainability in MNEs often demands revisiting the functioning of international value chains and targeting specific market segments, as shown in their example of US-based Kraft Foods, the grocery manufacturing and processing company: 'Sustainable sourcing in its value chain was a key part of Kraft Foods' coffee business unit . . . Applying sustainability standards from organizations such as Rainforest Alliance, Fair Trade, and UTZ Certified help boost crop yields and capacity – a critical need for a global food company dependent on reliable access to commodities . . . More often than not, however, "greening" a product is not the key to building new business in target segments, as Kraft discovered with its YES Pack commercial salad-dressing containers.[26] . . . What opened doors to commercial segments, though, was the package design. The bigger, easier-to-use pouches – which were less expensive to produce – were extremely popular with restaurants, giving Kraft a competitive advantage with lower costs.'[27]

5. *'Develop a clear business case for sustainability.'*[28] As regards implementation, companies should formally assess opportunities that can contribute both value to the business and positive environmental impacts. Here, key performance indicators (KPIs) should be linked to important and measurable goals and responsibilities, whereby middle management and – in the case of MNEs – foreign subsidiary managers should be actively involved. The example of US-based Timberland, an MNE active in footwear and apparel, shows how a firm can build new FSAs based on more generic expectations at the sectoral level: 'Timberland LLC leverages industry standards to tie sustainability efforts tightly to the bottom line. The company developed its own "nutrition label" that it calls Green Index. The index measures the climate impact, chemicals, and resources consumed in the manufacture of certain footwear products. Using the index, Timberland can compare a product's score to its profit margin. They could find out if shoes with higher environmental impact are better or worse for margin . . . Sustainable products may be more expensive to produce, but generate better margins.'[29]

6. **'Get the board of directors on board.'**[30] An MNE's board of directors is the main conduit for communication between senior management and investors as well as the firm's broader stakeholders. Especially when the latter become more important to the firm for it to maintain its licence to operate sustainably, the board of directors can perform a key role in communicating the seriousness of the sustainability endeavour. The authors note that the Sweden-based MNE Atlas Copco, specialized in manufacturing industrial tools and equipment, was at the forefront of this movement: '[It] . . . has become the first listed company whose board of directors has made an explicit statement identifying a significant connection between its business goals and the well-being of stakeholders other than its shareholders. . . . Atlas Copco is registered in Sweden and is legally governed by the Swedish Companies Act. This act requires that the Board of Directors governs the company to be profitable and create value for its shareholders. However, Atlas Copco recognizes going beyond this, [i.e.,] extending it to integrating sustainability into its business creates long-term value for all stakeholders, which is ultimately in the best interest of the company, the shareholders, and society.'[31]

7. **'Develop a compelling value-creation story for investors.'**[32] In some instances, investors may be pushing for stronger sustainability performance, but in other cases they may need to be convinced that such performance can positively influence the bottom line, or at least represents a precondition for the firm to have a licence to operate sustainably. For instance, 'Antoni Ballabriga, global head of responsible business at Banco Bilbao Vizcaya Argentaria (BBVA), the Spanish banking group, established a close working relationship between his sustainability group and IR [investor relations] to help develop a succinct sustainability value story for BBVA. The effort began as an information exchange, in which IR would reach out to Ballabriga's group when investors asked specific questions. As confidence built and investor demands increased, IR started asking Ballabriga to join earnings calls and other meetings with investors. Today, the relationship is a partnership, and the groups have jointly developed a process to create and update the investment story of how sustainability creates value and should be reflected in its share price.'[33]

8. **'Collaborate with a variety of stakeholders to drive strategic change.'**[34] MNEs may need to work on sustainability-related alliances with a diverse group of stakeholders, thereby resulting in an ecosystem of partnerships. But there is a challenge here, related to bounded rationality and bounded reliability. Especially MNEs operating in many countries may need to be very selective in terms of the stakeholders they co-opt in their sustainability strategies. Non-business stakeholders are typically more difficult to assess

as to the potential value they can bring to the MNEs, whether in terms of business value or contributions to environmental and social goals. Some non-business stakeholders may just want to close down MNE activities, or prevent firms from starting operations, especially in pollution-intensive industries dominated by large MNEs (e.g., the oil and gas sector), or simply earn bribes. Giving non-business stakeholders in-depth insight into value chain operations and business model functioning could also endanger proprietary knowledge and processes, and thereby the MNE's FSAs. Wishful thinking about sustainability-related, alliance ecosystems should not be confused with business reality. The authors note what they call a 'tragedy of the horizon', meaning that the short-term horizon often adopted by MNE senior managers for doing business and achieving growth and profits may not match the long-term horizon needed for addressing sustainability issues effectively.[35] But a similar tragedy could potentially unfold when trying to cater too much to unreasonable demands of stakeholders in the short run. This could reduce the firm's potential for growth and value creation in the long run.

In their classic article on greening for competitiveness, Porter and van der Linde highlighted, *inter alia*, the positive role of stringent, externally imposed environmental regulations, which could be instrumental to new FSA development. Kiron *et al.* augment Porter and van der Linde's idea by offering eight guidelines that could help MNE senior management integrate societal sustainability concerns into international business strategy. Here, the emphasis is twofold: paying sufficient managerial attention to internal organization so as to make a sustainability-oriented strategy successful and building sustainability-related collaboration with a variety of external stakeholders, far beyond responding to government regulations.

From an international business strategy perspective, MNEs will necessarily need to engage in new types of resource combinations, whereby they will partly build on complementary resources from non-business stakeholders in host countries. Kiron *et al.* found that the largest companies were most likely to have elaborate sustainability strategies. The non-location-bound FSAs commanded by MNEs may not be sufficient on their own to support sustainability strategies in high-distance countries. However, large MNEs' slack resources afforded by their size are more likely to permit a diverse set of strategies with a significant cost tag to be pursued in the realm of national responsiveness, and focused on the sustainability sphere.

As a second complement to Porter and van der Linde's piece, **Ans Kolk** and **Jonathan Pinkse**'s 2005 *CMR* article on climate change classifies and analyzes the strategies that firms can use to mitigate their climate change impact.[36]

Kolk and Pinkse suggest that flexible public policies in the climate change sphere are more prevalent now than in earlier years. This flexibility implies that managers have more choices available to them in adopting climate change impact mitigation strategies. Kolk and Pinkse focus on two strategic goals at the firm level: innovation and compensation. Innovation means, in line with Porter and van der Linde, that firms can improve their business performance through new FSA development, driving emissions reductions. Managers can pursue an innovation approach focusing either internally on their own production processes or on the firms they interact with in their supply chain, or outside their supply chain by exploring new product/market combinations. Alternatively, firms can use compensation approaches to essentially transfer/trade, often internationally, emissions or emission-generating activities.

In practice, Kolk and Pinkse observe that managers who perceive climate change as a business risk tend towards the compensation approach. In contrast, managers who see the potential business opportunities of climate change policy are more likely to adopt an innovation-based approach. To test the potential configurations of climate change impact mitigation strategies in practice, the authors analyzed data from companies included in the *Financial Times Global 500* that had participated in the Carbon Disclosure Project, an initiative pushed by institutional investors. The results of this analysis suggest that, including two types of inaction, firms fall into six broad types: cautious planners, emergent planners, internal explorers, vertical explorers, horizontal explorers, and emissions traders.

Cautious planners are firms preparing for action, but showing little activity related to any of the potential climate change strategic options presented above. As would be expected, these firms mention measures to reduce greenhouse emissions as a future possibility, but cannot provide any specific details on what mechanisms might be utilized to achieve this goal. The US-based electric utility FirstEnergy was a typical cautious planner. Initially, the firm reported efforts to reduce emissions; however, it was unclear about the results of these efforts, or the firm's current position in industry and targets to be achieved. In part, this position stemmed from FirstEnergy's view that there were only limited possibilities for process improvements in its operations. Subsequently, the firm started to promote strongly the idea of environmental sustainability and implemented a variety of sustainable initiatives and policies.

Like cautious planners, *emergent planners* have not yet implemented climate change measures. Unlike cautious planners, however, emergent planners have set targets for greenhouse gas reduction. US-based Bristol-Myers Squibb, a pharmaceutical firm, was an example of an emergent planner. It had well-developed

411

targets, but lacked long-term plans to reach those goals. 'The opportunities it identifies are not in the redesign of products or processes, but in the stakeholder recognition that the company receives for its environmental initiatives.'[37] Emergent planner firms like Bristol-Myers Squibb did not only have targets to reduce their own greenhouse gas emissions, but also extended these targets to suppliers. Subsequently, Bristol-Myers Squibb developed into a market leader in sustainability and intensified its stakeholder management in order to meet long-term goals.

Internal explorers are firms with a strong internal focus entailing a combination of targets and improvements in their production process. Firms in this category usually try to improve their energy efficiency in an effort to reduce CO_2 emissions. Nippon Steel is a classic example of an internal explorer. As early as the 1970s, it had set a goal of 20 per cent energy savings in reaction to the oil shocks. It similarly set a target of 10 per cent savings in reaction to climate change concerns to be achieved by 2010. In this particular example, however, the prior efficiency gains made subsequent energy reduction and emission targets more difficult to obtain. This pushed the firm to modify its supply chain for further efficiency gains and to acquire certified emission credits by transferring emission-reducing technology (one of its FSAs) to other countries in Asia that did not have targets for emission reductions. Nippon Steel thus evolved over time and became a hybrid vertical explorer/emissions trader. For an MNE such as Nippon Steel, the very ability to transfer its environmental FSAs is an FSA in and of itself. This FSA means the firm gained access to emission credits, thus increasing its strategic options to mitigate its climate change impact.

Vertical explorers are firms with a strong focus on environmental measures within their supply chains. 'The reason for a company to concentrate on upstream and downstream activities can be twofold: it relies on natural resources that are vulnerable to extreme weather conditions and/or its manufacturing process has relatively low climatic impact compared to the consumption of its products (for instance, the automotive industry).'[38] Unilever is an example of a vertical explorer because the firm's reliance on agricultural supplies exposes Unilever's production to risks from natural disasters such as floods and long-term drought. At the same time, the climate change impact of some of Unilever's products depends strongly on household consumer behaviour, for example, the water temperature used in consumers' washing machines.[39] These conditions have pushed Unilever to look for emission savings within its own supply chain by encouraging environmental standards among its suppliers and on the downstream side by utilizing life-cycle analysis in its product design.

The final two configurations, *horizontal explorers* and *emissions traders*, were the least common forms found in Kolk and Pinkse's sample (at 5 and 4 per cent, respectively). Horizontal explorers seek opportunities to mitigate their climate change impact in markets outside their current business scope. For example, Stora Enso, the Finnish forest products company, entered the green electricity market by developing biofuels from sawmill and logging residues. Emissions traders, on the other hand, trade on emission markets and participate in offset projects. 'This group of companies directly focuses on the opportunities of emissions trading and combines this option with an internal reduction target that has a global reach and with a favourable position towards new products and markets.'[40] Mitsubishi's early involvement in establishing a Japanese greenhouse gas market and its participation in emission reduction trading schemes in the United Kingdom made it a typical emissions trader.

Kolk and Pinkse note that of the six climate change profiles presented above, most companies fall into either the cautious planner or emergent planner category. This distribution indicates that most firms are still in the preliminary phase of planning their climate change impact mitigation strategies, which is probably because of the enormous bounded rationality challenges confronting senior MNE managers. Because it is highly uncertain what many countries' climate change policies will be, many managers understandably adopt cautious and non-committal approaches. Firms become less likely to pursue radical innovations, because policy uncertainty increases the risk that new FSAs will not be effectively deployable at home and abroad, and will not gain them first-mover advantage internationally.

Finally, although Kolk and Pinkse examine both the innovation and compensation approaches, it is important to realize that the innovation approach to addressing the climate change challenge is more likely to lead to the dual benefits of meeting emission targets and developing FSAs. In contrast, the compensation approach to climate change, while offering strategic flexibility that is important in high bounded rationality contexts, will not lead to direct FSA development, except for the firms that specialize in the compensation business, namely, the emission traders.

MANAGEMENT INSIGHTS

All three articles emphasize that environmental innovation can lead to the development of new FSAs. Implicit in linking environmental management with competitive strategies is the alignment of firm-level and societal interests, as also discussed more broadly in Chapter 17A. Porter and van der Linde have the important insight that environmental stewardship can be achieved through higher resource productivity, which in turn increases the competitiveness of the firm. Thus, the concept of resource productivity brings the profit-seeking interests of the firm into alignment with society's interest in environmental sustainability.

Porter and van der Linde also attempt to capture the role of bounded rationality in environmental strategies. For example, the authors address the following question: if efficiency gains from environmental initiatives are so prevalent, why would regulations ever be needed to encourage companies to adopt such initiatives? Wouldn't firms adopt the initiatives out of their own self-interest? Porter and van der Linde offer the following answer to this question: 'the belief that companies will pick up on profitable opportunities without a regulatory push makes a false assumption about competitive reality – namely, that all profitable opportunities for innovation have already been discovered, that all managers have perfect information about them, and that organizational incentives are aligned with innovating'.[41] Thus, environmental regulation is needed not only to align interests, but also to push companies towards reaching efficiency frontiers that they themselves cannot identify due to bounded rationality constraints.

The bounded rationality problem surrounding environmental issues is further illustrated by the difficulties of predicting the direction of environmental policies. For example, the idea that CO_2 would be considered a pollutant was not on most managers' radar screens three decades ago. The difficulty in predicting environmental trends is also illustrated by Monsanto's (acquired in 2018 by Bayer as a part of its crop science division) environmentally motivated shift from a chemical to a life sciences company. As a life sciences company, the US-based MNE developed genetically modified crops that reduced the need for pesticides and herbicides, thus producing what the firm thought was an environmentally friendly product. Unfortunately, bounded rationality constraints obscured the firm's ability to foresee the consumer, NGO, and government backlash against genetically modified crops. This backlash resulted in governments imposing strict regulations against the company's products, a one-third drop in Monsanto's market capitalization, and the dismissal of Robert Shapiro as the MNE's CEO. The Porter and van der Linde article correctly identifies that regulatory flexibility will minimize such firm-level risks; strict, inflexible regulations are unlikely to lead to resource productivity and innovation gains.

While Porter and van der Linde's piece captures the role of bounded rationality in firm-level decision making, the article has three important limitations. First, it does not address fully the impact of environmental regulations on location advantages in an international context. To address this limitation, Figure 17B.1 illustrates the role of environmental regulations as a potential source of location advantages.

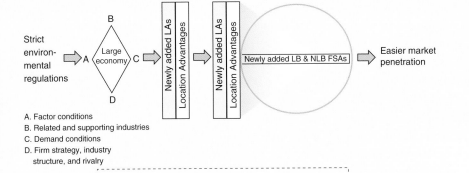

Figure 17B.1
The Porter and
multiple diamond
model perspectives
on environmental
strategy

A. Factor conditions
B. Related and supporting industries
C. Demand conditions
D. Firm strategy, industry
   structure, and rivalry

In the top panel, the vertical rectangular box on the right-hand side of the home diamond represents the new LAs resulting from strict environmental regulations in this large economy. These new LAs give rise to LB FSAs and NLB FSAs, represented by the horizontal rectangular box in the circle spanning the triangle, and should facilitate the MNE's international expansion.

In the bottom panel, the question marks in the rectangular boxes indicate it is highly uncertain whether strict environmental regulations in small open economies will give rise to new LAs, LB FSAs, or NLB FSAs. The dotted arrows, starting on the right-hand side, are suggestive of changes in relative strength of domestic and foreign diamonds, when environmental regulations are different in each country, the point being that small open economy governments (e.g., Canada) better be careful when imposing stricter environmental regulations than those prevailing in much larger trading partners (e.g., the United States).

The top part of Figure 17B.1 shows Porter and van der Linde's 'single diamond' perspective on environmental regulation. They suggest that strict environmental regulations should be viewed as a location advantage. This can then cascade into new location-bound FSAs for firms, which are encouraged to lower costs, innovate, and improve resource productivity. Ultimately, the pressures from environmental regulation may lead domestic firms to earn a first-mover advantage internationally as compared to firms from countries that lag behind in establishing stringent environmental regulations. Environmental regulations thus function as the source of new, internationally transferable FSAs, thereby making domestic firms more competitive abroad.

Porter and van der Linde's perspective is appealing for governments and firms in large, technologically advanced economies that can play a leadership role in setting the agenda for international negotiations on environmental regulation, or can otherwise influence the scope and substance of environmental regulation in a large number of other countries. If the domestic market is particularly large and attractive to foreign firms, it makes sense to set high environmental standards, thereby encouraging domestic firms to conform as quickly as possible, and providing incentives to foreign firms to follow these examples. In other words, this advice appears to be particularly appropriate for a country such as the United States, whose MNEs are largely home-market oriented, but also operate in host countries with less stringent environmental regulation.

However, the advice to enact stringent environmental regulation is dangerous for governments in small open economies that lack a large domestic market and do not wield any power, whether formal or informal, in setting international environmental standards. Here, it is an open question what the impact might be of stringent domestic regulations on business, both in terms of location advantages and FSAs, vis-à-vis other countries, especially important trading partners. This is shown at the bottom of Figure 17B.1. Indeed, Porter and van der Linde curiously admit themselves, in spite of their pleading for strict environmental regulation, that 'government cannot know better than companies how to address [resource inefficiencies and potential areas for technological improvement]'.[42] In a **double diamond** or **multiple diamond** world (see Chapter 3), in which the firm's competitiveness depends as much on what foreign governments do as on domestic regulation, unilateral imposition of strict environmental regulation by the home government would appear unwise. For example, in the case of Canada, the United States represents close to 75 per cent of the smaller country's exports. In this case, it is critical for the Canadian government and Canadian-based firms to understand US environmental regulations and to benchmark Canadian regulations against the US ones. This does not imply a loss of national sovereignty, nor an obligation to copy US standards. However, it does suggest that imposing stringent environmental regulations domestically, without understanding the equivalent regulations in the United States, might seriously hurt the competitiveness of Canadian-based firms when doing business in their largest host market. In other words, the actual development of FSAs by Canadian-based companies is highly uncertain, and the creation of first-mover advantages internationally is particularly doubtful.

The above does not imply that governments of small open economies should pursue the opposite strategy, namely lax regulations, often associated with earning the status of a **pollution haven**. In fact, the pollution haven approach, aiming to attract foreign MNEs using lax regulations, is not currently supported by conceptual or empirical analysis, both of which suggest that environmental regulations have little effect on MNE location decisions.[43] One reason why is that many MNEs from highly developed economies have some national responsiveness, but generally attempt to transfer their best practices across borders in the form of routines, so as to facilitate the operation, coordination, and control of their internal networks (i.e., to reduce bounded rationality and bounded reliability challenges). These MNEs require only that environmental regulations are within the substantial bandwidth that their routines require. Environmental regulations are not critical to these MNEs' location choices.

In fact, having environmental regulations far below what is considered appropriate internationally may lead to a negative country effect for domestic firms attempting to do business internationally, as experienced by Chinese firms in 2007. In that year, Chinese exports of contaminated food supplies and toxic or otherwise dangerous toys led some US politicians to coin the concept of 'Chinese roulette' to describe the alleged dangers facing US consumers when buying Chinese products. Bapuji and Beamish's subsequent studies on toy recalls and the product safety crisis completely discredited this narrative, and found that Chinese toy manufacturers were not at fault.[44]

A second limitation of Porter and van der Linde's article is the relative lack of focus on possible patterns of environmental FSA development. As discussed in Chapter 17A, in the broader context of corporate social responsibility, each of the ten patterns discussed throughout this book can be observed in a variety of MNE contexts. However, whereas the case for developing at least some FSAs in good corporate citizenship is compelling, this is less evident in the environmental sphere. Figure 17B.2 illustrates the patterns of developing transferable environmental FSAs. These non-location-bound, green FSAs may form through development Patterns I, II, V, VI, VII, VIII, or X. In all cases, the resulting FSAs are internationally transferable, though it may often be necessary also to develop location-bound FSAs in specific host country environments, as depicted by Patterns III, IV, VII, IX, and X. The importance of internationally transferring and deploying environmental FSAs, in the sense of imposing routines on the entire MNE network, is suggested by findings that a higher degree of multinationality is often associated with superior environmental performance. One explanation for such findings is that external pressures from international environmental regulations increase more rapidly than the firm's bargaining power.[45] However, an alternative and perhaps more credible explanation is that a higher degree of deploying routinized environmental practices across borders actually expresses the MNE's general superiority in institutionalizing its routines throughout its network, thereby leading to stronger performance, in both the economic and the environmental spheres.

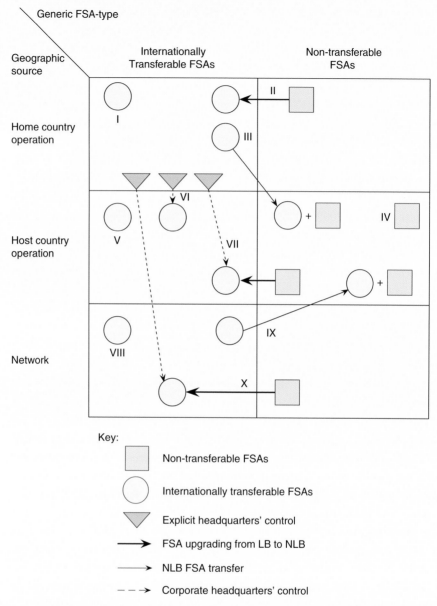

Figure 17B.2
Patterns of
environmental FSA
development
in MNEs

Key:

▢ Non-transferable FSAs

◯ Internationally transferable FSAs

▽ Explicit headquarters' control

⟶ FSA upgrading from LB to NLB

⟶ NLB FSA transfer

- - ▸ Corporate headquarters' control

There is a third limitation to Porter and van der Linde's work, related to the actual substance of environmental management in practice. Here, a distinction should be made among three categories of firms. The first category consists of firms in industries with distinctive, high-profile environmental issues (oil, electricity, automobiles). In these industries, environmental impact mitigation can be a source of competitive advantage. The second category consists of firms that specialize in goods or services instrumental to mitigating environmental impacts or anticipating, influencing, or responding to public policy/regulation. These two categories of firms must continually develop FSAs through *internal* investment, using the various FSA development patterns discussed above.

However, most firms fall into the third category: firms that can essentially *outsource* their environmental impact mitigation. MNEs faced with multiple national and regional regulatory regimes may do best to simply adopt the best available practices accessible in external markets. For example, if the MNE's legitimacy in a particular home country, from the perspective of the firm's stakeholders, arises from perceived purposeful action towards environmental impact mitigation and from measurable/measured improvements, this does not necessarily imply conventional FSA development: visible environmental commitment does not require the internal creation of new FSAs. In fact, the only FSA of MNEs in this category may be their proximity and easy access to multiple external markets providing best available practices. For example, improvement of environmental impacts in the production sphere may result from purchasing greener and productivity-enhancing technologies. Employees can be made more environmentally conscious by investing in externally provided employee training programmes (e.g., at the industry level). In order to develop organizational competencies in the environmental sphere that stretch across functional areas, the firm may purchase new tools in the market to facilitate internal communication (e.g., software and related support to measure impacts of virtual teamwork, leading to reductions in pollution costs). In the context of formal management systems and procedures, the firm may adopt externally developed tools where possible (e.g., the climate change impact measurement tools, developed by reputable audit companies, or the standardized trading processes introduced by intermediaries as in the case of carbon emission trading schemes). Finally, in the realm of strategic planning, senior management may monitor external developments on environmental mitigation policies and competitor strategies, but outsource all non-crisis environmental stakeholder management where possible (e.g., lobbying with industry associations).

Especially given the sometimes high country and regional specificity of government environmental policies, the above strategy of outsourcing, while not a conventional FSA, will give the MNE flexibility, thereby reducing bounded rationality and bounded reliability challenges in the environmental strategy sphere. It is indeed sometimes difficult to anticipate correctly when and how vote-needing politicians in several countries around the world will introduce specific, new environmental regulations, and what these regulations might entail substantively. In the face of this high political uncertainty, environmental complexity, and the substantial risk associated with making non-redeployable resource investments in the environmental sphere, reliance on external markets may be a wise strategy to pursue.

Strategic Challenges in the New Economy

Peter Hopkinson, *Markus Zils*, *Philip Hawkins* and *Stuart Roper*, in their *CMR* article, focus on how MNEs can exploit the market potential of circular economy (CE) opportunities in the global economy.[46] This is subject matter we already discussed in Chapter 14, in the context of foreign MNEs participating in eco-industrial parks in China. From a broad strategy perspective, the goal is to create at the same time new business value for firms and positive effects for society, given that resources available for consumption are finite. A CE strategy moves away from the traditional linear model of assembling resources, manufacturing and distributing products, and disposing of these products at the end of their useful economic life. A CE strategy can involve various approaches, including: the simple extension over time of product usage; the reuse of products through refurbishment and redistribution (without substantial rework of the products involved); the remanufacturing with new uses for existing products; and the recycling of resources embedded in products, for example, through re-melting metals embedded in discarded products.[47] One of the challenges to overcome in implementing a CE strategy, given many consumers' perception that 'new equals best', is how to market remanufactured products and products built around recycled ingredients or components. The authors describe how the Japanese MNE Ricoh developed a CE strategy over the course of four decades and make recommendations on how to think about and implement a successful CE business model.

In a *first stage*, between 1980 and 1994, Ricoh started with extending the usage of its products, mainly because of the somewhat artificial life cycle of copiers and printers. This life cycle typically lasted between eighteen and thirty-six months and was seldom longer than sixty months. The main reason was that most leasing contracts signed by customers were rather short, so as to give them the opportunity to upgrade to new equipment at the time of contract renewal. This systemic and industry-wide approach to upgrading resulted in a stockpile of returned copiers and printers that had not at all reached the end of their useful life. The main drivers of Ricoh's profits were contract renewals and the sales of consumables (e.g., toner cartridges). At the same time, there were increasing pressures in industry to engage in some form of reuse and to offer products with lower prices, for example, for home printers and copiers, where reuse and refurbishment could play a key role. Until the mid-1990s, Ricoh's asset reuse consisted mainly of refurbishment and redistribution, but this did not constitute one of its core businesses.[48]

In a *second stage*, from 1994 to 2004, Ricoh's operations in continental Europe and the United Kingdom developed actual design capabilities for CE, involving the massive recycling of materials: 'By the mid-2000s, a Ricoh remanufactured printer consisted of approximately 80% retained and reused materials from the original machine.'[49] In addition, 'Ricoh Europe invested in recovery and asset reuse infrastructure and consolidated operations at a few major sites to increase scale and reduce their reprocessing costs.'[50]

In a *third stage*, from 2005 to 2012, Ricoh's remanufacturing business expanded from covering only the European and UK markets, to include the Middle East, which led to the predictable challenges of operating in differentiated markets, such as: the level of requisite adaptation of these remanufactured products in the face of strong international market heterogeneity; the customers' differential brand perceptions and acceptance of remanufactured products' quality and reliability; and the dangers of cannibalization of sales between remanufactured products and fully new machines. As one response to these challenges, Ricoh created the 'Greenline' brand, targeting the public-sector market in the United Kingdom, as well as a price-sensitive customer segment, resulting in effective market segmentation and growth without cannibalizing new machine sales.[51]

As noted by the authors:

> The Greenline brand allowed Ricoh to harmonize a number of regenerative initiatives under a single umbrella. From a customer perspective, the value proposition brings together Ricoh certified product and service provision; attracting a competitive price point and the guarantee that all products, service parts, and consumables used in the provision of print will be returned to and reused within Ricoh's own global supply chain.[52]

Ricoh also established a new industry standard for remanufactured products, which was pivotal in changing customers' negative perceptions, whereby '[r]emanufacturing . . . guarantees the original specification and the only distinction is that for a remanufactured product, the packing indicates that the product may contain recycled or reused parts'.[53]

Finally, in a *fourth stage* starting in 2008, Ricoh was able to overcome the strong downward price pressures on its products, resulting from the great recession, by expanding into emerging markets, thereby increasing sales and gaining scale economies in these new markets. But as of 2012, two new challenges threatened Ricoh's traditional remanufacturing model. *First*, the rise of a more modular design of printers and copiers, thus facilitating the easy incorporation of new technologies. *Second*, the rising value of connectivity within or through single devices, via the use of convergent applications. Ricoh's Greenline-branded, older devices started to lose competitiveness as compared to new machine sales that would incorporate more modularity and connectivity. These new devices offered a lower total cost of ownership (TCO) for customers on two dimensions. On the one hand, they utilized fewer materials, thereby also creating stronger upstream efficiencies (e.g., in toner usage) and thus a better sustainability performance. On the other hand, they created additional value for customers by embedding new user applications directly within the same devices. This supported multi-functionality for the end users (e.g., scanning, faxing, texting, emailing, and saving documents and images using wireless Android).

In order to reinvent its remanufacturing model and make it competitive, Ricoh adopted a regionally differentiated approach focused on Europe, Asia, and the United States, respectively, each of which is responsible for managing its own '3R' (recover, reuse, recycle) community.[54] But these three communities all work under the umbrella of a global 'Business Solutions Group' based in Tokyo:

> Global best practice conferences are held annually at which the heads of each 3R community plus technical and commercial experts meet to discuss and deploy regional opportunity into global horizontal deployment of best practice. In the case of Europe monthly conference calls are held with the US community to share market intelligence and technical best practice (to avoid duplicating technical development and therefore waste cash).[55]

The authors describe, for instance, how 'the technology that was developed in the US to support the Latin American market for toner cartridge reuse (where price is always the main driver and piracy is rife) was deployed specifically in one European business group to help reduce service costs and make a previously unprofitable multi-million pound contract profitable'.[56]

Two points should be emphasized here. *First*, in spite of the supposed geocentric sustainability strategy (focused on sharing best practice, wherever it arises), Ricoh still appears to be managed largely as a Japanese, **international projector-type** MNE, whereby remanufacturing initiatives must credibly demonstrate their profit potential and be approved by the head office in Japan. *Second*, it is only because a global remanufacturing strategy is so difficult to implement that the firm operates with a triad-based, regional organization, complemented with some coordination between the regions. The firm's organization chart also indicates an even more fine-grained organization as a function of locational requirements.

In terms of guidelines useful to other MNEs, a 3R approach requires the joint attention upfront from two sets of individuals in the firm. *First*, engineering groups need to consider design items such as material choices, design durability, modularity of products, and software connectivity and compatibility. They also need to focus on the potential for scale economies and on promoting standards (possibly through pushing for regulations). *Second*, front-office groups that are close to marketing need to understand customer requirements for specific services (such as repairs and upgrading) and for product differentiation. It is important for upstream engineering experts and downstream customer experts to communicate together, especially in MNEs operating across national borders.

As an additional guideline, the authors note that remanufacturing will in most cases need to co-exist with making new products inside the firm: 'Going circular and mainstreaming from relatively small and well-defined niche operations in remanufacturing will create tensions and conflicts with the entrenched (linear) way of doing business.'[57] The authors suggest improving the status of circularity in the firm, by making it a clear goal to be contemplated in all future investment decisions. In addition, they propose – in a somewhat voluntaristic fashion – that tensions and conflicts could be viewed as opportunities for improving daily management operations towards circular practices.

As a last useful guideline, the authors recognize that many challenges related to achieving a more circular economy will require 'global cooperation between governments and businesses to ensure that key policy and system barriers to development are addressed'.[58] Industry standards indeed need to be established to guarantee product quality and to remove consumers' negative perceptions about remanufactured products. Here, international standards are critical for an MNE such as Ricoh. But given that CE development represents a global governance problem without enforceable global governance, substantial attention should perhaps be devoted to industry-level rather than government-mandated recognition of remanufacturing and CE activities. As one example, it is only as of 2011 that '[Infosource] (a market research organization for the office automation industry) has allowed remanufactured products to contribute to firms' overall market share figures'.[59] As to global governance, the question arises how any formal cooperation involving governments and firms would be structured. It is easy to propose global cooperation, but it is more likely that such cooperation will materialize at the regional level such as the European Union, or the level of a smaller number of countries.

In their classic article on the green competitiveness of firms, Porter and van der Linde highlighted the roles of both stringent, external environmental regulations, supposedly instrumental to the development of new FSAs, and improved internal resource productivity (e.g., by reusing waste products of one production process as feedstock for another process). Using an in-depth case study on Ricoh's CE business model, Hopkinson *et al.* added three insights to Porter and van der Linde's suggestions.

First, Hopkinson *et al.* clarified that an MNE's successful CE business model is the outcome of a long sequence of engagements with value-creating opportunities related to circular practices, using new types of resource combinations, and spanning different 'products, components, services, materials, and their by-products that [should] circulate at their highest value for the longest period'.[60] Especially across borders, the iterative nature of novel resource combination processes in the realm of CE may take substantial time before coming to fruition.

Second, in the value creation process, Hopkinson *et al.* highlighted the pivotal role of MNEs' proactive branding (and marketing) activities to overcome customers' negative perceptions about remanufactured products' quality, because 'rather than merely a sales opportunity, branding can be used to spread the message of, and philosophical support for a CE model both internally (among employees) and externally (among customers)'.[61] This is often a location-bound FSA that MNEs must develop in the various places where they operate around the world.

Third, Hopkinson *et al.* also caution about the potential tensions and conflicts between units in the MNE promoting the CE model and the units responsible for rejuvenating the firm's core businesses. Divided engagement and thus bounded reliability could endanger the firm's CE strategy: 'the best intentions of a CE model have been threatened by the significant advances in manufacturing efficiency' associated with the traditional linear business model.[62] However, internal competition inside the firm is a positive development in our view, because it highlights both the economic potential and the boundaries of CE models, which may again have very different application potential across geographic space as far as economic feasibility for the MNE is concerned.

Five Management Takeaways

1. Keep track of expected, new environmental regulations and assess not only their likely cost, but also their potential contribution to green FSA development.

2. Fight ill-conceived messages from external stakeholders that more stringent environmental regulations at home will lead to first-mover advantages abroad, since this is usually not true for firms based in small open economies.

3. Develop new FSAs through environmental innovation by considering the different consumer groups that might benefit from such innovation. This may include circular economy innovations, the potential of which is likely to vary across geographic space.

4. Analyze the scope of the MNE's environmental strategy (inside focus; vertical value chain focus; broader industry focus) to identify relevant environmental initiatives.

5. Beware of exaggerating the economic potential of environmental innovation initiatives, especially if the firm is unlikely to build unique expertise in this area and may be better off 'purchasing best practice solutions' in the external market.

Conclusion: The True Foundations of Global Corporate Success

This book has identified the limits of many insightful, but oversimplified, normative models of how to conduct international business strategy. As a general rule, those models do not spell out correctly the requirements for achieving international, let alone global, corporate success. The problem with most prevailing models is that they attempt to apply to all international business situations a set of prescriptions that are valid only for solving a narrow set of problems in narrow situational contexts. Each MNE and its senior leadership team have a particular history, access to a unique resource base, a specific position in industry, and their own vision of what constitutes desirable international expansion. With international business strategy, one size does not fit all.

What all MNEs do have in common, however, is that they all face opportunities and challenges inviting serious analysis, building on a small set of conceptual building blocks. These key building blocks include *firm-specific advantages* or *FSAs* (both *location-bound* and *non-location-bound*); *location advantages*; *value creation through resource recombination*; *complementary resources of other economic actors*; *bounded rationality*; and *bounded reliability*. These building blocks permit us to recognize and understand most international business opportunities and challenges facing senior MNE managers. Importantly, this small set of building blocks also allows us to identify the limitations of normative messages and models that prescribe how to conduct international business strategy.

Drawing on these conceptual building blocks, and their application throughout the book, we conclude by briefly touching on *seven themes*, each consistent with the observation that the world of international business strategy is far from flat, and unlikely to become much flatter in the foreseeable future. These seven themes are:

1. The observed dominance of regional over global strategies.
2. The 'new forms' of international expansion.

3. The tension between radical international innovation and internal coherence.
4. The challenges facing MNEs when trying to link effectively their back-office activities with the front office.
5. The need to qualify the importance of recombination capabilities.
6. The move towards private equity.
7. The bright and dark sides of the digital economy.

The last three issues are of particular importance for the era to come, in which gross global production will be unlikely to grow at more than 2 to 3 per cent per year, and MNEs will no longer have the option to expand into large emerging markets with double-digit macro-economic growth, namely, a growth level that represented 'requisite luxury' in periods following international economic crises such as the 2008 global recession and the 2020 COVID-19 pandemic. This reduced level of almost guaranteed macro-level growth will go hand in hand with unrelenting pressures to adopt new digital tools and to respond adequately to external stakeholder pressures.

Dominance of Regional over Global Strategies

Much international business strategy is conducted regionally, rather than on national or global levels. Past research has suggested there are only a few truly global firms (i.e., firms with a balanced distribution of sales and assets worldwide).[1] One study, looking at the *Fortune Global 500*, identified only thirty-six truly 'global' firms (i.e., firms having at least 20 per cent of their sales in each of three key regions of the world, namely Asia, the European Union, and North America) based on data published in 2017.[2] A number of other MNEs were close, but the vast majority of firms had a strong home region orientation, though many senior managers, as well as company directors and owners, typically want their firms to achieve a more balanced distribution of sales. A balanced geographical distribution of sales would signal worldwide customer acceptance of the firm's products and services.

The observed dominance of the home region in sales and assets has important implications for strategy. When engaging in strategic decision making, senior management committees and Boards of Directors of geographically diversified firms typically focus first on the geographic area that represents more than 50 per cent of sales and assets. The '50%+' (in most cases actually '75%+') geographic area is usually the main source of the firm's cash flows, as well as its knowledge-generation capabilities and its employees, and it typically is the cash cow allowing expansion into other geographic milieus and new product areas. Any senior executive at the corporate level, accountable to a diverse set of stakeholders, will devote prime attention to the business or set of businesses that represent the majority of sales and assets. This observation simply reflects rational managerial focus: a lack of emphasis on the firm's largest markets would imply a governance problem, with top management committees and Boards paying insufficient attention to what really matters, and paying excessive attention to 'pet projects' in 'pet destinations', at least if such pet projects are fraught with uncertainties and have only limited proven growth and profit potential.

In the above context of largely home-region-oriented sales (the precise definition of what constitutes the home region is obviously firm-specific), senior MNE managers then often also adopt a regional, rather than a national, approach to international strategy, particularly if the firm wants to expand into another key region of the world. When Asian or North American firms contemplate expansion to Europe, the main concern in boardrooms and top management committees is often 'How do we crack the EU market?' When European firms venture outside of Europe, the key question is now systematically 'How do we gain market share in Asia, and where in this geographic zone covered by the Regional Comprehensive Economic Partnership (signed on November 15th, 2020) should we set up a regional office (or regional offices)?' In the context of large host countries, it is correct that outsider MNEs may think primarily about the national host markets, such as the United States, China, and India, because of their relative size. But even then, organizational functioning often derives from a regional head office. The observation that most large MNEs have more than 50 per cent of their sales in their home region is likely to remain relevant in the future, especially in this era of global institutional fracturing and discrimination of outsiders in sectors considered sensitive, *inter alia*, from a national security, health, or 'supply certainty' perspective.[3] Thus, further sales and asset expansion within the home region will often continue to be easier than equivalent sales and asset growth elsewhere in the world.

The question arises whether the present internationalization patterns of emerging economy MNEs will change the above observations, especially as these firms often enter foreign markets to source knowledge that can only be accessed through M&As or alliances in host regions. Given substantial knowledge sourcing from other regions, many MNEs from emerging economies may still have the bulk of their foreign sales and assets in their home region, especially if these firms lack strong FSAs in managing an international, internal network.

The message for senior MNE managers, whether from highly developed nations or emerging economies, is simply not to overestimate the non-location-bound nature of their companies' FSAs, and to be very selective in their international expansion programmes. These managers must determine the correct geographical reach of their extant bundles of FSAs, as well as the requirements for investing in additional strengths when entering foreign environments. Too much adaptation will lead to excessive costs. Too much attention to desired scale and scope will prevent access to location advantages in host environments.

Too much focus on exploiting national differences will lead to vulnerable supply chains and severe coordination problems.

A continued strong focus on selling within a carefully selected geographic space, in accordance with the firm's limited resource base, may therefore be a wise path of action for the present majority of MNEs. This majority lacks the required levels of internationally transferable FSAs to reproduce globally whatever past success has been achieved in a restricted geographic area.

The 'New Forms' of International Expansion

The MNE's history, the environmental context within which it developed, and the resulting firm-level routines all play a key role in determining what constitutes desirable strategy for the future: no one formula can guarantee success. The increasing diversity of the MNE population provides ample evidence of this. While many MNEs continue to originate in the most highly developed economies and base their competitiveness on traditional FSAs such as advanced technology, an increasing number now comes from emerging economies such as China and India. In many cases, these firms are reaching out to exploit the strengths they have developed based on the location advantages of their home countries, whereas in the past, MNEs from Europe, Japan, or North America might have reached inside these countries to access those same location advantages (low labour costs, abundant natural resources, large pools of highly skilled but inexpensive ICT specialists, etc.).

For instance, Chinese companies have reached out to undertake large-scale investments in politically volatile environments, so as to secure the supply of raw materials. Chinese MNEs have for close to three decades benefited from their government owners' ability to influence these foreign environments through aid and diplomacy, as well as their relative insulation from the type of protests that might deter Western firms.[4] Indian ICT entrepreneurs have cast off the role of passive recipients of outsourcing/offshoring contracts. Their firms have established operations in developed countries' high-tech centres, thereby crafting their own direct customer linkages to improve service and capture a larger slice of the economic value created in the supply chain, namely, these firms have in some cases successfully moved up on the *smiling curve*.

For many firms in emerging economies, it is not proprietary R&D outcomes or brand names, or strengths in governing international supply chains that count the most, but rather the personalities, skill sets, and drive of their entrepreneurs, whether senior managers or owners. These individuals give emerging economy firms the ability to succeed abroad in direct competition with long-established MNEs from Europe, Japan, and North America. Perhaps in time they will develop the more traditional types of advantages in the same way that Korean firms such as Samsung, Hyundai, and LG have emerged with brand names and technology that are now well known around the world.

Developed economy MNEs need to carefully identify and nurture their own FSAs, to avoid being displaced by relative newcomers now engaged in sustainable patterns of value creation and value capture. The new forms of outsourcing/offshoring, going far beyond conventional cost-reduction purposes, are one expression of novel resource recombination by established MNEs.[5] A new focus is required on international ecosystems of contributors whose roles may extend far beyond those suppliers and distributors, to include a variety of innovation and co-creation activities across the entire value chain. This book's framework is entirely compatible with these 'new', unconventional types of FDI and other international activity by both established firms and newcomers, even if such expansion patterns cannot be accommodated within the simplistic rules of thumb that have emerged from much existing prescriptive research. In fact, this book has argued implicitly that most prescriptive models of the MNE are too 'MNE centric', meaning that success abroad always results from new forms of 'resources bundling', or 'recombination'.[6] Analysis of what will likely constitute a pattern of successful international expansion must therefore always consider the MNE's extant stock of FSAs, as well as the generic location advantages of the host countries entered and the particular complementary resources required from other economic actors and non-market actors such as governments and NGOs.

The Tension between Radical Innovation and Internal Coherence

Sustained international success will also require that senior MNE managers resolve the ongoing tension between the desire to take advantage of the vast array of opportunities offered in today's international marketplace, and the need to retain an appropriate level of control over the firm's geographically dispersed operations. Economic and political changes in the last two decades have raised hundreds of millions of people from subsistence and isolation to the point where their energy and creativity can begin to be harnessed for the advancement of material and social conditions around the world. On the one hand, there are good reasons for the firm to give its overseas operations the scope to engage creatively in unanticipated resource recombination to take advantage of these new opportunities. On the other hand, there are good reasons for the firm to craft and deploy routines to manage 'distance' and the 'liability of foreignness'. Striking this balance is a key challenge, and unfortunately senior managers cannot simply adhere to a single guideline given the diversity and rapidly shifting nature of individual parent–subsidiary relationships.

Final decisions on what to do and what not to do, what to internalize and what not, may need to be taken centrally, but subsidiary managers can and must be allowed to play a vital role in ensuring these decisions fully reflect locally available knowledge. This can best be accomplished through the promotion of *process* characteristics such as *respect* and *procedural justice* for subsidiary managers: these individuals should not be viewed primarily as a source of bounded reliability (or as an 'agency problem'), but rather as a critical resource for effective and efficient international business strategy development and execution. The fast-growing and highly profitable MNEs of the present and future will be those that are flexible enough to constantly re-evaluate and adjust this delicate balance between the dual need for both entrepreneurial freedom and internal coherence. The MNE's innovation process performance (and, more fundamentally, its resource recombination capability) must be looked at *in its entirety*, meaning from the initial appearance of creative ideas to the profitable delivery of new products to customers.[7] Here, senior managers should be careful not to place too much faith in the 'periphery', neglecting the businesses that are now providing the cash flows needed for future expansion, and experimenting on a grand scale with new governance models. Most large MNEs work with a mix of product and geographic divisions in a multidivisional governance system, with individual divisions usually responsible for the bulk of resource recombination activities. There are solid reasons for this, namely the needs for:

- specialization in decision making by corporate headquarters and the divisions;
- selectivity in inter-divisional interactions;
- standardized, quantitative monitoring and incentive systems;
- specific roles for corporate headquarters and the divisions in general innovation strategy; and
- careful and informed management of the tensions that may arise between incremental and breakthrough innovations.

The Tension between the MNE's 'Back Office' Activities and its 'Front Office' Needs

The tension between the 'back office' and the 'front office' in large organizations such as MNEs has sometimes been naively described as resulting from the difference between what the firm can reasonably deliver in an economic environment where cost discipline is critical and what the customer would ideally like to experience without paying for the real cost of superior quality.

The reality is more complex. The front office in large MNEs consists of individuals supposed to understand – and cater to – customer needs in local environments. In contrast, the back office is populated by individuals supposed to support the front office by providing rigorous, routinized data analysis (e.g., regarding which products and markets are the most profitable versus the least profitable), as well as a variety of services that make the supply chain run smoothly.

Unfortunately, many large firms, including MNEs in the services sector, are now characterized by the **tyranny of the back office**. This concept implies that individuals and groups in the organization (including most people working at the corporate head office) have become so divorced from the customer and from customer needs, that they become a cancer, negatively affecting the front office. The tyranny of the back office means killing all superior quality delivery in the MNE, especially in foreign subsidiaries. This point is different from the discussion of the previous theme, where internal coherence and **entrepreneurial discipline** were advocated so as to avoid diversifying into undesirable product areas or geographic markets.

Here, the problem is the rise of dysfunctional routines, often supported by sophisticated ICT systems, which ultimately do not allow front office employees to deliver customer service in a fashion that would deviate from standard protocol, but would at the same time optimize customer service quality. All readers of this book will have undoubtedly experienced this many times when using the services of an international airline or hotel chain, or engaging in international financial transactions. Individuals responsible for service delivery in foreign locations are forced to respect standard protocols, often at the expense of customer needs and without creating any real cost advantage or satisfying a legitimate quality requirement. The customers affected cannot interact directly with the individuals in the organization at the source of the front office dysfunction. The ultimate impacts on a firm's reputation can be disastrous, as exemplified by the song written by a disgruntled United Airlines passenger. His song, 'United [Airlines] Breaks Guitars', earned millions of YouTube viewings.[8]

A vicious cycle of bureaucratization results, whereby front office managers in particular become demotivated to communicate to the head office and to the more broadly dispersed back office what is going wrong in interactions with customers, or how customer experience can be improved. In other words, bounded reliability at the MNE's back office has strong negative effects. These negative effects result from senior managers in the back office giving priority to: (1) expedient internal network monitoring; (2) outputs that can be easily codified and are particularly visible (such as results from cost-cutting programmes, quarterly profit reports, or the evolution of the number of formal customer complaints); and (3) the pursuit of empire-building goals and the benefits of a rich social life commensurate with that of a large-company leader. Such goals typically go hand in hand with a systemic, substantive neglect of the front office. Customer service quality is the first victim. Front office managers experiencing a lack of respect from the back office, and often confronted with ill-informed

cost-cutting routines and more centralization, become demotivated and transform into bureaucrats themselves, as if they had been 'body snatched' by their
new back-office masters.

Interestingly, we observe here that bounded rationality in the back office ('let
us focus only on information that really matters') resulting from 'distance' vis-à-
vis the front office, leads the back office to lose its reliability in terms of
delivering what the front office needs. In turn, the front office becomes unreliable in the sense of not delivering the best service that could be delivered to
customers at a particular level of costs.

How to escape from the tyranny of the back office? A two-pronged
approach should be pursued. *First*, the CEO should be the voice of the
consumer. In other words, the CEO should educate both the back office and
the front office on what matters most in the organization as a precondition for
continued shareholder value creation. This requires a lot of 'wandering
around', both at home and internationally, and a diminished focus on looking
at quantitative data in an executive suite filled with back office suits.
Remember the famous words of Jack Nasser, a former Ford CEO, who started
his career with Ford as a financial analyst in the Australian subsidiary. He
testified before a US House Subcommittee and explained as follows the
absence of action by Ford in the United States (in contrast to action in several
developing countries), when faced with roll-overs of Explorer sports utility
vehicles equipped with Firestone tyres: 'We are a data driven company.'[9] Or to
put it in the words of Suresh Sethi (a manager from Modi, an Indian tyre
equipment company): 'Makers of autos and tires around the world were
overly concerned about price and market share. Not enough thought had
been given to safety . . . You buy a $30,000 vehicle . . . and what does the tire
cost? The companies were trying to save $1 per tire because $1 per tire adds up
to a lot. That is responsible for this.'[10] It is certainly a pity for any company to
focus on short-term profit outcomes at the expense of data related to customer
service quality, since the latter will ultimately determine the prospects of long-
term survival and financial sustainability.

Second, proper communication channels should be established between the
back office and the front office. More is required than procedural justice when
having a 'back office–front office' dialogue on a variety of routines shared across
the MNE (whether in the accounting, financial, customer service, ICT, etc. . . .
spheres). The back office employees must understand that their role is to support
the front office subject to a number of constraints (in the realm of cost discipline
and long-term strategy options). However, their role is not that of a mere
roadblock to effective front office functioning, with deviations from back-
office-crafted routines made impossible or being punished indiscriminately. All
large business organizations, and especially the world's largest MNEs, need a
'serving' back office rather than a 'self-serving' one. Fortunately, only MNEs with

a properly aligned 'back office–front office' organization are likely to survive in the long run, in line with the next theme below.

The Need to Qualify the Importance of Recombination Capabilities

Almost every significant challenge facing the world today, such as human overpopulation, shortages of natural resources, and climate change, requires us to reconcile global necessities and pressures with action taken at the local or individual level. Local and individual actions, which often lead to imperfect outcomes, create the need for scapegoats. As visible and strong evidence of the growing international interdependence among countries, the large MNE unwittingly and often undeservedly plays this scapegoat role, and thus becomes the subject of unjustified criticism and fear.[11]

Yet MNEs may actually offer society an array of governance models for addressing difficult global–local trade-offs, and might also perform a direct and constructive role in the resolution of the underlying problems. Large, internationally successful MNEs represent the only governance mechanisms specifically designed both to facilitate resource recombination across product and geographic space simultaneously, and to reconcile international and local pressures and priorities, thereby increasing world economic welfare.[12] MNE governance models could, therefore, subject to necessary qualification, serve as best practices for the future, public institutions of international and global governance that will become increasingly important, as pressure mounts from the type of problems described by the 'tragedy of the commons'.[13]

MNE managers often do play a direct role in improving not only economic efficiency, but also intercultural understanding, social justice, and environmental sustainability around the world. The principal reason they play this positive role is that when MNEs and their managers enter a foreign country, especially outside their home region, they are usually in a position of vulnerability, in spite of their non-location-bound FSAs. MNEs and their managers have five main types of vulnerability:

- to breakthrough, resource recombination efforts from existing or new international rivals;
- to the problems posed by running dispersed internal affiliate networks;
- to the actors providing complementary resources in a wide array of international cooperative business arrangements;
- to the decisions of sovereign governments, and a multitude of other stakeholders, including host country customers and employees; and
- to the scrutiny of the international media and internationally operating pressure groups.

The persistent vulnerability and contestable position of even the world's largest MNEs and their senior managers paradoxically guarantee that these firms make and will continue making positive contributions to improving human conditions globally. Vulnerability engenders humility, and humility creates openness to new ideas and new approaches; such humility can, in short, strongly encourage the firm's resource recombination efforts. Vulnerability-driven resource recombination invariably leads to change inside the MNE. This change may be resisted by the corporate immune system, but the internal dynamic of the process is usually to identify and respect the values that people in host environments treasure most. The change process thus ensures that some core values from the host environment are preserved, and possibly even spread internationally. Here, accountability to all relevant stakeholders, in any host environment, is much in line with the thinking of the late Elinor Ostrom, recipient of the 2009 Nobel Prize in economics, who advocated a system of *polycentric care for the commons*.[14]

Thus, senior MNE managers, especially those with extensive expatriate experience, function – perhaps unexpectedly – as agents of change in an imperfectly governed world. Often, they are willing to engage in a constructive dialogue with a multitude of stakeholders, including external pressure groups. Therefore, they can contribute immensely to the improvement of general, societal conditions while simultaneously pursuing their firms' interests. The possibility that MNEs can create a win-win situation for themselves and for the host nation should not be underestimated.

As the twenty-first century advances, the capability of resource recombination will become increasingly important. Brazil, China, India, and Russia will develop to become mature markets with macro-economic growth rates similar to the ones now characterizing most of the developed world. In this environment of low macro-economic growth, MNEs can meet the capital markets' expectations of double-digit levels of revenue and earnings growth only by continuously recombining resources across product and geographic space. In other words, MNEs must move continuously to new, fast-growing businesses that are related to their extant resource base. At present, few MNEs in the world have mastered the ability to reinvent themselves as a matter of routine. In addition, resource recombination in and by itself is not a panacea for success. During the 1980–2001 period, US-based General Electric was heralded as the shining example of a firm specialized in resource recombination and delivering superior value to shareholders. During this period, GE might not always have brought good things to life,[15] but it was acclaimed for its unique resource recombination capabilities. Unfortunately, even this proven ability to recombine resources did not guarantee continued success in the marketplace, as demonstrated by the firm's dismal economic performance between 2001 and 2020. Not every resource recombination initiative will necessarily be successful, and GE is a prime example of failure because of making a long series of wrong bets. Resource recombination is no substitute for understanding what are the external market values and for exercising proper entrepreneurial judgement on business opportunities, thereby trying to mitigate as much as possible bounded rationality and bounded reliability problems. This also means that much of the large strategy literature on corporate ambidexterity, namely, the 'proper' balancing of exploitation (building on routines) and exploration (engaging in resource recombination), is devoid of meaning for managerial practice, because not just any novel resource recombination initiative will pay off. The substance of exploration activities must fit with what the firm can execute upon and with what the market actually values. Only if MNEs can recombine resources effectively and efficiently can low macro-economic growth rates on a global scale be reconciled with high growth in revenues and earnings of individual firms, as expected by capital markets. But making sense of new product and geographic market opportunities is a tall order and requires a deep contextual understanding of how the firm can do things differently from the past and still be successful in a new environment.

In case resource recombination and the related innovation processes are rewarded by the market and lead to competitive success, this may still be associated with creating losing parties (e.g., the economic actors operating in the activities that are de-internalized and left behind by the MNE, as well as the groups dependent on such activities in specific locations). We are already witnessing today how senior MNE management is increasingly pressured by society to respect social justice objectives. One perspective that is gaining momentum across the planet is that employees and other longer-term stakeholders should enjoy the same treatment as equity capital. Senior MNE managers consider it legitimate to shed economic activities in order to secure the firm's long-term survival, profitability, and growth, thereby showing appropriate accountability towards holders of equity capital. Arguably, these managers should demonstrate the same accountability towards their employees and other longer-term stakeholders, who – just like capital owners dedicate equity capital – have dedicated themselves to the firm for prolonged periods of time. Just as senior managers must avoid capital destruction, they must also avoid the destruction of the lives of the very individuals who have put forward their best efforts to serve the firm's goals and, more broadly, the lives of all significantly affected by the firm's activities. The most effective way to protect employees and other longer-term stakeholders is usually to ensure their mobility and agility – by fostering their ability to shift easily to other jobs or to other activities in the economy. In practice, this implies continuous investment in training, retooling, and new skills development of employees, and the selective upgrading of external partners.

Contingent on a rational cost-benefit calculus, which should include the issue of maintaining a social licence to operate sustainably, it is likely that an increasing number of MNE senior managers will attempt to prove to society at large, especially in host environments, that resource recombination can indeed be a benevolent process. MNE managers from around the world must now rise to this challenge. ***Benevolent resource recombination*** legitimates the claim that the MNE is both a superior governance mechanism to achieve efficiency and an institution whose leadership can confidently be relied on as having the heart and compassion needed to improve the human condition. Benevolent resource recombination, informed by sound entrepreneurial judgement and deep knowledge of markets, is the key to both global corporate success and the further peaceful economic integration of nations.

The Move towards Private Equity

The previous point, which addressed the need for modern stakeholder management, must be somewhat qualified. MNE Boards of Directors and top management teams in market-based democracies are under tremendous pressure to focus on environmental, social, governance, and data stewardship or ESGD performance parameters. As noted above, MNEs can be a force for good in the world, in terms of improving both global economic efficiency and the human condition. External stakeholder pressures can undoubtedly be helpful in this regard, as many past cases convincingly demonstrate (e.g., Nike, Starbucks, IKEA, etc.). A problem arises, however, when stakeholder pressures become unreasonable and start negatively influencing the position of firms listed on public equity markets based on false or at least insufficiently contextualized information. An extreme solution is for owners and investors to take their firms private, so as to escape from the tyranny of ill-informed and ideology-driven stakeholders with whom fair debate on feasible ESGD performance improvements is impossible. Equity investors in publicly listed firms, and even financial institutions providing loan capital, can become subject to 'noise' that is not grounded in fact, but rather based on ideological precepts. Social media can further amplify attacks on high profile activities and investment projects, for their alleged weak ESGD performance, especially if these are initiatives emanating from foreign-owned MNEs.

Private equity can be a powerful antidote against the tyranny of unreasonable demands for ever-stronger ESGD performance that can threaten the MNE's growth and survival. Private equity firms similar to The Blackstone Group, The Carlyle Group, Kohlberg Kravis Roberts & Co. (KKR), and CVC Capital Partners may become increasingly important pillars for financing MNE activities in the global economy in the future, but not only because they allow economic activities to escape from a short-term focus on quarterly profits. These firms have often displayed superior capabilities in surgical cost cutting and reorganization so as to facilitate global competitiveness. Importantly, private equity can support unlocking value that is imprisoned in firms forced to focus more on externally imposed ESGD performance parameters than on economic value creation and capture through efficiency, market-driven resource recombination, and conventional good governance aimed at actually reducing bounded rationality and bounded reliability problems. A private-equity-driven governance approach may – perhaps paradoxically – also be stakeholder-centric, but with responses to stakeholder demands grounded in reason and facts, so as to generate a better business with an improved social licence to operate. Recent research has already demonstrated the positive spillovers of private equity investments in the global economy, in terms of increased productivity, employment, and capital investment in the affected industries.[16] Our prediction for the next decades is that the global economy will see vast increases in international activities being taken private as an effective governance tool to counter unreasonable stakeholder demands.

The Dark Side of Digital Globalization

The information and digital age (4th Industrial Revolution – IR4) refers to a number of disruptive technologies that are presently changing the dynamics of industries and markets. It means that digital resources are massively injected in the global economy. Digitalization refers to the conversion of 'things' (such as information, sounds, and shapes) into digital data. Such data can be stored, altered, and deployed an unlimited number of times, and at a low marginal cost. Digitalization revolves not only around digital data, but also digital technologies, as well as digital infrastructure, and dedicated business models (these elements can all be considered digital resources), and finally products and services. Each company has an evolving digital intensity: this refers to the relative weight of digital resources as compared to non-digital ones in the firm's overall resources reservoir. Companies in many industries are presently boosting their digital intensity (e.g., agri-business, automobiles, professional services).

Here, we can distinguish between 'going digitals' and 'born digitals'.[17] The former are existing brick-and-mortar businesses that are infusing digital technologies into their main activities. In contrast, born digitals try to create competitive advantage primarily on the basis of digital FSAs. They include internet search engines (e.g., ask.com, Baidu, Bing, DuckDuckGo, Google, Yahoo), internet social networks (e.g., Facebook, Instagram, LinkedIn, NextDoor, Twitter, WhatsApp, WeChat, YouTube), and internet-based sharing platforms (e.g., Airbnb, Dropbox, Google Drive, Khan Academy, Uber). Both going digitals and born digitals must identify, access, and utilize requisite complementary resources during their internationalization processes. The impacts of having to take on board complementary resources can be significant for internationally operating companies, as well as for their value chain or ecosystem partners.

The dark side of 'digital globalization' then refers to the costs and the negative consequences (both intended or unintended) of attempts to expand and do business internationally on the strength of digital resources.[18] The study of the dark side is important for three reasons. *First*, most normative messages coming from contemporary research in management and international business strategy, as well as from management consulting, herald the need for – and the benefits of – increased digital globalization. The extant scholarly and consulting literatures largely highlight the bright side of this phenomenon.[19] But the potential costs and negative consequences for firms that build on digital resources to internationalize and to do business in foreign markets deserve attention equal to that given to the supposed benefits. Careful analysis should be undertaken of the benefits and costs – and therefore of the boundaries – of digital globalization. *Second*, new economy firms can supposedly easily gain market share in their industry and reap high profits when expanding internationally, by deploying their home-proven digitally based FSAs. But many of these new economy firms actually struggle when trying to expand internationally. One reason is that digitally based FSAs need to be combined with more conventional resources, both vertically and laterally, when expanding abroad. Another reason is that digital firms are subject to new forms of government regulation. *Third*, conventional brick-and-mortar firms are often advised to increase their 'digital intensity', through developing or acquiring digital resources to compete effectively in the new economy (e.g., in the retail business). But here again, effective bundling of conventional resources with digital ones, and subsequent (or parallel) deployment of these resources across borders, is fraught with challenges.

Importantly, in addition to facing new resource combination challenges, MNEs may also need to revisit location choices. Even if international value chains could be managed more easily thanks to digitalization (which is debatable, as noted above), this does not necessarily create a level playing field among locations, as is sometimes assumed. Can small open economies actually thrive as loci for investment and employment by digital economy firms beyond having 'spoke status' in fragmented digital policy space? How will their location advantages change as a result of regional and multilateral agreements on regulating digital economy activities, and as compared with simply undergoing digital policy fragmentation or 'silent integration'? Issues of intellectual property protection and national security also abound when foreign MNEs deploy sensitive digital resources in a host country or access local digital resources (cf. the case of the Chinese firm Huawei being banned from fully participating in 5G networks in various countries). Finally, the pursuit of economic versus political strategies in the domestic and foreign milieus may also change because of the digital economy. The latter strategies will likely become more important in the future, given the infancy stage of government regulations, to address spillovers in the new digital space (e.g., crafting new liabilities of foreignness for potential entrants from hostile nations).

In addition, there can be *expected* negative spillovers of digitalization, resulting from MNEs gaining privileged access to big data on a worldwide basis through their dispersed customer base (e.g., sale of tractors collecting information on crop quality and quantity in agriculture). Finally, unexpected spillovers must also be addressed. With the progression of global digitalization, not all conventional value chain partners are likely to remain meaningful participants in global value chains. As one example, digitally enabled value chains can support MNE CSR strategies, but at the same time exclude second-tier and lower-tier suppliers from participating in 'digitalized value chains', *inter alia*, because they do not command advanced technologies.[20] In this particular case, the paradoxical outcome is the opposite of what is intended by base-of-the-pyramid guidelines, prescribing to MNEs to 'clean up their act', and to abide by the highest possible CSR standards, as may prevail in industry or in their home countries.

To conclude, a balanced managerial focus on the bright and dark sides of digital globalization is desirable. Some firms are simply better positioned than other ones, in terms of their extant capability reservoirs, both to exploit existing digital resources and to bundle non-digital resources and capabilities with newly acquired digital ones. In addition, resource recombination processes in foreign markets must take into account the complexities and uncertainties brought about by a variety of rapidly evolving government regulations and exigencies of non-market forces.

Notes

Introduction

1. In our own advisory and research work, we have interviewed many hundreds of MNE senior managers, and it has become abundantly clear to us that most academic research on international business strategy, by contrast, simply does not appeal to these practitioners.

2. Analysis of what is published in the *Journal of International Business Studies*, the leading academic outlet for research on international business, confirms this point. There are many schools of thought on the governance and functioning of MNEs. A superb synthesis of one core theory closely aligned with our framework, namely, internalization theory, can be found in Rajneesh Narula, Christian Asmussen, Tailan Chi, and Sumit Kundu, 'Applying and advancing internalization theory: the multinational enterprise in the 21st century', *Journal of International Business Studies* 50 (2019), 1231–52.

3. This reflects a view of the firm inspired by Edith Penrose's magnum opus, *The Theory of the Growth of the Firm*, 1st edn (Oxford: Basil Blackwell, 1959). For a discussion on the importance of Edith Penrose's work and the relevance of her work for multinational growth, see: Christos Pitelis (ed.), *The Growth of the Firm: The Legacy of Edith Penrose* (Oxford University Press, 2002); Alan M. Rugman and Alain Verbeke, 'Edith Penrose's contribution to the resource-based view of strategic management', *Strategic Management Journal* 23 (2002), 769–80; and Alan M. Rugman and Alain Verbeke, 'A final word on Edith Penrose', *Journal of Management Studies* 41 (2004), 205–17.

4. 'Federal Express spreads its wings: an interview with CEO Frederick W. Smith', *Journal of Business Strategy* 9 (1988), 15–20.

5. Justin Baer and Francesco Guerrera, 'The man who reinvented the wheel', *Financial Times* (3 December 2007).

6. Douglas A. Blackmon and Diane Brady, 'Orient Express: just how hard should a U.S. company woo a big foreign market? – In China, FedEx and UPS compete in contrasts; a risk-vs.-reward issue – planes at the Forbidden City', *Wall Street Journal (Eastern Edition)* (6 April 1998), A.1.

7. A. Hartman, J. Sifonis, and J. Kador, *Net Ready: Cisco's Rules for Success in the E-economy* (Toronto, ON: McGraw-Hill Ryerson, 1999).

Chapter 1

1. WTO, 'World Trade Statistical Review 2018'.
2. *Ibid.*; WTO, 'International Trade Statistics 2004'.

3. R. Dobbs, T. Koller, and S. Ramaswamy, 'The future and how to survive it', *Harvard Business Review* 93 (2015), 48–62.

4. A. M. Rugman and A. Verbeke, 'A perspective on regional and global strategies of multinational enterprises', *Journal of International Business Studies* 35 (2004), 3–18.

5. http://fortune.com/global500/.

6. A truly correct comparison would entail comparing the value added produced by an MNE (rather than its revenues) with country-level GDP.

7. http://fortune.com/global500/ and https://data.oecd.org/gdp/gross-domestic-product-gdp.htm.

8. *Ibid.*

9. B. Rosa and P. Gugler, 'Regional and global strategies of MNEs: (re)testing the Rugman and Verbeke study in a new decade', *Mimeo* (2018).

10. http://fortune.com/global500/.

11. Dobbs *et al.*, 'The future and how to survive it'.

12. Stephen Hymer wrote about the additional costs of doing business abroad in his doctoral dissertation, *The International Operations of National Firms: A Study of Direct Foreign Investment* (Cambridge, MA: MIT Press, 1976). This concept has since received considerable attention by international business scholars; see the outstanding synthesis by Lorraine Eden and Stewart R. Miller, 'Distance matters: liability of foreignness, institutional distance and ownership strategy', in M. A. Hitt and J. L. C. Cheng (eds.), *The Evolving Theory of the Multinational Firm: Advances in International Management* (Amsterdam: Elsevier, 2004), vol. 16. Obviously, MNEs can reduce the liability of foreignness by forging alliances, such as joint ventures, with local partners in host countries.

13. I view this observation of international FSA transfer, leading to economies of scope if the FSAs are transferred as intermediate goods, as the fundamental insight of modern international business theory.

14. An enormous literature exists on international entry mode choice, including the classic work of Peter J. Buckley and Mark Casson, *The Future of the Multinational Enterprise* (London: Macmillan, 1976); John Dunning, *International Production and the Multinational Enterprise* (London: Allen & Unwin, 1981); Jean-François Hennart, *A Theory of Multinational Enterprise* (Ann Arbor, MI: University of Michigan Press, 1982); and Alan M. Rugman, *Inside the Multinationals: The Economics of Internal Markets* (New York: Columbia University Press, 1981). Each of these five authors has continued to develop an impressive oeuvre on entry mode choice and international business strategy after the publication of the above studies. Academic outlets such as the *Academy of Management Journal*, the *Journal of International Business Studies*, *Management International Review*, and the *Strategic Management Journal* have published numerous articles on entry mode choice challenges.

15. Chris Bartlett and Sumantra Ghoshal, in their book *Managing across Borders: The Transnational Solution* (Boston, MA: Harvard Business School Press, 1989), made a distinction among three rather than four archetypes, probably for convenience of presentation and to keep their framework easily understood. They did recognize the international exporter (which they called the global firm), the international projector (which they called the international firm), and the multi-centred MNE (which they called the multinational firm). Unfortunately, they did not include the international coordinator in their framework, though many vertically integrated MNEs, especially in the resource-based sectors, conform exactly to that archetype. In addition, their terminology is confusing because the terms 'global', 'international', and 'multinational' had often been

used, before the publication of their book, by multiple other authors, but with very different meanings. In addition, the prescriptive model they propose, the so-called 'transnational solution', adds further to the confusion, because the term 'transnational' corporation is a generic term, used by the UN Centre on Transnational Corporations (UNCTC, set up in 1974 and presently an arm of the UN Conference on Trade and Development – UNCTAD) to describe all firms with operations outside their home country and engaging in FDI.

16. See, for example, Marc Levinson, *The Box: How the Shipping Container Made the World Smaller and the World Economy Bigger* (Princeton University Press, 2006).

17. NEC, Corporate Directory: www.nec.com/en/global/ir/library/annual/1996/corpo/corpo.html.

18. NEC, NEC Research Activities: www.nec.com/en/global/rd/labs/pdf/NEC_Research_Activities.pdf.

19. *Ibid.*, 11.

20. www.the-numbers.com/movie/Joker-(2019)#tab=summary.

21. Mira Wilkins and Frank Ernest Hill, *American Business Abroad: Ford on Six Continents* (Detroit, MI: Wayne State University Press, 1964), 18.

22. *Ibid.*, 50.

23. *Ibid.*, 100.

24. Geoffrey A. Fowler and Merissa Marr, 'Disney's China play; its new Hong Kong park is a big cultural experiment; will "Main Street" translate?' *Wall Street Journal* (16 June 2005), B.1.

25. *Ibid.*

26. *Ibid.*

27. Paul Wiseman, 'Miscues mar opening of Hong Kong Disney', *USA Today online* (10 November 2005).

28. Keith Bradsher, 'A trial run finds Hong Kong Disneyland much too popular for its modest size', *New York Times (Late Edition (East Coast))* (8 September 2005), C.1; Keith Bradsher, 'At Hong Kong Disneyland, the Year of the Dog starts with a growl', *New York Times (Late Edition (East Coast))* (4 February 2006), A.5; Henry Fountain, 'The ultimate body language: how you line up for Mickey', *New York Times (Late Edition (East Coast))* (18 September 2005), 4.4; Justine Lau, 'HK Disneyland gives Mickey Mouse lessons', *Financial Times* (London First Edition) (4 September 2006), 27.

29. BP company information, 2006: www.bp.com/en/global/corporate/who-we-are/our-history.html; Reuters Staff, 'BP to sign $20 billion LNG supply deal with China's CNOOC', *Reuters* (17 June 2014).

30. Logitech company information: www.logitech.com/lang/pdf/logitech_history_200703.pdf.

31. *Ibid.*

32. Frederik Philips, *45 Years with Philips* (Poole, UK: Blandford Press, 1978), 187.

33. *Ibid.*

34. Lafarge company information, 2005: www.lafargeholcim.com.

35. *Ibid.*

36. *Ibid.*

37. *Ibid.*

38. Mira Wilkins and H. G. Schröter, *The Free-standing Company in the World Economy, 1830–1996* (Oxford University Press, 1998). During the nineteenth century, freestanding companies represented a sizeable proportion of European firms. Thousands of British firms, and hundreds from the Netherlands and other European countries, were set up to operate

directly abroad. They were predominantly in the natural resource and service industries. Typically, their head office was very small, with a board of directors, a corporate secretary, and little else. The directors were given the mandate by the shareholders to select managers to head overseas investments and to monitor overseas operations. Basically, they were 'the men who stand to be shot at in the event anything goes wrong' (E. T. Powell, *The Mechanism of the City* (1910), 144–5, cited in Mira Wilkins, 'The free-standing company, 1870–1914: an important type of British foreign direct investment', *Economic History Review* 41 (1988), 264). Harrisons & Crosfield (H&C) was a typical freestanding company. Established in 1844 in Liverpool, H&C bought tea in China and India and sold it in Britain. H&C quickly expanded by opening branches in both tea-producing and tea-consuming countries, including, respectively, Sri Lanka and Malaya, and the United States, Canada, and Australia. Moreover, H&C diversified into the plantation business. In 1903, H&C invested in its first rubber plantation in British Malaya. Later investments in Malaya, Java, and the Dutch East Indies made it one of the largest plantation companies in Southeast Asia. The overseas branches of H&C, as agents for shipping and insurance, managed business on the spot and collected and transmitted information back to the London head office. The London head office was responsible for recruiting expatriates as well as providing plantation management services. For further reading on freestanding companies, see Mira Wilkins, 'The free-standing company, 1870–1914: an important type of British foreign direct investment', *Economic History Review* 41 (1988), 259–82; M. Wilkins and H. G. Schröter, *The Free-standing Company in the World Economy, 1830–1996* (Oxford University Press, 1998); Geoffrey Jones, *Multinationals and Global Capitalism: From the Nineteenth to the Twenty First Century* (New York: Oxford University Press, 2005); G. Jones and J. Wale, 'Diversification strategies of British trading companies: Harrisons & Crosfield, c. 1900–c. 1980', *Business History* 41 (1999), 69–101.

39. See, for example, Alvaro Cuervo-Cazurra and Mehmet Genc, 'Transforming disadvantages into advantages: developing-country MNEs in the least developed countries', *Journal of International Business Studies* 39 (2008), 957–979; Mauro Guillen and Esteban Garcia-Canal, 'The American model of the multinational firm and the "new" multinationals from emerging economies', *Academy of Management Perspectives* 23 (2009), 23–35; Ravi Ramamurti, 'What have we learned about EMNEs?', in Ravi Ramamurti and Jintendra Singh (eds.), *Emerging Multinationals from Emerging Markets* (Cambridge University Press, 2009).

40. I expanded on this point in the context of increased regionalization, whereby institutional arrangements such as the European Union and NAFTA (and its successor USMCA) have allowed firms to increase the geographic deployment potential of their location-bound FSAs. However, outside their home region, most large MNEs do appear to suffer from a rapid decay of the transferability, deployment, and exploitation of their FSAs, as reflected in their modest sales volumes, relative to total sales, in host regions; see Alan M. Rugman and Alain Verbeke, 'Regional and global strategies of multinational enterprises', *Journal of International Business Studies* 35 (2004), 3–18.

41. 'Japanese consumer goods: should we kow-tow to Kao?', *The Economist* 338 (1996), 60–1; Kao, company information: www.kao.com/global/en/about/outline/history.

42. Kao, Financial Report, 2019.

43. 'A tale of tellers in distant places', *The Economist* 316 (1990), 77.

44. *Ibid.*, 78.

45. Quentin Hardy, 'Banking: Citicorp seeks niche among rich in Japan', *Wall Street Journal (Eastern Edition)* (1 November 1993), B1.

46. William V. Rapp, 'International retail banking: the Citibank Group', Center on Japanese Economy and Business Working Paper Series, Columbia University (2000).
47. Toru Hanai, 'Citi agrees to sell Japan retail banking to SMBC', *Reuters* (31 November 2014); Data from *Zephyr*.
48. Eric Tegler, 'Designs a Europe', *Business Life* (October 2002), 37–40.
49. Yao-Su Hu, 'The international transferability of the firm's advantages', *California Management Review* 37 (1995), 73–88.
50. Yumiko Ono, 'U.S. superstores find Japanese are a hard sell', *The Wall Street Journal (Eastern Edition)* (14 February 2000), B.1.
51. Office Depot, company information, 2011: http://getfilings.com/o0000950144-99-002975.html.
52. Dhanya Skariachan, 'Office Depot selling Japan unit', *Reuters* (16 December 2010); Data from *Zephyr*.
53. Most international business opportunities and challenges for MNEs are thus positioned in a context situated between true globalization, which would allow the unfettered exploitation across borders of internationally transferable FSAs, and extreme localization, whereby only location-bound FSAs without international deployment potential would be relevant. This phenomenon can be called 'semi-globalization'; see Alan M. Rugman and Alain Verbeke, 'Extending the theory of the multinational enterprise: internalization and strategic management perspectives', *Journal of International Business Studies* 34 (2003), 125–37.
54. Pete Engardio and Peter Burrows, 'Acer: a global powerhouse', *Business Week* (1996), 95.
55. Martyn Williams, 'Acer to privatize Latin America PC Unit', *Computerworld* (13 January 2000).
56. Location advantages, and the differences in such advantages among nations, remain the foundation of modern international economics, with MNEs mostly treated as a black box; see James R. Markusen, 'International trade theory and international business', in Alan M. Rugman and Thomas L. Brewer (eds.), *The Oxford Handbook of International Business* (Oxford University Press, 2001), 69–87.
57. TMX Guide to Listing, 2020.
58. INVESTOPEDIA, '2019's 5 largest Canadian mining companies', *INVESTOPEDIA* (16 January 2020).
59. Hans Decker, 'Master craftsman, no college required', *The Wall Street Journal (Eastern Edition)* (18 March 1991), A14.
60. Michael Berger, 'Japanese firms testing more high-tech gadgets', *The Ottawa Citizen* (8 May 1989), D.2.
61. Karl Lohmann, 'The scents of the cities', *American City & Country* 114 (1999), 54.
62. E. S. Browning, 'At Guerlain, marketing makes scents – Paris perfumer's products no longer led by nose', *The Wall Street Journal (Eastern Edition)* (19 February 1991), B.7; Robert Graham, 'Town thrives most fragrantly: PERFUME by Robert Graham: despite competition from artificial fragrances, Grasse, with its remarkable ability to adapt, still has to be watched closely by other producers', *Financial Times* (21 October 1998), 3.
63. UNCTAD, *World Investment Report 2019* (New York and Geneva: UN Conference on Trade and Development, 2019).
64. Dan Primack, 'Biotech hotbeds: where are they, and how do you get one?', *Venture Capital Journal* (1 October 2004), 1.
65. https://sciencecenter.org/news/top-10-u-s-biopharma-clusters-2.

66. Primack, 'Biotech hotbeds', 1.

67. Vanessa Fuhrmans and Rachel Zimmerman, 'Leading the news: Novartis to move global lab to U.S. – Swiss drug maker follows other European companies shifting strategy abroad', *The Wall Street Journal* (7 May 2002), A.3.

68. *Ibid.*

69. *Ibid.*

70. Gary Sawchuk and Aaron Sydor, 'Mexico and Canada: changing specializations in trade with the United States', in Richard G. Harris (ed.), *North American Linkages: Opportunities and Challenges for Canada* (University of Calgary Press, 2003), 169.

71. The four motivations included here have been well documented in the international business literature: see John Dunning, *Multinational Enterprises and the Global Economy* (Reading, MA: Addison-Wesley, 1992).

72. 'ExxonMobil announces first production from Usan field offshore Nigeria', *ExxonMobil* (24 February 2012).

73. Deon Daugherty, 'ExxonMobil finds potential 1 billion barrel oil field offshore Nigeria', *Rigzone* (27 October 2016).

74. Matthew DiLallo, 'This red-hot oil stock delivered surprisingly good numbers in Q1', *The Motley Fool* (25 April 2019).

75. Philip F. Zeidman, 'The biggest market in the world', *Franchising World* 26 (1994), 60.

76. Richard Martin, 'China's size, economic boom lure US chains despite uncertainties', *Nation's Restaurant News* 29 (1995), 50.

77. Zeidman, 'The biggest market', 60.

78. Harichandan Arakali, Henry Foy, and Malini Menon, 'Amazon launches online shopping service in India', *Reuters* (2 February 2012).

79. Binu Paul, 'Amazon brings the curtains down on Junglee.com, finally', *Vccircle* (9 November 2017).

80. Katie Arcieri, 'Flipkart is No. 1 in India but faces formidable foe in Amazon, say experts', *S&P Global* (10 October 2019).

81. Vindu Goel, 'Amazon's plan to reach 500 million Indians: speak their language', *New York Times* (4 September 2018).

82. Euan Rocha and Nivedita Bhattacharjee, 'Amazon to acquire minority stake in an Indian supermarket chain operator', *Reuters* (22 August 2019).

83. 'Wal-Mart inks deal to enter India', *Forbes* (7 August 2007).

84. Simon Mundy and Peter Wells, 'Walmart confirms $16bn stake in India's Flipkart', *Financial Times* (9 May 2018).

85. 'Top 6 PC vendors in the world', *Chinadaily* (24 January 2019).

86. Justine Lau, 'Lenovo profits from IBM unit purchase', *Financial Times* (10 August 2005).

87. In principle, an MNE could restructure its existing network of affiliates and engage in rationalization investments without the prior occurrence of substantial environmental change, but in practice such environmental change is usually the key driver of restructuring.

88. Logitech Annual Report 2020.

89. L. Pun-Lee, 'Energy in China: development and prospects', *China Perspectives* 59 (2005), 14–25.

90. L. Hongyi, S. O'Hara, and K. Wysoczanska, 'Rationale of internationalization of China's national oil companies: seeking natural resources, strategic assets or sectoral specialization?', *Asia Pacific Business Review* 21 (2015), 77–95.

91. Keith Bradsher, 'Chinese company to buy Kazakh oil interests for $4 billion', *New York Times* (22 August 2005).

92. Hongyi *et al.*, 'Rationale of internationalization'.

93. 'Business: growing pains; Carrefour, Tesco and Wal-Mart', *The Economist* 375 (16 April 2005), 60.

94. Lisa Qixun Siebers, 'Carrefour's history and exit from China', *The World Financial Review* (5 August 2019).

95. Miriam Jordan, 'For many generic antibiotics, the supply line starts in New Delhi – little-known Ranbaxy makes a splash in look-alike drugs, seeks its own breakthroughs', *The Wall Street Journal* (28 December 1999), B.1.

96. *Ibid.*

97. Asian Business Review, 'Jollibee: the company that beat McDonald's', *Asian Business Review* (September 1997), 26–8.

98. Jessica Fenol and Joel Guinto, 'Jollibee chases McDonald's, KFC world crown with acquisition binge', *ABS-CBN News* (8 January 2019).

99. Gertrude Chavez, 'The buzz: Jollibee hungers to export Filipino tastes, dominate Asian fastfood', *Advertising Age International* (9 March 1998), 14.

100. *Ibid.*

101. Jon Viktor D. Cabuenas, 'Jollibee to open 500 new stores in 2019', *GMA News Online* (15 May 2019).

102. Pete Engardio, Manjeet Kripalani, and Alysha Webb, 'Smart globalization; being first and biggest in an emerging market isn't always the best way to conquer it. A better tactic: learn local cultures – and build a presence carefully', *Business Week* (27 August 2001), 132.

103. *Ibid.*

104. J. Matusitz, 'Disney's successful adaptation in Hong Kong: a glocalization perspective', *Asia Pacific Journal of Management* 28 (2011), 667–81.

105. Jason Cochran, 'Look at how different Shanghai Disneyland is from other Disney parks', *Frommers* (8 February 2018). Retrieved from www.frommers.com/slideshows/848246-look-at-how-different-shanghai-disneyland-is-from-other-disney-parks.

106. Brooks Barnes, 'In bow to "cross-cultural cooperation," Disney Shanghai opens gates', *New York Times* (17 June 2016), B.1. Retrieved from www.nytimes.com/2016/06/17/business/international/disney-shanghai-opens.html.

107. Allen J. Morrison and Kendall Roth, 'Developing global subsidiary mandates', *Business Quarterly* 57 (1993), 108.

108. *Ibid.*

109. Paul Ingrassia, 'Global reach: industry is shopping abroad for good ideas to apply to products – foreign research units use latest local technology; the case of Liquid Tide – on the fringes of the swamp', *Wall Street Journal* (29 April 1985), 1.

110. *Ibid.*

111. *Ibid.*

112. Julian Birkinshaw, 'Entrepreneurship in multinational corporations: the initiative process in foreign subsidiaries', unpublished PhD thesis, University of Western Ontario (1995).

113. Christopher Williams and Liaw Emily, '3M Taiwan: product innovation in the subsidiary', *Ivey Publishing* (3 November 2011).

114. Birkinshaw, 'Entrepreneurship in multinational corporations', 300.

115. *Ibid.*

116. Darren McDermott, 'Citibank uses Latin American lessons in Asia', *Wall Street Journal (Eastern Edition)* (29 December 1997), 1.

117. Oliver Gassmann and Maximillian von Zedtwitz, 'Trends and determinants of managing virtual R&D teams', *R&D Management* 33 (2003), 248.

118. Thomas W. Malnight, 'The transition from decentralized to network-based MNC structures: an evolutionary perspective', *Journal of International Business Studies* 27 (1996), 55.

119. Malnight, 'The transition to network-based MNC structures', 55.

120. Christopher A. Bartlett, Sumantra Ghoshal, and Julian Birkinshaw, *Transnational Management: Text and Cases*, 4th edn (Boston, MA: Irwin/McGraw-Hill, 2004), 478.

121. *Ibid.*

122. Robin Yale Bergstrom, 'Global issues demand taking teams global', *Automotive Production* 108 (1996), 61.

123. Bergstrom, 'Taking teams global', 61.

124. Benjamin Gomes-Casseres, 'Joint ventures in the face of global competition', *Sloan Management Review* 30 (1989), 17–26.

125. SEC report, 2006: https://sec.report/Document/0000950134-06-018709/h40158exv99w1.htm.

126. 'EnCana partnership worth $15 billion', *Times Colonist* (6 October 2006), A.17; Ian Austen, 'Conoco and EnCana plan oil sands venture', *New York Times* (6 October 2006), C.10; Diana Lawrence, Sheila McNulty, and James Politi, 'Energy groups to link in Canadian oil sands', *Financial Times* (6 October 2006), 30.

127. The bounded rationality concept was popularized by Herbert Simon, *Models of Bounded Rationality and Other Topics in Economics*, vol. 2: *Collected Papers* (Cambridge, MA: MIT Press, 1982), and *Models of Bounded Rationality*, vol. 3: *Empirically Grounded Economic Reason* (Cambridge, MA: MIT Press, 1997). Alain Verbeke and Wenlong Yuan provide an extension of the bounded rationality concept, with an application to the MNE context, 'Subsidiary autonomous activities in multinational enterprises: a transaction cost perspective', *Management International Review*, SI 2 (2005), 31–52.

128. David Leonhardt, 'It was a hit in Buenos Aires – so why not Boise? U.S. companies are picking up winning product tips from consumers in faraway places', *Business Week* (7 September 1998), 56.

129. Shelly Branch, 'Dulce de Leche takes a spot in vocabulary and pantries of U.S.', *Wall Street Journal* (12 October 2001), B.8.

130. Leonhardt, 'Picking up winning product tips', 56.

131. Ginny Parker, 'Wal-Mart gets high-cost lesson on low-price strategy in Japan', *Wall Street Journal* (2 February 2005), 1.

132. SkyTeam, Company information, 2020. Archived from www.skyteam.com/en/about/press-releases/press-releases-2020/oneworld-skyteam-and-staralliance-come-together-to-let-travelers-know-they-can-fly-with-confidence. Retrieved 11 October 2020.

133. Alain Verbeke and Sarah Vanden Bussche, 'Regional and global strategies in the intercontinental passenger airline industry: the rise of alliance-specific advantages', *Internalization, International Diversification and the Multinational Enterprise: Essays in Honor of Alan M. Rugman* (Amsterdam: Elsevier, 2005), vol. 11, 119–48.

134. Bartlett *et al.*, *Transnational Management*, 574.

135. Benjamin Gomes-Casseres, 'Competing in constellations: the case of Fuji Xerox', *Strategy and Business* (1997), 4–16.

136. See Oliver E. Williamson, *The Mechanisms of Governance* (Oxford University Press, 1996).

137. Liena Kano and Alain Verbeke, 'The three faces of bounded reliability: Alfred Chandler and the micro-foundations of management theory', *California Management Review* 58(1) (2015), 97–122.

138. Alain Verbeke and Nathan Greidanus, 'The end of the opportunism vs trust debate: bounded reliability as a new envelope concept in research on MNE governance', *Journal of International Business Studies* 40 (2009), 1471–95.

139. Alain Verbeke and M. Zaman Forootan, 'How good are Multinationality-Performance (M-P) empirical studies?', *Global Strategy Journal* 2(4) (2012), 332–44.

140. Dobbs *et al.*, 'The future and how to survive it'.

141. *Ibid.*, 50.

142. *Ibid.*

143. GE, *2018 Annual Report* (Boston, MA: General Electric Company, 2018).

144. Dobbs *et al.*, 'The future and how to survive it'.

145. *Ibid.*, 60.

146. J. B. Davis, 'Uncertain imitability', in M. Augier and D. J. Teece (eds.), *The Palgrave Encyclopedia of Strategic Management* (London: Palgrave Macmillan, 2018).

147. Dobbs *et al.*, 'The future and how to survive it', 60.

148. *Ibid.*, 60–1.

149. *Ibid.*, 61.

150. *Ibid.*

151. Tim Bradshaw, 'Apple retail boss Angela Ahrendts to leave after 5 years', *Financial Times* (5 February 2019). Retrieved at www.ft.com/content/555a0a7e-2990-11e9-a5ab-ff8ef2b976c7.

152. A. M. Rugman, *Inside the Multinationals: The Economics of Internal Markets* (New York: Columbia University Press, 1981); A. M. Rugman, *Inside the Multinationals 25th Anniversary Edition: The Economics of Internal Markets* (London: Palgrave Macmillan, 2006).

153. J. Hillemann and M. Gestrin, 'The limits of firm-level globalization: revisiting the FSA/CSA matrix', *International Business Review* 25 (2016), 767–75.

154. S. H. Prince, 'Catastrophe and social change: based upon a sociological study of the Halifax disaster', PhD dissertation, Columbia University (1920), 4.

155. A. Verbeke, R. Coeurderoy, and T. Matt, 'The future of international business research on corporate globalization that never was . . .', *Journal of International Business Studies* 49 (2018), 1101–12.

Chapter 2

1. C. K. Prahalad and G. Hamel, 'The core competence of the corporation', *Harvard Business Review* 68 (1990), 79–91.

2. *Ibid.*, 81.

3. *Ibid.*, 89.

4. *Ibid.*

5. P. Aversa, S. Haefliger, and D. G. Reza, 'Building a winning business model portfolio', *MIT Sloan Management Review* 58 (2017), 49–54.

6. *Ibid.*, 49.

7. *Ibid.*, 50.
8. *Ibid.*
9. M. C. Becker and F. Zirpoli, 'How to avoid innovation competence loss in R&D outsourcing', *California Management Review* 59 (2017), 24–44.
10. *Ibid.*, 25.
11. *Ibid.*
12. *Ibid.*, 29.
13. *Ibid.*, 30.
14. *Ibid.*, Figure 1, 31.
15. *Ibid.*, Figure 2, 32.
16. *Ibid.*, 31.
17. *Ibid.*
18. *Ibid.*, 39.
19. *Ibid.*, 25.
20. *Ibid.*
21. *Ibid.*, Figure 2, 32.
22. R. Casadesus-Masanell and J. Tarziján, 'When one business model isn't enough', *Harvard Business Review* 90 (2012), 132–7.
23. *Ibid.*, 133.
24. *Ibid.*
25. *Ibid.*, 134–5.
26. *Ibid.*, 133.
27. *Ibid.*
28. A. Verbeke, 'Will the COVID-19 pandemic really change the governance of global value chains?', *British Journal of Management* 31 (2020), 444–6.
29. 'Inside Samsung's fight to keep its global supply chain running', *Financial Times* (7 May 2020).
30. *Ibid.*
31. *Ibid.*
32. Verbeke, 'Will the COVID-19 pandemic really change the governance of global value chains?'.
33. 'Wizz Air chief hits out at UK quarantine plan for air passengers', *Financial Times* (3 June 2020).
34. J. Knowles, R. Ettenson, P. Lynch, and J. Dollens, 'Growth opportunities for brands during the Covid-19 crisis', *Sloan Management Review* 61 (2020), 1–5.
35. 'Why the unemployed in America could face a lost decade', *The Economist* (2 May 2020).
36. 'Silicon Valley was first to send workers home. It's been messy', *The Wall Street Journal* (16 March 2020).

Chapter 3

1. Michael E. Porter, *The Competitive Advantage of Nations* (New York: Free Press, Macmillan, 1990); Michael E. Porter, 'The competitive advantage of nations', *Harvard Business Review* 68 (1990), 73–93.
2. Porter, 'The competitive advantage of nations', 73.
3. *Ibid.*, 81.

4. W. C. Shih and S. Chai, 'What to know about locating in a cluster', *MIT Sloan Management Review* 57 (2015), 8–11.
5. *Ibid.*, 10.
6. *Ibid.*, 9.
7. *Ibid.*, 10.
8. *Ibid.*, 11.
9. David J. Teece, 'Foreign investment in Silicon Valley', *California Management Review* 34 (1992), 88–106.
10. *Ibid.*, 100.
11. *Ibid.*
12. Porter, 'The competitive advantage of nations', 92.
13. *Ibid.*, 93.
14. Porter, *The Competitive Advantage of Nations*.
15. R. Vernon, 'International investment and international trade in the product life cycle', *Quarterly Journal of Economics* 80 (1966), 190–207.
16. Leonard Waverman, 'Critical analysis of Porter's framework on the competitive advantage of nations', in A. Rugman, J. Van Den Broeck, and A. Verbeke (eds.), *Research in Global Strategic Management: Beyond the Diamond* (Greenwich: JAI Press, 1995), vol. 5, 67–95.
17. Alan M. Rugman and Alain Verbeke, *Analysis of Multinational Strategic Management* (Cheltenham: Edward Elgar, 2005), 206–22.
18. W. Kerr, 'Navigating talent hot spots', *Harvard Business Review* 96 (2018), 80–6.
19. *Ibid.*, 82.
20. *Ibid.*, 83.
21. *Ibid.*, 85.
22. A. Pande, 'How to make onshoring work', *Harvard Business Review* 89 (2011), 30.
23. *Ibid.*, 30.
24. *Ibid.*
25. *Ibid.*
26. W. Bedyński, 'Liminality: Black Death 700 years later. What lessons are for us from the medieval pandemic?', *Society Register* 4 (2020), 129–44.
27. 'The coronavirus could devastate poor countries', *The Economist* (26 March 2020).
28. 'Drive for cross-border solidarity to beat pandemic', *Financial Times* (15 May 2020); 'Multinationals fear rise in protectionism because of pandemic', *Financial Times* (10 May 2020).
29. 'US supply chains and ports under strain from coronavirus', *Financial Times* (2 March 2020).
30. 'US–China economic decoupling accelerates in first quarter of 2020', *Financial Times* (11 May 2020).
31. www.economist.com/leaders/2020/05/14/has-covid-19-killed-globalisation.
32. 'IMF warns of deepest economic plunge since 1930s', *Financial Times* (14 April 2020).
33. A. Verbeke, 'Will the COVID-19 pandemic really change the governance of global value chains?', *British Journal of Management* 31 (2020), 444–6.
34. *Ibid.*

Chapter 4

1. Pankaj Ghemawat, 'Distance still matters: the hard reality of global expansion', *Harvard Business Review* 79 (2001), 137–47.
2. *Ibid.*, 138.

3. *Ibid.*, 142.
4. *Ibid.*
5. *Ibid.*
6. *Ibid.*, 145.
7. *Ibid.*, 147.
8. *Ibid.*, 142.
9. Kate Taylor, 'The parent company of KFC and Taco Bell is acquiring Habit Burger Grill, a burger chain with a cult following', *Business Insider* (6 January 2020).
10. Ghemawat, 'Distance still matters', 142.
11. Till Vestring, Ted Rouse, and Uwe Reinert, 'Hedge your offshoring bets', *MIT Sloan Management Review* 46 (Spring 2005), 27–9.
12. Data from *Statista*.
13. Vestring *et al.*, 'Hedge your offshoring bets', 29.
14. *Ibid.*
15. F. Ancarani, J. K. Frels, J. Miller, C. Saibene, and M. Barberio, 'Winning in rural emerging markets: General Electric's research study on MNCs', *California Management Review* 56 (2014), 31–52.
16. *Ibid.*, 32.
17. *Ibid.*, 46.
18. *Ibid.*, 41.
19. *Ibid.*, 42.
20. *Ibid.*, 47.
21. *Ibid.*, 43.
22. *Ibid.*, 45.
23. *Ibid.*, 41.
24. *Ibid.*, 42.
25. *Ibid.*, 49.
26. This also implies that international experience may be largely useless if, for example, the institutional distance between the host country and the MNE's affiliates is particularly large. A similar conclusion was proposed by Verbeke and Yuan (Alain Verbeke and Wenlong Yuan, 'Subsidiary autonomous activities in multinational enterprises: a transaction cost perspective', *Management International Review* 45 (2005), 31–52) when assessing the economic potential of autonomous subsidiary initiatives in large MNEs.
27. Alan Rugman and Alain Verbeke, 'A perspective on regional and global strategies of multinational enterprises', *Journal of International Business Studies* 35 (2004), 3–18; Alan Rugman and Alain Verbeke, *Analysis of Multinational Strategic Management: The Selected Papers of Alan M. Rugman and Alain Verbeke* (Cheltenham, UK, and Brookfield, USA: Edward Elgar, 2005); Alan Rugman and Alain Verbeke, 'Regional multinationals: the new research agenda', in Peter Buckley (ed.), *What is International Business?* (New York: Palgrave Macmillan, 2005), 110–32.
28. Levi Strauss Annual Report, 2019: https://s23.q4cdn.com/172692177/files/doc_financials/2019/ar/873914_007_BMK_WEB_V2-(1).pdf.
29. Alan Rugman, Alain Verbeke, and Wenlong Yuan, 'Re-conceptualizing the classification of subsidiary roles in multinational enterprises', *Mimeo* (2005); *ibid.*
30. M. Corstjens and R. Lal, 'Retail doesn't cross borders', *Harvard Business Review* 90 (2012), 104–11.
31. *Ibid.*, 105.
32. *Ibid.*, 107.

33. *Ibid.*
34. *Ibid.*, 109.
35. A. M. Rugman and A. Verbeke, 'A perspective on regional and global strategies of multinational enterprises', *Journal of International Business Studies* 35 (2014), 3–18.
36. 'The outsourcers hoping to gain from the crisis', *Financial Times* (2 June 2020).
37. *Ibid.*
38. O. Petricevic and D. Teece, 'The structural reshaping of globalization: implications for strategic sectors, profiting from innovation, and the multinational enterprise', *Journal of International Business Studies* 50 (2019), 1487–512.
39. 'China is the world's factory, more than ever', *The Economist* (23 June 2020).
40. 'Japan models a new look for national security', *Financial Times* (13 May 2020).
41. 'China is the world's factory'.
42. 'National security regulator to take closer look at privacy risks in foreign investors' U.S. deals', *The Wall Street Journal* (13 February 2020).
43. 'U.K. bolsters foreign-takeover defenses as pandemic drives protectionist moves', *The Wall Street Journal* (22 June 2020).
44. 'Coronavirus accelerates European efforts to block foreign takeovers', *The Wall Street Journal* (10 April 2020).
45. 'Looking for M&A deals is risky now for both buyers and sellers', *Financial Times* (21 April 2020).
46. 'Protectionism spreads globally with the new coronavirus', *The Wall Street Journal* (29 May 2020).
47. 'Eastern Europe's Covid-19 recession could match its post-communist one', *The Economist* (30 May 2020).
48. 'China is the world's factory'.

Chapter 5

1. C. A. Bartlett and S. Ghoshal, 'Tap your subsidiaries for global reach', *Harvard Business Review* 64 (1986), 87–94.
2. C. A. Bartlett and S. Ghoshal, *Managing across Borders: The Transnational Solution*, 1st edn (Boston: Harvard Business School Press, 1989).
3. Bartlett and Ghoshal, 'Tap your subsidiaries for global reach', 88.
4. *Ibid.*
5. *Ibid*, 90.
6. *Ibid*, 89.
7. W. Chan Kim and Renée A. Mauborgne, 'Procedural justice, strategic decision making, and the knowledge economy', *Strategic Management Journal* 19 (1998), 323–38; W. Chan Kim and Renée A. Mauborgne, 'Implementing global strategies: the role of procedural justice', *Strategic Management Journal* 12 (1991), 125–43; W. Chan Kim and Renée A. Mauborgne, 'Effectively conceiving and executing multinationals' world wide strategies', *Journal of International Business Studies* 24 (1993), 419–48; W. Chan Kim and Renée A. Mauborgne, 'Procedural justice, attitudes, and subsidiary top management compliance with multinational's corporate strategic decisions', *Academy of Management Journal* 36 (1993), 502–26; W. Chan Kim and Renée A. Mauborgne, 'Making global strategies work', *MIT Sloan Management Review* 34 (1993), 11–27; W. Chan Kim and Renée A. Mauborgne,

'A procedural justice model of strategic decision making: strategy content implications in the multinational', *Organization Science* 6 (1995), 44–61.

8. Kim and Mauborgne, 'Making global strategies work', 14.

9. S. P. L. Fourné, J. J. P. Jansen, and T. J. M. Mom, 'Strategic agility in MNEs: managing tensions to capture opportunities across emerging and established markets', *California Management Review* 56 (2014), 13–38.

10. *Ibid.*, 21.

11. *Ibid.*

12. *Ibid.*, 22.

13. *Ibid.*, 24.

14. *Ibid.*

15. *Ibid.*, 22.

16. *Ibid.*, 23.

17. *Ibid.*

18. *Ibid.*, 30.

19. Alan Rugman, Alain Verbeke, and Wenlong Yuan, 'Re-conceptualizing the classification of subsidiary roles in multinational enterprises', *Mimeo* (2006).

20. Julian Birkinshaw and Neil Hood, 'Unleash innovation in foreign subsidiaries', *Harvard Business Review* 79 (2001), 131–7.

21. A more extensive analysis can be found in Rugman *et al.*, 'Re-conceptualizing the classification of subsidiary roles'.

22. 'Chinese torture', *The Economist* 347 (1998), 59–61.

23. *Ibid.*, 60.

24. *Ibid.*, 61.

25. David J. Teece, 'Foreign investment and technological development in Silicon Valley', *California Management Review* 34 (1992), 91.

26. Christian Zeller, 'North Atlantic innovative relations of Swiss pharmaceuticals and the proximities with regional biotech arenas', *European Geography* 80 (2004), 83–111.

27. Teece, 'Foreign investment in Silicon Valley', 94.

28. J. M. O'Brien, 'Logitech grows up', *Marketing Computers* 15 (1995), 77–81.

29. 'Logitech expands mouse manufacturing facility', *China Daily* (2005).

30. Logitech Annual Report 2020.

31. Joyce Chepkemoi, 'Who are the world's largest chemical producing companies?', *World Atlas* (10 June 2019).

32. BASF, *BASF History: We Create Chemistry 1865–2015* (2015) (Ludwigshafen: BASF SE).

33. H. Mueller, 'Activities of European chemical companies in China', in G. Festel, A. Kreimeyer, U. Oels, and M. von Zedtwitz (eds.), *The Chemical and Pharmaceutical Industry in China: Opportunities and Threats to Foreign Companies* (Berlin and New York: Springer, 2005), 23–46.

34. BASF Factbook 2020.

35. Junwei Wang, 'BASF to establish $10b site in Guangdong', *China Daily* (10 July 2018).

36. BASF Factbook 2020.

37. BASF, *BASF History*.

38. Alan Rugman and Simon Collinson, 'The regional nature of the world's automotive sector', *European Management Journal* 22 (2004), 471–82.

39. Bartlett and Ghoshal, 'Tap your subsidiaries for global reach', 94.

40. E. Meyer, 'When culture doesn't translate', *Harvard Business Review* 93 (2015), 66–72.

41. *Ibid.*, 68.

42. *Ibid.*, 69.
43. *Ibid.*
44. *Ibid.*, 70.
45. *Ibid.*, 71.
46. *Ibid.*
47. *Ibid.*
48. N. Kumar and P. Puranam, 'Have you restructured for global success?', *Harvard Business Review* 89 (2011), 123–8.
49. *Ibid.*, 127.
50. *Ibid.*, 126.
51. *Ibid.*
52. *Ibid.*
53. *Ibid.*
54. *Ibid.*, 127.
55. *Ibid.*, 126–7.
56. 'Will coronavirus pandemic finally kill off global supply chains?', *Financial Times* (27 May 2020).
57. W. Bedyński, 'Liminality: Black Death 700 years later. What lessons are for us from the medieval pandemic?', *Society Register* 4 (2020), 129–44.
58. 'Much of global commerce has ground to a halt', *The Economist* (21 March 2020).
59. A. Verbeke, 'Will the COVID-19 pandemic really change the governance of global value chains?', *British Journal of Management* 31 (2020), 444–6.
60. *Ibid.*
61. *Ibid.*
62. P. Caligiuri, H. De Cieri, D. Minbaeva, A. Verbeke, and A. Zimmermann, 'International HRM insights for navigating the COVID-19 pandemic: implications for future research and practice', *Journal of International Business Studies* 51 (2020), 697–713.
63. 'Manufacturers forge ahead with tech, R&D projects, despite capex cuts', *The Wall Street Journal* (12 July 2020).
64. *Ibid.*

Chapter 6

1. W. Kuemmerle, 'Building effective R&D capabilities abroad', *Harvard Business Review* 75 (1997), 61–70.
2. *Ibid.*, 62, 70.
3. M. E. Porter, 'The competitive advantage of nations', *Harvard Business Review* 68 (1990), 73–93.
4. Kuemmerle, 'Building effective R&D capabilities abroad', 62.
5. *Ibid.* (emphases in the original). Kuemmerle's sample had a slightly higher proportion of home-base-exploiting sites, representing 55 per cent of the labs studied compared with 45 per cent of home-base-augmenting labs.
6. *Ibid.*, 64.
7. *Ibid.*
8. *Ibid.*, 65.
9. The single most significant moment in modern communications history may well have been 6 August 1991, when CERN, the European Laboratory for Particle Physics located in

Switzerland, placed online the first website, thereby publicizing the new World Wide Web. Two years before that date, Tim Berners-Lee, a CERN Fellow, had started developing the Hypertext Markup Language (HTML) and the Hypertext Transfer Protocol (HTTP), as well as the first Web pages.

10. A. M. Rugman and A. Verbeke, 'Location, competitiveness, and the multinational enterprise', in Alan Rugman (ed.), *The Oxford Handbook of International Business* (Oxford: Oxford University Press, 2001), 150–77.

11. J. Birkinshaw and N. Fry, 'Subsidiary initiatives to develop new markets', *Sloan Management Review* 39 (1998), 51–62.

12. *Ibid.*, 52.

13. A. Verbeke and W. Yuan, 'Subsidiary autonomous activities in multinational enterprises: a transaction cost perspective', *Management International Review* 45 (2005), 31–52.

14. For a conceptual analysis, see Alan Rugman and Alain Verbeke, 'Extending the theory of the multinational enterprise: internalization and strategic management perspectives', *Journal of International Business Studies* 34 (2003), 125–37.

15. J. S. Engel, 'Global clusters of innovation: lessons from Silicon Valley', *California Management Review* 57 (2015), 36–65.

16. N. Furr and A. Shipilov, 'Building the right ecosystem for innovation', *MIT Sloan Management Review* 59 (2018), 59–64.

17. Engel, 'Global clusters of innovation', 39.

18. *Ibid.*, 40.

19. *Ibid.*

20. *Ibid.*, 43.

21. *Ibid.*, 44.

22. *Ibid.*

23. *Ibid.*, 45.

24. *Ibid.*

25. *Ibid.*

26. O. Petricevic and D. J. Teece, 'The structural reshaping of globalization: implications for strategic sectors, profiting from innovation, and the multinational enterprise', *Journal of International Business Studies* 50 (2019), 1487–512.

27. Engel, 'Global clusters of innovation', 52.

28. *Ibid.*, 53.

29. *Ibid.*

30. *Ibid.*, 54.

31. *Ibid.*, 55.

32. *Ibid.*

33. *Ibid.*, 57.

34. *Ibid.*, 45, 60.

35. A. M. Rugman and A. Verbeke, 'Multinational enterprises and clusters: an organizing framework', *Management International Review* 43 (2003), 151–69.

36. *Ibid.*

37. *Ibid.*

38. Kuemmerle, 'Building effective R&D capabilities abroad', 61.

39. *Ibid.*, 69.

40. *Ibid.*, 68.

41. Birkinshaw and Fry, 'Subsidiary initiatives', 51–62.

42. D. E. Westney, 'Cross-Pacific internationalization of R&D by U.S. and Japanese firms', *R&D Management* 23 (1993), 171–81.

43. K. J. Schaefer, 'Catching up by hiring: the case of Huawei', *Journal of International Business Studies* 51 (2020), 1500–515.

44. K. Wilson and Y. L. Doz, '10 rules for managing global innovation', *Harvard Business Review* 90 (2012), 84–90.

45. *Ibid.*, 86.

46. *Ibid.*

47. *Ibid.*, 87.

48. *Ibid.*

49. *Ibid.*, 88.

50. Furr and Shipilov, 'Building the right ecosystem for innovation'.

51. *Ibid.*, 59.

52. *Ibid.*, 61.

53. *Ibid.*

54. *Ibid.*, 60.

55. *Ibid.*, 61.

56. *Ibid.*

57. *Ibid.*, 62.

58. *Ibid.*

59. *Ibid.*

60. *Ibid.*

61. *Ibid.*

62. *Ibid.*, 63.

63. *Ibid.*

64. *Ibid.*

65. *Ibid.*

66. *Ibid.*, 64.

Chapter 7

1. K. Ferdows, 'Making the most of foreign factories', *Harvard Business Review* 75 (1997), 73–88.

2. *Ibid.*

3. *Ibid.*

4. *Ibid.*, 73.

5. *Ibid.*, 86.

6. *Ibid.*

7. *Ibid.*, 87.

8. *Ibid.*, 83.

9. *Ibid.*, 84.

10. W. C. Shih, 'What it takes to reshore manufacturing successfully', *MIT Sloan Management Review* 56 (2014), 55–62.

11. *Ibid.*, 55.

12. *Ibid.*, 59.

13. *Ibid.*

14. *Ibid.*, 60.

15. *Ibid.*, 61.
16. *Ibid.*, 62.
17. A. Ben-Ner and E. Siemsen, 'Decentralization and localization of production: the organizational and economic consequences of additive manufacturing (3D printing)', *California Management Review* 59 (2017), 5–23.
18. *Ibid.*, 8.
19. *Ibid.*, 6.
20. *Ibid.*, 12-13.
21. *Ibid.*, 13.
22. *Ibid.*, 15.
23. Ferdows, 'Making the most of foreign factories', 76.
24. These firms included Canada-based Nortel (filed for bankruptcy in 2009), US-based Lucent (merged with Alcatel SA of France in 2006, forming Alcatel-Lucent, and was subsequently acquired by Finland-based Nokia in 2016), and Cisco.
    Ian Austen, 'Nortel seeks bankruptcy protection', *New York Times* (14 January 2009); Vikas Bajaj, 'Alcatel and Lucent agree to merge in $13.4 billion deal', *New York Times* (2 April 2006); Nokia company information, 2016: www.nokia.com/about-us/news/releases/2017/03/23/nokia-has-filed-its-annual-form-20-f-for-2016-with-the-us-securities-and-exchange-commission-and-published-its-nokia-in-2016-annual-report.
25. Ritsuko Ando, 'Flextronics to buy Solectron for $3.6 billion', *Reuters* (4 June 2007).
26. Corporation company information, 2012: https://ir.sanmina.com/investor-relations/news/press-release-details/2012/Sanmina-SCI-Corporation-To-Change-Its-Name-To-Sanmina-Corporation/default.aspx.
27. L. Kano, 'Global value chain governance: a relational perspective', *Journal of International Business Studies* 49 (2018), 684–705.
28. M. Iansiti and K. R. Lakhani, 'Managing our hub economy', *Harvard Business Review* 95 (2017), 84–92.
29. *Ibid.*, 86.
30. *Ibid.*
31. *Ibid.*
32. *Ibid.*
33. *Ibid.*, 87.
34. *Ibid.*
35. *Ibid.*, 89.
36. *Ibid.*, 90.
37. *Ibid.*, 91.
38. *Ibid.*
39. *Ibid.*
40. *Ibid.*
41. *Ibid.*
42. *Ibid.*, 92.

Chapter 8

1. D. R. Lessard and J. B. Lightstone, 'Volatile exchange rates can put operations at risk', *Harvard Business Review* 64 (1986), 107–14.
2. *Ibid.*, 111.

3. *Ibid.*, 108.
4. *Ibid.*, 107.
5. *Ibid.*
6. *Ibid.*, 108.
7. *Ibid.*, 114.
8. *Ibid.*, 107.
9. U. Pidun, A. Richter, M. Schommer, and A. Karna, 'A new playbook for diversified companies', *MIT Sloan Management Review* 60 (2019), 29–38.
10. *Ibid.*, 29.
11. *Ibid.*, 30.
12. *Ibid.*, 36.
13. *Ibid.*, 31.
14. *Ibid.*
15. *Ibid.*, 33.
16. *Ibid.*, 35.
17. *Ibid.*
18. C. A. Bartlett and S. Ghoshal, 'Tap your subsidiaries for global reach', *Harvard Business Review* 64 (1986), 87–94.
19. G. Dushnitsky, M. Guerini, E. Piva, and C. Rossi-Lamastra, 'Crowdfunding in Europe: determinants of platform creation across countries', *California Management Review* 58 (2016), 44–71.
20. *Ibid.*, 44.
21. *Ibid.*, 57.
22. *Ibid.*
23. *Ibid.* For example, protection of legal rights at the national level promotes platforms adopting the lending model of crowdfunding. A more feminine national culture also appears to support the lending model. In contrast, a greater number of internet users supports the equity model of crowdfunding.
24. E. Heidari, M. Akhavannia, and N. Kannangara, 'To internationalize rapidly from inception: crowdsource', *Technology Innovation Management Review* 2 (2012), 17–21.
25. *Ibid.*, 18.
26. *Ibid.*
27. *Ibid.*
28. *Ibid.*, 20.
29. A. M. Rugman, *International Diversification and the Multinational Enterprise* (Lexington Books, 1979).
30. A. M. Rugman, 'Internalization theory and corporate international finance', *California Management Review* 23 (1980), 73–9.
31. Charles Goldsmith, 'Moguls rewrite script at Cannes as euro tanks', *Wall Street Journal (Eastern Edition)* (19 May 2000), B.1.
32. Lafarge, 20-F Report (26 March 2004).
33. www.lafargeholcim.com/files/atoms/files/04172019-finance-lafargeholcim_fy_annual_report-en.pdf
34. Michael H. Moffett, Arthur I. Stonehill, and David K. Eiteman, *Fundamentals of Multinational Finance* (Boston, MA: Pearson Education,), 244.
35. M. A. Desai and M. F. Veblen, 'Foreign exchange hedging strategies at General Motors: transactional and translational exposures', Harvard Business School: Case Study 9-205-095 (2006).

36. Equinor company information, 2018: www.equinor.com/en/about-us/about-our-name-change.html.
37. Statoil, Annual report (2005).
38. V. Govindarajan, S. Rajgopal, and A. Srivastava, 'A blueprint for digital companies' financial reporting', *Harvard Business School Publishing* (2018), https://hbsp.harvard .edu/product/.
39. *Ibid.*
40. *Ibid.*
41. *Ibid.*

Chapter 9

1. T. Levitt, 'The globalization of markets', *Harvard Business Review* 61 (1983), 93.
2. *Ibid.*, 92–102.
3. *Ibid.*, 99.
4. *Ibid.*, 98.
5. *Ibid.*, 97.
6. *Ibid.*, 100.
7. *Ibid.*, 94.
8. S. Li, F. Candelon, and M. Reeves, 'Lessons from China's digital battleground', *MIT Sloan Management Review* 59 (2018), 1–6.
9. *Ibid.*, 3.
10. *Ibid.*, 4.
11. *Ibid.*
12. *Ibid.*
13. *Ibid.*, 5.
14. *Ibid.*, 4.
15. *Ibid.*, 5.
16. D. Arnold, J. Birkinshaw, and O. Toulan, 'Can selling be globalized? The pitfalls of global account management', *California Management Review* 44 (2001), 8–20.
17. *Ibid.*, 16.
18. N. Capon and C. Senn, 'Global customer management programs: how to make them really work', *California Management Review* 52 (2010), 32–55.
19. *Ibid.*, 33.
20. *Ibid.*, 35.
21. *Ibid.*, 36.
22. *Ibid.*
23. *Ibid.*
24. *Ibid.*, 37.
25. *Ibid.*, 38.
26. *Ibid.*
27. *Ibid.*, 40.
28. Levitt, 'The globalization of markets', 94.
29. F. van den Driest, S. Sthanunathan, and K. Weed, 'Building an insights engine', *Harvard Business Review* 94 (2016), 64–74.
30. *Ibid.*, 66.
31. *Ibid.*

32. *Ibid.*, 67.
33. *Ibid.*, 69.
34. *Ibid.*
35. *Ibid.*
36. *Ibid.*
37. *Ibid.*
38. *Ibid.*, 70.
39. *Ibid.*
40. *Ibid.*, 71.
41. *Ibid.*, 72.
42. *Ibid.*
43. *Ibid.*
44. *Ibid.*, 67.
45. *Ibid.*, 72.
46. *Ibid.*, 73.
47. *Ibid.*
48. *Ibid.*
49. *Ibid.*, 74.
50. *Ibid.*
51. *Ibid.*

Chapter 10

1. J. S. Black and H. B. Gregersen, 'The right way to manage expats', *Harvard Business Review* 77 (1999), 52–63.
2. *Ibid.*, 53.
3. *Ibid.*, 61.
4. *Ibid.*, 53.
5. *Ibid.*, 58.
6. *Ibid.*, 54.
7. *Ibid.*, 62.
8. *Ibid.*, 58.
9. *Ibid.*, 60.
10. Geert Hofstede is Professor Emeritus of Organizational Anthropology and International Management at the University of Maastricht in the Netherlands. His comprehensive and influential study (e.g., G. H. Hofstede, *Culture's Consequences: International Differences in Work-related Values* (Newbury Park, CA: Sage Publications, 1984); G. H. Hofstede, *Culture's Consequences: Comparing Values, Behaviors, Institutions, and Organizations across Nations* (Thousand Oaks, CA: Sage Publications, 2001)) identified five independent dimensions of national culture differences. Hofstede's work has had far greater impact on later cultural studies than other frameworks. For example, Google Scholar indicated that Hofstede's 1984 book has been cited 4,334 times (accessed on 26 March 2007). At the same time, Hofstede's work has been criticized for being overly simplistic for having only five dimensions, ignoring intra-country cultural differences, etc. For a recent review of Hofstede's work and related empirical research, see Bradley L. Kirkman, Kevin B. Lowe, and Cristina B. Gibson, 'A quarter century of *Culture's Consequences*: a review of empirical research incorporating Hofstede's cultural values framework', *Journal of*

International Business Studies 37 (2006), 285–320. Hofstede analyzed a large database of employee values scores collected by IBM between 1967 and 1973, covering more than seventy countries. He first used only the forty largest countries, and then later extended the work to seventy-four countries through replications and extensions of the IBM study on different international populations. Hofstede developed a model that identifies five primary dimensions to differentiate cultures: Power Distance – PDI, Individualism – IDV, Masculinity – MAS, Uncertainty Avoidance – UAI, and Long-Term Orientation – LTO. PDI refers to the extent of equality/inequality between people in a country; IDV indicates to what extent individuals are integrated into groups; MAS focuses on the distribution of roles between the genders; UAI reflects the tolerance for uncertainty and ambiguity within a society; and LTO shows the degree to which the society values long-term, forward thinking. Hofstede's cultural values between countries have led to research on cultural distance and its impact on organizational outcomes. For example, as the cultural distance between countries increased, the tendency to choose a joint venture over an acquisition increased (B. Kogut and H. Singh, 'The effect of national culture on the choice of entry mode', *Journal of International Business Studies* 19 (1988), 411–32); as cultural distance increased, the amount of US FDI decreased (e.g., J. Li and S. Guisinger, 'The globalization of service multinationals in the "triad" regions: Japan, Western Europe and North America', *Journal of International Business Studies* 23 (1992), 675–96).

11. Y. Doz and C. K. Prahalad, 'Headquarters influence and strategic control in MNCs', *Sloan Management Review* 23 (1981), 15–29; C. K. Prahalad and Y. Doz, 'An approach to strategic control in MNCs', *Sloan Management Review* 22 (1981), 5–13.
12. Prahalad and Doz, 'An approach to strategic control in MNCs', 5.
13. Y. Doz and C. K. Prahalad, 'Headquarters influence and strategic control in MNCs', *Sloan Management Review* 23 (1981), 15–29; Prahalad and Doz, 'An approach to strategic control in MNCs'.
14. Doz and Prahalad, 'Headquarters influence and strategic control in MNCs', 28.
15. H. Bahrami, 'People operations at Mozilla Corporation: scaling a peer-to-peer global community', *California Management Review* 56 (2013), 67–88.
16. *Ibid.*, 67.
17. *Ibid.*, 68.
18. *Ibid.*, 67.
19. *Ibid.*, 71.
20. *Ibid.*, 72.
21. *Ibid.*, 68.
22. *Ibid.*, 73.
23. *Ibid.*, 76.
24. *Ibid.*, 77.
25. *Ibid.*, 78.
26. *Ibid.*, 79.
27. *Ibid.*, 79-80.
28. *Ibid.*, 81.
29. *Ibid.*, 83.
30. *Ibid.*, 71.
31. Black and Gregersen, 'The right way to manage expats', 54.
32. N. Anand and J.-L. Barsoux, 'What everyone gets wrong about change management', *Harvard Business Review* 95 (2017), 78–85.
33. *Ibid.*, 81.
34. *Ibid.*

35. *Ibid.*, 82.

36. *Ibid.*

37. *Ibid.*, 82–3.

38. *Ibid.*, 83.

39. *Ibid.*, 84.

40. *Ibid.*

41. *Ibid.*, 80.

42. E. Meyer, 'Being the boss in Brussels, Boston, and Beijing: if you want to succeed, you'll need to adapt', *Harvard Business Review* 95 (2017), 70–7.

43. G. Hofstede, *Culture's Consequences: International Differences in Work-related Values* (Beverly Hills, CA: Sage, 1980); G. Hofstede, 'The cultural relativity of organizational practices and theories', *Journal of International Business Studies*, 14 (1983), 75–89; B. Kogut and H. Singh, 'The effect of national culture on the choice of entry mode', *Journal of International Business Studies* 19 (1988), 411–32; I. R. P. Cuypers, G. Ertug, P. P. M. A. R. Heugens, B. Kogut, and T. Zou, 'The making of a construct: lessons from 30 years of the Kogut and Singh cultural distance index', *Journal of International Business Studies* 49 (2018), 1138–53; R. Maseland, D. Dow, and P. Steel, 'The Kogut and Singh national cultural distance index: time to start using it as a springboard rather than a crutch', *Journal of International Business Studies* 49 (2018), 1154–66.

44. G. Hofstede, *Culture's Consequences*; S. Beugelsdijk, B. Ambos, and P. C. Nell, 'Conceptualizing and measuring distance in international business research: recurring questions and best practice guidelines', *Journal of International Business Studies* 49 (2018), 1113–37.

45. *Ibid.*

46. M. F. Peterson and T. S. Barreto, 'Interpreting societal culture value dimensions', *Journal of International Business Studies* 49 (2018), 1190–207.

47. *Ibid.*

48. R. L. Tung and G. K. Stahl, 'The tortuous evolution of the role of culture in IB research: what we know, what we don't know, and where we are headed', *Journal of International Business Studies* 49 (2018), 1167–89.

49. Beugelsdijk *et al.*, 'Conceptualizing and measuring distance in international business research'.

50. Tung and Stahl, 'The tortuous evolution of the role of culture in IB research'.

51. *Ibid.*

52. Meyer, 'Being the boss in Brussels, Boston, and Beijing', 74.

53. *Ibid.*, 72.

54. *Ibid.*

55. *Ibid.*, 76.

56. *Ibid.*

57. *Ibid.*, 77.

58. *Ibid.*

Chapter 11

1. D. Arnold, 'Seven rules of international distribution', *Harvard Business Review* 78 (2000), 131–7.

2. *Ibid.*, 132.

3. *Ibid.*

4. *Ibid.*, 133.

5. *Ibid.*

6. *Ibid.*, 137.

7. *Ibid.*, 134.

8. *Ibid.*, 133.

9. *Ibid.*

10. L. Chevreux, M. Hu, and S. Gandhi, 'Why supply chains must pivot', *MIT Sloan Management Review: Frontiers* (2018), https://sloanreview.mit.edu/article/why-supply-chains-must-pivot/.

11. *Ibid.*

12. *Ibid.*

13. *Ibid.*

14. *Ibid.*

15. *Ibid.*

16. *Ibid.*

17. Hau L. Lee, 'Aligning supply chain strategies with product uncertainties', *California Management Review* 44 (2002), 105–19.

18. *Ibid.*, 108.

19. *Ibid.*, 118.

20. Here, we assume for simplicity that the required location-bound knowledge can actually be sourced externally – albeit not through simple market contracts. Such possibility of external sourcing is not always present, however, especially not in emerging or centrally controlled economies. We also assume that knowledge acquisition does not entail the acquisition of a host country firm. This assumption is reasonable because MNEs often are not interested in absorbing another company. Such absorption could involve internalizing – and perhaps subsequently needing to dispose of – unwanted assets, as well as needing to create a more uniform corporate culture after the acquisition, etc.

21. D. Simchi-Levi, W. Schmidt, and Y. Wei, 'From superstorms to factory fires', *Harvard Business Review* 92 (2014), 96–101.

22. *Ibid.*, 97.

23. *Ibid.*, 100.

24. *Ibid.*

25. *Ibid.*

26. *Ibid.*

27. *Ibid.*, 98–9.

Chapter 12

1. G. Hamel, Y. L. Doz, and C. K. Prahalad, 'Collaborate with your competitors – and win', *Harvard Business Review* 67 (1989), 133–9.

2. *Ibid.*

3. *Ibid.*, 134.

4. *Ibid.*, 138.

5. *Ibid.*, 135.

6. *Ibid.*, 137.

7. *Ibid.*, 139.

8. *Ibid.*, 135–6.

9. Erin Anderson and Sandy D. Jap, 'The dark side of close relationships', *MIT Sloan Management Review* 46 (2005), 75–82.

10. *Ibid.*, 79–81.

11. Prashant Kale and Jaideep Anand, 'The decline of emerging economy joint ventures: the case of India', *California Management Review* 48 (2006), 62–76.

12. *Ibid.*, 66.

13. H. Vantrappen and D. Deneffe, 'Joint ventures reduce the risk of major capital investments', *Harvard Business Review: Operations Management* (2016), https://hbr.org/2016/04/joint-ventures-reduce-the-risk-of-major-capital-investments.

14. *Ibid.*

15. *Ibid.*

16. *Ibid.*

17. *Ibid.*

18. *Ibid.*

19. *Ibid.*

20. *Ibid.*

21. *Ibid.*

22. *Ibid.*

23. *Ibid.*

Chapter 13

1. Pankaj Ghemawat and Fariborz Ghadar, 'The dubious logic of global megamergers', *Harvard Business Review* 78 (2000), 65–74.

2. *Ibid.*, 66.

3. *Ibid.*, 68.

4. *Ibid.*, 69.

5. *Ibid.*, 69–70.

6. *Ibid.*, 72.

7. *Ibid.*

8. James K. Sebenius, 'Case study: negotiating cross-border acquisitions', Sloan Management Review (Winter 1998), 27–41.

9. *Ibid.*, 40.

10. Andrew C. Inkpen, Anant K. Sundaram, and Kristin Rockwood, 'Cross-border acquisitions of U.S. technology assets', *California Management Review* 42 (2000), 50–71.

11. C. Chatterjee and D. Sokol, 'Don't acquire a company until you evaluate its data', *Harvard Business Review: Mergers & Acquisitions* (2019), https://hbr.org/2019/04/dont-acquire-a-company-until-you-evaluate-its-data-security.

12. *Ibid.*

13. *Ibid.*

14. *Ibid.*

15. *Ibid.*

16. *Ibid.*

17. *Ibid.*

18. *Ibid.*

19. *Ibid.*
20. *Ibid.*
21. *Ibid.*
22. *Ibid.*
23. *Ibid.*

Chapter 14

1. T. Khanna, K. G. Palepu, and J. Sinha, 'Strategies that fit emerging markets', *Harvard Business Review* 83 (2005), 63–76.
2. *Ibid.*
3. D. J. Arnold and J. A. Quelch, 'New strategies in emerging markets', *Sloan Management Review* 40 (1998), 7–20.
4. *Ibid.*
5. T. Khanna and K. Palepu, 'Why focused strategies may be wrong for emerging markets', *Harvard Business Review* 75 (1997), 41–51.
6. Khanna *et al.*, 'Strategies that fit emerging markets', 63–76.
7. *Ibid.*, 67.
8. *Ibid.*, 63–76.
9. Data from Bureau of Economic Analysis.
10. An example of biases in market selection comes from the 1950s work of MIT political scientist Harold Isaacs. He proposed that American firms favoured China over India because of America's romance with China that developed from the work of missionaries and scholars in China during the 1800s (Khanna *et al.*, 'Strategies that fit emerging markets', 64).
11. Khanna *et al.*, 'Strategies that fit emerging markets', 64.
12. *Ibid.*
13. *Ibid.*, 63–76.
14. The six indices used by the authors are: Growth Competitiveness Index ranking, Business Competitiveness Index ranking, Governance indicators, Corruption Perceptions Index ranking, Composite Country Risks Points, and Per cent weight in Emerging markets index.
15. Khanna *et al.*, 'Strategies that fit emerging markets', 65.
16. *Ibid.*, 66.
17. *Ibid.*, 67.
18. *Ibid.*, 74.
19. *Ibid.*
20. Laurie Burkitt, 'Home Depot learns Chinese prefer "do-it-for-me"', *The Wall Street Journal* (14 September 2012).
21. Khanna and Palepu, 'Why focused strategies may be wrong for emerging markets', 41–51.
22. S. Prashantham and G. S. Yip, 'Engaging with startups in emerging markets', *MIT Sloan Management Review* 58 (2017), 51–6.
23. *Ibid.*, 52.
24. *Ibid.*
25. *Ibid.*
26. *Ibid.*, 54.
27. *Ibid.*
28. *Ibid.*

29. *Ibid.*
30. *Ibid.*
31. J. A. Mathews, H. Tan, and M.-C. Hu, 'Moving to a circular economy in China: transforming industrial parks into eco-industrial parks', *California Management Review* 60 (2018), 157–81.
32. *Ibid.*, 159.
33. *Ibid.*, 160.
34. *Ibid.*, 162.
35. *Ibid.*, 165.
36. *Ibid.*, 163.
37. *Ibid.*, 165.
38. *Ibid.*, 166.
39. *Ibid.*, 169-171.
40. *Ibid.*, 171.
41. *Ibid.*, 172.
42. *Ibid.*
43. R. Florida and L. Hathaway, 'How the geography of startups and innovation is changing', *Harvard Business Review: Economics & Society* (2018), https://hbr.org/2018/11/how-the-geography-of-startups-and-innovation-is-changing.
44. *Ibid.*

Chapter 15

1. P. Ghemawat and T. Hout, 'Tomorrow's global giants? Not the usual suspects', *Harvard Business Review* 86 (2008), 80–8.
2. *Ibid.*
3. *Ibid.*
4. O. Gadiesh and T. Vestring, 'The consequences of China's rising global heavyweights', *MIT Sloan Management Review* 49 (2008), 10–11.
5. *Ibid.*
6. *Ibid.*
7. H.-T. Tsai and A. B. Eisingerich, 'Internationalization strategies of emerging markets firms', *California Management Review* 53 (2010), 114–35.
8. *Ibid.*
9. R. Mudambi, 'Location, control and innovation in knowledge-intensive industries', *Journal of Economic Geography* 8 (2008), 699–725.
10. See, e.g.: www.businessweek.com/magazine/chinas-new-protectionism-10272011.html.
11. M. Hensmans, 'Competing through joint innovation', *MIT Sloan Management Review* 58 (2017), 26–34.
12. *Ibid.*, 28.
13. *Ibid.*
14. *Ibid.*, 29.
15. *Ibid.*
16. *Ibid.*, 31.
17. *Ibid.*
18. *Ibid.*
19. *Ibid.*, 32.

Chapter 16

1. W. Kuemmerle, 'The entrepreneur's path to global expansion', *MIT Sloan Management Review* 46 (2005), 42–9.
2. *Ibid.*
3. This is, of course, fully consistent with the research findings several decades ago from the Uppsala school; see Johansson and Vahlne (J. Johansson and J. E. Vahlne, 'The internationalization process of the firm: a model of knowledge development and increasing foreign market commitments', *Journal of International Business Studies* 8 (1977), 23–32), as well as extensive follow-up work during the past thirty years.
4. W. R. Kerr, 'Harnessing the best of globalization', *MIT Sloan Management Review* 58 (2016), 58–67.
5. *Ibid.*, 60.
6. *Ibid.*, 63–64.
7. *Ibid.*, 64.
8. *Ibid.*
9. *Ibid.*, 65.
10. *Ibid.*
11. *Ibid.*, 66.
12. *Ibid.*, 63.
13. P. Muñoz and B. Cohen, 'A compass for navigating sharing economy business models', *California Management Review* 61 (2018), 114–47.
14. *Ibid.*, 115.
15. *Ibid.*, 114.
16. Airbnb is an online intermediary based in San Francisco, CA, in the United States, and it offers arrangement for tourists' lodging in the online rental marketplace all over the world.
17. Peerby is a start-up in Amsterdam, the Netherlands, and it operates an online platform for peer-to-peer renting services of household items in neighbourhoods.
18. BlaBlaCar is an online platform for ridesharing, established in France. It offers P2P connections in over twenty countries to drivers and passengers for intercity travel with shared costs.
19. Cohealo, based in Boston, MA, in the United States, is a leading company in medical equipment optimization. It provides a platform for sharing expensive medical equipment between hospitals.
20. Muñoz and Cohen, 'A compass for navigating sharing economy business models', 132.
21. *Ibid.*, 133.
22. *Ibid.*, 135.
23. *Ibid.*, 135–6.
24. *Ibid.*, 139.
25. *Ibid.*, 140–1.
26. B. M. Oviatt and P. P. McDougall, 'Toward a theory of international new ventures', *Journal of International Business Studies* 25 (1994), 45–64.
27. M. W. Rennie, 'Global competitiveness: born global', *The McKinsey Quarterly* 4 (1993), 45–52.
28. Oviatt and McDougall, 'Toward a theory of international new ventures', 49.

29. P. P. McDougall and B. M. Oviatt, 'International entrepreneurship literature in the 1990s and directions for future research', in D. L. Sexton and R. W. Smilor (eds.), *Entrepreneurship 2000* (Chicago, IL: Upstart Publishing, 1997), 291–320.

30. B. M. Oviatt and P. P. McDougall, 'Defining international entrepreneurship and modeling the speed of internationalization', *Entrepreneurship Theory and Practice* 29 (2005), 537–57.

31. P. P. McDougall and B. M. Oviatt, 'International entrepreneurship: the intersection of two research paths', *Academy of Management Journal* 43 (2000), 902–6; G. A. Knight and S. T. Cavusgil, 'Innovation, organizational capabilities, and the born-global firm', *Journal of International Business Studies* 35 (2004), 124–41.

32. A. Verbeke and L. Ciravegna, 'International entrepreneurship research versus international business research: a false dichotomy?', *Journal of International Business Studies* 49 (2018), 387–94.

33. *Ibid.*, 388.

34. S. T. Cavusgil and G. A. Knight, 'The born global firm: an entrepreneurial and capabilities perspective on early and rapid internationalization', *Journal of International Business Studies* 46 (2015), 3–16.

35. N. E. Coviello, 'The network dynamics of international new ventures', *Journal of International Business Studies* 37 (2006), 713–31.

36. Verbeke and Ciravegna, 'International entrepreneurship research versus international business research'.

37. *Ibid.*, 389.

38. *Ibid.*

39. *Ibid.*

40. Oviatt and McDougall, 'Defining international entrepreneurship'.

41. Verbeke and Ciravegna, 'International entrepreneurship research versus international business research'.

42. *Ibid.*, 390.

43. Muñoz and Cohen, 'A compass for navigating sharing economy business models', 133.

44. E. Heidari, M. Akhavannia, and N. Kannangara, 'To internationalize rapidly from inception: crowdsource', *Technology Innovation Management Review* 2 (2012), 17–21.

45. *Ibid.*

46. *Ibid.*

47. *Ibid.*

48. Kerr, 'Harnessing the best of globalization', 58–67.

49. A. M. Rugman, I. H. Lee, and S. Terjesen, 'International entrepreneurship in a world of broad triad regions: an international business perspective', in S. Fernhaber and S. Prashantham (ed.), *The Routledge Companion to International Entrepreneurship* (New York: Routledge, 2015), 202–18.

50. *Ibid.*

51. J. F. Hennart, 'The accidental internationalists: a theory of born globals', *Entrepreneurship Theory and Practice* 38 (2014), 117–35.

52. D. J. Isenberg, 'The global entrepreneur', *Harvard Business Review* 86 (2008), 107–11.

53. *Ibid.*, 109.

54. *Ibid.*

55. *Ibid.*, 110.

56. *Ibid.*, 111.

57. *Ibid.*, 109.

58. *Ibid.*

Chapter 17A

1. S. Vachani and N. C. Smith, 'Socially responsible pricing: lessons from the pricing of AIDS drugs in developing countries', *California Management Review* 47 (2004), 118.
2. D. Dunn and K. Yamashita, 'Microcapitalism and the megacorporation', *Harvard Business Review* 81 (2003), 47–54.
3. *Ibid.*, 53.
4. *Ibid.*
5. *Ibid.*, 50.
6. *Ibid.*, 51.
7. *Ibid.*, 52.
8. *Ibid.*
9. *Ibid.*, 48.
10. *Ibid.*, 50.
11. *Ibid.*, 54.
12. *Ibid.*, 53.
13. For a description of the Make Poverty History campaign, see www.makepovertyhistory .org. For an overview of a number of organizations specifically geared to fight poverty, see: www.humanrightscareers.com/issues/organizations-dedicated-to-fight-poverty/.
14. Dunn and Yamashita, 'Microcapitalism and the megacorporation', 53.
15. R. M. Locke and M. Romis, 'Improving work conditions in a global supply chain', *MIT Sloan Management Review* 48 (2007), 54–62.
16. *Ibid.*, 54.
17. *Ibid.*
18. *Ibid.*, 57.
19. *Ibid.*, 59.
20. *Ibid.*, 55.
21. *Ibid.*, 60.
22. Vachani and Smith, 'Socially responsible pricing', 118.
23. *Ibid.*
24. *Ibid.*, 120.
25. *Ibid.*, 121.
26. *Ibid.*, 119.
27. *Ibid.*
28. BBC, http://news.bbc.co.uk/2/hi/americas/6626073.stm, accessed on 4 May 2007.
29. Vachani and Smith, 'Socially responsible pricing', 127.
30. *Ibid.*, 131.
31. *Ibid.*, 133.
32. R. S. Kaplan, G. Serafeim, and E. Tugendhat, 'Inclusive growth: profitable strategies for tackling poverty and inequality', *Harvard Business Review* 96 (2018), 126–33.
33. *Ibid.*, 129–30.
34. *Ibid.*, 132.
35. *Ibid.*, 133.
36. A. M. Rugman and J. R. D'Cruz, *Multinationals as Flagship Firms: Regional Business Networks* (Oxford University Press, 2000).
37. 'Everyone is talking about ESG: what is it and why should it matter to you?', *Forbes* (8 November 2019) (www.forbes.com/sites/tinethygesen/2019/11/08/everyone-is-talking-

about-esgwhat-is-it-and-why-should-it-matter-to-you/#3c23bc4032e9); 'Integrated corporate governance: six leadership priorities for boards beyond the crisis', *Forbes* (18 June 2020) (www.forbes.com/sites/worldeconomicforum/2020/06/18/integrated-corporate-governance-six-leadership-priorities-for-boards-beyond-the-crisis/#301eff616ef5).

Chapter 17B

1. M. E. Porter and C. van der Linde, 'Green and competitive', *Harvard Business Review* 73 (1995), 120–34.
2. *Ibid.*, 120.
3. *Ibid.*, 128.
4. *Ibid.*, 122.
5. *Ibid.*, 133.
6. Rhône-Poulenc was merged with Hoechst AG to form Aventis in 1999, which was merged with Sanofi-Synthélabo to form Sanofi-Aventis in 2004. Sanofi-Aventis finally changed its name to Sanofi in 2011.
7. Porter and van der Linde, 'Green and competitive', 125.
8. *Ibid.*
9. *Ibid.*, 127.
10. *Ibid.*, 124.
11. *Ibid.*, 130.
12. GE Ecomagination, Annual report 2006; GE company information, retrieved from www.ge.com/news/reports/ecomagination-ten-years-later-proving-efficiency-economics-go-hand-hand.
13. GE Annual report 2019.
14. D. Kiron, G. Unruh, N. Kruschwitz, M. Reeves, H. Rubel, and A. M. Zum Felde, 'Corporate sustainability at a crossroads', *MIT Sloan Management Review* 58 (2017), 1–27.
15. *Ibid.*, 2.
16. *Ibid.*, 3.
17. *Ibid.*, 5.
18. *Ibid.*, 6.
19. *Ibid.*
20. *Ibid.*, 8–9.
21. *Ibid.*, 10.
22. *Ibid.*
23. *Ibid.*, 11.
24. *Ibid.*, 10–11.
25. *Ibid.*, 12.
26. The website Packaging Digest notes: 'The flexible four-sided pouch features grip handles and a pour spout; according to the company, the design makes it easier to handle the packaging and dispense the product. Further, the manufacturer states the Yes Pack offers a number advantages over rigid packs, including the ability to extract as much as 99 percent of the product without having to scrape out the last dregs (which yields two additional servings per gallon of dressing), reduced risk of cross-contamination, and ability to carry more than one pack at a time.'
27. Kiron *et al.*, 'Corporate sustainability at a crossroads', 12.

28. *Ibid.*, 14.
29. *Ibid.*
30. *Ibid.*, 15.
31. *Ibid.*, 16.
32. *Ibid.*, 17.
33. *Ibid.*
34. *Ibid.*
35. *Ibid.*, 19.
36. A. Kolk and J. Pinkse, 'Business responses to climate change: identifying emergent strategies', *California Management Review* 47 (2005), 6–20.
37. *Ibid.*, 13.
38. *Ibid.*, 14.
39. *Ibid.*
40. *Ibid.*, 15.
41. Porter and van der Linde, 'Green and competitive', 127.
42. *Ibid.*, 128.
43. A. M. Rugman and A. Verbeke, 'Corporate strategies and environmental regulations: an organizing framework', *Strategic Management Journal* 19 (1998), 363–75.
44. H. Bapuji and P. W. Beamish, 'Impacting practice through IB scholarship: toy recalls and the product safety crisis', *Journal of International Business Studies* 50 (2019), 1636–43.
45. Rugman and Verbeke, 'Corporate strategies and environmental regulations', 372.
46. P. Hopkinson, M. Zils, P. Hawkins, and S. Roper, 'Managing a complex global circular economy business model: opportunities and challenges', *California Management Review* 60 (2018), 71–94.
47. *Ibid.*, 73.
48. *Ibid.*, 75.
49. *Ibid.*
50. *Ibid.*, 76.
51. *Ibid.*, 77.
52. *Ibid.*
53. *Ibid.*
54. *Ibid.*, 84.
55. *Ibid.*
56. Hopkinson *et al.*, 'Managing a complex global circular economy business model', Unpublished Version, *Mimeo*, 25.
57. Hopkinson *et al.*, 'Managing a complex global circular economy business model', 88.
58. *Ibid.*, 89.
59. *Ibid.*, 90.
60. *Ibid.*, 91.
61. *Ibid.*, 85.
62. *Ibid.*

Conclusion

1. See Alan M. Rugman and Alain Verbeke, 'A perspective on regional and global strategies of multinational enterprises', *Journal of International Business Studies* 35(1) (2004), 3–18, as well as Alan M. Rugman and Alain Verbeke, 'Liabilities of regional foreignness and the

use of firm-level versus country-level data: a response to Dunning *et al.*', *Journal of International Business Studies* 38(1) (2007), 200–5. See also Alan M. Rugman, Chang Hoon Oh, and Dominic S. K. Lim, 'The regional and global competitiveness of multinational firms', *Journal of the Academy of Marketing Science* 40 (2012), 218–35.

2. Benjamin Rosa, Philippe Gugler, and Alain Verbeke, 'Regional and global strategies of MNEs: revisiting Rugman & Verbeke (2004)', *Journal of International Business Studies* 51(7) (2020), 1045–53.

3. Olga Petricevic and David J. Teece, 'The structural reshaping of globalization: implications for strategic sectors, profiting from innovation, and the multinational enterprise', *Journal of International Business Studies* 50(9) (2019), 1487–512.

4. See, e.g., Randall Morck, Bernard Yeung, and Minyuan Zhao, 'Perspectives on China's outward foreign direct investment', *Journal of International Business Studies* 39 (2008), 337–50.

5. See Arie Y. Lewin, Silvia Massini, and Carine Peeters, 'Why are firms offshoring innovation? The emerging global race for talent', *Journal of International Business Studies* 40 (2009), 901–25.

6. This same point was made explicitly in a brilliant paper; see Jean-François Hennart, 'Down with MNE centric theories! Market entry and expansion as the bundling of MNE and local assets', *Journal of International Business Studies* 40 (2009), 1432–54.

7. I have explored in more depth this challenge of reconciling the quest for new international opportunities with the requirement of internal coherence; see Alain Verbeke and Thomas Kenworthy, 'Multidivisional versus metanational governance of the multinational enterprise', *Journal of International Business Studies* 39 (2008), 940–56.

8. See www.forbes.com/sites/bruceupbin/2011/05/11/seven-signs-of-a-customer-focused-ceo/.

9. See www.stern.nyu.edu/om/faculty/zemel/ford_firestone.pdf.

10. *Ibid.*

11. Alan M. Rugman and Alain Verbeke, 'The world trade organization, multinational enterprise, and civil society', in Michele Fratianni, Paolo Svona, and John J. Kirton (eds.), *Sustaining Global Growth and Development*, 5 (Aldershot, UK, and Burlington, VT: Ashgate, 2003), 81–97; Alain Verbeke, Régis Coeurderoy, and Tanja Matt, 'The future of international business research on corporate globalization that never was . . .' *Journal of International Business Studies* 49(9) (2018), 1101–12.

12. See the insightful piece by Kasra Ferdows, 'Made in the world: the global spread of production', *Production and Operations Management* 6(2) (1997), 102–9.

13. The *tragedy of the commons* concept was popularized in a highly influential piece by Garrett Hardin, 'The tragedy of the commons', *Science* 162(3859) (13 December 1968), 1243–8.

14. Elinor Ostrom, 'Beyond markets and states: polycentric governance of complex economic systems', *American Economic Review*, 100 (2010), 1–33.

15. See, e.g., the extraordinary movie *Deadly Deception: General Electric, Nuclear Weapons, and Our Environment*, produced and directed by Debra Chasnoff, winner of the 1992 Academy Award for best short documentary, as well as the winner of the 1992 American Film & Video Festival Red Ribbon, the 1992 National Educational Film & Video Festival Silver Apple award, the 1991 CINE Golden Eagle, and the 1991 Chicago International Film Festival Gold Hugo.

16. Serdar Aldatmaz and Gregory W. Brown, 'Private equity in the global economy: evidence on industry spillovers', *Journal of Corporate Finance* 60 (2020) 1–23.

17. Lorraine Eden, 'The fourth Industrial Revolution: seven lessons from the past', in Rob van Tulder, Alain Verbeke, and Lucia Piscitello (eds.), *International Business in the Information and Digital Age*, vol. 13: *Progress in International Business Research* (Bingley, UK: Emerald Publishing, 2018), 15–35.

18. Alain Verbeke and Thomas Hutzschenreuter, 'The dark side of digital globalization', *Academy of Management Perspectives* (2020, forthcoming).

19. van Tulder *et al.*, *International Business in the Information and Digital Age*.

20. Rajneesh Narula, 'Enforcing higher labor standards within developing country value chains: consequences for MNEs and informal actors in a dual economy', *Journal of International Business Studies* 50(9) (2019), 1622–35.

Index